Government budgeting

Government

JESSE BURKHEAD

Maxwell Graduate School of
Citizenship and Public Affairs
Syracuse University

budgeting

New York
John Wiley & Sons, Inc.

London · Sydney

HJ
2051
B83
cop 3

EIGHTH PRINTING, MAY, 1967

Library of Congress Catalog Card Number: 56-8000

Printed in the United States of America

For my father

....

Preface..

Modern industrial society is characterized by an increasing quantity and variety of governmental activities. These activities are very often of a positive and purposive character that contributes to an improved standard of living and an extension of the limits of human freedom. Modern government is not simply a coercive mechanism which restricts and confines. Programs for resource development, slum clearance, and public health, to name a few, will contribute to the advancement of human dignity and personal liberty.

Government budgeting is one of the major processes by which the use of public resources is planned and controlled. To the extent that this is done well, governmental programs are brought increasingly to the service of the citizens, enhancing their material and cultural status.

The study of government budgeting is a study in applied economics—in the allocation of public resources. This study must look at operations and begin with organization and procedure, the routines which have been established for decision-making in government. It should extend to an examination of the influences, governmental and nongovernmental, that come to bear on the decision-making process.

Ours is both an organized society and a society of organizations. The significance of organization is nowhere more evident than in the public sector. Here organizational arrangements bring together the learning of all social scientists. The patterns for decision-making do not provide separate compartments for economic knowledge, for political knowledge, for social knowledge. These are merged in the organizational arrangements which have been established for the conduct of governmental affairs.

This volume is divided into four parts. The first is devoted to setting the stage, in historical, institutional and procedural terms. The last chapter in Part I is a brief description of the phases of the budget cycle, each of which is then examined in greater detail in Part III. Part II is concerned with the classification of budgetary data. This is given prominence here because of the author's conviction that the way in which revenue and expenditure are grouped for decision-making is the most important aspect of budgeting. The last part of the volume deals with specific budgeting problems, many of which cut across subjects examined elsewhere but are nevertheless capable of isolation for more detailed examination. The bibliography at the end of each chapter suggests readings relevant to the subject at hand. The suggestions are not intended to be comprehensive of the whole literature of budgeting.

There is considerable emphasis here, possibly an overemphasis, on budgeting in the national government of the United States. There is underemphasis on budgeting practices and procedures in state and local governments in this country. There is overemphasis on the work of the central budget office, and relative neglect of budgeting in departments and agencies. Some of these deficiencies are due to the limitations of the author's working experience and observation. Some are due to the inadequacy of available information. Many of the significant aspects of the budgetary process in governments in the United States have not been analyzed in the literature.

Every effort has been made to indicate the breadth of the subject. The frequent excursions into allied areas and allied disciplines indicate the scope of the problems here considered, even though not all of these ancillary areas are thoroughly explored.

A reasonable attempt has been made to document the vast amount of material which has been written on the subject of budgeting, particularly in the past twenty-five years. This has resulted in a quantity of footnotes which, it may be hoped, do not burden the text.

The author is very much in debt to a large number of patient and discerning readers. Carl W. Tiller has read and commented on most of these chapters. Alfred H. Landau, Richard B. Goode, Joseph A. Pechman, Grover W. Ensley, Herbert A. Klarman, Stein Rossen, O. H. Brownlee, and Robert S. Herman have each reviewed several chapters. My colleagues in the College of Business Administration at Syracuse University—Eric W. Lawson, William T. Jerome, and Walter G. Kell—have been generous with their time and counsel. But my greatest obligation is to my colleagues in the Maxwell Graduate School—Paul H. Appleby, Carl R. Bye, Melvin A. Eggers, A. M. McIsaac, Sidney C. Sufrin, Roscoe C. Martin, Guthrie S. Birkhead, Howard F. Miller, and Frederick C. Mosher. The Maxwell Research Center generously provided funds to help defray expenses. Angela P. Brown typed the manuscript. Polly Sperry Burkhead has made major contributions in editing, writing, and organizing.

Syracuse, New York
April 1956   JESSE BURKHEAD

Contents...........

Part I

The Budget and Modern Government

1.

The development

of modern budgeting

The modern budget system has accompanied the growth of representative government, and growth in the economic importance of governmental activities. In most countries, with the prominent exception of the United States, the budget system was established first at the national level and from there spread to provincial and local governments. Budgeting has not developed uniformly among all governments, however, nor is it traceable to a common set of influences which has operated in the same fashion in all countries.

The word "budget" originally meant the money bag or the public purse, which served as a receptacle for the revenue and expenditure of the state.[1] In Britain the term was used to describe the leather bag in which the Chancellor of the Exchequer carried to Parliament the statement of the Government's needs and resources. Eventually the term came to mean the documents which were contained in the bag—plans for government finances submitted for the approval of the legislature.

I. DEVELOPMENT OF THE BUDGET IN GREAT BRITAIN

The roots of the budget system in Britain are to be found in the emergence of Parliamentary control over the Crown. The budget developed as part of the growth of representative or popular control over the sovereign. The 12th article of the Magna Charta in 1217 stated:

[1] Henry Carter Adams, *The Science of Finance,* Henry Holt & Company, New York, 1898, p. 104.

2

No scutage or aid shall be imposed in the Kingdom unless by the common council of the realm, except for the purpose of ransoming the King's person, making his first-born son a knight, and marrying his eldest daughter once, and the aids for this purpose shall be reasonable in amount.

The barons at Runnymede were apparently not concerned with King John's expenditures, but they were very much concerned with the levies that he imposed on them. In fact, the long history of struggle for Parliamentary control of the purse was a struggle for control over taxation. The control over expenditure came much later, and as a by-product of the concern for the protection of taxpayers. In the Parliamentary contest with the Stuarts, for example, Charles II wished to impose taxes for the prosecution of a war against the Dutch. When Parliament consented to this, funds were specifically raised for this purpose and no other.[2]

With the Revolution of 1688 and the Bill of Rights of the following year came the provision:

Henceforth shall no man be compelled to make any gift, loan, or benevolence, or tax, without common consent by Act of Parliament.

To enforce this the Parliament reserved the right to authorize all expenditures made by the Crown. In asserting this right the House of Commons also asserted its supremacy over the House of Lords in the initiation of supply bills—the acts to authorize expenditure.[3]

Parliament did not at this time extend its authority over the purpose of expenditures; this would have been regarded as an unwarranted restriction on the power of the Crown. Only gradually were the details of expenditure controlled and specified. This specification extended first to the army, the navy, and ordnance.

The extension of Parliamentary control over government finance also came to embrace the supervision of the King's personal outlays. As a consequence of the events of 1688–89, the Civil List was established to separate the expenditures of the Crown from the expenditures of the state, and the Crown expenditures were limited to a specific amount. King George III, after 1760, gave up the greater part of his hereditary Crown revenues for an annual specified grant controlled by Parliament, and other modifications in the Crown's expenditures were made by successive Parliaments in the reigns of George IV and William IV. This was the foundation of the budget system—the complete financial control of the Crown by the Parliament.

[2] William F. Willoughby, Westel W. Willoughby, and Samuel McCune Lindsay, *The System of Financial Administration of Great Britain*, D. Appleton & Company, New York, 1922, pp. 29–30.

[3] E. Hilton Young, *The System of National Finance*, 3rd ed., John Murray, London, 1936, p. 37.

In 1787 another important element was added by the passage of the Consolidated Fund Act, which provided a single general fund for receiving and recording all revenue and expenditure. This laid the basis for a comprehensive financial statement of government activity. The Consolidated Fund Act was also significant in establishing a basis for accountability of public funds. From this there soon developed the complete statement of finances, published annually beginning in the year 1802. Not until 1822, however, did the Chancellor of the Exchequer present such a statement to the Parliament for its guidance and action.[4] This date may be said to mark the beginning of full-fledged budgeting in Great Britain. The financial statements thereafter set forth revenue and expenditure, and indicated the prospective surplus or deficit, together with the Government's financial plan.

Preceding the development of a formal government budget, Parliamentary practice had altered, as early as 1706, to provide that the House would consider no spending measures except those proposed by the Crown. This was formalized in Standing Order 66 of the House of Commons and has continued to be a basic feature of the British financial system. The significance of this procedure lies in the fact that it requires the executive to assume responsibility for the state of the Government's finances. The Parliament retains the authority to approve, reduce, or disapprove the proposed expenditure, but the executive must coordinate revenue and expenditure proposals. The financial plan is an *executive document,* proposed on the basis of executive authority. The legislature's power of approval does not alter the nature of executive responsibility. As a British authority has put it:

> . . . it cannot be too strongly impressed upon the student of constitutional law, that all the money spent upon public service is spent by the Crown; that all the money granted for the public service is granted by the Commons and that the Commons have imposed upon themselves a rule that they will not grant a penny unless it is asked for by a minister representing the Crown for a purpose specified in the terms of his request.[5]

In the execution of the budget the Parliament similarly has ultimate authority. The Crown is responsible for the effective and efficient collection and expenditure of moneys. These responsibilities are enforced by the Public Accounts Committee of the Parliament, established in 1862, and by an independent audit of government accounts prescribed by the Exchequer and Audit Act of 1866. Except for the important controls that are administrative in nature, these statutes completed the

---

[4] G. Findlay Shirras, *Science of Public Finance,* Vol. II, 3rd ed., Macmillan & Co., Ltd., London, 1936, p. 950.

[5] Sir William R. Anson, *The Law and Custom of the Constitution,* Vol. I, 5th ed., by Maurice L. Gwyer, Clarendon Press, Oxford, 1922, p. 285.

pattern of British financial control, which has continued largely unchanged to the present day.

The highly centralized responsibility for financial planning by the executive, so important in the British budget system, is a direct product
of the pattern of relationships between the Cabinet and the Parliament.
The Cabinet, as the central executive authority, is a committee of the
House of Commons.   In this role the Cabinet acts in many capacities.
As an executive, it provides an account of its stewardship—the manner
in which it has discharged its obligations for the conduct of the administration.   As an executive, the Cabinet formulates a statement of the
Government's needs and resources for the forthcoming period.   As members of the House of Commons, the Cabinet asks for the approval of its
program and defends and explains that program.   After approval is
granted, the Cabinet undertakes, in its executive capacity, to control the
administration of its program.

There is a difference between the Cabinet's responsibility for expenditure and for revenue.   The Commons is free to reduce expenditure; this
action does not reflect a loss of confidence in the Cabinet.   Similarly,
the Commons may reject a proposal for revenue and require the Cabinet
to return with an alternative.   But if the Commons moves to increase
expenditure, this does reflect a loss of confidence in the Cabinet and a
new Government must be formed.   The determination of the upper limit
of expenditure is regarded as the most critical of the Cabinet's budget
responsibilities.

The high degree of flexible, centralized responsibility inherent in these
relationships between the Cabinet and the House of Commons has made
the budget system in Great Britain extremely viable.   Indeed, the budget
system in Britain works so well, from the standpoint of centralized responsibility, that its success has had very great influence on developments
in other countries.[6]   At the same time, this centralization of responsibility, together with the increased complexity of governmental programs,
has reduced Parliament's role in budgeting to the point where there is
little effective legislative review of the details of the budget, either before
or after they are voted.[7]

The development of the budgetary system in Britain does not rest solely
on the formal pattern of responsibilities running between the Cabinet and

[6] It may be noted that the centralized responsibility in budgeting which characterizes the British system is utilized with substantially comparable effectiveness
in other Commonwealth countries.   See Robert MacGregor Dawson, *The Government of Canada,* University of Toronto Press, Toronto, 1948, pp. 425–433.

[7] Henry Higgs, *Financial Reform,* Macmillan & Co., Ltd., London, 1924, pp.
26–43; Eric Taylor, *The House of Commons at Work,* Penguin Books, Harmondsworth, Middlesex, 1951, pp. 221–225.

the Parliament. The budget has become a significant statement of governmental policy, and budgetary procedure has been important in the formulation of such policy. This development came after the "mechanical" features of the budget were well established.

Beginning with the Peel-Gladstone era, in 1840, " . . . the Budget became no mere statement of accounts, but was presented with a wealth of judgment, reflection, and imagination, which gave it . . . an indisputable place in the political economy of finance."[8] Much of this was due to the genius of Gladstone himself. There have been few finance ministers, before or since, of whom the following could be written:

> Just as Macaulay made thousands read history who before had turned from it as dry and repulsive, so Mr. Gladstone made thousands eager to follow the public balance-sheet, and the whole nation became his audience, interested in him and his themes and in the House where his dazzling wonders were performed.[9]

The first Gladstone ministry, from 1868 to 1874, was marked by "peace and retrenchment." Liberal Party reforms included the modification of "Tory landlordism," public education, and the Trade Union Act of 1871. In guiding these enactments Gladstone used the budget as a major instrument of control. The maxim "expenditure depends on policy" is apparently the product of this era, and Gladstone's policies, including his economy measures, found adequate expression in the budgets of this period. Gladstone thought that expenditure beyond " . . . the legitimate wants of the country is not only a pecuniary waste, but a great political and, above all, a great moral evil."[10] His feeling about the importance of the budget as an instrument of governmental policy is revealed in the frequently-quoted statement:

> Budgets are not merely matters of arithmetic, but in a thousand ways go to the root of prosperity of individuals, and relation of classes, and the strength of kingdoms.

MacGregor points out that the final triumph of the doctrine that "expenditure depends on policy" came with the era of expansionary finance that followed Gladstone's rule. Goshen, as Chancellor of the Exchequer from 1886 to 1892, ended the retrenchment efforts which had dominated the Liberal Party's program, and inaugurated an extension in the functions of the national government. The budget continued to be the major instrument for the expression of the Government's program; Parliamentary debate on Government policy centered on the budget.

[8] D. H. MacGregor, *Public Aspects of Finance,* Clarendon Press, Oxford, 1939, p. 12.

[9] Taylor, *op. cit.,* p. 211 (footnote).

[10] Quoted by MacGregor, *op. cit.,* p. 45.

The importance which the budget had acquired during a period of contraction and economy continued during a period of expansion.

II. THE BUDGET IN OTHER EUROPEAN COUNTRIES

The development of the budget system on the Continent is similarly part and parcel of the emergence of institutions of representative government. In Austria, for example, as early as 1766 there was a "budget" in the sense of an annual statement of the Crown's revenue and expenditure, but a budget system with executive responsibility for the preparation of a financial plan and with legislative authority for approval did not emerge until after World War I and the end of the Hapsburgs.[11]

In France there was only an occasional effort to assert a popularly controlled "budget right" prior to the Revolution. But beginning with a decree of June 17, 1789, it became a fundamental and enduring principle of French constitutional practice that "no tax whatever can be levied without the consent of the nation."[12] Since that time there have been only a few infractions of popular control over tax imposition, one of them committed by Napoleon, another by Louis Napoleon.

Expenditure control by the French National Assembly came much later than the control of taxation. It appears that for a number of years after the Revolution there was considerable uncertainty as to whether the Assembly ought to assert control over state expenditure, and a prevalent feeling that this prerogative belonged to the executive. The Constitutional Assembly demanded an accountability for funds but did not attempt to predetermine the objects of expenditure. In 1817, however, it was provided that the expenditure of each minister should not exceed the total of the appropriation accorded to him. In 1827 this control was solidified, and in 1831 the Assembly undertook to determine the detail of appropriations. Parliamentary control of the budget in France thus became complete on this date.

The budget as an annual statement of receipts and expenditures had been a feature of Parliamentary practice even before the National Assembly undertook to control the detail of appropriations. As early as 1815 such a statement became formalized when the Government presented each year a Budget Bill, which, upon enactment, became the Finance Act of that year.[13] Three conditions came to be associated with this pro-

[11] W. F. Willoughby, "The Budget," *Encyclopedia of the Social Sciences,* Vol. III, Macmillan Company, New York, 1930, p. 40.

[12] René Stourm, *The Budget,* translated by Thaddeus Plazinski, D. Appleton & Company, New York, 1917, p. 39.

[13] D. W. S. Lidderdale, *The Parliament of France,* Hansard Society, London, 1951, pp. 208–211.

cedure: the budget should be annual; it should be voted before the beginning of the financial year to which it applied; it should contain all financial provisions needed for the year. It came to be further characteristic of financial practice that items of revenue should not be earmarked for special purposes, but that all revenue should be paid into and paid out of a consolidated fund.

There are at least two significant differences between the budgetary system of Great Britain and the budgetary system of France. In Great Britain the Chancellor of the Exchequer has major responsibility for the preparation of the Government's financial plan. "Treasury Control" implies Treasury authority to modify the requests of other ministers. Appeal of the Chancellor's decisions to the Cabinet is possible but unlikely. In France the Minister of Finance has never exercised this degree of authority over the appropriation requests of his fellow ministers. Major budgetary decisions are made by the Cabinet, in which the Minister of Finance participates on a more or less equal basis with other ministers. The degree of centralized financial control possessed by the Chancellor of the Exchequer is partially lacking in France.

But of even greater significance is the budgetary authority possessed by the Parliament in France.[14] The Finance Committee of the Chamber of Deputies (now the National Assembly) has almost complete authority to reduce, increase, or eliminate items of proposed expenditure and taxation. Even individual deputies have considerable authority to introduce measures of expenditure and revenue, in spite of efforts to curtail this authority. Furthermore, the credits voted by the Assembly are specified and transfers among credits are prohibited, so that Parliamentary action determines much more of the detail of the budget than in Great Britain.

The characteristic feature of the British budgetary system—centralized responsibility for national finance—is lacking in the French system. Correspondingly, the Finance Committee of the Assembly has a large staff and examines departmental proposals more carefully than does the Estimates Committee of the House of Commons. Unfortunately, the Finance Committee does not always conduct its inquiry in a responsible fashion. The Committee and the Assembly may seek to harass the Government and even to bring about its downfall on budgetary matters. This will lead, not to a national election, as in Britain, but to a reshuffling of the cabinet. The larger measure of Parliamentary control exercised over the budget in France has not been accompanied by a larger measure of Parliamentary responsibility.

---

[14] Henry Laufenburger, *d'Economie et de Législation Financières, Budget et Trésor,* 3rd ed., Librairie du Recueil Sirey, Paris, 1948, pp. 24–44.

III. DEVELOPMENT OF BUDGETING IN THE UNITED STATES

A. The Period of Budgetary Disorganization in the Federal Government, 1789–1909

The budget system of Great Britain was not fully developed at the time of the American Revolution.[15]   There was no accepted British practice which could be emulated by the framers of the Constitution.   As a result, the Constitution requires only that, "No money shall be drawn from the treasury, but in consequence of appropriations made by law; and a regular statement and account of the receipts and expenditures of all public money shall be published from time to time." (Article I, Section 9.) Beyond this the Constitution requires that all revenue measures must originate in the House of Representatives.

The requirement for financial reporting was elaborated in the statute establishing the Treasury Department, which made it the specific duty of the Secretary of the Treasury " . . . to prepare and report estimates of the public revenue, and the public expenditures . . . " (1 *Stat. L.* 65). This was supplemented in 1800 by a statute directing the Secretary " . . . to digest, prepare, and lay before Congress . . . a report on the subject of finance, containing estimates of the public revenue and public expenditures, and plans for improving or increasing the revenues . . . " (2 *Stat. L.* 79).

In these important formative years Cabinet officials undertook direct and personal relations with the Congress in a manner very like the British practice.   Alexander Hamilton assumed a strong executive leadership in all financial matters and prepared estimates of need for expenditures and revenues. Except for the support he gave the Secretary of the Treasury, President Washington apparently had little hand in this; it was very largely the personal product of Hamilton's genius.[16]   As Henry Jones Ford has written:

> In the beginning all the branches of the government were bunched together in their quarters so that intercourse was ready and easy without formal arrangements, and the brief notices of the direct presence of cabinet officials appearing in the records give an inadequate notion of the real extent of the intimacy.   It was by direct, personal administrative initiative that the government was set in operation.   Only by such agency could the finances have received the radical treatment by which Hamilton almost at a stroke lifted the nation out of bankruptcy, established its credit and secured its

[15] For a description of early financial practices see Charles Bullock, "The Finances of the United States from 1775 to 1789," *Bulletin of the University of Wisconsin,* Vol. I, June 1895, pp. 117–273.

[16] See Leonard D. White, *The Federalists,* Macmillan Company, New York, 1948, pp. 323–347.

revenues. . . . His personal initiative transcended even the function of an English Chancellor of the Exchequer on which it was distinctly modelled, for he had no other compact party on which he could depend.[17]

In these first years the House of Representatives exercised its functions of criticism and control through a committee of the whole. In the case of appropriations, after discussion had been held, a specific committee was appointed to bring in a bill incorporating the views expressed by the committee. But by 1796 House procedure was altered. A Committee on Ways and Means was appointed, which was made a permanent standing committee in 1802. This marked the end of continuous executive direction of the government's finances. During Jefferson's reign the separation of Cabinet officials from the day to day work of Congress was made complete. Direct oral communication between the two branches of government gave way to written communication. Executive influence in legislation came to operate through and upon the developing committee structure of the Congress, and the executive lost much of its former initiative in the legislative process. Friction in financial matters between the Administration and the Congress increased, centering very often on the use of detailed appropriations to restrict executive discretion.[18]

With the emergence of organized political parties, executive influence on legislation came to be exercised by the President in his capacity as leader of a political party as well as in his capacity as head of the executive agencies of government. Some critics have viewed this enlarged role of the Presidency as a development which was not foreseen by the Constitution's fathers and as antithetical to their views.[19] In addition, there is evidence that some of the original members of the House felt that the Constitution required the executive's role in financial affairs to be one of reporting only, and that all proposals which were to be a "project of law" were to originate with the Congress.[20] Nevertheless, it was upon this expanded concept of the Presidency that the budget system eventually came to depend.

From 1802 to 1865 both revenue and appropriation authority were concentrated in the House Committee on Ways and Means. During this period the Secretary of the Treasury continued to present his annual report, and at the beginning of each session of the Congress, a Book of Estimates setting forth the expenditure requirements of the various departments and agencies. The Secretary's function was primarily clerical.

[17] Henry Jones Ford, "Budget Making and the Work of Government," *The Annals*, November 1915, pp. 4–5.

[18] Arthur Smithies, *The Budgetary Process in the United States*, McGraw-Hill Book Company, New York, 1955, pp. 53–54.

[19] Ford, *op. cit.*, pp. 5–9.

[20] Adams, *The Science of Finance*, pp. 122–123.

He classified the expenditure proposals and transmitted them to the Congress. He did not criticize, alter, reduce or coordinate the requests. Neither did the Cabinet serve as an agency for financial planning.

During this period the House Ways and Means Committee served as a planning mechanism, at least to the extent of providing an occasion for a comprehensive view of the state of the government's finances. This view emerged, however, only as one department after another had been heard. But beginning in 1865 a separate House Appropriations Committee was established, and thereafter such unity as had prevailed in Congressional review of the budget began to be dissipated. By 1885 there were eight committees of the House with authority to recommend appropriations. Later this was increased to ten in the House; the Senate, not far behind, delegated appropriating authority to eight of its standing committees.[21]

The period of extreme laxity in federal finance extended from about 1880 to 1909. One reason therefor is not hard to find. As James Bryce put it, in rather flowery language, in 1888:[22]

> Under the system of congressional finance here described, America wastes millions annually. But her wealth is so great, her revenue so elastic, that she is not sensible of the loss. She has the glorious privilege of youth, the privilege of committing errors without suffering from their consequences.

Also:

> . . . America lives in a world of her own. . . . Safe from attack, safe even from menace, she hears from afar the warring cries on European races and faiths, as the gods of Epicurus listened to the murmurs of the unhappy earth spread out beneath their golden dwellings. . . .

This was the period when the major financial problem faced by the Congress was the annual disposal of the large surpluses brought in by the tariff. President Cleveland, on December 6, 1887, sent a message to Congress which read:

> You are confronted at the threshold of your legislative duties with a condition of the national finances which imperatively demands immediate and careful consideration.
>   The amount of money annually exacted, through the operation of present laws, from the industries and necessities of the people largely exceeds the sum necessary to meet the expenses of the Government.
>   . . . This wrong inflicted upon those who bear the burden of national taxation, like other wrongs, multiplies a brood of evil consequences. The

[21] Vincent J. Browne, *The Control of the Public Budget,* Public Affairs Press, Washington, 1949, pp., 50–73.

[22] James Bryce, *The American Commonwealth,* Vol. I, Macmillan & Co., London, 1891, pp. 179, 303.

public treasury . . . becomes a hoarding-place for money needlessly with-drawn from trade and the people's use, thus crippling our national energies . . . and inviting schemes of public plunder.[23]

The President noted that the Treasury was building up a surplus which would probably mount to $140 million by the end of the fiscal year.

Rather evidently, this period of the "glorious privilege of youth" in financial affairs did not make for a rigid executive or legislative control over expenditures. It is not difficult to appreciate that a large number of Congressmen were anxious to increase the number of standing committees with authority over the expenditure of funds so easy to acquire. Neither is it difficult to understand that this period of Congressional history was characterized by extreme irresponsibility and wasteful extravagance in the form of ill-disguised raids on the Treasury. As one critic said, "The remarkable thing is not that the system breeds corruption, but that it should work at all."[24]

Congressional extravagances during this period were matched only by the profligacy of the executive departments. The practice developed of incurring "coercive deficiencies." Speaking of this, Wilmerding states:

> The departments governed their expenditures by the amounts of the estimates rather than by the amounts of the grants. If in any case less were granted than was estimated, the department or bureau affected, instead of revising its plans for the coming year to bring them within the financial limits of the reduced appropriation, continued them without change in perfect confidence that Congress would appropriate supplementary sums when they were requested rather than stop the service.[25]

The Congress undertook, with but limited success, to curb deficiencies in 1905 and 1906, but this practice was only one aspect of a generally lax and inadequate financial administration and could not be dealt with in isolation. The movement for a more general reform of federal financial practices did not begin to gain momentum until President Taft's administration.

B. The Development of Municipal Budgeting, 1900–1920

It is not possible to dissociate the influences which contributed to the development of the budget in the national government from the influences which contributed to the development of budgeting in American

[23] *Journal of the Senate of the United States,* 50th Cong., 1st sess., December 6, 1887, p. 8.

[24] Henry Jones Ford, *The Cost of Our National Government,* Columbia University Press, New York, 1910, p. 60. Also Rollo Ogden, "The Rationale of Congressional Extravagance," *Yale Review,* May 1897, pp. 37–49.

[25] Lucius Wilmerding, Jr., *The Spending Power,* Yale University Press, New Haven, 1943, p. 140.

cities.   But in point of time, the developments came first at the municipal level and the pressures for budgetary reform spread from there to the national government.   It may be that this is traceable to the influence of the "Muckrakers," such as Lincoln Steffens, Ida M. Tarbell, and Ray Stannard Baker, who centered attention on municipal corruption.

There are two historic dates in the development of municipal budgeting in this country.   The first is 1899, when the National Municipal League drafted a model municipal corporation act.   One of the prominent features of this model was a proposed budget system under the direct supervision of the mayor.   Since the League was very active in promoting local governmental reform, the model act had great influence; the budget system incorporated therein was adopted by numerous municipalities. The second date, of even greater significance, was 1906, which marked the establishment of the New York Bureau of Municipal Research, bringing together such able and aggressive personalities as William H. Allen, Henry Bruère, and Frederick A. Cleveland.   This group, with their staff, undertook immediate study and action in budgeting for New York City. Their first report, in 1907, was entitled "Making a Municipal Budget." Their proposals for budgeting for New York City's health program met with favor and were soon extended to other activities.[26]

The activities and orientation of the New York Bureau were of greatest importance in the development of the "good government" movement after the turn of the century.   They worked with a crusading zeal, and were highly motivated.   Waldo has said of this group:

> The Bureau Movement was a part of Progressivism, and its leaders were leaders of Progressivism.   They were tired of the simple moralism of the nineteenth century, although paradoxically they were themselves fired with the moral fervor of humanitarianism and secularized Christianity.   They were stirred by the revelations of the Muckrackers, but despaired of reform by spontaneous combustion.   They were sensitive to the appeals of and promises of science, and put a simple trust in discovery of facts as the way of science and as a sufficient mode for solution of human problems.   They accepted—they urged—the new positive conception of government, and verged upon the idea of a planned and managed society.   They hated "bad" business, but found in business organization and procedure an acceptable prototype for public business.   They detested politicians and were firm in the belief that citizens by and large were fundamentally pure at heart, desirous of efficient and economical government, and potentially rational enough to "reach up" to and support a vigorous government, wide in its scope, complex in its problems, and utilizing a multitude of professional and scientific skills.   They proposed to educate citizens to and assist them with this responsibility.   They were ardent apostles of the "efficiency idea" and leaders in the movement for "useful" education.   These last three notions— civic awareness and militancy, efficiency, and "useful" education—together

[26] A. E. Buck, *Public Budgeting,* Harper & Brothers, New York, 1929, p. 13.

form the core of the Efficient Citizenship movement. They caught the vision that "true democracy consists in intelligent cooperation between citizens and those elected or appointed to serve . . . . "[27]

In this approach to reform, the budget was conceived as a major weapon for instilling responsibility in the governmental structure: the budget system rests on popular control; the budget will publicize what government is doing and make for an informed and alert citizenry; the budget will destroy the rule of invisible government—the party bosses who are responsible to no one. To accomplish this, executive leadership must be institutionalized. "The atmosphere of democracy must be filtered and made to flow into useful channels by the power of leadership which may be made accountable."[28]

The growth of the budget system in American cities was hampered by the relatively inadequate executive powers possessed by most mayors. In the cities financial authority was typically concentrated in the city councils; the mayor did not possess more than the authority to sit with or to be represented in the finance committee of the council. Therefore, the adoption of the budget system necessitated a reorganization of city government and a redistribution of authority. Budget reform and governmental reorganization usually went hand in hand in efforts to improve the financial practices of the cities. This combination was a characteristic feature of the city manager movement. Indeed, the same pressures for reform that secured the introduction of the city manager in a number of American cities after 1910 were instrumental in securing the adoption of the budget system in other municipalities. Very often the reforms were the direct product of efforts by taxpayer-financed bureaus of municipal research.

It is difficult to assign a precise date, but it is appropriate to say that by the mid-1920's most major American cities had undergone a more or less thorough reform in municipal financial practices and had established some sort of a budget system. In the 1920's the pace of adoption was accelerated by the financial stringency which followed the passage of the

[27] Dwight Waldo, *The Administrative State,* Ronald Press Company, New York 1948, pp. 32–33.

[28] Frederick A. Cleveland and Arthur Eugene Buck, *The Budget and Responsible Government,* Macmillan Company, New York, 1920, p. 102. See also the discussion of the relationship of budgeting to democratic government, pp. 3–71. For additional writings expressing this point of view see *The Annals,* May 1912, especially, Herbert R. Sands and Fred W. Lindars, "Efficiency in Budget Making," pp. 138–150; J. Harold Braddock, "Efficiency Value of the Budget Exhibit," pp. 151–157; Henry Bruère, "Efficiency in City Government," pp. 3–22. Also, Edgar Dawson, "The Invisible Government and Administrative Efficiency," *The Annals,* March 1916, pp. 11–21.

18th Amendment and the corresponding loss of municipal revenue from the sale of alcoholic beverages. It was also accelerated by demands for increased municipal programs, such as paved streets to accommodate the automobile and new school buildings to accommodate an increase in school population.

In appraising the forces which accounted for this rather rapid adoption of the budget system in American cities, it should be noted that while the reformers were important, the zeal for good government significant, and the need for increased municipal outlays evident, these alone would not have been enough. The crucial element of support which led to the adoption of the budget system was pressure from the business community. Businessmen, who before 1900 had been largely indifferent to the state of governmental affairs, now became seriously concerned. This concern was the direct product of an increase in tax burdens. The way to reduce these burdens was to install a budget system to economize and reduce governmental expenditures. The slogan "more business in government" probably did more for budgetary reform than the agitation of the reformers against "invisible government." Budgetary reform came to be identified, realistically or not, with retrenchment in government, with a reduction in expenditures with a view to reduced taxes; not, as the reformers intended, with the strengthening of government for the more efficient conduct of programs of social welfare.

A second factor also contributed to the strong support by the business community for the adoption of a budget system in the cities. In many municipalities "boss rule," graft, and corruption had proceeded to the point where it was extremely difficult to carry on transactions with governments on a rational basis. Particularly in the award of construction contracts and in government purchasing, a reform looking toward a "businesslike" basis was necessary if others than the "insiders" were to be able to sell materials and supplies to municipalities. The increase in executive authority and responsibility inherent in the budget system was a major step in establishing this rational basis for the conduct of relations with business firms. Other reforms, such as competitive bidding, accompanied the budget system in a general rationalization of economic relations between the business community and governmental units.

C. The Commission on Economy and Efficiency, 1908–1912

Two sets of pressures converged on the national administration with the inauguration of President Taft in 1909. The first developed from the state of national finances, which, even for this rich, young nation in its "golden dwellings," came to border on crisis. The surpluses of President Cleveland's day were not as persistent after 1894. Deficits were incurred in two of the four years of President Theodore Roosevelt's second term. In the first year that President Taft was in the White House, the deficit was $89 million in a total budget of $694 million. Federal expenditures were running between $300 and $400 million in the 1890's. By 1909 they were nearly $700 million. The trends are shown in Table 1.

Not all of these increases in expenditure were traceable to graft and

TABLE 1
Federal Government Receipts and Expenditures, 1885–1912
(in millions)

Fiscal Year	Total Receipts	Total Expenditures	Surplus or Deficit*
1885	$324	$260	$+63
1886	336	242	+94
1887	371	268	+103
1888	379	268	+111
1889	387	299	+88
1890	403	318	+85
1891	393	366	+27
1892	355	345	+10
1893	386	383	+2
1894	306	368	−61
1895	325	356	−31
1896	338	352	−14
1897	348	366	−18
1898	405	443	−38
1899	516	605	−89
1900	567	521	+46
1901	588	525	+63
1902	562	485	+77
1903	562	517	+45
1904	541	584	−43
1905	544	567	−23
1906	595	570	+25
1907	666	579	+87
1908	602	659	−57
1909	604	694	−89
1910	676	694	−18
1911	702	691	+11
1912	693	690	+3

* May not add because of rounding.

Source: *Historical Statistics of the United States, 1789–1945*, U. S. Bureau of the Census, Washington, 1949, pp. 296–299.

corruption, extensive as these may have been. A much larger part of the increase was due to enhanced governmental functions, and, of course, to the outlays occasioned by the Spanish-American War. It was a period of national expansion. As Henry Jones Ford said, writing in 1910:

> Now American banking capital is taking nations in pawn. American commercial enterprise in invading every part of the world. A boycott in China sends shudders through the counting rooms of our cotton mills, and a hurry call for relief goes to Washington. National interests naturally look to the national government for protection. . . . In becoming a world power, we are already finding that the accompanying responsibilities are subjecting our governmental organization to strains that is unfitted to bear.[29]

With expenditures mounting rapidly, public concern increased and the proposals of the reformers were listened to more seriously. The assertion of Senator Aldrich in 1909 that the Congress in that year had enacted $50,000,000 of wasteful appropriations served as dramatic publicity.

A second set of pressures came from the antipathy to the graft and corruption itself. The factors which contributed to municipal budget reform also contributed to federal government reform. A number of those who had directed their crusading zeal against the malpractices of local government directed a similar zeal against laxness in federal administration and the corruption in the Congress. One of the most prominent of this group stated, in discussing the development of budgeting in the national government:

> This growing hostility to doing business in the dark, to "boss rule," to "invisible government," became the soil in which the "budget idea" finally took root and grew.[30]

The combination of these pressures began to produce some results. On March 4, 1909, an amendment to the Sundry Civil Appropriations Act provided that if appropriations exceeded revenues, the Secretary of the Treasury should immediately advise the Congress as to how appropriations could be reduced or additional taxes levied (35 *Stat. L.* 945, 1027). However, there is no evidence that the Secretary of the Treasury ever acted in conformity with this directive. On March 22, 1909, the Senate appointed a special committee to investigate the deficits. It reported that:

> . . . the application to the business of the government of improvements in systems and methods similar to those which have produced the high degree of business efficiency in the great business corporations of the country will

[29] Ford, *The Cost of Our National Government*, pp. 9–10.
[30] Frederick A. Cleveland, "Evolution of the Budget Idea in the United States," *The Annals*, November 1915, p. 22.

result in the saving of many millions of dollars annually and in a much higher degree of efficiency in the conduct of the government business.[31]

In December 1909 President Taft requested an appropriation of $100,000 " . . . to enable the President to inquire into the methods of transacting the public business . . . ." This request was granted by the Congress on June 25, 1910, and immediately thereafter the President appointed the Commission on Economy and Efficiency. In the meantime the Secretary of the Treasury, Franklin MacVeagh, had added his weight to the demands for procedural reform in national government finance, by pointing out in his *Annual Report* for 1909 that a budget system was necessary to reverse the trend " . . . toward an elimination of the responsibility of the executive branch."[32]

The Commission conceived its responsibilities broadly and for two years undertook investigations of (1) the budget as an annual financial program, (2) the organization and activities of the federal government, (3) personnel problems, (4) financial records and accounts, and (5) business practices and procedure in the government. One of the first things that the Commission did was to secure information from federal departments and agencies classifying expenditures according to objects purchased, such as personal services, materials, supplies, and equipment. On the basis of discussion with department heads and in consultation with the President, the Commission prepared a set of forms to be used by departments in the submission of annual budgetary data. In addition, the Commission prepared an organizational chart of federal government activity, the first that had ever been devised, and made numerous studies of overlapping and duplicating operations within the government.

In the summer of 1911 the new forms were transmitted to departments and agencies for their use in preparing the budget to be submitted at the January session of the Congress. However, since Congress required a different set of forms, the departments and agencies did not transmit the new set to the President until after the session was underway, and Congressional action in this session did not utilize the new classification. On January 17, 1912, President Taft sent to Congress a message on *Economy and Efficiency in the Government Service*.[33] On June 27, 1912, the report of the Commission on *The Need for a National Budget* was transmitted.[34]

These two documents were of greatest significance in the development

[31] Quoted by Ford, *op. cit.*, p. 105.
[32] *Annual Report of the Secretary of the Treasury for the fiscal year ending June 30, 1909*, p. 4.
[33] House Doc. No. 458, 62d Cong., 2d sess.
[34] House Doc. No. 854, 62d Cong., 2d sess.

of the budget system in the federal government and were of almost equal importance in the improvement of specific government management procedures. This was the first time in the history of the federal government that its organizational structure had been studied in detail, and the first time that detailed information had been assembled on the character of governmental expenditures. Of even greater significance was the fact that these documents represented an assumption of responsibility by the Chief Executive for financial planning and for the management of the "government's business," as it was then called.

President Taft's message was devoted to a description of the conditions which had called forth the Commission on Economy and Efficiency, a discussion of the work of the Commission, and the transmission of the organizational chart which they had prepared. Throughout the document Taft stressed the importance of establishing a national budget system as an instrument of executive management and control. The report stated, "The constitutional purpose of a budget is to make government responsive to public opinion and responsible for its acts."[35] The budget system was not conceived to be an instrument of economy and efficiency in a narrow sense. The President stated:

> We want economy and efficiency; we want saving, and saving for a purpose. We want to save money to enable the Government to go into some of the beneficial projects which we are debarred from taking up now because we cannot increase our expenditure.[36]

The report of the Commission on *The Need for a National Budget* was a similar broad-gauged document. The Commission had circulated a questionnaire to a large number of other national governments for the purpose of securing information on the operation of their budget systems. This information was apparently studied carefully; the Commission's report shows awareness of foreign government experience. In transmitting the report, President Taft stated, after reviewing the major defects in administrative organization which then characterized federal finances:

> The purpose of the report which is submitted is to suggest . . . a plan whereby the President and the Congress may cooperate—the one in laying before the Congress and the country a clearly expressing administrative program to be acted on; the other in laying before the President a definite enactment to be acted on by him.[37]

In the Commission's report the budget was conceived as serving a number of purposes—a document for Congressional action, an instrument of control and management by the Chief Executive, and a basis for

[35] House Doc. No. 458, p. 16.
[36] *Ibid.*, p. 17.
[37] House Doc. No. 854, pp. 4–5.

the administration of departments and agencies. On the latter point the Commission stated:

> In order that he [the administrator] may think intelligently about the subject of his responsibility he must have before him regularly statements which will reflect results in terms of quality and quantity; he must be able to measure quality and quantity of results by units of cost and units of efficiency.[38]

The Commission pointed out that the administrator's responsibilities could be implemented only when budget expenditures were classified in accordance with the activities undertaken by departments and agencies. To this end the *pro forma* budget incorporated in the report included an itemization of activity schedules as subdivisions of departmental and agency expenditures.

A major point of concern to the Commission was the constitutional issue—how a budget system would fit into a governmental structure based on the separation of powers. In considering this point the Commission suggested that the budget system was based on the constitutional theory of trusteeship. The government is the trust instrument; government officials are the trustees. Citizens, in their sovereign capacity, are the beneficiaries and creators of the trust. The President, as the principal government official, must be responsible for the budget. He should submit the budget message and the summary statements. The heads of departments and agencies should transmit data to the President; the President should have responsibility for prescribing the form of accounts. The Secretary of the Treasury should assist the President in discharging these obligations. The President's responsibility runs not only to the Congress, but to the public at large. The budget is the only effective means whereby the President can be made responsible for getting a definite, well-considered, comprehensive program before the people.

Unfortunately for the development of the budget system, the Congress was in no mood to undertake serious consideration of the President's recommendations. For general policy and political reasons a strong bloc of Democrats and Progressive Republicans opposed all of the President's recommendations in the 1912 session, including the recommendations for a national budget. In fact, shortly after the Commission's report was received, the Congress attached an amendment to the Sundry Civil Appropriations Bill, requiring the heads of departments and agencies to submit their appropriation requests at the specified time and in the form required by existing law—at no other time and in no other form. The President, however, insisted that he had constitutional authority to require that appropriation requests be submitted as he directed. Heads of departments and agencies therefore undertook to prepare two sets of ap-

[38] *Ibid.,* p. 164.

propriations requests—one in accordance with the requirements of the
Congress, and in the other in accordance with the requirements of the
President as set forth in the Commission's report.

In the meantime, the elections of 1912 resulted in defeat for President
Taft and returned a Congress controlled by the Democrats. When
President Taft submitted his new budget and budget message to the
Congress in February, no action was taken on it. President Wilson was
inaugurated in March. The Congress was convened immediately and
turned to problems deemed to be more significant than those of national
budgeting. Moreover, financial pressures on the federal government
were somewhat eased. Business conditions were good and the federal
government, with the passage of the 16th Amendment, had an additional
and important source of revenue in the personal income tax. No further
action was undertaken to establish a national budget system until after
World War I.

In spite of the fact that the work of the Commission on Economy and
Efficiency led to no immediate legislation, it had tremendous long-run
value. The prestige of the Commission and its strong backing by the
President made budgeting an issue of national significance. It stimulated attention to budgetary reform in municipalities and in the states.
It led to a very large volume of writings on the subject.[39] Eventually all
of this ferment produced results. Congressmen who had been hostile to
the budget system in 1912 came to support it. Business groups, particularly the National Chamber of Commerce, were concerned about budgeting; the Chamber conducted a referendum of its members as a means of
stimulating interest in this reform and reported, "The business interests
of the country today are practically a unit for this reform by the federal
government.[40] Support of a national budget system was incorporated
in the party platforms of the Progressives, the Republicans, and the
Democrats in 1916. The work of the Commission contributed greatly to
the eventual passage of the Budget and Accounting Act in 1921.

D. Budgeting in the States, 1910–1920

The belated concern with budgeting in state governments is primarily
attributable to the same factors which retarded the development of budgeting in the national government. The states did not face any serious
financial pressure until after the turn of the century. At that time total
state expenditures were less than $200 million, and revenues were gen-

---

[39] See the bibliography in William Franklin Willoughby, *The Problem of a
National Budget,* D. Appleton & Company, New York, 1918, pp. 193–213.

[40] Charles Wallace Collins, *The National Budget System,* Macmillan Company,
New York, 1917, p. 136.

erally adequate to meet expenditures. The general property tax, which was the major source of state revenue, had a stable yield with sufficient flexibility to meet expanding fiscal demands.

Furthermore, in the states there had been a number of changes in constitutional arrangements, which tended to move away from rather than toward the development of a budget system. Constitutional revisions had deprived state governors of some of the executive powers which they had originally possessed, and had also placed additional limitations on legislative action. Many important state officers with fiscal authority were elected officials, such as the state auditor or the state treasurer, and were not subject to control by the governor. In addition, heads of executive departments were often elected rather than appointed by the governor, with a further diffusion of executive authority. State appropriation systems also tended to limit the growth of executive budgeting; the objects and types of appropriations which might be enacted were often set forth in the constitution.

These restrictions on state governmental authority were an expression of the philosophy of popular government prevalent in this country in the 19th century, and to some degree still extant: the limitation of governmental authority will assure that it will not be exercised arbitrarily; the protection of the freedom of individuals requires rigid control over the scope of governmental action; the tyranny to be feared is the tyranny of arbitrary executive *and* arbitrary legislative action, and neither branch of government is to be trusted; the rights of citizens can be preserved only by limiting the responsibilities of government; one of the ways of accomplishing this limitation is to preserve a rigid separation of legislative and administrative power.

The prevalence of these attitudes and their embodiment in state constitutions meant that the introduction of the budget system necessitated major modifications in the structure of government and the division of governmental authority. The administrative system had to be "integrated," that is, the heads of state government departments must be made responsible to the governor, which meant that they could not be directly elected.[41] The reform known as "short ballot," introduced in the states after 1910, made for the concentration of authority in the governor, and made it possible for the governor to be held responsible for financial planning and administration.

Before the states came to adopt a thorough-going system of executive budgeting, there were experiments with boards of control. These were established in a number of states, notably Wisconsin, California, and

[41] William Franklin Willoughby, *The Movement for Budgetary Reform in the States,* D. Appleton & Company, New York, 1918, pp. 12–13; 183–186.

New York, and were typically composed of the governor and other administrative officers and legislative leaders. None of these experiments was successful in establishing the kind of executive leadership and responsibility that is basic to effective budgeting.[42]

The factors which eventually led to the establishment of state budgeting systems were not very different from those which were influential at the municipal and federal levels. After the turn of the century state governments began to encounter increasing financial difficulties. The general property tax was gradually abandoned as a source of state revenue in response to the demands of counties and municipalities for additional revenue sources. The abandonment of general property taxation by the states provoked pressure for efficiency and economy, and the budget system was viewed as a major instrumentality for achieving this objective. In addition, the same atmosphere of reform generated by the antagonism to "boss rule" and "invisible government" came to influence state legislatures, as it influenced municipalities and the federal government. As with municipalities, the activities of taxpayers' associations, trade organizations, and chambers of commerce were important in stimulating the demand for reform in state budgetary procedures. In fact, Willoughby contends that these groups deserve "chief credit" for the budgetary improvements in the states. Finally, the well-publicized work of the Taft Commission on Economy and Efficiency contributed substantially to public interest in the possibilities of effective budgeting.

The combined effect of these forces became evident in the states after 1910. The first state law authorizing the governor to draft a budget for submission to the legislature was enacted in Ohio in 1910. In 1911 Wisconsin and California provided for improvements in state financial procedure, with at least some of the appearance of a budget system. In 1913 six states enacted budgetary laws. It was not until 1916, however, that Maryland adopted a thorough system of executive budget-making. After this, reform spread rapidly; by 1920, 44 states had adopted some kind of improvement in budgeting. Twenty-three of these provided for an executive budget.[43]

One of the most significant of state actions during this period was the budget proposal which emerged from the New York State Constitutional Convention of 1915. The distinguished lawyer and statesman Elihu Root delivered an address to the convention, on the subject of "invisible government" as a perversion of democracy.[44] To restore re-

[42] *Ibid.*, pp. 186–194; Cleveland, "Evolution of the Budget Idea in the United States," pp. 31–32.

[43] Cleveland and Buck, *The Budget and Responsible Government*, p. 124.

[44] Extracts from this speech are reprinted in *The Annals*, March 1916, pp. x–xiii.

sponsible control over the institutions of government, reforms were needed, particularly budgetary reform.   The convention heard testimony from members of the Taft Commission on Efficiency and Economy, who also helped to work out constitutional provisions for a budget system. A prominent Congressman, Fitzgerald, who had opposed the budget system for the federal government, now reversed his stand and testified in favor of a budget system for New York State.

The budget system as proposed by the constitutional convention would have provided for strong gubernatorial leadership, with a severe limitation on the power of the legislature: "The legislature may not alter an appropriation bill submitted by the governor except to strike out or reduce items therein . . ." (Article V, Section 1, of the proposed constitution).   The new constitution for New York State was rejected by the electorate, however, apparently not because of opposition to the budgeting provision, but because of other, more controversial features.[45]   A second significant state action during this period was in Maryland, where the legislature submitted a constitutional amendment to the electorate in 1916.   This was approved, establishing a strong budget system in that state, including the feature of "no legislative increase" which had been incorporated in the New York proposal.   Only two other states, New Mexico and Utah, adopted this feature in establishing their systems. The experience of Massachusetts was also important in the development of state systems.[46]   In that state, budget proposals were debated for a number of years and finally a budget system was adopted by popular vote as an amendment to the constitution in 1918.   The Boston Chamber of Commerce was a leading proponent of the system.   The budget was "sold" to the voters as an economy measure that would keep down state expenditures and state taxes.

The movement for budgetary reform in the states developed very little that was new beyond what had been developed in the struggles for the establishment of municipal budgets.   As in the case of the cities, the "friends of budgeting" were of two divergent groups: the reformers, who wanted to make governmental institutions more responsible and responsive, and organized taxpayer groups, who were promoting retrenchment in expenditures and reduction in taxation.   Together, these groups were responsible for the rapid spread of the budget system.

The one significantly different feature which might have emerged from this reform movement was the New York State plan for "no legislative

[45] Willoughby, *The Movement for Budgetary Reform in the States,* pp. 152–167.

[46] This is described at length in Luther H. Gulick, *Evolution of the Budget in Massachusetts,* Macmillan Company, New York, 1920.

increase," which would have greatly strengthened the executive's role in budgeting. But this feature was not widely adopted. The "legislative increase" system has continued to be characteristic of American budget systems, with a corresponding division of budgeting responsibility between the legislature and the executive.

E. The Establishment of the National Budget System, 1918–1921

One of the most interesting of the many books and articles written on budgeting in the years immediately preceding the adoption of the federal budget system is *Budget Making in a Democracy* by Edward A. Fitzpatrick.[47] The author, an experienced government administrator, influenced by the Wisconsin experiments in executive-legislative cooperation in budgeting, apparently began to be concerned over two aspects of "the budget idea." His first concern was the increase in executive power which was a necessary concommitant of the establishment of a budget system. The second was concern because the budget system was being used as a tool for retrenchment, not as a means for improving the efficiency and quality of governmental services.

Fitzpatrick's condemnation of the executive budget was severe:

Without the executive budget the dominant Prussian military caste could never have permeated the German people with its immoral ideas and made Germany synonymous with organized terror and frightfulness. [Page ix.]

And further:

The so-called "executive budget" program proposes a shifting of the center of gravity of our government. Its tendency is toward autocratic executive power. It would achieve this change in government as a by-product to the budget scheme. [Page 292.]

Similarly, Fitzpatrick had very little faith in economy and efficiency as objectives of governmental policy. Economy always meant reductions, he pointed out, not an improved level of services, and the budget system was the means invariably proposed for retrenchment in public expenditures. Fitzpatrick quoted critically a Chamber of Commerce statement of 1915 that the most important thing about a budget was its balance. Balance, he pointed out, was too frequently produced by senseless economy and the elimination of necessary services.

By nature a "reformer," Fitzpatrick was thoroughly disenchanted with "the budget idea" by 1918. It is impossible to determine how widely his views were held and whether or not the strong conservative backing which the budget system attracted served to alienate other reformers.

[47] Macmillan Company, New York, 1918.

It would appear that the original group from the New York Bureau of Municipal Research did not alter its conception of the budget as an instrument for revitalizing government. Dr. Cleveland, writing in 1920, found that the budget was a part of the movement for popular control of government which began with the trust-busting activities of President Theodore Roosevelt, that a budget system for the national government would be a necessary strengthening of the Presidency, and the Presidency must become an office for hearing what the people wanted and acting in response to their wishes.[48]

In the developments from the end of World War I to the passage of the Budget and Accounting Act of 1921, the voices of the reformers were lost in the outcry for economy and efficiency. The arguments for strengthening executive functions as a means of strengthening popular government, the case for the budget as an instrumentality of responsible *and* responsive government—these arguments were heard less often. It seems to have been a foregone conclusion that a national budget would be established within a short time. Most of the "academic" argument centered on the relative roles of the Executive and the Congress within that system. Most of the debate in Congress centered on the necessity for reducing the nation's tax burdens. The Congress became as much interested in accounting control as a means to economy as in the establishment of an executive budget office. Budget execution came to be regarded as at least as significant as budget formulation.

In 1919 the House of Representatives appointed a Select Committee on the Budget. The Committee covered much the same ground that had been traversed ten years before by the Taft Commission on Efficiency and Economy. The only important opposition to an executive budget system came from Congressional "die-hards," such as Speaker of the House Joseph Cannon, who argued in very forcible terms that the Pharaohs and the Czars of Russia had an executive budget system, but that it had not been embodied in the American constitution, and

> . . . when Congress consents to the Executive making the budget it will have surrendered the most important part of a representative government, and put this country back where it was when the shot at Lexington was "heard 'round the world.' "[49]

This kind of opposition seems not to have been taken very seriously. A number of members of Congress, particularly the Chairman of the House Appropriations Committee, pointed out that an executive budget system would strengthen and improve the ability of the Congress to con-

---

[48] Cleveland and Buck, *The Budget and Responsible Government,* pp. 101–102.
[49] Quoted in Browne, *The Control of the Public Budget,* pp. 80–81.

trol national finances.[50]   Neither was serious consideration given to the
proposal of the reformers that an executive budget system required that
the privilege of the floor of Congress be extended to Cabinet members
for purposes of presenting and defending their budget requests.[51]

The Select Committee on the Budget reported favorably on an executive budget system.   Congressional discussion on the report emphasized
the importance of the budget in restoring sound finance.   As Senator
Medill McCormick, chairman of the Senate Finance Committee, put it,
"The business men of the country are crying out for a national budget."[52]
The budget was conceived as a means of reducing expenditures and reducing taxes, particularly the excess profits tax, which was the special
target of business criticism in this period.

The House of Representatives took favorable action on the report of
the Select Committee on the Budget on October 21, 1919.   The Senate,
however, did not act at this session, because of the pressure of time occasioned by debate on the Versailles Treaty.   At the opening of the next
session of Congress, in December 1919, President Wilson recommended
the enactment of a national budget system.   In May of 1920 the House
and Senate completed action on the measure.

Had it not been for a somewhat unusual circumstance, the new budget
and accounting act would have gone into operation in 1920.   As a part
of the reform of federal finance, the Congress incorporated in the bill
the establishment of a General Accounting Office, to be headed by a
Comptroller General.   This officer would be appointed by the President
but could not be removed by him.   The Budget and Accounting Act of
1920 was vetoed by President Wilson on the ground that appointment
and removal power could not constitutionally be separated.[53]

The national elections in the fall of 1920 centered on issues deemed
more significant than a national budget system—such as American participation in the League of Nations—but the platforms of both major
parties nevertheless strongly endorsed the budget system.   With the Re-
publican victory in the elections and with President Harding pledged to
a "businesslike" administration, the passage of the Budget and Accounting Act was assured.   It eventually became law, in much the same form
as had been vetoed by Wilson, on June 10, 1921.   In his first budget
message President Harding said that this was " . . . the greatest refor-
mation in governmental practices since the beginning of the Republic."

[50] Congressman Swagar Sherley, *Congressional Record*, 65th Cong., 3d sess.,
1919, Vol. 57, pp. 4608–4614.

[51] Cleveland and Buck, *op. cit.*, pp. 385–406.

[52] *Congressional Record*, 66th Cong., 2d sess., 1920, Vol. 59, p. 619.   See also
the Senate debate on April 30, 1920, *Congressional Record*, 66th Cong. 2d sess.,
Vol. 59, pp. 6349–6356.

[53] *Congressional Record*, 66th Cong., 2d sess., 1920, Vol. 59, pp. 8609–8610.

The atmosphere of the time and prevailing attitudes toward the newly established national budget system are well revealed in a statement made by General Charles G. Dawes, the first director of the Bureau of the Budget. The occasion was the initiation of the work of the Bureau. The heads of all departments and agencies and their bureau chiefs were assembled in the auditorium of the Department of the Interior on June 21, 1921. The meeting was opened by President Harding. General Dawes then spoke, and as he concluded his address, he turned to the President:

> I wish to say to you, sir, that the men before you realize the cares and perplexities of your great position. They realize that at this time the business of our country is prostrated, that men are out of employment, that want and desperation stalk abroad, and that you ask us to do our part in helping you to lift the burden of taxation from the backs of the people by a reduction in the cost of government.[54]

F. Conclusion: Some Observations on Budgetary Reform

In the United States the budget system developed almost a century later than in western Europe. This laggard development is attributable not to the inherent slowness of the American mind, but to the relative unimportance of the financial operations of government in relation to the operations of the economy in the years prior to the first World War. The pressures for a budget system in the cities and in state governments came as these governments expanded their activities at the turn of the century, and again in the 1920's. The pressures for federal reform were strong only when federal outlays increased faster than the increase in economic activity, and only when this differential rate of expansion produced stringency in federal government finance.

It seems to be characteristic of government in the United States, and possibly in other countries as well, that administrative reforms do not proceed until a near crisis is reached. This was certainly the case with the development of budgeting in governmental units in the United States, and it continues to be true even today for counties and other local governments which do not yet have a modern budget system. The fact that there are known improvements in financial administration which can be made with a minimum of effort, that taxpayers' burdens could be eased, and that governmental programs could be made more effective, is not enough. It takes more than this to produce the pressures which result in a reform as sweeping as the installation of a budgetary system.

There can be no doubt that a budgeting system is a major govern-

---

[54] Charles G. Dawes, *The First Year of the Budget of the United States,* Harper & Brothers, New York, 1923, pp. 18–19.

mental reform, particularly in governmental units in this country. The installation of a budget system is implicit recognition that a government has positive responsibilities to perform and that it intends to perform them. This assumption of responsibility requires a concomitant organization of executive authority and an increase in the relative importance of governmentally organized economic power in relation to privately organized economic power.

For this reason the development of budgeting in the United States ran head-on into the doctrine of the separation of powers. The divisions between executive and legislative authority in the constitutions and the practices of governments in this country had to be greatly altered before budget systems could be established. In this respect the establishment of budget systems in the United States was "revolutionary"; it was both a product of and a contribution to a fundamental change in the structure of government.

This "revolution" was brought about by a peculiar combination of reformers—the professional political scientists and public servants, who wished to transform government into a positive instrument for social welfare, and the conservatives of the business community, who wished to reduce governmental expenditures and lower tax burdens. Both of these divergent groups subscribed to budget reform under the heading of "economy and efficiency," that phrase which seems to have such powerful appeal in American politics.

In the period of American history in which the budget system developed, it was certainly inevitable and probably not undesirable that the hard-headed "realists" in the business community should take over from the "academic" reformers. But a budget system in government was not then and should not now be regarded as synonymous with an increase in governmental activities. A budget system is synonymous with a clarification of responsibility in government, whether the range of governmental programs is broad or narrow.

Selected Bibliography

Agger, Eugene E., *The Budget in the American Commonwealths,* Columbia University Press, New York, 1907.

Browne, Vincent J., *The Control of the Public Budget,* Public Affairs Press, Washington, 1949, esp. pp. 50–90.

Buck, A. E., *Public Budgeting,* Harper & Brothers, New York, 1929, pp. 10–24.

Cleveland, Frederick A., "Evolution of the Budget Idea in the United States," *The Annals,* November 1915, pp. 15–35.

Cleveland, Frederick A., and Arthur Eugene Buck, *The Budget and Responsible Government*, Macmillan Company, New York, 1920, esp. pp. 3–129, 333–406.

Commission on Economy and Efficiency, *The Need for a National Budget*, 62d Cong., 2d sess., 1912, House Doc. No. 854.

Fitzpatrick, Edward A., *Budget Making in a Democracy*, Macmillan Company, New York, 1918.

Ford, Henry Jones, "Budget Making and the Work of Government," *The Annals*, November 1915, pp. 1–14.

—— *The Cost of Our National Government*, Columbia University Press, New York, 1910.

Gulick, Luther H., *The Evolution of the Budget in Massachusetts*, Macmillan Company, New York, 1920.

Laufenburger, Henry, *d'Économie et de Législation Financières, Budget et Trésor*, 3rd ed., Librairie du Recueil Sirey, Paris, 1948, pp. 24–44.

Lidderdale, D. W. S., *The Parliament of France*, Hansard Society, London, 1951, pp. 206–230.

MacGregor, D. H., *Public Aspects of Finance*, Clarendon Press, Oxford, 1939, pp. 7–66.

Marx, Fritz Morstein, "The Bureau of the Budget: Its Evolution and Present Role," *American Political Science Review*, August 1945, pp. 653–684.

Message of the President of the United States, *Economy and Efficiency in the Government Service*, 62d Cong., 2d sess., 1912, House Doc. No. 458.

Smithies, Arthur, *The Budgetary Process in the United States*, McGraw-Hill Book Company, New York, 1955, pp. 49–76.

Stourm, René, *The Budget*, translated by Thaddeus Plazinski, D. Appleton & Company, New York, 1917, pp. 24–49.

White, Leonard D., *The Federalists*, Macmillan Company, New York, 1948, pp. 323–347.

Willoughby, W. F., "The Budget," *Encyclopedia of the Social Sciences*, Vol. III, Macmillan Company, New York, 1930, pp. 38–44.

—— *The Problem of a National Budget*, D. Appleton & Company, New York, 1918, esp. pp. 55–73; 130–157.

—— *The National Budget System*, Johns Hopkins Press, Baltimore, 1927.

—— *The Movement for Budgetary Reform in the States*, D. Appleton & Company, New York, 1918.

Willoughby, William F., Westel W. Willoughby, and Samuel McCune Lindsay, *The System of Financial Administration of Great Britain*, D. Appleton & Company, New York, 1922, esp. pp. 23–182.

Wilmerding, Lucius, Jr., *The Spending Power*, Yale University Press, New Haven, 1943, pp. 167–179; 205–283.

Young, E. Hilton, *The System of National Finance*, 3rd ed., John Murray, London, 1936.

2.

Economic characteristics of government

Economic activity is conducted in a number of organizational forms. Goods and services are produced by households, by business firms, and by governments. Within these broad categories there are many variations and overlaps. Some households, such as farm families, are also business firms, and members of the household make decisions with respect to the allocation of resources and the pricing of these resources. Business firms sometimes possess governmental characteristics and make the kinds of decisions which might be made by governmental organizations. A privately owned public utility, for example, may be granted the power of eminent domain, so that land that it wishes to acquire may be secured by condemnation and forced sale, even as in the case of roads that are to be built and maintained by government.

Organizational forms for the conduct of economic activity shade off, one into the other. Sharp lines do not always divide that which is household activity from that which is business firm activity, nor divide that which is governmental from that which is nongovernmental. Some of the most difficult questions of public policy, of administration, and of budgeting come from these borderline areas, where the shadings are almost imperceptible.

Nevertheless, and in full recognition of the continuum character of organizational forms and functions, it is possible and indeed necessary to delineate the special economic attributes of public activity, those attributes which characteristically mark it off from activity conducted by households

31

and business firms. Only in this way can the aspects of governmental activity which are of particular importance for the subject of public budgeting be analyzed. This approach necessarily neglects the many factors which the private and public sectors have in common, such as internal organization and hierarchy, and the role of leadership.

An examination of the characteristics of decision-making in the public sector, first by way of contrast with the private sector and then in the terms which have been suggested by economic theorists, will be followed here by an analysis of the political character of public sector decisions. The chapter closes with a case study in public expenditures, which is intended to illustrate both the special attributes of the public sector and the nature of decision-making therein.

I. THE PRIVATE AND PUBLIC SECTORS IN A MARKET ECONOMY

In economic terms, the relationship to the market is the most important feature differentiating public from private activity. This relationship requires different mechanisms for decision-making and different criteria for judging the efficiency of resource allocation in government.

A. THE ROLE OF THE MARKET

The private sector of the economy, composed of households, business firms, and mixtures of the two, conducts its activities in the market. Resources, that is, the services of labor and capital, are hired or purchased, in a greater or lesser degree of competition, from other firms or from households functioning as firms. Products are sold in the market, in a greater or lesser degree of competition with other firms. The market, whether it be competitive or monopolistic in varying degrees, records the prices which are determined. Labor and capital (factors of production) move toward those employments, that is, are "allocated" where they are demanded. The factors and the prices which are paid for them stand in a *quid pro quo* relationship. In the market economy, in a crude sense, "you get what you pay for." At the same time, business firms must sell their products in the market. The revenue so derived must be adequate to compensate the factors and retain them in their particular employment.

Economic activities in the private sector are dominated by the profit motive. Those activities are conducted which will produce a profit. The success or failure of economic activity is determined primarily by the volume and/or rate of profit. (The term profit is used here to mean the income which is paid to or accrued for the owners of equity capital in a business firm.) The techniques which have been developed for recording and measuring economic activity in the private sector—accounting statements—are primarily designed to measure profit in terms of net income or changes in net worth.   These techniques provide the materials for decision-making in business firms.   This has been nowhere better stated than by Wesley C. Mitchell in 1912:

> Money-making is systematized by accounting in which all the diverse elements in a complicated series of bargains are adequately expressed in terms of one common denominator—the dollar.   Thus a businessman is enabled to compare the advantage of granting long credits with the advantage of selling on closer margins for cash; he can estimate whether it would be cheaper to buy a higher grade of coal or to let his fireboxes burn out rapidly; he can set off the cost of additional advertising against the cost of more traveling salesmen.   And since profits are also expressed in dollars, the businessman can control all items of expense on the basis of their estimated contributions toward his gains.   In making money, nothing but the pecuniary values of things however dissimilar need be considered, and pecuniary values can always be balanced, compared and adjusted in an orderly and systematic fashion.[1]

Neither the foregoing statements nor the quotation from Mitchell are intended to suggest that business firms always seek to maximize their short-run profits or that all decisions by business firms can be reduced to a monetary calculus.   There may be nonprofit or social objectives which motivate modern business enterprise.[2]   It is obvious, however, that no business can pursue nonprofit objectives unless, at the same time, it is making a profit.   Otherwise it will not long continue in existence.

With the market as a recording mechanism, with accounting statements for measurement, and with profit as a guide, the business firm has the essential tools for decision-making.   The public sector stands in marked contrast.   Only selected aspects of governmental activities are in the market.   Accounting statements measure a much smaller portion of significant performance.   Government revenue is not expected to exceed government expenditure, leaving a surplus for the "owners."

An analysis of the implications of these fundamental differences between private and public economic activity might well start with an examination of the distinct organizational arrangements which public activity may assume.[3]

[1] Wesley C. Mitchell, *The Backward Art of Spending Money*, Augustus M. Kelley, New York, 1950, pp. 12–13 (reprinted from the *American Economic Review*, June 1912).

[2] See Neil W. Chamberlain, *A General Theory of Economic Process*, Harper & Brothers, New York, 1955, pp. 232–243.

[3] For a quite different approach to the differences between the public and private sectors see Earl R. Rolph, *The Theory of Fiscal Economics*, University of California Press, Berkeley and Los Angeles, 1954, pp. 20–37.

In the public sector activities are conducted in three major forms.   One of these has operating characteristics very much like those of business firms.   This is called government enterprise, and its activities range from the production and sale of documents to the production and sale of atomic energy.   It is partially in the market sector of the economy, purchasing its factors and selling its products there.   The volume of products sold and the prices at which they are sold may differ, however, from a comparable private operation.   In many of its organizational characteristics, government enterprise is private in nature, but in its policy characteristics it is public.   Its operating policies are a part of general public policy. Expenditures are not necessarily limited by revenue.   A cash surplus may or may not be an objective of management.

A second organizational form is the trust fund, which is customarily isolated, at least in part, from other governmental organization and is used for such purposes as the conduct of a contributory system of social insurance.   Trust funds are likely to be wholly nonmarket.   A fund's revenue may come from taxes similar to those imposed for financing general government.   Expenditures, apart from administration, are generally transfer payments to legally specified beneficiaries, who are not expected to provide goods and services in return.

The third organizational form is general government—the traditional activities conducted by departments and agencies for such purposes as the protection of persons and property, defense, the provision of educational and health services, and the maintenance of a judicial and legislative system.   General government operates in the market with respect to its factors of production.   It must purchase labor, services, and materials in the factor market in competition with business firms.   But its revenue is not derived from the sale of goods and services.   Moreover, and unlike business firms, it does not seek to maximize its revenue, that is, increase its receipts in order to increase its net income above costs.   There is no *quid pro quo* relationship between general government as producer and the consumer of general government product.   No specific price tags are attached to government goods.   Payments are compulsory, in the form of taxation, and specific services are not rendered for specific tax payments.   The cost of general government is opportunity cost—the goods and services which taxpayers might have enjoyed if government revenues had not been collected.

The market as a guide and the goal of profit are not available for the organization and disciplining of the public sector.   It is conducted, as Colm has suggested, in terms of the "budget principle":

The essence of the budget principle is that the services in this sphere are determined not by profit expectation and the willingness of individuals to spend their money for the purchase of such services, but by decisions reached through political and administrative procedures and based on common social objectives.[4]

Even though a government's budget may not be comprehensive of all public activities, for present purposes the terms public economy and budget economy will be used synonymously. In this budget economy, with decisions administratively and politically determined, financial considerations are of a different order. The complicated series of bargains in a political and administrative framework are not adequately expressed in terms of one common denominator, the monetary or any other.

B. THE TEST OF EFFICIENCY

The fact that governmental activities are organized in accordance with the budget principle means that the objective test of efficiency which is ever-present in the market economy is lacking here. There are no tangible and self-enforcing criteria for judging efficiency in the public sector; in fact, there is a great deal of fuzziness in the use of the term in connection with governmental activities.

For business firms financial efficiency can be judged in terms of rates of net profit—a measure which, as noted, is not available to government.[5] Operating efficiency can be quantified in terms of product output per unit of factor (labor and capital) input. Increases in efficiency are then measurable in terms of increases in productivity. But efforts which have been made to apply these concepts to government operations have not proved fruitful.[6] The product of general government very often is not

---

[4] Gerhard Colm, "Why Public Finance?" *Essays in Public Finance and Fiscal Policy,* Oxford University Press, New York, 1955, p. 9; see also Colm's "Theory of Public Expenditures," *The Annals,* January 1936, pp. 1–11.

[5] The importance of the market as a test of efficiency is shown in the practices of some large firms. In General Motors, where one division of the company buys parts from another division, it would be impossible to determine whether one division was efficient, or was living on the efficiency of other divisions. Therefore, General Motors requires that the car divisions buy accessories where they can be secured at lowest cost in the market, with no requirement that they be purchased from other General Motors divisions. In this way the separate divisions' profit figures are meaningful and an objective test of efficiency can be applied. (See Peter F. Drucker, *Concept of the Corporation,* John Day Company, New York, 1946, pp. 63–71.)

[6] See the careful analysis of the factors which are involved in computations of productivity in government in Solomon Fabricant, *The Trend of Government Activity in the United States Since 1900,* National Bureau of Economic Research, New York, 1952, pp. 84–102. Fabricant's conclusion is, *"Total* productivity, output per combined unit of all resources, appears to have risen in government. It is well to emphasize the uncertainties surrounding this conclusion. Unable to

measurable in these terms, simply because it is not sold. National defense, educational services, and the administration of justice cannot be counted in units which are homogeneous over time. Moreover, the measurement of productivity in government as an index of efficiency would be distorted in all cases where unprofitable operations had been transferred from the private to the public sector.

Chester Barnard has suggested that survival is the ultimate test of efficiency.[7] In general, and over a period of time, this is certainly applicable to the private sector. The more or less impersonal forces of the market will see to it that firms which operate unsuccessfully in terms of net profit do not survive. The market is the ultimate disciplining agency. In the public sector survival may provide some generalized criterion for judging the efficiency of a governmental system over time, but survival provides no test of the efficiency of particular governmental programs at any one time. For example, some governments may build manufacturing plants, absorb initial losses, and, when the plants are operating efficiently as measured in financial terms, sell them to private firms. There are many government emergency programs designed to deal with economic disaster or natural disaster, and planned for extinction as soon as they have been "efficient" in accomplishing their purpose. Survival is not the test here—the more rapidly the mission is accomplished, the sooner the program is terminated. Conversely, a governmental system may survive, or an administration may survive politically in spite of the fact that it conducts some particular programs very badly.

The difficulties in establishing an objective test of governmental efficiency make public operations a target for criticism which cannot easily be refuted. American political life is characterized by sweeping charges against "inefficient bureaucracy" and "wasteful government." These charges, often unsupported, are likely to continue because there is no way of comparing the financial efficiency of a private and a public venture. It is not now possible, and will never be possible, to make any general efficiency comparisons between the U. S. Treasury Department and the Department of the Interior, to say nothing of making efficiency comparisons between the Bethlehem Steel Corporation and the Treasury Department.

---

weigh all the factors affecting productivity, we cannot be sure what the net balance is . . . . Whether government productivity rose more or less rapidly than productivity in private enterprise is another matter, and one on which lack of information makes it idle to speculate." (Pp. 99–101.)

[7] Chester I. Barnard, *The Functions of the Executive,* Harvard University Press, Cambridge, 1946, pp. 40–44; 92–95. Barnard is careful to point out that the efficiencies of separate aspects of any organization are noncomparable.

Some kinds of partial comparisons can be made, and they may have a limited usefulness. In certain circumstances it may be possible to compare the cost and output of stenographers in the Treasury Department with the cost and output of stenographers engaged in similar operations in the Department of the Interior. Comparisons might be extended, without encountering formidable conceptual difficulties, to the stenographers of the Bethlehem Steel Corporation. But these comparisons of specific and measurable operations do not reveal the efficiency of operations as a whole. These will remain as noncomparable as the efficiency of the housewife, also in the nonmarket sector of the economy, and the efficiency of the housewife's husband in his activities in the market sector of the economy.

There remain the tests for efficiency of governmental operations that measure the improvement in comparable operations within the same agency over a period of time. These are important, and the techniques which are developing in this area are significant, although frequent technological and program changes limit their usefulness. (See Chapter 6.) The maximum development along these lines will not, however, provide unambiguous comparisons among government agencies or between the public and the private sectors.

Some have argued that the dissimilarities between the market economy and the budget economy are not as sharp as suggested here, and that the budget operates or should operate in the public sector to enforce efficiency in the same way that the market enforces efficiency in the private sector.[8] This argument claims too much for public budgeting. The budgetary process can make for better-informed judgments concerning the allocation of government resources and can encourage the more effective use of resources devoted to particular purposes. But public budgeting does not have access to the same kinds of objective tests which the market provides as a guide to resource allocation in the private sector. The maximum application of existing measurement techniques and those yet to be devised will not reveal government's contribution to the total economic, social, and political environment.

Decisions about the effectiveness of governmental operations will always be conditioned by such things as the attitudes of the persons and groups who are served by programs, by the success of programs in improving the material conditions of such persons and groups, by the attitudes of influential but non-affected persons and groups, and by the attitudes of

[8] Herbert A. Simon, *Administrative Behavior,* Macmillan Company, New York, 1947, pp. 172–197; Herbert A. Simon, Donald W. Smithburg, and Victor A. Thompson, *Public Administration,* Alfred A. Knopf, New York, 1950, pp. 488–512.

persons and groups who are adversely affected. Because judgments about governmental efficiency are so conditioned, the problems of measurement are and will continue to be elusive and difficult.

II. THE SIZE AND COMPONENTS OF GOVERNMENT

The budget principle does not expand into a neat set of rules for determining the kinds of activities which shall be deemed to be governmental in character, or for determining whether activities which are already deemed to be governmental in character shall be expanded or contracted. Fixed guidelines are not possible as long as there are changes in the structure of a society. An agrarian economy, for example, will call forth certain attitudes toward the role of government and the volume and variety of governmental functions. An industrialized economy will give rise to a different pattern of governmental needs. As John Dewey has said,

> Roughly speaking, tools and implements determine occupations, and occupations determine the consequences of associated activity. In determining consequences, they institute publics with different interests, which exact different types of political behavior to care for them.[9]

Similarly, changes in social structure will affect attitudes toward and the utilization of governmental power. For example, the responsibility of the family for its aged members will shape the nature of the government's welfare programs. The prestige, or lack of it, which attaches to government employment will shape a society's attitude toward the use of governmental authority.

The changing nature of the economic order and social attitudes, and the changing nature of government therein make for extreme difficulty in attempts to analyze the two overriding problems of budgeting: the determination of the size of the public sector, and the allocation of expenditures within the public sector.

A. Size of the Public Sector

Many of the factors which account for the size of the public sector are measurable, and numerous efforts have been made down the years to isolate these factors. As long ago as 1892, the German economist Adolph Wagner formulated the "law of increasing state activity": governments

---

[9] *Intelligence in the Modern World, John Dewey's Philosophy,* Joseph Ratner, ed., Modern Library, New York, 1939, p. 373.

tend to increase in size more than in proportion to the increase in population. He attributed this to urbanization and industrialization, and his "law" was buttressed by data on the ratio of population to land area.

In the 1930's, in a study of state and local government outlay, Colm identified four interrelated factors that account for variations in expenditure: the need for public services, the desire for superior public services, the resources available for governmental use, and the cost of public services.[10] More recently, Fabricant has undertaken an extensive statistical investigation of the quantity and variety of governmental activities in the United States, and Musgrave and Culbertson have conducted a similar although narrower survey.[11]

This kind of statistical investigation is useful and provides considerable ex post facto insight into the determinants of the size and scope of governmental activities. It does indicate secular trends, but it is not particularly helpful in the solution of the specific problems referred to here—the determination, at any particular time, that an activity should or should not be conducted by government, or that it should be expanded or contracted. These are, however, the decisions which must be made in public budgeting.

Economists, from time to time, have attempted to provide the needed canons for guidance. As is well known, Adam Smith laid down some hard and fast rules to regulate and limit the activity of the state. Expenditures could be appropriately made for defense, for justice, for public works and institutions, and for the dignity of the sovereign. The public works and institutions category could include outlays for the facilitation of commerce in general, particular branches of commerce, and institutions for the education of the youth and for the instruction of people of all ages.[12] Other kinds of governmental expenditures, such as for gov-

[10] Gerhard Colm, "Public Expenditures and Economic Structure in the United States," *Social Research*, February 1936, pp. 57–77. For a discussion of the factors which have contributed to the growth of all governmental expenditures, such as urbanization, economic insecurity, and the growth of humanitarianism, see Leverett S. Lyon and Victor Abramson, *Government and Economic Life*, Vol II, The Brookings Institution, Washington, 1940, pp. 1139–1146. For an approach to the delineation of the public and private sector on the basis of individual and collective wants see Theo Suranyi-Unger, *Private Enterprise and Governmental Planning*, McGraw-Hill Book Company, New York, 1950, pp. 9–33.

[11] Fabricant, *The Trend of Government Activity in the United States Since 1900*, esp. pp. 3–9, 42–83; R. A. Musgrave and J. M. Culbertson, "The Growth of Public Expenditures in the United States, 1890–1948," *National Tax Journal*, June 1953, pp. 97–115.

[12] Adam Smith, *The Wealth of Nations*, Modern Library, New York, 1937, pp. 653–768.

ernment enterprise, were unjustifiable. This kind of rigid formulation was most obviously inspired by Smith's desire to curb the governmental excesses of mercantilism and to attempt to ensure that England's emerging industrialism would not be hampered by the excessive taxation which accompanied excessive expenditure.

The least that can be said for the Smithian approach to determination of the size of the public sector is that it minimized the problems which must be solved by statesmen. Jean-Baptiste Say's famous dictum, "The very best of all plans of finance is to spend little," was an attitude which served to defeat the demands for additional governmental expenditures. But the rigidity of the Smithian approach could not long survive, particularly when the necessity for combating mercantilist tendencies in government ceased to be important. By 1848, John Stuart Mill could be concerned lest governmental interferences were " . . . overstepping the boundaries of the universally acknowledged functions . . . ," but he was not adamant and added[13]

> . . . there is scarcely anything really important to the general interest, which it may not be desirable, or even necessary, that the government should take upon itself, not because private individuals cannot effectively perform it, but because they will not.

By the last half of the 19th century western European governments were moving further and further from the Smithian ideal. Although there were occasional forceful restatements of the position, as in Herbert Spencer's *Social Statics*, first published in 1850, there was a general absence of attention to guiding principles for the determination of the kinds and quantities of activities which governments should undertake. It has been noted, for example, that in Parliamentary debates in Britain during this time, whether on the budget or on other matters, there was an avoidance of appeal to doctrine. Such terms as *laissez faire* were never used in support of policy positions.[14]

The decline of the Smithian principles as a guide for determining whether activities were properly governmental or nongovernmental left a void in the economics of political theory. Governments conducted more activities, assumed increasing responsibilities, and regulated more aspects of private economic activity. Many of these additional governmental activities were undertaken in efforts to modify or offset the economic consequences of a rapidly expanding economy. But they were

[13] John Stuart Mill, *Principles of Political Economy*, Ashley edition, Longmans, Green & Co., London, 1929, pp. 801, 978.

[14] D. H. MacGregor, *Public Aspects of Finance*, Clarendon Press, Oxford, 1939, pp. 14–20.

accompanied by few efforts at systematic rationalization of the things governments were doing. (The writings of the socialists are not in point here, since they were not interested in retaining the conduct of economic activity in private hands.)

An attempt to fill the void came in the last quarter of the 19th century, following the elaboration of marginalism as an explanation for consumer and market behavior in the private sector. In public finance these principles were first applied to taxation, then to government expenditures, and then to the equilibrating of private and public activities. Since this approach continues to have considerable influence in the writings of theoretical economics, under the general head of welfare economics, it will suffice to examine its current status rather than to attempt to trace its development. For this purpose Professor Pigou's third edition of *A Study in Public Finance* will be assumed to be authoritative. The problem which Pigou examines is that of maximizing the community's welfare:

> Expenditure should be distributed between battleships and Poor Relief in such wise that the last shilling devoted to each of them yields the same return of satisfaction. . . . This method of approach suggests an analogous test for determining how large government expenditure in the aggregate ought to be. If a community were literally a unitary being, with the government as its brain, expenditure should be pushed in all directions up to the point at which the satisfaction obtained from the last shilling expended is equal to the satisfaction lost in respect of the last shilling called up on government service.[15]

Pigou contends that this theoretical statement enables some useful deductions to be drawn. From these he concludes that: (1) the optimum amount of government expenditure is likely to be larger, with a given population, where the aggregate income of the community is larger; (2) if there are promising opportunities for public expenditure and less promising opportunities for private expenditure, the amount of public expenditure will be larger; (3) if income is relatively concentrated in the hands of a few rich persons, the amount of marginal sacrifice entailed in raising additional revenue will be less and public expenditure can be correspondingly larger; (4) if taxation is progressive, there will be less marginal sacrifice imposed on the community than if taxation is regressive.

But, as Pigou points out, there are limitations on this approach. The community is not a unitary being. The desire of some persons that the

---

[15] A. C. Pigou, *A Study in Public Finance*, Macmillan & Co., Ltd., London, 1951, p. 31.

community possess battleships will be influenced by what other persons are willing to provide in the way of battleships. Further, there are costs of administration in the collection of revenues and costs of compliance for taxpayers. Thus, taxes inflict indirect damage on taxpayers as a body, a damage which is not revealed in the sacrifice represented simply by the amount of tax which is paid. Taxes should not be pressed to the point where public satisfaction equates private dissatisfaction. A gap should be left to cover the amount of indirect damage.

The difficulties which Pigou points out, however, are not the whole of the problem of applying marginalism to the determination of the proper size of the government sector. This is not a full exploration of the case.

In the private sector it may be conceived that individuals apportion their expenditure among different goods so that the marginal return of satisfaction is the same for all resources that are employed. There is a market mechanism available for recording the results of this apportionment, and it is possible that by this means resource applications and satisfactions are balanced. But in the public sector the situation is quite different. Here the measurement of the satisfactions lost from the last shilling called up and the satisfactions derived from the last shilling expended must be politically determined. The decisions, once made, are implemented by coercion. Taxes are collected whether or not taxpayers are willing to be subjected to the loss of satisfactions; expenditures are made without specific regard to the *individual* satisfactions of benefited persons. The satisfactions derived from private expenditures may be presumed to be generally reflected in market values, although these satisfactions can never be compared directly. Neither can the satisfactions from public expenditures be compared, and there are no market values. Marginal social benefit and marginal social cost are attractive phrases, but they are devoid of explicit content.

There is an additional and important limitation which attaches to the comparisons of costs and benefits. In the initial elaborations of marginalism applied to the public sector it was assumed that government expenditures are always tax-financed. That is, public expenditures come from funds diverted from the private sector. In this capacity the government is resource-using, and its tax-expenditure operation means a corresponding loss in resource use in the private sector. But this condition, as has been stressed since Keynes, is relevant only when the economy is operating at relatively full employment. When there are unemployed resources in the private sector, their use by government is costless to the private sector in terms of lost product. In these circumstances the public sector may be increased in size by the use of nontax revenue such as borrowing, without a corresponding cost in resources foregone and with a resulting increase in total product. The initial increase in public activities may also generate secondary increases in the private sector. The size of the public sector may be increased, with a resulting increase in total economic activity and in the absolute amount of private activity. (See Chapter 3.)

B. Allocation of Public Expenditures

On what basis shall it be decided that government shall spend on X or Y—for battleships rather than poor relief? This presents some characteristics which differ from the "size" question.

Economists who have written about the allocation of public expenditures have generally attempted to argue that economic factors must be isolated from other influences, or have attempted to apply marginal analysis to this problem, or both.

There are those who argue simply that decisions affecting the distribution of government expenditures are political decisions, governed by noneconomic factors. This is put in various terms. Sometimes it is contended that political judgments are value judgments but that economic judgments are (or should be) stripped of normative elements.[16] It is argued that economics is concerned only with means and not with ends—the allocation of scarce resources toward societal goals which are otherwise determined. Or it is simply asserted that political factors are exogenous to the economics under consideration.

However the argument is put, economics and politics are always separated, and very often, at least implicitly, it is assumed that economics is a rational science, but that political influences are irrational, unpredictable, and frequently evil. Needless to say, this approach to public policy is embraced by almost no political scientist, but it does pervade much of what economists write about public finance, sometimes creeping in unobserved.

The approach to the allocation of public expenditures based on marginal principles is similar to that indicated above. To restate this argument: public expenditures should be allocated so that the additional satisfactions derived from the final unit of expenditure on each yields equal satisfactions—the principle of the equivalence of final expenditure.

It would be difficult to object to the statement that legislators and administrators are continuously engaged in balancing out satisfactions and dissatisfactions. The political process itself could even be described as an exercise in marginalism. But such a description would have only ex

---

[16] For a thorough dissection of this point of view as applied to public finance see Gunnar Myrdal, *The Political Element in the Development of Economic Theory*, Harvard University Press, Cambridge, 1954, pp. 156–190.

post facto validity. At the time when decisions are in process, marginal theory provides no guidelines for the allocation of public expenditures. The formidable obstacle which this approach encounters is that benefits from alternative government expenditures cannot be compared with one another. Those who have attempted to pursue this approach, whether in marginal terms or in terms of welfare economics, have frequently recognized the problem of noncomparability, but have concluded not that the approach is wrong, but that a scale of values must be developed. Guest, writing at the height of interest in marginalism as applied to problems of public finance, contended that we needed a new system of social accounting with which to weigh the price and nonprice factors. He thought that this system must result in a uniform pattern of measurement:

> These difficulties [in allocating public expenditures] can be cleared away only as it is made possible to think in definite quantitative terms of these other values that cannot be described adequately in terms of price. That such may be the case soon is to be most fervently hoped.[17]

This system of social accounting has not been developed and the problem of noncomparability remains unsolved. No amount of theorizing will be able to overcome this in a society addicted to plural values that cannot be measured in terms of price.[18]

III. BUDGETING IN A POLITICAL FRAMEWORK

The factors which determine the allocation of public expenditures are shaped by the machinery of government and by the private pressures which are brought to bear on the decision-makers. As V. O. Key stated, in commenting on the absence of criteria for determining whether X dollars should be allocated to activity A rather than to activity B,

> Perhaps the approach toward the practical working out of the issues lies in the canalizing of decisions through the governmental machinery so as to

[17] Harold W. Guest, *Public Expenditure,* G. P. Putnam's Sons, New York, 1927, p. 173.

[18] Compare Richard Abel Musgrave, "The Voluntary Exchange Theory of Public Economy," *Quarterly Journal of Economics,* February 1939, pp. 213–237; James M. Buchanan, "The Pure Theory of Government Finance," *Journal of Political Economy,* December 1949, pp. 496–505. For an attempt to revive a pure form of marginalism as applied to budgeting see Verne B. Lewis, "Toward a Theory of Budgeting," *Public Administration Review,* Winter 1952, pp. 42–54. The alternative budget scheme which Lewis suggests has considerably more usefulness than the theoretical framework in which he places it. See Chapter 10.

place alternatives in juxtaposition and compel consideration of relative values.[19]

The development of an adequate approach to decision-making in the allocation of public resources must recognize the interrelation of (1) the governmental machinery, and the administrator and legislator therein, in providing a mechanism for arriving at decisions; and (2) the influence of groups that are affected by public expenditures in shaping and molding the decision. Beyond these two, there is the influence of the facts—the measurement of specific benefits which have come and can come from specific expenditures.

The organizational structures which are established for decision-making and the procedures which are involved enter into all aspects of public budgeting and will be treated in other places in this volume.[20] At this point only two aspects of this complex will be examined—the political character of decision-making in government with specific reference to the position of the administrator, and the influence of interest groups.

A. ROLE OF THE ADMINISTRATOR

In the first important writings on public administration at the turn of the century, decision-making in government was analyzed in terms of a separation between "politics" and "administration." Writing primarily about American government, influenced by the formal separation of legislative and administrative authority, and motivated by a desire to support civil service systems, the early theorists stressed that policy was formulated primarily by the legislature and that it was the responsibility of the administrator to carry out this policy in accordance with certain principles which were intended to guide him.[21] Such policy determinations as were made within administrative agencies were the responsibility of appointed officials, subject to removal and control of elected officials. The formulation of policy rested exclusively with those who could be directly controlled by the electoral process.

In recent years a quite different approach has come to dominate the analysis of decision-making in government. It has been pointed out by

[19] V. O. Key, Jr., "The Lack of a Budgetary Theory," *American Political Science Review*, December 1940, p. 1142.

[20] For example, Chapter 10 deals with budgetary decisions at the agency level, Chapter 11 with the central budget office, and Chapter 12 with the legislature.

[21] See, for example, Frank J. Goodnow, *Politics and Administration*, Macmillan Company, New York, 1900, esp. pp. 1–22. For an excellent summary of the development of this doctrine of "separation of powers" as applied to public administration see Dwight Waldo, *The Administrative State*, Ronald Press Company, New York, 1948, pp. 104–129.

such observers as Appleby that a distinction between policy and administration is not descriptive of the operating reality of government; that the legislature makes policy, of course, but so do administrators; that the administrator is subject to many of the same kinds of political pressures in making his decisions as are the legislators; that policy is made where decisions are made; and that this is not confined to the upper reaches of the hierarchy of a government agency, nor to the corridors of the legislature.[22]

This approach to decision-making illuminates a good number of problems which, up to this time, had not been well understood. It emphasizes that power and authority in government do not reside in elected representatives alone, and it centers attention on the importance of securing responsibility in administration. The administrator is not responsible solely to elected representatives, to the chief executive, or to the Congress. The administrator operates—makes decisions—in an extremely complex pattern of responsibility. The materials for his decisions come from many and diverse sources, as Appleby says:

> The process of democratic public administration is one of group judgment at each hierarchal level, judgment of groups of levels, group judgment subject to review, modification, revocation, and punitive action in any one of the many higher levels as consequences of the judgment's having come to bear upon citizens and having become subject to the reaction of citizens. It is a process in which facilities of appeal and levels of review are more numerous, various, and open than in any other action-laden process yet devised. It is a process carried on in an environment more critical and more politically active and potent than the environment of any other administrative process. It is a process in which the pattern of responsibility runs to public representativeness of many kinds and roles, to subordinates, to associates in the same unit, to contiguous and related units with somewhat different responsibilities, to higher executive levels where repose broader responsibilities; it runs outward to special publics, outward from higher levels to other and larger publics, outward and upward from executive agencies to the Chief Executive, to the Congress, and to the general public.[23]

Further, there can be no separation of economics from politics in governmental decision-making. "The intermingling of economics and politics within the executive branch is just one aspect of the general intertwining of politics and administration."[24] Economic considerations are

[22] See, in particular, Paul H. Appleby, *Policy and Administration*, University of Alabama Press, University, Alabama, 1949, pp. 1–25; *Morality and Administration*, Louisiana State University Press, Baton Rouge, 1952, pp. 121–140.

[23] *Morality and Administration*, p. 251.

[24] Paul H. Appleby, "The Influence of the Political Order," *American Political Science Review*, April 1948, p. 274.

not of a higher order than political considerations. Both must be merged in the materials which are the basis of policy decisions. "If economists are to be of greater service in advising on public policy, they must recognize frankly the inseparability of economic and political analysis and gird themselves to do a better job."[25] The same point has been made by Congressman Cannon in commenting on United States government programs:

> . . . no economic program rightly called the federal government's will ever show much resemblance to an economist's dream—or even to the composite picture of the dreams of a thousand economists. The reason is obvious. Legislation is political business. It is the business of compounding distinct and divergent interests into progressively broader understandings and agreements.[26]

The pattern of responsibility which is inherent in any governmental program may be illustrated by a relatively simple example—an example which will also incidentally illustrate some of the difficulties in determining the efficiency of governmental operations.

Suppose that a city council, after reviewing the demands for various municipal services for the forthcoming year, authorizes a lump sum of $250,000 for the public library for operating purposes. Suppose that the librarian has freedom to determine his program within the limits of this appropriation and decides to curtail the purchase of new books, spending the funds which are saved on the encouragement of the use of the library. Lighting facilities are improved; the reading room is brightened up with curtains; some new chairs are purchased for the children's room; the periodicals are placed on open shelves. In addition, the librarian devotes his energies to publicizing the facilities of the library. He makes speeches in the public schools and before clubs and organizations. He arranges for book review luncheons. He sponsors a Great Books session every week in the library. Let it be assumed that his efforts are successful, and at the end of the year the use of the library is greatly increased. Whereupon, the community's demand for library facilities is enlarged, and in the next annual budget the city council sees fit to increase the appropriation to $300,000. The librarian can now purchase the new books that he did not buy the year before.

Has the librarian acted in an "efficient" fashion? As a result of his

[25] B~rtram M. Gross, in a review of *The Nineteen Fifties Come First* by Edwin G. Nourse, *American Political Science Review,* September 1951, p. 872. Nourse's views are somewhat different from those expressed here. See his *Economics in the Public Service,* Harcourt, Brace & Company, New York, 1953, esp. pp. 5–28.

[26] Clarence Cannon, "Congressional Responsibilities," *American Political Science Review,* April 1948, p. 308.

decisions the city ends up by spending more, not less, on the library. Citizens find that they devote more of their spare time to reading and less to other leisure-time activities. If they formerly patronized night clubs, thereby absorbing a quantity of police protection services, it may be that the number of police prowl cars can now be reduced.

This hypothetical case illustrates a number of the characteristics of the operations of the public sector and the role of the administrator therein.

First, it is evident that the administrator, as in this not extraordinary situation, may have great leeway in the determination of policy, that is, in the determination of what constitutes a "good" library.

Second, the resources which are available to the administrator are by no means rigidly limited. He can create the demand that additional resources be devoted to the program which is under his supervision. It may be noted that these additional resources might be diverted from other governmental programs, or they might represent a net addition to governmental resources, that is, the city council may authorize higher taxes in order to provide an increase in funds for the library.

Third, the community does not have a set of values that determine the amount of resources which will be used for the operation of libraries or any other governmental function. These values are operationally determined and are always in the process of being determined. The community decides that it wants a library. The librarian then shapes the community's demand for libraries by the way in which he administers. The kind and size of the library will be determined by the librarian's program and by the response of the community to that program.[27]

Fourth, the form in which the budget is presented and approved will determine the distribution of decision-making power between the administrator and the legislature. In the case here it was assumed that the librarian had considerable freedom to allocate the funds available to him. But if the city council were to specify in advance each detail of expenditure in the librarian's budget, his decision-making authority would be drastically limited.

Fifth, budget-making provides the occasion for periodic review and reassessment of community needs and resources. The community does and should change its mind about libraries from time to time. The periodicity inherent in budgeting provides the occasion for translating these policy changes into operating programs.

[27] See Norton E. Long, "Public Policy and Administration: The Goals of Rationality and Responsibility," *Public Administration Review*, Winter 1954, pp. 22–31. For a very different view of the determination of community values, and the role of the administrator therein, see Simon, *Administrative Behavior*, pp. 186–188; also, Clarence E. Ridley and Herbert A. Simon, *Measuring Municipal Activities*, International City Managers' Association, Chicago, 1938, pp. 1–9.

B. Interest Groups and the Budget

Decisions concerning the size of the budget, the distribution of revenues, and the distribution of expenditures are political decisions, which both reflect and affect the possession of power by economic groups and classes. The decisions that emerge and are called public policy are greatly influenced by the interplay and the resolution of forces which may be generally described as interest groups.[28] There are, of course, other influences at work. The analysis of interest groups does not constitute an inclusive approach to political behavior. The dynamics of personal leadership, the role of organized political parties, the influence of cultural values, creeds, and dogmas, the structure of an economic system—all of these and many more will shape that which is called public policy. Interest groups are singled out here because of their particular impact on budgetary decisions.

It was noted that the public sector is characterized by the absence of readily measurable criteria to guide the allocation of resources. It is not possible to determine, beyond the possibility of controversy, that X dollars spent on A will produce more "good" for society than X dollars spent on B. However, one of the ways by which it can be determined whether it is wise to spend X dollars on A rather than on B is to ask persons interested in A and B what they think.

This is one aspect of interest group activity which is of greatest importance for public budgeting, and which influences decisions made by administrators in the formulation of the budget and decisions made by legislators who modify and adopt the budget. Organizations and associations, whether they be representative of employees, manufacturers, or farmers, or representative of the vitreous china manufacturers of Syracuse, New York, or the growers of corn in Emmet County, Iowa, or

[28] Political scientists have written at length on this subject, and from various points of view. See, for example, the early work of E. Pendleton Herring, *Group Representation Before Congress,* John Hopkins Press, Baltimore, 1929; and *Public Administration and the Public Interest,* McGraw-Hill Book Company, New York, 1936. Also, Avery Leiserson, *Administrative Regulation,* University of Chicago Press, Chicago, 1942; David B. Truman, *The Governmental Process,* Alfred A. Knopf, New York, 1953; V. O. Key, Jr., *Politics, Parties and Pressure Groups,* Thomas Y. Crowell Company, New York, 1948. Apart from the earlier work of the institutionalists, such as Veblen and Commons, few economists in recent years have devoted very much attention to group and organizational problems. Important contributions, however, are Robert A. Brady, *Business as a System of Power,* Columbia University Press, New York, 1943; Kenneth E. Boulding, *The Organizational Revolution,* Harper & Brothers, New York, 1953; John Kenneth Galbraith, *American Capitalism,* Houghton Mifflin Company, Boston, 1952; Chamberlain, *A General Theory of Economic Process,* esp. pp. 259–281.

representative of predominantly noneconomic groups such as veterans and religious organizations, must and should make their views known on matters which affect them. In this way policy-making officials will become informed of the probable consequences of their decisions. This is a part of the adequate knowledge and consideration which officials must possess before their decisions can be made responsibly.

The fact that the interest groups have a legitimate role to play in relation to the formulation of governmental policy need not mean that the decision-maker is a helpless pawn in the hands of the dominant groups. In some cases the decision-making administrator may act solely to affirm the compromises that are reached by the interaction of forces beyond his control. But in other cases there is opportunity for the organization of compromise, for the sublimation of issues, for the invention of solutions, and for the assertion of what is deemed to be a larger and wider interest as a counter to what is deemed a narrower and special interest. When these possibilities exist, the administrator, as Redford has said,

> . . . should have competence in measuring possibilities and in discovering techniques for manipulating organism in terms of directive. It is the function of the political superstructure to see that he does not forget that his manipulative powers are subordinate powers, to be exercised in terms of the community purpose embodied in directives. It must also be the function of the political superstructure to provide some guiding concept of public purpose.[29]

In making decisions the administrator can play a partially independent role in the formulation of policy.[30] To him the public delegates some discretion. In some circumstances the administrator can assume active leadership in shaping and molding community support for or against specific proposals. The possibilities of this sort will vary in accordance with the program and in accordance with influences which are at work in the interest groups and in organized political parties. The relationship of the administrator to the community is not a static one.

---

[29] Emmette S. Redford, *Administration of National Economic Control*, Macmillan Company, New York, 1952, p. 231.

[30] There are important dissents to this view, particularly from those who emphasize that governmental decision-making is bound by the interest groups and their influence. See Earl Latham, *The Group Basis of Politics,* Cornell University Press, Ithaca, 1952, pp. 1–53, where it is contended that the characteristic which distinguishes government from other groups is that it is endowed with "officiality," an endowment which occurs only after interest group influences have been resolved and compromised. Also, Herbert Agar, *The Price of Union,* Houghton Mifflin Company, Boston, 1950, where this approach is applied to the analysis of political parties and their lack of principles.

IV. CASE STUDY: A NEW HIGH SCHOOL OR A SEWERAGE SYSTEM?

Some of the foregoing interrelations may be illustrated by a hypothetical case study. Although the elements of the problem are relatively uncomplicated, even this case will exhibit a fairly intricate pattern.

Let it be assumed that Central City, with a population of about 200,000, has a capital improvements program linked with its annual budget. After the Mayor and the City Council have determined the tax rate which it is feasible to collect, have counted the revenue from the state in the form of grants and gifts, have estimated what may be available from local nontax resources, and have pruned the operating budget of the city to its customary minimum, there remains this year $2 million for financing capital improvements.

As with most cities, this sum falls far short of the demands. The streets and highways are in a bad state of repair; motorists are complaining bitterly that their auto repair bills are excessive. The parents in the South Side Development, where juvenile delinquency is rampant, want playground facilities. The dreams for making Central City the air capital of the state will fade fast unless a new runway is constructed at the local airport. Water supplies are short and industry cannot expand unless new and expensive mains are built. The schools are badly overcrowded. The sewerage system is inadequate to handle the growth in the city's population; storm sewers do not take care of the overflow. Moreover, raw sewage has been dumped in the lake for the past several years because the treatment plant has broken down. The fish are dead and the lake can no longer be used for swimming.

In this situation let it be assumed that the Mayor is successful in reducing these demands to two: a new high school and a new sewerage system. Confronted with the necessity for a choice between these, the Mayor and the City Council will need, if it is not already in existence, an organizational structure for assisting in decision-making. This organization will be called the Capital Improvements Commission (CIC). The CIC has responsibility for recommending a solution to the Mayor, who in turn will transmit the recommendation, with or without modification, to the Council, which has the power of modification, approval, or rejection. Let it be further assumed that if the CIC does its work well, the Mayor and the Council will approve its recommendations without modification. The CIC must therefore have an organizational structure which is realistic in terms of its decision-making responsibilities.

This hypothetical case, while generally realistic in terms of municipal government, has been somewhat oversimplified. It has been assumed, in order to center attention on the allocation of expenditures, that the size of the public sector is fixed. In practice, this is not usually the case.

The CIC must establish an organizational structure which will enable it to perform three functions. These may be designated "expertise," "communications," and "responsibility." These functions need not be separated in terms of personnel. Those who are expert may also communicate with interested persons. Those who communicate may also be responsible for the decision. In the final stages of decision-making the functions merge, although in their initial performance they may be separated. In order to discharge its responsibilities the CIC needs a hierarchy—a commission made up of "representative" citizens and government officials and a staff made up of "experts"—and an interplay among levels of hierarchy.

The expertise function consists of *measurement* and *comparison*. Typically, it will be undertaken by the staff, by persons trained in economics, in sociology, in administration, and in engineering, or at least by persons who are competent to assess the importance of economic, sociological, administrative, and engineering considerations.

The measurements which should be undertaken are those which will show, first, what the city now has, and second, what it would get from additional expenditures. For existing school buildings this will require estimates of such items as pupils per room, the utilization of buildings, the present and prospective pupils distributed by age group and area within the city, and measurements of the age, condition, and useful life of school buildings. The possible consequences of the $2 million expenditure must also be measured, again in terms of such specifics as the resulting distribution of pupils per room and the listing of educational services which might be provided by the new building.

Comparisons must include those with the educational plants of other cities in the same state. The adequacy of governmental expenditures is always judged on a relative basis, and the only guidelines for this purpose are other jurisdictions that undertake comparable activities. A study of educational service levels in other cities may provide the materials on which the staff can construct an arbitrary "minimum needs requirement." The very elaboration of such a requirement and its publication will tend to influence community judgment and stimulate community effort to move toward this arbitrary requirement. In other circumstances the term "minimum" may have been pre-empted by the state department of education in its establishment of legal minimum service levels. Then the CIC staff may wish to develop a "desirable" level of educational services, a phrase almost as powerful in eliciting community response.

The measurement of what the city has and what it would get from additional expenditure on sewerage facilities may be more difficult and may require more ingenuity, but is nevertheless feasible. Here the task of establishing a standard and working toward its attainment is critical. Such a standard is not an absolute, but is determined by measuring the consequences of particular outlays designed to effect improvements. The specifics here are the reduction in the number of flooded basements, the reduction in the rate of communicable diseases, the increase in the fish population of the lake, and the possibilities of disease-free swimming. Again, comparisons with the sewerage facilities of comparable cities will be significant.

The measurements and comparisons developed by the experts are a very large part of the raw materials for decision-making, but they are far from all that is needed. Furthermore, these measurements and comparisons will necessarily be modified in the discharge of the communications and responsibility functions.

In the performance of the communications function the CIC must be sensitive to the interest groups which make up the community, conversant with their way of thinking, and able to establish a reciprocal exchange with them. In the hypothetical case here, this means that channels of communication must be kept open with all sorts of groups: the Mothers Club of Jones Junior High, the Parent-Teachers Association, the School Board, the State Department of Education, the League of Women Voters, the Isaak Walton League, the County Recreation Association, the County Medical Society, the Commissioner of Health, the City Engineer, and the Park Commission. County or state governmental agencies are likely to be in a position to influence Central City's expenditures; these agencies stand in relation to the CIC in much the same fashion as any other interest group.

Communication with interest groups that are concerned about and affected by specific public expenditures will provide additional suggestions for measurement and comparison. The Isaak Walton League may point out that unless sewage is discharged at a particular point in the lake, an important spawning bed will be destroyed. The measurement of this suggested consequence then becomes an assignment for the expert, and information can be assembled to determine whether this is a likely consequence, whether it could be avoided, and the cost of its avoidance.

The responsibility function is very closely linked with the communications function. The former consists in assuring that the proposed decision is realistic in terms of the political power structure of the community. These power structures may be adequately expressed by the interest groups whose views are well known. But they may also include less vociferous but powerful forces such as the realtors, the bankers, or a ward boss.

The CIC's performance of the responsibility function could be described simply as a matter of assuring the Mayor's political future by advancing the right decision.   By and large, and with few exceptions, good politics is good economics.   If the decision is to build the high school rather than the sewerage system, and this is based on a careful assessment of the consequences of the expenditure, then the new high school should help the Mayor's chances for re-election.   If the decision turns out to be wasteful of public resources, the Mayor may well lose.   The performance of both the communications and responsibility functions assures that the final decision will be accepted by the community and that it will be realistic in terms of the interests which are affected.

In the case here, the CIC has a partially independent role to play in its relations to the interest groups.   As was pointed out above, a governmental agency with responsibility for decision-making is not always a helpless pawn in the larger game of forces beyond its control.   An administrator is frequently in a position of community leadership where he can modify and counter the interest groups and develop additional sources of political strength.

The prestige and survival of the CIC will depend in large measure on the realism of its decisions—realism which will be determined by the objective consequences which flow from its decisions and by its pattern of relations with interest groups.   As Selznick pointed out in his study of "grass roots democracy" in the TVA, a governmental agency will necessarily engage in the "cooptation" of interest groups in order to avert threats to its stability or existence.   But this process of cooptation serves, at the same time, to limit the agency's freedom of decision-making; if the participation of the interest groups is carried too far, the leadership, perhaps even the authority, of the agency is destroyed.[31]

One of the ways by which a Capital Improvements Commission can avoid the dangers of the cooptive process is to formulate a Long-Range Plan for Municipal Improvements.   The very term itself connotes stability, foresight, and independence.   The Plan takes on a momentum of its own, and entrenched behind it the CIC can fight off those who would spend all of this year's capital improvement fund on X—X will be taken care of next year.   The Plan can provide an element of stability in decision-making.

The specifics that have been measured by the experts will not alone provide final answers.   The benefits from a sewerage system, set forth in terms of communicable diseases prevented, dry basements, and an increased fish population in the lake, cannot be added up and compared with the benefits from the high school, specified in terms of air for the pupils, a new school playground, and a better gymnasium.   The costs of

[31] Philip Selznick, *T.V.A. and the Grass Roots,* University of California Press, Berkeley, 1949, esp. pp. 3–16; 259–261.

each may be compared, but the benefits do not have a common denominator; the monetary calculus is not applicable here. The lists of benefits are the raw materials of decision-making, not the decision itself.

Armed with the lists of specifics and in possession of information on the attitudes of interest groups, the Commission must now reach its value judgments. The decision that it makes reflects the specifics and the interest group pressures, and also reflects the success that the Commission itself has had in influencing prevalent attitudes. The end product of the Commission's work—the decision to spend the $2 million on X rather than on Y—is the value judgment which has been shaped by the facts. This choice cannot be made on grounds of "efficiency"—that is, by simply selecting the "best" school building that can be obtained for the money or the "best" sewage treatment. The selection of the "best" is an intermingled fact and value judgment.[32]

It should be stressed that in a problem like this, as in most problems involving the allocation of public expenditures, "you start with what you have." This year's expenditures proceed from the base of last year's program. Next year's expenditures are structured by what is done this year. To this extent, at least, the economists who have approached public finance in terms of marginalism are on sound ground. The allocation problem necessarily deals chiefly with increments, with additional expenditures proceeding from expenditures which have been made.

The incremental character of the allocation makes the task of the Capital Improvements Commission (or any other agency charged with making similar decisions) much easier, because it opens the way for compromise. In practice this means that there are very few instances in which either the high school or the sewerage system will be completely neglected. The high school will have to be built for $1,800,000, while $200,000 is allotted for repairing the storm sewers, and the new disposal plant will wait for another budget.

Another consequence of "starting with what you have" stems from the complementary nature of many governmental expenditures. If a new high school is constructed, the additional school spirit engendered may lead to demands for a football stadium for the team. If the sewerage system is constructed and the lake improved, there will be a demand for a park or a new access road to bring more fishermen to the lakeshore. The decisions which are made this year will shape the decisions which must be made next year. Neither are public expenditures in any one direction necessarily subject to a diminishing marginal social benefit. The new high school may generate demands for new junior high schools and then for new elementary schools.

Above all, it should be stressed that decision-making in this area, as in

[32] Compare, Simon, Smithburg, and Thompson, *Public Administration,* p. 493.

other areas of governmental policy, is a product of organizational hierarchy. The staff assumes responsibility for certain types of decisions; the Capital Improvements Commission assumes responsibility for a different type of decision. As the materials for the final decision move up the hierarchy, wider and broader elements enter. The final decision is, or should be, a product of the complex economic, social, and political factors which affect the existence of a governmental unit.

To summarize, the foregoing hypothetical case study illustrates the following:

(1) There are three functions in decision-making about governmental expenditures: expertise, communications, and responsibility.

(2) The expertise function consists in measurement and comparison of the consequences of alternative public outlays, but such quantifications must be undertaken with full recognition that the end-product measurements of alternative A are not comparable with the end-product measurements of alternative B.

(3) The communications function consists in hearing the representations of interested and affected groups, or in ascertaining their views and feelings. These representations will suggest additional measurements and comparisons which should be undertaken in the performance of the expertise function.

(4) The responsibility function requires an appraisal of the political power groupings of the community, to test the realism of proposals in relation to these groupings, and to ascertain the quantity and quality of leadership required at a particular time. The responsibility function also includes facing criticism for the decisions that are made.

(5) In the final decision, expertise, communications, and responsibility are merged. Facts and values are no longer compartmentalized; facts shape values and values shape facts.

The realities of decision-making for governmental expenditures frequently depart from the foregoing hypothetical model, and are often particularly inadequate in the performance of communcations and expertise. The communications function is very often conducted within narrow limits. The interest groups that are already in existence and are in a position to make their influence felt will do so; they will be listened to. But the decision-makers are not likely to systematize the channels of communication to the point of making conscious efforts to ascertain the state of all interest groups feelings and wishes.

Neither is the expertise function well organized in most governmental units. Too often there is little attempt to measure specific consequences of alternative expenditures and, in particular, to experiment with new measurement techniques. (See Chapter 10.) The more widespread adoption of these techniques is hampered not solely by the present inadequacy of staff experts. Those who have responsibility for final decisions must be equipped to use the measurements and comparisons which are developed by a staff, and should encourage efforts at experimentation.

The model which has been developed here as a case study in governmental decision-making in a municipality has been simplified for purposes of exposition. Nevertheless, it has applicability to more complex situations.

Very commonly, even for municipalities, revenues are not absolutely fixed but are at least partially variable. It may be possible to have both the new high school and the sewerage system in the same year if taxpayers can be convinced of their importance. Also, it may be possible to have both by the flotation of bonds, with a more modest increase in annual taxes, spread over a longer period of time. Here the added element is the effect of the additional levies, and again, not only the measurable consequences but the attitudes of interested and affected groups. The problems involved in determining the size of the government sector in relation to the size of the private sector differ only in degree from those of determining the allocation of governmental outlays.

Similarly, the decisions about the allocation of expenditure for the national government and decisions about the size of the national government sector are not intrinsically different, but are much more complicated. For the national government the economic effects of expenditures and taxes on the size, distribution, and composition of the national income will be an important part of the measurements that make up the materials for final choices. Also, for a national government, the comparisons of performance in relation to other governments are much less significant than for state or local governments.

Decisions about the character of the public sector, its size, and its activities cannot be reduced to an exercise in abstract economics. Such decisions are a product of their context, which is an organizational context in a political framework.

Selected Bibliography

Appleby, Paul H., *Policy and Administration,* University of Alabama Press, University, Alabama, 1949, pp. 1–25, 93–120.
——— "The Influence of the Political Order," *American Political Science Review,* April 1948, pp. 272–283.

Banfield, Edward C., "Congress and the Budget; a Planner's Criticism," *American Political Science Review*, December 1949, pp. 1217–1228.

Brownlee, O. H., and Edward D. Allen, *Economics of Public Finance*, Prentice-Hall, New York, 1954, pp. 157–169.

Colm, Gerhard, "Why Public Finance?" *Essays in Public Finance and Fiscal Policy*, Oxford University Press, New York, 1955, pp. 3–23.

Dahl, Robert A., and Charles E. Lindblom, "Variation in Public Expenditure," *Income Stabilization for a Developing Democracy*, Max F. Millikan, ed., Yale University Press, New Haven, 1953, pp. 347–396.

Jones, Victor, "The Political Framework of Stabilization Policy," *Income Stabilization for a Developing Democracy*, Max F. Millikan, ed., Yale University Press, New Haven, 1953, pp. 583–624.

Key, V. O., Jr., "The Lack of a Budgetary Theory," *American Political Science Review*, December 1940, pp. 1137–1144.

Lewis, Verne B., "Toward a Theory of Budgeting," *Public Administration Review*, Winter 1952, pp. 42–54.

Nourse, Edwin G., *Economics in the Public Service*, Harcourt, Brace & Company, New York, 1953, pp. 5–28, 450–460.

Pigou, A. C., *A Study in Public Finance*, Macmillan & Co., Ltd., London, 1951, pp. 30–34.

Redford, Emmette S., *Administration of National Economic Control*, Macmillan Company, New York, 1952, pp. 220–271.

Simon, Herbert A., *Administrative Behavior*, Macmillan Company, New York, 1947, pp. 1–60; 172–197.

Simon, Herbert A., Donald W. Smithburg, and Victor A. Thompson, *Public Administration*, Alfred A. Knopf, New York, 1950, pp. 488–512.

Truman, David B., *The Governmental Process*, Alfrea A. Knopf, New York, 1953, pp. 3–65, 395–436, 501–535.

Vandermeulen, Alice John, "Guideposts for Measuring the Efficiency of Governmental Expenditures," *Public Administration Review*, Winter 1950, pp. 7–12.

Walker, Mabel L., *Municipal Expenditures*, Johns Hopkins Press, Baltimore, 1930, pp. 1–51.

3.

Fiscal policy and budgeting

One of the most important aspects of a public budget is its use as an instrumentality in the management of a nation's economy. The degree of management varies from country to country in accordance with the importance of the public sector in the combined total of public and private economic activity. The degree of management depends on the changes which can be made in the size or content of the budget to influence the quantity and character of economic activity. The economic management characteristic of budgeting is also the product of the political philosophy of a nation, and, in particular, of prevailing attitudes toward the role and responsibility of government.

The budget both reflects and shapes a nation's economic life. A government's budget is not passive. The revenues of the public sector will have specific effects on levels of income and economic activity in the private sector. The expenditures of the public sector will influence the kinds of economic activity conducted in the private sector, and will partially determine the level of total economic activity.

The budget is therefore more than a plan for administering the government sector. The kinds of governmental activity that are described in the budget will reflect the expressed needs of a nation for collective action by the state. The budget will also and necessarily reflect the relative distribution of economic and political power within the nation.

It is a reasonably good generalization that in most countries there is adequate recognition of the economic influence of the government's

59

budget. The budget is properly regarded as a tool of fiscal policy, that is, as an instrument for consciously influencing the economic life of a nation.

The economic management characteristic of budgeting does not pervade the budgets of all governmental units. In some countries, as in the United States, the national government's budget is an important tool of management and influence on levels of economic activity. The budgets of state governments, however, are rarely shaped with a view to their effect on levels of income and employment within the state. And local government budgeting in this country seems almost never to be influenced by a conscious intent to affect directly the level of local economic activity.

This concentration of fiscal policy considerations at the national level does not, however, prevail in all countries. In those countries with a federal system in which the states have broad responsibilities vis-à-vis the national government, as in Brazil and India, the state governments are of greatest importance in the formulation and execution of fiscal policy.

I. THE ELEMENTS OF FISCAL POLICY

A general appraisal of the budget and the budgetary process as a part of the larger area of fiscal policy is handicapped by the lack of commonly accepted and conventional definitions. The term fiscal policy does not have precise meaning, and there is no clear line to divide fiscal policy from public finance, from monetary policy, or from government economic policy. Neither is there agreement on the kinds of governmental actions which may properly be labeled as fiscal policy actions.

Historically the term is derived from the old French word *fisc*—the money basket or the treasury. The term therefore must have been originally synonymous with "public finance" as used in English to embrace the government's revenue, expenditure, and debt policies. But in current usage fiscal policy has a broader and different meaning, associated with governmental efforts to stabilize or stimulate levels of economic activity. This distinction between public finance and fiscal policy is a direct product of the antidepression experience of governments in the 1930's and the writings and influence of John Maynard Keynes. In the United States the widespread academic and popular use of the term was greatly stimulated by the publication of *Fiscal Policy and Business Cycles* by Professor Alvin H. Hansen.[1] During World War II the term fiscal policy came to mean the utilization of revenue, expenditure, and debt programs for achieving higher levels of total output and for preventing

[1] W. W. Norton & Company, New York, 1941. For Hansen's discussion of the changing nature of fiscal policy, see pp. 109–117.

inflation.[2] Over the past twenty-five years the emergence of the term "fiscal policy," as Ursula K. Hicks has pointed out, is generally attributable to the relative and absolute growth of the public sector.[3]

Defined in operational terms, fiscal policy as used here means the utilization of certain governmental activities and actions in the development and stabilization of the economy. These activities are the tools of fiscal policy—taxation, expenditures, and debt management. They must be coordinated and integrated with monetary and credit controls. The development of fiscal policy as a part of public economic policy can best be described by examining the recent utilization of these tools in the American economy.

A. TAXATION

In the tradition of classical and neoclassical economics, which dominated most of the thinking about public finance until the 1930's, taxation was viewed as a means of obtaining revenue for government, as a means of transferring resources from the private to the public sector. The more recent approach stresses that taxation does not serve solely to channel funds to finance government outlay. Taxation is also instrumental in controlling the volume of expenditure in the private sector.[4]

That taxation affects particular economic activity has long been recognized. Indeed, this is inherent in Justice Marshall's famous dictum, "The power to tax is the power to destroy." But within the past decade there has come to be general recognition that taxation can also be used to control the level of economic activity. This came to be most fully appreciated in World War II, when citizens were urged to make their tax payments to the government to prevent inflation. Income paid to the

[2] For discussion of the evolution of fiscal policy, its goals, and tools, see Arthur Smithies, "Federal Budgeting and Fiscal Policy," *A Survey of Contemporary Economics*, Vol. I, Howard S. Ellis, ed., Blakiston Company, Philadelphia, 1948, pp. 174–209; Gerhard Colm, "Fiscal Policy," *The New Economics*, Seymour E. Harris, ed., Alfred A. Knopf, New York, 1947, pp. 450–467; Gerhard Colm, "Fiscal Policy and the Federal Budget," *Income Stabilization for a Developing Democracy*, Max F. Millikan, ed., Yale University Press, New Haven, 1953, pp. 213–259.

[3] *British Public Finances*, Oxford University Press, London, 1954, pp. 141–142.

[4] Popular attitudes have changed since 1836, when Malthus wrote, "Yet taxation is a stimulus so liable in every way to abuse, and it is so absolutely necessary for the general interests of society to consider private property as sacred, that no one would think of trusting to any government the means of making a different distribution of wealth, with a view to the general good." (*Principles of Political Economy*, 2nd ed., William Pickering, London, 1836, p. 410.)

Treasury as taxes was not available for private expenditure on scarce commodities. And again in the fall of 1950, after the outbreak of hostilities in Korea, the Congress increased taxes, not solely to provide revenue, but for the purpose of restricting inflationary spending in the economy. Similarly, there has been considerable attention directed, both inside and outside Congress, to the possible stimulus to economic activity which may be expected from tax reduction. All of this evidences a drastic departure from "taxation for revenue only." Taxes will affect the level of private income, the distribution of that income, and the volume of private expenditures. Taxation can therefore be used as an instrumentality to affect the level of prices, as well as selectively to affect relative prices and the kinds and varieties of economic activity.

B. EXPENDITURES

Public expenditures, in the traditional view, were regarded as a subtraction from and a substitute for private expenditures. Government outlay was deemed desirable, generally speaking, only in those circumstances where the private sector could not conduct the activity.

Although exceptions were not unknown even in colonial times, these attitudes began to change most sharply in the 1930's as governmental expenditures were used to alleviate the distress of unemployment and to offset declines in economic activity in the private sector. Even in the middle 1930's, however, it was often argued that a dollar of public outlay was offset by a corresponding reduction of a dollar of private outlay and that full employment could not be achieved by government spending.

Today these views are seldom heard. Experience from 1938 to 1942 demonstrated conclusively that very large increases in governmental expenditures could abolish unemployment and push the economy not only to full employment, but beyond full employment to the point where additional expenditures, public or private, would be translated into price increases rather than increases in output.

Perhaps the best indication of the changed attitude toward government expenditure is evidenced by the now-familiar national income accounts. In this measurement of total income and expenditure, the government sector is treated like any other sector of activity. Government is conceived to be a recipient of income, and to make expenditures for goods and services in much the same way as households and firms. For purposes of measuring economic activity, the government accounts are an integral part of the national income account.

As with taxation, there is now widespread appreciation of the fact that the character and volume of government expenditures will affect levels of private income and its distribution and the prices and allocation of resources.

C. Debt Management

The sale, refunding, and retirement of government obligations was once viewed primarily as a financial operation. The success of debt management was judged by the rates of interest which were paid and by the ability of the Treasury to avoid frequent refunding operations. With few exceptions, this way of looking at debt management prevailed until the 1940's.

The appreciation of the fiscal policy significance of debt management is very largely a product of World War II, and may be illustrated by the experience of the U. S. Treasury Department in the sale of war bonds.

In April of 1942, when the major outlines of the government's war-time stabilization program were established, it was determined that war bonds should be sold with a view to minimizing the inflationary effect of governmental expenditures. This meant that every effort would be made to sell bonds to individuals rather than to banks, and that sales would be made under conditions which would discourage private expenditure on goods and services in short supply.

Early in this program the Treasury's War Savings staff seemed to regard this approach as suspect, and probably felt that more bonds could be sold if citizens were told that their dollars were providing the ammunition which their sons and brothers needed in the foxholes and on the beachheads. Nevertheless, perhaps at the urging of Treasury economists, the sales campaign came to stress increasingly the anti-inflationary aspects of the program, so that toward the end of World War II sales appeals were made more largely on economic than on emotional grounds. The populace was urged to buy war bonds *and* cut down consumer expenditures. It can hardly be doubted that this widely broadcast appeal made some contribution toward a greater understanding of the role of debt management in wartime.

The foregoing experience illustrates the fiscal policy significance of debt management, as opposed to narrower financial considerations. In selling debt obligations a government changes the composition of privately held assets—converts private assets from money to bonds. In some circumstances this conversion will alter the volume of private expenditure. Furthermore, the bonds that are outstanding are an instrument of economic management. They may be bought and sold by the treasury or the central bank under circumstances which, again, will vary the composition of private assets and rates of income and expenditure. This

makes debt management an instrument of monetary control, and means
that for many purposes the two cannot be separated.

D. MONETARY CONTROLS

It is customary to distinguish fiscal from monetary policy and to include taxation, expenditures, and debt management under the former and
measures designed to affect the cost and supply of funds for the conduct
of economic activity under the latter. Some types of monetary controls
are closely bound up with fiscal policy, but others are relatively independent. The following may be distinguished:

First, actions which are designed to affect the volume and cost of funds
which the banking system may make available to the private sector of the
economy.

Second, actions which are designed to affect the supply and the cost
of funds which may be available for financing specific types of transactions. Credit regulations which may determine the conditions for
financing the private purchase of housing or the purchase of consumer
durable goods fall in this latter category.

Third, government-initiated loan programs for influencing the quantity
or altering the cost of credit available for particular activities in the
private sector. Crop and seed loans for farmers, loans for rural elec-
trification, and government-guaranteed housing mortgages are examples
of this type of monetary action.

The first two types of monetary controls are customarily administered
centrally, typically by the central bank. The first is implemented primarily by varying the volume of reserves available to commercial banks.[5]
In countries where the government bond market is well developed and
the banks hold portfolios of government securities, the purchase and sale
of these securities by the central bank is an important means of altering
commercial bank reserves. Actions of this type are necessarily related
to the government's debt management program, and in some circumstances are conducted both by the central bank and by the treasury.
Debt management and monetary controls are intertwined and must be
directed toward common policy objectives.

Monetary policies of the second type are not as intimately linked with
the management of the public debt. In this case the purchase and sale
of government securities are not the implementing device. Rather, con-

[5] This generalized statement is not intended to be all-inclusive of the devices
which are available to a central bank for purposes of influencing commercial
bank lending. Other techniques include variations in standards of bank examination, and suasion of a more or less coercive character. For a full discussion see
Lester V. Chandler, *The Economics of Money and Banking*, Harper & Brothers,
New York, 1953, pp. 299–356.

trols are established by administrative regulations which prescribe in detail the types of transactions that may be financed in accordance with specified terms.

The third type of monetary action—governmental loan programs—is likely to require an increase in governmental expenditures in order to establish the initial loan fund for administrative expenses, and to offset losses which may be incurred. Loan programs are frequently administered by established departments and agencies rather than by the central bank. They are partially controlled by the budgetary process, usually to the extent of the initial appropriation and annual expenses, but the volume of loans is very often determined by considerations outside the range of budgetary policy.

The frequently used phrase "fiscal and monetary policy" connotes the close association of revenue, expenditure, debt management, and monetary policy. The association derives from the relationship between debt management and monetary controls, and between loan programs and expenditure policy. The relationship is much less close in the case of the second or specific type of monetary control.

It is evident that no hard and fast lines can be drawn either definitionally or operationally between fiscal policy and monetary policy. Definitional distinctions are not important. What is important is that both be formulated and administered in a consistent fashion.

Before examining the nature and importance of coordination in fiscal policy, it may be useful to sketch briefly the change in attitudes toward the use of aggregate monetary policy—the controls which are exerted by the central bank over the lending activity of commercial banks. In this case, unlike the other areas of fiscal policy, the change has not been all in one direction. Attitudes toward monetary controls which reached their peak in the 1920's were repudiated in the 1930's, but have come to be revived since the end of World War II both in this country and abroad.

In the 1920's, possibly in accordance with the relatively small scope of governmental operations in the United States and a substantially smaller need for governmental stabilization programs, an important role was assigned to monetary controls administered by the Board of Governors of the Federal Reserve System. During this period federal fiscal policy dictated a low level of federal expenditures, surplus tax revenues, and a maximum of debt retirement. Nevertheless, it was regarded as wholly proper for the Federal Reserve to undertake measures to counteract fluctuations in business activity. In general, and to oversimplify the philosophy and practice of central banking in this period, this called for a restrictive monetary policy in times of rising prices and employment, and a relaxation in the restrictions when economic conditions worsened.

Although monetary policy had not been particularly effective during World War I, in the 1920's the Federal Reserve acted as it was supposed to act, and with an apparent degree of success—in the inflation of 1920 and the recessions of 1921, 1924, and 1927. In spite of strenuous efforts to curb the stock market speculation of 1928–1929, however, little was accomplished and doubts began to emerge concerning the usefulness of monetary controls as a stabilization measure. These doubts were accentuated in the early 1930's, when the Federal Reserve undertook to raise interest rates to halt the outflow of gold. Unfortunately, this action served only to further reduce liquidity and restrict credit in the domestic economy. Then, after 1933 the "cheap money" policy of lowered interest rates and increased availability of credit was inaugurated. The results were disappointing; business conditions did not improve markedly under this stimulus. This experience is sometimes summed up in the phrase "liquidity is not enough," which implies that monetary measures are inherently weak in generating economic recovery.

The experience with monetary controls in the early 1930's continues to determine prevalent attitudes toward the use of these measures to combat a depression. Most economists will contend that monetary actions that take the form of lowered interest rates and an increased volume of available bank funds will undoubtedly encourage economic activity in particular areas, such as in residential construction. But there are few economists who would today contend, as was so widely believed in the 1920's, that monetary policy, taken by itself, is an adequate protection against a general recession in business activity.

The renascence in monetary policy has occurred since World War II and on both sides of the Atlantic.[6] Attitudes toward the use of monetary controls to curb inflationary activity, attitudes which had fallen by the wayside after the 1920's, have recently been revived and applied in governmental efforts to curb inflationary tendencies.

In this country the more intensive application of monetary controls required a realignment of governmental authority. The desire of the Federal Reserve to limit the volume of reserves available to commercial banks ran counter to the Treasury's concern to maintain low interest rates, since the latter could be implemented only by continued support of the government bond market through Federal Reserve open market operations. The conflict was resolved in the Federal Reserve's favor in

[6] See, for example, Joint Committee on the Economic Report, *Monetary Policy and the Management of the Public Debt,* 82d Cong., 2d sess., 1952; and "Monetary Policy: A Symposium," *Bulletin of the Institute of Statistics,* Oxford, April–May 1952, pp. 117–176; *The Revival of Monetary Policy,* International Monetary Fund, Washington, 1953.

1951, with a consequent increase in interest rates on government obligations and a corresponding increase in the ability of the Federal Reserve to control member bank lending.

This is not the place to argue the merits and demerits of the New Monetary Policy. There is and will be a continuing and understandable conflict between those who prefer lower and inflexible interest rates and those who prefer higher and more flexible interest rates, and between those who would place major reliance on monetary controls in a stabilization program and those who would assign them a minor role. But in any case, and regardless of their relative role, monetary controls must be administered in conjunction with fiscal controls.

E. Economic Coordination

The fifth element of fiscal and monetary policy is the coordinating operation. Economic coordination requires, first and foremost, the acceptance of governmental responsibility for economic stabilization. The changed attitudes in this regard, and the reality of federal responsibility, are well illustrated in the contrasting experiences of 1921 and 1949.

After World War I the American economy encountered a rather serious depression. Unemployment increased from 500,000 in 1920 to 4,700,000 in 1921. At the suggestion of Herbert Hoover, then Secretary of Commerce, President Harding convened a conference on unemployment in September 1921. In his opening remarks the President stated:

> The industrial depression which we are feeling is a war inheritance throughout the world. . . . Liquidation, reorganization, readjustment, re-establishment, taking account of things done, and the sober contemplation of things to be done, the finding of firm ground and the open, sure, and onward way— all these are a part of the inevitable, and he who thinks they might have been avoided by this plan or that, or this policy or that, or this international relationship or that, only hugs a delusion when reason is needed for a safe council. . . . I would have little enthusiasm for any proposed relief which seeks either palliation or tonic from the public treasury. The excess of stimulation from that source is to be reckoned a cause of trouble rather than a source of cure.[7]

One of the important conclusions of the conference was:

> . . . the first principle of American public life is reliance upon local initiative and obligation. . . . the problem of meeting the emergency of unemployment is primarily a community problem. The responsibility for leadership is with the Mayor and should be immediately assumed by him.

Presumably the mayors accepted their responsibilities more or less cheerfully and coped with their problems as best they could.

[7] Quoted in E. Jay Howenstine, Jr., "Public Works Policy in the Twenties," *Social Research,* December 1946, pp. 479–480.

In 1949 there was a moderate recession. Unemployment, which had averaged 2,000,000 in 1948, increased to 4,100,000 in July of 1949. It was not a generalized unemployment problem. Specific communities were most seriously affected; in some cases unemployment amounted to 20 percent of the working force. Nevertheless, and almost without delay, federal officials moved into action. Apparently there was little political pressure to force the mayors of the stricken cities to act, but there was much pressure on the Congressmen in these districts. As a result, the President established a procedure for channeling government contracts and procurement into the areas of most critical unemployment. A member of the White House staff was designated to select the critical areas and to coordinate federal efforts.[8]

Between the years 1921 and 1949 something had obviously happened in terms of popular attitudes toward the role of the federal government in dealing with economic conditions. This can be accurately described as an increased acceptance of central economic coordination and responsibility. It is symbolized in the passage of the Employment Act of 1946 (*P.L.*, 304, 79th Cong., 2d sess.), which stated:

> The Congress hereby declares that it is the continuing policy and responsibility of the Federal Government . . . to foster and promote free competitive enterprise and the general welfare, conditions under which there will be afforded useful employment opportunities, including self-employment, for those able, willing, and seeking to work, and to promote maximum employment, production, and purchasing power.

Economic coordination, as a part of fiscal policy, will be taken to mean here the conscious central planning which must be applied to taxation, expenditures, debt management, and monetary controls. Economic coordination does not imply an increase in the size of the public sector, or an increase in socialization or collectivization of economic activity. It does not require that resources be directly allocated by government decision. But it does require that the four operational areas of fiscal and monetary policy be brought together in a framework of consistent action. Fiscal policy, to be worthy of the name, must be conscious and intended, not a series of disjointed and contradictory actions with disjointed and contradictory economic effects.

This kind of economic coordination within a government requires an organizational structure developed for this specific purpose. The structure will, of course, vary from one government to the next, in accordance with the nature of governmental programs, with the character of the economy, and the relations between the executive and the legislature. Economic coordination may be undertaken by a central planning board

[8] *New York Times,* July 15, 1949, p. 1.

in a socialist country, where resources are allocated for specified purposes. It may be undertaken by a council of economic advisers in a predominantly private enterprise economy, where government directly controls a relatively small proportion of the nation's resources. But regardless of the variations in form and function, fiscal policy requires an organizational structure for its formulation and execution.

II. ECONOMIC POLICY AND FISCAL POLICY

Every governmental activity will have "fiscal policy effects" in the sense that every tax, expenditure, and debt management operation will exert influence, however small, on the level of national income and employment. But a definition of fiscal policy which is this broad destroys the significance of the term. Certain kinds of governmental programs are undertaken primarily with a view to their influence on the level of income and employment. Others are modified because of their probable influence on the level of income and employment. Only in those circumstances where government programs are designed or modified in accordance with their effects on these aggregates should they be termed a part of fiscal policy. As governmental programs come to be formulated increasingly in relation to these considerations, the boundaries of fiscal policy are extended.

In the case of governmental expenditures, fiscal policy consequences have sometimes been labeled "process effects" to distinguish them from the "product" effects of the outlay.[9] The latter are the end products in terms of streets, dams and bridges, fire protection and police protection, or guns and planes. The process effects are the consequences of government expenditure in terms of the resulting increases in income and employment, public and private.

The concern of fiscal policy with process effects of this type marks it off from what may be termed "government economic policy." The latter is far broader, and includes all manner of programs which reflect or are influenced by economic objectives or considerations. The number and variety of such programs was indicated by the U. S. Bureau of the Budget in 1945. The Senate Committee on Banking and Currency was holding hearings on the Full Employment Bill, later to emerge as the Employment Act of 1946. The Bureau was asked to submit a list of the probable postwar activities of the federal government as an aid in determining what might be done to maintain full employment and full production. The list was confined to those programs with a significant effect

[9] See Benjamin Higgins, *Public Investment and Full Employment,* International Labour Office, Montreal, 1946, pp. 23–25.

on the level of employment; additional programs which might have a direct or indirect influence on the size of the labor force, productivity, consumer expenditures, foreign trade, and the like, were excluded. Nevertheless, the listed "tool chest" of government activities amounted to several hundred programs.[10] All of the programs had fiscal policy effects, but it seems likely that very few of them had been, up to that time, in any way shaped or influenced by fiscal policy considerations.

More and more of economic policy is likely to become fiscal policy. The importance of stabilization objectives in governmental policy formulation, with the development of techniques for the appraisal of stabilization consequences, will mean that fiscal policy considerations will directly influence more and more governmental programs.

Just as fiscal policy is not conterminous with government economic policy, so it is that budgeting is not conterminous with fiscal policy. Procedures for the formulation of the budget provide the occasion for and require the formulation of revenue and expenditure policy. In fact, a budget may be defined in these terms—as a statement of revenue and expenditure for a future period. But the budgetary process does not necessarily require the formulation of the government's debt management program, nor the formulation of monetary policies. The organizational structure established for budget-making in a government may be utilized for decisions about debt management and monetary policies, but these latter decisions may also be undertaken by different organizations and even at a different point in time. The budget and the budget-making process do not necessarily serve as the economic coordinating mechanism for fiscal policy. But the organizational structure for coordination will necessarily permeate the budget-making mechanism. It may also extend well beyond it and be located at different places or levels in the structure of government.

Budgetary decisions, then, should be linked with other fiscal policy decisions. Similarly, if budgeting is to make its maximum contribution to fiscal policy, budgetary practices and policy must be flexible, so that revenue and expenditure can be modified in response to economic fluctuations. To achieve this kind of flexibility, governments should avoid restrictive budgetary practices such as the use of earmarked revenues, a device particularly characteristic of state budgeting in this country, by which specific revenues are assigned by statute to specific expenditures. Regardless of changes in program requirements and regardless of changes in economic conditions, the earmarking continues to channel revenue

---

[10] See Hearings before a subcommittee of the Senate Committee on Banking and Currency, *Full Employment Act of 1945,* 79th Cong., 1st sess., 1945, pp. 681–696.

toward the designated program. Earmarking may reduce taxpayer opposition to increased levies, but its harmful fiscal policy consequences are obvious—it hampers a government's ability to adapt revenue and expenditure to changing requirements.

Fiscal policy flexibility in budgeting can also be assured by built-in devices for stabilization. These operate on both the revenue and expenditure side. For revenues, built-in flexibility results from taxes on personal income and business profits, at graduated rates. Such levies will automatically dampen down fluctuations in economic activity. An increase in national income will produce a more than proportional increase in government tax revenue, thus operating automatically to restrict private expenditures. On the expenditure side, built-in flexibility will assure that reductions in national income will be countered, at least in part, by increases in government expenditures. Outlays for unemployment compensation and for agricultural price supports behave in this fashion. For United States financial operations the combined effects of built-in revenue and expenditure stabilizers are substantial.[11]

Built-in devices for stabilization assure that the budget will make an automatic contribution to a nation's fiscal policy. Beyond this, budget expenditures and budget revenues may be modified specifically with a view to their effects on the level of economic activity. The possibilities along these lines require that tax rates be adjusted in the same direction as changes in the national income, and that expenditures be adjusted in the opposite direction. In the case of the latter, an increase in program outlays when the national income declines, or their reduction when national income increases, may sometimes be difficult to secure. Program considerations may often outweigh in importance the considerations of process. By no means all budget expenditures are capable of modification in accordance with fiscal policy considerations. (See Chapter 12.)

III. CHARACTERISTICS OF FISCAL POLICY CONTROLS

The first and most important characteristic of fiscal policies is that they are aggregative in character, that is, they are intended to influence such magnitudes as the total volume of economic activity, the general level of prices, and the total of consumer spending. The controls utilized by fiscal policy may therefore be said to be indirect, in that they do not appear to influence specific transactions within the economy. The price of wheat, the price of steel, the wages of coal miners, are not intended to be directly affected by fiscal policy. The kinds of economic controls em-

[11] James A. Maxwell, *Fiscal Policy*, Henry Holt & Company, New York, 1955, pp. 100–117.

braced under fiscal policy are, therefore, in contrast with price regulations or the control of monopoly, which are direct in character and immediately influence particular prices and particular transactions.

This distinction between the indirect character of fiscal policy controls and the direct character of other types of economic controls is significant, although the distinction sometimes tends to blur in application.[12] Indirect controls may turn out to have direct effects. A general increase in personal income taxes designed to restrict the volume of consumer expenditure under inflationary conditions would be classed as an indirect control of economic activity. Nevertheless, such a tax increase will have direct effects in terms of its impact on expenditures for particular commodities and in terms of its restriction of particular incomes. Similarly, a general reduction in the volume of bank credit available to business firms will affect some firms differently than others, since not all concerns utilize bank credit to the same degree in financing their operations. In this case, what appears to be a general curtailment of the supply of credit becomes, in application, a specific curtailment of the economic activity of specific firms—a curtailment on those that do not possess their own reserves of liquid assets to be used for self-financing.

The direct effects of indirect controls are well illustrated by experience with consumer credit restrictions. A general regulation requiring larger down payments and higher monthly payments will not have a general effect. Those purchasers who are heavily dependent on consumer credit —generally lower and middle income groups—find their expenditures reduced. Upper income groups, not so dependent on credit facilities, are little affected.[13]

Although indirect measures have direct effects, their administration is impersonal, which gives them a kind of conservatism.[14] Fiscal policy attempts to regulate economic activity by controlling the aggregates of spending. The allocation of resources is very largely left to the private sector. The price system continues to serve in its traditional role as a guide to resource allocation among alternative employments.

Certain kinds of fiscal policies do not require an increase in the economic and political power of the public sector. Their implementation does not bring an increase in governmental organization. A tax system

[12] For a graphic presentation of the way in which indirect controls tend to shade into direct controls, see Robert A. Dahl and Charles E. Lindblom, *Politics, Economics, and Welfare,* Harper & Brothers, New York, 1953, p. 14.

[13] See *New York Times,* October 13, 1950, p. 40; October 15, 1950, p. 46.

[14] Smithies in *A Survey of Contemporary Economics,* p. 178. For a partial dissent see Paul A. Samuleson, "Principles and Rules in Modern Fiscal Policy: A Neo-classical Reformulation," *Money, Trade, and Economic Growth,* Macmillan Company, New York, 1951, pp. 162–170.

can be geared to collect either more or less revenue without substantial change in the number of tax collectors. Certain types of government expenditures, such as payments for social welfare purposes, can be increased or decreased without substantial alteration in the number of government employees. It may be noted that in terms of a transfer of economic activity from the private to the public sector, stimulation by means of a tax reduction is inherently more conservative than stimulation by means of an increase in governmental expenditures. In the former case, the increase in activity occurs in the private sector; in the latter case, the increase occurs in the public sector.

A second characteristic of fiscal policies—one which does not partake of a conservative character—is that they inevitably affect relative shares of national income: the distribution of income between the rich and the poor, and the distribution of income among farmers, wage earners, stockholders, bondholders, and business managers. This is also true of monetary policy, particularly where changes are effected in the rate of interest, thus altering the distribution of income between debtors and creditors.

The history of fiscal policy actions in the past several decades demonstrates that it is not possible to conduct a stabilization program without significant economic or social action to accompany it. An anti-inflation program, for example, does not so much curb income and expenditure in general as it curbs the income and expenditure of particular economic groups and particular income classes. An anti-inflation program will necessarily modify the distribution of economic and political power within a community. Similarly, an antidepression program must increase the relative income of particular economic groups. As Pendleton Herring has stated:

> The formulation of fiscal policy lies at the dead center of democratic government. It is the very essence into which is distilled the conflict between the haves and the have-nots. It represents the terms of compromise between powerful economic forces in the community. Utterly divergent economic forces are seeking to control the financial machinery of the government to promote their own ends.[15]

The fact that fiscal policy affects the distribution of economic and political power within a society makes it inherently controversial. Although it deals in aggregates, it does not affect all persons and economic groups equally. A great deal of fiscal policy involves taking money out of Peter's pocket and putting it in Paul's, at least on a relative basis. It can hardly be expected that Peter and Paul will always agree on how much should move from one pocket to the other. We can reasonably

[15] E. Pendleton Herring, "The Politics of Fiscal Policy," *Yale Law Journal,* March 1938, p. 728.

expect that citizens will continue to be interested and concerned not only about their own incomes and the incomes of others in their economic group, but also about the incomes of other persons and groups in society. At the same time, the difficulty of tracing the precise consequences of fiscal policies on the distribution of income sometimes tends to obscure their redistributional character and may well make them more acceptable and manageable on this account.

The conflicts in fiscal policy will persist. This persistence should be recognized and dealt with. Little contribution is made to the solution of stabilization problems by those who insist that the interests of farmers and urban consumers will always coincide, or by those who contend that there is never a conflict between employers and employees. Our economic order will continue to generate sharp disagreements among economic groupings and classes, and difficult questions of public policy can be resolved only by recognizing clearly the issues that are at stake.

It can be expected that in the throes of these controversies each particular group or class will seek to identify its interests with the general welfare and will seek to enlist public support on this ground. After all, the growers of lettuce can hardly expect to enlist widespread approval for a program of benefits for lettuce-growers if they contend simply that they would like a larger share of the national income. Rather, they must contend that lettuce is rich in vitamins, that eating it will cure insomnia, and that more lettuce must be consumed in the interest of the public welfare. To quote again from Herring:

> The concept of a fiscal policy designed to promote the economic welfare of the public as a whole is badly shaken when the incidence of a given policy is faced in terms of the groups affected. The general welfare concept is of little if any value as a tool of analysis; it is most effective as an instrument of exhortation. As a battle-cry for rallying sympathy and support to a given proposal it belongs in the same arsenal with "justice," "equity," and "fairness."[16]

Explicit recognition of conflict and controversy in the economic order, and in particular in fiscal policy, does not mean that the common ground of interest should be overlooked. Responsible consideration of the views of divergent interest groups and the resolution of conflict through political and administrative channels serves in itself to achieve harmony. The alternative to such responsible consideration could only lead to explosive disharmony. Then, too, to the extent that fiscal policy is successful in maintaining a high and stable level of economic activity, its very success will help to ameliorate conflict. It is easier to divide a large pie than

---

[16] *Ibid.*, p. 727.

it is to divide a small pie; there is less fighting over relative shares. When the national income is increasing in real terms, there is less conflict than when it is declining. Moreover, the last several years have witnessed the development of new techniques and organizational structures for the resolution of economic conflict. The escalator clauses in wage contracts, to protect employees from increases in the cost of living, are one example. With only an occasional exception, the contractual arrangements which have been worked out between the Atomic Energy Commission and business firms for the coordination of public and private enterprise are another.

A balanced approach to fiscal policy and indeed, to the whole of public policy, requires the most careful appraisal of both the harmony and conflict elements present in the economic order. An approach which overstresses either the harmony or the conflict is not likely to be successful in the solution of difficult problems.

A third characteristic of fiscal policy controls relates to the governmental level at which they are formulated and administered. For practical purposes, in the past several decades fiscal policy, as defined here in terms of the stabilization of economic activity, has been the concern of the federal government. State and local governments have not participated importantly in a positive program for stabilization. The reason for this lies in their operating characteristics, which are necessarily in a restricted framework.

It is true that state and local governments can often make modest contributions to the stabilization of employment in areas within their jurisdiction, and are increasingly examining the economic effect of their activities. But in the very nature of things, it cannot be expected that state and local governments will be dominated by stabilization considerations. The state government of New York, for example, could not, if it wished, assume responsibility for the level of income and employment of its citizens. New York State is not an independent economic unit; it is an open economy. The economic welfare of its citizens is determined in very large measure by the economic welfare of the citizens of the nation as a whole.

The economic limitations on state and local fiscal action are reinforced, in most jurisdictions, by constitutional and statutory provisions. The sources of taxation, the objects of expenditure, and the size and character of public debt are customarily limited in such a fashion as to tremendously hamper fiscal freedom. Also, state and local governments do not have access to the facilities of a central bank as does the federal government. They must be continually concerned about their credit rating, and must therefore operate in accordance with standards of liquidity and solvency that are in many respects comparable to those of business enterprise. State and local governments have a funds problem, which the federal government does not have.

The economic and governmental limitations on state and local fiscal policies do not mean that operations at these levels are uninfluenced by fluctuations in economic activity. State and local governments may not be able to modify these fluctuations, but they must adjust to them. Unfortunately, these adjustments very often run counter to the requirements of stabilization.

It may be hoped that this condition will be altered in the near future, and that the stabilization of economic activity will be an increasing concern of state and local governments. Optimism on this score cannot be justified, however, by citing successful accomplishment. The experiments of some states with public works reserves and other stabilization devices have been markedly unsuccessful. In spite of numerous proposals down the years to provide mechanisms for bringing state and local governments into a coordinated national fiscal policy, almost nothing has been achieved.[17]

IV. THE GOALS OF FISCAL POLICY

The literature of economics is replete with discussion of the ends that should be sought by using the tools of fiscal policy. Much of this discussion came at the end of World War II, in the writings on full employment and in the controversies on economic planning.[18] In this country the Congressional hearings on the Employment Act provided the occasion for an extensive consideration of the goals and tools of fiscal policy.[19]

An examination of this abundant literature reveals that any attempt to define the goals of fiscal policy presents a great many problems. Some of the difficulties are associated with the use of words in special

[17] See, for example, the proposals in Alvin H. Hansen and Harvey S. Perloff, *State and Local Finance in the National Economy*, W. W. Norton & Company, New York, 1944, pp. 121–140; 194–222. For a somewhat more optimistic view then expressed here see Mabel Newcomer, "State and Local Financing in Relation to Economic Fluctuations," *National Tax Journal*, June 1954, pp. 97–109.

[18] For example, William H. Beveridge, *Full Employment in a Free Society*, W. W. Norton & Company, New York, 1945, esp. pp. 17–38; Friedrich A. Hayek, *The Road to Serfdom*, University of Chicago Press, Chicago, 1944; Herman Finer, *Road to Reaction*, Little, Brown & Company, Boston, 1945; Barbara Wootton, *Freedom Under Planning*, University of North Carolina Press, Chapel Hill, 1945.

[19] Hearing before the House Committee on Expenditures in the Executive Departments, *Full Employment Act of 1945*, 79th Cong., 1st sess., 1945; Senate Committee on Banking and Currency, *op. cit.*

context—the kinds of semantic problems which beset so much of the popular writing in the social sciences. Other difficulties arise in the distinction between goals and values, and in the distinction between means and ends.[20] These difficulties are particularly serious when fiscal policy is broadly defined and viewed in the context of general governmental economic policy.

For present purposes the peace-time goal of fiscal policy in an advanced industrial economy will be defined simply as high-level stabilization of economic activity: jobs for all who wish to work, and a stable price level that does not arbitrarily impoverish some and enrich others. An underdeveloped economy or a war-time economy would necessarily have different fiscal policy goals.

The attainment of this peace-time goal must be measured in terms of the distribution of real goods and services. A high level of economic activity means a correspondingly high level of real income for the community as a whole. Success should be measured in terms of achievement in relation to what an economy has to work with, not in terms of its absolute level of real income.

The emphasis on stabilization as the goal of fiscal policy does not mean that economic growth is thereby neglected. An economy operates successfully only when the material conditions of existence are improving, and for large numbers of people. To assure this kind of successful operation, the output of goods and service must be increasing faster than population, so that per capita real income is rising.

The experience of the American economy indicates that in an advanced industrial society growth is both the inevitable accompaniment and the determinant of high levels of economic activity. This relationship may be explained by the manner in which the level of national income is determined. As Keynes demonstrated in theoretical terms, a substantial portion of the gross national product must be made up each year by either private investment or government deficit if the level of economic activity is to be maintained. For the years 1946 through 1954 this portion averaged about 14 percent of gross national product. In other words, the savings of households and business firms were matched by either private investment or government deficit to the extent of 14 percent of the nation's total expenditure on goods and services.

A part of the government deficit during this period represented net additions to the real assets of the economy—to its social capital measured in terms of dams, bridges, school buildings, and the like. Similarly, a part of the expenditures of households and firms for gross private domes-

[20] For an excellent discussion of some of these difficulties, see Dahl and Lindblom, *Politics, Economics, and Welfare,* pp. 25–28.

tic investment added to the nation's stock of real assets. These additions to capital plant, private and public, not only maintained the level of income but also accounted for the growth of the American economy and its increased productivity. This, in turn, provided for a substantial increase in per capita real income. The American economy, then, requires a large outlay each year for private investment or government deficit in order to maintain a high level of economic activity. At the same time, private investment and government expenditure provide the additions to plant and equipment which are necessary for increases in per capita real income.

It should be noted that this relationship between high levels of national income and economic growth does not obtain in all countries. In an underdeveloped economy there is sometimes a high level of economic activity, in that there is little evident unemployment, but the rate of savings and investment may be so very small that economic growth does not occur. The American economy does not behave in this fashion. The rate of saving and investment has been high in relation to population growth. This is both fortunate and unfortunate. A high level of activity in an advanced industrial economy will automatically produce economic growth. But an economy characterized by high savings and high investment is beset with particular difficulties in assuring that investment will be continuously forthcoming in order to maintain that same high level of activity.

Fiscal policy will be successful if it contributes to the stabilization of a high level of economic activity. For the American economy the most difficult task is not to assure growth itself, but to prevent depression with its waste of resources from unemployment, and inflation with its waste of resources from misallocation.

V. KEYNESIAN ECONOMICS AND FISCAL POLICY

The experience of governments, and the body of practice and literature which are called fiscal policy, had their origins in the Great Depression. The decade of the 1930's demonstrated that a private enterprise economy did not automatically return to equilibrium at full employment. This forced the re-appraisal of the economic consequences of governmental action, and led to techniques for economic stabilization. This development is customarily and properly associated with the work of John Maynard Keynes and the publication of *The General Theory of Employment, Interest and Money* in 1936.[21]

Although an examination of Keynesian economic lies outside the scope

[21] Harcourt, Brace & Company, New York.

of this volume, the influence of Keynes and the Keynesians must be explicitly recognized in the evolution of fiscal policy. Keynes provided a rationalization for the things that responsible governments were doing in their efforts to cope with the problems of unemployment and depression. That it may have been an ex post facto rationalization does not matter. The contribution of Keynes was to provide a framework for the analysis of the determinants of national income and the role of government therein.

For fiscal policy, the most important of the Keynesian propositions are the following:

(1) An advanced industrial economy does not necessarily come into equilibrium at full employment. At any one time, the volume of private investment may be inadequate, given the prevailing distribution of income and the consumption pattern of the community, to maintain a high level of income and employment.

(2) The traditional remedy for depression—cuts in money wage rates to reduce employers' costs—is not adequate. At best it is neutral, and at worst it may intensify a depression. Wages are both costs and the effective demand of wage earners. The stimulus to profit margins which may be occasioned by the wage reduction may be offset by the reduction in consumer expenditures.

(3) Governmental action can be undertaken to maintain a high and stable level of effective demand. In times of depression additional outlay by government is not offset by a corresponding reduction in private outlay. For the economy as a whole, the employment of unemployed resources is "costless" in that additional output and higher standards of living can be secured by increased governmental expenditure.

These Keynesian propositions, and others not as immediately relevant to fiscal policy, have had the greatest impact on governmental policy in Western Europe and in the United States. Many of the propositions have come to be a part of popular thinking about the way the economic system works, and the framework of Keynes' analysis is often used by those who profess an antagonism to anything Keynesian.

A set of propositions, however, or even a new framework of analysis would not likely have had the impact of Keynesianism had it not been for the tools which were developed for implementation. The major tool was national income accounting, the measurement of the components and aggregates of economic activity in a manner consistent with the theoretical analysis. Keynes' equation—the national income is equal to consumption expenditure plus investment expenditure $(Y = C + I)$—provided a framework for the measurement techniques that are basic to the formulation of programs of economic stabilization.

Although the Keynesian contribution to fiscal policy is very great and must be specifically recognized, the balance sheet is not composed entirely of assets. There are limitations which may be singled out as characteristic, and which attach to much of Keynesian analysis.

The Keynesian approach to economic problems is necessarily aggregative. This, in fact, is the most important characteristic of fiscal policies. But when attention is centered here, there is an inevitable neglect of structural relations within the economy. For example, the Keynesian approach to inflation conceives the problem in terms of an excess of demand over supply—"too much money chasing too few goods." Therefore, inflation control techniques center on limiting demand to the size of supply. In stressing the aggregative character of inflation, most Keynesians have generally neglected the other and equally crucial element in an inflationary situation, which is its differential character. Some prices rise faster than others, with resulting structural changes in the economy; the income of the sellers of goods and services increases differentially as compared with the income of aged pensioners; property income increases more than labor income, with a resulting increased concentration in the over-all distribution of income.[22]

A concern with the aggregates ignores this differential characteristic of inflation. Because it neglects the components, the Keynesian approach to economic stabilization leaves unanswered the policy questions dealing with economic conflict. In an inflationary situation Keynesian analysis cannot tell us which expenditures are to be cut, expenditures for consumer goods or expenditures for investment goods. Similarly, in times of depression the Keynesian prescription that effective demand must be increased will not tell us whose demand should be increased first and by how much. Should farmers' income be raised by government action, or wage-earners' income or stockholders' income? These questions, involving as they do the relative rather than the absolute shares of national income, cannot be answered by aggregative analysis.

A second serious limitation of Keynesian analysis and its application to fiscal policy is closely linked with the problem of aggregates versus components. Most Keynesians assume that the state is an economic entity above and beyond the private sector. Generally this assumption is implicit; a few have been explicit on the point. Polanyi has written:

> We shall meet plenty of difficulties in conducting the affairs of society at a state of ample employment. These troubles may be rightly considered as the price of ample employment. But the process undertaken in order to create sufficient circulation need involve and must involve no material

[22] See the author's "Changes in the Functional Distribution of Income," *Journal of the American Statistical Association,* June 1953, pp. 192–219.

sacrifice to speak of. *It should be, and can be, carried out in a neutral form, i.e. in a way requiring no materially significant economic or social action to accompany it.*[23]

What Polanyi is saying is that public policy can and must be above and beyond the conflicts over relative shares of the national income—that stable full employment is a goal which can be attained without affecting the interrelations of the components which make up the economic order.

This is an artificial and unrealistic view of the nature of the economic order and the role of the state therein. A government is first and foremost representative of the economic interest groups which make up a society. It is therefore, by its very nature, restricted by these interest groups and their motivations. In some circumstances government agencies and government programs take on an "independent" character; they develop a force and motivation of their own that may give the appearance of transcending the interest groupings of society. But this "independent" character is generally relative and short-lived. The persistent feature of governmental programs is their relation to power groupings, existent and emerging, within the economic order.[24]

The limitations of Keynesian economics are, in a sense, the limitations of fiscal policy itself. The preoccupation with aggregates to the neglect of structural relations, and an overemphasis on the independent role of the state to the neglect of economic groupings and power forces which make up the state, limit the usefulness of this approach to problems of public policy. These limitations can be overcome, however, by a balanced approach—by a recognition that structural relations in the economy will affect the shape of the aggregates, and by examination of the economic groupings which set the boundaries for action by government.

It is in the achievement of this balanced approach that budgeting assumes its greatest significance. Budgeting must inevitably be concerned with agency programs—with components as well as with aggregates, with programs that are shaped by the economic groups whom they serve. But the components must be put together in the framework of aggregates, and it is principally in this framework that government formulates and executes its fiscal policy. The budget process brings consistency and balance to the interrelations between components and aggregates. The budget itself is a direct reflection of the revenue, expenditure, and debt

[23] Michael Polanyi, *Full Employment and Free Trade,* Cambridge University Press, London, 1945, p. 29.

[24] For a relevant discussion in the context of public administration theory see Norton E. Long, "Power and Administration," *Public Administration Review,* Autumn 1949, pp. 257–264.

programs of a government, and should therefore constitute the expression
of a balanced fiscal policy.

Selected Bibliography

Bach, G. L., *Federal Reserve Policy-Making*, Alfred A. Knopf, New York, 1950,
pp. 32–50.
Colm, Gerhard, "Fiscal Policy," *The New Economics*, Seymour E. Harris, ed.,
Alfred A. Knopf, New York, 1947, pp. 450–467.
———— *Essays in Public Finance and Fiscal Policy*, Oxford University Press, New
York, 1955, pp. 113–150.
———— "Fiscal Policy and the Federal Budget," *Income Stabilization for a Develop-
ing Democracy*, Max F. Millikan, ed., Yale University Press, New Haven,
1953, pp. 213–259. (Also in *Essays in Public Finance and Fiscal Policy*,
pp. 188–219.)
Dahl, Robert A., and Charles E. Lindblom, *Politics, Economics, and Welfare*,
Harper & Brothers, New York, 1953, pp. 25–54.
Hansen, Alvin H., *Fiscal Policy and Business Cycles*, W. W. Norton & Company,
New York, 1941, pp. 109–117.
Hart, Albert Gailord, "Monetary Policy for Income Stabilization," *Income
Stabilization for a Developing Democracy*, Max F. Millikan, ed., Yale Uni-
versity Press, New Haven, 1953, pp. 303–345.
Herring, E. Pendleton, "The Politics of Fiscal Policy," *Yale Law Journal*, March
1938, pp. 724–745.
Hicks, Ursula K., *British Public Finances*, Oxford University Press, London, 1954,
pp. 140–169.
Little, I. M. D., "Fiscal Policy," *The British Economy 1945–1950*, G. D. N.
Worswick, ed., Clarendon Press, Oxford, 1952, pp., 159–187.
Maxwell, James A., *Fiscal Policy*, Henry Holt & Company, New York, 1955,
pp. 15–29, 100–117.
Millikan, Max F., ed., *Income Stabilization for a Developing Democracy*, Yale
University Press, New Haven, 1953, pp. 13–75.
Poole, Kenyon E., ed., *Fiscal Policies and the American Economy*, Prentice-
Hall, New York, 1951, pp. 1–54.
Samuelson, Paul A., "Principles and Rules in Modern Fiscal Policy: A Neo-
classical Reformulation," *Money, Trade, and Economic Growth* (in honor
of John Henry Williams), Macmillan Company, New York, 1951, pp. 157–
176.
———— "Full Employment versus Progress and Other Economic Goals," *Income
Stabilization for a Developing Democracy*, Max F. Millikan, ed., Yale Uni-
versity Press, New Haven, 1953, pp. 547–580.
Smithies, Arthur, "Federal Budgeting and Fiscal Policy," *Survey of Contemporary
Economics*, Vol. I, Howard S. Ellis, ed., Blakiston Company, Philadelphia,
1948, pp. 174–209.

4.

··

The budget cycle

Government budgeting, in its procedural aspects and time dimensions, expresses a pattern of responsibility derived from political power relationships. The responsibility function differs in the presidential and parliamentary systems and also among national, provincial, and local governments. These differences will be described in general terms, as a prelude to examination of the budget cycle. This will be followed by a postscript on the classical principles of budgeting.

Major portions of this chapter are an introduction to subjects to be discussed in later chapters, particularly in Chapters 10 through 14. This preliminary on the phases of budgeting serves to emphasize the continuous character of the budgetary process in modern government and the overriding importance of procedures.

I. THE RESPONSIBILITY FUNCTION IN BUDGETING

The historical development of modern budgeting suggests two significant generalizations concerning the distribution of budgetary responsibility.

First, the budget system developed as an instrument for democratic control over the executive. The power of the purse came to reside in the legislature in order to prevent the executive from imposing willful and arbitrary tax payments on his subjects. The budget is an expression of ultimate legislative authority.

Second, the budget system requires the development of a two-way pattern of responsibility, centering on the executive. One line of responsibility runs from the executive to the administrative agencies. The executive must be charged with general supervision of administrative affairs; executive authority must be able to control administration. Only then is it possible for the executive to prepare a financial plan; only then is it possible to execute the plan as adopted by the legislature. The second line of responsibility in a budget system runs from the executive to the legislature. In every democratic government the legislature may approve or reject the proposals of the executive; in some governments the legislature may also modify executive proposals. In the exercise of this authority the legislature must be able to hold the executive accountable—both for the execution of last year's financial plan and for the comprehensiveness of this year's program.

Many of the features which are usually said to characterize a budget system are the product of this pattern of two-way responsibility. A consolidated fund to receive and disburse all revenues is a prerequisite for the enforcement of the pattern of responsibility. Similarly, an accounting system for governmental programs, which must underlie budget statements, provides a basis for the execution of the budget. The annual statement of revenue and expenditure measures the flow of moneys through the consolidated fund, in accordance with the accounts maintained by the executive. These are the corollaries of a budget system; the essence of the system is the pattern of responsibility.

The budget system in parliamentary governments has very much the same pattern of responsibility as in governments where executive and legislative authority are separated. In Great Britain all grants of public money and all impositions of taxation must receive the initial approval of the Crown as expressed by one of its responsible ministers.[1] However, the House of Commons may not initiate budgetary proposals. This is the responsibility of the Chancellor of the Exchequer, who derives his authority from the Cabinet. The lines of responsibility are comparable to those in the national government of the United States—from the executive to the departments, and from the executive to the legislature. But in Britain the line of budgetary authority from the Cabinet to the House of Commons is continuous and is capable of precise definition.

The exercise of collective responsibility through the Cabinet means that the Chancellor of the Exchequer must present questions to the Cab-

[1] Eric Taylor, *The House of Commons at Work*, Penguin Books, Harmondsworth, Middlesex, 1951, p. 190.

inet for its consideration and is bound by the decisions made there.[2] His is presumably the most influential voice in financial affairs, but this influence is exercised in relation to the policy determinations of the Cabinet, and is derived from the fact that the Cabinet represents the majority party in the Commons and controls the legislative machinery. These relations between executive authority and legislative authority provide a degree of leadership and continuity in budget-making in Great Britain that is seldom attained in executive budgeting in American governments. The separation of powers does not facilitate the continuous influence of the executive in shaping and molding legislation. The Chancellor of the Exchequer, in the name of the executive authority, defends and explains the budget in the House of Commons. Through him the Cabinet assumes responsibility for its formulation, adoption, and execution.

On the other hand, the relations between executive authority and the administrative departments are not very different in Great Britain than in governments with well-established budget systems in the United States. The British Treasury does possess a wider scope for reviewing and planning than do most central budget offices in this country; its jurisdiction extends to revenue, expenditure, economic policy, personnel, and administration. In the performance of these responsibilities, however, it behaves in a manner similar to central budget offices with a more narrow range of responsibilities. In matters of expenditure it has the "watchdog" role and tends to review requests for funds with a view to reducing them. In matters of economic policy it serves as a staff agency for channeling questions for final decision to the Chancellor of the Exchequer and the Cabinet. In the execution of the budget it observes and reports on progress within programs.

Even as the location and performance of the responsibility for budgeting serve to characterize the differences and similarities between parliamentary and chief-executive budgeting, so will this account for some of the major differences in budgeting and budgetary procedure among national, state, and local governments in this country.

In the national government the responsibility of the President for the preparation and submission of the budget is well established, as is the position of the Bureau of the Budget to assist in the discharge of this responsibility. In the states, however, the governor's role is very often less clear, and even where the statutory responsibility of the governor for

---

[2] For a discussion of the pattern of collective responsibility see Sir Ivor Jennings, *The Queen's Government*, Penguin Books, Harmondsworth, Middlesex, 1954, pp. 118–125.

preparation and submission may be precisely stated, his position is often weakened by the absence of effective staff assistance in the preparation of the budget and in budget execution. In municipalities, the city manager form of government invariably centers complete control over budget preparation in the hands of the manager, and in the larger cities the budget director will report to the manager, not to the mayor. Lines of responsibility are less clearly fixed under the mayor-council system, even where there is a "strong-mayor" type of government. Here, and particularly in the larger cities, budget preparation may be shared with a board of estimates; budget-making authority is often diffused.

The central role of the executive in modern budgeting would suggest that the legislative budget system is not truly a budget system at all. Under this procedure, which is followed today in a great many county and rural governments in the United States, the legislative body—the county board of supervisors, for example—appoints a committee from its membership to prepare the annual budget. This committee receives requests for funds from each of the county department heads, and secures from the county treasurer or other financial officer a forecast of revenue. On this basis a document called a budget is prepared for submission to the whole legislature, or perhaps, if the county is a large one, to the finance committee. There is no principal executive officer who is responsible for the budget; there is no central budgetary review which assumes responsibility for the integrity of the estimates as submitted. The estimates are those of the departments, and the legislative budget committee assumes responsibility only for tabulation and summary.[3] Similarly, the legislative budget committee, under these circumstances, assumes no responsibility for the execution of the budget. This is left in the hands of the departments of the county. Under these circumstances the absence of executive authority with responsibility for either review or financial planning, or for execution, makes of budgeting little more than a bookkeeping operation.

The patterns of responsibility which characterize the budgetary process may be examined from a number of standpoints. As a legal institution, the budget is an expression of the constitution and statutes of a government, which endow the executive and the legislature with designated financial and managerial responsibilities. Viewed in terms of organization, the budget is an expression of decisions which are made hierarchally, with an interplay and mutual exchange between staff and line agencies, and between those who must provide executive leadership and those who must provide legislative leadership. As a matter of pro-

[3] See Lane W. Lancaster, *Government in Rural America*, 2nd ed., D. Van Nostrand Company, New York, 1952, pp. 117–122.

cedure, the budget is the product of a time sequence of decisions made in an organizational context. It is this time sequence, viewed organizationally, which will be examined in the remainder of this chapter.

The term "budget cycle" is not often used to describe the procedural character of budgetary systems of governments in the United States; this phrase is of Western European origin. The term "cycle," however, aptly emphasizes the periodicity of budgeting. It is of course true, as a cliché has it, that budgeting is a continuous process. Budget-making is not, or at least should not be, an annual affair; attention to the budget and budgetary formulation should influence the day-to-day decisions of management at all levels. But at the same time, this continuity is marked by specific phases of a cyclical character.

The examination of these distinct phases serves to center attention on the time dimension of budgeting. This latter is pervasive in its influence, limiting the decisions which can be made in the budgetary process and at least partially controlling the scope of activities. The actions of the legislature on last year's budget determine the programs which are now being conducted. Progress under the current year's budget shapes and bounds the programs which can be recommended in the budget now under preparation.

The time dimension also affects the interrelationship of programing and budgeting. If this were a static world, with closed economies uninfluenced by conditions beyond their borders, with technological change and population change proceeding at a constant rate, then the interrelationship of budgeting and programing would be relatively simple. Programs and plans would precede budgets, and budget-making would consist of the financial and managerial implementation of programs. But the "if" is unrealistic. Population, technology, and national income move unevenly. Sudden changes in their magnitude interrupt the smooth implementation and planning of governmental programs. Time schedules for the phases of the budget cycle must be altered to conform with immediate and pressing requirements. Unless there is some flexibility in the time dimension of budget-making, the crises and the "crash programs" cannot be managed.

The phases of the budget cycle can be generally identified as: (1) executive preparation and submission, (2) legislative authorization, (3) execution, and (4) audit.

Necessarily, these generalized phases are subject to substantial modification from one government to the next. In governments where executive budget-making is not well developed, legislative review dominates the whole of the budget cycle, and legislative decisions extend to the execution phase. In some governments the legislature's role is a minor one, and executive preparation dominates all phases. In still other cases execution and audit are mingled, either in time or in accordance with the governmental agencies responsible therefor.

II. THE BUDGET CYCLE IN THE UNITED STATES GOVERNMENT

No attempt will be made here to describe in detail the almost infinite possible variations in the phases of the budget cycle in various governments.[4] Attention will be centered on the complex operations of the cycle in one government—the federal government of the United States. Chart 1 shows the phases of the budget cycle and the branch and agency of government responsible therefore.

CHART 1
Phases of Budgeting in the U. S. Government

Preparation and submission	Executive	Departments and agencies Bureau of the Budget President
Authorization	Congress	House and Senate and their appropriations committees President's veto or signature
Execution	Executive	Bureau of the Budget Treasury Department Departments and agencies
Audit	Executive Congress	Departments and agencies General Accounting Office

A. PHASE I—PREPARATION AND SUBMISSION

Chart 2 details the preparation and submission of the budget by the executive. The time dimension listed is only approximate. Not only does it vary from year to year, but it varies from department to depart-

---

[4] There is a paucity of written materials on this subject. One of the few case studies at the state level is contained in L. Felix Joyner and John P. Stanley, "Budget Preparation in Kentucky," *State Government*, October 1951, pp. 252–253, 256; L. Felix Joyner, "Budget Preparation in Kentucky," *State Government*, June 1952, pp. 128, 137, and December 1952, pp. 273–274, 284. An examination of the phases of budgeting in the U. S. Government and shorter studies of procedure in Berkeley, California, the State of California, the State of New York, and the Secretariat of the United Nations are contained in O. Bakker, *The Budget Cycle in Public Finance in the United States of America*, W. P. Van Stockum & Zoon, The Hague, 1953. New York City's procedure is set forth and analyzed in A. E. Buck, *Budgeting and Financial Management of the City of New York*, Mayor's Committee on Management Survey, New York, 1951, pp. 46–68.

ment. For example, the Department of Defense in recent years has submitted its formal estimates to the Bureau of the Budget in October or November, not in September as indicated. Exact precision in timing the preparation of the budget does not and cannot exist.

CHART 2
Preparation and Submission of the U. S. Budget
(For Fiscal 1957)

Prior to April 1955	Bureau (unit) planning for fiscal 1957
April 1955	Budget call from departmental budget offices
May 1955	Consolidation of department's field budget with over-all budget for department
June 1955	Over-all budget policy development; clearance from President; revenue estimates from Treasury
	Bureau of the Budget; Director's policy letter; call for estimates; announcement of ceilings
July–August 1955	Departmental review, hearings and adjustments
September 30, 1955	Departments submit appropriation requests
September 30–November 15, 1955	Bureau of the Budget examiners' review
October 10–November 20, 1955	Hearings in the Bureau of the Budget
October–November 1955	Review by the Director of the Bureau of the Budget
November–December 1955	Presidential review
	Preparation of the budget message
	Preparation of the budget document
January 1956	Submission of the budget to Congress

The budget cycle in any government should be characterized by a flow-up and a flow-back of decisions. Certain kinds of decisions will be made at the operating level and will move up the organizational hierarchy to influence decisions there. At the same time, policy and program decisions will be made at the higher levels, to move down to the operating levels. This two-way flow is most obviously characteristic of the budget cycle in the United States government, and some of the relatively recent innovations in federal budgetary procedure have been undertaken with a view to the improvement of this two-way channel of communication.

As Chart 2 shows, the preparation phase starts at the operating levels, where units of bureaus and divisions initiate their budgetary planning more than 14 months before the beginning of the fiscal year to which the estimates are to apply. Very early in this process the departmental budget office begins its activity with a "budget call," which outlines policy decisions that may already have been made and transmits whatever technical information is necessary concerning the forms and reports to be provided by the units. As bureaus and divisions complete this initial work, the departmental budget office is in a position, in May for some departments and somewhat later for others, to prepare a consolidation of requests from the units, including the operations in the field (outside Washington), and is equipped with the information for subsequent relations with the Bureau of the Budget. In some agencies, where field operations are highly routinized and closely controlled by Washington, all budget preparation may be done centrally.

In May and June the Bureau of the Budget discusses with departments and agencies the nature of their probable requirements for the forthcoming year. These discussions are designed to provide the Bureau with information on the budgetary outlook. The Bureau is then in a position to advise the President as to the budgetary problems which are emerging, and to frame the questions which must be answered throughout successive stages of budget preparation.

The Bureau of the Budget now begins to put together, in June of each year, the pieces that make up the framework of budget policy for the forthcoming fiscal year. The initial conferences with departments and agencies provide an indication of their spending needs. The Bureau obtains a set of preliminary revenue estimates from the Treasury Department. These are based on a forecast of economic conditions and are, at this stage, predicated on the assumption that revenue laws and rates of taxation will continue in accordance with statutes previously enacted. At this point, the Bureau of the Budget may consult with the Council of Economic Advisers (CEA), with the staff of the Board of Governors of the Federal Revenue System, or the staff of the Department of Commerce on forecast levels of national income. It may consult with the Department of Agriculture on anticipated levels of farm prices and their probable impact on the budget. Very often, interdepartmental staff meetings will be arranged to pool available information and viewpoints on the economic shape of the future. The Treasury forecasts of revenue may also be subject to independent examination by staff of the CEA or the Bureau.

Concurrently with this examination of the economic outlook, the Director of the Bureau of the Budget will confer with the White House staff and with the President himself, to secure initial clearance on major program decisions, and to bring to the attention of the President the problems which are emerging and about which decisions must be reached at some later point in time. The over-all revenue and expenditure outlook can then be examined, at least in broad outline, and the Administration's fiscal policy for the forthcoming year can begin to take shape. This is how the "President's program" is formulated—it emerges and crystallizes as decisions are made; it does not spring full-blown from a planning staff that outlines it in advance (see Chapter 11).

With this background of interdepartmental and presidential consultation, the Bureau of the Budget initiates a major step in the "flow-back" of decisions. The Director issues a policy letter, which goes to the heads of departments and agencies. This letter customarily spells out, in general terms, the economic assumptions on which the budget is to be prepared. These indicate whether the level of national income is expected to rise or fall, and state the price level assumptions that are to serve as the basis for estimates of the cost of materials and supplies. The general policy indications may be translated into specific references to the possibilities for public works outlays for the forthcoming budget year, and agencies and departments may be apprised that they can expect to receive approval for an enlarged volume of construction projects, or that backlog projects must continue to be postponed.

In the policy letter the Director transmits to a number of department and agencies—about fifteen—a budget ceiling. This ceiling reflects an initial review of the department's requirements by the staff of the Bureau of the Budget, and any presidential decisions which may have been made affecting the agency's program. The ceiling now assumes the importance of a target. In effect, the Director of the Bureau is saying that in accordance with the President's program, it is anticipated that the department's budget submission will be within the announced ceiling. Programs which would force a break in the ceiling must be supported by special justifications. The estimates will not necessarily be rejected if they fail to come within the ceiling. Neither does the Director agree to approve all submissions within this ceiling; subsequent review may disclose places where reductions can be made.

A second aspect of the "flow-back" of decisions is the "Call for Estimates." This is a technical document issued in more or less permanent form, subject to occasional revision. The "Call for Estimates" notifies departments and agencies of the planned time schedule, the date for their submission of final estimates to the Bureau. It contains instructions on the form in which estimates are to be presented, and suggestions for the kinds of reports and written materials which are to accompany the submission. Instructions applying to the preparation of materials describing new programs are contained here.

During the months of July and August the departments and agencies conduct intensive examinations of their budgets in the light of any ceilings or policy directives which have been transmitted to them. During this period budget examiners from the Bureau are available for consultation on technical questions, to assist in providing the information which the Bureau requires. But the responsibility for departmental review, hearings, and adjustments is, of course, the department's. Budget officers in the departments work closely with the heads of divisions and with the secretary of the department, to bring the budget into line with the department's over-all policy objectives.

As the departmental estimates are prepared, they are submitted to the Bureau of the Budget, generally after the first of September. The estimates are then subjected to critical review by the budget examiners, who orient their examination toward the budget hearings and the questions which will be asked at that time. The period between submission of a budget to the Bureau and the hearings is relatively short; it is evident that unless examiners have been continuously following program developments, they will be unable, in this brief time, to bring to their review the necessary background of information.

Some of the examiners will begin budget hearings while others are still engaged in looking over the budget submissions of agencies under their jurisdiction. In general, the smaller agencies or those which have finished their submissions come first. The larger and more complex departments, such as Defense, are likely to be scheduled somewhat later, in November or even December rather than in October.

Prior to the hearings, each examining unit will prepare a brief agenda, which may be sent to the departmental budget officer and serves to outline the points that will be questioned most closely. The hearings are internal to the Bureau of the Budget, are conducted by the head of each examining unit, and are not open to the public. Senior budget examiners from each unit will attend, as well as Bureau of the Budget staff members who are not examiners but are interested in a particular program.

The budget officer of each department or agency is responsible for coordinating and organizing the defense of the estimates as submitted; he is assisted in this by members of his staff. The hearings may be opened with a statement by the head of a department or his deputy, who will be followed by the heads of operating bureaus and divisions. Hearings are conducted informally; the examiners will question particular items or ask for additional information; operating officials will attempt to justify their requests.

On the basis of the hearings and such additional information as has been submitted by the departments, the budget examiners prepare their recommendations for transmittal to the Director of the Bureau. Very often there will be consultation and interchange of views between the

Director and his staff prior to the final formulation of the examiners' recommendations. During this time there may also be informal consultation between the Director and the heads of agencies and departments.

The recommendations of the budget examiners are now subject to a more or less formal internal review by the Bureau of the Budget. This is the Director's Review, and it is conducted by a committee appointed for the occasion. The Deputy Director of the Bureau may act as chairman of the committee; the general Assistant Directors and the Assistant Director for Budget Review may make up the remaining membership. The Bureau's division chiefs will present their findings and recommendations. The Director's Review provides the opportunity for departments and agencies to appeal for a reconsideration of their estimates, and for the Bureau to coordinate the estimates of the various departments and agencies. A department or agency may also take a final appeal to the President, in an effort to reverse a Bureau decision.

The last stage of executive budget preparation takes place in November and December, concurrently with the Director's Review. This consists of presidential review of the budget as it is emerging from the Bureau of the Budget, and the preparation of the President's budget message.

Drafts of the message are initiated within the Bureau of the Budget late in October or in November. During November these are circulated among departments and agencies for comment, and by early December the budget message begins to be readied for White House examination.

Concurrently, the final estimates of revenue are prepared by the Treasury Department, with an "Explanation of the Estimates of Receipts" for inclusion in the budget document. With these estimates it is possible for the Bureau of the Budget, the Treasury, and the Council of Economic Advisers to prepare final policy recommendations for the President and, in particular, to recommend whether last-minute changes should be made in budget programs in order to affect the size of the budget deficit or surplus.

In the meantime, the Bureau of the Budget has begun to put the budget document together. Detailed estimates, narratives, and schedules are brought together and the summary tables are prepared. As the final estimates are determined for each department and approved by the President, the departments are notified of the decisions which have been reached.

The budget message and the budget document are readied for the Government Printing Office, and after printing, the document is formally transmitted by the President to the Congress, usually in the third week in January. Advance copies of the summary tables are made available to the press; in some years the President, together with the Director of the

Bureau of the Budget, have held a press conference on the day before the budget is formally transmitted. In other years the Director or the Secretary of the Treasury, or both, have held such a conference.

This completes the first phase of the budget cycle in the United States government.

B. THE BUDGET DOCUMENT

The President's policy with respect to existing programs and his policy with respect to new programs are both reflected in the budget document. The summary budget accounts distinguish between recommendations based on existing legislation and recommendations based on legislation which the President proposes. The necessity for this distinction arises from the fact that the Congress must treat these types of budget recommendations differently. Those based on existing legislation will require no further action by the standing committees of the Congress, and may be reviewed and approved or modified by the appropriations committees. New legislation requires two actions, one to authorize the program and the other to appropriate funds for its execution.

The President's budget is characterized by heavy emphasis on the government's outgo—on appropriations, obligations, and expenditures. There is much less attention to revenue and tax policy. The summary tables do show the relation between budget receipts and budget expenditures. But for many years the budget message did not deal with tax policy. Only since 1954 has the message contained more than a passing reference to taxation, and even recently this falls short of an extensive analysis.

The reason for this is that traditionally the Treasury Department has had responsibility for estimating revenues and for the staff work on the Administration's tax program. It is the Secretary of the Treasury who transmits this program to the Congress and who defends it before Congressional committees. Further, the Administration's tax program is customarily submitted to the Congress at a different point in time than the budget; the date varies, but it is more likely to be in February or March than in January. As a result of this organizational and time-sequence separation, the budget of the United States is primarily an expenditure document.

Even as an expenditure document the budget is not wholly comprehensive of the Administration's recommendations. Additional requests for supplementary appropriations will be transmitted while Congress is in session. These requests may arise from the changing nature of departmental and agency programs, changes which could not have been foreseen at the time the budget was prepared, such as the occurrence of droughts or floods or international crises. Requests may also arise from requirements which have not yet been enacted into legislation at the time of budget submission. For these latter, aggregate dollar amounts are indicated in the document and totaled as a part of budget expenditures, under the heading "proposed for later transmission." Also, the budget contains, as a separate expenditure category, a "reserve for contingencies" to cover the specific appropriations which Congress may be asked to provide during the forthcoming months. Budget submission, like budget preparation, is a more or less continuous process.

The foregoing account of executive budget preparation and submission in the United States government conveys a greater sense of precision and step-by-step scheduling than actually occurs. In practice, presidential decisions affecting major budget programs may occur at any time in the process or may be initiated wholly outside the budgetary routine. Programs with major budgetary implications may be formulated by departments and agencies, may receive the President's approval, and may be presented to the Bureau almost as a *fait accompli.*

Decision-making outside established budgetary channels is particularly characteristic of program and policy determinations for the Department of Defense. Since 1947 the National Security Council (NSC) has had statutory responsibility for advising the President on the integration of domestic, foreign, and military policies.[5] The NSC, since 1953, has been made up of the President, the Vice President, the Secretaries of State and Defense, the Director of the Office of Defense Mobilization, the Director of the Foreign Operations Administration, and such others as the President may designate from time to time. The Director of the Bureau of the Budget customarily attends NSC meetings. One of the early duties of the National Security Council was to advise the President on the size of the military budget, after reviewing in broad outline the programs of the Department of Defense, foreign aid programs, and the state of the civilian economy. This has been customarily accomplished during the summer months, and in some years has taken the form of a budget ceiling figure for the Department of Defense, similar in nature to the ceilings which are transmitted by the Director of the Bureau of the Budget to other specified agencies and departments. On other occasions the National Security Council recommendations have been made in program rather than financial terms.

Economic and fiscal policy considerations are similarly channeled into

[5] P. L. 253, 80th Cong., 1st sess. For a description, see Gus C. Lee, "The Organization for National Security," *Public Administration Review,* Winter 1949, pp. 36–44; Edward H. Hobbs, *Behind the President,* Public Affairs Press, Washington, 1954, pp. 125–155.

the budgetary process at many points. As noted, the Council of Economic Advisers and the Treasury will consult with the Bureau of the Budget prior to the Director's policy letter, and consultation continues through the period when the budget message is being prepared. Likewise, CEA, which has responsibility for preparing the *Economic Report of the President,* works with the Bureau of the Budget, the Treasury, and other agencies to assure that there is uniformity in the President's program and in the emphasis which is to be accorded to particular components of that program. The Office of Defense Mobilization will be directly involved in staff work relating to national security programs and their treatment as part of the President's program. Finally, both the *Economic Report* and the budget message must be coordinated with the state of the union message. These are the three major documents that outline the President's program, and they are submitted to the Congress at about the same time, in the first weeks of each session.

Given the complexity of the United States government and the need for asserting a centripetal force to counteract the continuous movement of government away from central control, it seems likely that more and more coordinating mechanisms will be established in the federal government. More and more policy and program decisions will require supplemental consideration outside the budgetary routine itself.[6] This tendency to utilize special coordinating mechanisms complicates and diffuses the program decisions which accompany the budgetary process. At the same time, it enhances the significance of budgeting as a final coordinating device.

C. Phase II—Legislative Authorization

Budget day in the United States Congress is an occasion of no particular significance. The drama associated with this event in Great Britain is wholly lacking here. In that country the Chancellor of the Exchequer's presentation of the budget is the announcement of the new tax rates that the Government recommends and that will almost certainly be adopted. The British housewife is naturally interested in the duties to be imposed on items of household expenditure; the British wage earner and businessman are interested in the tax rate to be levied on their in-

[6] The first Hoover Commission recommendations are a case in point. Although the Commission favored a strengthened Executive Office and improved staff and management aids for the President, it likewise recommended the creation of such new mechanisms as a Board of Impartial Analysis to review major public works construction projects and a National Monetary and Credit Council to co-ordinate domestic lending programs. (Commission on Organization of the Executive Branch of the Government, *Concluding Report,* Washington, 1949, pp. 53, 61.)

comes; taxes have always been the most controversial part of public finance. But in the United States the President's budget contains no spectacular announcements on taxation—and even if it did, the Congress would very likely adopt a modified tax program. Similarly, and again unlike Great Britain, congressional revision of expenditures is extensive and the President's recommendations are subject to considerable modification.

In its action on the President's recommendations, the Congress is limited by only one specific constitutional restriction—no appropriation for the army may run for more than two years.[7] Unlike revenue measures, which must be initiated by the House of Representatives, appropriation measures, so far as the Constitution is concerned, may be initiated by either chamber. In practice it has become traditional for the House of Representatives also to initiate appropriations; the Senate acts at a later point in time, and its action serves to modify the House action.

The House Committee on Appropriations is made up of 50 members, 30 from the majority and 20 from the minority party. Members of the House do not ordinarily serve on more than one committee; Appropriations is regarded as a key assignment. The committee chairman designates 13 subcommittees of from 6 to 14 members each; there is some duplication in subcommittee assignments, and for defense appropriations there are sub-subcommittees. The committee chairman schedules the hearings, after consultation with the chairmen of the subcommittees, and serves ex officio on each of the subcommittees. The whole committee has few responsibilities; the subcommittees and their chairmen have major authority.

Each subcommittee is responsible for reporting out one or two appropriation bills, the total number of which varies in any one session from 12 to 15. A single appropriation bill embraces the military functions of the Department of Defense, but other bills may cover a very large number of agencies, as with the Independent Offices Appropriation Bill. Unlike other legislation, which is introduced in draft form by individual Congressmen, appropriations measures are drafted in committee (see Chapter 12). Most of the subcommittees begin their hearings on the budget in January, although in nonelection years a few subcommittees may commence hearings even before the session is formally opened, on the basis of information provided by the Bureau of the Budget and the agencies. The hearings are seldom open to the public, and nonofficial witnesses are rare except at hearings on public works measures.

The subcommittees do not work with the budget document as such,

[7] Article I, Section 8. This has been modified in practice by the use of "no-year" appropriations for long-range procurement.

but rather with a "committee print" of the budget, which consists of the material from the document set up on sheets with a considerable blank space for notes. In addition, departments and agencies will submit supplementary information not contained in the document.

The responsibility for the presentation of the President's budget rests with the departments and agencies themselves, not with the Bureau of the Budget. No occasion is provided for a general presentation of the Administration's budgetary policy, and representatives of the Bureau are seldom present at the hearings. The budget officer of each agency and department organizes the testimony and the exhibits. He may enlist the support of his department head for the presentation of the initial testimony. The major support and defense of the estimates as submitted is undertaken by heads of bureaus and divisions.

Hearings are generally informal. The testimony is transcribed and made available for study by committee members, but off-the-record comments are permitted and all witnesses are given the opportunity to revise and extend their remarks for the record.

In the hearings committee members very often indicate their pleasure or displeasure with agency programs, in terms that suggest changes to be made during the forthcoming year. There are no sharp lines drawn between "policy" and "administration" here; the suggestions may touch on matters which the departments and agencies might regard as within their management prerogatives.

After the hearings the subcommittee goes into executive session for the "mark-up" of the bill, which consists in determining the appropriations to be recommended and any limitations to be attached to the use of funds for particular purposes. Each subcommittee has one or more clerks who assist in this process and in the preparation of the subcommittee report, which accompanies each appropriation bill. In this report the subcommittee will indicate the reasons for its actions, frequently with general observations on the nature of the programs which the department or agency is conducting, sometimes including suggestions on the way in which appropriations ought to be expanded in the forthcoming year. (See Chapter 12.) The appropriations measures themselves will usually incorporate specific limitations on certain kinds of program expenditures.

The subcommittee's report, together with the appropriation bill, is referred to the House Appropriations Committee, where it is seldom examined in detail or modified in any particular. The Appropriations Committee then reports the bill to the House, where it is a custom to advance the bill to debate within three days. This is accomplished by a resolution to resolve the House into a Committee of the Whole. The chairman of the subcommittee acts as floor manager for the bill, to present, explain, and defend the action of the Appropriations Committee. General debate is limited and it is unusual for the House to modify substantially the action of the Appropriations Committee. With the termination of debate, the appropriation bill is voted by the House. These votes are seldom a matter of record and absenteeism is usually high.

From the House of Representatives the appropriation bill goes to the Senate, where it is referred to the Senate Appropriations Committee, and in turn to its designated subcommittees. Some departure from this pattern has occurred in recent years, and it has become increasingly common for the Senate to begin its hearings before the House has actually completed its action. Nevertheless, final action by the Senate will almost always occur after final action by the House.

The Senate Appropriations Committee consists of 23 members, organized into 10 subcommittees. These subcommittees are much larger than in the House, with from 10 to 11 members of the Committee on each subcommittee. Unlike the House, one member may serve on more than one subcommittee. In addition, the subcommittees are supplemented by membership from other related standing committees of the Senate, such as Armed Services, Agriculture and Forestry, and Public Works.

Hearings before the subcommittees of the Senate Appropriations Committee are conducted in relation to the action taken, or contemplated, by the House. Procedure is similar to that before the House subcommittees. Again the agencies and departments present their testimony, followed by questions from members. Hearings are shorter, and the subcommittee action is very likely to be directed at the differences between the appropriations as requested by the President and the action which the House took—invariably reductions. The Senate thus tends to act as a court of appeal, and will very often restore a part or all of the reductions made by the House.

As in the House, the subcommittees, not the Appropriations Committee itself, wield the influence. The subcommittee marks up the bill, and with the help of its staff prepares a report. The Appropriations Committee, in turn, will rarely modify the action of its subcommittee and will transmit the bill to the Senate. Floor discussion is likely to be more extensive because of the privilege of free debate, and modifications on the floor are more frequent than in the House. Roll-call votes are, however, unusual.

The House bill and the Senate bill must be reconciled by a conference committee. This committee is empowered to adopt a final figure between the amount of appropriations approved by the House and the amount approved by the Senate. The conference committee draft is then reported to the House and to the Senate. Occasionally the con-

ference bill is rejected and sent back with instructions for further conference. More likely it will be accepted by both the House and the
Senate and adopted without substantial debate.

The "enrolled bill" is sent to the President for his approval or veto.
It is first referred to the Bureau of the Budget and from there to the
agencies and departments whose appropriations are affected by the legislation. These departments and agencies may then, if they so desire, prepare a memorandum recommending that the President veto the bill, or
that the President's signature be accompanied by a message pointing out
deficiencies in the legislation. These views are coordinated in the
Bureau of the Budget, and a final memorandum is prepared for the
President. (See Chapter 11.)

On the basis of this memorandum, and other information which the
President or his staff may solicit, the President rejects the bill or signs it,
with or without comment. Appropriations measures are rarely vetoed.
More frequently, the President will sign the measure but indicate his
disapproval of particular sections of the legislation. The Constitution
does not provide for an item veto of appropriation measures; they must
be accepted or rejected *in toto*. (See Chapter 12.)

If appropriation bills are not enacted by the beginning of the fiscal
year, it is customary for the Congress, by joint resolution, to authorize
departments and agencies to incur obligations at the same rate as during
the preceding fiscal year.

On the first day of each month during the session the *Congressional
Record* prints a summary of appropriation measures as of that time. At
the end of each session the clerks of the appropriations committees prepare for inclusion in the appendix to the *Congressional Record* a summary of appropriations measures adopted. Some weeks later a comprehensive document is published, under the title *Appropriations, Budget
Estimates, Etc.*, containing the complete text of all appropriation measures, schedules comparing the budget recommendations of the President
and actions taken by the Congress, the chronological history of appropriations actions taken by the House and the Senate, and other pertinent
information.

The Bureau of the Budget may publish a mid-year review shortly after
the close of each session, in August or September. This review will contain revised estimates of receipts for the fiscal year under way and estimates of expenditures which reflect the actions taken by the Congress.

D. Phase III—Execution of the Budget

Congress generally extends budget authorizations directly to the spending agencies and departments, not to the President nor to the Bureau of

the Budget. The only prominent exceptions to this practice are for programs of foreign military and economic aid, where funds are appropriated to the President. In all cases, however, before spending agencies may incur obligations or make expenditures, they must initiate action to secure release of the authorization from the Bureau of the Budget.[8]

The procedure for the release of budget authorizations is known as apportionment; its major purpose is to regularize the rate of obligation in order to minimize the need for deficiency or supplemental appropriations. Briefly, this works out as follows.

Within fifteen days after the approval of a budget authorization by the Congress, the specified agency must transmit a request for apportionment to the Bureau. This request outlines the agency's need for funds over the forthcoming fiscal year, and suggests an apportionment, usually on a quarterly basis. An apportionment on the basis of specified projects or activities may also be used to supplement or as a substitute for a time-period basis. The apportionment request is reviewed by the Bureau of the Budget, and the agency is notified of the decision. Apportionments are cumulative in that amounts not used in one period are available for obligation in a later period of the fiscal year.

At the end of each month agencies must report the current status of their budgetary authorizations, and the cumulative apportionments, obligations, expenditures, and unliquidated obligations, as well as unobligated and unexpended balances. These reports, sent to the Treasury and to the Bureau of the Budget, provide the basis for a re-examination of apportionment status. Agencies may at any time initiate a request for a change in apportionments in order to adapt their programs to altered conditions. The Bureau acts on such changes in the same manner as on the original request for apportionment. The Bureau must also examine the status of apportionment requests each quarter to ascertain whether modifications are necessary.

In addition to its apportionment power, the Bureau of the Budget has authority to establish reserves against appropriations. These are established for the following purposes: (1) to provide for emergencies which may arise later in the fiscal year and would otherwise require a deficiency appropriation, (2) to bring obligating authority into line with changed conditions in the interests of economy, and (3) to control appropriations which extend over a period of years in order that obligational authority will be available in the future. The establishment of reserves against

[8] Portions of the material which follow are reproduced, without substantial modification, from the author's "Budget Execution and Government Accounting in the United States," in *Government Accounting and Budget Execution*, United Nations, 1952, pp. 73–90.

appropriations does not necessarily mean that the reserved portion will be unavailable to the agency. If conditions change during the fiscal year so as to justify the use of the reserve, the agency may request that the Bureau make the reserve available.

The second step in the process of budget execution in the federal government is allotment, which extends budgetary authority to administrative units within agencies and departments. Allotment is under the control of the agencies and is customarily administered by the budget office of each agency, acting on authority of the agency head. Allotment consists in the extension of obligational authority to units or divisions of departments, usually on a monthly or quarterly basis. It may also be extended in terms of objects of expenditure or activities within administrative units. The allotment must be harmonious with the apportionment from the Bureau of the Budget, but the allotment is internal and the Bureau has no supervision over its terms or procedures. The allotment system within agencies and departments is often controlled by a system of internal reporting on a monthly basis. This permits the agency budget office to review the rate at which budget authorizations are being employed and to intervene, if necessary, to prevent overobligation.

The foregoing pattern of budget execution in terms of apportionments by the Bureau of the Budget and allotments by agencies and departments may be termed administrative control. Its general purpose is to assure that programs are conducted in conformity with the policies of the Executive Office of the President and in conformity with agency policy. In addition, budget execution in the federal government has a corollary pattern of fiscal controls administered by the Treasury Department and the agencies. Fiscal controls consist of the maintenance of accounting records to show appropriations, obligations, and disbursements, thus assuring that budget execution is conducted within the framework of legal authority, in accordance with the constitutional prescription that "No money shall be drawn from the Treasury, but in consequence of appropriations made by law . . . ." (Article I, Section 9).

After appropriation bills have been signed by the President, the Secretary of the Treasury directs the Treasurer of the United States to establish a credit equal to the aggregate amount of the appropriation. These credits are made available to disbursing officers through accounts maintained in Federal Reserve Banks. Departments and agencies may now incur obligations, that is, enter into contracts for goods and services.

As public creditors present bills for payment, the appropriate administrative officers in each agency certify the payment and direct the disbursing officers to issue checks to liquidate the obligation. The certifying officers who sign vouchers for payment are liable for performance in accordance with statutes and regulations, and are responsible for the adequacy of balances available to meet the payment. Disbursing officers do not have responsibility for the legality of payments. All disbursement officers maintain accounts, which are subject to audit.

All receipts—from taxation, customs duties, and other revenue sources —are deposited by administrative officers to the credit of the Treasurer of the United States, in accounts in Federal Reserve Banks.

In addition to the accounts maintained centrally by the Treasurer, each department and agency has general ledger accounts to record apportionments of appropriations and allotments, as well as obligations, unexpended balances, and revenues, if any. In most organizational units the allotment accounts are the basis for the daily record of operations, and reports based on these accounts provide information for higher supervisory levels.

The receipts and expenditures of the federal government, as reflected in the accounts maintained by the Treasurer, are reported in summary form in the *Daily Treasury Statement*. A *Monthly Treasury Statement* presents a comprehensive account of federal financial activity; some information is also contained in the monthly *Treasury Bulletin*. After the close of each fiscal year the Treasury publishes the *Combined Statement of Receipts, Expenditures and Balances of the United States Government*. This document, which in other countries would be called the "closed accounts," is prepared on the basis of appropriations and shows, for each account, disbursements and unexpended balances. The *Combined Statement* is transmitted to the Congress at the beginning of each session, which is six months after the close of the fiscal year.

E. Phase IV—Audit

General responsibility for compliance with the legalities of appropriation is in the hands of the agencies and departments to whom appropriations are made. The Congress, however, has an independent check through the General Accounting Office (GAO), headed by the Comptroller General.

The General Accounting Office has responsibility for the settlement of accounts—for "closing the books" of administrative officers charged with responsibility for the custody of public funds. The audit precedes and leads to settlement. In addition, in recent years GAO has had major responsibility for the supervision of the accounting systems installed in agencies and departments, and for determining the extent to which accounting and other financial reporting throughout the government result in full disclosure of the receipt and expenditure of public funds.

The GAO conducts a number of types of audit, of which three are particularly significant. The first is the general audit, directed toward the examination of the accounts of administrative officers who have been entrusted with public funds. This includes both certifying officers and disbursement officers, and the audit takes the form of examining the legality of all transactions undertaken. Where expenditures or receipts have been illegally or improperly handled, recovery procedures are instituted against the responsible officers.

The second major audit is the commercial type, which is employed for government corporations and other government enterprise which may maintain accounts on a commercial basis. Here the GAO has no power to disallow erroneous or illegal payments, but is empowered to report these to the Congress.

The general audit is gradually being replaced by a third type—the comprehensive audit. This examination by the GAO emphasizes the audit of the system of accounting rather than the transactions, although the latter will be examined selectively. It is utilized where agencies and departments have established their own systems of internal control.

The Comptroller General submits an annual report of his activities to the Congress, and may also conduct special investigations of the financial affairs and administration of departments and agencies. Both the annual report and the reports of investigations are submitted to the House and Senate Committees on Government Operations. Since the GAO does not maintain accounting records on the financial activities of departments and agencies, it has no responsibility for reporting on the revenue and expenditure of the federal government.

F. Conclusion: The Character of the Budget Cycle

The time span from the beginning of budgetary planning in agencies and departments to the final execution of the budget is about 27 months. Approximately nine months of this period is consumed by executive preparation and submission; approximately six months by congressional review and authorization. This extended period tends to make budgeting unresponsive to changing program requirements and changing economic conditions (see Chapter 10).

It should not, however, be concluded that the long time period required for budgetary planning and congressional review makes for complete rigidity and unresponsiveness. Major program decisions involving substantial increases or reductions in total outlay are sometimes reached in the last days before the budget is submitted to the Congress. Modifications in presidential recommendations are possible thereafter by the use of requests for supplemental appropriations. When the exigencies of the situation demand it, some flexibility can be found; it is not inherent.

The budget system of the United States government is based on the responsibility of the President for preparation and submission; the Bureau of the Budget derives its authority from the President. The President is also responsible, in his joint capacity as chief of the administrative agencies and the head of a political party, for securing favorable consideration of his budget by the Congress. The President's authority for preparation and submission of the budget is well established; the authority and prestige of the Bureau of the Budget is secure. But the President's responsibility for securing favorable congressional consideration is much less clearly defined.

At the same time, a description of the budget cycle in the United States government as one in which the President recommends and the Congress modifies and adopts is a great oversimplification. There are occasions on which the President will personally and publicly intervene to support a specific appropriation that is under congressional attack. On other and more numerous occasions the President will work with political party leaders in the Congress to secure favorable action on a measure which he regards as significant in relation to his program. Similarly, during the time when the budget is being prepared and the major outlines of the President's budget policy are emerging, there will be conferences with congressional leaders, to secure their reactions and enlist their support for specific programs, although not for the budget as a whole. Neither is congressional influence on the Administration restricted to that which can be channeled through to the President. The secretaries of departments, particularly where programs are strongly influenced by local interest groups, as in Agriculture and Interior, are very likely to consult with Congressmen and with members of the appropriations committees about program and budgetary policy. Subcommittee hearings provide a further opportunity for the transmittal of direct congressional influence, both on the budget under consideration and on future budgets. The budgetary process in the United States government does not follow a simple pattern of checks and balances, with a sharp division of authority between the executive and the legislative.

Woodrow Wilson, in attacking the mechanistic views of Montesquieu on the nature of government, once described the interrelations of the Administration and the Congress in terms which could well apply to the budgetary process:

> The trouble with the theory [checks and balances] is that government is not a machine, but a living thing. It falls, not under the theory of the universe, but under the theory of organic life. It is accountable to Darwin, not to Newton. It is modified by its environment, necessitated by its tasks, shaped to its functions by the sheer pressure of life. No living thing can have its organs offset against each other as checks, and live. On the contrary, its life

is dependent upon their quick cooperation, their ready response to the commands of instinct or intelligence, their amicable community of purpose.[9]

III. A NOTE ON THE PRINCIPLES OF BUDGETING

In the development of the literature on budgeting toward the close of the 19th century, there was a great deal of attention devoted to the enunciation of principles intended to guide the formulation, adoption, and execution of the budget. As early as 1885 Leon Say outlined such desiderata in terms of the requirements that the budget possess unity, that it be annual, that it be prepared in advance of legislative action, and that it represent an accountable person.[10] Somewhat later, Stourm suggested that all budgetary principles could be embraced under the headings of universality (comprehensiveness), and accuracy (reliability).[11] Other writers in this tradition laid great stress on the principle of budget balance.[12]

This emphasis on principles served a useful purpose in the development of the literature and practice of budgeting. It provided a framework in which the writers on governmental financial practice could organize their materials. The principles selected were those generally descriptive of features in the best budgetary systems of that time. In their stress on ideal arrangements, these writers undoubtedly hoped to encourage the more widespread adoption of these practices. The very enunciation of principles tends to discourage that which is unprincipled.

In 1935 Sundelson, after a careful review of the British and Continental writings on budgeting, set forth an outline of principles intended to encourage greater attention to budgetary theory in this country. These were as follows:[13]

I. Relation between the budgetary system and the fiscal activities of the political unit
   (a) Comprehensiveness
   (b) Exclusiveness
II. Treatment by the budgetary mechanism of the factors included in the system
   (a) Unity

[9] Woodrow Wilson, *Constitutional Government in the United States,* Columbia University Press, New York, 1917, p. 56.
[10] Cited in J. Wilner Sundelson, "Budgetary Principles," *Political Science Quarterly,* June 1935, p. 237.
[11] René Stourm, *The Budget,* translated by Thaddeus Plazinski, D. Appleton & Company, New York, 1917, pp. 144–168.
[12] See G. Findlay Shirras, *The Science of Public Finance,* Macmillan & Co., Ltd., London, 1936, Vol. I, pp. 82–83; Vol. II, pp. 968–974. For a discussion of this principle in relation to the development of economic theory see Chapter 17.
[13] *Sundelson,* "Budgetary Principles," p. 243.

Since much of the literature of budgeting contains reference to these or similar principles, it may be desirable to indicate briefly their historical meaning. *Comprehensivness* requires that the budget should embrace all of the financial activity of a government, that there should be no extrabudgetary funds or finance outside the control of the budgetary process. *Exclusiveness* means that the budget should deal only with financial matters, not with substantive legislation. *Unity* requires that the budget be presented in gross terms—that is, total revenues and total expenditures should be set forth, not net revenues and net expenditures. *Annuality* requires that budgets be presented each year and that they cover only one fiscal year. *Accuracy* means that revenues and expenditures should be correctly, although conservatively, estimated. *Clarity* and *publicity* are self-explanatory.

These principles may be useful as a means of examining some aspects of the budgetary process.[14] But if viewed as commandments, they are hopelessly unrealistic. Governments with excellent budgetary systems continuously violate many of these rules. Indeed, some of these, such as the principle of unity, cannot be adapted to a government where activity is carried on in multiplicity of organizational forms, including trust funds and government enterprise.

There is probably only one principle which is likely to be useful—that of operational adequacy. The budget cycle and the budgetary process must be capable of coping with the governmental problems at hand. This means that there must be an emphasis on flexibility and adaptability, not an emphasis on an ideal that is intended to be unchanging.

[14] See Harold D. Smith, *The Management of Your Government,* McGraw-Hill Book Company, New York, 1945, p. 85. Smith suggests an alternative set of principles, emphasizing the executive management aspects of budgeting (pp. 90–94).

Selected Bibliography

Bakker, O., "The Budget Cycle in Public Finance in the United States of America," *Public Finance*, Vol. VI, 1951, pp., 273–305, 342–375; Vol. VII, 1952, pp. 279–315, 386–438. (Also published as a separate volume by W. P. Van Stockum & Zoon, The Hague, 1953.)

Buck, A. E., *Public Budgeting*, Harper & Brothers, New York, 1929, pp. 301–428.

——— *The Budget in Governments of Today*, Macmillan Company, New York, 1934, pp. 79–113.

International City Managers' Association, *Municipal Finance Administration*, Institute for Training in Municipal Administration, Chicago, 1937, pp. 82–146.

Naylor, E. E., *The Federal Budget System in Operation*, Washington, 1941, pp. 73–151.

Selko, Daniel T., *The Federal Financial System*, Brookings Institution, Washington, 1940, pp. 118–185.

Smith, Harold D., *The Management of Your Government*, McGraw-Hill Book Company, New York, 1945, pp. 82–99.

Stourm, René, *The Budget*, translated by Thaddeus Plazinski, D. Appleton & Company, New York, 1917, pp. 144–168.

Sundelson, J. Wilner, *Budgetary Methods in National and State Governments*, J. B. Lyon Company, Albany, 1938, pp. 47–84, 133–145, 265–349, 389–475, 525–561.

——— "Budgetary Principles," *Political Science Quarterly*, June 1935, pp. 236–263.

Part II

Budget
Classification

5.

Functions, organizations, and objects

Budget data on expenditures and revenues must be organized in such a way that their significance may be understood and that comparisons may be facilitated. Budget classification is a means to observation and gives to information on government operations the form and structure essential for analysis and inference.

The search for an ideal single classification for the budget is a mistaken and fruitless search. A budget classification may serve more than one purpose, but the usefulness of classification techniques can be judged only in relation to their operational character, their ability to facilitate the decision-making that characterizes and comprises the various phases of the budget process. These decisions determine the role, scope, and complexity of governmental operations, and the activities which must be classified and budgeted.

Classification is the structural key to conscious and rational government budgeting. The manner in which the items of revenue and expenditure are grouped will be determined by, and also will determine, the character of the decisions that can be made in the budgetary process. These decisions result from a constant interplay of questions and answers among levels in the hierarchy of government. The purpose of budget classification is to help focus the questions and to clarify and detail the answers. The classification must not bracket the important questions; it must center on them.

The complex economic and political characteristics of the public sector

110

yield complex decisions in the budgetary process. Families, in their household budgeting, frequently have difficulty arranging and controlling expenditures and revenues to reconcile diverse and often conflicting needs and desires. Such difficulties are geometrically compounded in the budget process in government, the operating vehicle through which a multitude of separate interests and welfares constantly seek reconciliation and stable adjustment. Meaningful and adequate classification of budget data is the basis for the adjustment process.

I. CLASSIFICATION REQUIREMENTS

Governmental activity is conducted by departments and agencies, which administer programs designed to serve public functions. Program authorizations to these departments and agencies, and appropriations to conduct these programs, are made by the legislature. Programs must be administered legally, that is, in conformity with constitutional and legislative requirements. The program is the operational center of governmental activity. Budget accounts must be arranged to facilitate program formulation, execution and accountability. Budget accounts must be sufficiently flexible and sufficiently numerous to serve in all phases of the budget cycle.

Four general purposes may be served by a classification system.[1] First, budget accounts should be arranged to facilitate program formulation. The chief executive, or the finance minister, has responsibility for proposing that the legislature authorize the government to conduct certain operations during the forthcoming fiscal year. These proposals are based on the responsibilities which the government has assumed, and are shaped by its political, social, and economic philosophy. Budget accounts must be set up in such a way as to show clearly the program decisions that have been made, and the changes recommended from year to year. The requirements for program formulation also impose on the executive the necessity for showing, in the budget accounts, the means of finance. Changes in expenditures should be related to changes in revenue. Recommended alterations in the amount and distribution of taxes should be set forth. In other words, the requirements of program formulation extend to both the revenue and expenditure sides of the budget.

Second, budget accounts must be established in such a way as to contribute to effective budget execution. The program administrator must know the amount of financial resources available to him and the re-

---

[1] See *Final Report of the Committee on the Form of Government Accounts* (Cmd. 7969), His Majesty's Stationery Office, London, 1950, pp. 9–12.

sponsibilities he is expected to assume. Since effective budget execution requires efficiency in the use of resources, budget accounts must facilitate efficiency comparisons. It should be noted, however, that efficient governmental operations cannot be secured alone by a budget classification system. Additional management techniques such as unit cost accounting and work reporting are necessary supplements, as well as such broader requirements as effectively trained and motivated personnel.

Third, budget accounts must be established to serve the purpose of accountability. Specific organizational units and specific persons within these units must be charged with responsibility for the collection of revenue, the obligation of funds, and the disbursement of moneys. Budget accounts should be maintained in such a way that these responsibilities can be defined accurately and precisely. Accountability is customarily enforced by means of an audit. Therefore, budget accounts and the responsibility fixed thereby must be arranged so that they can be effectively checked by persons other than those who have immediate legal responsibility. As with program execution, budget accounts may be the basis for establishing accountability, but techniques for assuring accountability are not limited to the control of the accounts themselves.

Fourth, budget accounts should be established in such a way that it is possible to analyze the economic effects of governmental activities in all cases where there has been an assumption of responsibility for economic stabilization or resource development. These are the process effects of fiscal policy, as distinguished from product effects. (See Chapter 3.) Included here are the impact of governmental revenue and expenditure on the aggregates of national income and employment, the effects of governmental activity on the distribution of income within an economy, and the government's contribution to capital formation. For units of government with limited responsibilities, this type of budget classification is of lesser significance and is probably not worth the effort that it entails, but for a national government this type of classification may be of greatest importance.

There is an almost infinite variety of ways in which budgetary data may be classified. A single item of government expenditure—a typewriter, for example—might be classified in accordance with the time of purchase, the place of purchase, the program for which it was purchased, the agency which purchased it, the type of accounting used to record the purchase (cash, accrual), the legislative appropriation which authorized the purchase, and so on. Any one of these may be useful for specific budgetary purposes in a specific government. However, certain general classification techniques are broadly useful; these will be examined here and in the chapters that follow. Some of these techniques are widely practiced and widely understood. Others are of recent origin and are only beginning to be put into operation.

Some types of classification systems are directed primarily toward expenditures, with little emphasis on the revenue side of the budget. In other cases, accounting for revenue is of cardinal importance. Revenue accounts will be examined here only where they are an essential part of the classification system.

The remainder of this chapter will be devoted to classification by function, organizational units, and objects of expenditure. Chapters 6 and 7 will deal with program and performance budgeting; Chapter 8 with the capital budget. An economic character classification of governmental activity will be examined in Chapter 9.

II. FUNCTIONAL CLASSIFICATION

A functional classification is concerned primarily with governmental expenditures, and is designed to facilitate program formulation at the chief executive's level and at the level of legislative review. The functional classification sets forth, on the expenditure side, the broad programs which the government is conducting, in terms of the economic or interest groups which are served.[2]

The functional classification is the "citizens' classification," since it provides general aggregative information on government operations that can be set forth in the "short budget" type of presentation. This is the classification used in the *Federal Budget in Brief*, published annually by the U. S. Bureau of the Budget, designed to familiarize the general reader with the outlines of the President's budget. It is similarly used by the Minister of Finance in France in the presentation of the annual citizen-type budget (*Le Budget*), and by most governments which publish an annual report to the taxpayers.[3]

The functional classification is ideally suited to the analysis of governmental activities over time, particularly when the categories are broad. Utilizing this classification it is possible to measure changes in the nature

[2] Unfortunately, the terms function and functional have a wide variety of meanings in the literature and practice of budgeting. For example, A. E. Buck uses the terms functions and subfunctions to describe specific activities or programs within departments and agencies (*Public Budgeting*, Harper & Brothers, New York, 1929, pp. 181–188.) This type of classification will here be labeled performance budgeting, and every effort will be made in this and succeeding chapters to restrict the use of the term functional classification to the aggregate, general-purpose presentation.

[3] For a discussion of the experience of the state of Washington with this kind of budget summary see Roger A. Freeman, "What Price State Government?" *National Tax Journal*, March 1953, pp. 19–37.

TABLE 2

Bureau of the Census Functional Classification of State and City Expenditures

State General Expenditure

Public Safety
  Correction only
Public welfare
  Old-age assistance
  Aid to dependent children
  Aid to blind
  Aid to disabled
  Public assistance, n.e.c. *
  Other (including all public welfare
    administration)
Education
  State institutions of higher education
    Operation of commercial activities
    only
  Intergovernmental expenditure
  Other
Highways
  Regular state highway facilities
  State toll highway facilities
  Intergovernmental expenditure
Health and hospitals
  State hospitals and institutions for
    the handicapped
  Other

Nonhighway transportation
Housing and community redevelopment
Natural resources
Employment security administration
General control
Miscellaneous and unallocable
  Veterans' services
  Intergovernmental expenditure,
    n.e.c. *
  Function not specified
Interest
Other
Liquor stores expenditure
Insurance trust expenditure
  Employee retirement
  Unemployment compensation
  Workmen's compensation
  Other

City General Expenditure

Police
Fire
Highways
Sanitation
Public welfare
  Public assistance
  Other
Education
  City operated schools

Libraries
Health and hospitals
  Own hospitals
  Other
Recreation
General control
General public buildings
Interest on general debt
Other and unallocable

* N.e.c., not elsewhere classified.

Source: U. S. Bureau of the Census, Governments Division, *Compendium of State Government Finances in 1953*, Washington, 1954, pp. 6–7; *Compendium of City Government Finances in 1953*, Washington, 1954, p. 11.

of governmental programs and changes in the distribution of governmental activity, by program and at different levels of government.[4]   This is the kind of information that encourages citizens to form intelligent judgments about the scope of government and to appraise the merits of arguments about the relative size of the public and the private sectors.

[4] Solomon Fabricant, *The Trend of Government Activity in the United States Since 1900*, National Bureau of Economic Research, New York, 1952, pp. 42–83.

The functional classification is widely applied for purposes of intergovernmental comparisons. The U. S. Bureau of the Census uses for such purposes classifications composed of categories sufficiently broad to be generally applicable, with enough subcategories to provide meaningful comparisons. The Census Bureau's functional classification for states and cities is set forth in Table 2.

The use of functional classification for taxonomic purposes should be distinguished from its use for budgetary purposes, even though the two overlap at particular points. The Bureau of the Census classifications, as shown in Table 2, are more purely taxonomic—that is, they are designed primarily for comparison, not as a framework for decision-making in the budgetary process. Fabricant has set forth a generalized functional classification of this type, composed of but five categories: (1) maintenance of order, (2) promotion of economic activity, (3) production to meet current needs, (4) development of the nation's capacity to defend itself and satisfy its needs, and (5) distribution of the nation's income. As Fabricant notes, however, these classes are not mutually exclusive. A great many governmental activities contribute to more than one of the five objectives. Education, for example, " . . . is justified as essential to the maintenance and development of the country, it produces a currently needed service, supervision of child play, and it is a vehicle by which national income is transferred."[5]

When the number of functional categories is increased, it becomes easier to find a specific slot for each activity. The functional classification used by Chatters and Hoover in *An Inventory of Governmental Activities in the United States* contains 15 major groups and some 400 subgroups; this takes care of most, but not all, of the problems of activities which serve more than one function.[6]

Where the functional classification is designed primarily for budgetary purposes, it will necessarily vary from one government to another in accordance with the prevailing political and social philosophies. For example, a functional classification in a city government might well separate public health from other social welfare activities if the administration wished to stress its importance. Similarly, "recreation" might be a designated functional category in one city because officials wished to emphasize it, but in another city it might be submerged in the function entitled "maintenance of parks and playgrounds.[7]

The United States government uses the functional classification for

[5] *Ibid.,* p. 50.

[6] Carl H. Chatters and Margorie Leonard Hoover, published by the Municipal Finance Officers Association, Chicago, 1947.

[7] For a generalized functional classification intended to be widely applicable to all governmental units, see United Nations, *A Manual for the Classification of Government Accounts,* New York, 1956.

both budgetary and informational purposes. As a broad summary classification, it serves as the framework for the President's budget message.[8] Each functional category is discussed in the message, with emphasis on proposed changes in broad program areas.

The major functional categories in the United States budget are as follows:[9]

Major national security
International affairs and finance
Veterans' service and benefits
Welfare, health, and education
Agriculture and agricultural resources
Natural resources
Commerce and manpower
General government
Interest

These major functions are the basis for the classification of aggregate expenditures in summary Table 1 in the budget document. In addition, a number of subfunctions are delineated for each major function; these are summarized for informational purposes in a special analysis in the budget document.[10] For example, the subfunctions listed under "International affairs and finance" are:

151. Conduct of foreign affairs
152. Economic and technical development
153. Foreign information and exchange activities

Within each of these numbered subfunctions there is a further designation of the participating agencies and departments. Subfunction 152 lists expenditures from funds appropriated to the President, independent offices expenditures, and expenditures by the Departments of Agriculture, Commerce, Defense, State, and Treasury. This provides additional in-

---

[8] A functional classification for the federal government was first proposed in 1912 by the Taft Commission on Economy and Efficiency. Such a classification was used in U. S. budgets from 1924 to 1936 but was then abandoned in favor of a mixture of functions and organizational units. It was re-established in the 1948 budget. For a description of the techniques employed see *Budget of the United States Government for the fiscal year ending June 30, 1948*, pp. 1353–1355.

[9] *The Budget of the United States Government for the fiscal year ending June 30, 1956*, p. A5.

[10] In the fiscal 1956 budget this is Special Analysis B; Special Analysis K sets forth a ten-year comparison of budget receipts and expenditures, utilizing the functional classification.

formation on the organizational basis for functional categories without making the classification unduly complex.

A functional classification has certain characteristics not common to other types of classifications. First, to show effectively what a government is doing, in broad program terms, the major titles in the classification must cut across agency and departmental lines. There are very few governments where functions, broadly defined, are conducted by only one agency or department. The functional classification, to be accurate, must therefore break down the major programs of agencies and, where necessary, reshuffle these. If it is desirable to show a specific agency or department's contribution to the total function, subfunctions may be used.

Second, the functional classification does not identify public works as a separate category. A specific public works outlay, such as a bridge, would fall under transportation; the construction of a military installation would fall under national defense or national security. Public works are therefore viewed not as significant in themselves, but as important only in their relation to the interests served by governmental programs.

Third, the functional classification should present only expenditures, not appropriations or obligations. This arrangement of budgetary data is intended to show "what government is doing," and the best way to measure this is in terms of the actual outlays in the past and estimated expenditures for the budget year. Information on appropriations and obligations is of course significant in a budget document, but it need not fall within the framework of a functional classification. An attempt to record more than expenditures in a functional classification will make for a cumbersome presentation and will tend to defeat the objectives of simplicity and clarity.

Fourth, the general government category should be kept as small as possible, which means that general overhead items should be allocated to functional categories even if this requires some statistical estimating. Interest on the public debt, however, should probably remain a separate nonfunctional category. It is both difficult to allocate among the functions for which it was incurred, and in addition, considerable attention usually centers on this item.

Fifth, there will always be activities which serve more than one function. A veterans' hospital is both "Veterans' service and benefits" and "Welfare, health, and education." Schools for servicemen's children overseas are both 'National security" and "Welfare, health, and education." A functional classification, or any classification for that matter, will necessarily require a number of arbitrary decisions. It is important to have an unduplicated total of expenditures, and this means that each governmental activity can be counted once and only once. Multiple-purpose expenditures will always be difficult to classify.

Although the functional classification places major emphasis on expenditures, it must include a revenue statement. In accordance with the primary purpose of this presentation—to provide an over-all view of government programs in a concise summary account—the revenue statement should center attention on major categories of receipts, and omit the detail.

In the United States budget there are only seven major revenue categories:

> Individual income taxes
> Corporation income and excess profits taxes
> Excise taxes
> Employment taxes
> Estate and gift taxes
> Customs
> Miscellaneous receipts

Additional detail on these categories is provided elsewhere in the budget document; the seven are undoubtedly adequate for describing the general structure of federal government receipts.

In any government the most difficult problem encountered in functional classification is the identification and reporting of programs in accordance with the form of governmental organization; that is, the identification of general government, public enterprise, and trust funds and their integration in a summary statement.

This problem can best be examined in relation to the functional classification employed by the United States government in Table 1 of the budget document, the "Summary of Budget Receipts and Expenditures." A description of the structure of the budget is necessary, however, before the nature of this summary statement can be analyzed.

The so-called "conventional" or "administrative" budget of the United States government embraces general government activities and the activities of government corporations. Trust funds are outside this budget. The financial transactions of trust funds are reported in the budget document, and a part of their revenues are reflected in a subtotal of budget revenues. But trust funds are not included within the definition of total budget receipts and net budget expenditures.

The exclusion of the trust funds from the budget has both a legal and an operational justification. Legally, the funds are not owned by the government. Instead, the government acts as trustee, administering the funds in behalf of beneficiaries designated by statute. Most of the large trust funds were established for social welfare purposes—the Old Age and Survivors Insurance Trust Fund, the Unemployment Trust Fund, the Railroad Retirement Account, and federal employees' retirement funds. Others are for the benefit of particular groups, such as the veterans' life insurance funds or those who will ultimately benefit from donations to the National Archives gift fund. Trust fund revenues are not available to meet the general requirements of the federal government. They are not appropriated funds; expenditures are made by the trustee for designated purposes. They require no specific budgetary action by either the executive or the Congress.

On the other hand, the omission of trust fund activity from the budget obscures the total of the federal government's fiscal activities. The trust funds are, after all, governmental in character and established for a public purpose. The major funds were legislated into existence by Congress. A statement of the government's financial activity will not be comprehensive if they are omitted, and when a budget classification is designed to reveal the economic impact of governmental activity, they must be included (see Chapter 9).

The exclusion of the trust funds from the United States budget, in accordance with the foregoing legal distinction, means the definition of deficit or surplus is the difference between "Total budget receipts" and "Net budget expenditures," shown in Table 3. The deficit, measured in accordance with these concepts, becomes the amount of funds which must be provided, other than from budget revenue, to meet the expenditures of general government and public corporations. The deficit does not measure the total borrowing requirements of the federal government; these will be determined by the deficit *plus* changes in cash balances. But even if cash balances were constant from one fiscal year to the next, the deficit would not measure the volume of borrowing required from the public, since surpluses from the trust funds may be borrowed to meet the cash requirements of the budget. This kind of borrowing is intragovernmental in character; no additional securities are sold to private persons or firms.

Even as the trust funds may be appropriately excluded from the budget on legal grounds, so may public enterprise be included on legal grounds. Some federal government enterprise is conducted in departmental form—the Post Office Department, for example; other enterprises are conducted in corporate form—such as the Tennessee Valley Authority and the Federal Housing Administration. But whether corporate or noncorporate, these enterprises are owned by the federal government and their budgets are controlled by congressional appropriations (see Chapter 16).

TABLE 3
Summary of Budget Receipts and Expenditures, U. S. Government
(Based on existing and proposed legislation. In millions)

Description	1954 Actual	1956 Estimate Under Existing Laws and Authorizations or Recommended	Proposed for Later Transmission	Total
BUDGET RECEIPTS				
Individual income taxes	$32,383	$32,500	......	$32,500
Corporation income and excess profit taxes	21,523	15,984	$1,050	17,034
Excise taxes	10,014	8,328	1,022	9,350
Employment taxes	5,425	7,095	......	7,095
Estate and gift taxes	945	970	......	970
Customs	562	570	......	570
Miscellaneous receipts	2,320*	2,486	......	2,486
Subtotal	73,173	67,933	2,072	70,005
Deduct				
Transfer to Federal old-age and survivors insurance trust fund	4,537	6,175	......	6,175
Transfer to railroad retirement trust fund	603	625	......	625
Refund of receipts	3,377	3,396	−191	3,205
Total budget receipts	$64,655	$57,737	$2,263	$60,000
BUDGET EXPENDITURES				
Major national security	$46,523	$39,068	$1,390	$40,458
International affairs and finance	2,166	1,504	336	1,841
Veterans' services and benefits	4,289	4,684	......	4,684
Welfare, health, and education	2,248	2,217	95	2,312
Agriculture and agricultural resources	7,497	7,647	......	7,647
Natural resources	1,391	1,180	29	1,209
Commerce and manpower	7,355	7,037	130†	6,908
General government	1,212	1,350	219	1,569
Interest	6,470	6,378	......	6,378
Reserves for proposed legislation and contingencies				
Net cost of classified pay increase			125	125
Other			200	200
Total budget expenditures	79,151	71,067	2,265	73,332
Deduct applicable receipts	11,379	10,923	......	10,923
Net budget expenditures	$67,772	$60,144	$2,265	$62,408
Budget deficit	$3,117	....	......	$2,408

* Includes $9 million of internal revenue not specifically classified.
† Deduct, includes proposed postal rate increase of $400 million.

Source: *Budget of the United States Government for the fiscal year ending June 30 1956* p. A5. (The column for fiscal 1955 is omitted.)

In combining the operations of general government with the operations of public enterprise in a functional classification, the program receipts of the enterprises occasion the difficulty. These receipts include such revenue as the sale of postage stamps by the Post Office Department, the repayment of mortgages to the Federal Housing Authority, and revenue from electric power sold by the Tennessee Valley Authority. Program receipts are income to the federal government, available for financing expenditures. Some receipts are available only for specific program expenditures, but in other cases they may be available for general expenditure requirements. In every case program receipts reduce the volume of funds which would otherwise need to be taxed or borrowed to finance aggregate government expenditures. Therefore, such program receipts must be reflected in the budgetary totals and increase the surplus or reduce the deficit, no matter how these concepts are defined.

Table 3 shows the manner in which program receipts are handled in the functional classification in the budget. The item "Total budget expenditures" is the gross outlay of general government and government enterprise. Program receipts, called "applicable receipts," are then deducted from this gross figure to arrive at "Net budget expenditures."

This is one logical way to effect the combination of general government and enterprise activity, but there are others. In fact, at least four possibilities are available for the treatment of program receipts in a functional classification, including the one used by the United States government. These possibilities are demonstrated in Table 4. For the purposes of this table it has been uniformly assumed that general government receipts are 100, general government expenditures 110, and that government enterprise has gross receipts of 30, expenses of 20, and a net surplus of 10.

The first possibility, shown as Procedure I in Table 4, is to make net program receipts a category of budget receipts, separated from tax revenue but identified and included in the total of budget receipts. This emphasizes the revenue-producing or tax-gathering character of government enterprise, and would be most appropriate where enterprises charge prices intended to bring a surplus into the treasury, as in the case of the fiscal monopolies for salt or matches on the Continent, or state liquor monopolies and some municipally owned electric power companies in this country. In this procedure an increase in government enterprise activities, where and to the extent that the increase is matched by additional enterprise revenue, will not be revealed in the summary accounts.

A second possibility, one which was used by the United States government in budgets from fiscal 1947 to fiscal 1954, is to treat program receipts as a negative expenditure, that is, to deduct them from gross expenditures in each functional category. This makes expenditures by functions a

TABLE 4
The Treatment of Government Enterprise in a Functional Classification

Procedure I

Net program receipts	10	General government expenditures	...
Budget receipts	100	(itemize by functions)	...
Total receipts	110	Total expenditures	110

Procedure II

Receipts (excluding net program	...	General government expenditures	...
receipts)	...	(itemize by functions less net	...
	...	program receipts)	...
Total receipts	100	Total expenditures	100

Procedure III

Receipts (excluding net program	...	General government and enter-	...
receipts)	...	prise expenditures (itemize by	...
	...	functions)	...
Total receipts	100		...
			130
		Less: gross program receipts	30
		Total expenditures	100

Procedure IV

General Government

Receipts	100	Expenditures (itemize by functions)	...
			...
			...
		Total	110

Government Enterprise

Gross receipts (itemize by func-	...	Gross expenditures (itemize by	...
tions)	...	functions)	...
	...		...
Total receipts	30	Total	20
		Net program receipts	10

Consolidated Account

Net program receipts	10	General government	
General government receipts	100	expenditures	110
Total receipts	110	Total expenditures	110

combination of gross and net activity. Where a specific function includes enterprise activity operating at a profit, this profit will be deducted from the gross expenditures of general government for this specific function, to record a gross-net complex. But where a specific function includes no enterprise activity, expenditures will be recorded at gross. This procedure tends to reduce the budget totals. Enterprise activity which is self-supporting is not reflected in the summary statements; enterprise activity which shows a profit reduces budget expenditures; only the enterprise losses increase the total of expenditures. This procedure shows clearly the total volume of expenditure which must be financed by taxation or borrowing.

Procedure III in Table 4 is the one now employed by the United States government. This makes each functional category a gross category, to record total general government and enterprise expenditure. The total or gross program receipts are then deducted to make the total of government expenditures a net figure. This procedure has the advantage of showing both the total expenditures of a government, without regard to the organizational form in which expeditures are made, and the net expenditures reflecting the influence of enterprise receipts. Again, as in Procedure II, net expenditures measure the cost of government as a whole in terms of taxpaying and borrowing. What is lost is the cost of each function. Under Procedure III it is not possible to determine the net cost of a function such as "Agriculture and agricultural resources," which may include substantial deficits or surpluses incurred by government enterprise (Commodity Credit Corporation) to support agricultural prices. The emphasis is on the aggregate and not on the components.

A final possibility, shown as Procedure IV, is to isolate as a separate section of the functional classification all enterprise activity, and report it on a gross basis. Each enterprise can be "functionalized" so that it is possible, by independent calculation, to determine the net cost of specific functions. This procedure requires a consolidation account, to bring together the net results from enterprise activity and the gross receipts and expenditures of general government. By isolating enterprise activity this procedure serves to center attention on it. Therefore, in a government where enterprises are significant, this technique provides the most comprehensive reporting, in summary form, for enterprise activity.

An attempt to combine trust funds with general government in a functional classifiation, or to combine trust funds with general government and enterprise to show the total of financial activities, gives rise to problems comparable to those encountered in the combination of enterprises and general government. As a technical matter, the possibilities for bringing the trust funds into a functional classification are identical with those shown for enterprises in Table 4. Viewed as a technical matter, a separate section for trust funds, itemized functionally and reported on a gross basis, is the most informative classification system that can be used. However, the problems here are not wholly technical in nature.

The treatment of both government enterprise and trust accounts within the framework of a functional classification must be determined in relation to the purposes of that classification. If the objective is to present a statement which is all-inclusive and provides a maximum of information, then, certainly, the form in which government activity is conducted should be identified and the sectors of government brought together in a consolidated account. But if the major objective of the classification is to provide an easily understood statement with a maximum of usefulness for purposes of citizen understanding, the functional classification should be as uncomplicated as possible. The United States government has chosen a relatively uncomplicated functional classification, with the omission of trust accounts and with no attempt to show the total volume of government enterprise activity.[11]

The summary account classifications for any government should include a public debt statement relating the budget surplus or deficit to changes in public debt. Such a statement can be presented in summary form to accompany the functional classification of aggregate revenue and expenditure. Table 5 shows a simplified statement of this kind, used by the United States government in its summary accounts for a number of years.

TABLE 5
Public Debt Summary Statement, U. S. Government

	1953 Actual	1954 Estimate	1955 Estimate
Public debt at beginning of year	$259,105	$266,071	$269,750
Change due to budget deficit (+)	+9,389	+3,274	+2,928
Other changes in public debt	−2,423	+ 405	+ 322
Public debt at end of year	266,071	269,750	273,000

Source: *Budget of the United States Government for the fiscal year ending June 30, 1955*, Table I, p. A5.

A more detailed statement would itemize separately the changes in public debt attributable to the surplus or deficit, to changes in cash balances of various kinds, and to intragovernmental borrowing.[12] This

[11] For a combination of functional classification and classification in accordance with the form of government, see United Nations, *A Manual for the Classification of Government Accounts.*

[12] See "Effect of Financial Operations on the Public Debt," *Budget of the United States Government for the fiscal year ending June 30, 1956*, p. A7.

may be supplemented, where information is available, by a statement showing changes in the distribution of public debt among classes of bond-holders.[13]

Finally, it should be emphasized that a functional classification is undoubtedly the best possible form of budget presentation for summary account purposes in almost every government. Citizen groups and governments that are interested in raising the level of popular understanding of the activities of a government should seek to strengthen and improve this type of classification. The responsibility of a government for communicating with its citizens does not, of course, start and stop with budgetary information. There are many other channels, such as the annual reports of departments and agencies, that are of importance.

III. CLASSIFICATION BY ORGANIZATIONAL UNITS

Every budget classification system must include a presentation of government accounts based on organizational units, that is, a presentation which reflects the departmental and agency structure of a government. The organizational units are the "doers" in government, who plan and execute budget programs. Their needs must be served by a classification system. Budget preparation is initiated by organizational entities within a government, and all later stages of the budget cycle—review, submission, legislative examination, budget execution, and audit—must be based on the organizational framework. The major budget summary accounts are best presented on a functional basis, which cuts across agency and departmental lines, but the second most important basis for summary account presentation is an organizational classification.

An organizational classification is of greatest significance for legislative authorization. An appropriation measure authorizes a specific department or agency to incur obligations or to make disbursements for specified purposes. An organizational classification underlines the ultimate legal authority which must be extended by the legislature.

A summary classification of government operations on the basis of organizational units should include a statement of revenues. This is likely to be the same revenue statement that accompanies the functional classification. The outlay side of the account may be presented on the basis of either expenditures or obligational authority. In fact, these may be combined in a single statement, and if the customary three-year summaries are used—the previous year, the current year, and the budget year—the right-hand side of the accounts will then contain six columns.

[13] See United Nations, *Budgetary Structure and Classification of Government Accounts,* New York, 1951, pp. 44–45.

TABLE 6
Summary of Budget Expenditures by Agency, U. S. Government
(Based on existing and proposed legislation.   In millions)

		1956 Estimated		
Agency	1954 Actual	Under Authorizations Enacted or Recommended in This Document	Proposed for Later Trans- mission	Total
Legislative branch	$59	$83	......	$83
The Judiciary	28	33	*	33
Executive Office of the President	9	9	......	9
Funds appropriated to the President	5,477	4,743	$613	5,356
Independent offices				
Atomic Energy Commission	1,895	1,910	90	2,000
Veterans Administration	4,316	4,615	90	4,705
Other	3,739	2,994	248	3,242
General Services Administration	808	969	......	969
Housing and Home Finance Agency	1,440	1,264	......	1,264
Department of Agriculture	5,963	6,013	......	6,013
Department of Commerce	1,083	1,223	*	1,223
Department of Defense				
Military Functions	40,336	33,000	1,000	34,000
Civil Functions	708	618	14	632
Department of Health, Education, and Welfare	1,983	1,960	95	2,055
Department of the Interior	571	572	19	591
Department of Justice	183	201	1	202
Department of Labor	357	512	4	515
Post Office Department	2,686	2,811	270†	2,541
Department of State	156	148	2	150
Treasury Department	7,339	7,356	35	7,391
District of Columbia (general fund)	13	34	......	34
Reserves for proposed legislation and contingencies	......	....	325	325
Total budget expenditures (gross)	$79,151	$71,067	$2,265	$73,332
Deduct applicable receipts‡	11,379	10,923	......	10,923
Net budget expenditures	$67,772	$60,144	$2,265	$62,408

* Less than one-half million dollars.

† Deduct, includes proposed postal rate increase of $400 million.

‡ Receipts of public enterprise funds (government-owned corporations, the postal service, and other revolving funds, the receipts of which come primarily from outside the Government).

Source: *Budget of the United States Government for the fiscal year ending June 30, 1956,* p. M19.   (The column for fiscal 1955 is omitted.)

In the United States government it has been customary in recent years to present an organizational unit summary for both expenditures and obligational authority, and to distinguish in this presentation the recommendations that are transmitted in the budget as presented to the Congress and those proposed for later transmission. Table 6 shows the statement which is used to summarize budget expenditures.

In the organizational summary, enterprise operations are treated in the same fashion as in the functional presentation, that is, program receipts are deducted to arrive at "Net budget expenditures." An alternative procedure might be preferable here, however, in order to emphasize the enterprise character of specific governmental organizations. This alternative would require a grouping of those agencies or departments primarily engaged in enterprise activity in one section of the account, listing their transactions on a net basis. For the federal government, this would mean grouping together and reporting on a net basis the financial operations of such agencies as the Export-Import Bank, the Tennessee Valley Authority, and the Post Office Department.

An organizational classification compiled to show expenditures should be consistent in the treatment of intragovernmental transfers. There are two options here. The transfer may be shown as an expenditure of the paying agency, or it may be shown as an expenditure of the receiving agency. The practice of the federal government, and the basis on which Table 6 is compiled, is to record expenditures to the paying agency. This procedure underlines the legal authority which the Congress extends to agencies and departments. It emphasizes the work done for an agency, rather than the work done by an agency. This is an appropriate emphasis in a classification not organized around either functions served or programs conducted.

IV. CLASSIFICATION BY OBJECTS OF EXPENDITURE

The most widely used form of classification for budget expenditures is that based on objects. In this country its introduction accompanied the wave of municipal budget reform measures initiated by the work of the New York City Municipal Research Bureau (see Chapter 1). The first comprehensive budget for a New York City department, that for the Department of Health in the year 1907, was presented on this basis. The Taft Commission in 1912 presented accounts for all federal government departments and agencies on an object basis.[14] In fact, these object

[14] Report of the Commission on Economy and Efficiency, *The Need for a National Budget,* House Doc. No. 854, 62d Cong., 2d sess., (1912), pp. 234–235, 351–365.

classifications were even summarized, so that it was possible to determine the total amounts expended by the federal government for personal services, for travel, for printing and binding, and so forth.

It is not surprising that the object classification was regarded in these years as a major improvement in budgeting. It served admirably to establish a tight control over expenditures and limited sharply the discretion of government officials. The object classification was the direct product of an era when both legislators and the citizenry at large were filled with distrust for administrators. It was a great technical step forward in budgeting, since it permitted the installation of government accounting systems which could be linked with budget accounts, and thus limit defalcations.

This is the principal purpose served by an object classification: the control of expenditures at the departmental or agency level. There is no object classification for revenues.

The object classification centers attention on the accounting aspect of governmental operations in terms of things bought. Since departments and agencies within a government, and among governments, tend to buy the same things—personal services of specified grades, laundry soap, brooms, filing cabinets, and the like—it is possible to set up a system of accounts that is uniform throughout the whole of a government. Further, with little modification the system of accounts used in one government can be used in another government. The government of Syracuse, New York, conducts very different programs than the government of the State of California, but it tends to buy the same things. The object classification has therefore led to a strong emphasis on the accounting aspects of financial administration in government. Very often, with this classification, accounting has dominated budgeting.

The object classification is used in almost every state government in this country and in the vast majority of local governments, and is also used as a supplementary classification by the federal government.[15] This classification is frequently called the "line-item" budget. This is an appropriate term, since the objects of expenditure are very often specified in great detail, leading to the familiar cumbersome budget so characteristic of American governmental units.[16]

The New York State object classification is representative of this type

[15] Activity schedules have generally replaced object classification in the U. S. budget document. However, an appendix to the budget is transmitted annually to the Congress, entitled *Obligations by Objects and Detail of Personal Services*.

[16] For a critical appraisal of the line-item budget in New York City, see Robert M. Haig and Carl S. Shoup, *The Financial Problem of the City of New York,* Mayor's Committee on Management Survey, New York, 1952, pp. 437–449.

of budget presentation and will serve here as an illustrative case. Each department in the state government must submit its budget request to the New York State Division of the Budget, on standard itemized forms. For the typical department there are three major schedules covering its operations:

    I. Personal Service
    II. Other Maintenance and Operation
    III. Maintenance Undistributed
    IV. Total Departmental Operations (I, II, III)

In addition, all requests for equipment, both new and replacement, are budgeted separately through the Capital Construction Fund. Payments to local units of government—grants and subventions—are also handled separately.

Each of the three major operational schedules must be itemized in considerable detail. The personal service schedule requires a listing of each title and position, by divisions and units within the department, together with the present salary, proposed salary, and the name of the incumbent.[17] All position reclassifications are noted separately. The schedule for "II. Other Maintenance and Operation" is itemized as follows:

    02 Traveling Expense
    03 Automotive Expense
    04 General Office Supplies and Expense
    05 Printing and Advertising
    06 Communication
    07 Fuel, Light, Power, and Water
    08 Food
    09 Clothing and Clothing Materials
    10 Household, Laundry, and Refrigerating Supplies and Expense
    11 Medical, Surgical, and Laboratory Supplies and Expense
    12 Farm and Garden Supplies and Expense
    13 (Obsolete)
    14 Special Supplies and Expense
    15 Repairs
    16 Rentals
    17 Special Departmental Charges

Each of these line entries is in turn broken down. For example, there are 13 subitems under "Repairs" and 4 subitems under "Rentals."

[17] State of New York, Division of the Budget, *Instructions for Preparation of Budget Requests, 1954–55.*

Schedules III and IV provide somewhat greater flexibility than Schedule II, but again, specific itemization is required.

An object classification of this type, as used in New York State, serves certain budgetary purposes and serves them well. It provides a strong central control over departmental expenditures. Where the objects of outlay are specified in detail, and where the budget as adopted by the legislature incorporates this detail, the administrative discretion of department heads is greatly reduced. The object detail, by its very nature, limits the freedom of administrative action. Where the budget office or the chief executive establishes the classification and enforces the execution of the budget in accordance with the details, decision-making power in budget execution is effectively transferred from the department head to the budget office or chief executive.

The object classification may also serve to strengthen the legislature in relation to the operating departments, although frequently with rather perverse effects. By its nature an object classification is readily understood. It is easy to grasp the significance of a proposed increase of 10 percent in printing and binding or a salary reclassification for John Jones. Therefore, the legislature can and often will review and alter the minutiae of expenditure. The overattention to detail inherent in the object classification undoubtedly encourages overattention to detail at all levels of budget review, with a consequent inattention to the larger issues which ought to be presented in the budget but which remain buried in the object detail.

In spite of these limitations, or perhaps because of them, the object classification has two distinct advantages not possessed by other types of budget classifications. The first of these is accountability. An object classification below the departmental level establishes a pattern of accounts that can be controlled and audited. Funds cannot be obligated except for the objects specified. Each object of expenditure is subject to a separate pattern of documentation. The control of inventory is facilitated by careful documentary control. This, however, is a narrow definition of accountability. The object classification cannot provide the basis for accountability in the sense of measuring the performance of a governmental unit or progress in the administration of a particular program.

A second advantage possessed by the object classification is that it provides useful information for personnel management. The status of existing personnel and proposed changes thereof are clearly set forth. Personnel requirements are closely linked with other budgetary requirements, and the control of positions is used as the lever to control the whole of the budget. On the other hand, it should be noted that there are other means of assuring effective personnel administration that do not require the detailed control inherent in the line-item personnel classifications. In many governments the personnel detail is a hang-over from days when the legislature controlled patronage. With the development of the merit system and salary classification boards, the personnel detail is obsolete and hampers rather than contributes to effective legislative decision-making.

The object classification is not useful for summary account purposes— for aggregating across departmental lines. Little interest attaches, for program purposes, to the total expenditure of a government for clothing and clothing materials as compared with medical, surgical and laboratory supplies.

Where it appears desirable to limit the discretion of department heads or other operating officials, and where it is of utmost importance to ensure detailed accountability, the object classification is most useful. But it may be hoped that even in governments where these considerations are paramount, alternative classifications will be provided to improve the materials on which decisions are made.

By way of conclusion it should be noted that budget classification systems may be distinguished according to their method of preparation. Some classifications are of an *accounting* nature, that is, are based on the specific accounts used to control and record financial transactions, both revenue and expenditures, for governmental agencies. Other classifications are *statistical* in character. These may be compiled by the budget officer of a department or agency, or by the central budget office, or by a central statistical office. A statistical classification will necessarily be based on the accounts of revenue and expenditure, but the data may be partially estimated and may cut across account lines. Typically, therefore, an accounting classification has more accuracy than a statistical one, but the margin of error which attaches to a statistical classification need not limit its usefulness.

Budget classifications are also distinguishable on the basis of their *aggregative* or *nonaggregative* character. Some classification systems add to significant totals. The total of governmental revenue or the total of governmental expenditures is an essential feature of the classification. Other classifications place their emphasis on the components; they may be additive only for a specific governmental program or for a governmental agency, but not for governmental activity as a whole. The aggregative classifications may be prepared on either an accounting or a statistical basis. These are, by definition, the only type that is useful for summary account purposes.

Above all, a budget classification system is purposive, and its usefulness must be judged by its purposive character. These relationships are

CHART 3

The Purposes and Types of Budget Classification Systems

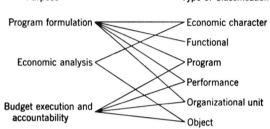

summarized visually in Chart 3, which sets forth the types of classifications that have been examined in this chapter and serves as a preliminary to the classification systems discussed in succeeding chapters.

Selected Bibliography

Buck, A. E., *Public Budgeting,* Harper & Brothers, New York, 1929, pp. 177–229.
Final Report of the Committee on the Form of Government Accounts (Cmd.
7969), His Majesty's Stationery Office, London, 1950.
Dalton, Hugh, *Principles of Public Finance,* 4th ed., Routledge & Kegan Paul,
Ltd., London, 1954, pp. 139–150.
Kilpatrick, Wylie, "Classification and Measurement of Public Expenditures," *The
Annals,* January 1936, pp. 19–26.
Municipal Finance Officers Association, *Simplified Municipal Accounting,* Public
Administration Service, Chicago, 1950, pp. 127–138.
Shirras, G. Findlay, *Science of Public Finance,* Vol. I, Macmillan & Co., Ltd.,
London, 1936, pp. 84–147.
Walker, Harvey, *Public Administration in the United States,* Farrar & Rinehart,
New York, 1937, pp. 244–248.

6.

Performance budgeting[*]

The budget reforms introduced in the United States in the postwar period under the head of "performance" are of great significance and have ushered in a new era in budget-making in this country.

At a broad definitional level, performance budgeting can be most appropriately associated with a budget classification that emphasizes the things which government does, rather than the things which government buys. Performance budgeting shifts the emphasis from the means of accomplishment to the accomplishment itself. The kind of classification required must therefore be very different from one based on objects of expenditure classified according to type. The object classification shows *what* government purchases but not *why;* accordingly, it does not show the nature of governmental programs, or accomplishments under those programs.

I. THE DEVELOPMENT OF PERFORMANCE BUDGETING

Some of the reforms which are now called performance budgeting have their antecedents in budget practice dating back for many years. The earliest of these was the experimentation with cost-data budgets in the

* This chapter was originally published, in substantially its present form, in *Revûe de Science et de Législation Financières,* April–June, 1955, and is reproduced here with the permission of the editors.

Borough of Richmond, New York City, in the years 1913–1915.[1] Under the auspices of the New York Bureau of Municipal Research, detailed classifications were devised for three public works functions—street cleaning, sewerage, and street maintenance. Each of these was divided into about ten subfunctions, called work classifications. Physical units of measure, such as miles of streets flushed, were set forth in the budget, together with unit costs, total costs, and a distribution of outlays by objects of expenditure for each of the subfunctions. These schedules, further classified on a quarterly basis, were written into the appropriation acts and legislated by the board of aldermen. The resulting budget was overdetailed and highly inflexible, and the practice was soon abandoned.

During the 1920's the literature of budgeting contained occasional references to this experience and to a performance approach to budget-making.[2] In many governments what came to be called a project budget or a program budget is similar to what is now termed a performance budget.

For the federal government, as early as 1912 the Taft Commission on Economy and Efficiency stressed the importance of budgeting in accordance with the subjects of work to be done. Little of a comprehensive nature was done along these lines, however, until the project budgeting and the activity schedules of the U. S. Department of Agriculture in 1934. About the same time, the Tennessee Valley Authority undertook a thorough budget classification in accordance with program and accomplishment. TVA's program budget system continues to be one of the most outstanding examples of this approach to budgeting (see Chapter 7). Other federal agencies began to develop activity schedules within program budgets during the war years.

In the postwar years the federal government provided an increased impetus to performance budgeting. In 1946 the Navy Department presented its fiscal year 1948 budget both on the traditional object basis and on a program basis. This work was combined with a simplification of the appropriation structure for the department.[3] These efforts carried over into the newly organized Department of Defense, and from there influenced the work of the Commission on Organization of the Executive

[1] A. E. Buck, *Public Budgeting*, Harper & Brothers, New York, 1929, pp. 170–171, 273–275, 460–463; Henry Bruère, "The Budget as an Administrative Program," *The Annals*, November 1915, pp. 176–191.

[2] Lent D. Upson, "The Other Side of the Budget," *National Municipal Review*, March 1923, pp. 119–122, and "Half-Time Budget Methods," *The Annals*, May 1924, pp. 69–74; A. E. Buck, "Measuring the Results of Government," *National Municipal Review*, March 1924, pp. 152–157.

[3] Frederick C. Mosher, *Program Budgeting*, Public Administration Service, Chicago, 1954, pp. 79–80.

Branch of the Government (Hoover Commission). In the meantime the Bureau of the Budget had completed a reclassification for summary account purposes—the functional classification—and the General Accounting Office, the Treasury Department, and the Budget Bureau were engaged in the first steps in a basic improvement of accounting procedures in the federal government. In this climate of reform, and encouraged by the Bureau of the Budget, agencies and departments introduced activity schedules as a supplement to the detailed object classifications.

These developments in federal budgeting laid the basis for the work of the first Hoover Commission; the Commission in turn provided major stimulus for further advance. The term "performance budget" lent appeal to the recommendations for budgetary reform. The Commission stated in its report on *Budgeting and Accounting*, as "Recommendation Number 1":

> We recommend that the whole budgetary concept of the Federal Government should be refashioned by the adoption of a budget based on functions, activities, and projects: this we designate a "performance budget."[4]

This recommendation was supplemented by the proposals of A. E. Buck in the Commission's Task Force Report. There it was stated:

> A program or performance budget should be substituted for the present budget, thus presenting in a document of much briefer compass the Government's expenditure requirements in terms of services, activities, and work projects rather than in terms of the things bought. Such a budget would not detract from congressional responsibility and should greatly improve and expedite committee consideration.[5]

In the Commission's report, examples of performance budgeting were set forth, and there was some discussion in generalized terms of the kind of budget that was intended. It may properly be inferred that the Hoover Commission's thinking about performance budgeting was shaped primarily by its concern for improving congressional review—for reducing the number and improving the presentation of the programs with which the appropriations committees must deal.

In 1949 a further step was taken in the amendments to the National Security Act, where it was provided that the budget estimates of the Department of Defense:

> . . . shall be prepared, presented, and justified, where practicable, and authorized programs shall be administered, in such form and manner as the

[4] Commission on Organization of the Executive Branch of the Government, *Budgeting and Accounting,* Washington, 1949, p. 8.
[5] Task Force Report, *Fiscal, Budgeting, and Accounting Activities,* Washington, 1949, p. 43. See also A. E. Buck, "Performance Budgeting for the Federal Government," *Tax Review,* July 1949, pp. 33–38.

Secretary of Defense, subject to the authority and direction of the President, may determine, so as to account for, and report, the cost of performance of readily identifiable functional programs and activities, with segregation of operating and capital programs.[6]

The Act provided for the establishment of a comptroller in the Department of Defense and comptrollers in each of the three military departments. The latter were " . . . responsible for all budgeting, accounting, progress and statistical reporting, and internal audit . . . , and for the administrative organization structure and managerial procedures relating thereto." This legislation, known as Title IV of the National Security Act, was significant as an expression of congressional approval for performance budgeting. Its significance was enhanced by the establishment of the comptroller function in the armed forces, with assigned responsibility for implementing the budget reclassification.

A year later the Congress enacted the Budget and Accounting Procedures Act of 1950 (*P.L. 784,* 81st Cong., 2d sess.). Although the term performance budget does not appear in the statute, it was provided that, "The Budget shall set forth in such form and detail as the President may determine . . . functions and activities of the Government . . . any other desirable classifications of data . . . " The President was given explicit authority to prescribe the " . . . contents, order, and arrangement of the proposed appropriations and the statements of expenditures and estimated expenditures contained in the Budget. . . . " From the report on the bill it is evident that the Congress intended to encourage the extension of performance budgeting in the federal government (*House Report* No. 2556, 81st Cong., 2d sess.). In 1955 the second Hoover Commission reviewed and praised the progress that had been made in the development of performance budgeting, and recommended that further steps be taken in this direction.[7]

Interest in performance budgeting in American municipalities antedates some of these developments. In 1939 the Municipal Finance Officers Association presented a model accounting classification, which emphasized activity classifications within functions. This emphasis was continued in reports in 1942 and again in 1953 and has had considerable influence on municipal practice.[8]

[6] *P.L. 216,* Section 403, 81st Cong., 1st sess. For a discussion of the background of this legislation see Mosher, *op. cit.,* pp. 37–42.

[7] Commission on Organization of the Executive Branch of the Government, *Budget and Accounting,* Washington, 1955, pp. 11–15; Task Force Report, *Budget and Accounting,* Washington, 1955, pp. 27–32.

[8] National Committee on Municipal Accounting, *A Standard Classification of Municipal Revenues and Expenditures,* Municipal Finance Officers Association, Chicago, 1942; MFOA, *Municipal Budget Procedure and Budgetary Accounting,*

In the years since World War II a substantial number of cities have undertaken budgetary reforms along program and performance lines. In Richmond, Virginia, the city manager form of government was adopted in 1948, a new budget director was appointed, and a thorough reorganization of budgets and accounts was undertaken.[9]   San Diego and Los Angeles also completed major budget reclassifications along performance lines, and it has been reported that performance budgeting is operative in such diverse municipalities as Cleveland; Kansas City, Missouri; Denver; Detroit; Rochester, New York; Long Beach; Wichita; Phoenix; Providence; Slater and Lebanon, Missouri; New Haven, Windsor and Manchester, Connecticut; Anchorage, Alaska; Berkeley and Oxnard, California; and Saginaw, Michigan.[10]   A performance budget has been strongly recommended for New York City.[11]

The states have lagged somewhat in this development.   Oklahoma has incorporated some performance features in its budget, as have Michigan, Connecticut, Illinois, California, and Oregon.   Maryland, one of the pioneers in budgetary reform at the time of World War I, seems to have made the greatest progress.[12]   In New York State the Governor's budget message in January 1954 noted that the budget for that year included some of the features of a performance or program type of budget for selected departments.   The Governor stated:

> We propose to test carefully every aspect of this type of budgeting on a
> limited scale in selected individual departments or units of a department

---

Chicago, 1942; National Committee on Governmental Accounting, *A Standard Classification of Municipal Accounts,* MFOA, Chicago, 1953.

[9] John A. Donaho, "The Performance Budget," *Municipal Finance,* February 1950, pp. 103–106.

[10] Listed in Report of the Temporary State Commission to Study the Organizational Structure of the City of New York, *Four Steps to Better Government for New York City,* 1953, pp. 132–133. See also Orin K. Cope, "Performance Budgeting," *Tax Digest,* December 1950, pp. 415–418; Samuel Leask, Jr., "Performance Budgeting in Los Angeles," *Tax Digest,* February 1953, pp. 52–53; 70–71; George A. Terhune, *An Administrative Case Study of Performance Budgeting in the City of Los Angeles, California,* Municipal Finance Officers Association, Chicago, 1954; Catheryn Seckler-Hudson, "Performance Budgeting in Government," *Advanced Management,* March 1953, p. 7; Connecticut Public Expenditure Council, *Taxpayers News,* July–August 1954, p. 3.

[11] Mayor's Committee on Management Survey, *The Financial Problem of the City of New York,* New York, 1952, pp. 487–491; *Four Steps to Better Government for New York City, op. cit.,* pp. 19–23, 58–70.

[12] Commission on Administrative Organization of the State, *The Maryland Budget System,* Baltimore, 1951; John Wood Logan and John A. Donaho, "The Performance Budget and Legislative Review," *State Government,* July 1953, pp. 185–187.

before applying it in a more generalized way.   The steps which we are taking conflict in no way with our time-tested type of budgetary presentation.   It is entirely within the realm of possibility that the best features of a performance-type budget combined with our traditional type of budget may prove to be one of the truly new and effective tools in contemporary public fiscal management.[13]

It can hardly be doubted that as experience grows in the federal, state, and local governments, additional jurisdictions will introduce budgetary improvements in accordance with performance or program concepts.

Like a good many other governmental reforms, performance budgeting has been promoted by diverse interests seeking diverse ends.   Public officials, harrassed by tax-ridden citizens, have found in performance or program budgeting a technique for explaining and justifying their con- tribution to the community.   As one school administrator has put it:

Instead of thinking of money alone . . . citizens should hear children singing in the spring concert, travel with the crippled child in early morning from his home to his special unit, feel that school roofs are tight and walls are safe, see the pupils in the corridors washing their dirty hands and drying their clean ones, accompany in spirit the injured child to the hospital for treatment, and see salmon fishing in Alaska with children in the fifth grade.   A top per- formance budget paints pictures in words that justify the expenditure.[14]

At the same time, the partisans of "economy and efficiency" have been most ardent advocates of the performance budget, and large numbers of persons have become instilled with the hope that its introduction will lead to immediate tax reductions and effect substantial savings in govern- ment operations.

If there is a single element that is more important than any other as an explanation for the wave of interest in performance budgeting, it is undoubtedly to be found in the very complexity of modern government. Where citizens and legislators are generally familiar with what govern- ment is doing, where programs are financed from a single source of funds, where an administrator has a relatively small number of programs under his jurisdiction, there is little need for performance budgeting. But modern government is not like this.   Multipurpose programs and multipurpose agencies are commonplace, and the organizational and program lines get badly tangled.   The traditional object classification

[13] State of New York, *The Executive Budget*, Vol. I, Albany, 1954, p. 24.   The development of performance budgeting in New York State has been encouraged by the work of the Temporary Commission on Fiscal Affairs of State Government. In its report of February 1954, the Commission recommended that " . . . all aspects of performance budgeting be explored over the next year" (p. 24).

[14] Harold E. Akerly, "For Better Public Relations Use a Performance Budget," *Nation's Schools*, February 1951, p. 37.

does not readily lend itself to unraveling them. In this situation performance reporting and budgeting can make a major contribution.

II. THE CHARACTERISTICS OF PERFORMANCE MEASUREMENT

There is no precise definition for performance budgeting; it has come to mean something different in every jurisdiction which puts it into operation. In particular, there has been a tendency to make program budget and performance budget synonymous terms, and this has contributed a good deal to the terminological confusion.

In an attempt to clarify what is meant here by program and performance, definitions will proceed along organizational and hierarchal lines. For present purposes, program will be defined in relation to a higher level of organization than performance. A program embraces a number of performance units. A department or agency may conduct or participate in several different programs, whereas organizational (performing) units below the bureau or division level within a department conduct the derivative activities and are directly responsible for performance. Program costs are broad summary costs which may be built by aggregating the costs of performance units. On the other hand, a program budget might stop with broad program costs; it need not be extended to or built on performance units, and in some cases performance detail may serve no useful purpose.

Program and performance may also be distinguished according to their time dimension. Budgetary programs are inherently forward-looking, a projection of the economic and social policies of a government. Performance must be based on the past—on the record of prior accomplishment. In the preparation of budget estimates, program determinations should precede and set the framework in which the measurement of performance can be undertaken.

In accordance with these definitions, a program budget serves a different purpose than a performance budget. A program budget is useful for review and decision-making at and above the departmental level. It is adapted to the requirements of over-all budgetary planning—to central budget office review, review by the chief executive, and by the legislature.[15] The performance budget may also provide useful information for review, but in addition, it must serve management purposes at and below the departmental level. Performance classification and analysis

---

[15] Roland N. McKean, of RAND Corporation, has suggested, in correspondence with the author, that program review in terms of costs and benefits, even where the latter are difficult to measure, is the greatest gain which can come from this kind of budgeting.

seek to measure the cost and accomplishment of detailed activities, and by so doing improve the implementation of programs.

In the discussion which follows, the term performance classification will be used to describe a specific technique for organizing and reporting budget data for administrative units within departments and agencies. The nature of this classification will be examined prior to an appraisal of its role and significance in the budgetary process.

A performance classification differs from other classifications. The intent of a performance classification is to assure that the things bought by a government are no longer to be counted or classified solely by type, as things in themselves, but are to be organized and aggregated according to the activities they serve. Objects bought and used are viewed as activity factors or components, and the object is deemed significant and classified in relation to what it is used for, not in relation to its specific character.

At some point any budgetary system must be concerned with things bought, with objects. The difference between a performance classification and the traditional object classification lies in the way things bought are viewed and grouped. In a performance classification a ton of cement is potentially a section of a road, a dam, or a concrete building and is so classified. The emphasis is on process, or on purpose or achievement. A ton of cement in combination with other materials, some equipment, and the physical activity of men, becomes a specific end product for the implementation of program decisions. Performance classification provides the link between the things bought and the things done or accomplished. This is what has become obscured in the traditional object classification as government activities have moved from the simple and small to the complex and large. In a performance classification expenditure data are reorganized to assist, rather than confuse and detract from, management responsibilities. It is then possible to relate the myriad of things bought to the myriad of things done or to the end products effected.

The end products or things done may be reports filed, roads built, infantrymen trained, tons of food transported, acres of trees planted, tax returns audited, labor disputes mediated, school lunches provided, pennies minted—in fact, any tangible thing that government does. This tangible quality of the end products which may be listed in a performance classification is of greatest significance. Herein lie both its potentialities and its limitations.

It is always possible to identify an end product in a government activity; the things that are done are always recorded in some fashion or other. The difficulty is that frequently the objective things that are done are nonsignificant as a measure of accomplishment under a program.

For example, every labor dispute mediated by a government agency is recorded in the files of that agency. In a given fiscal year it is always possible to count the number of disputes which have been mediated; the information is available and easily measurable. Unfortunately, this is largely irrelevant information for budgetary purposes. In some years the disputes may be difficult to settle; in other years easy. In some years there might be but one case mediated, but this might significantly affect the national economy. In another year there might be no disputes at all because the disputes of the previous year had been so very well settled that all labor-management issues had been disposed.

On the other hand, there are many governmental activities where the end products are identifiable, measurable, *and* significant. Tons of garbage collected, gallons of water provided, and numbers of trout hatched are meaningful measures of performance for the governmental units which conduct these activities. And, of course, there is the middle range of governmental activities, where the measurable and identifiable end products are only reasonably significant in determining accomplishment. Numbers of children graduated from the eighth grade, or property tax assessments completed, or building inspections performed are examples of this sort.[16]

What it comes to, then, is that performance classification based on end products can often create an illusion—the illusion that program content and accomplishment can be measured by the discrete things that are done by a government. This is by no means the case. Regardless of whether or not the end product in a performance classification is meaningful in terms of program content and accomplishment, it cannot measure performance in any value sense.

The facts of performance are not judgments about programs and should not be regarded as such. Value judgments are made in the minds of men. These may partially rest upon the number and type of things done, but they can reside in them only by imputation. Therefore, it is useless to search for a homogeneous end-product unit that will measure "better education," "better defense," or "more economic and efficient personnel recruitment." The best that can be done is to measure a variety of specific accomplishments, which may facilitate judgment as to whether governmental services are improving, in relation to the costs of such improvement.

[16] For a spirited defense of the end-product approach as applied to military budgeting see David Novick, *Which Program Do We Mean in "Program Budgeting"?* RAND Corporation, Santa Monica, 1954 (processed). Novick, however, does not discuss the problem raised here, the significance of the end products in measuring performance.

Performance classification in and of itself does not assure more desirable government programs at a lower cost, although this is frequently implied in discussions of the subject. At best, performance classification provides factual evidence which may be of assistance to all levels of management in determining effectiveness. Performance data, when properly grouped in relation to larger programs, can also be of assistance to legislators and citizens as they select desirable government activities and programs. Performance classification can point up the concrete things done and the dollar cost of these, but the value judgments about them are made in the politic mind—and, for society, in the political process.

III. SELECTING THE PERFORMANCE UNIT

Just as it is difficult to generalize about the difference between program and performance, so is it difficult to generalize about the technique of performance classification. The complex nature of performance is implicit in some of the definitions that have been used. To quote from an unpublished memorandum prepared by the U. S. Bureau of the Budget:

> A performance budget is one which presents the purposes and objectives for which funds are required, the costs of the programs proposed for achieving those objectives, and quantitative data measuring the accomplishments and work performed under each program.[17]

As this definition implies, measuring accomplishment and measuring work performed are not the same thing. Work performed is the process or the activity; accomplishment is the end product and, as noted, the end product may or may not be a significant measure of the character of the program.

In the selection of the performance unit it will always be possible, however, to discover a number of government programs where the end product is significant and measurable. Municipal government programs frequently have performance characteristics of this type. Garbage collection is such a case. It is relatively easy to ascertain the specific number of tons of garbage collected in a municipality during a fiscal year and, on the basis of a number of years' experience, to forecast tonnage for the forthcoming budget year. The trucks and manpower used for collection are not likely to be devoted to any other activity, and therefore the costs per ton can be computed and accurate full-cost budgets set forth in these terms. Certain problems of homogeneity may still remain, however, and

---

[17] Quoted in Chester E. Glassen, *Development of the Performance Budget Structure in the Department of the Army* (unpublished master's thesis), Syracuse University, 1953, p. 34.

may be sufficiently serious to partially invalidate the year-to-year comparability of the performance measurements. The volume of commercial garbage, which is relatively easy to collect, may change in relation to the volume of residential garbage, which is more expensive to collect. Some homes may install garbage disposal units, making the stops for pick-up less numerous this year than last.

There are other government programs that produce specific and significant end products—a reforestation service which plants a specified number of trees in a given period, a reclamation service which adds each year to the number of acres of arable land in a given area, or a highway department which constructs a number of miles of new roads. Again, homogeneity problems will enter. In one year the trees may be planted on the hillsides, in another year in the valleys. Acres of reclaimed land may be of better quality in one year than the next. The new roads this year may be better (or worse) than the ones last year. Technological changes also intrude with improved methods, and get mixed with the changing nature of the end product, to produce performance units which are noncomparable in cost terms over a period of time.

Nevertheless, the end-product approach to selecting the performance unit can provide significant information on program content in a number of cases, and can serve as a relatively firm basis for budgetary planning. Where it can be used, it provides information of great service to management. It permits a determination of whether program costs are increasing because more work is being done or because costs are higher for the same volume of work. The measurement of activity costs cannot do this.

The end-product approach, however, cannot dominate performance classification for the reason already noted—definable, homogeneous, and significant end products do not exist in a great many cases. For many programs the work process or the activity must serve as the performance unit. This situation is well illustrated in the case of a staff function such as a personnel office.

The general responsibility of a personnel office is to contribute to an improvement in the level of skills, effectiveness, and morale of employees subject to its jurisdiction. It implements this responsibility through its programs for recruitment, examination, training, and employee relations and by means of continuous studies of job classification. It may also be charged with the administration of welfare and retirement programs; it will customarily devote a considerable part of its energies to maintenance of employee records. For a personnel office there are no end products which will effectively measure the discharge of these responsibilities. The same general situation obtains in governmental research programs.

In ordnance development the number of tests and experiments conducted during the year is a meaningless performance unit.

In these cases performance must be measured in terms of activities. For a personnel office, activities might be described as follows:

01 General administration
02 Recruitment and examination
03 Reclassification
04 Training
05 Maintenance of records
06 Employee relations
07 Research in classification
08 Administration of welfare programs

To each of these activities dollar cost figures should be attached for past, current, and future fiscal years. In the budget justification each activity should be described and, where possible, changes in work load indicated.

Performance classification in terms of activities will provide a great deal of information about "what government is doing," will center management attention on program, and should help to make management cost-conscious. Activity classification can be refined to great detail if this is desired.[18] Refinement, however, runs the risk of obscuring the major outlines of an agency program and of transforming budgeting to a detailed exercise in accounting.

What activity costs can do is to show the relative dollar emphasis on the components of a program. But like an end-product classification, activity costs cannot, in themselves, provide the value judgments which are necessary for budgeting. The dollar figures in the above example for "04 Training" will not tell the personnel director of the central budget office or the legislator whether the training programs this year are better than the ones last year. The costs of "01 General administration" may be lower this year than last because personnel officers are unavailable for hire at the prevailing salary rate. The total of activity costs will show only what it costs to conduct the whole program. The success of the personnel office in improving the morale and effectiveness of employees will have to be determined primarily by administrators who see the results of what the personnel office does. And this is more likely to be based on what is observable around the office than on what appears in the activity schedules.

With all their limitations, the activity schedules are nevertheless likely to serve as the unit of performance measurement in most governmental

[18] See Municipal Finance Officers Association, *Performance Budgeting for Libraries*, Chicago, 1954.

programs. They are flexible and usually fit in well with existing organizational structures. Activity schedules have served as the unit of measurement in much of the performance budgeting work that has been done in the federal government. Table 7 shows such a schedule for Marketing Research and Service, Agricultural Marketing Service, U. S. Department of Agriculture.

The obligation basis of reporting used by the federal government in these schedules shows the commitments which have been or may be undertaken for the conduct of the activity during the fiscal year. Obligational authority permits agencies and departments to award contracts, hire personnel, and place orders for materials and supplies. Obligations do not measure the liabilities incurred; these depend on the delivery of materials or the provision of personal services. And neither do obligations nor liabilities measure the cost of an activity in terms of the rate at which goods and services are used. Federal government activity schedules are useful for control purposes, since obligations are incurred in point of time before costs are incurred, but these schedules are not an accurate measure of activity costs.[19]

In the federal government a further problem is encountered in combining the activity schedule with a listing of the sources of funds, as illustrated in Table 7. In this case the program for Marketing Research and Service is financed from three sources: appropriations directly to the Agricultural Marketing Service, reimbursements from the Commodity Credit Corporation, and reimbursements from other agencies. These sources are separately designated and totaled. To find the total of obligations for any one activity it is necessary to add the amounts which may be provided from one or more of the three sources of funds. This makes the activity schedule complex, just as the sources of financing for federal programs are complex.

In the federal government the term activity has been broadly applied to mean, under various circumstances, process, purpose, and project. For example, the budget presentation for the Soil Conservation Service, U. S. Department of Agriculture, lists under "Flood prevention" the activity of "Preliminary examinations and surveys."[20] This is a process

[19] In some federal agencies which conduct commercial-type operations, accounting reforms within the past several years have introduced accrual accounting side by side with obligation accounting. This permits an accurate determination of the costs of activities, and a reconciliation of activity costs and obligations. (See T. E. Russell, "An Accounting System with Accrual Features for an Agency Operating on an Annual Appropriation." *Federal Accountant,* September 1953, pp. 1–5.)

[20] *Budget of the United States Government for the fiscal year ending June 30, 1956,* p. 371.

TABLE 7

Obligations by Activities, Marketing Research and Service, Agricultural
Marketing Service, U. S. Department of Agriculture

Description	1954 Actual	1956 Estimate
Direct Obligations		
1. Marketing research and agricultural estimates		
(a) Marketing research	$3,884,253	$5,469,200
(b) Economic and statistical analysis	862,850	1,309,200
(c) Crop and livestock estimates	3,667,596	4,202,600
Subtotal	8,424,699	10,981,000
2. Marketing services		
(a) Market news service	3,399,294	3,653,000
(b) Inspection, grading and classing, and standardization	6,223,386	6,002,000
(c) Freight rate services	155,074	161,000
(d) Regulatory activities	1,560,676	1,549,000
(e) Administration and coordination of State payments	28,529	50,000
Subtotal	11,366,959	11,415,000
3. Obligations under reimbursements from non-Federal sources	240,174	348,900
Total direct obligations	$20,031,832	$22,744,900
Obligations Payable Out of Reimbursements from Commodity Credit Corporation		
2. Marketing services		
(b) Inspection, grading and classing, and standardization	$1,267,032	$1,645,000
Obligations Payable Out of Reimbursements from Other Accounts		
1. Marketing research and agricultural estimates		
(a) Marketing research	64,389	10,000
(b) Economic and statistical analysis	381	2,900
(c) Crop and livestock estimates	14,414	16,000
Subtotal	79,184	28,900
2. Marketing services		
(a) Market news service	48,421	700
(b) Inspection, grading and classing, and standardization	149,323	192,000
Subtotal	197,744	192,700
Total obligations payable out of reimbursements from other accounts	276,928	221,600
Total obligations	$21,575,792	$24,611,500

Source: *Budget of the United States Government for the fiscal year ending June 30, 1956,*
p. 377. (The column for fiscal 1955 is omitted.)

approach to classification. The same activity schedule also lists "General basin investigations in the Arkansas–White–Red River and New England–New York areas." This is a project approach. The Veterans Administration's activity schedule in the program for Inpatient Care, Maintenance and Operation of Hospitals, shows a threefold breakdown. (1) neuropsychiatric hospitals, (2) tuberculosis hospitals, and (3) general medical hospitals.[21] This is a purpose classification.

In a complex government there is no other solution. It is not possible to define all activities in terms of purpose, process, or project. Under these circumstances the activity schedule must retain flexibility in the measurement of components of programs.

Whether the unit of performance is established on the basis of end products or on the basis of activities, it is easier to develop this type of budgeting if programs and organizational structures are synchronized within departments and agencies, and within divisions or bureaus of these departments and agencies.

In every government a number of programs are conducted jointly by two or more administrative units. This means that administrative responsibility is divided and the hierarchal lines of authority are not clear. Neither specific activities nor specific end products can be assigned to individual organizations, and the responsibility for performance cannot be readily determined. In other cases a single administrative unit will conduct a number of different programs. Here the costing becomes difficult and requires the allotment of employee time by the use of time slips or some other form of record-keeping where such detail is justified.

Difficulties in the synchronization of organizational structure and program arise most frequently in those governmental units where professional skills are recognized organizationally. A state public service commission is a typical example. Here the commission may be organized in terms of an engineering division, an accounting division, and a legal division. Personnel from all three divisions will work on rate cases and on the enforcement of service standards. In fact, working teams specifically drawn from each division may be assigned to specific cases. The end product is a regulatory order; the activity is utility regulation. Both the end product and the activity are of a joint character. Performance for the commission as a whole cannot be broken down into specific programs, without a detailed and cumbersome costing system, unless separate divisions are created for electric companies, gas companies, street railways, and so forth, with a rearrangement of engineers, accountants, and lawyers in these divisions.

[21] *Ibid.*, p. 157.

Important as performance classification may be, it would be unwise to recommend that all governmental agencies should be reorganized in the interests of defining performance units. The measurement of performance should contribute to effective administration, not impede it. An organizational structure based on professional skills may make performance classification difficult or even impossible, but it may be the best way to administer the organization. In every case it is effective administration which is the goal, not the classification as such.

The relationship of performance classification to other types of classifications is shown in generalized form in Chart 4. As defined here, a

CHART 4
Performance Classification

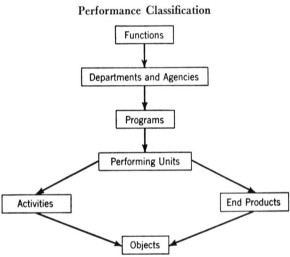

program classification is broader than a performance classification, and each program embraces a number of performing or organizational units. Chart 4 shows that performance can be measured in terms of either activities or end products, and that objects of expenditure can be grouped on either basis.

These relationships are further elaborated in Table 8, based on the hypothetical but typical municipal function, "Provision of streets and roads." The hypothetical case is relatively uncomplicated and is intended to demonstrate the interrelationships of function, program, performance, and object classifications.

As Table 8 demonstrates, it is possible to move with relative ease from a functional classification which cuts across agency and departmental lines, to programs, to performance. Also, no difficulties are encountered in using the object classification to supplement the performance schedules. The total expenditure for objects will equal the total expenditure for performance unit "01.45 Storm sewer repairs."

TABLE 8
Performance Classification in a Classification System

			Department or Bureau	Number of Units	Total Cost
Function	01.	Provision of streets and roads			
Program	01.1	Street construction	Bureau of Streets		$ xxx
	01.2	Street lighting	Bureau of Streets		xxx
	01.3	Traffic control	Traffic Department		
			Police Department		xxx
	01.4	Street maintenance	Bureau of Streets		xxx
Performance	01.41	Streets cleaned (miles)		xx	xxx
	01.42	Resurfacing (miles)		xx	xxx
	01.43	Inspections		..	xxx
	01.44	Bridge and tunnel reconstruction		..	xxx
	01.45	Storm sewer repairs (number)		xx	xxx
Objects of		(a) Personal services	$ xxx		
expenditure		(b) Materials and equipment	xxx		
		(c) Other expense	xxx		
		Total	xxx		

At the same time, the example illustrates that performance data cannot always be extended to significant end products. In this case it has been assumed that street maintenance inspections are not homogeneous over time, and that they are a mixture of inspections of streets constructed, streets maintained, storm sewers, and the like. Therefore, this performance unit must be established on an activity basis. The same lack of homogeneity has been assumed for the performance unit "01.44 Bridge and tunnel reconstruction." That is, it has been assumed that bridges and tunnels in a typical city differ greatly in size and in the costliness of reconstruction.

In practice the administrator is the person best equipped to make the arbitrary assumptions and decisions as to whether an end product or an activity is the better unit for measurement. If the maximum potentialities of performance budgeting are to be realized, its applications must be worked out flexibly. Nothing is gained in budgetary classification by overrefinement of detail. In fact, the overrefinement of detail is a positive evil—it detracts from the importance of program and destroys the perspective of decision-makers. Performance budgeting should not become a victim of self-strangulation.

IV. THE MEASUREMENT OF COST

The uniform measurement of the full cost of end products or activities is logically required, to convert a system of performance *reporting* into a performance *budget*. The distinction is this: performance reporting is the identification of activities or end products and the measurement of changes therein. This may be done either in terms of work units or in terms of dollar figures. Performance budgeting goes beyond this. The identification of programs and the measurement of changes therein are set forth on a cost basis so that performance costs are equal to total costs for budgetary purposes. Performance reporting is selective; performance budgeting is comprehensive. Most governments are likely to find that a full-cost performance budget is impractical.

For performance budgeting to be complete it must embrace the supporting agency accounts, to provide a harmonious accounting framework starting with appropriations and continuing through the accounts that are used for recording obligations and disbursements. These must all be established and maintained on a basis of performance within programs, so that they may be used by management for purposes of observing and controlling the rate of budget execution.

Performance *reporting,* as defined here, need not extend to a reclassification of financial accounts. Performance data can be developed by management independently of the budget and control accounts, and dollar figures may or may not be attached thereto.[22]

This kind of performance reporting has long been used in government operations, particularly in the justification of budgetary requests. It has also been used as a management control for measuring cost and progress in those operations where work is homogeneous and routine. In such cases, the technique consists of identifying units of work load and showing changes in the quantity of such units as a basis for analyzing financial requirements. The management control and budgeting for institutional care—hospitals and correctional establishments—has often been developed on this basis. The number of patients per hospital, the number of beds per hospital, or the number of inmates per prison are measured and projected as a basis for budgetary requests and for cost control.

A simplified example of this kind of performance reporting is shown in Table 9, which reproduces data from the budget presentation of the U. S. Forest Service.

Performance reporting of this type is valuable in providing information

[22] The definition of performance reporting used here is more restrictive than that employed in other materials on this subject. See U. S. Treasury Department, *Performance Reporting,* Washington, May 1950; Eugene R. Elkins, *Program Budgeting,* Bureau for Government Research, West Virginia University, Morgantown, 1953, pp. 27–38. For a discussion of performance measurement for nonbudgetary purposes see William A. Gill, *A Performance Analysis System,* International Institute of Administrative Sciences, Brussels, 1953.

TABLE 9

Main Workload Factors in Resource Development, U. S. Forest Service

(in acres)

Description	1954 Actual	1956 Estimate
Planted to trees (annual)	22,750	22,000
Planted to trees (cumulative)	1,372,084	1,416,084
Still to be planted (total)	4,000,000	4,000,000
Reseeded to range grasses (annual)	41,491	40,000
Reseeded to range grasses (cumulative)	550,638	630,638
Still to be reseeded (total)	3,449,362	3,369,362

Source: *Budget of the United States Government for the fiscal year ending June 30, 1956,* p. 359. (The column for fiscal 1955 is omitted.)

on program and accomplishment. It is not a performance budget as the term is used here.

In the development of the cost figures which make up a performance budget, all costs should be included.[23] Ideally, this requires an accrual system of accounting for the measurement of past program costs, and estimates on an accrual basis for the budget year. In turn, this would mean that inventory should be maintained on an accrual basis and that the portion of capital equipment used up in each fiscal period should be charged to the performance costs for that period.

The requirements for full costing in terms of accrual accounting are more than most governments are prepared to meet. Government accounts are traditionally maintained on the basis of obligations, showing the commitments which are or may be undertaken during the year, or on a cash disbursement basis, showing the amount of goods and services paid for during the year. A shift to accrual accounting, which would show the goods and services used during the year, is invariably difficult and costly, and most governments will avoid it unless there is a clear demonstration that outstandingly better management results will thereby be attained.

In the absence of accrual accounting, the measurement of performance

[23] There is considerable difference of opinion on this point. It has been contended by one prominent practioner of performance budgeting that its use has been restricted by adherence to cost accounting techniques (Orin K. Cope, "The Performance Budget," *Tax Digest,* December 1952, p. 420). For a contrary view see A. Winston Sykes, "Performance Budgeting in Municipal Governments," *N.A.C.A. Bulletin,* December 1951, pp. 475–485; also U. S. Bureau of the Budget, *The Accounting Basis for Performance Budgeting and Improved Management,* Washington (processed, undated). The second Hoover Commission also laid great emphasis on the cost accounting support for performance budgeting (Commission on Organization of the Executive Branch of the Government, *Budget and Accounting,* pp. 13–15; Task Force Report, *Budget and Accounting,* pp. 30–31).

cost becomes most difficult in government programs where capital expenditures are a significant part of total costs, and where the capital outlay portion is not constant from year to year. A state highway department is one example; a municipal public works department is another.

In cases of this sort the ideal measurement would be full annual cost per mile of highway or per mile of streets and roads, with mile of highway or mile of street defined precisely in terms of a standard construction unit of specified composition, width, and durability. It would then be possible to charge to each year's budget the costs incurred in that year, as each mile of highway or street was used up, and it would be possible to determine whether the highway plant was in better condition at the end of the fiscal year than at the beginning and by how much.

This ideal condition is not likely to be attained. Apart from the problems encountered in accrual accounting, there are conceptual problems. A standard highway unit this year is not a standard highway unit next year. In practice, therefore, the measurement of performance costs that are a mixture of current and capital outlays must be based on activities, with a separation of outlays for maintenance and repair from outlays for new construction, and with no effort to annualize all capital costs. Under these circumstances performance budgeting becomes a technique for decision-making about different kinds of activities. The segregation of capital outlays is desirable, not for purposes of arriving at cost figures, but for purposes of improving decision-making in budgeting (see Chapter 8).

Apart from highways and some other types of public works programs, the conflict between traditional cash accounting and the cost measurements required for effective performance budgeting are not always sharp. In a great many general government departments and agencies, the difference between cash and accrual accounting as reflected in the treatment of inventory or in depreciation on capital assets is not likely to be significant. Where the bulk of an agency's expenditure is composed of wage and salary payments, the difference between cash and accrual measurements will not be of sufficient importance to invalidate the cash basis for purposes of performance budgeting. For government enterprise, accrual accounting is very likely to be employed for all accounting and budgeting purposes; no change in the basis of reporting is required for purposes of performance budgeting.

There are other problems in cost measurement. The activities of any agency will include certain common staff functions such as personnel and accounting, and an unapportioned activity which must be classified as general management or executive direction. Costs recorded for these staff functions are not always capable of explicit further breakdown in terms of specific activities. However, the usefulness of performance budgeting is not substantially diminished by the presence of unapportioned cost items of this sort, provided that the composition of the unapportioned element remains reasonably constant from one year to the next. That is, the composition of activities or end products must remain roughly comparable to facilitate the cost comparisons which are the rationale for performance budgeting.

The measurement of program costs is sometimes complicated by the existence of joint products and activities, a problem similar to that of apportioning general management expense. An agency engaged in a specified number of activities may wish to add an additional activity. This will require only slight additions to cost. In the case of a central statistical agency, for example, a new type of data may be added to existing data-gathering activities at small additional (marginal) cost. A reapportionment of the cost of activities to include the additional one will make programs partially noncomparable from one year to the next.

It is evident from the foregoing cases and examples that full cost measurement is impossible in all circumstances. Whether it is of sufficient importance to force a complete reorganization in government accounting, and whether it is worthwhile to attempt to refine performance costs, are questions that must be answered in relation to the needs of particular governmental units, and in particular, in relation to the requirements of administrators, whose interests must be served by performance budgeting.

V. THE INSTALLATION OF PERFORMANCE BUDGETING

By way of summary, it might be well to set forth the steps that are involved in the installation and operation of a performance budgeting system. These are as follows:[24]

First, the central budget office and the administrators of departments and agencies must cooperate in the identification of work programs that are meaningful for management purposes. The central budget office should attempt to preserve uniformity in terminology and should provide some general advisory service at this stage, but program identification is the administrators' responsibility.

Second, programs, once identified, should be examined in relation to organizational structure. Where it appears desirable in the interests of more effective administration, some organizational realignments may be called for to assure a greater harmony between program and hierarchy.

[24] For other discussions of installation procedure see Donaho, *Municipal Finance,* February 1950, pp. 103–106; Cope, *Tax Digest,* December 1950, pp. 415–418; Frank A. Lowe, "How to Initiate a Performance Budget Program," *Performance Budgeting and Unit Cost Accounting for Governmental Units,* Municipal Finance Officers Association, Chicago, 1954, pp. 1–7.

Third, the units of performance should be identified within each program. In some cases this unit will be a specific end product; in most cases it will be an activity. In every case the unit should be as homogeneous as possible over time.

Fourth, consideration should be given to the full measurement of performance costs. In some circumstances it will be desirable to introduce accrual accounting for inventory and capital expense.

Fifth, a system of internal reporting should be established so that progress under the program can be measured throughout the fiscal year. Accomplishment must continuously be compared with plans.

Sixth, the legislation that authorizes the budget should be drafted in program terms. Appropriation structures should be simplified so that each program, where possible, is financed from a single appropriation.

Seventh, the accounts maintained to control and record the disbursements of moneys should be established on a program basis, subdivided by performance units. This, together with a simplification of appropriation structures, will establish a single set of accounts to support all phases of the budget cycle.

During the installation phase the central budget office must be available for assistance and consultation, but the administrators themselves must have major responsibility for the definitions if the performance budget is to accomplish its purpose of orienting management toward program. The applications cannot be worked out in the central budget office and imposed on the agencies.

At the same time, the agencies are not wholly independent in the development of performance units and performance costing. The central budget office must assure some pattern of uniformity throughout the whole of a government. A standard terminology needs to be employed, so that such concepts as program, subprogram, and activity have a uniform meaning in relation to the organizational hierarchy. For example, it might be decided that departments and bureaus of departments would conduct programs and subprograms, and that units of performance would be established within the subprograms. A uniform coding system must be developed to accompany such a standard classification.

It should be emphasized that performance classification is not useful for the summary budget accounts. Performance classifications are agency-level and division-level. For a large government the number of budgeted programs might amount to several hundred, and the number of budgeted activities or end products to several thousand. These may be meaningfully summarized only in terms of broad functions and organizational units.

Despite all of the difficulties that may be encountered in the installation of a performance budgeting system, it has one very great advantage in that it can be introduced in a step-by-step process over a period of years. There is no necessity for a rapid conversion to performance classification in any government. The techniques developed in the departments and agencies where the task is relatively simple can be adapted to the more difficult areas. As one writer has said, "The performance budget process in government . . . is not a destination but a pilgrimage. . . . "[25]

VI. THE CONSEQUENCES OF PERFORMANCE BUDGETING

The development of performance budgeting has been characterized by a widespread popularization of the term, by definitional variety and operational flexibility in its application, and by a relatively slow rate of progress in adoption. The reason for this is not hard to find. Performance budgeting is extremely difficult and requires an almost complete reorientation in the administrator's "way of life." It has been said that, "The budget is a psychological device to make people in an administrative organization think. . . . "[26] But a reorganization in thinking takes time and can be accomplished only if those who must do the thinking are flexible and receptive and understand the reasons for reorganization.

The most important consequence of performance budgeting is that it increases the responsibility and accountability of management. A performance classification provides an additional tool of analysis, which should enforce on administrative units a consciousness of their contribution to departmental programs and the cost of their contribution. The program analysis required should provide perspective for the department head, and the cost-consciousness it entails should facilitate the administrator's control over his financial operations. The performance budget enhances the role of management, but at a price—budgeting may no longer be treated as a peripheral assignment, but is now at the center of management responsibility, and the administrator must be willing to assume this responsibility. This should lead to an improvement in the quality and quantity of budgeting at the level of operations.

A second consequence of performance budgeting is a necessary reorganization of the role and duties of the central budget office. This kind of budgeting shifts detailed responsibility and decision-making authority to the operating agencies and away from the central office. This changes the nature of central office review. The review function should now be directed toward the program itself and changes therein, and to

[25] Seckler-Hudson, *Advanced Management*, March 1953, p. 32.
[26] Quoted in John A. Perkins, "Preparation of the Local Budget," *American Political Science Review*, October, 1946, p. 949.

the coordinating of individual programs with the total program of the administration. The central office may now devote a larger measure of its effort to studies of organization and procedure within agencies and to the reorganization of work methods. Performance budgeting, once the installation phase is completed, should strengthen the organization and management work of the central budget office. At the same time, the identification of programs should reveal overlaps and duplications, and thus provide the raw materials for continuing studies with a view to improved efficiency.

The third consequence of performance budgeting is a change in the nature of legislative review and authorization. The traditional object classification presents data to the legislature in terms which are readily understood, even though these readily understood objects of expenditure may be unimportant for purposes of reviewing the nature and content of programs. Its use has made program analysis by the legislature exceedingly difficult. Under a performance budgeting system, costs are summarized by program and the legislature must, of necessity, concentrate on the review of program need in relation to goals and accomplishments. Expenditures and costs are an integral part of this review and not an unrelated maze of figures. The legislator is better equipped to analyze and question proposals for expenditure, and the administrator is likewise better equipped to support and defend them. The program budget helps the legislature to make major budgetary decisions with respect to the size and type of program and the relation of one program to another. At the same time, the performance detail is available if legislators decide to examine units of operation.

This requires a reorientation in legislative thinking and practice, which is not likely to be accomplished without some difficulty. Where legislators are accustomed to review the objects of expenditures, they may well feel uncomfortable about a kind of budgeting that shifts decisions about program detail to the administrators. Legislative experience in Maryland, however, seems to indicate that the transition can be successful. It has been reported that members of the General Assembly in that state now have more confidence in their ability to make budgetary decisions and are more aware of the financial implications of substantive legislation.[27]

An improved legislative review can be a significant by-product of a performance budget system. However, performance budgeting and the effort that is required for its installation will be fully justified if it succeeds in strengthening the role of budgeting as a tool of management.

[27] Logan and Donaho, *State Government,* July 1953, p. 187.

Selected Bibliography

Buck, A. E., "Performance Budgeting for the Federal Government," *Tax Review,* July 1949, pp. 33–38.

Burrows, Don S., "A Program Approach to Federal Budgeting," *Harvard Business Review,* May 1949, pp. 272–285.

Commission on Organization of the Executive Branch of the Government, *Budgeting and Accounting,* Washington, 1949, pp. 1–17, 77–84.

Cope, Orin K., "The Performance Budget," *Tax Digest,* December 1952, pp. 419–422, 432.

——— "Performance Budgeting," *Tax Digest,* December 1950, pp. 415–418.

Donaho, John A., "The Performance Budget," *Municipal Finance,* February 1950, pp. 103–106.

Elkins, Eugene R., *Program Budgeting,* Bureau for Government Research, West Virginia University, Morgantown, 1955.

Gill, William A., *A Performance Analysis System,* International Institute of Administrative Sciences, Brussels, 1953.

Leask, Samuel, Jr., "Performance Budgeting—Los Angeles," *Tax Digest,* February 1953, pp. 52–53, 70–71.

Logan, John Wood, and John A. Donaho, "The Performance Budget and Legislative Review," *State Government,* July 1953, pp. 185–187.

Mosher, Frederick C., *Program Budgeting,* Public Administration Service, Chicago, 1954, pp. 78–123.

Municipal Finance Officers Association, *Performance Budgeting and Unit Cost Accounting for Governmental Units,* Chicago, 1954. (Contains: Frank A. Lowe, "How to Initiate a Performance Budget Program"; Orin K. Cope, "Operation Analysis—The Basis for Performance Budgeting"; Joseph M. Cunningham, "Accounting and the Performance Budget.")

——— *Performance Budgeting for Libraries,* Chicago, 1954.

——— *Administrative Uses of Performance Budgets,* Chicago, 1954.

National Committee on Governmental Accounting, *A Standard Classification of Municipal Accounts,* Municipal Finance Officers Association, Chicago, 1953.

Novick, David, *Which Program Do We Mean in "Program Budgeting"?* RAND Corporation, Santa Monica, Calif., 1954 (processed).

Ralston, Robert Jr., "Performance Budgeting in Connecticut," *GRA Reporter.* Governmental Research Association, March–April 1951, pp. 1–2, 8.

Seckler-Hudson, Catheryn, "Performance Budgeting in the Government of the United States," *Public Finance,* Vol. VII, 1952. pp. 327–345.

——— "Performance Budgeting in Government," *Advanced Management,* March 1953, pp. 5–9, 30–32.

Sherwood, Frank, "Some Non-cost Accounting Approaches to Performance Budgeting," *Public Management,* January 1954, pp. 9–12.

Sykes, A. Winston, "Performance Budgeting in Municipal Governments," *N.A.C.A. Bulletin,* December 1951, pp. 475–485.

U. S. Treasury Department, *Performance Reporting,* Washington, May 1950.

7.

Applications of performance concepts

The previous chapter described the development of performance budgeting in the United States and discussed general problems which are encountered in its installation and operation. This chapter will be devoted to a consideration of the manner in which four governmental organizations utilize a budget system with program or performance characteristics: the Tennessee Valley Authority, the U. S. Department of the Army, the City of Richmond, and the City of Los Angeles.

It will be evident from these cases that a performance budgeting manual applicable to a large number of governmental units cannot yet be written. Performance concepts must evolve from the political and administrative framework of specific governments to serve specific needs; only after considerable experience, if ever, will generalized principles be evident. In particular, the size and complexity of the operations of a governmental unit will have the greatest influence on the development of performance concepts.

I. TENNESSEE VALLEY AUTHORITY[1]

The budget system of TVA, in the first years after the organization of the corporation in 1933, was developed somewhat independently of budgeting practices employed in other federal agencies. These were

[1] This section is based on Donald C. Kull, *Budget Administration in the Tennessee Valley Authority,* University of Tennessee, Knoxville, 1948; budget presentations for TVA in *The Budget of the United States Government;* Kull, "Decen-

158

years in which government corporations enjoyed considerable autonomy in their relations with the executive branch, and years in which TVA, in particular, had considerable freedom in working out its own management procedures. From its beginning TVA was characterized by a willingness to experiment with management techniques; it was headed by an administrative group that was anxious to do some pioneering. Although its budgets were submitted to the U. S. Bureau of the Budget for review as early as fiscal 1935, this review did not deprive TVA of its procedural freedom.[2]

Today the TVA budget involves the control of annual expenditures and receipts amounting to hundreds of millions of dollars. Fiscal year 1955 expenditures exceeded $400 million, and receipts exceeded $200 million. Salaried personnel in this year totaled about 24,000, including 10,000 temporary construction workers. TVA's budget system, developed in 1937 and 1938, is an integral part of TVA's general philosophy and practice of decentralized management. The TVA budget office is a small one—it currently includes only about six professionals—and is located in the General Manager's Office. Most of the detail work is carried out in the divisional budget offices. The central office serves primarily as an agency for broad program review and as a means of channeling budgetary problems to the General Manager and the Board of Directors for decision. Budgeting, like program planning, is intended to come from the bottom up, and the two are closely meshed. All budget estimates originate at the operating level and move up to the General Manager and the Board, where they are examined with a particular view to the internal consistency of TVA's total program.

The program budget system in TVA is intended to serve management purposes within the corporation, at the operating level and at the level of top policy review. It was not devised primarily for purposes of congressional review, although it has also turned out to have considerable usefulness for these purposes. The program classifications form the basis for much of the discussion and analysis in TVA's annual report.

TVA operations are budgeted in terms of four major programs:

1. Navigation, flood control, and power
2. Fertilizer and munitions
3. Resource development
4. General service

tralized Budget Administration in the Tennessee Valley Authority," *Public Administration Review*, Winter 1949, pp. 30–35; correspondence with L. J. Van Mol, Chief Budget Officer, Tennessee Valley Authority.

[2] C. Herman Pritchett, *The Tennessee Valley Authority*, University of North Carolina Press, Chapel Hill, 1943, pp. 229–241.

Each of the first three major programs embraces a number of subprograms. For example, "Resource development" includes as subprograms:

1. Agricultural resources development
2. Forest resource development
3. Tributary watershed development
4. Topographic mapping

These are further subdivided, so that "Agricultural resource development," for example, includes:

1. Economic analyses of valley agriculture
2. Agricultural development in problem areas
3. Research on forage crops and animal industry
4. Soil survey
5. Agricultural engineering research and demonstrations
6. Part-time farming studies

Expenses incurred under the heading "Administrative and general expenses" are prorated among the four major programs but are not generally assigned to the subprograms. The other important common service activity of TVA—the operation of multipurpose reservoirs—is similarly prorated to the navigation operations, flood control operations, and power operations categories of expense.

The administrative structure of TVA does not coincide with its program structure. Divisions are generally organized along lines of professional specialization or subject-matter jurisdiction, and any one division may participate in one or more major programs.

> Departments [now divisions] are encouraged to think in terms of programs and to participate jointly and freely in program formulation, definition, and refinement. Central management devotes considerable attention to problems of program definition, authorization, and review. . . . The program approach keeps management's attention focused on the objectives of TVA. . . . Program budgeting avoids the organizational approach with its emphasis on historical precedent and self-preservation.[3]

Therefore, although programs and their subdivisions are the basis for preparation, submission, and review of budgets within the corporation, other classifications must accompany the budget process. These include summaries of expenditures by divisions; summaries to show the source of TVA funds, whether from appropriations, from operating receipts, or as reimbursements from other government agencies; summaries to show the character of expenditure, whether for current expense or for asset acquisition; and the object classifications required by the U. S. Bureau of the Budget and the Congress.

[3] Kull, *Budget Administration in the Tennessee Valley Authority*, pp. 19–20.

Major programs are linked with organizational units through the activity account. An activity is defined as the smallest practicable division of work operations within an organizational unit. Organizational units may be large or small, and one organizational unit may conduct a number of activities. The activity account does not cross organizational lines. In those cases where different organizational units are conducting closely related operations, a separate activity account will be set up for each unit. Every effort is made to avoid prorating administrative expenses among activity accounts. Therefore, "general supervision" or "general expense" may be established as a separate activity within the administrative unit. As an example of activity accounts, "Economic analyses of valley agriculture" embraces three:

1. General economic analyses
2. Research in agricultural and industrial development
3. Other general expense distributed to economic analyses of valley agriculture

Since the activity accounts can be grouped in terms of either programs or divisions, they may be used as the basis for the preparation of program budgets. Divisional budget staff, and ultimately the central budget office, group the departmental activities into programs. These are analyzed and budget recommendations are submitted to the General Manager.

Generally speaking, the TVA has not emphasized the development of a unit of performance that extends to the measurement of end products. In some instances, work-cost estimates appear to be meaningful and are incorporated in budget justifications. In other cases there is a specific end product, as in fertilizer production, and unit costs can be measured; here the activity accounts are extended to serve as the basis for cost accounting. In still other cases, as in dam and reservoir construction, supplementary accounts that go beyond activity accounts are employed for costing purposes.

TVA's program budget system also serves as the basis for budget execution. After Congress has authorized the budget for the forthcoming year, the Board of Directors allocates funds on the basis of major program requirements. Within these allocations the General Manager then approves budgets for each organization, again in program terms, and assigns to each administrator the maximum obligations which he may incur in the forthcoming year. In every case the amounts approved are based on the budget submission, modified by whatever changes may have been made by the U. S. Bureau of the Budget or by the Congress. Within the limits of the approved budgets, there remains a considerable area for management discretion in the expenditure of funds.

Internal reporting is based on programs, divisions, and activity accounts. The TVA Division of Finance issues monthly financial statements. These statements include a detailed comparison of actual costs with budgets as approved by the General Manager. The Budget Office utilizes these statements for control purposes and as a means of checking on progress in each program and subprogram. Divisional administrators similarly utilize the financial reports and, in addition, will typically maintain an internal reporting system on work progress which fits specialized management needs.

The high degree of budgetary flexibility which this system possesses is derived from the utilization of the activity account. Programs are based on activities, and activities are classified and cross-classified to reveal the information necessary for successive stages of budgetary review and for budget execution. This necessarily leaves the detailed work of budget-making to the operating level, where the activity account is supplemented by end-product performance budgeting in some but not all organizational units. TVA recognizes the value of work-load and end-product data, but has not developed these unless it was very clear that they were sufficiently uniform and meaningful to be representative of the performance of an activity. The major emphasis is on programs and program costs; secondary emphasis is given to unit costs.

To some extent TVA's budget system is an outgrowth of its corporate status. This means that TVA may use the "business-type" budget statements prescribed by the Government Corporation Control Act of 1945, which provide more flexibility than the budget presentations used by administrative departments and agencies (see Chapter 16). The corporate form also gives TVA somewhat greater freedom in budget execution than is possessed by departments and agencies. More important than corporate status, however, is TVA's management philosophy, with its emphasis on the budgetary responsibilities of divisions and decentralized management.

II. THE UNITED STATES DEPARTMENT OF THE ARMY[4]

As noted in Chapter 6, the armed services were among the pioneers in budget reclassification along program lines in the years immediately after World War II. These early efforts were given additional encouragement

[4] This section is based on Frederick C. Mosher, *Program Budgeting,* Public Administration Service, Chicago, 1954, esp. pp. 47–123; U. S. Senate, Committee on Armed Services, *Implementation of Title IV, National Security Act of 1947, as*

and a legal basis by the enactment of Title IV of the National Security Act in 1949. Congress apparently intended that this title would provide an improved machinery for budgeting and financial control in the armed services, and that henceforth it would be possible to ascertain the costs of specific activities. In addition, the enactment would prevent over-obligation and deficiency appropriations, fix responsibility for funds and costs, and improve the basis for budget review within the Department of Defense and by the Bureau of the Budget and the Congress. Title IV was aimed specifically at a clarification of the lines of financial responsibility by the elimination of overlapping appropriations and multiple sources of funds.

The enactment of Title IV seems to have reflected a feeling on the part of Congress that it had lost control over military expenditures, or perhaps it was derived from a newly found will to control them. In any event, there is no doubt that Title IV grew out of a totally different setting for military budgeting from any which Congress had previously faced. Formerly, in peacetime, military expenditures were cut back and the armed services were largely left alone to ration out their funds as best they could. In wartime, viewpoints shifted sharply and the citizenry and the Congress assumed a generally uncritical attitude toward military expenditure in an effort to give all military commanders everything they wanted and needed.[5] The fears and suspicions of waste and extravagance in the armed forces were quietly put to one side.

But after World War II, the prospect of large military expenditures continuing through a long period of mobilization, led to a new emphasis on cost reduction in the armed services and a new concern for the impact of these expenditures on the national economy. It was evident that previous budgetary practices, developed when military budgets were both small in themselves and small in relation to the national income, needed to be drastically revised. Title IV contemplated nothing less than a financial and managerial revolution in the armed services.

Amended, "Interim Report of the Preparedness Subcommittee No. 3" and "Hearings before the Preparedness Subcommittee No. 3," 83d Cong., 1st sess., 1954; Chester E. Glassen, *Development of the Performance Budget Structure in the Department of the Army* (unpublished master's thesis), Syracuse University, 1953; Arthur Smithies, *The Budgetary Process in the United States,* McGraw-Hill Book Company, New York, 1955, pp. 229–325.

[5] Mosher quotes the statement of Representative D. Lane Powers, of the House Appropriations Committee, in 1943: " . . . I am taking the word of the General Staff of the War Department, the people who are running the show. If they tell me this is what they need for the successful prosecution of this war and for ultimate victory, I am for it. Whether it staggers me according to its proportions or not, I am still for it." (*Op. cit.,* p. 25.)

The Department of the Army continues to be the largest of the three branches of the service in terms of personnel, and the second largest in terms of expenditures. For fiscal 1956 the Army was expected to maintain about 1,300,000 military personnel, hire about 400,000 civilian personnel, and spend about $10 billion. It can be unequivocally stated that there is no single governmental operation anywhere which is more complex. The Army's activities are conducted in all governmental forms— as general government, as enterprise, and through trust and revolving and management funds. Its operations are geographically far-flung, with a complicated pattern of administrative relations between the field and Washington. And above all, its operations and activities must be brought into line with other programs of the Department of Defense, and budgets for the Department of Defense must be geared to the budget and budgetary policy of the government as a whole.

The classification of military expenditures has always posed and will continue to pose extremely troublesome problems. One of these arises from the kinds of budgetary information which the Congress typically desires. Although military expenditures are all directed to a single function or purpose—defense and armed strength—and although this function has nationwide significance, the component activities may have specific and local significance quite unrelated to this aggregate purpose. The employment level and prosperity of the 10th Congressional District may depend heavily on expenditures at the air base. For this reason a member of the House Appropriations Committee may want to know the total outlay for a military installation in his district, and whether that outlay is increasing or decreasing as compared with last year. Also, Congressmen have been generally much concerned with the personnel requirements of the Army, and the relationship between civilian personnel and military personnel. Unfortunately, a classification which produces this kind of information, either on installation cost or on personnel requirements, may have little importance for other budgetary purposes. A given installation, from the management standpoint, may not be a budgetary unit and may have budgetary significance in relation to a different grouping of expenditures, such as the training of troops or the conduct of research. To satisfy the justified and legitimate interests of Congressmen, it therefore becomes necessary to undertake extensive cross-classifications and statistical estimates of expenditures on different groupings, with a corresponding multiplication of auxiliary account classifications.

A further difficulty encountered in Army budgeting is related to the nature of its organizational structure, which is based on the command concept. By virtue of history, tradition, and operational reality the Army gives command (managerial) responsibilities to officers for a specific installation, division, or headquarters. Each one of these commands will embrace numerous kinds and varieties of operations. The commands, in turn, are supported by the various technical services, which supply the goods and services consumed as free issue. This makes for a division and dissipation of responsibility in expenditure (see Chapter 10). Who is responsible for the efficient procurement and use of blankets—the quartermaster who buys them, stores them and supplies them, or the troop commander who uses them? Similarly, who has responsibility for the hospital on the post—the post commander or the Surgeon General? Obviously, the command concept is effective for command purposes, but it cannibalizes financial responsibility.

Budgeting stands in a different relationship to program planning in the Army, and in the other military services, than it does in civilian agencies. Program planning in the military is bounded by strategic and tactical considerations, which in turn are bounded by logistics. The determination of military programs is thus heavily dependent on an expertise function which cannot be decentralized. Strategic considerations must be determined at the top and directed down through the command structure. Only the details of military decision-making can be left to decentralized discretion. It is not possible to merge budgeting and planning at the lowest hierarchal levels and carry this merger through successive stages of review. In the military, programing must always start at the top and must precede budgeting.

There is a particular problem with costs in the military that makes the application of performance budgeting concepts most difficult. Performance classification stresses the measurement of cost and changes in cost from one fiscal period to the next. But the kinds of defense activities which are undertaken are not very much influenced by relative costs. Guided missiles and hydrogen bombs are not proscribed because they are costly. The armed services are not inherently cost conscious. The military is understandably anxious to be fully prepared for all contingencies, regardless of the cost of such preparations. You never know when the seventh lining will be needed for the uniform which the adequately dressed infantryman wears in Alaska. The success of a military operation is very often determined by what it has to start with. The Army likes to have a great many things accumulated which might turn out to be useful sometime. A budget which concentrates attention on cost in relation to performance may well conflict with these traditions of preparedness.

The budget system of the Department of the Army must be examined against this background of complex activities, an organizational structure which divides financial responsibility, the necessity for program planning partially independent of budgeting, and a *modus operandi* which is not inherently in sympathy with cost control. The development of performance budgeting, beginning in 1949, had been preceded by the definition of primary programs established for planning purposes and designed to facilitate review and coordination by the Joint Chiefs of Staff. The primary programs cut across organizational lines and embrace more than one year. Program planning, based on this structure, was intended to start at the top, flow down the hierarchy for specific scheduling, return to the top for review and approval, and then form the basis for program execution. Unfortunately, on a number of occasions the preparation of program documents has been delayed past the point of usefulness for budgetary purposes.

There are now sixteen primary programs for the Army:

1. Troop program
2. Command and management
3. Military personnel
4. Civilian personnel
5. Intelligence
6. Training
7. Research and development
8. Industrial mobilization
9. Matériel
10. Supply, distribution, and maintenance
11. Services
12. Installations
13. Construction
14. Joint projects
15. Army national guard
16. Army reserve and ROTC

The program budget structure was developed independently of the primary programs. Here the major consideration was to reduce the number of appropriation titles, and to break each title into a limited number of specific budget units. The budget programs were to facilitate legislative review. After the major classification structure was established, the subdivisions were arranged so that they would fit into the major budget program classifications. This has necessarily led to some improvisation in the subclassifications.

Although the primary program classification was developed prior to and independently of the program budget classification, the two have tended to come together in terms of definitions, organizational relationships, and timing. Many of the personnel of the program advisory committees are identical with the personnel of the budget advisory committees. Beginning in 1953 positive steps were undertaken to assure a greater procedural coordination of the two. It is anticipated that over the next several years it will be possible to develop primary program documents annually for each of the foregoing sixteen classifications. These will be prepared to facilitate review, including presidential review and decision. Then, budget execution plans will be set forth to reflect the funds needed for each of the primary programs. After the budget is authorized by Congress, the execution plans will serve as a basis for requests for apportionment from the Bureau of the Budget.

The program budget system of the Army is based on its performance-type appropriation structure, which is made up of eight titles, a reduction of thirteen from the previous number. These eight are as follows:

1. Military personnel costs
2. Maintenance and operations
3. Procurement and production
4. Military construction
5. Army national guard
6. Reserve personnel requirements
7. Research and development
8. Military construction, civilian components

Within these appropriations there are 46 budget programs. These, in turn, are subdivided into about 140 projects, and some of the projects are further divided into subprojects. At each army installation these projects and subprojects may be further subdivided into station operating accounts. There is no uniformity in the criteria used for the subclassifications. At varying levels the subdivisions may be established on the basis of subject matter dealt with, pre-existing organizational structure, or even objects of payment. The object classification is also utilized, with the traditional distinctions among personal services, travel, transportation, and the like.

Typical program budget classifications in the Army are as follows:

Appropriation: Procurement and Production

Programs: Vehicles (noncombat)
           Industry preparedness measures
           Weapons
Projects: Artillery
           Chemical weapons
           Small arms

Appropriation: Military Personnel

Programs: Subsistence
               Travel of the Army
               Pay of the Army
Projects: Pay and allowances of enlisted personnel
               Pay and allowances of Cadets of USMA
               Warrant officers
               Pay and allowances of officers
Subprojects: Commissioned officers
               Army nurses and WMSC

Within each project and subproject, capital outlays are differentiated from operating expense, but the definition of military capital is not uniform throughout the Army.   In some cases capital includes procurement items which may be used up within a year; in other cases the distinction is made on the basis of unit cost or the time required for getting the item into production.[6]

Procedural relationships in the development of primary programs and in the development of budget programs are not uniform throughout the whole of the Army.   In some cases budget programs are worked out at the higher echelons and the decisions flow down to the operating levels. In other cases there is a good deal of decentralized budget-making and hierarchal review more nearly comparable with procedures in federal civilian agencies.   There has been a general emphasis on shifting the preparation of budget estimates to the units responsible for using Army equipment and supplies, and away from units responsible for furnishing equipment and supplies.

Program budgeting in the Army has been accompanied by a reassignment of budgetary responsibility within the organizational structure. This is particularly significant since Army organization does not generally coincide with Army primary programs.   Organizational units may contribute to more than one program; the technical services participate in almost all of the primary programs.   To strengthen the relationship between organization and program, budget program directors have been given increased responsibility and control.   The influence of the technical services has been reduced to some extent in the preparation but particularly in the presentation and defense of the Army budget.   The

---

[6] It seems likely that the capital classification was introduced in an effort to follow the recommendations of the Hoover Commission, and in accordance with the requirements of the 1949 amendments to the National Security Act.   However, the significance of any designation of military capital is highly questionable (see Chapter 8).

supervisory and coordinating influence of the Joint Chiefs of Staff has been substantially increased. Since appropriations and programs are Army-wide in character, only the General Staff divisions are now in a position to make basic budgetary decisions.

Program budgeting in the Army has contributed to increased emphasis on program costs in broad terms. Better information is now available on such matters as the cost of specific additions to the military establishment, the cost and subject matter of additional research and development, and the location and cost of military construction. There is an improved integration of budgetary decisions and policy decisions.

The budget reforms introduced in the Army since 1949 have included the simplification of appropriation structures. This permits the appropriation committees of the Congress to see somewhat more clearly the relationship between what they are voting and what is to be done. Each of the basic budget programs is now financed from a single appropriation title. This is a distinct contribution to financial clarity.

It is difficult to assess the over-all degree of improvement which has been made in Army budgeting and financial procedures as a result of the efforts to introduce performance concepts.[7] The program classification which is used is not geared to specified military objectives. Financial considerations do not enter into military programing at an early point in the procedure. Beyond doubt, some financial savings have been effected, but it is not possible to measure an increase in cost-consciousness in such a complex organization. The basis for a more effective congressional review may have been laid, but appropriations committee hearings would not indicate either that the committees are now wholly satisfied or that there has been a major shift away from the minutiae and toward program and accomplishment.[8]

It would not be wise to expect too much from performance budgeting as applied to the military. There are some things which it cannot do. Performance classification in a municipality may tell citizens whether

[7] For a more complete appraisal see Mosher, *Program Budgeting,* pp. 90–123; Smithies, *The Budgetary Process in the United States,* pp. 232–237, 257–277. Suggestions for further improvement are also contained in Advisory Committee on Fiscal Organization and Procedures, *Financial Management in the Department of Defense,* Office of the Secretary of Defense, Washington, 1954. The present discussion omits from consideration some important budgetary, accounting and organizational developments which have accompanied and influenced the program budget system. These include the funding system, the role of the military comptrollers, and the use of working capital funds. (For further discussion see Chapter 10.)

[8] See Subcommittee of the Committee on Appropriations, House of Representatives, *Department of the Army Appropriations for 1955,* 83d Cong. 2d sess., 1954, for example, pp. 260, 792–840; Smithies, *op. cit.,* pp. 232–237.

their hospitals are better this year than last and by how much, but performance classification in the military cannot be expected to tell us whether we are better defended this year than last. Military technologies change too rapidly; a unit of defense is not homogeneous over time; neither is it possible to know how many units are needed until they are needed.

This is an area in which the citizen and the Congressman must always expect to feel somewhat helpless. The knowledge that police patrol cars have been substituted for foot patrolmen (with resulting cost savings) may shed some light on an increase in the number of crimes in a city. The knowledge that we have fewer but better equipped planes (at a lower total cost) does not tell us whether we are better defended. National defense is not definable in such immediate terms; its adequacy cannot easily be measured and translated into quantities which are capable of broad understanding. The Department of Defense and the President are planning for the unknown and the unwanted. When it comes to the specifics, military programs and budget programs based on military programs must incorporate value judgments, which are uncertain even for the expert.

III. RICHMOND[9]

Richmond, Virginia, is a city with a population of 230,000 (1950 census) and a current general fund budget of about $30 million. The performance budget system has been developed there since 1948, primarily in response to the needs of the City Manager, who first assumed office in that year. These needs were two-fold. The Manager required better data on duplications and overlaps in operations of city departments, in order to effect savings in some programs, make these savings available to other programs that required expansion, and at the same time avoid the deficits which had been persistent in the city's budgets in prior years. Second, the Manager needed an improved basis for budget presentation to the citizenry and to the City Council in order to secure their cooperation in the development of effective city government.

[9] This section is based on John A. Donoho, "The Performance Budget," *Municipal Finance*, February 1950, pp. 103–106; William R. Harton, Jr., Edward M. Holmes, Jr., and John A. Donaho, "Performance Budget in Public Health Management," *American Journal of Public Health*, February 1953, pp. 259–264; Thomas E. Cunningham, *Performance Budgeting in Richmond, Virginia* (unpublished master's thesis), Syracuse University, 1954; *Budget, City of Richmond*, various years; Budget Bureau, City of Richmond, *Manual of Budget Instructions and Regulations*, January 1952; correspondence with Glen R. Peterson, Richmond Budget Bureau.

Apart from some few agencies headed by elected officials and agencies reporting directly to the City Council, the Richmond budget system gives over-all control of administration to the City Manager. The Budget Bureau is a part of the executive office of the Manager. Performance budgeting was not developed in response to the needs of departmental administrators, although as a by-product it has undoubtedly contributed to more effective management at this level.

The orientation of performance budgeting in Richmond is clearly set forth in the *Manual of Budget Instructions and Regulations:*

> The Program and Performance Statements for each work program are the explanation to Council and to the people of what each work program is to accomplish. It is in answer to the question—"What performance can I as a citizen expect from this work program if I put up the dollars requested? [Sec. 11.]

This approach—in terms of work programs and activities and their justifications—has meant that the Richmond budget lays stress on what has been defined here as performance reporting. These performance reports are written in terms of departmental programs. Work-load and unit-cost data are used wherever possible and desirable, but major emphasis has not been placed on the definition of work units and the detailed attribution of costs to these units.

The performance budget system was initiated in Richmond by the central budget office, which analyzed the operations of all city departments, in consultation with these departments, and defined some 200 work programs for the city as a whole. These programs were then made the basis for an accounting reorganization for all account classifications. As the system was eventually installed, these revised accounts also served as the basis for a quarterly allotment system to permit the City Manager to control the execution of the budget.

Programs were defined with emphasis on the understandable and recognizable, and in such a way that they did not cross agency and departmental lines. For example, the work program for the Department of Personnel was established as follows:

240101 General administration
240102 Recruitment, examination, certification, and placement
240103 Training
240104 Classification and pay plan
240105 Service records and reports
240106 Medical and welfare service
240107 Workmen's compensation
240108 Employee relations
240109 Retirement

Each of the nine work programs is supported by a concise narrative statement describing the nature of the work and, in cases where they can be measured, the volume of work and unit costs. These last may apply to only a part of one of the nine programs. For example, under "240102 Recruitment, examination, certification, and placement" the budget shows:

	Actual 1952–1953	Estimate 1953–1954	Budget 1954–1955
Employee placements	1262	1100	900
Unit cost	$14.87	$12.43	$19.10

In some instances the nine programs are subject to further breakdown. For example, "Medical and welfare service" is divided into three subprograms: (1) maintenance of employee efficiency, (2) maintenance of employee health, and (3) retirement and rehabilitation programs. Within the department the subprograms and activities do not necessarily coincide with organizational lines. A single personnel administrator may participate in one of more work programs; the narrative statements indicate in approximate terms the allocation of man-years to each program. The Budget Bureau experimented with the use of daily service reports for all employees who divided their time among programs, but this proved to be unduly burdensome and was abandoned. The Budget Bureau now relies on unit chiefs for estimates of time allotments, supplemented by occasional sample surveys.

The recapitulation for the Department of Personnel includes a summary classification by character and object, as follows:

Personal services, Permanant
     Temporary
Supplies and materials
Equipment, maintenance, and replacement
Equipment, new
Rents and utilities
Printing and binding
Travel
Grants, subsidies, and contributions
Other contractural services
Unclassified

This set of accounts is used by all departments and agencies of the city. The object schedules are not approved as such by the City Council, but they are used for allotment purposes in the execution of the budget.

Appropriations by the City Council are in lump sum. For the Department of Personnel the appropriation ordinance text reads as follows:

> For salaries, wages, and other expenses, including the acquisition of new equipment, necessary for the conduct of the work programs of the Department of Personnel as set forth in the General Fund Budget..... ($————).

For all departments and bureaus the Office of the Director of the Budget also requires the submission of supplementary schedules covering the detail of personal services and of operating expenses. These, however, are intended primarily for budget office review, and are included in the budget presentation only in summary form.

The budget summary is compiled on the basis of expenditures, defined to include amounts encumbered, committed, or obligated, as well as payments actually made during the fiscal year. This means that program costs are measured in terms of obligations rather than in terms of amounts of goods and services consumed or used up during the fiscal period. To the extent that obligations are not incurred uniformly, or to the extent that inventories of materials are not consumed uniformly from one fiscal period to the next, this basis for measuring expenditures falls short of a precise annual measure of program costs. The discrepancies, however, are not regarded as significant for purposes of program review.

The budget structure of Richmond is based on a number of funds. In addition to the general fund, there are funds for utilities and for schools. In effect these three are considered together in the review by the City Council, as one budget. The capital budget is reviewed as a separate document. Some performance data are incorporated in the school budget, but performance concepts are not employed for utilities or for the capital budget. The Richmond budget does not include a consolidated financial statement showing the revenue and expenditure for all funds.

All capital programs fall into a sixteen-title classification. Each of these titles is broad and may cover a number of specific projects. For example, a designated street improvement will be listed as a primary project in the capital budget, and funds appropriated here to the department of public works for engineering and construction. In addition the street improvement may require outlays for new traffic signals. This will be budgeted as a secondary project and will be shown in the summary statements of the department of public safety, as an expenditure from capital funds. There are no summary statements in the budget presentation that bring together both primary and secondary project costs.

In most cases the capital programs within departments are organizationally distinct. Within the Department of Public Works, Bureau of Engineering, street improvements are done by the Division of Construction, while the maintenance of streets is undertaken by the Division of Maintenance. This emphasis on organization and activity makes for effective program administration and program review. It does not, however, provide data on the totals of current and capital costs for a given function. Information on the full costs of specified miles of usable streets for the City of Richmond would require a consolidation of current and capital outlays for the street program as a whole.

Richmond's program budget and performance data are the basis for review by the Budget Bureau, the Manager, and the City Council. Richmond's budget system is also designed for control over budget execution, but the classifications used here are not solely those of program and performance.

As noted, budget authorizations are extended by the City Council in lump sum. Before obligations may be incurred by agencies, the authorization (called an appropriation unit) must be allotted by the Budget Bureau. This allotment is based on the object-character classification which accompanies the budget presentation. But the allotment does not extend to all of the items in the classification; for most agencies the allotment is a two-way division between personal services and other expenses. The administrator has more freedom in outlays for "other expenses" than for personal services. The Director of the Budget is required by law to make allotments on either a monthly or a quarterly basis. Transfers between personal services and "other expenses" can be made only on the approval of the Director of the Budget and the City Manager. Supplementary controls are used for personnel vacancies and for the purchase of motor vehicles.

Allotment in terms of the object-character classification is combined with a periodic financial and program review during the budget year. The Director of Finance provides monthly reports to the City Manager, and each agency prepares for the Budget Bureau a quarterly report on program and performance. Hearings are then held quarterly for a review of progress in relation to program, and each agency is, in effect, rebudgeted for the remaining quarters of the fiscal year. Surplus funds may be put in reserve. Deficiencies within an appropriation unit may be met by transfer from one program to another. Transfers among agencies may be made only with the approval of the City Council and only in the fourth quarter of the fiscal year.

The Richmond Budget Bureau is continuously engaged in an attempt to improve the quality of performance reporting by a redefinition of work units. At the same time, there has been no effort to force such data on the agencies. Emphasis has been placed not on unit costs and cost accounting, but on work-program data. Except for capital projects, programs are defined to coincide with departmental and agency organization. The staff of the Budget Bureau has become increasingly engaged in organization and methods analysis in agencies, viewing this as a necessary supplement to performance budgeting.

IV. LOS ANGELES[10]

Performance budgeting in the City of Los Angeles was initiated in 1950 on the basis of recommendations by the Commission for Reorganization of the Los Angeles City Government, which appears to have been influenced by the work of the Hoover Commission and its recommendations for the federal government. Subsequently, the City Council proposed a charter revision which, approved by the electorate, provided for the establishment of a City Administrative Officer with responsibility for budgeting. The Administrative Officer was appointed in 1951, and under his direction the planning and installation of a performance system was inaugurated. The budget for the city for the fiscal year 1952–1953 was presented and adopted on a performance basis. This rapid introduction of performance techniques was a substantial achievement in a large and complex municipal government; Los Angeles has a population of nearly two million and a budget of about $140 million.

In the planning stage, the budget staff studied the city charter to ascertain the permissible classification basis, and found that in the general provision for classification by functions there was adequate legal basis for a performance budget. Whereupon budget staff were assigned to departments and bureaus to:

> . . . secure data relative to the activities performed, the personnel assigned to such activities, the type of work performed, the legal basis for the work performed, the availability of statistical information concerning the work loads handled, and the possible units of measurement which could be used.[11]

After these investigations were made, the budget staff reviewed and analyzed the activities and subactivities which had been identified, and

[10] Information here is based on George A. Terhune, *An Administrative Case Study of Performance Budgeting in the City of Los Angeles, California*, Municipal Finance Officers Association, Chicago, 1954; Frank Sherwood, "Some Non-cost Accounting Approaches to Performance Budgeting," *Public Management*, January 1954, pp. 9–12; Samuel Leask, Jr., "Performance Budgeting—Los Angeles," *Tax Digest*, February 1953, pp. 52–53, 70–71; Frank A. Lowe, "How to Initiate a Performance Budget Program," *Performance Budgeting and Unit Cost Accounting for Governmental Units*, Municipal Finance Officers Association, Chicago, 1954; City of Los Angeles, *Budget, 1954–1955;* correspondence with Frank A. Lowe, Assistant City Administrative Officer, Los Angeles.

[11] Terhune, *op. cit.*, p. 3.

then prepared a comprehensive coded classification of functions, sub-functions, departments, activities, and subactivities.

The general functions for the city as a whole were established as:

10 General government
20 Protection to persons and property
30 Health and sanitation
40 Highways, bridges, and structures
50 Cultural and recreational services
60 Employee pensions and retirement
70 Bond redemption and interest
80 Miscellaneous

Each general function was further divided into a number of subfunctions. For example, "20 Protection to persons and property" included such sub-functions as fire protection, police protection, traffic engineering, and legal service. Subfunctions were linked with departments as follows:

21.   Structural Regulation
   21.1   Building and safety department
      21.10   Departmental administration
      21.11   Building permits and inspections
         21.110   Administration
         21.111   Plan checking
         . . . . . .
         21.115   Building inspection
            21.1150   Administration
            21.1151   Inspections

In the foregoing classification four-digit titles are activities; five- and six-digit titles are subactivities. A subactivity was defined as any unit or op-eration which constituted a functional level at which adequate work measurement could be undertaken.

Following the development of the activity and subactivity classifica-tions, the budget staff undertook an extensive study of the ways in which performance could be measured. Although some cost accounting was in operation in Los Angeles, particularly in public works, it was decided not to undertake an extension of traditional unit cost methods to all de-partments, but to measure performance in terms of man-hours per work unit. This decision and its implementation represents the unique con-tribution of Los Angeles to the theory and practice of performance budgeting.

The decision to utilize man-hours per work unit as the basis for measuring performance was reached, first, because of dissatisfaction with traditional unit costs, and second, because the man-hour approach was much more simple and uniform in application from activity to activity. It was found that unit costs were unsatisfactory not only because costing techniques are complicated, but because during periods of rising prices and wages the results are noncomparable from year to year unless adjusted by a price index. It was further found that personnel costs were about 83 percent of the total municipal budget, and that the ratio of personnel costs to materials costs in most activities was reasonably constant.

This approach required the determination of a work unit for each subactivity and the determination of personnel time devoted to the production of this work unit. The budget staff encouraged the departments to select the work unit, guided by the criteria that it must be countable, that it must express output and reflect work effort, that it must have consistency and must be expressed in familiar terminology. Then the man-hours attributable to the subactivity and the work unit were ascertained from personnel records on the basis of annual full-time employee equivalents. By dividing the gross total man-hours by the number of work units, man-hours per work unit were obtained. These computations were developed for each subactivity for the past year, the current year, and the budget year.

In a number of cases it was discovered that work units were not measurable or significant, since personnel requirements were fixed in terms of organizational structure or by the requirements for maintaining operations regardless of work load. The police and fire departments were the principal nonmeasurable activities. With the exception of these departments, the nonmeasurable activities in the budget amounted to only 12.45 percent of all personnel costs.

The tabulations of personnel requirements in terms of man-hours per work unit became the measure of performance in the budgets of each department. Additional itemized supporting schedules of other outlays, such as expenses and equipment, were included in the budget presentation but not as a part of performance measurement. Each departmental budget was then summarized by activity and by character or class of expenditure, as shown in Table 10. The departmental summary thus reflects the full costs of conducting activities. The performance data which support the departmental summary show man-hour costs per unit of performance. These data are reviewed by the Administrative Officer and his staff and are available for review by the City Council. The budget document itself summarizes the activity recapitulation, and includes schedules on positions and salaries and work program statistics. Work

TABLE 10

Recapitulation by Activity, City of Los Angeles

Function: Protection to Persons and Property

Subfunction: Structural Regulations

Department: Building and Safety

(1) Code	(2) Activity Description	(3) Personnel Required	(4) Regular Salaries	(5) Overtime	(6) Expense	(7) Equipment	(8) Land and Improvements	(9) Total
21.10	Administration							
21.11	Building permits and inspections							
21.12	Plumbing permits and inspections							
21.13	Electrical permits and inspections							
21.14	Heating and refrigeration permits and inspections							
21.15	Elevator permits and inspections							
21.16	Boiler and pressure vessels inspection							
21.17	Maintenance and operation fire and police signal systems							
21.18	Examiners							
	TOTALS							

Source: George A. Terhune, *An Administrative Case Study of Performance Budgeting in the City of Los Angeles, California*, Municipal Finance Officers Association, Chicago, 1954, p. 8.

program statistics for the Building and Safety Department are shown in Table 11.

TABLE 11
Work Program Statistics, Building and Safety Department, City of Los Angeles

	Actual 1952–1953	Estimated 1954–1955
Building inspections	383,626	418,000
Conservation inspections	. . . . . .	98,000
Plumbing inspections	258,766	244,000
Electrical inspections	249,030	256,000
Heating and refrigeration inspections	80,221	82,500
Elevator inspections	10,061	10,600
Boiler and pressure vessels inspections	31,708	35,100
Total inspections	1,013,412	1,144,200
Building plans checked	30,902	29,000
Circuit miles (fire alarm and police signal system)	18,700	20,600
Electrical laboratory tests	1,898	1,800

Source: City of Los Angeles, *Budget, 1954–1955*, p. 22. (The column for 1953–1954 estimates is omitted.)

In the first year of performance budget operation in Los Angeles the installation phase was characterized by numerous conferences between the Administrative Officer and his staff and the departments in an effort to reach agreement on definitions and measurements of activities, sub-activities, work units and man-hours. In a number of cases the departments developed additional records and reporting systems in order to provide the necessary information. Even in the first year of operation, however, it was reported that a number of savings were effected in some departments in the process of analyzing budget requests in relation to projected work load.[12]

In order to assure that performance concepts carried over into budget execution, the City Administrative Officer and his staff established a system of quarterly work programs in terms of projections and accomplishments, to be prepared by the department and bureau heads after appropriations were enacted by the City Council. The work program was projected on a base of estimated work units, man-hours per unit, and personnel requirements. To check on progress under the work program the City Administrative Officer instituted a monthly report on personnel utilization.

Beginning in 1954, with the budget for 1954–1955, Los Angeles initiated a Capital Improvement Expenditure Program. As presented

[12] Terhune, *op. cit.*, p. 10.

in the budget document, this consists of a listing of specific capital out-lays to be financed from the general fund and other funds. The listed projects are under the supervision of the Department of Public Works, with the exception of specific library and recreation and parks projects, and many of the projects are undertaken by Public Works personnel. No effort has been made to develop performance data for such capital improvements, nor to provide consolidated schedules covering both op-erations and maintenance and outlays for capital improvements by ac-tivities. The Capital Improvement Expenditure Program is a nonper-formance section of the Los Angeles budget. The capital program, with its listing of priorities, has, however, contributed to a more effective scheduling of engineering design time in the Bureau of Engineering.

The outstanding feature of the Los Angeles budget system is its de-velopment of man-hours per work unit as the basis for performance measurement. This unit has the advantage of universality and relative simplicity. It avoids the danger of overrefinement inherent in the cost accounting approach to performance budgeting. To the extent that changes in costs of activities or end products are adequately reflected in changes in labor costs, comparisons from one year to the next are greatly facilitated.

Even though performance budgeting in Los Angeles was initiated and installed primarily by the staff of the City Administrative Officer, the system should encourage departmental administrators to examine their operations more carefully. Over a period of years this should lead to a considerable increase in both cost-consciousness and a concern with ac-complishment throughout the whole of the Los Angeles government.

V. CONCLUSION: VARIETIES OF PERFORMANCE BUDGETING

The experience of the four jurisdictions which have been examined demonstrates that the more complex the operations of government, the more complicated program and performance budgeting become. At the same time, the more complex a government, the greater the need for a budget classification that centers attention on accomplishment and facili-tates a budget review that must proceed through successive stages of decision-making.

The classification of governmental expenditures in terms of "what government does" is subject to a variety of interpretations. The ac-complishments of government can be measured at several levels and in many different ways; not all of these can be quantified into budget sched-ules. In TVA the level of measurement is both program and activity cost; budgeting and planning are closely linked. In the Department of the Army budgeting follows planning; program outlines are first established and then performance units are measured wherever possible. In Richmond the emphasis is on activity costs within departments and agencies; performance reporting is brought into the budget narratives with an emphasis on units of work but not on cost accounting. In Los Angeles performance is measured at the level of operations; man-hours per work unit are measured in detail; broad program costs are not emphasized.

It may be hoped that experiences with performance budgeting will continue to multiply, and that there will be an effective sharing of these experiences. Budgetary reform along performance lines is certain to improve the coordination of budgeting and planning. The extent to which refined performance detail will be useful for this or other fiscal purposes is yet to be determined.

8.

The capital budget

There are so many kinds and varieties of capital budgets that a general definition or a general description of procedures is impossible. This much is universally true: a capital budget as used by a government is not primarily a mechanism for recording and measuring changes in assets. A capital budget does not account for what an economist might like to measure as additions to social capital or what a businessman measures as additions to net worth. The division of a government's budget into two parts—current and capital—is undertaken primarily for policy and procedural purposes. At minimum, the identification of capital outlays centers attention on a kind of expenditure that requires a specialized pattern of decision-making.

The capital budget is a variety of double budget. It is in some ways similar to those budgets which distinguish between recurring and nonrecurring expenditure, or between ordinary and extraordinary expenditure.[1] Double budgets, almost without exception, have had their origin in attempts to justify loan finance, so that the extraordinary portion, or the nonrecurring portion, or the capital portion could be identified to serve as a rationalization, sound or unsound as the case might be, for government borrowing.[2]

[1] Matti Leppo, "The Double-Budget System in the Scandinavian Countries," *Public Finance*, Vol. V, 1950, pp. 137–147. For a general review of prewar experience with double budgets see J. Wilner Sundelson, *Budgetary Methods in National and State Governments*, J. B. Lyon Company, Albany, 1938, pp. 146–198.

[2] This was the experience of the U. S. government, which used an "emergency"

The capital budget groups transactions according to "character," which has been traditionally defined to mean a distinction based on the time element.[3] In this schema the denotation of capital is a part of a broad grouping which also isolates for separate treatment on the expenditure side, current expenses, fixed charges, and debt redemption. This kind of character grouping is often used for major headings within which the traditional object classification spells out the detail.

The separation of capital and current activities is not a controversial issue in all sectors of government. Trust funds almost never have capital expenditures, nor do they customarily have capital receipts. Government enterprise, on the other hand, will invariable engage in capital transactions in a manner comparable with that of private enterprise. Indeed, government enterprise typically maintains its accounts on a commercial basis, which requires a distinction between current expense and capital expense and embraces a balance sheet showing financial condition at the end of the fiscal period.

The questions and difficulties with capital budgeting arise in the general government sector. To illustrate the varying purposes that may be served by a capital budget for general government activities, the following will be examined: the experience of American municipalities, New York State's Capital Construction Fund, and the development of capital budgeting in Sweden. Discussion of a controversial case—the United States government—will conclude the chapter.

I. CAPITAL BUDGETING IN AMERICAN MUNICIPALITIES

Municipalities in this country, whether large or small, conduct their operations in an institutional framework that has common features. These features have called forth certain budgetary techniques. The capital budget is one of these.

A municipality has responsibility for the orderly development of public facilities within its boundaries. Typically, it does not assume responsibility for economic stabilization, that is, for coping with inflation or deflation, and it does not attempt to vary its rate of expenditure or taxation

---

budget category from 1933 to 1938. The emergency was the depression, and expenditures so classified were financed by borrowing. By this technique the Administration may have allayed some fears about unsound finance and thus facilitated an expansionary fiscal program. See J. Wilner Sundelson, "The Emergency Budget of the Federal Government," *American Economic Review,* March 1934, pp. 53–66.

[3] A. E. Buck, *Public Budgeting,* Harper & Brothers, New York, 1929, pp. 209–211. This kind of character classification should be distinguished from an *economic character* classification, which will be discussed in Chapter 9.

in order to affect employment within its jurisdiction (see Chapter 3). But municipalities do have responsibility for community development, and should order their outlays for facilities so as to contribute to the realization of their economic potential. Most American municipalities are very much interested in economic growth, which is part of civic consciousness, and this means that the construction and maintenance of schools, recreation facilities, streets and roads, water and sewerage systems, must be adequate to support the development of the local economy. Further, local economic development is contingent, at least in part, on the level of local tax burdens. The construction of public facilities must therefore be accompanied by strict attention to local tax burdens. The city fathers will continually search for the optimum—a level of public services adequate to attract and support economic development, at a cost which does not impose undue burdens on that development.

Municipalities operate with limited fiscal resources. Their revenues are circumscribed by state constitutions and by state legislatures. There are limits on the tax rates that may be imposed, limits on the subjects that may be taxed, and limits on the bonded indebtedness that may be incurred. Municipalities must conduct their affairs in accordance with traditional canons of sound finance, and moreover, these canons will likely be enforced either by a specific state agency with authority for supervising local finance, or by investment bankers. These latter are in an enforcement position because, with no central bank at its disposal, the municipality must turn to the investment bankers for loan finance. Municipalities must therefore conform with conventional standards of fiscal capacity, which are in many ways similar to the standards of fiscal capacity enforced on business corporations that undertake to sell their securities to the public.

The attention municipalities must pay to cost in relation to development, and their operation within a pattern of limited fiscal resources, give rise to attitudes which will sometimes support the deficit financing of municipal public improvements. In a growing city it is impossible to pay for a large volume of public works from current tax revenue without a sharp and unpalatable increase in the tax rate.[4] Further, current financing of major improvements means that the present generation is providing major improvements that future generations will use. The new municipal auditorium lasts for fifty years; it is a nonrecurring outlay. As a matter of equity, should not future users contribute to its cost?

[4] James A. Maxwell, "The Capital Budget," *Quarterly Journal of Economics,* May 1943, pp. 453–455.

This widespread attitude toward local improvements and their cost distribution over time serves to justify loan finance, apart from considerations about the regularization of tax rates. In some cases where specific nonrecurring public improvements can be financed by charges against the users of the facilities, this approach goes one step further to justify the establishment of special public corporations known as authorities (see Chapter 16).

The conflict between the need for municipal improvements and the reality of limited fiscal resources centers community attention on the capital improvements program. It is the battleground of the interest groups who are anxious for more and better schools, for a water system to support new manufacturing enterprise, and for improved parking facilities. The operating budget of a city government tends to remain reasonably constant, with annual changes determined largely by the growth of population and by fluctuations in the price level. Year in, year out, the most difficult budgetary decisions faced by the mayor and the city council will involve the construction or acquisition of new facilities, not the expenses recorded in the operating budget.

In this framework a substantial number of cities have found that a capital budget greatly facilitates financial planning and budgetary decision-making.[5] The capital budget, as it is typically used, provides a vehicle for financial planning and for the regulation of local tax rates. It thus contributes to financial solvency, and at the same time assures that over a period of years needed improvements will be constructed. The capital budget, when linked with a long-range improvement plan, enables local government officials to deal with and yet exert some control over the representations of the interest groups.

Many of the capital budget systems now in operation in American cities were established in the 1940's and are the combined product of the depression and World War II. The former event forced a number of cities to the verge of bankruptcy and brought home forcibly the consequences of the unplanned and often overzealous public works programs of the 1920's. In the 1930's came an increased local concern with planning and zoning, developments which were encouraged by federal grants. World War II was a period in which municipalities were unable to maintain their physical plants in good operating condition; war's

[5] In a survey in 1953 the Municipal Finance Officers Association found that 25 percent of the cities reporting claimed to possess a formal procedure for reviewing capital programs. This was apparently a smaller percentage than had been anticipated. (Frank P. Sherwood, "Capital Improvement Planning: A Report," *Municipal Finance*, May 1954, p. 132.)

end, with its release of manpower, materials, and prosperity, brought both the need for capital expenditures and an improved ability to finance them.[6]

In practice, the capital budget in American cities is usually presented in a separate section of the annual budget, but is prepared on a different organizational base than the remainder of the budget. Department heads and the central budget officer follow distinctive procedures for capital items; additional organizational entities, such as the city planning commission or a citizen's commission, are typically involved in budgeting for capital items. Frequently the capital budget is linked with the operating budget in summary statements. Each capital expenditure is supported by a statement of need, a statement of cost, and usually by a statement of anticipated performance—that is, intended accomplishment. The capital budget is thus something more than a statement of annual capital expenditures. At the same time, as used by municipalities, it does not include a balance sheet to show the city's assets and liabilities. It is therefore, in only a very limited way, analogous with capital accounting as employed by business firms.

The procedures for capital budgeting in American municipalities are not at all uniform. Nevertheless, certain generalized steps may be outlined.[7]

First, a full-fledged capital budget procedure starts with a long-range physical improvements plan, sometimes called the Master Plan, which seeks to look ahead from 10 to 25 years and chart the growth of the community in broad terms on the assumption of normal peacetime development. This kind of a physical plan is very often the product of a considerable community effort, including the contribution of civic groups as well as official planning commissions, who join together in outlining

[6] George G. Sipprell, "A Capital Budget Program," *Municipal Finance,* February 1949, pp. 14–20 (the experience of Buffalo); Virgil H. Hurless, "Obtaining Improvements through Balanced Financing," *Municipal Finance,* May 1954, pp. 136–139 (the experience of Milwaukee).

[7] There is considerable literature on capital budgets in municipalities, either descriptive of existing practices or prescriptive of what ought to be done. The classic treatment is to be found in National Resources Planning Board, *Long-Range Programming of Municipal Public Works,* Washington, 1941. See also International City Managers' Association, *Local Planning Administration,* 2d ed., Chicago, 1948, pp. 268–288; Arnold E. Furlong, "Capital Budget," *Municipal Finance,* August 1947, pp. 38–42; S. M. Roberts, "Long-Term Capital Improvement Budgeting," *Public Management,* August 1948, pp. 226–230; Paul van T. Hedden, "Capital Budgeting," *Proceedings of the Annual National Planning Conference,* American Society of Planning Officials, Chicago, 1952, pp. 146–149. The issues of *Municipal Finance* for February 1949 and May 1954 are devoted to various aspects of capital budgeting and programing.

the prospects for growth and change. The long-range physical plan places particular stress on land use and control, and seeks to lay down the broad outlines within which the city zoning commission can regulate the details of subdivisions and building codes. This kind of physical planning for a community is directed both toward public improvements and toward control over the private use of property. Where it is successful, the planning process is invariably endowed with formal legal status in the city charter or ordinances, extending to a statement of general objectives and the specific responsibilities of participating organizations and officials. The preparation of the Master Plan is regarded as an executive responsibility, although very often it will be submitted to the city council. It is not enacted into law.[8]

Second, and this is where the budgeting phase is initiated, the municipality creates an organizational structure for preparing a capital improvements plan. The planning period is typically six years, and the planning process starts with a listing of all needed or desired public improvements. These are proposed by department and agency heads within the city government. In addition, civic organizations, charitable organizations, and even fraternal and veterans groups are sometimes asked to submit their proposals, together with justifications. These projects are then transmitted to a city planning commission or other officially designated group, or possibly to a special citizen's group appointed by the mayor or the city manager. This committee must screen the proposals, investigate costs and interrelations, and establish a priority list.

Third, a financial analysis of the city's revenue and expenditure requirements, present and anticipated, must be prepared. This is customarily the responsibility of the city finance officer, or the city budget officer. Sometimes the planning commission, with the assistance of expert staff, undertakes the financial analysis as well as the establishment of the priority list. A complete financial analysis will extend to an examination of the city's debt status, the possibilities for future additions to the property tax base, sources of new revenue, and the like.

Fourth, the financial analysis must be coordinated with the priority list of projects. This may be a responsibility, again, of the city financial officials or of the planning commission.[9] Such coordination is frequently a complex matter, since it may involve not only the city, but the

[8] For further discussion see Robert Averill Walker, *The Planning Function in Urban Government,* University of Chicago Press, Chicago, 1950.

[9] There appear to be sharp differences of opinion and practice on this point. In some cities the planning officials are not concerned with timing or financing and leave this to the budget office. Others argue that planning must become involved in financing if it is to be realistic. See Frank Lombardi, "The Planning Agency and Capital Improvement Programs," *Journal of the American Institute*

county, school districts, and other governmental units operating within the city, and it requires a careful examination of the specific financing possibilities available for specific projects—such as special assessments for streets and sidewalks, user charges for sewerage, and state or federal aid for housing, airports, or slum clearance. On the basis of these considerations, the priority list is revised, preparatory to incorporating the capital improvements program in the annual budget.

Fifth, the first year's total of capital improvement projects now becomes the capital budget for the annual city budget. As such, these projects are likely to be brought under further review by the budget officer, the mayor, and the city council, sometimes with substantial modification. The relation of capital projects to the city's operating budget must be examined at this point, to assure that funds are available for maintenance and operation of capital facilities once they are constructed. In succeeding years the plan is extended by one year, and the list of priorities from the previous year becomes the starting point for a re-examination of projects in relation to the development of the community and for modifications in the six year plan. In some cities the basic physical plan is also subject to a thorough re-examination every five or six years. The possibilities for maintaining citizen interest in planning and capital budgeting depend heavily on their periodic participation in the procedure and also on the manner in which city officials present to the council and the public the capital improvements plan and budget.

That part of the capital improvements program which makes up the annual capital budget is usually set forth in a separate section of the city's budget document, with summary tables showing the distribution of projects by function and department. The summary tables may also show prior costs and future costs for projects, or these may be set forth in supporting schedules. The capital budget presentation also includes a summary of the sources of finance.

In terms of budget classification the critical schedule is the one which shows the relationship between the project and the annual budget. Table 12 illustrates such a schedule, adapted from the forms used in Wichita, Kansas.

Capital budgeting, as practiced in American municipalities, has one

of Planners, Spring 1954, pp. 95–101; William Stanley Parker, "Capital Improvement Programs," ibid., pp. 192–195.

One authority suggests that the organizational relationship between the planning commission and the budget office is one of the most critical future problems that cities will face in their capital improvements programing. See Coleman Woodbury, ed., The Future of Cities and Urban Redevelopment, University of Chicago Press, Chicago, 1953, pp. 670–671.

TABLE 12
Six Year Program for Municipal Capital Improvements, 1953–1958, Selected Activities

Department or Division and Projects	Total for 1953–1958	Method of Financing*	1953	1954	1955	1956	1957	1958	Annual Staff and Maintenance Requirements
V. Service Department									
C. Sewage Disposal									
1. Sludge processing plant	$70,000	G.O.	$35,000	$35,000					
2. Enlarge and improve primary	85,000	G.O.		85,000					
3. Refuse incineration and power plant	1,200,000	G.O.		200,000	$400,000	$200,000	$200,000	$200,000	$20,000
4. Sewage pumping stations	7,500	G.O.	7,500						
Total	$1,362,500		$42,500	$320,000	$400,000	$200,000	$200,000	$200,000	$20,000
D. Street and Sewer Division									
1. Equipment shed	$25,000	G.O.		$25,000					$200
2. Maintenance building	7,000	O.B.			$7,000				100
3. Reconstruction and resurfacing	816,055	G.O.	$189,575	168,480	92,000	$150,000	$106,000	$110,000	
Reconstruction and resurfacing streets	846,500	A.B.	12,500	145,000	193,000	115,000	181,000	200,000	
Total	$1,694,555		$202,075	$338,480	$292,000	$265,000	$287,000	$310,000	$300

* Code: A.B., special assessment bonds; G.O., general obligation bonds; O.B., operating budget.

Source: Adapted from Municipal Finance Officers Association, *Long-Term Financial Planning*, Chicago, 1948, p. 3.

disadvantage. It is an attitudinal disadvantage, but one which appears to be deeply embedded. The capital budget technique has come to be closely associated with a financial program of borrowing for public improvements. There is no objective reason why this should be the case. The technique is inherently neutral with respect to the means of finance. The classification of annual capital expenditures and the procedures established to arrive at decisions about capital items do not require that outlays be financed by bonds. It is possible for a municipality to set aside a specific sum from current tax revenue each year, this sum to be applied to capital improvements. Nevertheless, a number of cities that are strongly addicted to pay-as-you-go for capital improvements avoid the use of a capital budget for fear that it will involve them in loan finance. Conversely, cities which are growing rapidly utilize the capital budget for the very reason that it expedites their borrowing program.[10]

With its emphasis on procedures for decision-making and financial analysis, the capital budget as used in American cities does not reflect any careful effort to define capital or capital improvement. The criteria are rough and are phrased in such terms as large size, long life, fixed nature, or nonrecurrent. Major replacements and reconstruction are usually included in the definition of capital, while equipment items which wear out in two or three years are usually excluded. Schools and public buildings, sewerage and water supply are inside the capital budget, but police patrol cars are outside. Capital budgeting becomes construction budgeting or public works budgeting, with a strong emphasis on the engineering aspects. In fact, the advantages of capital budgeting include the regularization of the designing phases in a municipality and improved engineering for projects. The time span is extended for the preparation of surveys, plans, and specifications and for the acquisition of land for public improvements.

It is not customary for a city which uses a capital budget to maintain depreciation accounts for public assets. The operating budget is not charged with the annual depreciation on the total of public property. It is not possible to determine whether the city has an increased value of assets at the end of the year as compared with the beginning of the year. Property records, of course, will be maintained by departments in any reasonably well-managed city, but the preparation of municipal balance sheets is not customary. Insofar as the two may be separated, capital

[10] Fred W. Lawrence, "The Capital Improvement Program—A Challenge to a Small City," *Municipal Finance*, May 1954, pp. 144–148 (experience in Modesto, California). Pay-as-you-go versus loans for municipalities is one of the hardy perennials of controversy in the field of local finance. For a discussion of some of the elements in the controversy, see National Resources Planning Board, *Long Range Programming of Municipal Public Works*, pp. 27–41; also Chapter 17.

budgeting in American municipalities emphasizes planning, not budgeting. It is a highly useful technique for centering attention on a class of expenditures which is difficult to evaluate and difficult to finance.

II. NEW YORK STATE'S CAPITAL CONSTRUCTION FUND

In World War II New York State accumulated substantial surpluses from an excess of general fund revenue over expenditure. Even though state tax rates were reduced, wartime prosperity brought in more revenue than could be expended, given the shortage of personnel and materials. During the war it was recognized that there would be a need for postwar improvement in state facilities, and it was anticipated that there would be postwar unemployment. The surpluses would be useful in meeting both problems.

The postwar unemployment did not materialize, but the demands for state-financed capital construction did. Many state properties, because of inadequate wartime maintenance, were in need of major repairs and reconstruction. There were demands on every hand for state construction of highways, housing, hospitals, and higher education facilities. A Postwar Reconstruction Fund was established in 1943 as a means of providing for orderly consideration of these demands, and to minimize the necessity for borrowing.[11] The fund was initiated with a transfer of about $460 million from general fund surpluses. In 1949 the Postwar Reconstruction Fund was renamed the Capital Construction Fund (CCF).[12]

New York's Capital Construction Fund, like the capital budgets of American municipalities, is characterized by the way in which it has served to facilitate the consideration of proposals for capital outlays.

The requests for CCF projects are originated by department heads in the state government at the same time as other budget requests. For each project proposal departments prepare a separate justification on a specific form; this includes all items of equipment. The project requests are not processed by the regular budget examiners in the Division of the Budget, but by an engineering unit in the Division. There is an initial screening, based on the justifications as submitted and on information which Division staff secure from conferences with the departments and from field investigations. This may eliminate about half of the dollar volume of projects requested. After the initial screening the remaining

[11] Lynton K. Caldwell, *The Government and Administration of New York*, Thomas Y. Crowell Company, New York, 1954, pp. 239–240.

[12] The material which follows is drawn very largely from interviews with officials in the New York State Division of the Budget.

projects are submitted to the Department of Public Works, which prepares a detailed report on each, covering cost, feasibility, urgency, and
construction time required. The report by Public Works is advisory
only; it is submitted to the Division of the Budget, which retains sole
authority to make budget recommendations to the Governor.[13]

On the basis of the reports made by Public Works, the Division now
begins to assign priorities to the projects which might be included in the
budget to be submitted by the Governor. To supplement the information already in its possession and to enlist the cooperation and understanding of the departments, the Division of the Budget initiated in the
fall of 1953 a series of hearings on capital projects. These were conducted by the Director of the Budget, and were attended by Division
staff, department personnel, and the State Architect. After the hearings
final priorities are established.

In the meantime, the research staff of the Division has begun to estimate
the revenue that might be made available to the Capital Construction
Fund. This revenue is of varied character; the major source is appropriations from operating funds. For example, if general fund revenues are exceeding expenditures, over and above what has been anticipated,
it may be possible to appropriate a part of this excess to the Capital Construction Fund for the following year.[14] Other CCF revenue may derive from sales of property and investments by the state, and surpluses
from such miscellaneous state funds as the grade crossing elimination
fund and the dwelling relocation fund. Finally, CCF may be augmented
by proceeds from bond issues.

The provisional estimates of revenue available to CCF are now related
to the project costs in accordance with the priorities which have been
established by the Director of the Budget. As the budget moves toward
final preparation in January, the estimates of revenue for the forthcoming
year are firmed up and the requirements of the operating budget are
known. At this point it becomes necessary to make major policy decisions
on CCF projects and to determine whether or not additional loan finance
will be requested for particular programs. As with other aspects of
budgetary policy in New York State, final decisions are made by the
Governor, after consultation with the Director of the Budget and legis-

[13] For a description of the general responsibilities and operating characteristics
of the Division of the Budget see Frederick C. Mosher, "The Executive Budget,
Empire State Style," *Public Administration Review*, Spring 1952, pp. 73–84;
Caldwell, *op. cit.*, pp. 229–253.

[14] The New York state budget is divided into sections—state purposes and
local purposes. These two make up the general fund, and are financed from the
aggregate of total revenue. Revenues are not earmarked for state purposes or for
local purposes.

lative leaders. The decisions reached here are incorporated in the Governor's Budget Message, transmitted in January. The budget document contains a tabular presentation of the status of the fund and a detailed listing of recommended projects.

As a classification technique, the total expenditures from CCF are a reasonably good approximation to the concept of "gross government investment," since they include all new construction, equipment, and wages and salaries paid to the Department of Public Works for planning and surveying. This falls short of a measure of total state investment, however, since expenditures from funds outside the general fund are not included. The most important of such exclusions are the authorities, including the Thruway Authority. In fact, the New York State budget, like most other state budgets, is seriously deficient as a comprehensive statement of total financial activity.

Generally speaking, the Division of the Budget, in its staff work on proposed Capital Construction Fund requests, does not attempt to define precise criteria for judging the relation of benefits to costs for particular project proposals. In some cases needs can be quantified, as with patients in mental hospitals, current and prospective, or with highways, where it is possible to measure the quantity of highway use and highway facilities. But in other areas broad standards of urgency, largely subjective, must necessarily be applied in the abence of more precise measures.

One of the technical tools available for judging the construction needs of state government departments is a property listing, maintained by the engineering staff of the Division of the Budget since the late 1930's. This listing shows, for each facility owned by the state, the date of construction and its original cost, together with the cost of subsequent major repairs. For many facilities there are maps and aerial photographs. The listing does not extend to current asset values, nor does it include current engineering appraisals of remaining useful life. Such appraisals are made only when requests for major rehabilitation or replacement of the structure are initiated by departments. Therefore, these property records are in no sense a balance sheet of state assets, nor could they easily be converted to one. It is estimated that it would cost the state from $500,000 to $1 million to bring the property list up to date in terms of estimated current asset values and remaining useful life. The expenditure of a sum of money of this magnitude has not yet appeared to be justified.

New York State's Capital Construction Fund is not a device for justifying loan finance, although it may help to maintain a reasonably close scrutiny over the state's borrowing and thus contribute to a strong credit rating, which in turn holds down interest costs and tax rates. The

CCF is more procedural than financial. The separation of capital expenditures is undertaken to provide decision-making assistance to elected and appointed officials within established budgetary routines. The techniques employed assure that expert judgment will be utilized, almost to the exclusion of the views of the interest groups, who must make their representations directly to the Governor.

The CCF procedure centers political responsibility for the state's capital improvements program, with the exception of the independent authorities, clearly and definitely in the Governor's office. Decisions are not shared with a citizen's commission nor with a state planning commission.[15]

III. THE CAPITAL BUDGET IN SWEDEN

There are probably no governments in the world where budgetary techniques are more highly developed than in the national governments of the Scandinavian countries, and where budgetary techniques have been as closely integrated with budgetary policy. Many of these policy and technical developments have come to be associated with the use of the capital budget. In some respects this association is inappropriate. Budget procedure and classification in these countries go far beyond what can appropriately be described in connection with the techniques for listing and controlling capital outlays.

The budgetary practices of Denmark, Norway, and Sweden have important common features. For present purposes attention will be centered on Sweden, whose budget system has received the most attention in this country. Although major emphasis will be laid here on the treatment of capital in the Swedish system, it will be necessary to describe related matters, which are, in part, a digression into fiscal and economic policy.

Modern technical and policy developments in budgeting in Sweden are firmly rooted in the concern and responsibility of the national government for economic welfare. This is a concern which dates back at

---

[15] The contrast with Maryland, another state where capital improvement planning is well developed, is particularly sharp at this point. In that state there is a formal annual review of capital requirements by the Maryland State Planning Commission, composed of legislators and designated state government department heads, assisted by Planning Commission staff. The Commission submits a published report to the Governor, recommending the inclusion of a specified list of projects in the budget. (Maryland State Planning Commission, *1956 Fiscal Year Long-Term Capital Improvement Program*, Baltimore, 1954.) The Maryland procedure is generally in conformity with the recommendations of the National Municipal League in its *Model State and Regional Planning Law* (New York, 1954).

least to World War I, when a State Unemployment Commission was established to inquire into the causes and remedies of a depression from which Sweden was then suffering.[16] Subsequently, unemployment commissions were established in 1921–1922, in 1924, and again in the early 1930's. In every case professional economists served on these commissions or contributed to the analysis and the findings. The reports of the commissions had considerable impact on national policy and were customarily implemented by the Swedish Parliament.

The depression was not severe in Sweden until late in 1930, but after that date unemployment began to increase sharply, and acting on the recommendations of the Unemployment Commission then in existence, the state undertook substantial outlays for public works and for grants to assist municipalities in work projects. Taxes were increased in the years 1930–1932 in an attempt to maintain a balanced budget in accordance with then prevailing notions of sound finance. Nevertheless, the tax increases were not sufficient to cover the increase in outlays, and deficits occurred in the state budget in the fiscal years 1932 and 1933.

During these years of depression there were sharp debates, inside and outside the Parliament, on the merits of budget balance and on the extent to which the state should assist in coping with unemployment. These conflicts were resolved by the 1933 elections, which brought the Social Democratic Party to power, pledged to an expansionist policy. As a result, the state further increased its public works activities and social welfare outlays. Total government expenditure increased by about 40 percent from fiscal 1929–1930 to 1934–1935, with large deficits in fiscal 1934 and 1935. In the meantime, the Unemployment Commission in 1931 had invited four economists to submit monographs analyzing the character of the economic problems which Sweden faced. One of these monographs, prepared by Gunnar Myrdal, discussed the economic effects of public financial policy, and became the basis for continued political and theoretical discussion, eventuating in a major budgetary reform in June of 1937.[17]

During this period, possibly as a result of the expansionist budgetary policy and deficit financing, Sweden's economy made a substantial recovery. From 1933 to 1937 unemployment fell from 164,000 to 18,000.

[16] Lewis L. Lorwin, *National Planning in Selected Countries*, National Resources Planning Board, Washington, 1941, p. 94.

[17] Other economists who contributed to the work of the Unemployment Commission were Hammerskjold, Ohlin, and Johansson. The theoretical discussion on economic policy which their work produced led to the "Stockholm School" of economics. See Bertil Ohlin, "Some Notes on the Stockholm Theory of Savings and Investments," *Economic Journal*, March 1937, pp. 53–69, and June 1937, pp. 221–240.

In 1937 industrial production exceeded 1929 levels by 46 percent.[18]   By
fiscal 1936 the earlier deficits had been turned to surpluses, which continued for the next three years.   In these circumstances it was possible
to ascribe a good deal of this recovery to budgetary policy, although this
would certainly involve some oversimplification.[19]   Nevertheless, the economic recovery that accompanied deficit financing facilitated the Parliamentary adoption of the budget reform bill of 1937.   This action, in
effect, formalized Ohlin's statement of 1935:

> The idea that the budget must be balanced *each year,* and that otherwise infla-
> tion is bound to ensue, is one of those popular maxims which are true in
> certain circumstances but not in others.   The fact that they have been
> preached as a general gospel without qualifications, especially by bankers, has
> done much harm.   For if an economic policy is believed to be unsound the
> practice of it cannot fail to call forth certain unfavorable "confidence reac-
> tions."   In Sweden, fortunately, influences of this kind have been very slight.
> It is time to learn the lesson of recent experience that intelligent and sound
> public finance does not require the budget to be balanced each year but only
> over a number of years, including both good and bad business conditions.[20]

In terms of policy the 1937 law was significant in that it officially
abandoned the principle of annual budget balance and substituted a
policy of attempting to balance the budget over the business cycle—the
deficits of depression years to be matched by the surpluses of prosperity
years.   Again, to quote Ohlin:

> In order to prevent the Minister of Finance from forgetting the deficit in
> a past depression, rules were laid down that if a deficit appeared one year,
> he must enter 20 percent of that deficit as a debit item to be covered by
> revenue in the next year.   If a deficit arose in the second year too, the
> government should put as an item to be covered by income during the third
> year 40 percent of the annual deficit (20 percent of the first deficit and 20
> percent of the second).   By applying this rule, it was hoped to remove a
> deficit from the world eventually.   The 20 percent rule is not a very rational
> thing, of course.   However, it placates the conservative opinion, and the
> whole thing went through in the Riksdag without any opposition at all.[21]

The Swedish economists apparently felt that concessions had to be made
to the traditional budget-balancing views of the community.   In 1939

[18] Lorwin, *op. cit.,* p. 113; Ernst Wigforss, "The Financial Policy During Depression and Boom," *The Annals,* May 1938, pp. 25–39.

[19] *Fortune,* "That Wonderful Swedish Budget," September 1938, pp. 65ff.

[20] Bertil Ohlin, "Economic Recovery and Labour Market Problems in Sweden:
II," *International Labour Review,* May 1935, p. 685.

[21] Bertil Ohlin, *The Problem of Employment Stabilization,* Columbia University
Press, New York, 1949, pp. 67–68.

Myrdal stated, "We must, therefore, not only make a virtue of the sins but also incorporate them in the regular fiscal system in order to avoid the adverse confidence reaction."[22]

As it turned out, cyclical budget balancing was never wholly practiced. In 1938–1939 there was a substantial budget surplus; then, with the outbreak of war in Europe, Sweden, although neutral, undertook heavy defense expenditures. This led to budget deficits during the war years, even though the economy was operating under conditions of generally full employment.

In addition to a new fiscal policy, the budget reform of 1937 prescribed a new budgetary structure for the Swedish national government, and it is to this structure that the term capital budget is applied. The conceptual basis for the capital budget is expressed in the phrase "financial soundness," which is measured in terms of the influence of the government's transactions on the net assets of the state.[23] The net assets of the state are not changed when borrowings are applied to the acquisition of assets, since additional debt liability is matched by assets, leaving the "net worth" of the state intact. Net asset are changed (downward) when expenditures exceed revenue on current account. This emphasis on changes in net assets leads to a sharp distinction between current and capital transactions; the budget deficit or surplus is defined solely in relation to the current account. Capital expenditures can then be appropriately financed by borrowing, without making the state "poorer."

At the same time, an accurate measurement of net asset position requires that the current budget be charged with the annual depreciation on all assets owned by the state. This volume of annual depreciation must be covered by current taxation if asset values are to be preserved. The final results of governmental financial operations, both current and capital, are combined in a single financial statement, but the totals of revenue and expenditure in this consolidated account lose their significance as a measure of deficit or surplus.

This approach to financial soundness, as measured by changes in the state's net assets, is reinforced in the Swedish governmental system by what may be termed the concept of the custodianship of assets. Cabinet ministers in Sweden have a very high degree of individual responsibility for the property and funds under their jurisdiction; this responsibility is

[22] Gunnar Myrdal, "Fiscal Policy in the Business Cycle," *American Economic Review*, March 1939, Part 2, p. 187.

[23] United Nations, *Budgetary Structure and Classification of Government Accounts*, New York, 1951, pp. 68–69; Erik Lindahl, *Studies in the Theory of Money and Capital*, Farrar & Rinehart, New York, 1939, pp. 352–355.

not a collective responsibility as in some parliamentary regimes.[24]   Each minister has traditionally been charged with the preservation of the assets under his supervision.

Before examining additional aspects of Sweden's budget structure, it would be well to complete the chronology of developments in budgetary policy and procedure.

In 1944 the government appointed a Post-War Economic Planning Committee, with the responsibility for recommending changes in governmental policy designed to cope with a possible postwar depression.[25]   On the basis of the recommendations of this committee, a further reform was adopted in 1947.   The principal consequence of this was the introduction of "emergency budgets," to be voted by the Parliament but to be implemented by the government only in case of need.   There are two such emergency or standby budgets.   The first is the "emergency budget for national defense," which takes the form of approximate appropriations that may be exceeded by the government in the event of a war crisis. The second is the "general emergency budget," which embraces appropriations for public works and other income-creating government expenditures, to be undertaken when the government attempts to counteract an appreciable decline in the level of production and employment.

The general emergency budget is a formalization and extension of the public works reserve procedure used in a number of governments since the late 1920's.   In differs from these primarily in its close link with the general budget structure and procedure of the Swedish government.

The 1947 budget reform retained the distinction between the current budget and the capital or investment budget.   The emergency budget thus becomes a waiting list for the capital budget.   When a budget year has passed without a depression, the most urgent of the projects are taken from the emergency budget and included in the capital budget for the following year.   Then additional projects are included in the revised emergency budget.   This assures both an extended planning period for public improvements and a continuously revised and current emergency reserve.

Since 1947 there has come to be less emphasis on financial soundness in Sweden's budgetary policy and an even greater emphasis on the use of the budget for stabilization purposes.   The budget is still intended to be balanced over the business cycle, but this is less significant than in the 1937 budget philosophy.   As stated in an official summary of the Swedish

[24] Carl Murray, "Budget Execution and Government Accounting in Sweden," *Government Accounting and Budget Execution,* United Nations, New York, 1952, pp. 60–61; Fritz Morstein Marx, "The Divided Budget in Scandinavian Practice," *National Tax Journal,* June, 1955, pp. 194–195.

[25] Ohlin, *The Problem of Employment Stabilization,* pp. 73–88.

budgetary system, " . . . the question of the balancing of the working budget over the long range must be examined from a broader viewpoint than that which inspired the 1937 budget reform."[26] Currently, the emphasis is not on rules of budget balancing but on the procedures by which the economic outlook and economic policy are built into budgetary policy.

The interrelating of economic and budgetary policy work out as follows. Each fall the Minister of Finance, who has responsibility for the government's budget policy, recommends, and the government appoints, a National Budget Delegation. This group is made up of representatives from government departments and the major political parties, and economists from the staff of the Economic Research Institute, a government agency that operates independently of the Ministry of Finance. The Institute prepares a careful analysis of recent economic developments, with particular attention to changes in governmental financial activity, the level of private investment and consumer expenditures, and the export-import position. On the basis of this and other information, the Budget Delegation prepares a National Economic Budget—a comprehensive forecast of national income and expenditure for the forthcoming year.[27] These materials, the Institute's survey and the National Economic Budget, are now made available to the Minister of Finance, who submits the government's budget and economic policy recommendations in January of each year. Revenue estimates prepared independently by the General Accounting Office are similarly submitted to the Finance Minister.

Budget and economic policy recommendations are shaped in relation to this National Economic Budget. For example, a forecast decline in private investment would presumably lead the Minister of Finance to recommend an expansion in the state's investment activity or a reduction in taxes to stimulate domestic investment. A forecast shortage of foreign exchange might lead to recommended tax reductions for exporters. The budget document and policy recommendations submitted to the Riksdag contain the Institute's economic review, the revenue forecast, and the National Economic Budget projection, so that the quantitative and analytical materials which shape budgetary and economic policy are available for consideration by both the Riksdag and the general public.

[26] Quoted in United Nations, *Budgetary Structure and Classification of Government Accounts*, p. 69.

[27] Petter Jakob Bjerve, "Government Economic Planning and Control," *Scandinavia Between East and West*, Henning Friis, ed., Cornell University Press, Ithaca, 1950, pp. 73–97; Murray *op. cit.*, pp. 61–62; Erik Lindahl, "Swedish Experiences in Economic Planning," *American Economic Review*, May 1950, pp. 15–17. Doris Olson of the Foreign Operations Administration has also supplied materials for this section.

The budget committees of the Riksdag may modify the government's recommendations. The Minister of Finance will, in turn, be called on to defend his recommendations. In the debate on both the budget and economic policy, it is customary for the Minister of Finance to insist that all proposed changes be interpreted in relation to the National Economic Budget—that is, judged by their impact on levels of income, expenditure, and employment for the forthcoming period. The National Economic Budget does not, of course, have the force of law—it is not possible to legislate a forecast—but it nevertheless serves as a basis for appraising and adopting the government's budget, and also serves as the basis for specific governmental actions such as domestic materials allocations or controls over imports.[28]

As has been noted, the procedures which link the budget and government economic planning are supported by a budget classification which facilitates an analysis of the economic impact of governmental activities. This budget classification, whose most important structural characteristic is a division between current and capital account, has a number of other features.

First, the Swedish budget is comprehensive of all state financial activity except the social insurance funds. All supplementary budgets, such as for special funds and public enterprises, are shown separately but are consolidated into a summary account for the government as a whole.

Second, all government activities conducted in the form of public enterprises maintain commercial-type accounting, with operating and capital accounts. The operating deficit or surplus is carried into the current budget of the state. In addition, all governmental agencies which maintain or operate capital facilities are organized with separate funds, to provide an accounting for their activities; these funds also incorporate a distinction between current and capital.[29] This includes the General Real Estate Fund, which charges rent to all government agencies occupying structures under its jurisdiction, and which has responsibility for maintaining and repairing these structures.

Third, depreciation accounts are maintained by all government enterprises and funds, including the General Real Estate Fund. This practice is intended to facilitate the valuation of assets, and therefore the ascer-

---

[28] For a discussion of the techniques used in the preparation of the National Economic Budget and an appraisal of results see Ingvar Ohlsson, *On National Accounting*, Konjunkturinstitutet, Stockholm, 1953, pp. 273–312.

[29] Public enterprise in Sweden is organized in a form resembling the joint stock company, which differs somewhat from the public corporation as used in Great Britain and the United States. (See Hakan Stromberg, "The Public Corporation in Sweden," *The Public Corporation*, W. Friedmann, ed., The Carswell Company, Ltd., Toronto, 1954, pp. 324–337.)

tainment of the financial soundness of the state. Balance sheets showing the values of state assets on the basis of original cost less depreciation are compiled for each fiscal year. This, it may be noted, will not give an accurate current value for assets when the price level and hence replacement costs are rising, as in the postwar years. Since all capital assets are under the jurisdiction of enterprises and funds, and since the operating results of the enterprises and funds, reflecting annual depreciation charges, are carried forward to the state's current account, the current account surplus or deficit reflects depreciation charges.

Fourth, certain capital expenditures which are deemed to be "unproductive," that is, nonrevenue producing, are charged against the current budget as expenditures. These include all military assets except those few cases where the military constructs permanent buildings which might be converted to other government uses. Also included here are outlays for public roads. In other cases that portion of the capital outlay which is deemed unproductive will be charged off. In every case the capital expenditures included in the current account are excluded from the assets on the state's balance sheet.

Fifth, surpluses or deficits on current account are recorded in a Budget Equalization Fund. This fund shows cumulative totals, a practice intended to reveal changes in the net asset position of the state over a period of years.

Sixth, the investment activities of the state are shown in the consolidated account of state funds and enterprises which appears in the summary budget accounts. This budget summary shows net investment, not gross investment. Gross investment includes capital outlays made from internal funds, such as depreciation allowances and revenues from the sale of assets. This is not carried forward to the consolidated account. Therefore, the net investment figure equals the amount of borrowing which must be undertaken to finance investment. The Riksdag votes an investment authorization and a loan authorization, but the borrowing operations themselves are conducted by the National Debt Office, which is independent of the Ministry of Finance.

Seventh, the government maintains considerable flexibility in the execution of investment expenditures. If economic conditions change during the fiscal year, authorizations need not be utilized, and even where investment projects are initiated, the rate of expenditure is subject to considerable variation. The rate of current account expenditure may also be modified in accordance with changing economic conditions.

Sweden has carried to a very high level the use of the budget for purposes of economic stabilization and the integration of budget-making with other aspects of economic policy. There is no evidence, however, that the Swedish government regards the budget as the only stabilization measure available. The structure and classification of the government accounts have by no means been subordinated wholly to economic planning considerations, but are intended to serve purposes other than economic analysis. In fact, the Economic Research Institute in recent years, on the ground that the budget accounts are not sufficiently refined for its purposes, has prepared a separate classification of government transactions for analyzing the impact of the public finances. On balance, nevertheless, there is no doubt that economic policy considerations have had great influence on Swedish budgetary classification and procedure.

IV. SUMMARY: PURPOSES OF CAPITAL BUDGETING

These three cases—American municipalities, New York State, and Sweden—illustrate the general purposes which may be served by capital budget classification and procedures.

First, as a double budget the capital budget can be a convenient device for segregating a kind of government expenditures that need a specialized type of review and analysis. This review may provide a particular expertise, or it may provide a broad citizen participation not available in the ordinary budgetary mechanism.

Second, capital budgeting and its procedures, linked with long-range public works planning, can effectively serve as an instrument for orderly resource development and maintenance. This will aid financial planning, serve to regularize expenditure over a period of years, and thus preserve the credit standing of a government.

Third, a capital budget can be used to show changes in the net asset position of a government, indicate trends in the accumulation and preservation of social capital, and provide information useful in estimating the government component of national wealth.

It is evident from the foregoing listing that there are two major types of capital budget which ought to be distinguished. The first is the kind used in American cities and in New York State, where annual capital expenditures are grouped. The second is the kind used in Sweden where, in addition to the grouping of annual capital expenditures, depreciation accounts are maintained so that asset values can be summarized. The Swedish variety permits balance sheets to approximate government asset condition; the American variety does not. Since property inventories and depreciation accounting are difficult and expensive to install, this means that the Swedish-type capital budget is considerably more complicated than the American type.

For either type of capital budget there is an attitudinal factor which seems to accompany its use. If citizens know that a portion of governmental expenditures adds to the community's stock of assets, they tend to feel more content about the level of expenditures. This feeling will facilitate an expansion in public outlay. Citizen fears about wasteful expenditure are allayed by the countervailing sentiment that capital expenditures are not wasteful. This consideration may be important in implementing a fiscal policy to counteract depressions, but it might be hoped that stabilization programs could be grounded on other and broader public understandings.

V. A CAPITAL BUDGET FOR THE UNITED STATES GOVERNMENT

There have been recurrent suggestions that the federal government of the United States adopt a capital budget.

Beyond doubt, a capital budget can provide the financial framework for resource planning and development. This purpose alone justifies its use and extension in municipalities. However, the federal government does not have clearly defined responsibilities of this kind. There is no six-year plan for national development, nor is there likely to be one in the foreseeable future. The nature of federal responsibility for resources is very different than in an underdeveloped country where the national government accepts such responsibility and attempts to implement it.

In the United States much of the responsibility for resources and community development resides with state and local governments. This is the case with education, transportation facilities, public health and recreation, and to a lesser degree with conservation, navigation, and flood control. The federal government may encourage a number of these activities through grants-in-aid, but this encouragement is neither comprehensive nor continuous. Although federal expenditures are about two-thirds of total government expenditures, its ownership of assets is much less significant. This ownership has been estimated at 30 percent of the nation's physical, nonmilitary government assets.[30] Unless there is a fundamental rearrangement of governmental responsibilities among federal, state, and local units, which may be put down as unlikely, a capital budget for the federal government could not be comprehensive of responsibilities for resource development.

[30] J. E. Reeve, et al, "Government Component in the National Wealth," *Studies in Income and Wealth,* Vol. XII, National Bureau of Economic Research, New York, 1950, p. 487. (Based on data for December 31, 1946; monetary gold and silver are excluded from the computation.)

On the other hand, it may well be that a capital budget for the federal government could contribute to a regularization and extension of procedures for a "shelf of public works." The U. S. Bureau of the Budget has had centralized authority over public works planning since 1943 (*Executive Order* 9384). It has procedures established for a six-year planning program for public works in all departments and agencies. The Bureau publishes an annual survey of public works activities and a summary of these plans.[31] The Bureau's coordinating role has been limited, however, by lack of funds and personnel, and the planned reserve would appear to be wholly inadequate.[32] A more adequate public works reserve could, of course, be established without a capital budget, but the latter would undoubtedly encourage the former.

With the federal government's limited responsibility for resource development, public interest and attention cannot center on capital expenditures to the same degree as in state and local governments. Instead, attention centers more on broad interests served, as expressed in a functional classification which sets forth amounts expended in major program areas. In this focus of attention the separation of current and capital outlay is distinctly subsidiary, and in the process of budgetary review and Congressional consideration such a separation may be diversionary and may even have perverse results.

In fact, something like this has occurred in recent years as certain kinds of capital items which were wholly or partially self-liquidating have been moved out of the budget to be financed privately. The budget totals have been thereby reduced, but without a corresponding reduction in ultimate financial liabilities.[33] There is always the danger that where capital outlays are listed separately and emphasized in budget schedules, these items may come to be regarded as postponable or subject to special financing. Instead of concentrating on the analysis of program, review may concentrate on the analysis of capital.[34]

[31] See *Budget of the United States Government for the fiscal year ending June 30, 1956*, pp. 1175–1188.

[32] The reserve, planned to a stage where construction could be started, for federal civil public works for fiscal 1956, is reported at $1.9 billion, with some planning completed on an additional $3.4 billion (*ibid.*, p. 1177). The full expenditure of these amounts could make only a modest contribution to offsetting a major decline in the level of economic activity.

[33] See Sidney G. Tickton, *The Budget in Transition*, National Planning Association, Washington, 1955.

[34] The first Hoover Commission recommended that capital expenditures be differentiated within the scope of a performance budgeting classification. (Commission on Organization of the Executive Branch of the Government, *Budgeting and Accounting*, Washington, 1949, pp. 15–16.) The Commission did not discuss this recommendation is detail, nor indicate the basis on which the distinction was to be made, nor suggest the purposes which were intended to be served thereby.

The federal government does not need a capital budget in order to preserve its credit rating. It does not operate in a framework where the Constitution imposes restrictions on borrowing and taxing. Its ability to borrow is not affected by asset acquisition, as is the case with municipal governments. The federal government is not subject to the solvency criteria which investment bankers enforce on local governments. In fact, the financial soundness of the federal government can be interpreted only in terms of the soundness of the United States economy as a whole.[35]

One of the reasons that the capital budget has seemed attractive is its businesslike appearance. In order to compute annual costs and therefore to compute annual profit, business firms use a capital budget in that they maintain their accounts in terms or current and capital income and outlay. This is fitting, proper, and conventional. Asset accounting in the private sector is the only way by which it is possible to compute accurately the volume of profit from current operations. With this technique the cost of capital attributable to current operations can be allocated; in this way it is possible to show the financial condition of the firm. The concept of the custodianship of assets did not originate with the Swedes. Its roots are to be found in the double-entry bookkeeping practices of the Medicis.

The fact that capital accounting is necessary for the measurement of profits (and losses) in the private sector does not, in and of itself, mean that it should be lifted over and applied to the public sector.[36] Public activities are not operated to secure for the owners the greatest return on net worth. To attempt to make government more businesslike by introducing profit-measurement techniques from the private sector will only lead to confusion. For business firms a capital expenditure is one which does not turn over into cash within the accounting period. The flexibility of the commitment is the criterion for separating capital and noncapital outlays.[37] If there is justification for capital budgeting in government, it cannot be found in analogy with the private sector.

[35] In the debate on the Revenue Act of 1954 Senator George put this point as follows, "When we return home, our constituents will ask us what budget it was that we wished to balance, and whether it was the unbalanced Federal budget . . . or whether we wished to have the home budgets balanced, and thus increase the capacity of the American people to purchase the products which can be turned out by our mills and our factories." (*Congressional Record*, 83d Cong., 2d sess., June 30, 1954, p. 9298.)

[36] For a different view see Morris A. Copeland, "The Capital Budget and the War Effort," *American Economic Review*, March 1943, pp. 38–49.

[37] Joel Dean, *Capital Budgeting*, Columbia University Press, New York, 1951, p. 4. For a discussion of the techniques which may be used for arriving at capital expenditure decisions in the private sector, see Dean's article, "Measuring the Productivity of Capital," *Harvard Business Review*, January-February 1954, pp. 120–130.

The Committee on the Form of Government Accounts in Great Britain summarized this point very well:

> The Government administration is expected to maintain an efficient service as required by Parliament, and considerations of cost, while important, must not be allowed, in themselves, to hamper the achievement of those ends; private business, on the other hand . . . is primarily concerned with financial results, which are in the end the tests of efficiency. . . . What we seek to guard against is the generalized and uncritical supposition that a principle or a method properly applied in business accounting must necessarily be suitable for the very different purposes of Government accounting.[38]

Although this limitation—the unsuitability of private sector techniques applied to the public sector—is serious enough to warrant hesitation in the adoption of capital budgeting for the federal government, there are further discouraging technical complications.

It is not possible to formulate a precise rule for the identification of capital expenditures. This problem is common to both the private and the government sector, but for the individual firm the profit criterion and income tax regulations provide conventional benchmarks to facilitate the necessarily arbitrary decisions as to what is or is not capital. For government there are no such criteria, and any system of capital budgeting which is intended to rest on a clear definitional basis is impossible. It cannot be conclusively determined, one way or the other, that expenditures for jet aircraft are current or capital, or expenditures for the training of troops, or for overseas installations. Similar conceptual problems are encountered in the nonmilitary area in determining the current or capital nature of outlays for roads, for soil conservation, for flood control. Expenditure for education can be as productive of long-run increases in the national income as the construction of dams and bridges. Any category labeled "capital expenditures" is bound to be an extremely artitrary category.[39]

Comparable problems are encountered in the valuation of public assets where an effort is made to list government property in a balance sheet and maintain depreciation accounts, that is, where the Swedish-type capital budget is used. It is not possible to arrive at a market value where assets will never be sold, and valuation on the basis of cost of reproduction less depreciation is formidable in the case of military assets, public roads, and national monuments, to note only a few examples.[40]

[38] *Final Report of the Committee on the Form of Government Accounts* (CMD. 7969), His Majesty's Stationery Office, London, 1950, p. 7.

[39] For a further discussion see Gerhard Colm and Marilyn Young, *The Federal Budget and the National Economy*, National Planning Association, Washington, 1955, pp. 86–100.

[40] This point is put somewhat more strongly by the Committee on the Form of Government Accounts: "The fact is that no element of homogeneity can be

A capital budget for the federal government might contribute to greater citizen contentment about federal expenditures and thus rationalize either an increase in expenditures or a reduction in taxes. This seems to have been the thinking of one Senator, who in 1947 asked the Bureau of the Budget to prepare a listing of capital expenditures in the budget then under congressional consideration.[41] Possibly as a follow-up to the information provided by the Budget Bureau on that occasion, the budget document has contained since fiscal 1951 a listing of "additions to federal assets" in a special statistical analysis.[42] This analysis presents considerable information about the character of expenditures. For 1956, for example, it shows that "additions to federal assets" in the proposed budget amounted to $19 billion, of which $17 billion were for national security purposes. This information may be of some comfort to ordinary taxpayers, but it is highly doubtful that congressional budget decisions were much influenced by this knowledge. The important thing about national security expenditure is its adequacy, not its division between current and capital outlay.

The interest in a capital budget as a means of expanding federal outlay dates back, in this country, to the late 1930's.[43] Beyond doubt, a capital budget can serve as a satisfying ritual to support deficit financing.[44] Unfortunately, where this is its justification, the results are not wholly salutary. Capital outlays are not the only and certainly may not be the best way to counteract a downturn in economic activity. If a government is undertaking an all-out program, there are a good many current expenditures which ought to be increased or current taxes which ought to be reduced, and this can be done rapidly and flexibly. A capital budget might well lead to overemphasis on public works. To confine antidepression spending to durable goods or capital facilities is unduly restrictive.[45] The current or capital character of the expenditure is not

---

found among Government assets, ranging from battleships to trunk roads, which would give any meaning to a monetary total of the values thereof or to fluctuations from year to year in such a total." (*Op. cit.*, p. 75.)

[41] *Congressional Record*, 80th Cong., 1st sess., July 10, 1947, pp. 8596–8602 (Senator Wayne Morse). The proposals of Beardsley Ruml would also appear to fall in this category. See *A Budget Reform Program* and *Budget Reform—Round Two*, The Seventh Company, New York, 1953.

[42] See Special Analysis D, "Investment, Operating, and Other Budget Expenditures," *Budget of the United States Government for the fiscal year ending June 30, 1956*, pp. 1153–1164.

[43] Chapter 17; Morris A. Copeland, "Public Investment in the United States," *American Economic Review*, March 1939, Part 2, pp. 40–41.

[44] Sherwood M. Fine, *Public Spending and Postwar Economic Policy*, Columbia University Press, New York, 1944, pp. 40–42.

[45] Gerhard Colm, "Comment on Extraordinary Budgets," *Social Research*, May 1938, pp. 176–177.

significant in determining the effect of governmental activities on the *current* level of national income.[46] And certainly there is no reason to assume that at any one time the volume of deficit financing required is exactly equal to the volume of government capital expenditures.

A capital budget may be even more hazardous in time of inflation. Once the feeling is established that it is proper to borrow for capital outlays, there is danger that this attitude will carry over to inflationary periods and the canons of "sound" finance will now serve to perpetuate government contributions to inflationary pressure when economic stabilization requires substantial aggregate surpluses. If budgetary policy is to make a maximum contribution to stabilization, decisions to borrow or tax should be made independently of the current or capital character of government outlay. It would be necessary for the federal government to introduce a capital budget without introducing at the same time a rationalization for borrowing to finance the capital outlay.[47]

Apart from considerations relating to stabilization policy, it may be useful, particularly for some types of governmental activities, to show net asset position and changes in this position over time. This is done, of course, with the enterprise operations of the federal government which are conducted in corporate form. Business-type budgets are used, with commercial accounting practices applied to asset acquisition and the measurement of depreciation. In recent years this type of accounting and budgeting has been extended to some noncorporate enterprise operations in the federal government, such as the Bureau of Engraving and Printing in the Treasury Department (see Chapter 12).

An extension of capital budgeting beyond such enterprise-type operations would require the organization of a general real estate fund in accordance with the Swedish prototype. It may be that this technique would encourage greater attention in the federal government to the maintenance of public assets, and would lead to improved property

[46] Richard Abel Musgrave, "The Nature of Budgetary Balance and the Case for the Capital Budget," *American Economic Review,* June 1939, pp. 262–267; Maxwell, *Quarterly Journal of Economics,* May 1943, p. 463.

[47] The following statement is reproduced without comment from the Honorable Finance Minister's Budget Speech, Burma, August 1952: "The Budgets I had presented in the years previous to 1951–1952 had all been deficit Budgets, and they have accordingly been described as unbalanced Budgets. The reason, however, for showing a deficit in these years has been no other than that both current and capital expenditures had been lumped together in one Statement during all those years. This form of presentation was, however, altered with the Budget for the financial year 1951–1952, and with this change both the receipts and expenditure on current account have been shown separately from the receipts and expenditure on capital account. As a result, it has been possible to produce a surplus Budget in the current account for 1951–52, while the capital account showed a deficit."

management. These benefits might offset the high cost of installation and the difficulties encountered in attaching valuations and depreciation rates to federal assets. The interests of improved property management can be at least partially served, however, by an inventory of assets which need not extend to current valuations. Such an inventory was prepared in 1937 and another was completed in 1955 by the General Services Administration. This and other techniques could make for improved property management independently of a capital budget.[48]

Finally, a capital budget may provide information useful in estimating the government component of national wealth. This is a very different kind of consideration from the foregoing budgetary and policy-formulation purposes. On this point it should be noted that there has been a substantial and growing interest in recent years in the measurement of national wealth for purposes of economic analysis.[49] This kind of measurement, including the government component, is useful for analyzing asset ownership patterns and their changes over time, for estimating war damages, for analyzing economic growth, and for other purposes. But the usefulness of wealth measurements for economic analysis does not mean that the federal government should install a capital budget system. Estimates for the government sector can be derived statistically, utilizing budget data, without forcing budgetary procedure and classification into a mold designed solely for this purpose. Here is the place where the statistical summaries of federal investment expenditures already included in the budget document are most useful.

The case for a capital budget for the federal government is not persuasive. Further information on the economic character of federal expenditures is much needed, and this kind of information can be developed as a part of an economic character classification which will include the measurement of annual capital outlay. But this ought to be a statistical measurement, and not one built into the budget schedules of all departments and agencies. Business-type budgets with asset accounting and depreciation allowances are now used for all corporations and for some departmental activities which are commercial in character. Their use

[48] Commission on Organization of the Executive Branch of the Government, *Real Property Management*, Washington, 1955, esp. pp. 23–26.

[49] In *Studies in Income and Wealth*, National Bureau of Economic Research, New York: Raymond W. Goldsmith, "Measuring National Wealth in a System of Social Accounting," Vol. XII (1950), pp. 23–79; J. E. Reeve, et al, "Government Component in the National Wealth," Vol. XII, pp. 461–526; Goldsmith, "A Perpetual Inventory of National Wealth," Vol. XIV (1952), pp. 5–61, esp. pp. 42–46 on findings; Simon Kuznets, "On the Measurement of National Wealth," Vol. II (1938), pp. 3–64, the classic treatment of this subject, is somewhat more critical of the usefulness of wealth estimates than the foregoing.

will undoubtedly be extended to other enterprise-type activities in the administrative agencies. An extension beyond this to the whole of general government activities is of questionable value.

Selected Bibliography

Bjerve, Petter Jakob, "Government Economic Planning and Control," *Scandinavia Between East and West*, Henning Friis, ed., Cornell University Press, Ithaca, 1950, pp. 49–111.

Colm, Gerhard, "Comment on Extraordinary Budgets," *Social Research*, May 1938, pp. 168–181.

Final Reports of the Committee on the Form of Government Accounts (Cmd. 7969), His Majesty's Stationery Office, London, 1950, esp. pp. 28–33, 74–76.

Copeland, Morris A., "The Capital Budget and the War Effort," *American Economic Review*, March 1943, pp. 38–49.

———— "Public Investment in the United States," *American Economic Review*, March 1939, Part 2, pp. 33–41.

Drummond, J. M., *The Finance of Local Government*, George Allen & Unwin, Ltd., London, 1952, pp. 43–61, 112–137.

Fortune, "That Wonderful Swedish Budget," September 1938, pp. 65ff.

Hansen, Alvin H., *Fiscal Policy and Business Cycles*, W. W. Norton & Co., New York, 1941, pp. 189–207.

International City Managers' Association, *Local Planning Administration*, 2d ed., Chicago, 1948, pp. 268–288.

Lindahl, Erik, "Swedish Experiences in Economic Planning," *American Economic Review*, May 1950, pp. 11–20.

———— *Studies in the Theory of Money and Capital*, Farrar & Rinehart, New York, 1939, pp. 351–384.

Lorwin, Lewis L., *National Planning in Selected Countries*, National Resources Planning Board, Washington, 1941, pp. 93–120.

Marx, Fritz Morstein, "The Divided Budget in Scandinavian Practice," *National Tax Journal*, June 1955, pp. 186–200.

Maxwell, James A., "The Capital Budget," *Quarterly Journal of Economics*, May 1943, pp. 450–465.

Municipal Finance, February 1949, May 1954 (whole issues).

Murray, Carl, "Budget Execution and Government Accounting in Sweden," *Government Accounting and Budget Execution*, United Nations, New York, 1952, pp. 60–72.

Musgrave, Richard Abel, "The Nature of Budgetary Balance and the Case for the Capital Budget," *American Economic Review*, June 1939, pp. 260–271.

Myrdal, Gunnar, "Fiscal Policy in the Business Cycle," *American Economic Review*, March 1939, Part 2, pp. 183–193.

National Resources Planning Board, *Long-Range Programming of Municipal Public Works*, Washington, 1941.

Ohlin, Bertil, *The Problem of Employment Stabilization*, Columbia University Press, New York, 1949, pp. 65–88.

Ohlsson, Ingvar, *On National Accounting*, Konjunkturinstitutet, Stockholm, 1953, pp. 273–312.

Roberts, S. M., "Long-Term Capital Improvement Budgeting," *Public Management*, August 1948, pp. 226–230.

Tennessee State Planning Commission, *Dyersburg Capital Budget*, Nashville, 1950.

Thompson, Spencer, "The Investment Budget," *Public Policy*, Harvard University, Cambridge, 1941, pp. 63–77.

United Nations, *Budgetary Structure and Classification of Government Accounts*, New York, 1951, pp. 68–81.

Wigforss, Ernst, "The Financial Policy During Depression and Boom," *The Annals*, May 1938, pp. 25–39.

9.

Economic character classification

An economic character classification is intended to provide materials useful in reaching decisions about governmental policies that affect the composition and level of economic activity. Governments that have assumed at least some responsibility for the prevention of inflation and deflation, for resource development, and for stabilizing employment within their jurisdictions will find that an economic character classification is a very useful tool. Governments with limited responsibilities in these areas will find that an economic character classification, while it may possess some academic interest, is not sufficiently useful to be worth the effort required.

In the United States the federal government has used limited kinds of economic character classifications for budgetary and other fiscal policy purposes. In all likelihood these classifications will be broadened and used increasingly in the formulation, adoption, and execution of stabilization programs. State and local governments, with very limited commitments to stabilize income and employment within their jurisdictions, are not likely to need an economic character classification. In other countries, where national governments have at least as much responsibility for the growth and stabilization of the economy as in this country— Sweden and the Netherlands, for example—an economic character classification of governmental activities has become an essential part of the materials of fiscal planning. And in underdeveloped countries an economic character classification is a prerequisite to the formulation of

212

practicable programs for an increase in capital formation and an improvement in standards of living.

I. ATTRIBUTES OF ECONOMIC CHARACTER CLASSIFICATION

An economic character classification is not economic policy but is a part of the materials for policy-making. As such, it has a number of limitations, which should be specifically recognized.

This classification does not or should not purport to measure the whole of a government's impact on levels of economic activity. It measures a part of that impact and measures this only in approximate terms. It can furnish information about the contribution of government to the national income, and whether that contribution is increasing or decreasing. It can give an indication of the relative portion of a nation's capital formation provided through the government sector. It can indicate, by comparisons among fiscal periods, whether government is contributing to inflationary pressures because its activities are demand-increasing, or whether governmental activities are generally deflationary. It can also provide information about the form in which the impact of governmental activities is transmitted—whether through transfer payments or through the direct use of resources.

An economic character classification can record only those governmental influences measured by changes in the volume and composition of governmental revenue and expenditure. The regulatory activities of government may affect relative prices, the volume of securities issued, or the kinds of goods that can be marketed. Such regulations have a significant impact on the level and composition of economic activity. Certain financial programs of the government, such as guarantees for residential mortgages, may have a decidedly stimulating effect on the total of private construction. These effects will not be revealed by measuring the volume and composition of government expenditures. Similar examples could be multiplied to cover the influence of the central bank, of banking regulations generally, of the tariff, and other facets of governmental operations in a complex economy.

An economic character classification does not, in itself, provide an estimate of the effects of governmental activities on the distribution of income,[1] nor the effects on its division among sectors of the economy

---

[1] For pioneering efforts along these lines see Tibor Barna, *Redistribution of Incomes Through Public Finance,* Clarendon Press, Oxford, 1945; John H. Adler, "The Fiscal System, the Distribution of Income, and Public Welfare," *Fiscal Policies and the American Economy,* Kenyon E. Poole, ed., Prentice-Hall, New York, 1951, pp. 359–409 Alan T. Peacock, ed., *Income Redistribution and Social*

(agriculture, manufacturing, etc.). This kind of information is of great importance in the formulation of fiscal policy, for both expenditures and taxation, but its development requires additional and different information than is served up by this single classification.

Within the scope of what an economic character classification can measure, there are further qualifications to its usefulness as a tool of analysis. A grouping of governmental receipts and expenditures by economic character provides approximations only. An increase of $2 billion in federal expenditures for goods and services, with tax revenue constant, may produce very different changes in national income, depending on the composition and consequences of the $2 billion outlay. Some part of this expenditure may lead to additional outlay in the private sector, but some part of the $2 billion might lead to an offsetting restriction of private expenditures. Both kinds of effects are possible, for example, in resource development. A river valley development program may stimulate private investment in agricultural machinery, but the same program may discourage private investment that would otherwise have occurred in electric power facilities. In the language of income analysis this means that separate multipliers may attach to specific kinds of governmental expenditures, but the present state of our knowledge does not permit the isolation and identification of such multipliers. In view of these limitations, it might be well to describe this kind of classification as an economic impact budget, and to recognize that the impacts cannot be measured with any high degree of refinement.[2] To measure the *total* influence of the government's budget is an impossible task.

The successful utilization of an economic character classification requires an awareness that the government's budget does have an impact on the economy, and an appreciation that this impact is one of the factors which must be taken into account in the formulation of budgetary policy. An economic character classification is useful only at the top policy level. It is not necessarily useful for the line official, who is concerned with program formulation and execution. For example, the administrator who is charged with providing housing for construction workers is not primarily concerned with the fact that the housing is new or old, but with its adequacy. It may be a matter of indifference to him whether he buys previously built structures or builds new structures. But this dis-

---

Policy, Jonathan Cape, London, 1954, which contains Alfred H. Conrad, "Redistribution through Government Budgets in the United States, 1950," pp. 178–267.

[2] This term is proposed by John Sagan, Jr., "An Analysis of Federal Budgets," *Current Economic Comment,* University of Illinois, August 1951, pp. 45–60.

tinction is important in an economic character classification. The purchase of old structures does not add to current levels of national income; the construction of new housing does. Similarly, a welfare department should separate administrative expenses from transfer payments because they have different program significance, not because they have different economic effects. Economic distinctions therefore need not be incorporated in budget classifications at the management level, where program, performance, and the objects of expenditure are stressed. An economic character classification must necessarily be statistical and should be prepared by the central budget office or a central statistical office.

At the same time, an economic character classification should not be isolated from other budgetary classifications. If such a classification is to contribute to an awareness of the economic consequences of budgetary decisions, it must be integrated into the budget-making process and must provide information on *economic* consequences in the same way that other classifications provide information on *program* consequences—information which is needed for central budget office review, and for review by the chief executive and by the legislature.

II. ECONOMIC CHARACTER CLASSIFICATION AND NATIONAL INCOME ACCOUNTING

There is always an operational interplay between the development of economic statistics and the emergence of economic problems. Economists become interested in measuring the totals of economic activity when the economy encounters difficulty in maintaining its previous totals, as in the depression, or when public policy requires a sudden increase in the total, as during World War II.

The interest in analysis of the economic importance of governmental activities dates specifically from the depression of the 1930's, the efforts of governments to cope with that depression, and the rise of Keynesian economics to provide a theoretical framework for dealing with economic stabilization. Most of the practical work and the conceptual development in this area has been carried on by national income statisticians. National income accounting is the parent "discipline"; economic character classification of governmental activities is one of the healthy progeny. Like most progeny, it has enjoyed some independent developments.

Before examining these developments, it should be noted that in recent years there has come to be an increasingly widespread use of national income data at a number of points in the budgetary process. In the federal government a preliminary forecast of probable levels of national

income typically accompanies the Bureau of the Budget's "Call to Estimates" (see Chapter 4). Forecasts of unemployment are used in estimating budget expenditures for a number of programs where either administrative expenses or program outlay are geared to changes in employment, as in the administration of benefits for old age and survivors'
insurance and grants to the states for the administration of unemployment
compensation benefits. Estimated budget expenditures for farm price
supports depend on a forecast of national income and a further forecast
of demand for agricultural commodities. Estimates of losses from loan
guarantees are related to predictions about business conditions during
the budget year. And, of course, revenue estimating in the federal
government, and increasingly in state and local governments, is based on
forecasts of national income and its relevant components (see Chapter
15).

The foregoing uses of national income data are a part of the program-
planning aspect of budget-making, and well-qualified budget officers and
budget examiners can be expected to use this kind of information. An
economic character classification, however, is designed to provide additional and different kinds of information. A brief review of the development of this technique in the United States government will serve to
illustrate these distinctions and extensions.

A. DEVELOPMENTS TO 1946

The development of technique and applications in the parent body of
knowledge—national income accounting—have been well summarized
elsewhere and need not be repeated here.[3] In the specific examination of
the government's contribution to changes in national income, important
pioneering work was done by economists on the staff of the Federal Reserve Board and introduced in testimony before the Temporary National
Economic Committee in 1939.[4] This work consisted of estimates of the
income-increasing expenditures and income-decreasing receipts of government. A similar approach was used by Villard at about this same
time.[5] Income-increasing expenditures were defined as government outlay "likely to be spent for current output"; income-decreasing receipts,
as government revenue "likely to restrict current output." Separate

[3] See Carl S. Shoup, "Development and Use of National Income Data," *A
Survey of Contemporary Economics*, Vol. I, Howard S. Ellis, ed., Blakiston
Company, Philadelphia, 1948, pp. 288–313.

[4] *Investigation of Concentration of Economic Power*, 76th Cong., 1st sess.,
Hearings Part 9, pp. 3528–3529, 4011, 4017.

[5] Henry Hilgard Villard, *Deficit Spending and the National Income*, Farrar &
Rinehart, New York, 1941, pp. 261–294.

series for expenditures and receipts were prepared, and these were aggregated to provide a net income-increasing expenditure series, designed to show the impact of changes in governmental fiscal activities for the federal government and for all governmental units in the United States. The major limitation of this approach was that it attempted to reduce all of government's influence on economic activity to a single figure.

During the defense and World War II period, forecasts of national income and governmental activities as a component thereof played an important part in setting war production goals and in formulating fiscal programs. A major conceptual advance was made at this time in the use of GNP—the gross national product—as a measure of aggregate output. Forecasts of production potential in these terms permitted the establishment of realistic goals for the increase in total government expenditure and its components. Within this framework, estimates of inflationary pressure in the civilian sector were developed in terms of the "inflationary gap."[6]

The war years also brought the first official efforts to improve the classification of federal government activities with a view to an increased usefulness for purposes of economic analysis. In January 1943 the Bureau of the Budget included in the budget document for fiscal 1944 a special analysis of cash receipts from and payments to the public. This statement, which has continued in subsequent budget documents, shows the flow of money between the public and the federal government as a whole, where the government sector is defined to include federal funds and trust and deposit funds, with intragovernmental transactions consolidated. The statement is therefore a cash consolidated account and more comprehensive than the conventional or administrative budget.

Table 13 shows this statement, as reproduced from the 1956 budget. The public is defined to include individuals; banks, including the Federal Reserve and Postal Savings Banks; all business firms; state, local, and foreign governments; and international organizations.

This type of summary account is considerably more meaningful for purposes of analyzing the economic impact of federal activities than are the conventional budget summaries. Not only is it more comprehensive, but the basis of reporting is more uniform. Certain items counted as expenditures in the conventional budget summary, such as accrued interest on the public debt, are reported here on a cash basis. The elimination of intragovernmental transactions makes the totals and changes

[6] See Gerhard Colm, "Experiences in the Use of Social Accounting in Public Policy in the United States," *Income and Wealth*, Series I, Bowes & Bowes, Cambridge, 1951, p. 79; Shoup, *op. cit.*, pp. 305–309.

TABLE 13

Federal Government Receipts from and Payments to the Public

(Excluding major intragovernmental and noncash transactions. In millions)

Description	1954 Actual	1955 Estimate	1956 Estimate
Federal Receipts from the Public			
Individual income taxes	$32,383	$30,700	$32,500
Corporation income and excess profits taxes	21,523	18,466	17,034
Excise taxes	10,014	9,073	9,350
Employment taxes	5,425	6,080	7,095
Estate and gift taxes	945	930	970
Customs	562	570	570
Deposits by States, unemployment insurance	1,246	1,200	1,400
Veterans life insurance premiums	426	414	406
Other budget and trust receipts	2,530	2,598	2,724
Refunds of receipts (−)	−3,418	−3,382	−3,256
Total Federal receipts from the public	$71,636	$66,649	$68,793
Federal Payments to the Public			
Major national security	$46,681	$40,814	$40,625
Veterans' services and benefits	4,963	5,026	5,170
International affairs and finance	1,583	1,201	1,207
Welfare, health, and education	6,452	7,706	8,269
Agriculture and agricultural resources	2,601	3,149	2,283
Natural resources	1,228	1,151	969
Commerce and manpower	2,727	4,110	3,709
General government	1,445	1,441	1,573
Interest	4,688	4,715	4,622
Deposit funds (net) *	−115	−16	51
Reserves for proposed legislation and contingencies	. . . .	100	325
Deduction (−) from Federal employees' salaries for retirement funds	−430	−436	−502
Change in clearing account for outstanding checks, etc.	46	64	−67
Total Federal payments to the public	$71,868	$69,026	$68,235
Excess of Federal receipts from the public	. . . .	. . . .	$558
Excess of Federal payments to the public	$232	$2,377	. . . .

* Excludes deposit funds of Government-sponsored enterprises.

Source: *Budget of the United States Government for the fiscal year ending June 30, 1956,* p. 1133.

therein more significant as a measure of the government's impact on the flow of funds to the private sector.[7]

[7] For a detailed explanation of the concepts used in this table see *Budget of the United States Government for the fiscal year ending June 30, 1953,* p. 1142; for a reconciliation of this statement with the national income and product accounts of the U. S. Department of Commerce see Karl O. Nygaard, "Economic Impact

In January 1945 an even more significant step was taken in the development of an informational base for fiscal policy decisions. In the budget for fiscal 1946 the Bureau of the Budget included a presentation of "The Government's Budget and the Nation's Budget," a form of national income accounting based on summary transactions by major sectors: consumers, business, international, and government.[8] This statement was continued in the 1947 budget and then, with the organization of the Council of Economic Advisers, was transferred to the *Economic Report of the President,* where it has since served as a framework for the analysis of economic developments under varying titles—"The Nation's Economic Budget," or "The Nation's Economic Accounts." In the 1954, 1955, and 1956 *Economic Report of the President* this type of account presentation was considerably de-emphasized, appearing as an appendix table entitled "The Nation's income, expenditure, and saving."[9] The form of the account, however, has remained substantially unchanged over the years, regardless of the prominence with which it has been presented. Table 14 shows the presentation from the 1955 *Economic Report.*

The data used in this account, hereafter referred to as the Nation's Budget in accordance with its original title, are derived from the U. S. Department of Commerce, but the form of presentation differs substantially from the official form in which national income estimates are published. The Department of Commerce emphasizes the balance between income and product for the economy as a whole; the Nation's Budget emphasizes changes in the major transactor sectors. The sector approach permits the ready isolation and identification of changes in economic activity and their relation to changes in gross national product. It is a more manageable form of national income accounting for fiscal policy planning and, in particular, for determining the impact of changes in total governmental activity. The Nation's Budget is geneologically a direct descendant of both national income accounting and government budget procedures.[10]

---

of Federal Government Programs," *Survey of Current Business,* March 1952, pp. 8–14.

[8] For a description of this technique and a statement of the underlying philosophy see Grover Wm. Ensley, "A Budget for the Nation," *Social Research,* September 1943, pp. 280–300; Gerhard Colm, "The Nation's Economic Budget, A Tool of Full Employment Policy," *Studies in Income and Wealth,* Vol. X, National Bureau of National Research, New York, 1947, pp. 85–93; Colm, "From Estimates of National Income to Projections of the Nation's Budget," *Social Research,* September 1945, pp. 350–369.

[9] See *Economic Report of the President,* 1956, p. 170.

[10] Gerhard Colm, *Essays in Public Finance and Fiscal Policy,* Oxford University Press, New York, 1955, pp. 241–286.

TABLE 14
The Nation's Income, Expenditure, and Saving, 1952–1954
(Billions of dollars)

Economic Group	1952 Receipts	1952 Expenditures	1952 Excess of Receipts (+) or Expenditures (−)	1953 Receipts	1953 Expenditures	1953 Excess of Receipts (+) or Expenditures (−)	1954 Receipts	1954 Expenditures	1954 Excess of Receipts (+) or Expenditures (−)
Consumers									
Disposable personal income	236.9	.....	......	250.1	.....	......	253.6	.....	.....
Personal consumption expenditures	.....	218.4	......	.....	230.1	......	.....	234.0	.....
Personal net saving (+)	.....	.....	18.4	.....	.....	20.4	.....	.....	19.6
Business									
Gross retained earnings	34.3	.....	......	35.1	.....	......	37.3	.....	.....
Gross private domestic investment	.....	50.7	......	.....	51.4	......	.....	46.1	.....
Excess of investment (−)	.....	.....	−16.3	.....	.....	−16.3	.....	.....	−9.0
International									
Net foreign investment	.....	−0.2	......	.....	−1.9	......	.....	−0.6	.....
Excess of receipts (+) or investment (−)	.....	.....	0.2	.....	.....	1.9	.....	.....	0.6
Government (Federal, State, and local)									
Tax and nontax receipts or accruals	91.1	.....	......	95.9	.....	......	90.1	.....	.....
Less: Transfers, interest and subsidies (net)	16.7	.....	......	17.3	.....	......	19.9	.....	.....
Net receipts	74.3	.....	......	78.6	.....	......	70.2	.....	.....
Total government expenditures	.....	93.9	......	.....	102.5	......	.....	97.4	.....
Less: Transfers, interest, and subsidies (net)	.....	16.7	......	.....	17.3	......	.....	19.9	.....
Purchases of goods and services	.....	77.2	......	.....	85.2	......	.....	77.5	.....
Surplus (+) or deficit (−) on income and product account	.....	.....	−2.8	.....	.....	−6.6	.....	.....	−7.3
Statistical discrepancy	0.6	.....	0.6	1.0	.....	1.0	−4.0	.....	−4.0
Gross national product	346.1	346.1	......	364.9	364.9	......	357.1	357.1	.....

* Preliminary estimates by Council of Economic Advisers.
Note: Detail will not necessarily add to totals because of rounding.
Source: *Economic Report of the President*, Washington, 1955, p. 142.

The Nation's Budget, as it has been used by the Bureau of the Budget, and particularly by the Council of Economic Advisers, has been a highly useful tool of analysis. However, the accounts presented are for the calendar year just terminated. There has been no effort to publish an official forecast of the Nation's Budget for the future; hence, there is no established relationship between the budget of the United States government and the forecast of national income on which it must be based.

B. Developments Since 1946

The success which government economists enjoyed in their use of national income forecasts during World War II and the development of the technique known as econometric models was reflected in a feature of the Full Employment Bill introduced in the Congress in 1945. This bill would have required that the Administration prepare an annual forecast of national income, modeled along the lines of the Nation's Budget, and accompanying estimates of employment and unemployment. The Administration would then have been required to recommend a program designed to deal with any possible "gaps" in the level of income or employment, or designed to cope with estimated inflationary pressure. Forecasts would have been mandatory and would necessarily have served as the basis for policy recommendations. This requirement, however, was eliminated from the Employment Act of 1946 as it was finally adopted. Instead, the Act stated that the President should transmit an annual report setting forth "current and foreseeable trends" and levels of total expenditure, public and private, needed to promote "maximum employment, production, and purchasing power." (*P.L.* 304, 79th Cong., 2d sess.)

About the time the Employment Act was adopted, returns were coming in on an experience which resulted in a severe set-back for economic forecasting in the United States. The event was the effort by government economists to predict the level of income and employment for the postwar reconstruction period, and the set-back was the failure of the pessimistic predictions to materialize.[11] Regardless of the fact that this failure might be excused on the ground of the formidable difficulties encountered in forecasting economic activity in such a transitional period, and regardless of the improvements which have since been made in econometric techniques, there is no doubt that this experience substantially hampered the subsequent official publication of national income forecasts by the federal government.[12]

During the postwar period one additional effort to improve the eco-

[11] For an excellent analysis of these efforts see Michael Sapir, "Review of Economic Forecasts for the Transition Period," *Studies in Income and Wealth,* Vol. XI, National Bureau of Economic Research, New York, 1949, pp. 273–351. Contained herein are footnote references to the abundant literature on this subject. See also, Elmer Clark Bratt, "A Reconsideration of the Postwar Forecasts," *Journal of Business of the University of Chicago,* April 1953, pp. 71–83.

[12] For a discussion of econometric techniques see Everett E. Hagen, "The Role of Economic Forecasting in Income Stabilization," *Income Stabilization for a Developing Democracy,* Max F. Millikan, ed., Yale University Press, New Haven, 1953, pp. 190–200.

nomic quality of information available for fiscal policy purposes has been included in the budget document. This is the publication, since fiscal 1951, of an analysis of investment, operating, and other budget expenditures. A summary statement of this account is shown in Table 15. The account sets forth significant information about the character of federal expenditures and, in particular, about the current or capital nature of outlays. It provides information useful for economic analysis, including estimates for the forthcoming budget year, but it is not a full-scale economic character classification.

TABLE 15
Summary of Investment, Operating, and Other Budget Expenditures
Fiscal 1956 Estimate (in millions)

	Gross Expenditures	Applicable Receipts	Net Expenditures
Additions to Federal assets:			
Civil	$9,086	$7,073	$2,013
Major national security	16,934	. . . . . .	16,934
Expenditures for other developmental purposes:			
Civil	2,071	16	2,055
Major national security	1,649	. . . . . .	1,649
Current expenses for aids and special services:			
Civil	9,974	1,042	8,931
Major national security	3,716	. . . . . .	3,716
Other services and current operating expenses:			
Interest	6,378	. . . . . .	6,378
Other civil	5,043	2,792	2,251
Major national security	19,910	*	19,910
Reserves for legislation and contingencies	325	. . . . . .	325
Deduct: Unallocated reduction in estimates			
(Major national security)	1,750	. . . . . .	1,750
	$73,332	$10,923	$62,408

* Less than one-half million.

Source: *Budget of the United States Government for the fiscal year ending June 30, 1956*, p. 1155 (fiscal years 1954 and 1955 are omitted).

A second important development has come, not from the Administration, but from Congress. Since its organization in 1946, the Joint Committee on the Economic Report has maintained a strong interest in forecasting and in the use of econometric techniques for analyzing the role of government. The staff of the Joint Committee has prepared materials on both short and long-range projections, in the Nation's Budget frame-work.[13] These have undoubtedly encouraged congressional committees to appraise specific legislation in terms of its impact on the economy, and have encouraged the Administration to improve the statistical basis on which fiscal policy recommendations are formulated.[14]

Much has been accomplished in the improvement and use of statistical information available for budgetary and fiscal policy purposes in the federal government. Further developments are in no sense pioneering efforts, but can build on the substantial progress of the last two decades. Two things are now needed: first, an increased official interest in the economic data base from which budget-making and fiscal policy must proceed; and second, the development of a systematic economic character classification to accompany the federal budget.

The United States government has lagged behind many other national governments in its official use of the Nation's Budget technique. In the Scandinavian countries the integration of forecasts and budgeting has been highly developed (see Chapter 8). In the Netherlands a thorough-going system of national budget forecasts, as a part of the government's budget presentation, has been used since the end of World War II.[15] In Great Britain since 1941 the White Paper on *National Income and Expenditure* has been published annually, preceding the budget presentation.[16]

It is not entirely clear why the United States government should fall

[13] For example, Joint Committee on the Economic Report, *Joint Economic Report*, 84th Cong., 1st sess., Washington, 1954, esp. pp. 89–93; *The Sustaining Economic Forces Ahead*, 82d Cong., 2d sess., Washington, 1952; *Potential Economic Growth of the United States During the Next Decade*, 83d Cong., 2d sess., Washington, 1954.

[14] In addition to the work that has been done in the mainstream of fiscal policy formulation, the U. S. Bureau of Labor Statistics made major contributions to structural analysis in "Full Employment Patterns, 1950," *Monthly Labor Review*, February 1947, pp. 163–190, and March 1947, pp. 420–432. Private organizations have also made significant studies of economic goals and objectives. The National Planning Association has published two: *National Budgets for Full Employment*, Washington, 1945, and *The American Economy in 1960*, Washington, 1952. The Twentieth Century Fund published an extensive survey of trends and prospects for all sectors of the economy, including government, in J. Frederic Dewhurst and associates, *America's Needs and Resources*, New York, 1947, pp. 459–510; *ibid.*, 1955, pp. 577–662.

[15] J. Tinbergen, "Government Budget and Central Economic Plan," *Public Finance*, Vol. IV, 1949, pp. 195–199; G. Stuvel, "Recent Experiences in the Use of Social Accounting in the Netherlands," *Income and Wealth*, Series I, pp. 160–177.

[16] See E. F. Jackson, "The Recent Use of Social Accounting in the United Kingdom," *Income and Wealth*, Series I, pp. 148–159.

behind western European countries in this development. National government expenditures in relation to the total of national income are not markedly different in these western European countries than in the United States. Neither are the problems of forecasting for the United States economy instrinsically more difficult. Admittedly, this economy is dynamic and unstable, but the foreign trade and foreign investment component is smaller in relation to the total of national income than is true in Sweden, the Netherlands, or Great Britain. Therefore, forecasts for the United States are less likely to be upset by exogenous factors than in these countries. Neither is it at all clear that the United States government, as a practical matter, assumes less responsibility for levels of economic activity than is the case in these western European countries, or that there is less American concern about economic affairs.

Perhaps the explanation for the failure to extend the use of the Nation's Budget lies in the fact that the American economy has functioned without a major economic crisis since World War II. There have been no acute shortages of foodstuffs or foreign exchange to provide an impetus for a sharpened governmental concern about the components of national income. There is a natural reluctance for a private enterprise economy to accept more than the necessary minimum of government planning. In the American economy the minimum is lower than in less successful economies.

Whatever the reason for this state of relative backwardness, there can be no doubt that a more explicit use of the Nation's Budget could improve the formulation of economic policy in the United States, both when the economy is running well and when it is running badly. An extension of this technique would make for more rational and conscious decision-making and would increase the awareness of the economic consequences of specific public policies. Properly used, the Nation's Budget can show the conflicting claims on an economy—the demands for consumers goods, for investment goods, for government goods. It can show the sources of savings for capital formation and the dependence of an economy on foreign trade. The Nation's Budget can indicate the sectors of inflationary or deflationary pressure, and thus point to where fiscal and monetary measures may be employed for coping with instability. If the Council of Economic Advisers were to shift the Nation's Budget presentation to a fiscal year basis and use it as a framework for analysis, there would tend to be a much closer relationship between economic policy and budgetary policy. As Smithies says, "The Economic Reports should illuminate the budget rather than attempt to avoid discussion of it."[17]

[17] Arthur Smithies, *The Budgetary Process in the United States,* McGraw-Hill Book Company, New York, 1955, p. 202. Smithies, however, is generally skepti-

The contribution which budgetary classification can make to an improved data base for economic policy purposes is in the development of a thorough-going economic character classification of governmental activities.[18] This is not a substitute for a more explicit use of the Nation's Budget, but a supplement to it; an improved economic character classification would encourage the further use of the Nation's Budget. An incidental by-product of such a classification would be the eradication of overemphasis on a single budget balance in terms of surplus or deficit. An economic character classification yields several significant balancing items, each of which must be appraised in context.

III. NATIONAL INCOME ACCOUNTING AND BUDGET CLASSIFICATION

An economic character classification of governmental activity must build on the conceptual base which has developed in recent years for national income accounting, but at the same time it must not be rigidly bound by its techniques and conventions. National income accounts have usually been developed independently of any specific policy-making purpose they were intended to serve.[19] Emphasis has been placed on estimating the flow of goods and services at market prices in an economy during a period of time, and on securing an unduplicated total of final products and the corresponding factor and nonfactor costs. Necessarily and properly, with this approach government activities in national income accounts are not measured with a view to defining their governmental character or with a view to grouping those transactions which may be influenced by governmental decisions. Instead, government activity is measured within a conceptual framework primarily devised for recording and analyzing the flow of total economic activity. The transactor groups that make up the components of national income are not based wholly on the organizational form in which economic activity is conducted.

cal of the use of forecasting techniques. See his discussion at *ibid.,* pp. 441–443, and "Long-Run Projections and Government Revenue and Expenditure Policies," *Studies in Income & Wealth,* Vol. XVI, Princeton University Press, Princeton, 1954, pp. 365–371. For a different view, which argues that forecasts should be distinguished from a maximum employment projection and that the latter should be geared with the budget, see Gerhard Colm and Marilyn Young, *The Federal Budget and the National Economy,* National Planning Association, Washington, 1955, pp. 3–4, 54–63.

[18] In 1954 the Joint Committee on the Economic Report recommended that both the budget and the President's *Economic Report* should include additional statistical information. (83d Cong., 2d sess., *House Report* No. 2628.)

[19] Ingvar Ohlsson, *On National Accounting,* Konjunkturinstitutet, Stockholm, 1953, pp. 25–34.

Some examples will serve to underscore this point. In a number of national income accounting systems, including the one used by the U. S. Department of Commerce, government enterprise is counted in the private business enterprise sector. The current output of government enterprise cannot be identified as such, although capital investment by government enterprise is brought together with other purchases of goods and services by government.[20] This particular treatment suits the purpose of providing an unduplicated total of government and private economic activity. At the same time, it obscures the peculiarly governmental character of public corporations and other commercial-type public activities.

Similarly, national income accounts do not always distinguish government investment. The U. S. Department of Commerce treatment of government purchases of goods and services groups all outlay for current and capital goods, without differentiation. Conceptually, this would appear to mean that only the private sector undertakes investment. Again, this treatment may be appropriate for the measurement of total national output, but it is unsatisfactory for purposes of measuring the nature and significance of governmental activities.[21]

An economic character classification is primarily designed for measuring and forecasting changes. It brings to budgetary classification the techniques and distinctions useful for economic analysis—a grouping of governmental activities that is significant for fiscal policy planning and budgetary purposes. It should not be restricted by the conventions which control measurements by the national income statisticians.[22]

Neither should an economic character classification be bound by the conventions of established government accounting. As Myrdal has said:

> Any budget has ample possibilities of concealed deficits in all its corners: hidden reserves which can be mobilized, incomes which can be accounted to

[20] U. S. Department of Commerce, *National Income,* 1954 Edition, Washington, 1954, p. 49.

[21] These and other problems of the measurement of governmental activities in the framework of national income accounting have received extensive treatment in the literature. For example, Gerhard Colm, "Public Revenue and Public Expenditure in National Income," *Studies in Income and Wealth,* Vol. I, National Bureau of Economic Research, New York, 1937, pp. 175–227; Gottfried Haberler and Everett E. Hagen, "Taxes, Government Expenditures, and National Income," *ibid.,* Vol. VIII, 1946, pp. 1–31; Simon Kuznets, "Government Product and National Income," *Income and Wealth,* Series I, pp. 178–244; Ingvar Ohlsson, "Treatment of Government Economic Activity in the National Accounts," *ibid.,* Series III, pp. 224–259 Carl S. Shoup, *Principles of National Income Analysis,* Houghton Mifflin Company, Boston, 1947, pp. 231–288.

[22] See Julius Margolis, "National Economic Accounting: Reorientation Needed," *Review of Economics and Statistics,* November 1952, pp. 291–304.

an earlier year, costs which can be formally postponed without implying a real saving. . . . It is this play with fictitious economies, branched out into all items of the budget to conceal an actual deficit from the general public and sometimes, also, from the legislators, which makes an economist feel so hopeless in dealing with budgetary matters.[23]

This feeling of hopelessness can be overcome when an economic character classification is competently prepared by the central budget office, or by a central statistical office working closely with the budget office, and where the classification is developed as a part of established budget procedure and published in the budget document.

There are some who feel that it is possible to devise a single comprehensive and uniform treatment of government activity which will serve the purposes of national income accounting and economic and budgetary policy purposes, and that all interested parties should work toward this end. This is probably asking too much, given both the rivalries of statisticians, who themselves often behave like an interest group, and given the necessarily divergent purposes to be served by the measurement of government activity. However, it is not asking too much to urge that somewhere in every government the differing measurements be brought together and reconciled. In the United States government this would mean a reconciliation of the budget accounts and the statement of cash receipts from and payments to the public, both published in the budget document, and the Department of Commerce statement of government activities.[24]

IV. SIGNIFICANT GROUPINGS FOR ECONOMIC ANALYSIS

An economic character classification should be comprehensive of all of the financial transactions of a government. It need not be restricted to those that are excluded from a conventional definition of the budget for legal or traditional reasons. It may appropriately include social insurance trust funds, which might be extrabudgetary in character, and may also include the operations of autonomous government enterprise.[25] An economic character classification is therefore likely to be more com-

[23] Gunnar Myrdal, "Fiscal Policy in the Business Cycle," *American Economic Review*, March 1939, Part 2, p. 183.

[24] For a pioneering effort along these lines see Marilyn Young, "Three Federal Budgets: A Reconciliation," National Planning Association, Washington, 1955 (mimeo).

[25] J. R. Hicks contends in *The Problem of Budgetary Reform* that it is the unsatisfactory treatment of public enterprise, both the trading services and the nationalized industries, which makes the United Kingdom budget meaningless as an economic document and thus necessitates an improved classification of governmental activities. (Clarendon Press, Oxford, 1948, esp. pp. 5–22.)

prehensive, with a broader definition of government than other types of budgetary classifications.

The greater comprehensiveness which characterizes this kind of classification does not, however, solve the problems of drawing lines between that which is governmental and that which is nongovernmental. The limits of "governmental" are simply extended to uncover a new set of borderline cases.

It is not possible to establish the scope of an economic character classification on the basis of what is controllable by a government. Behavior characteristics in terms of those activities which may be increased or decreased may be significant for some purposes, but these provide no firm guide to what may properly be included. Expenditures made for veterans' benefits which are wholly within the responsibility of the national government may be less controllable or variable than expenditures by a mixed-ownership corporation which makes loans to farmers. Interest on the national debt may be less controllable than central banking operations that appear to be independent. The ability of the central government to influence an agency or program is not a useful criterion to assist in drawing a line between the public and private sectors.[26]

What it comes to is that there are no criteria for drawing these lines, other than arbitrary ones, particularly as applied to the classification of government enterprise. This will necessarily be the case, given the continuation and even multiplication of complex economic relationships between government and business firms and households.

An economic character classification should be based on the government accounts and should therefore cover the fiscal year, not the calendar year as is customary in national income accounting. For maximum usefulness it should show, as do all budget summaries, the year completed, the current year, and the budget year. This classification must build on a recognition of the form in which government activity is conducted—whether as general government, enterprise, or trust funds. A consolidation account can bring together the financial results of the three sectors and facilitate the computation of meaningful aggregates.

It should be stressed that an economic character classification is statistical in nature; it need not be accurate to the last dollar in the same way that other budget classifications must account for each dollar of expenditure or revenue. The purposes of economic analysis are not served by this kind of precision. Therefore, significant magnitudes may properly be estimated.

[26] For a somewhat different view see A. R. Prest, "Government Revenue and the National Income," *Public Finance,* Vol. VI, 1951, p. 244.

In the discussion which follows, attention will be directed to only the major groupings which ought to be incorporated in an economic character classification. Refinements are always possible and can be introduced where information is available or where more extensive cross-classifications are desirable.[27]

A. CAPITAL ACCOUNT

It was suggested in Chapter 8 that a distinction between current and capital transactions in the general government sector is useful for budgeting purposes in some but not all governments. But for an economic character classification the distinction between current and capital is generally useful. Its significance is most apparent in an underdeveloped country, where the government is continually seeking ways and means to increase the volume of domestic capital formation. Here the measurement of government capital expenditure will serve as an indication of past accomplishment and provide a basis for planning the government's role in capital formation. Even in an advanced industrialized country, where there is likely to be more concern with stabilization than with development, the measurement of the volume of government capital formation will provide useful information for such purposes as analyzing the effect of governmental activities on the construction industry, measuring changes in the public control of asset formation, and assisting in estimates of the government component of national wealth.

As noted, trust funds typically do not undertake the construction of new assets, and government enterprise usually maintains commercial-type accounts which incorporate a distinction between current and capital outlays, so that the problem of separating current from capital expenditures is critical only in the general government sector.

The economists' definition of capital formation for national income purposes includes (a) new construction, (b) producers' durables, that is, machinery and equipment, and (c) additions to inventory. Ideally, this definition should be applied to the general government sector, but in practice it will usually be desirable to exclude additions to inventories because of the difficulties encountered in obtaining information of this kind. The omission is not likely to lead to a serious distortion, provided that major inventory accumulations, such as stockpiles of strategic materials and surplus agricultural commodities, are administered and accounted for by government enterprises.

[27] For an extensive discussion, with appropriate attention to the refinements of an economic character classification, see United Nations, *A Manual for the Classification of Government Accounts*, New York, 1956. Also, William H. White, "Measuring the Inflationary Significance of a Government Budget," Internati[·]nal Monetary Fund, *Staff Papers*, April 1951, pp. 355–378.

The exclusion of additions to inventories for the general government sector will mean that capital expenditures should be subdivided into two major groups—new construction, and machinery and equipment. Construction should include transportation facilities such as roads, canals, harbors, and airports, and projects for the permanent improvement of natural resources, such as flood control, reclamation, and reforestation.[28] Major repairs and alterations that extend the life expectancy of capital assets or increase their usefulness should be included as a capital expenditure, but ordinary maintenance and repairs should be treated as a current expenditure.

The major classification problem encountered, for both new construction and machinery and equipment, is the choice of a workable line of demarcation between current and capital. There are two possibilities. A line can be drawn on the basis of revenue-producing and nonrevenue-producing, or a line can be drawn on the basis of life expectancy.[29]

The revenue-producing criterion is extremely restrictive, since very little of the total of government additions to plant and equipment contributes directly to government income. Furthermore, many assets which are not directly productive of revenue may be indirectly productive. An improved highway system in and around metropolitan areas may contribute more to economic growth and increased tax revenues than a four-lane toll road. The use of the revenue-producing criterion will exclude important additions to the nation's stock of real assets.

A division based on life expectancy emphasizes the difference between final product which is used up during the accounting period and final product which produces benefits that accrue partly in the future. This criterion is admittedly arbitrary, but at least it conforms with the practice of most countries that have attempted to separate current and capital expenditures in the general government sector. Some departure from strict annuality is probably called for; small items of expenditure, regardless of life expectancy, should be treated as current outlay; the dividing line might be placed at three years for larger items. As J. R. Hicks has stated, "Useful and intelligible accounts could be constructed with the line drawn in several different places."[30]

Arbitrary decisions must also be made in the treatment of outlays for national defense. In the capital budget classification in Sweden, national defense installations are generally regarded as a current expenditure

[28] United Nations, *Concepts and Definitions of Capital Formation*, New York, 1953, p. 14.
[29] United Nations, *Budgetary Structure and Classification of Government Accounts*, New York, 1951, pp. 14–17.
[30] Hicks, *The Problem of Budgetary Reform*, p. 57.

regardless of their life expectancy. This can be justified on the ground that military installations are not productive assets yielding a flow of goods and services which add to the future (real) volume of national income.[31] On the other hand, from the standpoint of immediate economic impact, it matters not whether government expenditures are productive in any long-run social sense. Government outlay for military structures affects the construction industry in much the same way as private outlay for new plant or buildings. Although military capital may be difficult to define and estimate, it may properly be included with other types of general government capital in an economic character classification. Even here, however, it may be appropriate to exclude military equipment and additions to stores on the ground of their doubtful character as durable assets.

Within the capital account there should be a distinction between direct investment and indirect investment. The former consists of the outlays made by government for the purchase of new assets—currently produced plant and equipment which are to be used directly for government purposes. Indirect investment consists of government loans or grants to encourage private capital formation.[32] Where it is reasoned that indirect investment—lending activity to the private sector—gives rise to capital formation which would not otherwise have occurred, the economic effects on national income of direct and indirect government investment are likely to be very much the same. But operationally the two are different. Indirect investment leaves the control of the new asset in private hands; direct investment adds to government control over resources. For the United States government, where lending activity is significant, the differentiation between direct and indirect investment serves to throw light on the complex ways in which the government influences the total level of investment.

Direct and indirect investment both add to the volume of capital formation for the economy as whole. They are both in the category of real investment, as distinguished from financial investment. The latter consists of capital transfers—the purchase of previously produced assets, such as buildings and equipment, or the purchase of privately issued securities or private mortgages. These do not add directly to current levels of national income, and while they may appropriately be included in a capital account, they must be identified as financial in nature.

[31] United Nations, *Budgetary Structure and Classification of Government Accounts,* pp. 16–17.

[32] For a discussion of these and other capital transactions in a somewhat different framework than is suggested here, see C. Lowell Harriss, "Government Expenditure: Significant Issues of Definition," *Journal of Finance,* December 1954, esp. pp. 355–358.

Capital account receipts in the general government sector consist of two major items: repayments of loans made to the private sector and capital transfers. The former is financial disinvestment to the government, and therefore properly a capital receipt. However, when households and business firms repay loans, particularly of the amortized type, the effects on disposable private income are not measurably different than when taxes are paid.

Capital transfers arise where government sells previously produced assets to the private sector—both fixed assets, such as land and buildings, and current assets, such as war surplus. Capital transfers are not related to the flow of current productive activity and income creation. This kind of government revenue does not draw down private income or restrict private expenditure. It is a financial receipt, just as government purchases of existing assets are financial investment.

It has sometimes been argued that death duties are capital transfers and should therefore appear as capital revenues. This practice is followed in Denmark's budget. Since it is by no means clear, however, that death duties are always paid out of capital rather than income, this would seem to be an unjustified treatment. The receipts from a capital levy—the once-over tax on asset values used in some western European countries—would be more clearly in the category of capital transfers, as a government revenue that does not directly affect the level of current national income.

Generally speaking, there cannot be complete reciprocity between the current and capital accounts of government and the current and capital accounts of the private sector. It is not possible, in every case, to classify as a capital receipt of government only those transactions which affect private capital accounts, nor to classify as a current revenue of government only those taxes which are paid out of private income accounts.[33] Government, in its fiscal capacity, frequently acts as a converter. That which is private income may be paid to government and transformed into government capital.

An economic character classification should look primarily at the government accounts, not at government's effects on private accounts. As Hicks says:

> The first object of a public accounting system . . . is to give a clear and intelligible picture of the government's own transactions. For this purpose it must be based upon criteria which arise out of the government's own transactions, not upon criteria which are relevant only to the other side of those transactions which concern the private sector of the economy.[34]

[34] Hicks, op. cit., p. 63.

[33] Leo T. Little, "Direct Taxation and the Inflationary and Deflationary Effects of Fiscal Policy," Accounting Research, July 1950, pp. 443–488.

B. Current Account

Expenditures in the current account may be broken down into three major categories: outlays for goods and services, transfer payments, and subsidies. Government expenditure for goods and services on current account takes the form of wage and salary payments to persons (households), and purchases of noncapital goods from business firms. Where possible, these two should be distinguished within the broader category.

Transfer payments by government consist of outlays which are not matched by current services provided by the recipients. This is a kind of unilateral economic activity. Government transfer expenditures are not resource-using. Therefore, transfers do not add directly to current levels of national output, but they do add to private incomes and may be significant in affecting both the level of personal income and its distribution.

Subsidies are difficult to define and difficult to handle consistently in an economic character classification. One type of subsidy is " . . . a charge incurred by a public authority with the object of enabling the general public to buy a commodity or service at less than the price which would otherwise have to be paid."[35] These may be paid directly to producers by a general government agency, and can be identified and labeled as a subsidy in general government current expenditures. Payments to domestic airlines for the transport of airmail and the outlays to merchant marine shipowners for operating purposes would fall in this category. The more difficult cases, for classification purposes, arise where a public enterprise incurs a deficit as a means of aiding a group of producers or consumers.

Trading activities in foodstuffs in Great Britain, where losses are sustained in order to hold down prices to consumers, are an example of this type of subsidy. In the United States, agricultural price support activities are handled in the same fashion, except that here the effect of the government corporation deficit is to increase, not reduce, prices to consumers. In any event, all subsidies, no matter what form they take, affect relative prices, and may be thought of as a sort of negative indirect tax.

Apart from the general government subsidies which may be specifically classified as such, it might be possible to distinguish, within the public enterprise sector, those deficits which are incurred for purposes of conscious subsidy, and those which are unplanned, in the sense that they

---

[35] Richard Stone, "Definition and Measurement of the National Income and Related Totals," *Measurement of National Income and the Construction of Social Accounts,* United Nations, Geneva, 1947, p. 33.

arise from the unanticipated failure of income to match expenditure. The effect on levels of national income and prices is not very different in the two cases, but the planned deficits are likely to be the center of attention for economic policy purposes.

The current revenue account should include all taxes, with the exception of those which are paid from private capital. Taxes paid from private income may be assumed to restrict the volume of current private expenditure on goods and services. It has become conventional in national income accounting to distinguish between direct and indirect taxes. The latter, but not the former, are supposed to affect relative prices of goods and services. Indirect taxes include sales taxes and customs and excise duties, while direct taxes include those levied on business and personal net income. This division has become sufficiently conventionalized that it is appropriate to incorporate it in an economic character classification of current revenue, even though both are alike in that they draw down private income.

Nontax revenue should also be distinguished from tax revenue in current account receipts. Again, the distinction is somewhat conventional, since nontax revenue such as fines will have economic effects very similar to those of taxes. This type of revenue is imposed on a different set of considerations than tax revenue, however, and thus may be appropriately identified. It should also be possible to identify the revenue from the incidental commercial-type activity conducted in the general government sector, such as fees imposed by hospitals and educational institutions, or income from the sale of documents.

C. Public Enterprise and Trust Funds

In the structure of accounts suggested here for an economic character classification, all enterprise activity which is organizationally distinct should be grouped together. The net results from this sector can then be brought together with general government and trust funds in a consolidated account.

A number of general government departments and agencies will conduct incidental enterprise activity not organizationally separated from the administrative activities of the department. For purposes of an economic character classification, it is usually unwise to attempt to separate out such incidental commercial-type activity; the enterprise sector can appropriately be confined to those activities which are separately organized as such, usually in the corporate form.

Within the public enterprise sector it may be appropriate to distinguish among trading, financial, and production ventures, where a government has enterprise activity of all three major types. When public corporations maintain their accounts on a commercial basis, no serious problems of separating capital and current outlays are likely to be encountered. The net results of these activities can be consolidated with the other sectors, and certain gross expenditures, such as for capital formation, can be identified for aggregating purposes.

The trust fund sector in most governments is likely to consist primarily of social insurance activities. The current account should distinguish the transfer payments to beneficiaries from payments for administrative expenses. Taxes levied for social insurance purposes should be classified as a current account revenue. If trust fund accumulations are used for direct investment in real assets, or are loaned to the private sector, such transactions should be shown in a separate capital account. But if accumulations are invested solely in general government securities, no capital account is necessary.[36]

D. Other Classification Issues

In some countries the national government is engaged in activities that involve receipts and expenditures from abroad. Export duties may be paid by firms from overseas balances, and the proceeds may be applied to interest on foreign-held debt. Expenditures may be incurred for overseas military installations and thus in no way increase the level of domestic income. Where foreign transactions are of sufficient importance to affect the significance of the totals of government activity, it is desirable to carry through the accounts the distinction between "at home" and "abroad" receipts and expenditures. Unless these transactions are significant, however, the complications involved in this differentiation are such that the separation is not justified.

In an economic character classification a particular problem is posed by the inclusion or exclusion of central banking operations. A case can be made for inclusion, on the ground that the central bank typically conducts transactions that may be controlled by the government and that these transactions have the same kinds of economic effects as those lending operations conducted by government corporations. On the other hand, central banks engage in other transactions, such as loans and advances to commercial banks, which are of a markedly different character than the lending operations of government corporations. Needless to say, the inclusion of central banking operations in the scope of an economic character classification introduces very great com-

[36] For a classification which links national insurance accounts and general government accounts along lines which are comparable with those suggested here, see Alan T. Peacock, *The Economics of National Insurance,* William Hodge & Co., Ltd., London, 1952, pp. 38–40.

plications. In most cases it is probably better to make an exclusion and restrict the scope of this classification more nearly to a budgetary framework.

In the preparation of an economic character classification an accounting problem arises in the measurement of general government activities. In most countries the revenue and expenditure of general government departments and agencies are accounted for on either a cash basis or an obligation basis. In cash accounting, revenues are booked as received and expenditures are booked when checks are issued. Obligations record the amount of liabilities for expenditures as these liabilities are incurred. Budget estimates are conventionally prepared on either one or both of these bases, which means that the general government accounts will not show the rate at which goods and services are used up. On the other hand, government corporations maintain their books on an accrual basis, so that revenues are booked when they are earned and expenditures are booked as goods or services are consumed. National income accounts are also prepared on an accrual basis, and if an economic character classification is to have maximum usefulness in relation to these accounts, there ought to be a uniform measurement.

There is no easy way of handling this problem. It would hardly be appropriate to shift the whole of the general government sector to an accrual basis of accounting in order to serve the purposes of an economic character classification. Public enterprises need accrual accounting for the measurement of operating results. Therefore, the most that can be done under these circumstances is to make whatever statistical adjustments are necessary to avoid major discrepancies in the accounts for the general government sector.

V. A SIMPLIFIED SET OF ACCOUNTS

Table 16 illustrates the general principles on which an economic character classification could be constructed. It is compiled in accordance with the groupings which have been suggested, incorporating a set of assumptions intended to make the structure of accounts as simple as possible. The classification is intended to be generally applicable to the kinds of activities conducted by the United States government.[37]

In the interests of drastic simplification, intragovernmental transactions among the sectors have been held to a rigid minimum. Only

[37] These accounts have been established along the lines indicated in United Nations, *A Manual for the Classification of Government Accounts* and *Budgetary Structure and Classification of Government Accounts*.

one such transaction is shown; it is assumed that the trust funds hold general government obligations and receive interest thereon. This is shown as I-B-4 and III-A-3; this transaction cancels out and is therefore eliminated in the consolidated accounts. The accounts do not include a type of intragovernmental transaction that is frequently important, in which general government makes loans or advances to public enterprise. Such transactions would be entered in a separate section of the general government capital account. Also omitted are public enterprise transactions in the securities of general government. It has been assumed that the trust funds undertake no capital expenditures on their own account and engage in capital transactions only with general government. That is, the trust funds do not buy and sell securities, government or otherwise, from the private sector, and their surpluses

TABLE 16
Simplified Accounts for an Economic Character Classification

I. GENERAL GOVERNMENT

Current Account

A. Receipts
1. Direct taxes
2. Indirect taxes
3. Other taxes
4. Interest and dividends
5. Sales of goods and services
6. Fines and miscellaneous
7. Total

B. Expenditures
1. Purchases of goods and services
   a. From households
   b. From business firms
2. Transfer payments
   a. To other governments
   b. To persons
3. Subsidies
4. Interest to trust funds
5. Interest to households and firms
6. Total

C. Surplus or deficit on current account (A − B)

Capital Account

D. Receipts
1. Sales of assets
2. Other (*e.g.*, capital transfers)
3. Total

E. Expenditures
1. New buildings and other construction
   a. Civilian
   b. Military
2. Machinery and equipment (civilian)
3. Total: gross capital formation
4. Purchases of existing assets
5. Total: additions to government assets

F. Surplus or deficit on capital account (D − E)

(*Continued*)

Table 16 (*Continued*)

II. PUBLIC ENTERPRISE

Current Account

A. Receipts
   1. Sales of goods and services
   2. Interest and dividends
   3. Increase (+) or decrease (−) of inventories of goods in process

B. Expenditures
   1. Wages and salaries
   2. Other purchases of goods and services
   3. Interest to households and firms
   4. State and local tax payments
   5. Total: payments
   6. Depreciation allowances
   7. Decrease (+) or increase (−) in inventories of purchased goods
   8. Total: expenditures

C. Surplus or deficit on current account (A − B)

Capital Account

D. Receipts
   1. Depreciation allowances
   2. Sales of own securities
   3. Sales of obligations issued by households and firms
   4. Repayment of obligations issued by households and firms
   5. Total

E. Expenditures
   1. New buildings and other construction
   2. Machinery and equipment
   3. Additions to inventory (A-3 and B-7)
   4. Total: gross capital formation
   5. Purchases or redemption of own securities
   6. Purchase of obligations issued by households and firms
   7. Total: expenditures

F. Surplus or deficit on capital account (D − E)

III. TRUST FUNDS

Current Account

A. Receipts
   1. Employer taxes
   2. Employee taxes
   3. Interest from general government
   4. Total

B. Expenditures
   1. Administrative expenses
   2. Transfers or payments to beneficiaries
   3. Total

C. Surplus or deficit on current account (A − B)

Table 16 (*Continued*)

IV. CONSOLIDATED ACCOUNT: OVER-ALL FINANCIAL RESULTS
Current Account

A. Receipts
1. General government (I-A-7)
2. Surplus of enterprise (II-C)
3. Trust funds (III-A-4 —
   III-A-3)
4. Total
C. Surplus or deficit on current account (A — B)

B. Expenditures
1. General government (I-B-6 —
   I-B-4)
2. Trust funds (III-B-3)
3. Total

Capital Account

C. Surplus from current account
D. Receipts
1. General government (I-D-3)
2. Enterprise (II-D-5)
3. Total
F. Consolidated surplus or deficit
   (C + D — E)

E. Expenditures
1. General government (I-E-5)
2. Enterprise (II-E-7)
3. Total

V. CONSOLIDATED ACCOUNT: ADDITIONS TO PRIVATE SECTOR INCOME
Current Account

A. Receipts
1. General government (I-A-7)
2. Surplus of enterprise (II-C)
3. Enterprise depreciation
   (II-B-6)
4. Trust funds (III-A-4 —
   III-A-3)
5. Total

B. Expenditures
1. Current purchases of goods and
   services
   a. General government (I-B-1)
   b. Trust funds (III-B-I)
2. Transfer payments
   a. General government (I-B-2)
   b. Trust funds (III-B-2)
3. Subsidies (I-B-3)
4. Interest (I-B-5)
5. Total

C. Net additions on current account
   (B — A)

Capital Account

D. Receipts
1. Repayment of obligations issued
   by households and firms
   (II-D-4)

F. Net additions to private income
   (C + E — D)

C. Net additions on current account

E. Gross capital formation
1. General government (I-E-3)
2. Enterprise (II-E-4)
3. Total

(*Continued*)

Table 16 (*Continued*)

VI. SUMMARY ACCOUNT: CHANGES IN PUBLIC DEBT*
  A. Surplus or deficit in
     1. General government current account (I-C)
     2. General government capital account (I-F)
     3. Total general government
     4. Public enterprise current account (II-C)
     5. Public enterprise capital account less depreciation (II-F − II-D-1)
     6. Less: net sales of own securities (II-D-2 − II-E-5)
     7. Total public enterprise
     8. Total surplus (+) or deficit (−) (3 + 7)
  B. From government sources
     1. Changes in cash balances (increase −)
                                  (decrease +)
     2. Enterprise depreciation (II-B-6) (+)
     3. Total borrowing requirements (A-8 + B-1 + B-2)
  C. Trust fund surplus (+) or deficit (−)
  D. Changes in debt held by the public (− increase)
                                        (+ decrease)

* It is assumed that public enterprises may sell obligations of their own which are not counted as part of the public debt.

are invested in general government bonds. If trust funds were to engage in capital transactions with the private sector, real or financial, it would be necessary to establish for them a capital account similar to the one shown for public enterprise.

To keep the accounts as straightforward as possible, it has also been assumed that all lending activity—indirect government investment—is conducted by public enterprise and not by general government. The accounts for the public enterprise sector embrace both lending activities and production and trading activities, as well as real investment. The general government sector includes some incidental commercial-type activity (I-A-5 and I-B-1) ; this is reported at gross rather than at net, in accordance with the procedures generally used in other budgetary classifications. Inventory accumulations are confined to the enterprise sector and no adjustments have been made for the differences between cash and accrual reporting. That is, it has been assumed that public enterprise net results measured on an accrual basis may be consolidated directly with general government on a cash basis. Since the general government current account does not carry depreciation charges, the surplus or deficit (I-C) will overstate the increases, or understate the decreases, in general government net worth. To make this item an accurate measure of changes in general government net worth, it would be necessary to include depreciation allowances as a current expenditure, with a corresponding receipt entry in the general government capital account.

No effort has been made to indicate, for either receipts or expenditures, the detailed itemization which is possible in an economic character classification. For example, item I-B-1 (general government purchases of goods and services on current account) does not show a breakdown of outlay for employee compensation separate from other current expenditures, although this would be useful information. Similarly, no effort has been made to include the complicated pattern of debits and credits necessary for an effective tabulation of social insurance contributions paid by government employees into a government trust fund.

In the capital account it has been arbitrarily assumed that it is appropriate to classify certain military expenditures as capital. Where this practice is followed, it is still possible to charge military capital against the current account, with appropriate adjusting entries in the consolidated account. This permits an aggregation of gross government capital formation, civilian and military, but suggests that military capital is an appropriate item of current expense.

Sections IV, V, and VI of Table 16 are constructed to yield two separate consolidations and a summary public debt account. In the consolidations the current activities of the enterprise sector are treated on a net basis; gross receipts are shown only in the sector account.

The first consolidation (IV) shows the over-all financial results of government activity. Current and capital account distinctions are maintained, and both financial and real investment are included. Therefore, the consolidated surplus or deficit (IV-F) is, in effect, a cash consolidated account, showing the relations of the government with the public, where the latter is defined to include households, business firms, the central bank, commercial banks, and state and local governments. Item IV-F is a measure of the government's cash surplus or deficit during the fiscal period, as affected by both goods and service transactions and financial transactions.

The second consolidation (V) shows the government's influence on private income accounts. Again, current and capital account distinctions are maintained to show the type of transaction by which private income is influenced. In this account all indirect investment, as distinguished from direct investment, is omitted. Also omitted are purchases and sales of existing real assets, which add to or substract from government assets, but which do not affect private income accounts. Repayments of loans, however, are treated as a subtraction from private sector income and these are regarded as having an effect on private income and private demand comparable to that of tax payments. Item

F in account V thus becomes the best single measures of changes in the government's contribution to inflationary or deflationary pressure. Where F is a larger positive magnitude, as compared with a previous fiscal period, *net* government additions to private income are increasing. Where F is smaller than in a previous period, government is exerting a deflationary influence on levels of private income.[38]

The summary account (VI) brings together the financial results on a sector basis to identify the surplus or deficit of general government, public enterprise, and the trust funds. The current or capital nature of the deficit or surplus is subordinated here to the sector identification. Line VI-A-8 (total surplus or deficit) makes allowance for enterprise sales of their own securities, assumed to be omitted from the public debt. Additional entries would be required if the enterprises purchased general government obligations directly from the treasury rather than from the public. With the incorporation of changes in treasury cash balances, the summary account adds to changes in debt held by the public, on the assumption that holdings by the trust funds are counted in public holdings.

The economic character classification presented here produces three balancing concepts: over-all financial requirements, the government's net contribution to private income accounts, and net changes in government debt held by the public. All of these are significant measures of the government's influence on levels of economic activity.

VI. CONCLUSION: TOOLS FOR ECONOMIC ANALYSIS

In almost every country in the world, budgetary policy is now a well-recognized major tool for the development and stabilization of the economy. This recognition is both explicit and implicit.

Where the recognition is explicit and the role of government is that of conscious leadership and planning for economic growth and stability, policy decisions which are "sound" can be made only on an informa-

[38] For an demonstration that an increase in governmental expenditures, when balanced by an increase in governmental revenue, will also produce an increase in national income, see Henry C. Wallich, "Income-Generating Effects of a Balanced Budget," *Quarterly Journal of Economics,* November 1944, pp. 78–91. Also, Trygve Haavelmo, "Multiplier Effects of a Balanced Budget," *Econometrica,* October 1945, pp. 311–318; G. Haberler, "Some Monetary Implications of Mr. Haavelmo's Paper," *ibid.,* April 1946, pp. 148–149; R. M. Goodwin, "The Implication of a Lag for Mr. Haavelmo's Analysis," *ibid.,* pp. 150–151; Everett E. Hagen, "Further Analysis," *ibid.,* pp. 152–155; Haavelmo, "Reply," *ibid.,* pp. 156–158. Other references and a qualifying argument are contained in William J. Baumol and Maurice H. Peston, "More on the Multiplier Effects of a Balanced Budget," *American Economic Review,* March 1955, pp. 140–148.

tional base which is adequate. Budgetary policy cannot be effective in these circumstances unless information is available for appraising the impact of governmental activities. In discussing the future of public accounting in Great Britain, Ursula K. Hicks put this point as follows:

> Once these gaps in the statistics have been filled—as they will no doubt be filled—the Cabinet will have before it a scientific basis for a comprehensive plan, which will in principle enable it to keep the economy in a state of full activity without resort to direct control over the private sector or to authoritarian planning of the whole. In 1939 the mere idea of such an instrument of policy would have seemed chimerical; today it is on a fair way to being achieved. The idea has not, however, lost any of its fascination by greater familiarity; on the contrary its possibilities appear greater as its outlines become better recognized.[39]

An improved budgetary classification for purposes of economic analysis should provide relevant data to help fill these gaps. Other analytical techniques have also been developed by economists in recent years, techniques which can be expected to assist in the improvement of public decision-making. Input-output analysis has made and will continue to make important contributions, particularly in the scheduling and programing of military requirements.[40] The analysis of moneyflows for the economy may eventually throw light on a number of questions affecting the role of government.[41]

Economists are not, however, the sole possessors of understandings and techniques that assist in the analysis of changes in the structure and character of the economy. Their expertise must be merged with understandings of other kinds—social, political, psychological—and these latter are especially useful in exploring the explicit factors which limit the achievement of a society's implicit economic goals.

[39] Ursula K. Hicks, *Public Finance,* Nisbet & Co., Ltd., London, 1947, p. 386.

[40] Wassily W. Leontief, *The Structure of the American Economy, 1919–1939,* 2nd ed., Oxford University Press, New York, 1951; Leontief and others, *Studies in the Structure of the American Economy,* Oxford University Press, New York, 1953.

[41] Morris A. Copeland, *A Study of Moneyflows in the United States,* National Bureau of Economic Research, New York, 1952.

Selected Bibliography

Colm, Gerhard, *Essays in Public Finance and Fiscal Policy,* Oxford University Press, New York, 1955, pp. 241–286.

———— "Experiences in the Use of Social Accounting in Public Policy in the United States," *Income and Wealth,* Series I (International Association for Research in Income and Wealth), Bowes & Bowes, Cambridge, 1951, pp. 75–97.

Colm, Gerhard, and Marilyn Young, *The American Economy in 1960,* National Planning Association, Washington, 1952.

Ensley, Grover Wm., "A Budget for the Nation," *Social Research,* September 1943, pp. 280–300.

Hagen, Everett E., "The Role of Economic Forecasting in Income Stabilization," *Income Stabilization for a Developing Democracy,* Max F. Millikan, ed., Yale University Press, New Haven, 1953, pp. 169–211.

Hicks, J. R., *The Problem of Budgetary Reform,* Clarendon Press, Oxford, 1948.

Hicks, Ursula K., *Public Finance,* Nisbet & Co., Ltd., London, 1947, pp. 368–387.

Kuznets, Simon, "Government Product and National Income," *Income and Wealth,* Series I (International Association for Research in Income and Wealth), Bowes & Bowes, Cambridge, 1951, pp. 178–244.

Ohlsson Ingvar, *On National Accounting,* Konjunkturinsitutet, Stockholm, 1953, esp. pp. 8–39, 79–84, 185–191.

—— "Treatment of Government Economic Activity in the National Accounts," *Income and Wealth,* Series III (International Association for Research in Income and Wealth), Bowes & Bowes, Cambridge, 1953, pp. 224–259.

Prest, A. R., "Government Revenue and the National Income, *Public Finance,* Vol. VI, 1951, pp. 238–252.

Shoup, Carl S., "Development and Use of National Income Data," *A Survey of Contemporary Economics,* Vol. I, Howard S. Ellis, ed., Blakiston Company, Philadelphia, 1948, pp. 288–313.

—— *Principles of National Income Analysis,* Houghton Mifflin Company, Boston, 1947, esp. pp. 231–288.

Tinbergen J., "Government Budget and Central Economic Plan," *Public Finance,* Vol. IV, 1949, pp. 195–199.

United Nations, *A Manual for the Classification of Government Accounts,* New York, 1956.

—— *Budgetary Structure and Classification of Government Accounts,* New York, 1951, pp. 3–50.

Part III

The Phases of Budgeting

10.

Agency budget-making

Someone has said that a budget is a device for securing money from a legislature. The author of this rather cynical definition was, perhaps, the budget officer of an agency. From the agency's standpoint a budget is frequently regarded as a necessary evil—a burdensome routine which must be got through as the price of existence. This kind of attitude, it may be hoped, is not everywhere prevalent among government administrators. Budget-making may not be the most enjoyable of the administrator's duties, but in addition to providing the justification for an appropriation, it ought to make some positive contributions to management.

One of these positive contributions is the injection of cost-consciousness. This must occur at the operating level and must be associated with the systematic review of program needs and accomplishments. Cost-consciousness is not the same as retrenchment. Where the head of an agency and his budget staff conduct a review, with operating officials, of the nature of work programs and the administrative techniques which have been utilized, there should be a resultant and increased concern with the effective employment of public resources.

Beyond this, and as a corollary, budget-making in agencies should provide the occasion for evaluating agency policy—an investigation of the program areas which should be expanded or contracted, and the investigation of new programs which are required—in short, program planning.

246

Program planning and budgeting, however, are not identical. In point of time, planning comes first. Mosher has put the distinction as follows:

> Planning involves first the conceiving of goals and the development of alternative courses of future action to achieve the goals. Second, it involves the reduction of these alternatives from a very large number to a small number and finally to one approved course of action, *the program*. Budgeting probably plays a slight part in the first phase but an increasingly important and decisive part in the second. It facilitates the choice-making process by providing a basis for systematic comparisons among alternatives which take into account their total impacts on both the debit and the credit sides. It thus encourages, and provides some of the tools for, an increasing degree of precision in the planning process. Budgeting is the ingredient of planning which disciplines the entire process.[1]

Further, planning almost always involves more and different persons and a more long-run point of view. The concern with developments over a period of years is the planner's concern. The budgeteer in the agency must focus on the fiscal year at hand, to annualize the work of the planner. As a disciplinary ingredient, the budgeteer imposes a conservative influence on the planner by questioning financial implications and forcing cost comparisons.

The achievement of a workable partnership between budgeting and planning requires that budget officers be more than clerks. Failure to recognize this accounts for the underdevelopment of budget-making in many governments. Budgetary responsibilities must be assigned down into the organizational hierarchy, but the downward movement must not be a dissipative one; all levels of management should be involved, but not all employees. In some governments the failure to bring budgeting and management together at the operating level is unfortunately attributable to the presence of a strong budget office attached to the chief executive, which sometimes, and erroneously, feels that the development of agency budget staff is a threat to its authority.

In efforts to raise the level of budgetary skills throughout an agency, there are risks that effectiveness can be impeded by overspecialization. In some governments budgeting can become so complex and so subdivided as to accounting and statistical skills that its integration with program planning and evaluation is threatened. Budget-making in agencies should not become the peculiar province of procedural specialists who have no interest in or familiarity with the substantive programs that the agency is conducting. An agency budget office needs account-

---

[1] Frederick C. Mosher, *Program Budgeting*, Public Administration Service, Chicago, 1954, pp. 48–49; see also Robert A. Walker, "The Relation of Budgeting to Program Planning," *Public Administration Review*," Spring 1944, pp. 97–107.

ants, statisticians, and procedures analysts; it must provide a working climate in which these specialist skills are applied in a generalist context.

I. THE AGENCY BUDGET OFFICE

The budget cycle is initiated at the agency level. The estimates prepared here move to the central budget office and to the chief executive for review and coordination, and from there to the legislature for authorization. The budget, as modified by the legislature, returns to the agency for execution. The agency's experience in carrying out the budget is then subject to audit.

The agency is the starting point for budgeting and the means of implementation. Its responsibilities in this latter phase are examined in Chapter 13. In its role of budget-making the agency must develop specific channels of communication, internal and external. Its procedures must be such as to pose the alternatives which are the essence of budgetary decision-making. The informational base for preparing the estimates must be adequate.

A. CHANNELS OF COMMUNICATION

In smaller governments, budgeting at the agency level poses no special organizational and procedural difficulty. The heads of departments or their deputies will meet with the central budget officer or his staff; decisions and points at issue will be referred to the chief executive; no great attention to lines of communication is needed. In a large government, where the budget function is highly developed and the agency budget office is placed near the top of the organization, there is need for conscious attention to multiple channels of communication. The first such channel is upward to the head of the agency. The budget office is a staff office, with responsibility to clarify policy issues for review by the agency head, and with responsibility to see to it that decisions are made (see Chapter 11). The second channel of communication is to the operating bureaus. The agency budget office must be in a position to understand the substantive problems of line administrators and to assist in translating programs into financial requirements. The third channel of communication is likewise internal to the agency—the channel to the other staff offices, such as personnel, and to staff units in charge of planning or units in charge of organization and methods analysis.

Every agency budget office will also have a channel of communication with the central budget office. In this relationship the agency budget officer shares a common professional interest with the central staff—a mutual concern for good technique and a budget which can be defended before the legislature. At the same time, the agency budget officer is an advocate of the interests of his agency, an interpreter of agency problems, and a defender of the integrity of the estimates which have been worked out with the operating officials of his agency.

In some circumstances the agency budget officer also has a most important channel of communication to the legislature. Departmental and agency budget offices are generally well staffed and strong in the United States government because they must deal with congressional committees on appropriations. In fact, in this milieu the ability of an agency budget official may be judged very largely on the basis of his success in handling the pattern of more or less continuous negotiations with the Congress. The agency budget officer in these relationships runs the risk of becoming a policy official, identified with a particular administration. It is not easy to be politically effective in a nonpolitical way. Yet, unless this is achieved, career status is jeopardized. Political acumen divorced from political activity would seem to be what is required.

B. Examination of Alternatives

There is a widespread suspicion that budget-making at the operating level consists of a deliberate overestimate of requirements in anticipation of a percentage cut equivalent to the overestimate, which will leave the operating bureau with what it really needed at the outset. Some of this kind of behavior is probably inevitable, but to the extent that it prevails it tends to nullify the significant policy-making work of the agency budget officer.

There is also a suspicion in some quarters that administrators have a tendency to be imperialistic, that government officials have an inborn desire to spend more of the taxpayers' money, to hire more people, to build more buildings. Sometimes this charge is couched in more gentle terms; it is suggested that administrators tend to overestimate simply to be on the safe side, so that they will be able to retain some leeway in program administration. Again, there is no doubt that these charges and suspicions are justified in particular cases. The overzealous and overambitious are not unknown in our society, or in any society. But it would be difficult to demonstrate that these tendencies are more widespread in government than elsewhere. Very often, what looks like an overweening ambition may turn out to be responsive administration. The government official who seeks to expand his program may do so because he sees the need, because he would like to do a better job, because he is close to the beneficiaries of his program operations.

Where agency budgeting is done responsibly, much of what is done can be described in terms of the examination of alternatives. This examination should extend to both a review of the purposes of programs and a review of the means of accomplishment.

The governmental responsibilities assigned to an agency—the statutes under which it operates—will naturally limit the programs which may be proposed. But beyond this, the top levels of departmental administration do not, or should not, attempt to stifle the proposals of line administrators. For example, in the U. S. Department of Agriculture, where budgetary practice has long been highly developed, the department head, acting through the budget officer, does not impose financial ceilings on the initial proposals of the bureaus. There is no effort to " . . . dam the flow of estimates at their sources . . . ."[2] Rather, the budget office prefers to have before it for review purposes all of the plans and hopes of the bureaus so that it can better sift, filter, and revise. To assist the agency budget office in the review of program alternatives, it has been customary in the Department of Agriculture to ask each bureau to present its requests for increases in the order of priorities. To make sure that the bureaus do not put all of their requests for increases in the category of highest priority, it has been required that the total increases for each bureau be divided into four equal parts, and that an equal amount be listed in each of the four columns. This gives to the policy-making department officials an indication of the comparative importance attached to particular programs by the bureaus themselves. In this way, the examination of alternatives can proceed on the basis of the informed judgment of line management.

Program alternatives must, of course, be set forth in program terms. The budget classification employed must group outlays in terms of costs and accomplishments. A program or project type of grouping must be used as the basis for all budget-making within the agency if policy review is to be effective (see Chapter 6). Where projects within an agency are of the same general type, it may be possible to measure benefits in relation to costs. These measures will provide a quantitative base from which value judgments can be made.

In the earlier examination of the economic characteristics of the public sector it was concluded that it is not possible to compare directly the benefits derived from expenditures for different types of programs; decisions as to whether to spend funds for a high school or for a sewerage

    [2] Verne B. Lewis, "Budgetary Administration in the Department of Agriculture," in John M. Gaus and Leon O. Wolcott, *Public Administration and the United States Department of Agriculture,* Public Administration Service, Chicago, 1940, p. 423.

system cannot be made by direct measurement (see Chapter 2). However, within any one homogeneous program category, it is possible and indeed necessary to undertake cost-benefit studies as a basis for the choices which must be made in the preparation of an agency budget. A state highway department, for example, can measure the costs of specified highway improvements in relation to the probable volume of traffic to be affected. In this way it can establish priorities and prepare its budget on the basis of a reasonably firm appraisal of relative needs.

Some of the most significant work that has been done in the use of cost-benefit ratios has been developed for the appraisal of river basin projects in the United States government. Here the Federal Inter-Agency River Basin Committee has set forth procedures for the necessary measurement, in an effort to provide a uniform assessment of desirability.[3] Benefits are estimated from the point of view of the national economy to include private benefits over the life of the project. Costs are estimated to include those incurred by the government, for initial construction and subsequent operation. Projects are deemed to be justified only when the ratio of benefit to cost exceeds 1:1.

The use of the benefit-cost ratios has been fraught with unresolved difficulties in the definition of primary, secondary, and intangible benefits, with difficulties in the choice of an appropriate discount rate for valuing future benefits, with disagreements among federal agencies in the application of the procedures, and with some hostility from congressional committees.[4] Nevertheless, the measurements have undoubtedly contributed to a more effective appraisal of projects within departments and agencies. Experience with the benefit-cost computations illustrates both the usefulness and the limitations of a measurement approach to decision-making.

The examination of alternative means available for the accomplishment of a given program must proceed along lines somewhat different from the review of alternative programs. Here the budget officer should possess sufficient knowledge of operations, and of methods and procedures, to be able to challenge badly conceived projects and to ask the kinds of questions which call forth the orderly processes of administration. This is where budget review and organization and method analysis tend to merge, and it is here that the reviewing officer who has had operating experience can be most effective in questioning and criticizing management techniques.

[3] Subcommittee on Benefits and Costs, Report to the Federal Inter-Agency River Basin Committee, *Proposed Practices for Economic Analysis of River Basin Projects,* Washington, 1950.

[4] Arthur Smithies, *The Budgetary Process in the United States,* McGraw-Hill Book Company, New York, 1955, pp. 335–346.

Consequently, the review of the means of accomplishment differs from the review of alternative programs, although the two will often be examined together, with the latter proceeding from the former. Insofar as these can be separated in the routine of budgetary review, it is the analysis of alternative program proposals which is probably in greatest need of improvement in most governments.

Verne B. Lewis has made suggestions for improved program review by means of an alternative budget system.[5] Lewis points out that in building a budget a number of procedures can be employed. One of these is the open-end budget, which permits subordinate officials to submit an estimate for whatever amount is deemed necessary to conduct present and proposed programs. This procedure leaves to the higher levels of budget review the whole responsibility for selecting among alternatives, but provides review officers with no factual or even value-judgment basis for making such a selection. Another budget-building procedure is the fixed-ceiling approach, in which the central budget office establishes a maximum on the estimates early in budget preparation and prevents operating officials from submitting new plans and proposals. The fixed ceiling provides no assurance that the maximum for one bureau has not been set too high and for another too low.

Lewis suggests that instead of these an alternative budget system be used.

> Under this procedure, each administrative official who prepares a budget estimate, either as a basis for an appropriation request or an allotment request after the appropriation is made, would be required to prepare a basic budget estimate supplemented by skeleton plans for alternative amounts. If the amount of the basic estimate equals 100, the alternatives might represent, respectively, 80, 90, 110, and 120 percent of that amount. The number of alternatives might vary with the situation. Ordinarily, three alternatives would seem to secure a sufficient range of possibilities.[6]

Ten percent increments would not be an invariable rule; larger or smaller ones might be employed in particular cases. For each alternative the budget proposals would show not only cost but the benefits to be provided in the form of new services or expanded services. Benefits could be described in general terms or quantified with precision, depending on the nature of the program.

The great advantage of this kind of budget-making is that informa-

---

[5] "Toward a Theory of Budgeting," *Public Administration Review,* Winter 1952, pp. 42–54. For a discussion of the marginal utility economics which Lewis employs see Chapter 2.

[6] *Ibid.,* p. 49.

tion is made available to the agency budget office on the consequences of alternative decisions, and made available by those persons who are presumably in the best position to ascertain the consequences—the operating officials. In this way budget review in the agency will not only encompass new programs but also extend to a review of the less urgent elements in existing programs. So often, review concentrates almost all of its attention on proposed increases, with less attention to the costs and benefits from programs which are stable. The alternative budget system would also provide the information necessary for making budget reductions, if and when these should prove necessary, with minimum danger of slashing those programs in which benefits are great in relation to costs.

Lewis suggests that in the United States government the alternative budget system might be used at all stages of budget review, including that by the President and the Congress. If this were done, program alternatives would have to be successively grouped into larger aggregates through the various phases of budget preparation.

Alternative budget presentations would appear to be most useful at the agency level, although in a complex organization such as the Department of the Army, the preparation of three budgets might prove to be impossibly burdensome. In a large government, review by the chief executive and the legislature can probably be accomplished equally well on the basis of a unified program and performance classification.

C. BUDGETARY INFORMATION

Whether the agency budget office conceives its responsibilities for program review broadly or narrowly, it must nevertheless produce a consistent and integrated budget proposal for review by the head of the agency and for submission to the central budget office. The possibility of achieving a high degree of consistency and integration depends in large measure on the way in which budgetary data are developed and the hierarchal levels at which they are developed.

The amount of information, quantitative and qualitative, that may be either incorporated or reflected in an agency's budget in a large organization is almost infinite. The kinds of information might include, but certainly need not be restricted to, the following:[7]

1. Legal and procedural framework
2. Pertinent program legislation, enacted and proposed
3. Pertinent executive and administrative programs, approved and proposed

---

[7] The author is indebted to Frederick C. Mosher for this outline.

4. Government-wide, agency-wide, or unit policies and procedures
5. Environmental factors (outside budgetary control)
   a. Social facts, trends, forecasts
   b. Economic facts, trends, forecasts
   c. Political factors
   d. Geographical facts, trends, forecasts
   e. International situation and forecasts
   f. Special factors affecting agency program
6. Wage and price factors—present levels, trends, and forecasts
7. Internal organization, functions, activities, and methods, including projected changes thereof
8. Budget experience, current and preceding years
9. Operating experience and plans
   a. Quantity
   b. Quality
   c. Speed
10. Personnel experience and forecasts, especially
    a. Turnover
    b. Promotions and transfers
    c. Condition of morale
    d. Condition of labor market
11. Cost data

The mere compilation of this mass of information does not make a budget. Information must be classified and arranged. Some of it must be reduced to dollar amounts. Some of it must appear in written justifications in support of the budget. Other information is for background purposes only.

From the foregoing outline it is evident that some of the information necessary for budget-making is known primarily at the operating or bureau level, some of it is known only at the level of agency policy, and some is known only to the central budget office or to the chief executive. Items 4, 5, and 6 are data which should be provided by the central budget office; items 7, 8, 9, 10, and 11 may be provided by the agency. The major prebudget work which must be undertaken by the agency budget office is the development of budget assumptions and their transmittal to the operating levels where budget-building starts. For example, the chief executive might be responsible for assumptions about the volume of public construction that will be recommended for the forthcoming budget year. The central budget office would estimate trends in the costs of materials and supplies. The policy determination plus the cost estimate would then serve as the basis for specific estimates of construction projects proposed by departments and agencies. In a large agency the budget office will not prepare specific estimates; this is left to the divisions and bureaus.

Where budget assumptions are prepared by the central budget office, it is the responsibility of the agency budget staff to transmit these to operating levels. Where budget assumptions are developed at the agency level for use by operating bureaus, they must be harmonious with the directives which have come from the central budget office.

In a complex organization, particularly one with field offices, where generally similar activities are conducted in more than one location and administered by differing organizational units, agency budgeting can be greatly facilitated by the use of factorial estimating.[8] This consists of the careful analysis and computation of average costs per activity or costs per unit of work. It finds its widest application in budgeting for the armed services, where it is possible, on the basis of experience reinforced by tables of organization, to derive factor costs for an entire activity in terms of work units. In the Air Force, for example, it has been found that the factor "flying hours" is a reliable index to use in computing gasoline consumption, maintenance and replacement costs, and certain kinds of training costs. Other factors have been developed for budgeting for warehousing operations and facilities maintenance. Where such computations can be safely employed, budgeting becomes multiplicative rather than additive. Budgets can be constructed in financial terms on the basis of work-load estimates or average costs of activities.

Factorial budgeting requires careful and intensive central analysis of costs and changes therein, but it greatly simplifies the process of budget preparation. Factor costs are averages, of course, and subject to the limitations of averages. But their use will help to avoid a common pitfall of agency budget preparation—the tendency to overrefine. A budget is an estimate; it is not reality. No budget will be executed exactly as planned. It is wasted effort to build, from the bottom up and in great detail, a budget which will be subject to modification as operating conditions change. As Smithies says:

> Budgeting involves estimates of an uncertain future. But because of the influence of accountants, budgets—in government at any rate—are prepared in a degree of detail that is quite unwarranted by the uncertain assumptions on which the estimates are based. A major source of government waste could be eliminated if estimates were prepared in no greater detail than was justified by their accuracy.[9]

[8] Mosher, *Program Budgeting*, pp. 140–165.
[9] Smithies, *The Budgetary Process in the United States*, p. 44.

Factorial techniques have the further advantage of facilitating budget review by the agency budget office. Where reliable cost factors can be developed, they serve as an index for judging past performance. Specific operations that are out of line can be quickly detected. At the same time, the line administrator finds his budgetary attention focused on program level and the volume of operations.

D. BUDGET OFFICE ORGANIZATION

Where agency budget-making has developed as a major instrument of administration, there has been a tendency to bring within the orbit of the budget office a number of closely related management and fiscal functions. In these circumstances, budgeting is regarded as but one of

CHART 5
U. S. Department of Agriculture, Office of Budget and Finance

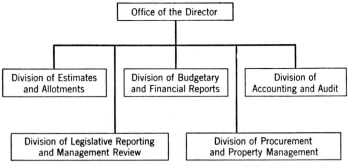

Source: U. S. Departent of Agriculture, *Report of the Director of Finance, 1951,* Washington, 1951, pp. 8–9.

a number of coordinate staff functions, along with accounting, financial reporting, and the analysis of organization and management (see Chapter 11).

The structure of the Office of Budget and Finance in the U. S. Department of Agriculture illustrates this kind of organizational grouping, as set forth in Chart 5. As the chart suggests, the traditional review of estimates is handled by only one of the five divisions of the office—the Division of Estimates and Allotments, which examines the proposals submitted by the bureaus of the Department of Agriculture and directs the preparation of justifications, schedules, and other materials that must go to the U. S. Bureau of the Budget and to the Congress. This division also prepares recommendations for the allotment of funds in the execution of the budget.

The Division of Budgetary and Financial Reports maintains a unified and consolidated system of reporting within the department on both financial and program developments, and has charge of the preparation of consolidated financial statements and their interpretation for budgetary purposes. The remaining divisions have responsibilities distinctly auxiliary to budget review. The Division of Accounting and Audit maintains selected control accounts on some departmental funds and supervises the installation and operation of accounting systems throughout the department. It also serves as a liaison with other agencies in the development of auditing procedures. The Division of Legislative Reporting and Management Review combines activities which are department oriented—studies of organization and procedure—with a centralized liaison arrangement with the Congress. The Division of Procurement and Property Management handles matters of department-wide concern in accounting, management practices, and purchase of land, buildings, equipment, and supplies.

This kind of strong agency budget office does not develop overnight. The Department of Agriculture Office of Budget and Finance is the product of many years' experimentation in the development of top-level staffing arrangements. It is also the product of the organizational genius of an outstanding federal civil servant.[10] A good part of the strength of this office has been its ability, down the years, to operate successfully in a dual capacity—as a staff arm of the Secretary of Agriculture, and as an authoritative spokesman for the Department of Agriculture in relations with other government agencies and with the Congress, with the latter proceeding from the former.

In its budget-making responsibilities the Department of Agriculture Office of Budget and Finance continuously emphasizes its staff role. Final budget and policy decisions are not made in this office but by the Secretary of Agriculture, and Budget and Finance reports to the Secretary. Before 1953 this was a direct reporting channel. In that year a reorganization of the department grouped all staff functions, including Budget and Finance, under an Administrative Assistant Secretary. Since this office is regarded as a career civil service position, nonpolitical in character, its creation has not altered the character of Department of Agriculture budgeting.

[10] For background see Lewis in *Public Administration and the United States Department of Agriculture*, pp. 412–445; Robert A. Walker, "William A. Jump: The Staff Officer as a Personality," *Public Administration Review*, Autumn 1954, pp. 233–246; Norman M. Pearson, "The Budgeting Function in the Department of Agriculture," *Public Administration Review*, Winter 1943, pp. 24–41; W. A. Jump, "Budgetary and Financial Administration in an Operating Department of the Federal Government," *Materials on Budgeting*, Vol. V, Catheryn Seckler-Hudson, ed., American University, Washington, 1944, pp. 123–138.

In the discharge of its responsibilities for budget review within the department, and to assist the Secretary in budget policy decisions, it has been customary for the Secretary to designate an *ad hoc* budget review committee from among the assistant secretaries. This committee provides top-level department-wide consultation on all major budget policies, and concretizes issues for the Secretary's consideration. This procedure assures that each of the program interests of the department will be represented in policy formulation.

E. THE COMPTROLLER FUNCTION AND BUDGETING

The conception of agency budget-making as an instrument of top-level staff in policy-coordinating dictates the kind of organizational structure possessed by the Office of Budget and Finance in the U. S. Department of Agriculture. As noted, budgeting is the keystone of the office; accounting, property management, and organization and methods studies occupy a subsidiary role. A different conception of the role of agency budget-making is exemplified in the application of comptrollership to government. Here budgeting is not pre-eminent but is orga1iza-tionally combined with statistical reporting, accounting, finance, and audit. In the federal government there is an office of comptroller in the Post Office Department, the General Services Administration, the Atomic Energy Commission, the Veterans Administration, the Foreign Operations Administration, and the Departments of Defense, Army, Navy, and Air Force. The Tennessee Valley Authority also has a comptroller, but in this case the functions of the office are not combined with budgeting. The strengthening of the comptroller approach to departmental management was encouraged by the Budget and Accounting Procedures Act of 1950 and by the recommendations of the second Hoover Commission.[11] It may be anticipated that there will be further developments in this direction.

The consolidation of budgeting and the comptroller (controller) function comes from private industry and has been borrowed from there for application in government.[12] As it has developed in business, controllership is an outgrowth of accountancy, with emphasis on the use of accounting records as a guide to the future. The controller in a business firm is a top advisory official, reporting to the general manager or to the board of directors, or both, with responsibility for interpreting account-

[11] Commission on Organization of the Executive Branch of the Government, *Budget and Accounting*, Washington, 1955, pp. 32–34; Task Force Report, *Budget and Accounting*, Washington, 1955, pp. 60–61.

[12] For a history of this development in American industry see Thornton F. Bradshaw and Charles C. Hull, *Controllership in Modern Management*, Richard D. Irwin, Chicago, 1949, pp. 11–27; also Mosher, *Program Budgeting*, pp. 193–202.

ing policy in relation to business policy and for advising on the financial consequences of business decisions. The controller in private business is not a policy official, but occupies an independent advisory role. He will typically either have charge of the preparation of the firm's budget or will have responsibility for reviewing it.

The most significant application of comptrollership in governments in this country is in the U. S. Department of Defense, where its development coincided with the introduction of performance budgeting (see Chapter 7). Mosher has described the influences leading to its adoption in the post World War II period as follows:

> The comptrollers represent and even epitomize several related basic motifs in the ethos of military management since the war: the rise to eminence of the fiscal and financial factors, functions, and organizations; the struggle of the principles and techniques of scientific management with those of traditional military and Federal management; the emulation of, and growing dependency upon, business and business practices; the establishment of the phrase "efficiency and economy" as a commandment, not merely a slogan; and, in a still confused way, the search for a formula (or perhaps merely a wedge) for more effective civilian control of the military.[13]

These pressures, objectives, and hopes contributed to the establishment of a comptroller of the Air Force in 1946, and one in the Army early in 1948. This development was given statutory approval by the enactment of amendments to the National Security Act in 1949, prescribing a civilian comptroller for the Department of Defense and comptrollers for each of the services (*P.L.* 216, 81st Cong., 1st sess.). The comptroller organizations in the Army and Air Force were thereupon realigned, and comptrollers were established for the Department of Defense and the Navy. The resulting organizational arrangements are shown in Chart 6.

Since 1949 the comptrollers have had great influence on budgeting and all other aspects of fiscal management in the military establishment. Under their leadership accounting systems have been improved, significant steps have been undertaken in performance budgeting, and improved management practices have been initiated. The comptrollers have had strong backing from their superiors and from the Congress.[14] The comptroller in the Department of Defense is an Assistant Secretary, with a civilian staff. This office has had the major responsibility for reviewing and integrating the budget of the Department of Defense. Within each of the services the organization and duties of the comptroller's office vary. In the comptroller's office in the Army, for example,

[13] Mosher, *Program Budgeting,* pp. 191–192.
[14] U. S. Senate, Committee on Armed Services, *Implementation of Title IV, National Security Act of 1947, as Amended,* "Hearings before the Preparedness Subcommittee No. 3," 83d Cong., 1st sess., Washington, 1954.

CHART 6
Comptroller Organizations in the U. S. Department of Defense

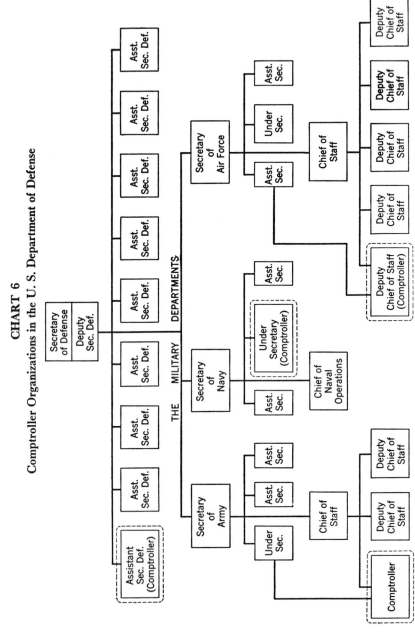

Source: U. S. Senate, Committee on Armed Services, *Implementation of Title IV, National Security Act of 1947, As Amended*, "Hearings before the Preparedness Subcommittee No. 3," 83d Cong., 1st sess., 1954, p. 171.

a Division of Program Review and Analysis has served as the principal staff agency for merging progress reporting and budget planning.[15] This merger has not been formalized to the same degree in the other services.

The experience with comptrollership in the Department of Defense is not yet adequate for an assessment of its impact on budgeting. The responsibilities of the comptrollers are not wholly fixed, and their relationships, one to another and to the chiefs of staff, are not fully delineated. There is some danger that, in the long run, budgeting and program planning in the military will be overwhelmed by the statistical, accounting, and financial management aspects of comptrollership.[16] But if this can be avoided and the generalist approach to budgeting strengthened, the comptroller's office will at least assure that budgeting will be regarded as a top-management responsibility.

II. BUILDING THE BUDGET

An agency budget is an expenditure budget or an expenditure-appropriation budget, but it is not an income-expenditure budget. An agency budgets on the assumption that revenues will be available to cover its estimated expenditures; the agency is not directly concerned with how these revenues are to be provided. This latter is the concern of the central budget office, which must at some point examine budget expenditure in relation to budget revenue and recommend that the chief executive propose a deficit, a surplus, or a balanced budget. There is one exception to this general orientation to expenditure rather than to income-expenditure in departments and agencies. For some government enterprise and for commercial-type activities within departments and agencies, there is a partial balancing of income and outgo. But for general government activities, budget-making is concerned exclusively with expenditures and the appropriations necessary to authorize expenditures.

There is one other significant difference between budget-making in the agencies and budget-making by the central budget office. For the agencies there is, or should be, a consistent relationship between budget preparation and budget execution. The planning done in the preparation of the budget will lay the basis for the management of programs which are eventually authorized. This is budget-making for operations

[15] Raymond S. McLain, "Applying Sound Management Principles to Comptrollership in Large Organizations," *Advanced Management,* November 1953, pp. 5–7.

[16] Smithies, *The Budgetary Process in the United States,* pp. 260–261; 283; Mosher, *op. cit.,* pp. 225–229.

which are underway or for new programs which are to be integrated with existing programs. The central budget office does not have this kind of management concern with operations. Its responsibilities in budget execution are much more limited.

In the agencies, it has been said that the appropriation act is the hub of budgeting. The whole of the budget submission centers on the proposed appropriation. Financial data are submitted in support of the appropriation. Information about the activities of the agency is classified to show what the agency is doing and the way in which this justifies a continuation of its activities.

A. The Components

The elements in an agency budget presentation are three: the proposed appropriation, the schedule of proposed financial activities, and the justification. The first element consists of last year's appropriation language, with bracketed or italicized insertions to show the proposed changes in language and amount. The schedule of financial activities may not be one, but many, in accordance with the nature of agency operations. The justification is program description, in tabular or narrative form.

Chart 7 is taken from the U. S. Bureau of the Budget's *Instructions for the Preparation and Submission of Annual Budget Estimates.* As indicated, the preparation of the estimate in this form provides a basis for ready comparison of the appropriation in the budget year with the appropriation in the current and prior fiscal years.

In every government the schedules of proposed financial activity will depend on the classification system employed, and will be both summary and supporting. They will include, but not be limited to, an agency summary on the basis of organizational units, showing obligations which are proposed for each of the bureaus of the agency. These, in turn, may be itemized by objects of expenditure, with supporting detail on personnel. Where program budgeting is used, the organizational unit schedules may be cross-classified on this basis, with activity costs or schedules of detailed performance. The income and expenditure of any commercial-type activities financed from working funds will be reported on separate schedules.

Regardless of the classification employed for major emphasis, which should probably be on a program basis, financial statements must include one prepared on an organizational unit basis and one prepared on the basis of "inputs"—the means of accomplishment.[17] Responsibility

[17] John D. Millett, *Management in the Public Service,* McGraw-Hill Book Company, New York, 1955, pp. 208–209.

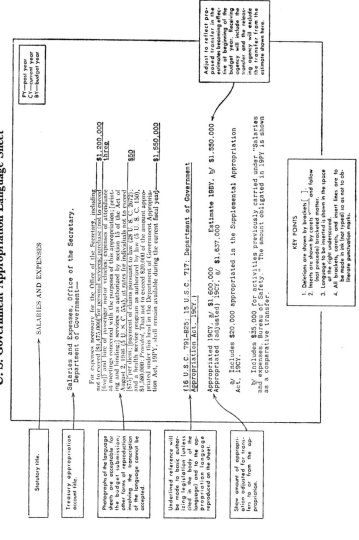

CHART 7

U. S. Government Appropriation Language Sheet

Source: U. S. Bureau of the Budget, *Instructions for the Preparation and Submission of Annual Budget Estimates*, Washington, 1954, Exhibit 31.

for management can be fixed only in organizational terms. Programs, even where they cut across organizational lines, must at some point be recast in organizational terms.

The schedule of inputs shows what will be bought—the personal services, materials, and supplies necessary to actuate the program. This is the traditional object classification, and unwieldy as it may be for some purposes, such as for legislative review, at the agency level it is the necessary bridge between program goals and program accomplishment.

The third component in an agency budget presentation is the justification—the materials specifically designed to show the need for appropriation.[18] This will be made up of narrative statements describing the work of the agency and its general objectives. In the United States government the narrative is, technically, separate from the justification, but general practice is to combine the two. Specific narratives may be prepared for individual bureaus. Major changes in agency programs and new programs are usually described in greater detail than existing programs. In addition to the narrative statements, the budget justification must contain tabular summaries showing sources of expenditure in relation to previous and proposed obligational authority. Where sources of funds are complicated by transfers of appropriations, by deficiencies, or by supplementals, this should be shown in the tabular summary. Very often the justification schedule is shown in terms of a base figure. This is computed by starting with last year's appropriation, adding supplemental and deficiency appropriations if any, and subtracting nonrecurring appropriation items. From this base, increases or decreases are shown, to emphasize the importance of proposed changes.

If a budget justification is to be more than an essay with a price tag attached, it should be grounded in cost data.[19] Even if a government does not employ the kind of program or performance budgeting which requires the presentation of obligation schedules on a cost basis, it will be possible to use cost data as a part of the justification (see Chapter 6). A discussion of work loads and selected units costs may be included in

[18] See Robert H. Rawson, "The Formulation of the Federal Budget," *Public Policy*, Graduate School of Public Administration, Cambridge, 1941, pp. 104–106.

[19] For case studies see Society for the Advancement of Management, Washington Chapter, Case Studies of the Budget Planning Round Table, American University Press, Washington, 1945: *Budget and Fiscal Program of the Civil Aeronautics Administration*, pp. 11–12; *Budgetary and Financial Administration in the United States Forest Service, Department of Agriculture*, pp. 17–22; *The Budget as a Tool of Management within the Federal Housing Administration*, pp. 13–18. For a discussion with specific reference to municipal budgeting see Samuel M. Roberts, "The Management Aspects of Budgeting," *Municipal Finance*, February 1949, pp. 28–32.

the narrative statement. In the United States government the Bureau of the Budget has been encouraging agencies to develop cost-type budget statements, either as a part of the justification or as a substitute for the schedule of obligations by activities.[20] An illustrative statement is shown in Chart 8. Where all of the activities of an agency can be described on the basis of cost, a reconciliation table will be required, to show the relation of costs to proposed appropriations. Cost data provide a basis for effective budgetary review by the central budget office and are sometimes useful in legislative review. In addition, these data can serve as the basis for the allotment of obligational authority once the budget has been authorized. The use of cost data is an important technique for linking budget preparation and budget execution.

Where work-load data are used, it may be possible to incorporate schedules in the budget justification to show distribution over time, that is, the quarterly or even monthly rate of obligations which the agency expects to incur. The scheduling of work within a fiscal year may be wholly the responsibility of the agency, but the work schedule will show the rate at which funds are required during the period of budget execution. The development of such schedules as a part of agency budget-making will lay the basis for the allotments which are to come during the phase of budget execution.

B. Revolving Funds

Budgeting at the agency level can very often be facilitated by the establishment of revolving funds, which provide a financial segregation of activities that generate receipts available for continuous use. Revolving-fund revenue is not included in general revenue, and fund expenditures are reflected in total expenditures for the agency only to the extent of the excess of expenditure over revenue. Appropriations to cover the net expenditures of such funds are itemized separately within the appropriations for the agency.

Revolving funds can be used for the segregation of activities which involve transactions with the private sector. In the United States government these are called public enterprise funds. Those which derive their receipts from inside the government are intragovernmental funds, and management funds are those which are used to pool activities financed by two or more appropriations.[21] Canteens or post exchanges

---

[20] Cost-type budget statements were given strong endorsement by the second Hoover Commission (Commission on Organization of the Executive Branch of the Government, *Budget and Accounting*, pp. 13–15).

[21] *Budget of the United States Government for the fiscal year ending June 30, 1956*, p. A3.

CHART 8
U. S. Government Cost-Type Budget Statement

Appropriation title: Salaries and Expenses, Bureau of Research, Department of Government

OBLIGATIONS BY ACTIVITIES

Description	19PY actual	19CY estimate	19BY estimate
Direct Obligations			PY—past year CY—current year BY—budget year
Costs by activities:			
1. Market analysis..........	$3,104,205	$2,728,000	$2,517,400
2. Product manufacture..........	984,026	882,800	874,800
3. Operation of facilities..........	790,449	757,200	750,000
4. Security..........	292,966	287,200	283,000
5. Administration..........	118,641	124,800	124,800
Total costs..........	5,290,287	4,780,000	4,550,000
Net change in inventories, undelivered orders, etc....	−34,806	−30,000	−40,000
Net change in equipment, excluding depreciation.........	140,910	15,000	10,000
Total direct obligations.........	5,396,391	4,765,000	4,520,000
Obligations (Costs) Payable Out Of Reimbursements From Other Accounts			
6. Miscellaneous work performed.........	191,275	120,000	50,000
Obligations incurred.........	5,587,666	4,885,000	4,570,000

This entry is computed as follows:

	Inventories	Accrued annual leave	Undelivered orders	Total
At 6/30/19PY-1	$787,565	−$588,294	$180,153	$379,424
Adjustments in 19PY	......	......	−9,917	−9,917
At 6/30/19PY	761,751	−600,875	173,825	334,701
Net change	−25,814	−12,581	3,589	−34,806

This entry represents the change from start to end of the year in those current assets and current liabilities which enter into obligations before they become costs, or vice versa, such as inventories, undelivered orders, and accrued annual leave. The data will be shown on one or more lines, depending upon the content and significance of the items.

This entry will consist of the equipment purchased, less the value of equipment which has been included in costs (either through depreciation or charge-offs or both).

Source: U. S. Bureau of the Budget, *Instructions for the Preparation and Submission of Annual Budget Estimates*, Washington, 1954, Exhibit 72.

in the armed forces or in government hospitals may be financed in this way. Revolving funds may also be established for the purpose of budgeting and controlling intragovernmental activities such as central purchasing or central storekeeping. Here the fund revenue is provided by the sales of goods or services within the government, and is charged to the user or ordering agency. Both of these types of funds are typically financed from an initial appropriation, but thereafter the fund is expected to be self-supporting with no further effect on budget expenditures. The initial appropriation is nonrecurring, and the activity may thereafter be excluded from budgetary statements and from budgetary review.

Trust funds administered by departments and agencies constitute an additional kind of special budgetary fund (see Chapter 5). Here the department acts as a trustee over funds which it does not own; payments from the trust fund are often subject to annual appropriation by the legislature, but are more typically under a permanent appropriation. Where the trust agreement specifies the purposes for which expenditures are to be made, there is little need for budgetary control, but in the interests of comprehensiveness there should be an annual reporting, in the agency's budget presentation, of trust fund receipts and expenditures.

The revolving funds established to assist in budgeting for inventory and for intragovernmental purposes are most significant for budgetary control. In every government the effective use of resources requires that certain kinds of goods and services which may be used by a number of agencies be provided centrally as a common service. In these cases both the service-providing and the service-using agency should establish a pattern of budget presentation that reflects the interagency character of the activity.

In the United States government an agency's purchase of goods and services on a contractual basis is budgeted as an obligation by the using agency, and the schedules of obligations reflect all such activities—as a charge against the agency ordering and using the commonly provided service. At the same time, the service-providing agency must budget its total expenditures. Where goods and services are provided by one agency to a number of agencies, it is desirable to establish a revolving fund to record the transfers from user agencies and the expenditures made by the service-providing agency. Working capital may be needed to finance inventory maintained by the servicing agency or to finance the lag between expenditures for materials, supplies, and personnel and the receipt of payment. In addition, the service may be partially supported by an appropriation—usually labeled a "subsidy" in these circumstances—and this should be shown in the budget schedules of the servicing agency. The net effect of the service activities on the budget totals can then be computed. Table 17 shows this kind of a summary budget schedule for the revolving and management funds of the Department of the Army. The funds *provided* by operations are those paid in by the user agencies—in this case, other branches of the Army. The funds *applied* represent the expenses of conducting the activity.

TABLE 17

Summary Statement of Revolving and Management Funds,
U. S. Department of the Army, Fiscal 1955

	New Authorizations	Funds Provided (by Operations)	Funds Applied (to Operations)	Net Effect on Budget Expenditures
Army industrial fund				
Reappropriation (current authorization)	$149,650	$443,585	$468,585	$25,000
Army management fund	....	2,435,000	1,335,000	1,100,000*
Army stock fund	....	2,129,400	1,737,400	392,000*
Replacing engineer supplies	....	....	4,000	4,000
Replacing medical supplies	....	....	....	....
Replacing ordnance and ordnance stores	....	....	180,000	180,000
Replacing quartermaster supplies	....	....	1,997	1,997
Replacing Signal Corps supplies and equipment	....	....	15,000	15,000
Army account of advances	....	....	403	403
Consolidated working fund	....	26,126	46,126	20,000
Total, Department of the Army	149,650	5,034,111	3,778,511	1,245,600*

* Deduct, excess of repayments and collections over expenditures.

Source: *Budget of the United States Government for the fiscal year ending June 30, 1956*, pp. 508–509.

In the Department of Defense, since 1949, there has been an extension of the use of special funds for purposes of costing and control of activities.[22] For commercial-type activities such as arsenals, shipyards, repair facilities, and printing plants, working capital is provided by what is called an industrial fund. For the acquisition and replenishment of items of common use, working capital is provided by a stock fund, a device which has been used by the Navy since 1893 and extensively since 1917. Such funds were established originally by the transfer of unobligated balances of appropriations.

In operation these funds are managed along commercial lines. Orders are placed by the user agencies and charged against their appropriations. The working capital is used to finance the acquisition and holding of inventory or the provision of goods and services until after the orders have been filled, at which time the fund is debited with the payment from the user agency. In the case of industrial funds it then becomes possible to arrive at standard cost figures for each item of output.

[22] *Implementation of Title IV, National Security Act of 1947, as Amended*, "Hearings before the Preparedness Subcommittee No. 3," pp. 126–130, 180–185; Melvin K. Zucker, "Industrial Fund Accounting in the Defense Department," *N.A.C.A. Bulletin*, January 1953, pp. 635–643.

This may make possible a comparison of the efficiencies of analogous activities within the Department of Defense, and may even permit some comparisons with the costs of private firms—at least to the point of determining whether specific supplies can be obtained at lower cost outside the Department.

In the Department of Defense the stock and industrial funds have made an important contribution to overcoming the difficulties in the practice of "free issue." Under procedures which have recently been established, the user agency is charged with matériel, not the supplying agency. This should at least provide the basis for a concern over costs on the part of defense installations. The working capital system thus becomes a double-edged weapon.[23] It puts pressure on the consuming units to economize in their use of equipment. It also puts pressure on the supplying units to keep their costs in line with similar industrial-type operations.

The use of working capital funds may appear to complicate agency budgeting. Actually, once these are established, they can simplify both budgeting and accounting. In terms of budget preparation and review, a great mass of detail is segregated for separate treatment. With the accounting system in operation, changes in the costs of supply can be quickly ascertained; attention can be directed to analyzing efficiency on the basis of performance through a post-audit of operations. Budgetary review should then center on the user agencies and their requirements, although there is always some danger that these separate pockets of funds will not be scrutinized carefully.[24]

C. The Time Span of Budget-Making

It is axiomatic that government budget-making should be flexible and capable of adaptation to changes in governmental responsibilities. But in many governments the procedures—the phases of the budget cycle—are so rigid and so time-consuming that adaptation is difficult.

The United States government is an outstanding case in point. Here the executive phase is particularly lengthy. Agency budget-making generally takes about five months, although the military requires fifteen months. Central budget office and Presidential review take another four months. Congressional review requires about six months.

This elongated time span brings difficulties of two sorts. First, it makes program planning less realistic in those cases where little operating experience in the current fiscal year is known before budgets must

[23] Mosher, *Program Budgeting*, p. 244; Smithies, *The Budgetary Process in the United States*, pp. 316–325.

[24] Task Force Report, *Budget and Accounting*, pp. 70–71.

be prepared for the forthcoming year. Budget planning must start even before the action of the Congress on the current budget has been completed. This leads to a great deal of waste motion. Detailed budget preparation is made obsolete by subsequent changes in policy.

The second difficulty arises, not on the program side, but on the fiscal policy side. If the budget is to be modified in accordance with the requirements of economic stabilization, such modification cannot be undertaken a year or more in advance. Economic forecasts are not this reliable. Budgetary changes which are to produce modifications in the level of national income and employment may need to be planned and proposed within the space of a few months.

The requirements for maintaining flexibility for program purposes are not uniform for all government agencies nor for all programs within these agencies. The traditional administrative functions of government do not change very much from year to year. An extended time span for budget-making is not likely to lead to serious programing difficulties for "old line" activities such as revenue collection or customs administration. But programing difficulties may be very serious in the national military establishment, where budgetary requirements must be modified by changes in strategic considerations, by changes in technology, and by the performance of suppliers.

Recent critics, concerned about the elongated time span for budgeting in the United States government, have proposed sweeping changes in procedure with a view to shortening the budget preparation phase. For the military, Mosher has suggested a procedure which would shorten the timetable by a full year.[25] Budgets for the armed services would be prepared initially on a broad program basis, and reviewed by the Bureau of the Budget and the President and presented to Congress on this basis. After presidential decisions had been made and during the time that the Congress was engaged in review, the armed services would prepare a detailed administrative budget, which would be modified and readied for budget execution by the time Congress had completed action at the beginning of the fiscal year.

Smithies has proposed a reorganized time table for the whole of the budget.[26] He suggests that executive budget preparation begin in December or January and end in March, and that the budget be prepared on a statistical or factorial basis and presented to the Congress on a program basis for review and authorization. Congressional examination of the detail would be handled through a review of performance. Similar proposals were made by a task force of the second Hoover

[25] Mosher, *op. cit.*, pp. 237–244.
[26] Smithies, *op. cit.*, pp. 178–192, 218.

Commission.[27] The possibilities for shortening the time span rest, however, on a fundamental point—the willingness of Congress to enact appropriations which are supported only by a general presentation of program outlines. Unless the Congress is willing to abandon the detail, it will be difficult to compress the period of budget preparation and review.

The economy in time, as such, is less important than flexibility and adaptability. It is most obviously not possible to budget for the unpredictable. The most accurate of budget preparation techniques cannot fully eliminate deficiency appropriations and unobligated balances. However, if traditional time schedules cannot be modified and if the emphasis in budget preparation and budget authorization cannot be shifted to a program basis, then flexibility must be secured in the execution of the budget. Within limits, it is possible to compensate for the unpredictables after the budget is authorized, if it cannot be done in advance (see Chapter 13).

In every government the time span of budgeting should be examined with a view to its differential application among departments. There is no reason why stable departments may not remain safely committed to a longer time span. But for unstable programs, such as the military or public works, every effort should be made to budget closer to the beginning of the fiscal year. This requires a classification of government programs in accordance with their stability over time, and an acceptance of differing procedures by all participants, including legislatures.

The necessity for maintaining flexibility in accordance with fiscal policy considerations may dictate further modifications in budgeting with respect to time. In public works, for example, the executive might be permitted to propose modifications in legislative authorizations at any time up to the beginning of the fiscal year. Further flexibility could be secured by authorizing the chief executive to control, within limits, the rate of spending for designated works projects. Tax rates should also be capable of variance in accordance with fiscal policy considerations. Unless a government is operating in conformity with rigid standards of budget balance, there is no reason why both revenues and expenditures cannot be modified on reasonably short notice. Flexibility in budget-making can be increased by experimentation with multiple procedures.

III. GOVERNMENT BUDGETS AND BUSINESS BUDGETS

An earlier chapter compared the operating characteristics of government with the operating characteristics of private firms (Chapter 2).

[27] Task Force Report, *Budget and Accounting*, pp. 21–25.

There it was contended that the absence of a market for government product had a controlling influence on the operating behavior of the public as compared with the private sector. Government requires a nonmarket guide for the allocation of resources; the budgetary process provides this guide. But in the private sector the market is ever-present, and budgeting by business firms is done in relation to the market rather than as a substitute for the market. A brief examination of budget-making in business firms will serve to reveal the implications of this fundamental distinction.

In most industrial economies, management techniques have generally developed first in the private sector, and then have been transferred to and modified in application to the public sector. Budgeting, however, has worked the other way. Its development came first in the public sector, and its application by private firms has been relatively recent. Some firms have used this technique since World War I, but its more widespread adoption did not come until the late 1930's. Its use, although growing, is still restricted to larger firms.

There are necessarily infinite patterns of variation in the technique, purposes, and comprehensiveness of business budgets. It is nevertheless possible to generalize some major characteristics.[28]

In terms of procedure, the budget cycle in a business firm is comparable to that in government: preparation and submission, authorization, execution, and audit. The terms to describe these phases are customarily the same, except for the final one, which could more aptly be called an appraisal of results than an audit. This appraisal serves as the basis for budget formulation for the following year. The audit in business is directed to the accounts and their accuracy, not to results. Similarly, the organization for budget-making does not differ in its essentials as compared with that of government. In a business firm, major responsibility for the preparation of the budget will be assigned to a top-level staff officer, usually the controller. He will be assisted by a "central budget office," which in turn will work closely with the operating departments. Where the procedure is well articulated, there will be the same kind of flow-up and flow-back of decision-making. Initial budgetary goals are worked out by top management as a part of basic product and market

[28] The literature is voluminous. See, for example, J. R. Bartizal, *Budgeting Principles and Procedures,* Prentice-Hall, New York, 1950; Walter Rautenstrauch and Raymond Villers, *Budgetary Control,* Funk & Wagnalls Company, New York, 1950; J. Brooks Heckert and James D. Willson, *Business Budgeting and Control,* Ronald Press Company, New York, 1955; William H. Newman, *Administrative Action,* Prentice-Hall, New York, 1951, pp. 429–443; American Management Association, *A Program of Financial Planning and Controls* (case study of the Monsanto Chemical Company), New York, 1953.

decisions. For example, it might be determined that an effort would be made to capture a larger share of the existing market for a particular product. This would require a different sales forecast than if it were decided that the firm would attempt to hold the line in relation to the industry.

The major budgetary goals established by the higher echelons of management are discussed at the operating level, and the final budget is a product of an interplay among levels of hierarchy. The preparation of the budget becomes the occasion for a review of the policies of the firm and their statement and restatement in financial terms.

The budget will be authorized by the general manager or by the board of directors. Departments are notified of the decisions which have been made, and work plans are executed in accordance with the budgets for each department. A reporting system is used to check on performance, and there is a periodic budgetary review.

So much for the characteristics in common. There are, however, some important differences in procedure, and some even more important differences in the objectives that are served by the budget in the public and in the private sector.

All phases of budgeting in private firms are geared to performance in terms of profit. As one authority says, "Budgeting is planning how to spend money to produce maximum profits."[29] The programs proposed and the results achieved by individual departments within the firm can be judged in relation to this criterion.[30] In a business firm, profits are increased by adding to revenue and/or holding down expenses. But governments try to hold down their expenses in order to reduce their income, that is, in order to lower the revenue taken from the community in taxation. Governments are not deemed to be successful or efficient when their revenues increase. But business firms are very often judged to be successful when their revenue and expenditure increase together, even though profit rates may be unchanged.

The budget has a different significance as a coordinating device in business firms than it does in government. The necessity for coordinating the activities of the separate departments in a firm (marketing, production, research, etc.) arises from the need for assuring that each department makes its maximum contribution to the welfare of the whole organization. The availability of the profit criterion for making judg-

---

[29] Charles C. James, "The Basis of the Flexible and the Variable Budget in an Expanding Economy," *Advanced Management,* September 1952, p. 6.

[30] For example, in the Monsanto Company the yardstick for budgeted performance is the rate of return on gross assets in each division of the company. (American Management Association, *op. cit.,* pp. 8-10.)

ments about program levels for most departments greatly simplifies the decision-making process. The value judgments which are so treacherous in government—the pervasive difficulties of choosing between expenditure on program X and on program Y—are not as serious in private budgeting. On the other hand, the need for coordination among the departments of a firm is greater than the need for coordination among the bureaus of a government department. In a department of agriculture it is possible for a bureau of plant and animal industry to be somewhat "on its own." Its program level is not *uniquely* determined by the program levels of other bureaus within the department. But in private firms the program of the marketing department is determined by the program of the manufacturing department, and vice versa. The necessity for coordination in budget preparation among the departments is greater; the requirement for coordination in execution is paramount. Unless the manufacturing department fulfills its budget, the marketing department will fall short of its budgeted goals. Coordination must be achieved with respect to timing as well as with respect to program level; in business firms, budgeting must be based on both product and period. Commodities must be produced in specified time periods so that they will move through distribution channels in other time periods. Inventory policy is a matter of timing as well as of absolute level.

The interdependence of the separate departments of private firms has made budget procedure an important device for securing a pattern of collective decision-making and behavior. The budget in business has been described as a "psychological tool of administration," a phrase which is probably intended to stress its usefulness as an educational device for thinking about interrelationships in a large firm.[31] In some firms, therefore, participation in budget-making is widely based, perhaps more widely based than in most government organizations. The preparation of the budget becomes an occasion for restating program and performance objectives, and widespread participation of employees is enlisted with a view to planning for the maximum utilization of both equipment and manpower.

The sharpest differences in budgeting in the public and in the private sector come in budget execution. By and large, and with only occasional exceptions, once a government budget is authorized, a department or agency may plan its work program for the budget year with the knowledge that its income is assured. At this point, budget expenditures do not depend on budget income. But in private firms budget execution takes on the greatest significance. Expenditures must be continually ex-

[31] Newman, *Administrative Action,* pp. 431–432.

amined not alone in relation to goals and accomplishments, but in relation to realized levels of income in specified time periods. Government budgeting assumes that income is controlled; private budgeting assumes that it is not, and that operating expenditures must adapt to income.

In any private firm the budget must be based on a forecast of revenue from sales. This forecast shows the total amount of operating income available to the firm during the budget year, and therefore the amount which may be allocated to each department of the firm. As the year progresses, budget income may not conform with realized income. Sales may exceed or fall short of the budget figure. If sales exceed the expected volume, the component budgets of some departments have to be altered; outlays for manufacturing operations, for example, must be increased. If sales fall short of the budget, downward adjustments must be made in a number of departmental programs in order to avoid losses for the firm as a whole. The budget is not only a coordinating device for the preplanning of activities; it is, more significantly, a control device for regulating and continuously adjusting expenses to income.

Budget planning and formulation must therefore rest on careful studies of cost behavior, in terms that are familiar to the student of economics under the heading of the differences between fixed and variable cost. The relationship of cost to income is not the same for each of the departments of a firm. Advertising outlays, for example, may be independent of the current level of sales. Research activities or capital expenditures may also be deemed of sufficient importance to require no alteration within the budget year. On the other hand, marketing costs and production costs may be budgeted as a direct function of changes in the level of the firm's income.

The execution of the budget therefore requires that the budget office have periodic reports from each department on expenditures in relation to the budget plan, and reports on sales. Progress under some auxiliary budgets, such as the cash budget or the profit and loss budget, can be measured only by the central staff. All of the auxiliary budgets must be analyzed for presentation to top management, which has the responsibility for determining the adjustments that must be made in expenses. Management in a large firm can use budgeting as a technique to assist in separating those decisions which must be made centrally and those decisions which can be left to departmental managers. Top supervision can be retained, but with a large measure of decentralized decision-making, in accordance with the nature of the activities and their impact on the budget.

The importance of the continuous adjustment of expenses to income via the budget has led some firms to adopt a multiple-budget system. In some applications of this technique, a probable budget is prepared, based on the most likely forecast of revenue. Alternative budgets, with forecast levels 10 percent above and 10 percent below the probable are also prepared. During the budget year one of the alternative budgets may then be utilized, in accordance with actual sales. A flexible budget may also be employed to facilitate the necessary expense adjustments, especially in the items of overhead. With this technique a graph is prepared for every department, to show the relationship of each expense item to income at varying levels of income. Actuals can then be interpolated from the chart for any realized level of income.[32] A flexible budget may take more time to prepare than alternative budgets, but it will presumably require less revision in the execution phase. However, as one critic has suggested, flexible budgets have their operational limits. "In seeking a flexible standard for control purposes most of the planning and coordinating benefits of budgeting are sacrificed."[33]

The use of a business budget for controlling operations is somewhat different from its use for purposes of eliciting performance. In the latter case the original budget is established, not so much on the basis of the probable, but on the basis of the maximum. The budget then serves as a target for attainment and as a technique of management pressure to enlist maximum effort on the part of employees.[34] In some firms a budget is established not only for the sales department as a whole, but for each member of the sales force. Standard costs per unit of product are very often developed as part of the budgeting and accounting system, or when developed independently, they are used for budgetary planning and the control of performance.

Budgeting has proved to be a highly useful management tool for private firms, particularly where large business units are engaged in the production of a variety of commodities. With further developments in the applications of business budgeting, both the private and public sectors could profit from a mutual exchange of experience in the techniques of organization and procedure. The purposes of budgetary control, however, will necessarily remain different in the two sectors, and the transferability of methods is thus inherently limited.

[32] See Rautenstrauch and Villers, *Budgetary Control*, pp. 184–197. A further distinction between flexible and variable budgets is developed by James, *Advanced Management*, September 1952, pp. 2–3.

[33] Newman, *op. cit.*, p. 441.

[34] For an analysis based on case studies of the budget as a pressure device see Chris Argyris, "Human Problems with Budgets," *Harvard Business Review*, January–February 1953, pp. 97–110; James L. Peirce, "The Budget Comes of Age," *Harvard Business Review*, May–June 1954, pp. 58–66.

Selected Bibliography

James, Charles C., "The Basis of the Flexible and the Variable Budget in an Expanding Economy," *Advanced Management*, September 1952, pp. 2–8.

Jump, W. A., "Budgetary and Financial Administration in an Operating Department of the Federal Government," *Materials on Budgeting*, Vol. V, Catheryn Seckler-Hudson, ed., American University, Washington, 1944, pp. 123–138.

Lewis, Verne B., "Budgetary Administration in the Department of Agriculture," in John M. Gaus and Leon O. Wolcott, *Public Administration and the United States Department of Agriculture*, Public Administration Service, Chicago, 1940, pp. 403–460.

———— "Toward a Theory of Budgeting," *Public Administration Review*, Winter 1952, pp. 42–54.

Mosher, Frederick C., *Program Budgeting*, Public Administration Service Chicago, 1954, pp. 124–249.

Millett, John D., *Management in the Public Service*, McGraw-Hill Book Company, New York, 1955, pp. 202–228.

Peirce, James L., "The Budget Comes of Age," *Harvard Business Review*, May–June 1954, pp. 58–66.

Rautenstrauch, Walter, and Raymond Villers, *Budgetary Control*, Funk & Wagnalls Company, New York, 1950.

Roberts, Samuel M., "The Management Aspects of Budgeting," *Municipal Finance*, February 1949, pp. 28–32.

Shipman, George A., "Notes on the Management Aspects of Agency Budgeting," *Materials on Budgeting*, Vol. IV, Catheryn Seckler-Hudson, ed., American University, Washington, 1945, pp. 140–145.

Society for the Advance of Management, Washington Chapter, Case Studies of the Budget Planning Round Table, American University Press, Washington, 1945: *Budget and Fiscal Program of the Civil Aeronautics Administration; Budgetary and Financial Administration in the United States Forest Service, Department of Agriculture; The Budget as a Tool of Management within the Federal Housing Administration; Wartime Budgetary Practice of the United States Coast Guard; Development of Budgetary Administration within the General Accounting Office of the United States Government.*

U. S. Senate, Committee on Armed Services, *Implementation of Title IV, National Security Act of 1947, as Amended*, "Hearings before the Preparedness Subcommittee No. 3," 83d Cong., 1st sess., Washington, 1954.

Walker, Robert A., "The Relation of Budgeting to Program Planning," *Public Administration Review*, Spring 1944, pp. 97–107.

———— "William A. Jump: The Staff Officer as a Personality," *Public Administration Review*, Autumn 1954, pp. 233–246.

11.

The central budget office

In the preparation of the budget the central office has two responsibilities, program review and management improvement. Program review is the examination of agency operations from a central vantage point, the knitting together of the pieces of governmental operations into a whole. Program review is concerned with such questions as: What is the relative importance of this program as compared with other programs? At what level should this program be conducted? What are the benefits which will be derived here as compared with alternatives? What revenues are available for the support of this program and for all programs?

Management improvement consists in the optimization of a given program—the effective allocation of resources for the achievement of stated objectives. Management improvement is concerned with such questions as: Can this program be conducted at a lower cost? Will improved work methods contribute to a more effective program? Will a realignment of responsibilities contribute to a higher level of performance?

In its operating capacity the central budget office will necessarily undertake program review and management improvement simultaneously, and will translate its findings and conclusions into financial terms.

The activities of a central budget office may embrace other responsibilities than these two. But these are the fundamentals of the preparation process, and their characteristics will be examined here as an introduction to a specific description of the operations and structure of a

278

major budget office—the U. S. Bureau of the Budget. The work of the central office in budget execution will be examined in Chapter 13.

I. THE NATURE OF BUDGETARY REVIEW

Program review and management improvement are usually conducted jointly. In some of their aspects the two are indistinguishable; in other aspects they are clearly separated and may be undertaken at different points in time and by different organizational entities within the central office.

A. PROGRAM REVIEW

Executive authority in any government must be supported by an organizational pattern which moves decisions upward to a higher and broader level of consideration. The budget process is a major channel by which this is accomplished. Fritz Marx has observed:

> In the United States . . . the budget process has become a prime mechanism for achieving assent to a proposed plan of governmental operations to be carried out during the fiscal year. . . . In other countries, budgeting has never supplied a channel for policy determination which compares even remotely with its importance in American government.[1]

In the upward movement of decisions, budgetary procedure serves as something more than the transmission of information. Review consists, or should consist, of crystallizing the issues which are involved, of separating the less important from the more important, and of indicating to the higher levels of executive authority the ramifications and consequences of alternative courses of action within a complex of aggregate actions and policy. For example, the program of a department of agriculture for the stabilization of farm prices must be reviewed in relation to its impact on foreign trade, an impact which the department of agriculture may not perceive, or which may be perceived better by the department of foreign affairs or the department of commerce. Outlays for national defense must be reviewed not only in relation to the provision of security, but in relation to levels of national income and employment, considerations which are not the primary concern of the department of defense.

Program review in this connotation means not the imposition of authority from above, but an intermeshing of the parts—the subjection of the discrete elements to a broader view.

[1] Quoted in Gerhard Colm and Marilyn Young, *The Federal Budget and the National Economy*, National Planning Association, Washington, 1955, p. 18.

... departmental policy should be an integral part of what is known as "general policy." General policy is not an imaginary "whole," an airplant, it is the interweaving of many policies. Whether we are talking of the individual man, or individual department, the work should never be sacrifice, it should always be contribution. We want every possible contribution to the whole.[2]

This kind of control, in the interests of general policy, must continuously be asserted in any government. Close observers of the governmental process have noted that program administrators have an almost inherent tendency to move away from the center. Their attention is necessarily focused on their own operations and the consequences of these operations. A conscientious administrator is anxious to live up to his responsibilities, which he conceives in program terms. This concern tends toward segmentation and compartmentalization.[3] The inevitable out-movement of responsibility must be countered by continuous reintegration.

Program review therefore becomes both reconciliation and centralization. Budget examiners cannot be expected to possess the insight of program administrators with respect to requirements and missions. Similarly, the administrators cannot be expected to provide the overview.[4] Both the program administrator and the budget examiner are fostering meritorious interests; the interests of both must be considered in achieving a maximum contribution to the whole.

This makes the budget examiners' role that of the generalist, not that of the specialist. The point has been well put as follows:

In most instances, questions are raised with an examiner not because he has *more* information than the man who asks the questions (although there are times when he will have), but rather because he has information of a *different* kind than his questioner. The examiner "knows" how a given expansion in program, shift in program emphasis, or shift in proposed means of accomplishing a program would be viewed by the budget director, the controller, or the Governor if it were called to their attention. At least, his institutional vantage point puts him in a position to predict the relative preferences of his own superiors more accurately than can the agency per-

[2] Mary Parker Follett, "The Process of Control," *Papers on the Science of Administration,* Luther Gulick and L. Urwick, eds., Institute of Public Administration, New York, 1937, p. 164.

[3] Charles McKinley, "Federal Administrative Pathology and the Separation of Powers," *Public Administration Review,* Winter 1951, pp. 18–20; Herbert Emmerich, *Essays on Federal Reorganization,* University of Alabama Press, University, Alabama, 1950, pp. 33–60.

[4] Frederick J. Lawton, "The Role of the Administrator in the Federal Government," *Public Administration Review,* Spring 1954, p. 117.

sonnel, who are politically and administratively much farther removed from the center of Executive policy-making.[5]

As Schubert and McIntyre indicate, central budget office review must be conducted with a full awareness on the part of budget examiners of the nature of the political program of the executive. Program review is a political process conducted in a political framework; this is one of the sensitized areas of decision-making. Its political character is not altered by the fact that review is customarily conducted *in camera;* public hearings at which interest groups are represented are unusual in the work of the central budget office in any government. The interest group representations that directly and immediately influence executive program proposals are far more likely to be channeled to bureau chiefs, department heads, and the chief executive. This practice is common at the state level in this country, where the governor will often serve as the focus of interest group pressures. The impact of such representations is then communicated, directly or indirectly, to those who would appear to be far removed from the political scene. As Appleby has said, speaking of the budget, "It is not made in a public arena, but the public is somehow well represented. This is one of the most mystifying of governmental phenomena."[6]

Program review has been examined thus far in terms which would suggest that all of the activities of a government are subject to this process. This is far from the case. Major portions of a government's expenditures and revenues are effectively removed from budget review. Several classes of cases may be distinguished.

First, there are the expenditures of branches of the government coordinate with the executive—the judiciary and the legislature. A great many constitutions and budgetary statutes remove these estimates from review by the executive. In the United States government the President must include in the budget, without revision, the estimates of Congress and of the Supreme Court, although estimates for the remainder of the federal judiciary may be reviewed. In New York State the appropriation requests of the judiciary and the legislature may not be modified by the Governor, but he may recommend their modification by the legislature.[7]

Second, by virtue of organizational arrangements or custom, as the case may be, a part or all of the revenue program may be reviewed by

[5] Glendon A. Schubert, Jr., and Donald F. McIntyre, "Preparing the Michigan State Budget," *Public Administration Review,* Autumn 1953, p. 243.

[6] Paul H. Appleby, "The Influence of the Political Order," *American Political Science Review,* April 1948, p. 281.

[7] For other examples see A. E. Buck, *Public Budgeting,* Harper & Brothers, New York, 1929, pp. 340–342.

staff other than the central budget office. This is the case in the United States government, where the Bureau of the Budget has little practical authority over revenues; the Treasury Department has traditionally served in this capacity. In a great many states the revenue program, particularly where new tax levies are contemplated, is so sensitive an area that the governor will work closely with legislative leaders in the initial stage of formulation. A government's debt policy may also be outside the scope of budget office review. Decisions to draw down cash balances or to borrow, and subsidiary decisions on the type of borrowing to be undertaken, like tax policy decisions, are critical and high-level and yet may not be reviewed by budget staff.

Third, program review may not extend to some significant and major outlays because of their unalterable character. The standard example here is interest on outstanding public debt, which cannot be altered because it is contractual in nature and is handled under a permanent appropriation. Again, where statutes provide for transfer payments to beneficiaries of welfare programs or for veterans' benefit programs, there is little or no central budget office review. Here a previously enacted law is controlling, and while it may be that the executive is in a position to review these programs and recommend statutory revision, such recommendation is not likely to emerge from the budgetary process.[8] A similar class of cases obtains where a national government mandates programs to be carried out by state governments, or where state constitutions and statutes impose on their own legislatures and on municipalities restrictions with respect to borrowing and taxing. Grants-in-aid that require matching by the unit of government receiving the funds likewise tend to remove programs from review and decision by the grantee jurisdiction.

Fourth, program review may be denied the central budget office by virtue of special funds and earmarked revenues. In many states all motor vehicle revenues flow into a segregated fund not subject to central budget office control. The revenue from hunting and fishing licenses may be applied to programs for game and fish conservation. Invariably, earmarking and segregation of this type represent an attempt, not to introduce an improved pattern of fiscal management, but to protect and isolate the beneficiaries of specific governmental programs. In New

[8] The growing significance of the "relatively uncontrollable" items in the federal budget has found expression in an expenditure classification used in the budget message, entitled "Summary of Net Budget Expenditures Indicating Controllability." In fiscal 1956 about one-fourth of the total is described as " . . . permitting little or no administrative discretion through the budget process." (*Budget of the United States Government for the fiscal year ending June 30, 1956*, pp. M23–M25.)

York State, where there are relatively few special funds of this sort, about one-third of the state's expenditures are nevertheless beyond the scope of budget office review. In California the proportion is probably closer to two-thirds.

Fifth, and closely linked with the foregoing, are the programs sponsored by strong departments and strong clientele. The power centers of a government are not confined to the chief executive. Budget review may be more shadow than substance where strongly entrenched agencies are in a position to virtually defy the central budget office, or to appeal beyond the executive to the legislature. The most frequently noted case of this sort is the behavior of the Corps of Engineer in the U. S. Department of the Army, which has successfully by-passed the Bureau of the Budget on numerous occasions.[9] Since power centers within a government change over time, it cannot be expected that a central budget office will deal, from one year to the next, with identical distributions between controllable and uncontrollable programs. That which is uncontrollable this year may be controllable next, and the reverse may also be true.

The thoroughness of program review can therefore be described in terms of both breadth and depth. The relatively fixed programs in a budget may be substantial, but the budget office may still be in a position to exert major influence over remaining programs. Conversely, the depth of review may not be great, but the central office may have a large proportion of the financial activities of a government within its purview.

B. Management Improvement

Expenditure for governmental programs is always limited. The limits may lie in difficulties of transferring resources from the private sector via taxation; in constitutional restrictions on outlays, either aggregate or specific; in the attitudes of citizens. Therefore, every central budget office feels that it must economize and cut back program requests. Although there may be isolated cases where budget examiners have recommended increases in outlays beyond those requested by administrators, these are most exceptional circumstances; the pressure is in the other direction.

This pressure to cut back is one means of encouraging management improvement. Central budget office review will always urge departments and agencies to conduct the same program with fewer resources, will always assume that a continued drive for economy will yield more

[9] David B. Truman, The Governmental Process, Alfred A. Knopf, New York, 1953, pp. 410–415; Commission on Organization of the Executive Branch of the Government, Task Force Report on Natural Resources, Washington, 1949, pp. 26–27.

efficient operations. This process is very like that in the private sector, where there is more or less continuous pressure for cost-cutting in business firms that are in a competitive market. But in government the discipline of the market is lacking because government product is not sold. The pressure for management improvement which can come from central budget office review may be regarded as a kind of substitute for market pressure and profit maximization.

To be truly effective in management improvement, the pressure for economy must be transmitted by budget examiners possessed of intimate knowledge of agency operations. It cannot be forced by arbitrary reductions. Sir John Woods quotes a letter from the Permanent Secretary of the Board of Trade to the Permanent Secretary of the Treasury, written in 1872:

> Economy and efficiency must be worked out from within and cannot be forced upon an office by the Treasury from without. And the wholesome state of things is when the best men in each office look to the Treasury as their helper against claims and proceedings which they better than anyone know to be improper.[10]

Budget review which is to contribute to efficiency must be based on mutual confidence and respect, not on the ability of the central budget office to enforce its decisions by the sheer weight of its organizational position.

Budget examiners are in a position to make major contributions to management improvement in a number of specific ways. One of these is in a judicious handling of new programs. A seasoned budget examiner will proceed cautiously in putting pressure on the administrators of new operations, and will recognize that a shake-down period is necessary. The examiner does not have operating responsibility; he will not be brought into judgment for the success or failure of the program. Therefore, he must lend encouragement and advice, but avoid the kind of pressure which might characterize review of well-established programs.

The examiner can also make a significant contribution to management improvement if he is acquainted with ways and means to "save money by spending money." Suggestions for the mechanization of work procedures fall in this category. Up-grading of personnel and improved salary classifications may also be available for the ultimate improvement of the level of operating efficiency. The budget examiner should be in a position to sacrifice short-run expenditures for long-run economy.

Above all, the budget examiner, if his range of assignments or experi-

---

[10] Sir John Woods, "Treasury Control," *The Political Quarterly*, October—December 1954, p. 376.

ence is broad, is in a position to relate the management problems which he is reviewing to the management problems of other departments. The seemingly mundane but frequently complex organization of a mail room, a filing system, a stenographic pool, or payroll records may fall in this category. Beyond this, the examiner has the responsibility for initiating action to establish interdepartmental committees and special review procedures for programs which may be the joint concern of a number of departments. The interrelation of operations is the particular province of the central budget office.

Apart from the management improvement which is a direct product of budget examination, many central budget offices have special staff to conduct studies of organization and methods. It can be argued that organization and methods work is an operating responsibility best left to the agencies themselves, and that a central budget office is not the place from which to conduct management improvement studies. This argument rests on what is conceived to be a traditional distrust running from the agencies to the central budget office, and an alleged feeling that any proposals for management improvement which emanate from that office will always be undertaken with a view to reduction in staff and in appropriations. Better cooperation between a central organization and methods office and the agencies, it is contended, will ensue if budgeting and management improvement are divorced.

On the other hand, it can be contended that the translation of results from management improvement studies is effected only through the budget, and that budget examiners themselves should spend at least a part of their time in specific studies of work methods in agencies and departments. The second Hoover Commission, in fact, urged that examiners from the U. S. Bureau of the Budget be assigned to work continuously in the agencies.[11]

Both approaches may be employed, and the success of either probably depends more on the personnel involved than on organizational location. In New York State a major responsibility of the Division of the Budget is organization and management work in the departments. Some New York State departments have their own management improvement staffs, but in every case their work is closely geared with that of the Division. On the other hand, the U. S. Bureau of the Budget, in recent years, has conducted very few major management improvement studies; the tendency in the federal government seems to be toward a strengthening of this work in the agencies themselves, with some coordinating and stimulating influence in the hands of the Bureau, which

[11] Commission on Organization of the Executive Branch of the Government, *Budget and Accounting,* Washington, 1955, pp. 5–7.

has direct responsibility only for interagency matters.[12] Arthur Smithies has proposed that the Bureau of the Budget greatly strengthen its influence in this area by way of an annual President's Report on Executive Performance.[13] This would be based on departmental reports covering program objectives, unit costs, and the measures which had been undertaken for management improvement. It would, in addition, describe the actions which the Executive Office had undertaken to improve management in departments and agencies. This kind of report would undoubtedly encourage the Congress to a more systematic review of performance, in a context broader than that of economy, as that word is customarily interpreted.

Aside from the special studies of management improvement which are conducted under the auspices of a central budget office, it is not possible, in operational terms, to separate program review from management improvement in the work of the budget examiner. Decisions about the level and extent to which programs should be conducted are bound up with decisions about the efficiency of programs. If a program can be managed with greater economy in the use of resources, it may be possible to expand its level of operations and increase the number of things done or the number of persons served. Conversely, budget examiners may know that a given program is costly, but the importance of the program may nevertheless necessitate its expansion.

C. ORGANIZATIONAL PATTERNS

The definition of a budget function in terms of program review and management improvement does not mean that budget offices do or should confine their activities to these two functions. Any central budget office with review authority will necessarily undertake both of these, but in addition it will typically conduct, for one reason or another, additional activities which may or may not be specifically related to a narrow definition of the budget function.

In Great Britain, for example, and in most other Commonwealth countries, the Chancellor of the Exchequer and the Treasury have a unified command over all financial and economic planning. Most of the organization and methods work is conducted by the Treasury, not by the departments. The government's economic policy and budget policy are closely coordinated by central staff, as are personnel, purchasing, and accounting. In governments in the United States there is no uniformity whatsoever in organizational arrangements, either in the

[12] President's Advisory Committee on Management, *Report to the President,* Washington, 1952, pp. 14–18.

[13] Arthur Smithies, *The Budgetary Process in the United States,* McGraw-Hill Book Company, New York, 1955, pp. 208–213; Commission on Organization of the Executive Branch of the Government, *Budget and Accounting,* pp. 7–8.

CENTRAL BUDGET OFFICE

location of the budget office with respect to the chief executive or in the range of central office responsibilities.

In all but seven of the American states the governor has responsibility for the preparation and submission of the budget. The exceptions are Arkansas, Florida, Indiana, Montana, North Dakota, South Carolina, and West Virginia.[14] Four states that have an executive budget system have no central budget office—Arizona, Vermont, South Dakota, and Wyoming.[15] The best staffed of the state budget offices are New York and California, but other states in which budget offices are reasonably well developed include Michigan, Maryland, Connecticut, Wisconsin, Kentucky, North Carolina, and Illinois.

There seems to be a general tendency toward strengthening the governor's control over fiscal affairs. Very often this takes the form of fiscal integration in a department of finance and administration, headed by a gubernatorial appointee, and bringing together responsibilities for budget, central accounting, purchasing, and personnel. About 25 states have central departments of this type.

Some states, however, have developed reasonably successful budgetary procedures which are far outside this pattern.[16] In Texas, since 1949, executive budgeting responsibility has been shared with a Budget Board headed by the Lieutenant Governor, with the speaker of the House and six other legislators as board members. The Budget Board has a staff which conducts joint hearings with the staff of the executive budget office; together the two work on special budgetary assignments.[17] In California there is a strong budget staff attached to the governor's office, but budget review here is supplemented by the Legislative Auditor and his staff. The Auditor prepares a separate and lengthy review of the governor's budget, for independent submission to the legislature.[18]

Organizational diversity among the budget offices in the states is ex-

[14] Eugene R. Elkins, *State Fiscal Organization in West Virginia*, West Virginia University, Morgantown, 1954, pp. 45–46.
[15] Frank M. Landers and Howard D. Hamilton, "A Survey of State Budget Agencies," *Public Finance*, Vol. VIII, 1953, p. 400.
[16] American cities likewise have diversified patterns of budgetary responsibilities. In municipalities with a "strong-mayor" charter the chief executive will typically supervise the preparation and submission of the budget. City managers invariably have responsibility for the budget. But the recent mayor-manager systems do not uniformly give budget review authority to the manager. (See Wallace S. Sayre, "The General Manager Idea for Large Cities," *Public Administration Review*, Autumn 1954, pp. 253–258.)
[17] Vernon A. McGee, "A Legislative Approach to State Budgeting," *State Government*, August 1953, pp. 200–204.
[18] Robert A. Walker and Floyd A. Cave, *How California is Governed*, Dryden Press, New York, 1953, p. 138; Joseph P. Harris, "Needed Reforms in the Federal Budget System," *Public Administration Review*, Autumn 1952, p. 247.

ceeded only by their diversity of responsibilities. In Maryland, for example, budgeting is joined with centralized purchasing in a Department of Budget and Procurement. In Virginia the maintenance of buildings and grounds is a part of the duties of the budget office. There are also differences, even among the stronger budget offices, in the extent to which economic and fiscal planning is merged with the budget process. The budget offices in New York and California probably come closest to such a unification of staff responsibilities. In other states fiscal planning is more likely to be undertaken by the governor and his immediate staff, or directly by the governor in consultation with legislative leaders, and with little staff assistance.

On one point there is almost complete uniformity among the states. Wherever there is a budget office, it has statutory responsibility for organization and methods studies. Unfortunately, the lack of staff sometimes prevents the performance of this duty.

Perhaps the only generalization that can safely be made about the implementation of the budget function in governments in the United States is the one which Rowland Egger suggested in discussing budgeting in Virginia: "Power is not enough." Regardless of organizational patterns, and regardless of the statutory authority possessed by a central budget office, it is staff that counts.[19] The effectiveness of budgeting depends almost entirely on the competence of the staff.

II. THE U. S. BUREAU OF THE BUDGET

The evolution of the Bureau of the Budget since 1921 can be described in terms of the changes which have occurred in the performance of the two major attributes of budget preparation—program review and management improvement. The emergence of the Bureau's significance in program review is synonymous with the emergence of the Executive Office of the President in the federal government. In management improvement the Bureau's responsibility has changed over the years from a narrow concern with efficiency and economy to a broader concern for effective administration.

A. DEVELOPMENT OF THE BUDGET FUNCTION

The origins of the United States budget system were examined in Chapter 1, where it was pointed out that the Budget and Accounting Act of 1921 was the combined product of a strong retrenchment movement directed toward the federal government and a reform movement de-

[19] Rowland Egger, "Power Is Not Enough," *State Government,* August 1940, pp. 149–151; 160–162.

signed to make all government more responsible and responsive. During the first decade in the history of the Bureau the former influence predominated. The first director, General Charles G. Dawes, conceived the role of the Bureau to be:

> . . . simply a business organization whose activities are devoted constantly to the consideration of how money appropriated by Congress can be made to go as far as possible toward the accomplishment of the objects of legislation. If it functions properly, it has not and can never have any purpose but that of the Executive and Congress in seeking the imposition, throughout the government administration, of correct business principles in routine business administration.[20]

And further,

> . . . one must remember that the Bureau of the Budget is concerned only with the humbler and routine business of government. Unlike cabinet officers, it is concerned with no questions of policy, save that of economy and efficiency. No cabinet officer on the bridge with the President, advising as to what direction the ship of state should sail—concerned with matters of policy of the highest importance, but at the same time under our Constitution charged with responsibility for a limited portion of the common machinery of the ship—will properly serve the captain of the ship or its passengers, the public, if he resents the call of the Director of the Budget from the stoke hole, put there by the captain to see that coal is not wasted.[21]

In his relations with departments and agencies General Dawes attempted to draw sharp lines between that which was policy and that which was administration, and to confine activities to the latter, to emphasize the "impartial, impersonal and non-political" character of the Bureau. Sometimes it was difficult to maintain this distinction. There were occasions when Dawes found it necessary to conceive his responsibilities more broadly.[22]

Regardless of Dawes' occasional long-run and broader interests, the immediate emphasis was to see that "coal is not wasted." To this end, a large number of interdepartmental committees were organized, such as the Federal Liquidation Board, the Federal Purchasing Board, and the Federal Traffic Board. A Business Organization of the Government met in Washington twice a year. This was made up of all department and agency heads and bureau chiefs, and their budget and finance officers.

[20] Charles G. Dawes, *The First Year of the Budget of the United States,* Harper & Brothers, New York, 1923, p. 118.

[21] *Ibid.,* p. xi. Both of the foregoing quotations are cited by Vincent J. Browne, *The Control of the Public Budget,* Public Affairs Press, Washington, 1949, pp. 91, 93.

[22] See Fritz Morstein Marx, "The Bureau of the Budget: Its Evolution and Present Role, I," *American Political Science Review,* August 1945, p. 675; Don K. Price, "General Dawes and Executive Staff Work," *Public Administration Review,* Summer 1951, pp. 167–172.

The meetings were addressed by the President and the Director of the Bureau, who reviewed accomplishments in retrenchment and stressed the possibilities for new reductions.[23] Outside Washington, in cities where federal agencies were operating, there were Federal Business Associations for the exchange of information on techniques for economy. Each department and agency of the government submitted an annual report on the savings which had been effected during the year.[24]

Special clubs were set up among federal employees, with membership restricted to those who effected reductions in expenditures. These had such names as the One Per Cent Club, the Loyal Order of Woodpeckers, and the Correspondence Club, and were dedicated to the zealous encouragement of retrenchment.[25] All of these activities were in addition to the work of the Coordinating Service and the Bureau of Efficiency, which operated independently of the Bureau of the Budget during this period.[26]

It is difficult to assess the significance of this tremendous emphasis on retrenchment in isolation from other political and economic influences at work during this period. The record itself is very impressive. Federal expenditures in fiscal 1921 were $5.1 billion, and in fiscal 1922 were $3.4 billion. The Dawes approach to the responsibilities of the Bureau of the Budget epitomized the dominant sentiments of the time and reinforced them. Even though the American economy was not working particularly well in these first years—there was first inflation and then unemployment in 1921–1923—this did not lead to vigorous and expanding governmental programs. Instead, the feeling toward government was one of apathy. This was a period which Pendleton Herring has described as one when we raised a tired feeling to the dignity of national policy.[27]

[23] See, for example, the *Second Annual Report of the Director of the Bureau of the Budget,* Washington, 1923, pp. 22–23, 30–32.

[24] The following is quoted from the Bureau's own report in 1924: "Pencils.— The bureau has given special attention to economy in this direction. Only one pencil at a time is now issued to any one and he is expected to turn in the unused portion of the last one received. The results justify the practice. Our item of expense for pencils is materially less." (*Third Annual Report of the Director of the Bureau of the Budget,* Washington, 1924, p. 217.)

[25] A. E. Buck, "Financial Control and Accountability," *Fiscal Management in the National Government,* President's Committee on Administrative Management, Washington, 1937, p. 5; *Sixth Annual Report of the Director of the Bureau of the Budget,* Washington, 1927, p. 17.

[26] Horace W. Wilkie, "Legal Basis for Increased Activities of the Federal Budget Bureau," *George Washington Law Review,* April 1943, pp. 268–269.

[27] "Executive-Legislative Responsibilities," *American Political Science Review,* December 1944, p. 1154.

Of General Dawes' success in establishing the prestige of the Bureau among executive agencies there can be no doubt; the Bureau got off to an extremely good start. Dawes enjoyed close personal relations with President Harding, and by his continued insistence on the Bureau's staff role in relation to the President was able to create for the Bureau a position independent of the Treasury Department, where it was organizationally located. At the same time, the physical attachment of the Bureau to the Treasury probably contributed to its prestige in the business community and to a general understanding, both inside and outside government, of the nature of its work. The concept of program review may sometimes be difficult to explain, but finance is more readily appreciated. In the next several years it was occasionally necessary to reassert the Bureau's position, but the authority of the President to submit the budget was secure. The departments and agencies were no longer free to present their own estimates directly to the Congress.[28]

Dawes had equal success in his relations with the Congress. The work of the appropriations committees was reduced; Congressmen came to rely on the estimates as presented. This is evidenced by a statement of the chairman of the Senate Committee on Appropriations in 1923:

> The Budget law has demonstrated its worth. It helps separate the chaff from the grain. It gives accuracy, as well as integrity, to estimates, which results in less work on the part of Congress. Under the old system congressional committees were obliged to spend a great amount of time on extravagant and questionable estimates. . . . Now that estimates mean something, the work of all is accelerated.[29]

Dawes left the Bureau of the Budget after only one year, but the imprint of his philosophy continued to dominate during the succeeding decade—not alone because of Dawes himself, but because this approach to the role and functions of the Bureau was appropriate to the 1920's. It was in keeping with this philosophy that the Bureau staff itself continued to be small—numbering from 30 to 40; for the Bureau, parsimony began at home. The major criticism which can be directed against the

---

[28] In 1925 President Coolidge stated to a meeting of the Business Organization of the Government, "At our last meeting I had occasion to call attention to the fact that under the law the only lawful estimates are those which the Chief Executive transmits to Congress. . . . in a few instances officials of the executive branch of the government advocated before the committees of Congress the appropriation of amounts in excess of those recommended in the executive estimates. Both the letter and the spirit of the budget and accounting act prohibit such action." (Quoted in Buck, *Public Budgeting*, p. 361).

[29] Francis E. Warren in the *Congressional Record*, March 4, 1923, p. 5601, quoted in Edward H. Hobbs, *Behind the President*, Public Affairs Press, Washington, 1954, p. 27.

Dawes approach is the failure of the Bureau to take the initiative in governmental reorganization.[30]   This could have been done within the scope of the budgeting philosophy of that period.

From this time and into the 1930's the Bureau of the Budget continued to conceive its role primarily as that of management improvement, to be accomplished by a budget review which emphasized reductions in expenditures.   Even the New Deal did not at first bring a change in the Bureau's role, nor an increase in its staff.   Many of the emergency relief and recovery programs in the first years after 1933, in fact, by-passed the Bureau.   Responsibilities for public works planning and coordinating, which might have been lodged here, were given to newly created agencies, such as the National Resources Committee and its successor agency, the National Resources Planning Board.   During these years the Bureau came to operate more nearly like a Treasury bureau, and less like a staff agency to the President.

The change came with the monumental report of the President's Committee on Administrative Management, the Reorganization Act of 1939, and the subsequent executive orders which moved the Bureau from the Treasury to the Executive Office and changed it from an agency concerned with management improvement in a narrow sense to an agency concerned with program review.[31]   These changes were, of course, the outgrowth of an enlarged variety and quantity of federal programs in the 1930's and the belated recognition that improved mechanisms for governance were required.   The Committee made an outstanding contribution to this end by a careful analysis of the President's role as general manager of the executive agencies.   Its recommended solution, in large part adopted, strengthened the whole structure and operations of the federal government.[32]

The philosophy underlying these changes was that presidential leadership must be supported by more adequate staff, with a view to improving the President's capacity for effective management and for policy formulation.   The far-reaching implications of a strengthened Executive Office

[30] Marx, *American Political Science Review*, August 1945, pp. 676–677, 683.

[31] A report which in many respects paralleled that of the Committee on Administrative Management was submitted by the Brookings Institution in 1937 to the Senate Select Committee to Investigate the Executive Agencies (*Senate Report* 1275, 75th Cong., 1st sess.).

[32] President's Committee on Adminstrative Management, *Administrative Management in the Government of the United States*, Washington, 1937, esp. pp. 15–20.   The statute authorizing executive reorganization was enacted by Congress in 1939 (*P.L.* 19, 76th Cong., 1st sess.); Reorganization Plan No. 1 was transmitted to the Congress April 25, 1939; *Executive Order* 8248, September 8, 1939, established the internal structure of the Executive Office.

have been adequately and extensively discussed in the literature; only the budgetary implications need be examined here.[33]

The importance of the Bureau of the Budget as a staff agency was clearly set forth by the President's Committee in 1937. The following quotation is representative of its thinking:

> If the Bureau of the Budget is to be developed into a serviceable tool for administrative management to aid the President in the exercise of over-all control, it needs greater resources and better techniques. . . . The Director of the Bureau of the Budget is one of the few Government officers in a position to advise the President from an over-all, as opposed to a bureau or departmental, point of view. He should therefore be relieved to the greatest possible extent from the minor details of administration. He should be released for duties of maximum importance to the President. . . . The Bureau of the Budget as a managerial agency of the President should therefore be made responsible for the execution, as well as the formulation, of the budget as a national fiscal plan.[34]

In recommending that budgeting be regarded as a Presidential function, the Committee implicitly rejected a proposal of its task force that the Bureau be strengthened within the Treasury Department.[35] This latter had been urged on the ground that there should be an organizational grouping of executive agencies to correspond with their functional activities, and that therefore budgeting, tax policy formulation, revenue collection, and accounting should be brought together.[36] The Committee did not specifically recommend that the Bureau be transferred from the Treasury Department, but its stress on the presidential aspect of budgeting leaves no doubt that this was regarded as more important than a grouping of financial functions.

The transformation of the Bureau of the Budget from an agency with narrowly conceived functions to one with broad responsibilities for pro-

[33] See, for example, Arthur W. MacMahon, "The Future Organizational Pattern of the Executive Branch," *American Political Science Review*, December 1944, pp. 1179–1191; Fritz Morstein Marx, *The President and His Staff Services*, Public Administration Service, Chicago, 1947, pp. 1–16; George A. Graham, "The Presidency and the Executive Office of the President," *Journal of Politics*, November 1950, pp. 599–621; Clinton L. Rossiter, "The Constitutional Significance of the Executive Office of the President," *American Political Science Review*, December 1949, pp. 1206–1217; Emmerich, *Essays on Federal Reorganization*, pp. 61–90; Don K. Price, "Staffing the Presidency," *American Political Science Review*, December 1946, pp. 1154–1168.

[34] President's Committee on Administrative Management, *op. cit.*, pp. 17–18.

[35] Buck, *Fiscal Management in the National Government*, pp. 1–30.

[36] A similar proposal was repeated a decade later to the Commission on the Organization of the Executive Branch of the Government (Hoover Commission), and again rejected. See Task Force Report, *Fiscal, Budgeting, and Accounting Activities*, Washington, 1949, p. 41.

gram review and the improvement of management was accomplished within about two years' time, under the direction of Harold D. Smith.[37] New staff was employed; from fiscal 1940 to fiscal 1943 the Bureau's appropriation increased from $670,000 to almost $2,000,000. By the end of 1940 five divisions were established: (1) Estimates, for the review of department and agency budget submissions; (2) Fiscal, for the economic analysis of programs; (3) Legislative Reference, for clearing legislative proposals of agencies and departments and reviewing their reports on legislation enacted but not approved by the President; (4) Administrative Management, for conducting studies of organization and work methods; (5) Statistical Standards, for coordinating federal statistical programs. This divisional organization continued without important modification until 1952.[38]

The expanded and strengthened Executive Office of the President and the Bureau of the Budget therein were put to a major test by the organizational and program problems faced during the defense period, beginning in the summer of 1940. From this time and continuing through the first two years of World War II, the Bureau discharged major assignments in establishing emergency agencies, in planning and budgeting for military outlays, and in formulating programs for inflation control.[39] As war mobilization proceeded, the Bureau began to share an increased number of these responsibilities with other agencies in the Executive Office—the Office of Economic Stabilization, the Office of War Mobilization, and its successor agency, the Office of War Mobilization and Reconversion. World War II tested and proved the soundness of the Executive Office philosophy and the role of the Bureau as a major agency of presidential management.

In the years since World War II the Bureau of the Budget has not changed in size, nor in the scope and variety of its activities. The changes that have occurred are those of emphasis and can be described in terms of a deepening of its more traditional functions and a narrowing of its activities in program planning and review. The narrowing that has taken place has not meant a constriction in the Bureau's activities; rather, its program influence and coordinating role has been

[37] For Smith's approach to budgeting see *The Management of Your Government*, McGraw-Hill Book Company, New York, 1945; Arthur N. Holcombe, "Over-all Financial Planning through the Bureau of the Budget," *Public Administration Review*, Spring 1941, pp. 225–230.

[38] For a discussion of the responsibilities of these divisions see Fritz Morstein Marx, "The Bureau of the Budget: Its Evolution and Present Role, II," *American Political Science Review*, October 1945, pp. 880–893.

[39] See Bureau of the Budget, *The United States at War*, Washington, 1946, pp. 43–101, 235–273.

shared more widely with other agencies, particularly with agencies in the Executive Office.

The deepening that has occurred has been primarily the product of specific legislation that strengthened the Bureau in the performance of its task of budget review and execution. In 1945 the Government Corporation Control Act gave to the Bureau authority to review the budget submissions of wholly owned government corporations; the estimates for these corporations became part of the President's budget. (*P.L.* 248, 79th Cong., 1st sess.). In 1950 the Budget and Accounting Procedures Act strengthened the President's authority, and therefore that of the Bureau, in budget classification and formalized the Bureau's role in the improvement of government accounting systems. (*P.L.* 784, 81st Cong., 2d sess.). The General Appropriation Act of 1951 gave the Bureau additional authority to apportion appropriations and to establish reserves against appropriations. (*P.L.* 759, 81st Cong., 2d sess.). Beyond this statutory strengthening, the Bureau's role in legislative clearance has become more firmly established in recent years, and its authority to review all Executive Orders continues to be a significant general management responsibility.[40]

The narrowing or sharing of the Bureau's responsibility for program review is the result of the creation of additional agencies within the Executive Office. The first of these, apart from the wartime agencies, was the Council of Economic Advisers, established under the Employment Act of 1946. (*P.L.* 304, 79th Cong., 2d sess.). The Council developed a close pattern of working relations with the Budget Bureau, and in particular with the Fiscal Division. At the same time, the Council initiated a separate pattern of working relations with agencies and departments, with the President, and with the White House staff in the development of economic policy. The creation of the National Security Council and the National Security Resources Board in 1947 (*P.L.* 253, 80th Cong., 1st sess.) provided further agencies of program planning and coordination, both for the military and for related civilian programs. These were formally brought into the Executive Office in 1949. With the outbreak of hostilities in Korea, the Office of Defense Mobilization was added to the Executive Office, again with program planning duties (*Executive Order* 10193, December 16, 1950).

The 1949 recommendations of the Commission on Organization of the Executive Branch of the Government (Hoover Commission) un-

[40] The only other postwar statute affecting the Bureau's power was the Classification Act of 1949, which required the Director to enforce a systematic review by agencies of their operations and to maintain efficiency award systems in each agency (*P.L.* 429, 81st Cong., 1st sess.). This authority was transferred to the Civil Service Commission in 1954.

doubtedly contributed to this narrowing of the Bureau's program review and planning functions, and to a concentration on estimates work. A task force of the Commission filed a report which was sharply critical of what it regarded as nonbudgetary activities.[41] The Commission itself, in a tone not quite as sharp, recommended that the work of the Administrative Management, Fiscal, and Estimates Divisions be coordinated to place greater emphasis on the review and revision of estimates.[42]

CHART 9
Executive Office of the President, Bureau of the Budget

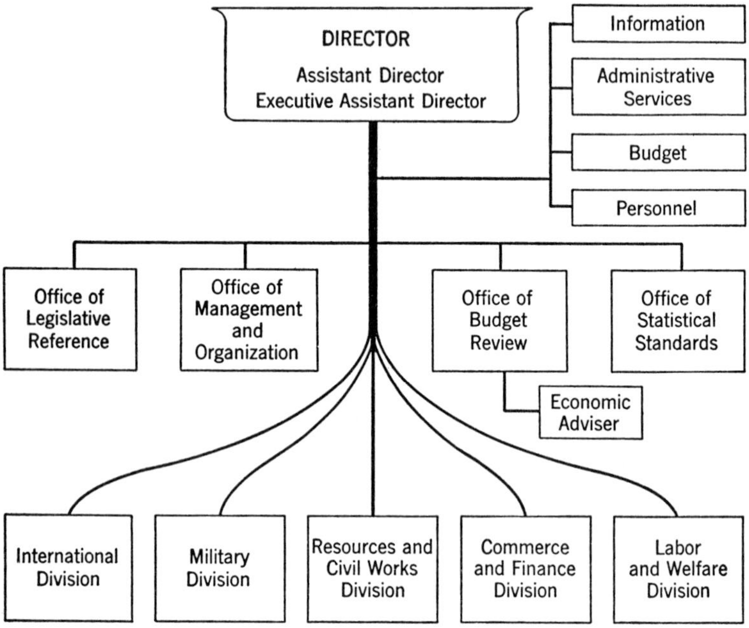

Possibly in response to this recommendation, and perhaps in implicit recognition that the Bureau's program review functions had come to be more widely shared with other agencies, the Director of the Bureau effected an internal reorganization in 1952. The result was an organizational structure that emphasized the estimates function. The Fiscal Division was abolished, and personnel from this division and from Administrative Management were transferred to five realigned divisions combining estimates, management improvement, and economic analysis. The resulting organization is shown in Chart 9.

[41] *Fiscal, Budgeting, and Accounting Activities, op. cit.,* esp. pp. 45–60.

[42] Commission on Organization of the Executive Branch of the Government, *Budgeting and Accounting,* p. 23.

B. The Organization of the Bureau of the Budget

The structure of the Bureau of the Budget is a relatively simple one, as Chart 9 shows. The basic framework is five program divisions and four offices, plus the "housekeeping services"—budget, personnel, administrative services, and information. Until 1953 the Bureau supported a limited field service; this was abolished by the Director in that year.[43] During World War II a Committee on Records of War Administration was organized, staffed by a small unit in the Bureau of the Budget. This was reactivated during the Korean emergency under the designation Defense History and operated for a short period under the Bureau's auspices as a unit outside the basic division and office structure.

The five program divisions are the major channels through which the Bureau conducts its normal working relations with agencies and departments in the federal government.[44] Each of these divisions is in charge of reviewing estimates and following program developments in agencies and departments grouped in broad but roughly homogeneous areas. Division personnel may work on a wide range of assignments, including management improvement, proposed changes in agency functions, and program review and coordination—all activities related to and contingent on the review of estimates. In 1955 about 216 out of some 430 Bureau employees were assigned to the divisions.

The four offices conduct activities which are Bureau-wide in character. The Office of Legislative Reference reviews for the President all legislative proposals emanating from agencies and departments, and coordinates the views of agencies on enrolled bills.[45] This responsibility dates back to 1921, and although it has been subject to a number of vicissitudes, it is now very well established as a major Budget assignment. Its performance requires close liaison with the White House. Its end product is a determination that a legislative proposal is or is not "in accordance with the President's program." Legislative Reference, particularly as it applies to new legislation, is thus a staff agency for forging the President's program and enforcing discipline within the executive branch in its re-

---

[43] For a description and analysis of the activities of the Bureau's field service see Earl Latham, "Executive Management and the Federal Field Service," *Public Administration Review,* Winter 1945, pp. 16–27.

[44] U. S. Bureau of the Budget, *Functions and Organization,* Washington, 1952, p. 2 (processed).

[45] For a historical account and appraisal of this power see Richard E. Neustadt, "Presidency and Legislation: The Growth of Central Clearance," *American Political Science Review,* September 1954, pp. 641–671; Hobbs, *Behind the President,* pp. 56–62; Carl R. Sapp, "Executive Assistance in the Legislative Process," *Public Administration Review,* Winter 1946, pp. 10–19.

lations with the Congress. The staff of the Office of Legislative Reference is small, numbering about 13 professionals. Necessarily this means that Legislative Reference must work closely with the program divisions of the Bureau; legislative clearance thus serves as a coordinating influence within the Bureau.

The Office of Management and Organization numbers about 28 professional employees. This office has dual and interlocking lines of communication and assignment. The first line runs through the divisions of the Bureau toward specific management improvement studies, which may be conducted within the Bureau divisions or by agencies in cooperation with budget examiners in the divisions. The other line of work assignments is interagency in character; the Office of Management and Organization conducts government-wide surveys, which may embrace not only work methods and organization but also personnel, fiscal, and accounting activities. All reorganization plans which the President transmits to Congress are prepared or received by this office.[46]

The Office of Budget Review, and the Economic Adviser attached thereto, assumes leadership within the Bureau for the preparation of the budget message, the *Federal Budget in Brief*, and other documents. This office undertakes the initial preparation of the policy statement and budget assumptions to accompany the Call to Estimates, and serves as the focal point in relations with other agencies in the development of the Administration's economic policy, and with congressional committees concerned with economic and fiscal policy. The Office of Budget Review also has charge of the classification of expenditures used in the budget document, and appropriation structure and language. The legal adviser for the Bureau is located here. In general, this office has responsibility for a uniform application of the Director's and the President's budgetary policies.

The Office of Statistical Standards reviews and approves all forms and reporting plans used by the federal government for gathering data.[47] Questionnaires and other statistical forms may not be issued to the public without prior approval by Statistical Standards.[48] Although originally charged with a reduction in the number of forms and questionnaires

[46] For a discussion of the importance of the reorganization plans in relation to the prestige of the Bureau, see Charles S. Hyneman, *Bureaucracy in a Democracy*, Harper & Brothers, New York, 1950, pp. 345–346.

[47] The first federal coordinating agency in statistics was the Central Statistical Board, created in 1933. This activity was transferred to the Bureau in the reorganization of 1939. See Stuart A. Rice, "Coordination of Federal Statistical Programs," *American Journal of Sociology*, July 1944, pp. 22–28.

[48] For a description of the legal basis for this authority see Wilkie, *George Washington Law Review*, April 1943, pp. 295–297.

issued by government agencies, over the years most of the work of this office has come to be concerned with the improvement of data-gathering procedures and the development of standard definitions and classifications. Very often the examination of an agency's data-gathering program involves budgetary considerations, and on all such questions personnel in Statistical Standards become, in effect, budget examiners.

This description of the organizational structure of the Bureau of the Budget in terms of assigned responsibilities of divisions and offices conveys an impression of compartmentalization and segmentation which does not actually exist. Organizational lines within the Bureau have always been reasonably flexible, and none except the most critical observers have accused the Bureau of lack of internal teamwork or *esprit de corps*. Although the Bureau is wholly committed to the Executive Office philosophy, it has necessarily developed a concern for its own institutional status and a natural instinct to preserve itself regardless of the political party which happens to control the White House or the Congress.[49]

C. BUDGETING AND PROGRAM PLANNING

An evaluation of the role and effectiveness of the U. S. Bureau of the Budget must look beyond the boxes on an organizational chart and the sums of money saved by critical budget examiners, to an analysis of the relationship of budgeting to executive program planning. This relationship will be examined first in connection with the Administration's fiscal policy. Some general conclusions about program planning in the Executive Office will then be suggested.

The core functions of the Bureau—the review of estimates and management improvement—do not in themselves provide either the occasion or the mechanism for the development of the Administration's fiscal policy. Management improvement is concerned mainly with the efficiency of governmental work methods, and only secondarily with the programs themselves. Similarly, the review process centers attention on the level of the program and on program interrelationships, but not always on program development. An examination of the specific area of fiscal policy will serve to make this distinction clear.

In accordance with the definition of fiscal policy suggested earlier, there are embraced here the government's activities in taxation, expenditures, and debt management. (See Chapter 3.) Monetary controls are administered very largely by the Board of Governors of the Federal Reserve System. The Board, quasi-governmental in character, is

[49] Arthur Maass, "In Accord with the Program of the President?" *Public Policy*, Graduate School of Public Administration, Cambridge, 1953, p. 83.

outside the pattern of Budget influence and, indeed, sometimes outside the pattern of presidential influence.

Budget review as it relates to taxation and debt management illustrates the limitations of the estimates process as a means to the formulation of fiscal policy. In the federal government the Administration's tax policy has traditionally been proposed by the Secretary of the Treasury; the Secretary is regarded as the Administration's spokesman in this area. To assist him in the research and analysis which goes into the tax program, the Secretary has an Analysis Staff. The estimates for this unit are reviewed by budget examiners in the Bureau of the Budget, but the review is concerned with the numbers of professional staff, with their work load and their interrelations with other agencies. The examiners are not concerned with the policy recommendations that emerge from the research of the Analysis Staff. This is regarded as internal to the Treasury and not subject to budget review. The same situation obtains in the review of Treasury activities concerned with the management of the public debt. It is appropriate for budget examiners to ask questions about the numbers of persons engaged in the formulation of debt management policies, but it is not appropriate to ask questions about the policies themselves. Insofar as tax policy and debt management policy are to be brought into a coordinated Administration fiscal policy, this must be accomplished by other mechanisms.

For expenditures, program planning and coordination by the Bureau of the Budget is much more complete. Here the traditional review procedure and legislative clearance are effective in uncovering conflict areas and differences in viewpoint among departments. The Bureau can then arrange conferences for reconciliation and secure a workable degree of harmony among agencies, both in cases where it is important simply to establish agreement and in cases where major policy issues are at stake.[50] This kind of program coordination, always limited and bound by existing legislation and by strongly organized interest groups, is and must be a necessary accompaniment of budget-making. The budget policy statement, the Call to Estimates, and the preparation of the budget message all provide further occasions for ensuring harmony where expenditures are involved.

In some areas program coordination by the reduction of conflict has been highly effective, as in the construction and operation of federal hospitals, formally coordinated by the Bureau through a Federal Board of Hospitalization. In other areas of expenditure where program coordination is equally needed, the Bureau has been much less successful, as in resource development projects (see Chapter 8).

[50] Maass, *op. cit.*, pp. 80–82.

CENTRAL BUDGET OFFICE

CENTRAL BUDGET OFFICE

301

In these program activities the Bureau is necessarily in the position of a policy-reviewing agency, not a policy-proposing agency. Coordination in terms of eliminating conflict and securing assent within the executive branch certainly has a positive value, and the line between program development and program coordination is often a very thin one. But the line is there, and the Bureau of the Budget, effective as it is in coordination, is not in the same position with respect to program development.

As a consequence of the way in which the Bureau has evolved and the limitations inherent in budget review as a mechanism for program development, the economic policy of the Administration must emerge from a substantially larger framework than can be provided by the Bureau. This framework must not be bound by the economizing orientation which seems inescapably to mold the outlook of budget examiners.[51] It may be that this combination of circumstances—the inherent limitations on the economic policies that can be reviewed by the Bureau, the existence of strong policy-proposing agencies outside the framework of the Executive Office, and the inevitable tendency to an economizing outlook—makes it impossible for Budget to assume the leadership in economic planning and fiscal policy. Whatever the reasons, the fact is that the Bureau is now but one, and not necessarily the most important one, of several agencies concerned with the formulation of the Administration's fiscal policy.

The Bureau of the Budget does not now possess, nor is it likely to possess, a broad range of command over budgeting and fiscal policy. There is no discernible trend in this direction. The pattern of the Executive Office has moved quite the other way.

Apart from the emergency agencies in World War II, the significant step that started the Executive Office down the path of internal proliferation was the establishment, in 1946, of the Council of Economic Advisors as an agency independent of Budget. The CEA immediately took over, as it was required to do by statute, a number of the responsibilities formerly undertaken by the Fiscal Division of the Bureau. CEA, as might be expected, had many growing pains and some internal dissension in working out its relations with other agencies, with the President, and with the Congress.[52] Not only has it survived, however, but it ap-

[51] Some critics contend that its emphasis on economy and the conservation of funds and its concern for institutional survival makes the Bureau of the Budget incapable of exerting leadership in the development of positive economic and fiscal programs. See Herman Miles Somers, *Presidential Agency*, Harvard University Press, Cambridge, 1950, p. 212; Maass, *op. cit.*, p. 82.

[52] The literature on CEA and its organizational role is voluminous. See, for example, Edwin G. Nourse, *Economics in the Public Service*, Harcourt, Brace &

pears to have been strengthened by the change of Administration in 1953 and will continue to be a major factor in the formulation of federal fiscal policy. The trend toward proliferation of authority over economic and fiscal policy within the Executive Office is further evidenced by the responsibilities of the National Security Council and the Office of Defense Mobilization, and by the recent tendency to create special commissions and planning groups inside and outside the Executive Office.

The existing structure of the Executive Office does not always provide all of the mechanism for positive program planning. On numerous occasions the Administration has established additional machinery solely in the interests of coordination. In 1950 the Secretary of Agriculture was designated as the coordinator for the Administration's economic policy, and was assigned specific responsibility in that year for reconciling the budget message, the state of the union message, and the *Economic Report*.[53] In 1953 the President created an Advisory Board on Economic Growth and Stability, headed by the chairman of the Council of Economic Advisers and made up of selected heads of departments and agencies.[54] This was undertaken in order to make the " . . . work of the Council of Economic Advisers more effective at the top policy level of the executive branch. . . . " In 1954 a subcabinet of deputy secretaries of departments was established in the interests of coordination.

It may be that the Council of Economic Advisers will eventually become a general staff for fiscal and economic planning, but its effectiveness to date has been limited by its lack of operating roots. At the same time, the Bureau of the Budget has become even more firmly grounded in the review of program expenditures but has moved away from economic policy formulation. Its program-formulation responsibilities are exercised largely by way of the legislative reference function. The other significant area for the exercise of positive responsibility— the preparation of reorganization plans—is episodic and has only occasional relation to the continuous process of program development.

The question which remains is this: Are additional mechanisms re-

Company, New York, 1953; Edwin G. Nourse and Bertram M. Gross, "The Role of the Council of Economic Advisers," *American Political Science Review*, April 1948, pp. 283–295, Hobbs, *Behind the President*, pp. 94–124; Bertram M. Gross and John P. Lewis, "The President's Economic Staff during the Truman Administration," *American Political Science Review*, March 1954, pp. 114–130.

[53] Nourse, *op. cit.*, 268–269.

[54] See Message to Accompany Reorganization Plan No. 9, *Economic Report of the President*, Washington, 1954, p. 137. For a description of the work of CEA under the Eisenhower Administration see Ronald C. Hood, "Reorganizing the Council of Economic Advisers," *Political Science Quarterly*, September 1954, pp. 413–437.

quired for the federal government, and particularly for the Executive Office—mechanisms to accomplish what, for want of a better term, may be described as "an integrated economic and fiscal policy"? Such integration would require policy review to assure harmony among taxation, expenditure, and debt management, and would ideally go beyond this to policy development. Such integration would seek to bring together, at far more points than is now done, the Administration's economic policy and the process of budget review.

Many suggestions have been made for such additional mechanisms. Some of these pertain only to fiscal and monetary policy.[55] Some call for the creation of a new Office of Economic Coordination within the Executive Office.[56] Other critics have suggested that new coordinating mechanisms be established for a program planning and review broader in scope than that customarily embraced under economic and fiscal policy.[57] Others argue for an attempt to restore cabinet leadership with collective responsibility.[58] Still others contend very forcibly that efforts to strengthen executive organization for economic planning are futile without corresponding and parallel emphasis on further coordinating mechanisms running between the Administration and the Congress.[59] Finally, there are those who would strengthen the programing responsibilities of the Bureau of the Budget itself.[60]

Proposals to establish additional mechanisms to achieve the coordination of budgeting and fiscal policy or the integration of economic and fiscal policy or positive program development sound attractive. In point of fact, coordination, integration, and program development are elusive concepts; regardless of how much specific content they may comprise on particular occasions, they are extremely difficult to achieve. This much is certain: Any effort to broaden the concept of budget and program review in the federal government cannot be undertaken in isolation from the whole pattern of policy formulation by the Executive.

[55] A number of economists have advanced organizational proposals designed to effect closer working relations in the monetary and fiscal areas. See, for example, Eric W. Lawson, "A Federal Department of Finance—A Proposal," *Journal of Finance*, March 1952, pp. 1–9; G. L. Bach, *Federal Reserve Policy-Making*, Alfred A. Knopf, New York, 1950, pp. 186–207.

[56] Thomas I. Emerson, "Administration of Stabilization Policy," *Income Stabilization for a Developing Democracy*, Max F. Millikan, ed., Yale University Press, New Haven, 1953, pp. 691–701.

[57] Somers, *Presidential Agency*, pp. 203–233.

[58] Herman Finer, "The Hoover Commission Reports," *Political Science Quarterly*, September 1949, pp. 405–419.

[59] R. G. Tugwell, "The Utility of the Future in the Present," *Public Administration Review*, Winter 1948, pp. 49–59.

[60] Smithies, *The Budgetary Process in the United States*, pp. 213–222.

The evident need is for national planning in accordance with the definition of the term used by Millett:

National planning today simply means careful management in reviewing and timing government activity as a whole. Just as the purpose of national budgeting was to bring about greater orderliness and central review of expenditure programs, so national planning means the same type of central management for the underlying plans upon which expenditures are based. . . . National planning is synonymous with Presidential management.[61]

This kind of national planning and the organizational structure necessary for its effectuation will come, belatedly perhaps, when the pressures from citizenry point out that its absence is an expensive luxury which can no longer be afforded. It does not emerge when the price level is reasonably stable, when there is little unemployment, when international crises are confined to police actions.

It is not possible to forecast the future organizational pattern that will produce this kind of national planning, nor the place of budgeting therein. On the basis of experience, it is safe to predict that institutional arrangements within the Executive Office will continue to be flexible, varying in accordance with changing needs and the changing personalities of the presidents and their immediate advisers. It is also safe to predict that budget review will eventually be broadened and merged more specifically and more continuously with other aspects of executive programing.

[61] John D. Millett, *The Process and Organization of Government Planning,* Columbia University Press, New York, 1947, pp. 179–180.

Selected Bibliography

Browne, Vincent J., *The Control of the Public Budget,* Public Affairs Press, Washington, 1949, pp. 91–164.

Buck, A. E., "Financial Control and Accountability," *Fiscal Management in the National Government,* President's Committee on Administrative Management, Washington, 1937, pp. 1–30.

——— *Public Budgeting,* Harper & Brothers, New York, 1929, pp. 283–300, 339–370.

——— *The Budget in Governments of Today,* Macmillan Company, New York, 1934, pp. 79–99.

Chester, D. N., "Machinery of Government and Planning," *The British Economy 1945–1950,* G. D. N. Worswick, ed., Clarendon Press, Oxford, 1952, pp. 336–364.

Commission on Organization of the Executive Branch of the Government, Task

Force Report, *Fiscal, Budgeting, and Accounting Activities*, Washington, 1949, pp. 35–84.

——— *Budgeting and Accounting*, Washington, 1949, pp. 21–44.

Dawes, Charles G., *The First Year of the Budget of the United States*, Harper & Brothers, New York, 1923.

Egger, Rowland, "Power is Not Enough," *State Government*, August 1940, pp. 149–151, 160–162.

Gross, Bertram M., and John P. Lewis, "The President's Economic Staff During the Truman Administration," *American Political Science Review*, March 1954, pp. 114–130.

Hobbs, Edward H., *Behind the President*, Public Affairs Press, Washington, 1954, pp. 21–76.

Holcombe, Arthur N., "Over-All Financial Planning through the Bureau of the Budget," *Public Administration Review*, Spring 1941, pp. 225–230.

Hyneman, Charles S., *Bureaucracy in a Democracy*, Harper & Brothers, New York, 1950, pp. 325–354.

Landers, Frank M., and Howard D. Hamilton, "A Survey of State Budget Agencies," *Public Finance*, Vol. VIII, 1953, pp. 399–413.

Maass, Arthur, "In Accord with the Program of the President?" *Public Policy*, Graduate School of Public Administration, Cambridge, 1953, pp. 77–93.

Marx, Fritz Morstein, "The Bureau of the Budget: Its Evolution and Present Role," *American Political Science Review*, August 1945, pp. 653–684; October 1945, pp. 869–898.

——— *The President and His Staff Services*, Public Administration Service, Chicago, 1947.

Nash, Bradley D., *Staffing the Presidency*, National Planning Association, Washington, 1952.

Neustadt, Richard E., "Presidency and Legislation: The Growth of Central Clearance," *American Political Science Review*, September 1954, pp. 641–671.

Rawson, Robert H., "The Formulation of the Federal Budget," *Public Policy*, Graduate School of Public Administration, Cambridge, 1941, pp. 78–135.

Smithies, Arthur, *The Budgetary Process in the United States*, McGraw-Hill Book Company, New York, 1955, pp. 198–225.

Wilkie, Horace W., "Legal Basis for Increased Activities of the Federal Budget Bureau," *George Washington Law Review*, April 1943, pp. 254–301.

12.

Legislative authorization

The role of the legislature in budgeting is shaped by several coordinate influences. The first, in point of time, derives from executive authority, which proposes the programs that the legislature must review, modify, and adopt. The second derives from the internal organization of the legislative body, which will determine the importance attached to budgetary actions and the relationship between budgetary and other legislation. The third influence is the legislators themselves and their individual and collective interests and abilities in fiscal affairs.

The budget-making authority of the chief executive requires the assumption of responsibility for the integrity of the estimates as submitted, and for the analysis of program requirements and their translation into financial terms. It is the executive who will administer the programs that are eventually authorized. His budgetary review of all programs and policies in a systematic fashion helps to make executive authority commensurate with executive responsibility. At the same time, a budget system does not subtract from the authority of a legislature. Centralized executive responsibility for budget preparation and submission will facilitate budget authorization by the legislature and enable it to center attention on program review and policy considerations. This will avoid the segmentation of effort and attention to detail that would otherwise result. The legislature can be most effective when it brings its influence to bear on a budget which has already had careful review by the executive.

306

In almost all legislative bodies some kind of committee system is used. The committee which reviews the budget and makes recommendations thereon may be called the committee on estimates, the committee on ways and means, the committee on appropriations, or the committee on finance. Whatever its title, the quality of its work will be, in part, a product of the prestige it enjoys in relation to other legislative committees. Legislative budget-making will be of high quality and conscientiously done, and the budget committee will attract the best of legislative talent, only if the budget is a vehicle for important public policy decisions. Conversely, if most issues are decided by other, nonbudgetary committees, and if the budget committee is concerned only with regularizing decisions that are made elsewhere, legislative budget-making is not likely to be conducted at a high level.

Internal organization will influence a legislature's ability to coordinate fiscal and program aspects. It is much easier, for example, to secure this coordination with a unicameral organization. In counties and municipalities, where the legislature consists of but one body, there is very often a single finance committee, or at most a revenue committee and an appropriations committee. In contrast, a bicameral organization will typically have four fiscal committees, one for revenue and one for appropriations in each chamber. Moreover, independent deliberation by two chambers means that conference committees must be appointed for purposes of reconciliation. Unified consideration of the budget becomes difficult.

In the legislature, as in the executive, and probably not more so, budget-making is a political process, conducted in a political arena for political advantage. The legislature, like the budget, will reflect the integrating forces in a government which produce something that may be called city or state or national policy. The legislature, like the budget, will also reflect partisan interests and sectional interests. The budget is a periodic readjustment and reconciliation of these numerous and conflicting influences. Often, the apparent equilibrium is far from stable; accordingly, every budget will offer a new opportunity to modify and alter the relations among interests and regions. It is unlikely that major political realignments will occur in the process of budgetary review, but the promotion of "pet projects," vote trading, and some whittling away at the larger issues may take place. The knowledge that budget authorizations must necessarily be enacted sometime during the legislative session is a constant temptation to attach substantive legislation to a budget bill. These "riders" may be universally condemned by all financial experts, but they are certain to continue to provide an additional channel for political maneuvering in a dynamic society.

The budget as an expression of public policy reflects a variegated pattern of influences. Stephen K. Bailey, in summarizing an analysis of the passage of the Employment Act of 1946 by the United States Congress, stressed this unbelievable complexity:

> Legislative policy-making appears to be the result of a confluence of factors streaming from an almost endless number of tributaries: national experience, the contributions of social theorists, the clash of powerful economic interests, the quality of Presidential leadership, other institutional and personal ambitions and administrative arrangements in the Executive Branch, the initiative, effort, and ambitions of individual legislators and their governmental and non-governmental staffs, the policy commitments of political parties, and the predominant culture symbols in the minds of both leaders and followers in the Congress.[1]

Complex it is, but chaotic it is not. The stream of influences is endless and the final result may sometimes be in doubt. But in any legislative body, budget-making, like all policy-making, is a continuous process. It is always bounded by previously-enacted programs, by this year's level of operations, by pressures for restricting the scope of governmental activities, by the resources of taxpayers. These are very often measurable and predictable boundaries.

I. LEGISLATIVE RESPONSIBILITIES IN BUDGET-MAKING

The actions of a legislative body in authorizing the budget can be generally grouped under two heads: the formulation of policy, and the oversight of administration. Policy-making by legislatures can be separated, at least conceptually, into two subheads: the determination of programs and program levels, and what may be called the determination of the aggregates—the over-all relationship between revenues and expenditures. The actions of appropriations committees and legislative bodies will encompass all of these in varying proportions.

A. POLICY FORMULATION: AUTHORIZING PROGRAM LEVELS

The consideration and enactment of the budget by a legislature may not be the occasion upon which policy is made. In one of Winston Churchill's phrases, "finance is the servant and not the master." Financial policy is very often little more than a reflection of policies arrived at through nonfinancial procedures.

In the United States government and in most state governments the authorization of a program by a legislature precedes the appropriation of funds for the program. In every government, departments and agencies

[1] Stephen Kemp Bailey, *Congress Makes a Law*, Columbia University Press, New York, 1950, p. 236.

are established by statute and endowed with responsibilities which may be specifically or broadly defined by that statute. Where responsibilities are specifically defined, the authorizing statute, in effect, controls program level and appropriation. Where responsibilities are broadly defined, decision-making in the appropriating process is correspondingly broad.

These differences may be illustrated by example. A state legislature may enact and the governor may sign a measure to provide for the construction and operation of a specified number of hospitals. Further, the legislation may have been specific in terms of the kinds of facilities to be provided and the number of patients to be served. It may have included a cost figure. In this case the budget committee has little margin for decision-making, and its approval of the financial authorization is routine.

Conversely, the legislation may have been written in broad terms. In this case it is mandatory for the legislature's budget committee to approve funds for the hospital, but the budget committee will have latitude for decision-making about the number of patients to be served and the kinds of facilities to be provided. The budget committee, in effect, fills in the details of the original legislative intent, and these may be very significant details.

Once the hospitals are in operation, the administrator in charge must return to the legislature for an annual review and budget authorization. The administrator now has experience in the implementation of the original legislative intent as expressed in the statute and in the budget authorization. This experience and the administrator's proposals for its interpretation and modification are reviewed by the legislature's budget committee. The interrelationship among the original legislation, the subsequent budget authorizations, and the actions and proposals of the administrator—this continuous interpretation and reinterpretation of legislative intent—illustrates the continuous overlap of administrative and legislative authority.[2]

Appropriations actions by the United States Congress are replete with examples of the varying degrees of overlap of authority expressed in authorizing statutes, executive implementation, and the appropriation measure. Agricultural price support programs are controlled by statutes that prescribe the level of support to be undertaken and authorize the Commodity Credit Corporation to make the necessary purchases to hold farm prices at this level. The House and Senate Appropriations Committees have no practical authority in this area; to withhold funds would

[2] For a general discussion of this relationship see Bertram M. Gross, *The Legislative Struggle*, McGraw-Hill Book Company, New York, 1953, pp. 154–161.

be unthinkable. The statutory action controls the budget authorization and, in fact, price support programs are financed by a kind of budget authorization which does not pass through the hands of the appropriations committees.

A very different relationship between the basic statute and the budget authorization obtains for the national military establishment. Here the statutes are broad and seldom specify the number of troops to be maintained in any one year, the number of vessels to be floated, or the number of planes to be kept operative. These decisions are made in large measure by the appropriations committees, after examining the budgets of the Department of Defense, hearing the testimony and reviewing the operating experience of officials in the Department, and relating defense expenditures to over-all budgetary requests and revenues.[3]

Lying between the cases in which the authorizing statute controls the appropriating action and the cases that offer a virtual *carte blanche* are the many programs for which the kinds of operations are specified but not the level of operations. The National Bureau of Standards has continuing statutory responsibility for the development of standards of physical measurement in the fields of physics, mathematics, chemistry, metallurgy, and engineering. But specific projects are subject to annual review and decision in the budgetary process.

The fact that some programs are not subject to constant budgetary review and that government budgets thus come to be at least partially uncontrollable has been viewed with great concern by some authorities. Arthur Smithies, for example, feels that this is one of the most serious defects in budgetary procedure in the United States government. He suggests that financial considerations should be overriding and that the House Appropriations Committee should have authority to propose, in appropriations measures, amendments to substantive legislation.[4]

There is no doubt that strongly entrenched programs limit the over-all effectiveness of budgetary review. But in these circumstances "uncontrollable" is probably a misnomer. These outlays can be controlled, but they may be irreducible. In many cases programs are so well established, so strongly supported by interest groups, and so much a part of accepted public policy that frequent and searching budgetary review, extending to annual examination of substantive legislation, would be somewhat pointless. If there is widespread agreement, inside and outside the legislature, that veterans should receive pensions for service-connected disabilities,

[3] For an analysis of decision-making in the military appropriations process see Elias Huzar, *The Purse and the Sword,* Cornell University Press, Ithaca, 1950, esp. pp. 132–206.

[4] Arthur Smithies, *The Budgetary Process in the United States,* McGraw-Hill Book Company, New York, 1955, pp. 175–178. For case studies of agriculture and veterans' programs with a view to their uncontrollability, see pp. 360–391.

and agreement on the amounts of the payments, there is no need for extensive hearings before appropriations committees on the merits of funds for veterans' pensions. A change in policy toward veterans is not likely to come from appropriations committees. Here finance is the servant, and a fairly servile servant besides.

If the number of such nonreviewable programs is constantly increasing, this is merely evidence that the role of national governments is changing. The traditional core of governmental expenditures has grown considerably since the days of Adam Smith. Effective budgetary review and control are still possible, but legislative and executive responsibilities towards this end may have to be reinterpreted and redirected.

The ability of the legislature adequately to review the executive's budget and to enforce modifications therein will depend in some measure on the expertise which can be provided by the legislators themselves or summoned in their behalf. In the face of the growth and complexity of modern government, legislatures in western Europe and in the United States have not generally added staff to assist in legislative budget-making. Instead, they have come to depend increasingly on the executive for advice and guidance. It has been argued that this tends to handicap the legislature vis-à-vis the executive. However, in governments based on a separation of executive and legislative powers, it is not at all clear that this handicap can be overcome simply by building strong legislative staffs.

Legislative review of the budget depends first and foremost on the way in which budget programs are presented by the executive. A budget classification which sets forth revenue and expenditure data that can be readily understood and analyzed strengthens the legislature's position. A budget presentation which is overdetailed and is not supported by clearly descriptive narratives produces legislative ineptitude, frustration, and resentment. Clarity in budget presentation carries over to clarity in appropriation structure. Not only is it important for the legislature to have information on the nature of agency operations, it is also necessary for the legislature to be able to trace the relationship between organizational structure and sources of funds. This requires continuous attention, on the part of both the executive and the legislature, to the simplification of appropriation structures.

B. Policy Formulation: Determination of the Aggregates

The actions of a legislature in providing funds for a series of specific programs, when combined with the enactment of revenue measures, will add up to something which may be called the authorization of the budget as a whole. There is, however, a critical difference between a legislature's action in examining the specifics and a legislature's action in examining the aggregates. In the former case, examination proceeds in terms of a program in relation to itself and to other programs; an appropriations committee will act in much the same way as an agency budget office in the performance of its review functions. Here, policy formulation is the determination of the level of the program and the examination of the financial resources which are being applied for the support of program objectives.

In the examination of the aggregates, the policy formulated is fiscal policy—the determination of the level of government operations as a whole, and the interrelation of revenue and expenditure. One of the important end results is the authorization of a deficit or surplus in the total budget.

It is in the merger of aggregates and specifics that legislative budget procedure as it operates in Britain and in most other parliamentary governments has its greatest strength. In Great Britain the budget is both an executive proposal and a "project of law" for enactment by the Parliament. The budget is a reflection both of executive decisions about the level of specific programs and of executive decisions about aggregate fiscal policy. As the Parliament proceeds through the readings and debate on the budget, both programs and aggregates are subject to examination. The same concern with programs and aggregates obtains in Sweden, where, moreover, there is continuous parliamentary examination of the relation of the government's budget to the forecast of national income (see Chapter 8).

In American governments there is generally adequate legislative occasion for the determination of the level of programs. In local governments and in state governments the aggregates will also come in for review, not because legislative budget-making here is more "broad-gauged," but because of the strictures which are imposed in terms of maintaining a balanced or near-balanced budget (see Chapter 17). But in the federal government the Congress does not examine the budget as a whole; revenues are authorized at a different point in time than appropriations; the budget is enacted piecemeal. The budget is never a single "project of law," but a series of executive proposals, which must then be translated into specific appropriation acts, whose summation may or may not be related to the enactment of revenue legislation. In fact, the failure to look at the aggregates, to achieve the over-all view, is usually said to be a major weakness in United States budget practice.

C. THE OVERSIGHT OF ADMINISTRATION

The legislature's review of the executive's budget provides a major occasion for examination of the character and quality of administrative actions. Such examination is inherent in the review of programs, and every legislature has at least some watch-dog responsibility. The success or failure of administrative actions is a part of the materials for decisions about the level at which programs should be conducted. The quality of administration is a proper concern of the legislature.

But there is a difference between direction, and supervision or surveillance.[5] Supervision consists in a continuing concern on the part of the legislature with the details of administration and, in particular, with the specific content of administrative decisions. Direction, on the other hand, implies a much less intimate concern with the details and is centered on "major" rather than "minor" issues.

A legislature which is aggressive, or which lacks respect for executive authority, or which is interested in enhancing the influence of legislators via aggrandizement will attempt to supervise administration by way of budgetary review and authorization. A legislature which is dominated by the executive, or which recognizes its inherent inability to administer, or both, will confine itself to broad direction of administration. In some governments there has been a discernible trend away from supervision and toward direction, and the direction has tended to become increasingly broad and general. In the British Parliament, for example, the Committee on Supply does not have sufficient time to examine all estimates in detail.[6] The complexity of governmental operations is such that administration is increasingly examined ex post facto by the Public Accounts Committee.

One of the traditional techniques by which a legislature supervises administration is the itemization of appropriations. This is accomplished by specifying in detail in the budget authorization the objects of expenditure that may be undertaken by the executive. The application of this technique certainly increases the volume of legislative supervision. At the same time, it tends to be destructive of responsible administration and invites special-interest detail.

The issue here is by no means of recent vintage. In 1797 in the United States Congress, Albert Gallatin, then a representative from Pennsylvania, proposed an amendment to an appropriation bill, restricting expenditure to objects specified therein. In opposing this amendment Mr. John W. Kittera of Pennsylvania stated:

Suppose a boat should be overset with tents in the lake, or a magazine blown up, the losses could not be repaired, because, though there might be surplus

[5] The degrees of oversight and distinctions therein are discussed by Gross, *The Legislative Struggle*, pp. 136–138.

[6] Lord Gilbert Campion, "Parliamentary Procedure, Old and New," *Parliament: A Survey*, George Allen & Unwin, Ltd., London, 1952, pp. 161–162.

sums in the Treasury from other items in the establishment, yet, if this
amendment prevailed, they could not be touched.[7]

Alexander Hamilton put the issue even more strongly:

> The exigencies of the public service are often so variable, that a public agent
> would frequently find himself full-handed for one purpose, empty-handed
> for another; and if forbidden to make a transfer, not only the service would
> suffer, but an opportunity, with very strong temptation, would be given, to
> traffic with the public money for private gain; while the business of the
> government would be stagnated by the injudicious and absurd impediments
> of an over-driven caution.[8]

Nevertheless, the "absurd impediments of an over-driven caution"
predominate in many governments.

Rigid itemization as practiced in American governments is a hangover
from an era when legislatures and the citizenry generally had great distrust of administrative authority, and when administrative authority may
well have merited this distrust.   Where these conditions do not obtain
and where administrative authority is responsible, detailed itemization of
appropriations restricts administrative efficiency and probably tends to
perpetuate executive irresponsibility.   Itemization encourages an attention to staying within the letter of the appropriation and discourages
attention to the development of program goals and objectives (see
Chapter 13).

In some governments in this country the legislature's excessive itemization and its occasional tendency to indulge in an extravagant specific
appropriation is partially offset by the item veto.   This provision made
its first appearance on the American scene in the constitution of the
Confederate States of America and has since been adopted by 40 of the
states.   It permits the governor to strike out a single item in an appropriation without invalidating the remainder.   The legislature may override the veto, in most states, only by a two-thirds majority.   In some
instances the govenor has authority to reduce items as well as veto them.[9]

As it has operated in the states, the item veto is very often a significant
addition to the governor's fiscal authority.   It permits him to counter
excessive supervision by the legislature.   The threat of its use enables the
governor to make his influence continuously felt on the legislature's budgetary actions.   Further, the item veto has been used frequently to strike
out expenditures deemed wasteful.

[7] Quoted in Fred Wilbur Powell, *Control of Federal Expenditures,* Brookings
Institution, Washington, 1939, p. 158.

[8] *The Works of Alexander Hamilton,* Vol. VIII, Henry Cabot Lodge, ed.,
G. P. Putnam's Sons, New York, 1904, p. 309.

[9] A. E. Buck, *Public Budgeting,* Harper & Brothers, New York, 1929, pp. 413–
416.

On the other hand, the possibilities for its abuse are ever-present. Individual legislators who, for a variety of reasons, may be antagonistic to the governor can insert appropriation items favorable to their constituents, knowing in advance that the governor will strike them out, to his resulting political disadvantage. The possibility of veto may thus discourage fiscal discipline on the part of individual legislators; conversely, the governor may abuse the item veto by using it as a weapon against individual legislators and their projects.

It is by no means clear that an item veto is, under all circumstances, a desirable feature in executive-legislative budget relations. In the United States government there is no reason to assume that it would be a practicable addition to the authority of the President, who has tended to use his general veto power on a highly selective basis in major political controversies with the Congress. Its more widespread use might tend to reduce its importance.[10] This is apart from the fact that an item veto would probably require a constitutional amendment.[11]

Before proceeding to an examination of the nature and variety of legislative budget authorization, it may be well to summarize the foregoing considerations.

The general responsibilities of a legislature in budgeting are (1) the formulation of policy with respect to program level, (2) the formulation of over-all fiscal policy, and (3) the oversight of administration. In the discharge of these responsibilities, legislatures have seldom adapted their institutions to conform with the changing nature and the increased volume of their tasks. Parliamentary procedures apparently tend to be ingrained. Departure from traditional practice is difficult, and indeed, for most governments, the legislative machinery for budget-making has been very little changed over the past century. The contrast with the machinery of executive budget-making is sharp. In every modern government there has been increased centralization of executive budget authority and increased staffing for the central budget office, with frequent reorganizations of budgeting and financial procedures. No comparable centralization has occurred in legislatures; the trend here has been toward decentralization of budget-making authority. In some legislatures there have been modest additions to the staffs of appropria-

[10] Pendleton Herring, *Presidential Leadership,* Farrar & Rinehart, New York, 1940, pp. 76–77.

[11] Such an amendment was introduced in the 83d Cong., 2d sess. (1954), as *Senate Joint Res.* 30 by Senator Harry Flood Byrd. Hearings were held by a subcommittee of the Senate Committee on the Judiciary. These did not indicate that the proposal commands widespread support in the Congress. A similar resolution was introduced in the 84th Cong., 1st sess. (1955), as *Senate Joint Res.* 52, with a companion measure in the House.

tions and financial committees, but these additions have been far less significant than the comparable additions to the staffs of central budget offices.

It should hastily be observed that this "failure" of legislatures to expand their budget-making authority by expanding their budgetary personnel may not be a failure at all. Attempts to match and keep up with executive budgetary developments might well be a perversion of legislative authority. It may be that legislatures would do better to strengthen their existing authority by increased general oversight of executive budgetary procedure and program level, and by a search for new budget-making techniques designed to enhance the role and prestige of the legislature in carrying out its own budget-making responsibilities.

II. BUDGET AUTHORIZATION BY THE U. S. CONGRESS

As was noted in Chapter 4, the Congress of the United States does not review the President's budgetary policy in its total dimensions. No occasion is provided for an examination of aggregate revenues and expenditures, nor for the interrelation of expenditure programs. Indeed, the term budget authorization, which in most governments would embrace both revenue measures and appropriations, in the United States government applies only to the expenditure side of the budget.

A. TYPES OF BUDGET AUTHORIZATIONS

Action by the Congress on appropriations takes the form of from twelve to fifteen appropriation measures, each one of which may cover several departments and agencies. Within each appropriation measure there are a number of separate appropriation titles, numbering about 375 in all. (In recent years there has been considerable progress in the simplification of appropriation titles, which at one time numbered about 2,000.) These appropriation titles are geared to the organizational structure of departments and agencies and to the type of outlay. A large bureau within a major department will typically have one appropriation for administrative expenses, and if it conducts public works programs or administers major grants, one for each of these.

Budgetary authorizations by the Congress may permit departments and agencies to incur obligations, to make expenditures, or both. Obligational authority permits departments and agencies to award contracts, to make commitments for wages and salaries, and to order materials and supplies. Expenditure authority permits departments and agencies to direct the issuance of checks or the payment of cash to liquidate obligations. Appropriation measures combine obligational and expenditure authority, although in some types of budgetary authorizations these may be separated.

Budget authorizations by Congress include the following major types:[12]

(1) Ordinary current appropriations are for a definite, specified amount, but vary in accordance with the period of availability. One-year appropriations are commonly used for salaries and other current expenditures of departments and agencies. Multiple-year appropriations are often used for nonrecurrent expenditures. No-year appropriations are available indefinitely and are used primarily for construction projects.

(2) Annual indefinite appropriations are indefinite in amount but specified as to purpose. These are used for the allocation of earmarked revenues and for such purposes as covering the deficit of the Post Office Department.

(3) Permanent appropriations are those under which funds become available from year to year without specific action by the Congress. Interest on the public debt is paid under a permanent appropriation.

(4) Contract authorizations permit obligations to be incurred, but do not provide the funds to liquidate the obligation. This type of authorization has been used frequently for military and naval procurement, but in recent years its use has been increasingly limited in favor of multiple-year and no-year appropriations.

(5) Appropriations to liquidate contract authorizations are a separate type of budget authorization, which must be enacted subsequent to a contract authorization.

(6) Authorizations to expend from public debt receipts are sometimes used in lieu of appropriations when it is anticipated that the outlay may be repaid at a future date. For example, moneys for the lending program of a government corporation may be provided by this type of authorization; it has also been employed for the United States subscriptions to the International Bank and the International Monetary Fund. In these cases, funds are provided by Treasury borrowing. In addition, there may be authorization to expend from corporate debt receipts; a government corporation is authorized to conduct the borrowing. These authorizations are usually provided in substantive legislation and are not typically reviewed by the appropriations committees.

In addition to these six basic types of budget authorizations, there are, in some circumstances, *reappropriations* of unobligated balances of previous one-year or multiple-year appropriations which would otherwise expire. Similarly, there may be *reauthorizations of contract authority* and *reauthorizations to expend from public debt receipts.*

[12] *Budget of the United States Government for the fiscal year ending June 30, 1956,* p. A4; Michael S. March, "A Comment on Budgetary Improvement in the National Government," *National Tax Journal,* June 1952, pp. 160–161.

All of the foregoing types of budget authorizations are a control on obligations, and only indirectly a control on expenditures. Obligational authority is generally extended for a specified period, as with the annual appropriation or the multi-year appropriation. When this period expires, the obligational authority expires. Once the obligation is incurred, however, goods and services may be charged against the commitment for a period of two years after the close of the fiscal year, a procedure that dates back to 1874. The carryover of obligated but unexpended balances means that expenditures in any one year may be made from obligational authority extended in any one of three fiscal years. Only after the two-year period has elapsed does the obligated but unexpended balance revert to the Treasury. The Treasury lumps these balances together and continues to honor bills presented by public creditors, under a procedure for certified claims. From time to time these obligated but unexpended balances are written off the books.

This system results in an inconstant and fluctuating relationship between the volume of appropriations which Congress makes each year and the volume of federal government expenditures for that year. The new obligational authority which Congress *extends* for the budget year may exceed or fall short of the obligations incurred by departments and agencies in that year, since obligations may be incurred against previously extended authority. Moreover, expenditures depend on the rate at which goods and services are provided to administrative agencies. In any one year these may be greater or less than the amount of obligations incurred by the agencies. The variations between annual appropriations and annual expenditures are extreme for such outlays as military procurement, which involve a long lead-time between contracts and delivery.

The relative importance of expenditures anticipated from current and from prior authorizations is shown, for fiscal 1956, in the following data:[13]

	Millions
Out of new obligational authority	$37,923
Out of appropriations to liquidate contract authorizations	892
Out of authorizations to expend from subsequent year appropriations	147
Out of balances of prior expenditure authorizations	25,020
Out of balances of revolving and management funds	1,573 *
Expenditure in the year (net)	$62,408

* Deduct.

It is evident that in its action on the 1956 budget Congress was legislating with respect to only slightly more than 60 percent of the expenditures

[13] *Budget of the United States Government for the fiscal year ending June 30, 1956,* p. A6.

which would be made in fiscal 1956. About 40 percent of the expenditures in the budget year came from obligational authority extended by previous congressional action. At the same time, actions on the 1956 budget predetermine a significant portion of expenditures for later years.

Critics have pointed out that this system makes it extremely difficult for Congress to impose an annual control on expenditures. Several years ago Herman C. Loeffler contended that the dichotomy between obligations and expenditures was the major weakness in the federal budgetary system.[14] Loeffler argued that it not only complicated the budgetary planning which Congress was expected to review but, in addition, it made for "an unbelievable lack of internal cohesion" in the budget document itself. The reason for this is that the President's budget message and the major summary tables are presented in terms of expenditures, but the supporting detail on department and agency programs emphasizes obligations proposed for authorization in the forthcoming year. Loeffler suggested that nothing short of a drastic revision in appropriation practices would remedy the difficulties. This would include the use of contract authorizations for all multi-year programs, with annual appropriations linked to expenditures to cover only the amount of goods and services expected to be delivered to each department during the year, a lapsing of all appropriations at the end of each fiscal year, and the establishment of a 90-day period for the payment of bills submitted after the fiscal year.

The confusion is most severe in the national defense and public works areas, where there is considerable lag between authorization and obligation, and where the rate of deliveries of goods, and hence the rate of expenditure by the federal government, is dependent on the planning and production schedules of private firms.[15] Michael S. March, in rebuttal to Loeffler's proposals, suggested that in these cases contract authorizations should be abandoned and obligational authority extended each year. The time limit on the obligational authority would be specified as one year, two years, or three years, and the uniform three-year practice that now prevails would be discontinued.

More recently the second Hoover Commission has proposed a major modification in appropriation practices, along lines similar to those suggested by Loeffler.[16] Agency budgets would be presented in terms of

[14] Herman C. Loeffler, "Alice in Budget-Land," *National Tax Journal,* March 1951, pp. 54–64.

[15] March, *National Tax Journal,* pp. 155–173; Loeffler has further comments at *ibid.,* pp. 174–175.

[16] Commission on Organization of the Executive Branch of the Government, *Budget and Accounting,* Washington, 1955, pp. 17–25: Task Force Report, *Budget and Accounting,* Washington, 1955, pp. 33–41.

annual accrued expenditures, defined as the charges incurred for goods and services received. All congressional appropriations would be annual, to cover accrued expenditures. Long term procurement would be handled under contract authorizations reviewed and extended annually by the Congress. The practice of obligating from unexpended balances of prior-year appropriations would be abandoned.

The introduction of the concept of accrued expenditures would bring government financial practices much closer to the accounting concepts employed in private business. It would not, however, automatically restore the power of the purse, as the Commission seemed to feel. Accrued expenditures would vary in accordance with the rate of delivery of goods and services. Neither are accrued expenditures synonymous with program costs; the latter depend on the rate at which goods and services are consumed by government agencies, not on the rate of deliveries. Even if transition difficulties could be overcome, not all problems would be solved.

Significant steps have been taken in recent years to overcome some of the foregoing disparities by establishing a clarified relationship between obligations and expenditures. The major emphasis in department and agency budgets continues to be on schedules of obligations. But in most cases the agency presentation now contains a reconciliation table to show the "bridge" between obligations and expenditures. The goal here is to assure that congressional committees are aware, at all times, of the sources of expenditure in relation to current and prior obligational authority. The departments and agencies and the Bureau of the Budget certainly have responsibility for a budget presentation which reveals this relationship. The congressional committees likewise have a responsibility to recognize that a part of this year's commitments will have to be paid for in future years.

The system of budget authorization employed in the United States government does tend toward confusion. In the public mind, the budget is associated with expenditures. When Congress "cuts" the budget, the impression prevails that expenditures are reduced. Actually, Congress may only be "cutting" obligational authority; budget expenditures for the forthcoming year may be little affected.

Disposing of this popular misconception may be difficult. The point at which control must be exercised is much earlier than the stage at which checks are issued to pay the bills.[17] Control must come first in the basic statute authorizing the program. Then it must come when obligational authority is extended and when the use of previously extended

[17] See the statements of Elmer Staats quoted in George B. Galloway, *The Legislative Process in Congress*, Thomas Y. Crowell Company, New York, 1953, p. 137.

obligational authority is examined. Only if the expenditure implications are consciously and continuously traced through can there be a realistic grasp on the purse strings. This means that congressional committees must ask for and the agencies must provide understandable schedules to show the relationship between the authorization under consideration and the expenditures which agencies expect to make.

B. Congressional Influences on Program and Administration

As an old cliché has it, "It is the function of the executive to propose, of the legislature to dispose." The observer of the legislative scene might hope that things were this clear-cut. Such is not the case; proposals and disposals get mixed up.

No attempt will be made here to describe and analyze the multifarious influences which shape congressional action on the budget, and, in particular, no effort will be made to examine the specific influence of interest groups and their impact on budget authorizations.[18] Rather, attention will be directed to, first, the general character of congressional budget action and the ways in which it differs from review by the Bureau of the Budget and the President; and second, to the devices employed by the Congress for the control and influence of administration.

1. National and Local Interests. In his budget-making responsibilities, the President of the United States necessarily reflects and shapes his recommendations in accordance with the functional interests of departments and agencies, viewed in a context of national interests. The President's proposals are an embodiment of his own political and social philosophy and that of the political party which he heads, and, in addition, of the program and operating requirements of departments and agencies.

The Congress, however, is composed of representatives elected on a geographical basis, with responsibilities necessarily conceived in terms of the interests of constituents. An individual Congressman looks at the budget with concern for the welfare of his region, or district, or state, as well as with concern for national interests. The combined views of many Congressmen will thus reflect an approach to budgeting that is broader geographically but narrower functionally than the approach to budgeting which the President will employ.[19] Both approaches are necessary in a society that is complex and dedicated to pluralistic values. Either one alone could give rise to provincialism or distortion.

[18] For an excellent summary description with case studies see David B. Truman, *The Governmental Process*, Alfred A. Knopf, New York, 1953, pp. 352–394.

[19] For a statement of this difference with respect to agricultural programs see Bela Gold, *Wartime Economic Planning in Agriculture*, Columbia University Press, New York, 1949, pp. 526–527.

In the application of its local concerns to a national budget, the Congress will necessarily engage in some reshaping and remolding. Very often this process takes the form of increases in specific appropriations for specific projects in a Congressman's district. Where individual Congressmen are powerful or strategically placed, as on appropriations committees, there is a resultant dipping into the "pork barrel."[20] In the semantics of American politics the "pork barrel" is an extremely sinful kind of thing. But it should be recognized as an inevitable and at times a desirable device for reshaping national policy.

The aggregates of a budget may be an expression of a national interest, but the components will have specific regional and local impact. The national income or the national prosperity is a complex. Viewed in one way, it is the summation of economic activity conducted in localities, and the national prosperity depends on the sum of local prosperities. It is hardly immoral or sinful for a Congressman to be concerned with local unemployment, with the income of local contractors, or with the economic development of his state or district. To condemn this would deny the relationship between the aggregate and its geographic units. The budget of the United States government will be a realistic expression of national interests only when there is room for its modification in accordance with local concerns.

Looked at in another way, however, and translated into the realm of congressional actions, the relationship between local prosperities and the national prosperity is not always additive. Not every district can have a new dam, a new highway, a new hospital. That which one district gets is very often at the expense of another district. One Congressman's gain may be another's loss. There is a serious element of conflict in "local interest" legislation—a struggle of district versus district and state versus state. This conflict may sometimes resolve only at the expense of the national interest. Too many localities may win, local pressures may force the aggregates above levels desirable in the national interest. For example, if the economy were operating at full employment, an excessive sum of local spendings would make for inflationary price rises.

Given the existing organization and procedure for budget-making in the Congress, the possibilities for the incorporation of local concerns—the possibility for access to the "pork barrel"—are not uniformly distributed. Not all Congressmen are in a position to make their influence

[20] Appropriations for the improvement of rivers and harbors and for flood control are most often subject to this kind of expression of local interest in federal expenditures. For documentation see the case study of congressional behavior and the Rivers and Harbors Flood Control Act of 1950 in Stephen K. Bailey and Howard D. Samuel, *Congress at Work*, Henry Holt & Company, New York, 1953, pp. 166–193.

felt. As Arthur W. Macmahon has stated, in examining the general relations between Congress and the Administration in budgeting:

> It is not the Congress, not the House or Senate, not even the appropriations committee as a whole that should be thought of as abstractions, set against administration. The reality is a handful of men from particular states or districts, working with a particular committee clerk on a multitude of details.[21]

The conflict among and the concern for both local interests and national interests gives rise to the common phenomenon in which Congressmen will argue most vehemently for economy, efficiency, balanced budgets, and other virtuous causes, and simultaneously vote larger appropriations for specific projects for their districts. This is not a peculiarly American trait. A British financial authority is supposed to have said in the last century, "If you want to raise a certain cheer in the House of Commons, make a general panegyric on economy; if you want to invite a sure defeat, propose a particular saving." This kind of behavior, whether British or American, should not be condemned as either hypocritical or schizoid. The legislator who reacts in this way is simply expressing the realities of his existence. In point of fact, his role reflects a duality. He must continually blend a concern for national viewpoints and national issues with a concern for local issues. Most Congressmen would appreciate the wisdom of Mansfield's remarks:

> . . . it is plain that of all the great powers of government the most elastic and the most congenial is the spending power. It is adaptable to the widest variety of objectives—to wage war, to buy peace, to regulate the acreage of agricultural crops, to build highways, to stabilize the price of peanut butter. It is susceptible of countless techniques of application—by adding to the public payroll, by contracts for the services of private enterprise, by grants-in-aid to states and cities, by outright gifts, by conditional loans. It is supported by the taxing and borrowing powers of the wealthiest of nations. It is subject to no constitutional restraints of consequence. And if there are economic limits on its exercise, they have not yet been measured. The disbursement of government funds is one of the great harmonizers of divergent interests.[22]

The amount by which Congress increases budget expenditures in order to satisfy local and particularist concerns cannot be quantified. Senator Douglas suggests that the Senate is much more exposed to pressures of this sort than is the House, since there are more interest groups in a state than in any one congressional district. The historic tendency of the

[21] Arthur W. Macmahon, "Congressional Oversight of Administration: The Power of the Purse; I," *Political Science Quarterly*, June 1943, p. 181.

[22] Harvey C. Mansfield, "Fiscal Accountability," *Elements of Public Administration*, Fritz Morstein Marx, ed., Prentice-Hall, New York, 1946, p. 578.

Senate to increase appropriations over and above those enacted by the House may be a confirmation of this greater degree of exposure.[23]

2. TECHNIQUES OF CONGRESSIONAL INFLUENCE. Congressional decisions about the level at which programs are to be conducted find their legal expression in the budget authorizations which are enacted. These are written in general terms that do not prescribe the programs which the agency is authorized to undertake. For example, the appropriation for the Securities and Exchange Commission for fiscal 1955 reads as follows:

> Salaries and expenses: For necessary expenses, including not to exceed $500 for the purchase of newspapers; not to exceed $125,000 for expenses of travel; and services as authorized by section 15 of the Act of August 2, 1946 (5 U.S.C. 55a); $4,750,000.....................................$4,750,000.

There is a tacit understanding that SEC will conduct its program for the forthcoming year in accordance with its budget justifications as submitted to the committees on appropriations. But there is nothing in the statute which requires this. Such understanding does not have a legal status.

The specific items contained in the SEC appropriation do have, however, the force of law. These are known as *limitations* and operate to restrict the amount of obligations that may be incurred in accordance with the terms mentioned. For some agencies the number of specified limitations may be very large, and may attach to the use of funds for the purchase of books and newspapers, for travel, for construction, or for the purchase of real estate. Limitations apply only to the appropriation in which they are contained, and do not become a permanent provision of law.[24]

Apart from the appropriating legislation itself and the limitations which may be set forth there, congressional influence on programs and their administration is transmitted at the time of the hearings and in the reports of subcommittees of the appropriations committees.

Appropriations committee hearings are very often extended and searching in character.[25] It is not unusual, in the case of a major department or agency, for the subcommittee to conduct hearings over the course of six or eight weeks, particularly in the House. During these proceedings the members of the subcommittee will have adequate opportunity to

[23] Paul H. Douglas, *Economy in the National Government*, University of Chicago Press, Chicago, 1952, pp. 58–59. For a history of the Senate's alleged profligacy see George H. Haynes, *The Senate of the United States*, Vol. I, Houghton Mifflin Company, Boston, 1938, pp. 460–464.

[24] For a discussion of the unwritten rules governing limitations, see Galloway, *The Legislative Process in Congress*, pp. 99–100.

[25] For an excellent general discussion of committee hearings and committee actions see Gross, *The Legislative Struggle*, pp. 284–336. For a case study see Bailey and Samuel, *Congress at Work*, pp. 357–381.

express themselves, and these expressions may be disregarded only at the risk of incurring the subcommittee's displeasure in the following year, with a consequent reduction in appropriations. The fact that the subcommittee is dealing with the agency and not with the Bureau of the Budget means, of course, that such suggestions are likely to be particularly effective. This is face-to-face contact with program administrators, not a generalized influence transmitted through an intermediary.

The reports of each subcommittee of the appropriations committees accompany the bill as it goes to the appropriations committee. These reports are prepared after the hearings, by the clerk of the subcommittee and his staff, if any, under the general supervision of the chairman of the subcommittee. It is here that the subcommittee clerk is most influential. The reports are extralegal, but have strong influence. Macmahon has described them as follows:

> In the reports are mingled many shades of suggestions, of precise recommendations, of doubts, of warnings, of commendations, and of rebukes. It is the difficult task of administrators to construe the reports and to identify the commands and interdictions which the committee intends to have an intrinsic force, not merely advisory value.[26]

Congressional influence on administration does not stop with the hearings, the subcommittee reports, and the final legislation. James MacGregor Burns has said:

> The appropriations committeemen are not content to state their views once a year and then leave the administrators to their own devices. Knowing the importance of sustained direction, many of the legislators bolster their formal powers with informal meetings with administrative chiefs around the year. These meetings may take place at lunch, in the congressman's or administrator's office, or more formally in the committee room. The appropriators often take a paternalistic attitude toward agencies under their wing. They feel free to offer directions and suggestions, and usually they expect their conception of administration to be followed out. . . . this type of legislative oversight has increased measurably in recent years.[27]

On some occasions the continued oversight of administration has extended to the requirement, either in the bill or in the subcommittee report, that specific transactions be reviewed by the subcommittee before their consummation by the administrator.

The volume and degree of congressional oversight of administration by the foregoing techniques vary greatly from agency to agency, from year to year, and in accordance with the personalities of both appropriators and administrators. Its evident importance should be taken into account in assessing the contentions of those who argue that Congress has lost control of the budget.

[26] Macmahon, *Political Science Quarterly*, June 1943, p. 389.

[27] *Congress on Trial*, Harper & Brothers, New York, 1949, pp. 105–106.

Congressional budget-making centers on the subcommittees. Although all committees of Congress are solely advisory in character, in point of fact it is here that decisions are made and influences transmitted. The House Appropriations Committee and the Senate Appropriations Committee seldom review or modify, in any important detail, the work of their subcommittees. Established procedures are such that there is little occasion for modification. It is usually a matter of days from the time that the subcommittees complete their work to the time that the appropriation bill comes to the floor of the House or Senate for debate. The pressure at this stage in the legislative process also makes for inadequate floor discussion in both the House and the Senate. Very often the important subcommittee reports have been available for examination for only a few hours.

It is unlikely that these procedures will be altered. It cannot reasonably be expected that the whole membership of the House or even of the Senate will be informed and interested in all appropriation measures; the immensity of legislative tasks will require a continued sharing of work assignments. If reforms in congressional budget-making are called for, they must surely build on existing committee and subcommittee structure and operation.

C. Reform in Congressional Budget Procedures

The cries for reform in congressional fiscal procedures come from many sources. Sometimes the criticisms are put in lurid language—"the budget is out of control" or "the Administration has usurped the powers of the Congress." Gross says, "These charges of usurpation, however, are usually nothing but a means of arguing or agitating against action which is opposed on substantive grounds.[28]

Sometimes the criticisms are more measured and accompanied by modest suggestions for the strengthening of congressional review of the budget. More often than not the author of the criticism proposes a gadget—a procedural reform intended to bring order out of chaos, to slash expenditures, to at last make government efficient and economical.

Not all of this concern is recent. In 1897 Rollo Ogden asked a question equally appropriate today:

What has led to this strange impairment of the power of the purse? Why has Congress, inheritor of the right wrested from the king to control national expenditure, become seemingly unable to control it, not as against King or President, but as against itself?[29]

[28] *Op. cit.*, p. 156.
[29] Rollo Ogden, "The Rationale of Congressional Extravagance," *Yale Review,* May 1897, p. 39.

The more recent restlessness and uncertainty about the role and effectiveness of Congress in budget-making would appear to be a direct product of the growth of the federal government itself. In fiscal 1940 federal expenditures were 12 percent of the national income; in fiscal 1955 they were almost 22 percent of the national income. The *relative* growth of government in the United States has been primarily federal in character. The sheer size of the federal establishment, and therefore its potential for good or evil, is disturbing and disconcerting to large numbers of persons. The question of control assumes more serious proportions, and the traditional machinery may well appear to be inadequate for the enlarged task.

The post-war dissatisfaction with Congress's ability to control the budget has varied in accordance with the political relations between the Congress and the Administration. During the Truman Administration, when the Congress, regardless of the political party in power, was more conservative than the Administration, there were numerous efforts to reform congressional budget-making. In these years congressional distrust of the Administration was extreme, and the fears of government encroachment and unhappiness about the size of government produced a very large volume of concern over the budget-making role of the Congress. After January 1953, when the Administration appeared to be as conservative as the Congress in its fiscal outlook, there was much less concern. The Congress seemed to be satisfied that the President and the Bureau of the Budget were bending every effort toward economy and efficiency.

But these factors—the difficulties of accommodating to the realities of a large federal government and the derivative expression of political controversy—are not the whole of the story.

The budgetary process in the United States government, in its present character, will in itself continue to give rise to dissatisfaction because the patterns of responsibility are not clearly fixed. Once the budget leaves the hands of the President, decision-making is diffused. Neither the President nor the Director of the Bureau of the Budget defends or explains the budget to the Congress. This is left to the heads of departments and agencies, and to the heads of bureaus under them. The committee structure of the Congress tends to produce additional diffusion. The generalist approach to budgeting which the Executive provides gives way to the particularist approach of the members of congressional subcommittees. It is not surprising that the Congress should feel, and that critics of the Congress should continually point out, that the over-all approach has been lost in the mass of details. To some extent this diffusion is due to piecemeal consideration without subsequent reintegration, to procedural failure. But there are indications that the problem transcends procedures. It may be inevitable that the legislative body of a pluralistic society will have trouble in focusing responsibility and producing rigidly consistent policies when the society itself can simultaneously embrace a number of partially conflicting goals.

The significant reforms in Congressional budgeting, either attempted or proposed in the years since World War II, include: (1) the Legislative Budget experience of 1946–48, (2) the Omnibus Appropriations Bill for fiscal 1951, and (3) the proposals for a Joint Committee on the Budget.

1. THE LEGISLATIVE BUDGET. In 1946 the Congress enacted the Legislative Reorganization Act (*P.L.* 601, 79th Cong., 2d sess.). Contained therein was Section 138, which created a Joint Committee on the Legislative Budget, composed of all members of the House Ways and Means Committee, House Appropriations Committee, Senate Finance Committee, and Senate Appropriations Committee. The Joint Committee was directed to meet early in each session, examine the President's budget as submitted, and frame a concurrent resolution for adoption not later than February 15 by both houses of the Congress. The resolution was to establish a ceiling on appropriations and a ceiling on expenditures, which were then intended to be binding on the work of the appropriations committees during the remainder of the session. Section 138 also required that the resolution set forth an estimate of revenue and a provision that surpluses, if any, should be devoted to the reduction of the public debt.

This section seems to have been motivated by a number of considerations. Important among them was a zeal for retrenchment. At war's end federal expenditures were very high, judged by prewar standards, and there was widespread concern over the federal debt. It was hoped that a strengthened congressional review and strong congressional action on the totals of the budget would assist in the retrenchment process.

The retrenchment drive was accompanied by considerable antagonism toward the fiscal practices of the Executive. The Committee on the Reorganization of Congress had stated in its report:

> The executive has mingled appropriations, brought forward and backward unexpended and anticipated balances, incurred coercive deficiencies, and otherwise escaped the rigors of congressional control.[30]

It was intended that the legislative budget procedure would curb these administrative transgressions and re-establish congressional control over

[30] *Congressional Record,* 79th Cong., 2d sess., Vol. 92, p. 10047.

the purse strings.[31]   It was also intended that the provisions requiring the fiscal committees of the Congress to join together in a budget consideration would furnish the over-all joint revenue-expenditure deliberation necessary for a fiscal policy determination.

Section 138 did not work out well. In the 1947 session the Joint Committee on the Legislative Budget met and appointed a subcommittee of twenty to bring in a recommendation. After considerable debate here, and in the whole committee (made up of 102 members), it was agreed to cut expenditures and appropriations by $6 billion. A resolution to this effect was adopted by the House, but amended by the Senate. The conference committee appointed to reconcile the differences could not agree, and the legislative budget was thus inoperative in the 1947 session.

In the 1948 session the Legislative Budget Committee reached agreement within the scheduled time, and the House and Senate passed the concurrent resolution. The maxima were not observed, however, and final action on appropriations measures exceeded the legislative ceilings. In the 1949 session it was agreed to postpone the legislative budget provisions until May 1, but this date passed without action by the Congress. No subsequent efforts to revive Section 138 have gone beyond the discussion stage, and although the provision has not been repealed, it has been pronounced a "dead letter" by influential Congressmen.[32]

This experience bolsters the observation that no single procedural gadget will reform congressional budget machinery. Apart from all considerations about the underlying philosophy of Section 138, it is evident, and was pointed out by critics in advance, that Congress is not in a position early in the session to establish a rigid ceiling on budgetary expenditures and appropriations. Not until the components have been carefully examined by the subcommittees, can the Congress know where program levels should be established and what the aggregates must be. There must be an interplay between the components and the aggregates, not a predetermined total.

[31] For further examination of Section 138 see the author's "Federal Budgetary Developments: 1947–48," *Public Administration Review*, Autumn 1948, pp. 267–270. Other and differing interpretations of this experience are Avery Leiserson, "Coordination of Federal Budgetary and Appropriations Procedures under the Legislative Reorganization Act of 1946," *National Tax Journal*, June 1948, pp. 118–126; Clinton Fielder, "Reform of the Congressional Legislative Budget," *National Tax Journal*, March 1951, pp. 65–76; Galloway, *The Legislative Process in Congress*, pp. 103–105.

[32] See, for example, John Phillips, "The Hadacol of the Budget Makers," *National Tax Journal*, September 1951, pp. 256–257; Clarence Cannon, "Congressional Responsibilities," *American Political Science Review*, April 1948, p. 316.

The positive accomplishment of Section 138 was that it did, during the years in which attempts were made to apply it, provide the occasion for full-scale congressional debate on the budget as a whole, and hence on the fiscal policy proposals of the Administration. Subcommittee actions on the components did not previously and do not now provide this kind of general consideration. This is worthy of an attempt at salvage.

2. THE OMNIBUS APPROPRIATION BILL. In 1947 a subcommittee of the Committee on Rules and Administration of the Senate held hearings on a proposal to include all general appropriation bills in one consolidated appropriation bill. This proposal had been introduced by Senators Byrd and Butler as a necessary supplement to Section 138 (*Senate Concurrent Res. 6, 80th Cong., 1st sess.*). The sponsors of the resolution contended that it would give to both houses of the Congress an opportunity for the examination of revenues and expenditures together. Under the terms of the resolution, the consolidated (omnibus) appropriation bill would be supported by committee reports showing the relation of appropriations to expenditures for the fiscal year and the probable carry-over of expenditures into future years. It was hoped that this would provide the Congress with additional weapons in efforts to reduce expenditures and hence either federal debt or tax rates.

The Byrd-Butler resolution was reported favorably by the Senate Committee on Rules. No further action was taken by the Senate in that year, but in 1949 the Senate approved the measure.[33]

In 1949, after the demise of Section 138, the Chairman of the House Committee on Appropriations announced that beginning in January 1950 the House would " . . . discontinue the practice which has been in effect since the early days of the Congress, of reporting appropriations piecemeal in separate, unconnected and uncorrelated individual bills, and will submit the annual appropriations in one consolidated omnibus appropriation bill."[34] This the House did, but the resulting delay was considerable. The omnibus bill did not reach the Senate until May 10, and was not enacted by that body until August 4. Conferences meant further delay, and the bill was not finally signed by the President until September 6, two months after the beginning of the fiscal year.

In the next session of Congress the House Appropriations Committee took the almost unprecedented step of voting down its chairman on the continued use of the omnibus bill. It was apparently felt that, in addi-

[33] *Senate Concurrent Res.* 18, 81st Cong., 1st sess.; *Senate Report* No. 616. For a discussion of this experience see Dalmas H. Nelson, "The Omnibus Appropriations Act of 1950," *Journal of Politics,* May 1953, pp. 274–288.

[34] Quoted from the *Congressional Record* by Phillips, *op. cit.,* p. 257.

tion to the delay which seemed to be inherent, the consolidation of all appropriation measures in one bill tended to concentrate undue influence in the hands of the chairmen of the appropriations committees, to the detriment of the members of the subcommittees. This action underlines the significance of the specifics and the corresponding authority of the subcommittees in congressional budget-making.

In the years since 1950 there have been numerous efforts to revive the omnibus bill, particularly on the part of the Senate. In 1951 the Committee on Rules and Administration favorably reported a resolution which would have required its use (*Senate Report* No. 842, 82d Cong., 1st sess.). In 1953 a similar and expanded resolution was reported favorably by the same Committee (*Senate Report* No. 267, 83d Cong., 1st sess.). On both occasions there were strong dissents from individual members of the Rules Committee. Furthermore, very little support has been forthcoming from the House of Representatives for the omnibus bill. The House, in fact, is in a different position than the Senate in this matter. It may force the Senate to consider appropriation measures in a consolidated form if it chooses to, but the Senate may do no more than urge the House to move in this direction.

The opponents of the omnibus bill, although expressing desire for retrenchment, contend that the consolidation of appropriation bills will not accomplish this end.[35] The size and complexity of the omnibus bill make for less debate on the floor of the House. Since the work of the Senate is delayed until all of the House subcommittees complete their action, there is less time for examination in that body. The shortage of time encourages the "meat-ax" technique—across-the-board cuts of a flat percentage, which leave to the President and the heads of departments the responsibility for making reductions in specific programs.[36] Furthermore, it is contended that the omnibus bill invites "pork-barrel" amendments and substantive riders. The presidential veto power is put in jeopardy because the bill necessarily comes late in the session and the President will hesitate to delay further the provision of funds for the whole of the executive branch. In fact, two successive Directors of the

[35] Phillips, *op. cit.*, pp. 258–262.

[36] The flat percentage cut was used by Congress in 1949 on the General Appropriation Act of 1950, but has not since been employed. The Administration objects to its use on the ground that if the Congress wishes to reduce expenditures it should indicate where those expenditures should be reduced. Some Congressmen object to the technique on the ground that it gives the President additional authority. The controversies were well explored in hearings in 1949. See U. S. Senate, Committee on Expenditures in the Executive Departments, *Reduction of Government Expenditures*, 81st Cong., 1st sess.

Bureau of the Budget have pointed out that the use of an omnibus bill ought to be accompanied by an item veto to retain the President's authority to approve or disapprove appropriations.[37]

It is difficult to assess the merits of the conflicting arguments on the omnibus bill. There is no doubt that it would provide the occasion for an over-all view. Whether this advantage would be more than offset by other and more significant disadvantages is difficult to determine. One year's experience, and that in the year of hostilities in Korea, does not provide conclusive evidence. Any action to enforce a general examination of the budget as a whole is commendable, but there may be other ways to accomplish this.

3. THE JOINT COMMITTEE ON THE BUDGET. In 1913, in House debate on the proposals of the Taft Commission, Representative Fitzgerald stated:

> Everyone who is familiar with the history of the enactment of the various statutes compelling the furnishing of the information required by the law knows that it has been a continual struggle on the part of Congress to compel the executive departments to furnish the necessary data to enable the Congress to make proper appropriations, and that there has been ample authority, if the Executive desired to exercise it, to furnish the most complete information possible.[38]

In 1946 Congressman Jensen, of the House Appropriations Committee, said in testimony before the Joint Committee on the Organization of Congress:

> The fact is that we do not have sufficient information on which to base the amounts we should allow for the respective items, so when we start marking up the bill, we make cuts arbitrarily, which is not the best or proper way to appropriate. We may cut one item too much and maybe another item not enough and there may be some items that we will trim down that should not be trimmed down. . . .
>
> These men from the departments that line up across the table from us, and there are generally from six to a dozen from every branch of the respective departments, those gentlemen are schooled in the art of justifying their requests, they have spent years at it and we are so busy with a thousand and one things to carry on our duties here in Congress. . . .
>
> When they come before us . . . we are obliged to take their word. . . . in the end, we appropriate blindly, so to speak.[39]

The legislature's search for information on which to legislate, its distrust of the information which is provided, its suspicion that the admin-

[37] Senate Report No. 267, 83d Cong., 1st sess., Part 2, pp. 11–12; Frederick J. Lawton, "Legislative-Executive Relationships in Budgeting as Viewed by the Executive," Public Administration Review, Summer 1953, pp. 169–176.

[38] Congressional Record, 63d Cong., 1st sess., Vol. 50, p. 2156.

[39] Quoted by Huzar, The Purse and the Sword, pp. 383–384.

istration is withholding information—these seem to be the hardy perennials of legislative-executive relationships. The possibilities for distrust are no doubt accentuated in a government which separates executive and legislative powers.

The Budget and Accounting Act of 1921 contained two provisions intended to assist the Congress in eliciting information. The first was the requirement that the Bureau of the Budget furnish, on request from appropriations committees, such reports as were desired. Also, the Act provided that the Comptroller General should make reports and investigations as directed by either house of Congress or by the revenue or appropriations committees. Neither of these provisions seems to have been adequate for congressional needs. The appropriations committees make few such requests of the Bureau of the Budget, and although the Comptroller General's power to make special studies and reports was strengthened by the Legislative Reorganization Act of 1946, and such reports have been provided in substantial numbers since that time, they seem to be of limited use to the appropriations committees.[40]

The failure of existing channels to provide the kind of information which the Congress feels it needs has led to recurring proposals for new staffing arrangements for the appropriation committees. Some of these proposals date back before World War II.[41] More recently, proposals of this type have centered on the creation of a Joint Committee on the Budget.

The model for such proposals is the Joint Committee on Internal Revenue Taxation, which has been in successful operation since 1926.[42] It is composed of members of Congress who serve on the House Ways and Means and Senate Finance Committees, but most of its work has been carried on by a small professional staff, which conducts studies of revenue measures proposed and pending and serves in an advisory capacity on technical and policy matters to the two standing committees. The Joint Committee staff has provided an expertise in revenue legislation which the Congress has very much needed.

[40] Section 206 of the Legislative Reorganization Act provides: "The Comptroller General is authorized and directed to make an expenditure analysis of each agency in the executive branch of the Government (including Government corporations), which, in the opinion of the Comptroller General, will enable Congress to determine whether public funds have been economically and efficiently administered and expended." The Comptroller General submitted about 300 such reports in the years 1947–1953, to the appropriations committees and to the committees on government operations of both houses.

[41] Victor Jones, *The Legislature and the Budget*, Bureau of Public Administration, University of California, Berkeley, 1941, pp. 15–17.

[42] For a description of the work of this committee see Roy Blough, *The Federal Taxing Process*, Prentice-Hall, New York, 1952, pp. 63–64.

A bill to establish a Joint Committee on the Budget was introduced in 1950 by Senator McClellan.[43]   No action was taken in this session, but extensive hearings were held in the Senate in 1951.[44]   In 1952 the bill passed the Senate, was reported favorably by the House Rules Committee, but failed of passage in the House.   In 1953 and in 1955 similar measures were adopted by the Senate, but the House did not take action.[45]   The intent of the proposal was stated as follows:

> This committee believes that S. 833 offers at least a sound approach to the solution of these problems in that the legislative branch would be definitely provided with the equipment to permit it to examine carefully every item of expenditure so that appropriations may be limited to only and much, as no more than [sic], is actually necessary to provide the minimum funds essential to successful operation of the Government.[46]

The bill provided for a Joint Committee of 14 members, 7 from the House Appropriations Committee and 7 from the Senate Appropriations Committee, with a staff of approximately 50 employees.   The Joint Committee was empowered to recommend hearings which would combine the membership of the House and Senate Appropriations Committees.   Beyond these organizational arrangements, it was required that any committee reporting legislation to authorize appropriations must include in its report an estimate of the probable expenditures to be incurred over the forthcoming five-year period.   The bill provided that the Comptroller General could be asked by the chairman of the Joint Committee to undertake specific surveys.   The bill also provided for the repeal of Section 138 of the Legislative Reorganization Act.

The appropriations committees do need, as Huzar has put it, a "better organization of their curiosity."[47]   Enlarged staffing might provide this; the few years in which the Senate Appropriations Committee utilized separate professional staff would seem to bear this out.[48]   There

[43] For an analysis of this bill and its intended accomplishments see Joseph P. Harris, "Needed Reforms in the Federal Budget System," *Public Administration Review*, Autumn 1952, pp. 245–247; for a critical view see Smithies, *The Budgetary Process in the United States*, pp. 95–99.

[44] Committee on Expenditures in the Executive Departments, *To Create a Joint Committee on the Budget*, 82d Cong., 1st sess.

[45] *Senate Report* No. 295, 83d Cong., 1st sess. (S. 833); *Senate Report* No. 352, 84th Cong., 1st sess. (S. 1805).

[46] *Senate Report* No. 295, *op. cit.*, p. 2.

[47] Huzar, *The Purse and the Sword*, p. 391.

[48] Thomas J. Graves, "The Professional Staff of the U. S. Senate Committee on Appropriations," *Notes & References*, Governmental Research Association, May 1948, pp. 1–4.   There has been an increase in the clerical staff of the House Appropriations Committee since 1947 but no effort to develop a separate professional staff (Gladys M. Kammerer, *Congressional Committee Staffing Since*

are, however, some difficulties which must be faced in the use of staff such as is contemplated for a Joint Committee on the Budget. These are not peculiar to budgeting, but are encountered in all kinds of legislative work.

A committee of the American Political Science Association, in a general examination of legislative-executive relations, has stated:

> One approach . . . is to concentrate on improving the legislature so as better to equip it to carry on the long-standing tug-of-war with the executive. Indeed, it would seem that many who are preoccupied with streamlining the lawmaking assembly have only this aim in view, which, if realized, could only serve to intensify the interminable struggle between the legislature and the executive.[49]

Improved staffing for legislative committees may create an atmosphere of independence and lead to a deterioration in working relations with the executive. Committees can never come to rely fully on their own staffs for information. The detailed knowledge of operations which is necessary for effective legislation—and effective budget-making—can come only from the agencies themselves. The province of any legislature is to provide a lay judgment on these programs and operations. As Macmahon states,

> Something of the value of the mingling of special and non-special minds might be lost if the politician-legislator dealt with administration only through an intermediate legislative bureaucracy.[50]

A second difficulty in the use of staff for congressional appropriations committees is that the Congress itself has not evolved consistent working relations with its professional employees. Gross says on this point:

> The services provided by the professional staffs of committees cannot be described by any general formula. In some cases staff members make a valiant effort to stand apart from the legislative struggle and provide objective assistance to both sides. When this happens, they pass into the background whenever a really "hot" issue comes up. The genuine staff work, which is necessarily controversial, is thereby left to the staffs of executive agencies and private organizations. In other cases, staff members are required to take sides or do so of their own choosing. When this happens the more imaginative ones are in a better position to mobilize and direct the staff operations of friendly agencies and organizations. The others tend to serve as transmission belts—with some leeway for initiative and judgment—between members of Congress and non-congressional groups.[51]

1946, Bureau of Government Research, University of Kentucky, Lexington, 1951, pp. 3–7).

[49] Belle Zeller, ed., *American State Legislatures*, Thomas Y. Crowell Company, New York, 1954, p. 164.

[50] Macmahon, *Political Science Quarterly*, June 1943, p. 187.

[51] Gross, *The Legislative Struggle*, pp. 282–283.

The general uncertainty about the role of staff in the legislative process applies as well to budget-making, and perhaps accounts for the fact that the House Appropriations Committee has employed very few permanent staff members. Instead, temporary assistance is obtained on a reimbursement basis from executive agencies. Representative Cannon has argued that this permits more flexibility and economy in staff assignments and prevents the professional staff from becoming a power center with their own independent motivations.[52]

In addition to a better organization of its curiosity, Congress needs a better organization of its obligations. The creation of a Joint Committee on the Budget would not bring an automatic solution to all problems of congressional budget-making. But if some satisfactory way could be found to define the role of the staff in relation to the appropriations committees and in relation to the executive, the Joint Committee would have a reasonable chance for successful operation. Feelings and attitudes are important in these circumstances. If a Joint Committee on the Budget is established with a view to improving working relations with the executive, then its possibilities for success are enhanced. If it is established with a view to substituting a congressional staff for the Bureau of the Budget or for the budget offices of departments and agencies, further frustration will result. A Joint Committee on the Budget *could* provide a vehicle for strengthening the influence of the Bureau of the Budget in the process of congressional review. It *could* provide the mechanism for assembling information on expenditure commitments over time—data on the long-run costs of government programs, not now available.

Policy determination can be improved where machinery is available for channeling information to the right point and in the right form. The establishment of a Joint Committee on the Budget would provide a further vehicle for bringing the Joint Committee on the Economic Report more nearly to the point where broad economic and fiscal considerations can influence congressional budget-making.[53] A Committee on

---

[52] Committee on Expenditures in the Executive Departments, *To Create a Joint Committee on the Budget,* p. 26. Difficulties in the use of expert staff in the legislative process are not confined to Congress. For a Canadian viewpoint see J. A. Corry, "Adaptation of Parliamentary Processes to the Modern State," *Canadian Journal of Economics and Political Science,* February 1954, pp. 7–8.

[53] The National Planning Association has suggested that the responsibility for reviewing the economic aspects of the budget might be assigned to the Joint Committee on the Economic Report, which would be retitled the Joint Committee on Economic and Fiscal Policy. (Gerhard Colm and Marilyn Young, *The Federal Budget and the National Economy,* National Planning Association, Washington, 1955, pp. 5, 64–67.)

the Budget would presumably hold hearings and discuss the economic outlook and the interrelations of budgetary and economic policy. Cooperation between a Committee on the Budget and the Joint Committee on the Economic Report should improve the effectiveness of both in providing a general review of federal budgeting and fiscal policy, but a review which is synchronized with program requirements.[54]

4. STRENGTHENING POLITICAL PARTIES. Reform in congressional budget-making procedures will not occur in isolation from other congressional procedures and in isolation from the general pattern of relations between the executive and the Congress. This point has long been recognized by political scientists and by many influential Congressmen who have studied the changing pattern of Executive-Congress relationships.[55] The strengthening of democratic institutions in the United States depends on the strengthening of responsibility in government. Those who make decisions must be accountable for their actions. An increased concern for national welfare, it is contended, must come by strengthening the instruments of political life which are national in character—the Presidency and the major political parties. Stephen K. Bailey says:

> . . . the strengthening of party cohesion in Congress would unquestionably enhance the collective power and prestige of that vital institution. The present splintering of decision-making leads to inevitable confusion and frustration among our national legislators. . . . Congress must have the continuing right of introducing, revising, and enacting legislation, but these functions should be carried on in such a way that the public can pin responsibility unequivocally.[56]

Those who sponsor this approach argue that the strengthening of national political parties by the establishment of party councils with authority to develop a consistent party program would lay the basis for im-

[54] The Committee for Economic Development has suggested the establishment of a Joint Budget Policy Conference to review the fiscal and economic implications of the President's budget, but without the assistance of additional staff and separated from the work of the appropriations committees. This is probably less workable than the McClellan proposal, since, like Section 138, it would attempt to separate aggregate economic considerations from program considerations. (Committee for Economic Development, *Control of Federal Government Expenditures*, Washington, 1955, pp. 25–28; Smithies, *The Budgetary Process in the United States*, pp. 192–197.)

[55] Report of the Committee on Political Parties, American Political Science Association, "Toward a More Responsible Two-Party System," *American Political Science Review*, Supplement, September 1950; Gross, *op. cit.*, pp. 77–91; Elbert D. Thomas, "How Congress Functions under its Reorganization Act," *American Political Science Review*, December 1949, pp. 1179–1189.

[56] Bailey, *Congress Makes a Law*, pp. 239–240.

provements in relations with the executive agencies. The President himself would then be in a position to work more closely with party leaders in the Congress, both on the budget and on other matters of policy. This, in turn, would tend to ameliorate " . . . the interminable struggle between the legislature and the executive. The best solution would seem to be to avoid the supremacy of either branch but to devise the conditions of a working partnership that would assure greater harmony without destroying the essential independence of either."[57]

Unfortunately, it is difficult to be optimistic about the possibilities of strengthening the major political parties. There is little evidence in recent history to suggest that party cohesion has increased. The multivalued character of the major parties seems to be continually predominant.

5. PROSPECTIVE DEVELOPMENTS. A decade ago Leonard D. White said,

> The details of the business of government have escaped the competence of legislative committees and chairmen; the possibility of deciding policy by settling details, once perhaps feasible, has disappeared; and in the future, legislatures perforce must deal with administration on the basis of principle and generality if they are to deal with it effectively and in the public interest.[58]

What was true in 1945 is at least as true today. The oversight of administration by the Congress, as by other legislative bodies, must inevitably tend to become more general in character where it is undertaken as a precondition for appropriations. In all likelihood the Congress will come eventually to a detailed review of program operations only after the event—a post-audit of performance.

A redirection of congressional attention toward "principles" and "generality" will undoubtedly bring, at some point, the adoption of some such institution as the Joint Committee on the Budget. This would strengthen Congress in its efforts to review program levels and, perhaps even more important, would provide the machinery which the Congress was searching for under Section 138 of the Legislative Reorganization Act and in the Omnibus Appropriation Bill. Congress needs, and should have, an occasion for a fiscal policy review of the President's budget, coordinated with program review. This does not mean simply a strengthening of Congress or a reform in congressional procedures. It

---

[57] Zeller, *American State Legislatures,* pp. 164–165.

[58] Leonard D. White, "Legislative Responsibility for the Public Service," *New Horizons in Public Administration,* University of Alabama Press, University, Alabama, 1945, p. 6.

means a further effort to develop a working partnership with the Executive.

Selected Bibliography

Banfield, Edward C., "Congress and the Budget; A Planner's Criticism," *American Political Science Review*, December 1949, pp. 1217–1228.

Buck, A. E., *The Budget in Governments of Today*, Macmillan Company, New York, 1934, pp. 185–224.

Fielder, Clinton, "Reform of the Congressional Legislative Budget," *National Tax Journal*, March 1951, pp. 65–76.

Galloway, George B., *Reform of the Federal Budget*, Public Affairs Bulletin No. 80, Library of Congress Legislative Reference Service, Washington, 1950.

———— *The Legislative Process in Congress*, Thomas Y. Crowell Company, New York, 1953, pp. 91–143, 655–664.

Harris, Joseph P., "Needed Reforms in the Federal Budget System," *Public Administration Review*, Autumn 1952, pp. 242–250.

Huzar, Elias, *The Purse and the Sword*, Cornell University Press, Ithaca, 1950.

Leiserson, Avery, "Coordination of Federal Budgetary and Appropriations Procedures under the Legislative Reorganization Act of 1946," *National Tax Journal*, June 1948, pp. 118–126.

Loeffler, Herman C., "Alice in Budget-Land," *National Tax Journal*, March 1951, pp. 54–64.

Macmahon, Arthur W., "Congressional Oversight of Administration: The Power of the Purse; I," *Political Science Quarterly*, June 1943, pp. 161–190; II, September 1943, pp. 380–414.

March, Michael S., "A Comment on Budgetary Improvement in the National Government," *National Tax Journal*, June 1952, pp. 155–173.

Nelson, Dalmas H., "The Omnibus Appropriations Act of 1950," *Journal of Politics*, May 1953, pp. 274–288.

Phillips, John, "The Hadacol of the Budget Makers," *National Tax Journal*, September 1951, pp. 255–268.

Smithies, Arthur, *The Budgetary Process in the United States*, McGraw-Hill Book Company, New York, 1955, pp. 89–100, 175–197.

Zeller, Belle, ed., *American State Legislatures*, Thomas Y. Crowell Company, New York, 1954, pp. 163–188.

13.

....

Budget execution

To the extent that budget programs are presented clearly, that they express work programs which are realistic, that the legislature has made its intent clear in the modification of these programs, and only to this extent can there be an organized system for carrying out the budget. Preparation and execution are separate and distinct phases of the budget cycle, but unless each builds on the other, governmental administration will fail to utilize the full potentialities of the budget as an instrument of governance.

The carrying out of the budget is an executive responsibility. This is clearly recognized in parliamentary governments, where the legislature discharges its function when it authorizes the budget and again when it reviews the record of accomplishment in program, legal, and financial terms. In the United States the lines are not so clear-cut, and the history of budgeting is replete with cases in which the legislative body intervenes in execution, to modify decisions it has previously made, to influence administrative actions, to interpose independent checks on specific transactions. But even here the trend is discernible toward increased executive control in this phase of budgeting. The growth and complexity of administration make further executive direction inevitable.

The procedure for budget execution, which will shape and influence decision-making, evolves in accordance with the distribution of power within a government. The authority of the legislature vis-à-vis the administration will be reflected in budget execution. Within the adminis-

340

tration the role of the chief executive and of his staff agencies, in their control of operating departments and agencies, will be manifest in the techniques which are employed to carry out the government's financial plan.

Some writers on budgeting have stressed, above all, the importance of strong central authority for effective budget execution. A. E. Buck, for example, said in discussing state and local budget systems in this country:

> . . . the lawmakers . . . gave little or no thought to the position of the executive with respect to the various agencies of the administration. This was particularly true in state governments where these agencies were often arranged in a haphazard and disjointed fashion, their administrative officers, in many instances, not being even remotely under executive control or supervision. . . . Although the executive might prepare a satisfactory financial plan for the legislative body under these circumstances, he could not hope to be able to enforce the plan once it had been adopted. No wonder the budget system in many of these cases has been little more than a farce. . . .[1]

Further, strong central control maintains budgetary equilibrium throughout the fiscal year:

> If this is not done, the budget will fail in a large measure to accomplish its purpose, which is to produce stability in the government's finances by making both ends meet.[2]

Although this approach to budget execution, with its emphasis on budget balance, planned and administered, must be regarded as excessively narrow, reflecting an undue concern with rigid financial considerations, there is need for a substantial measure of *current* central direction and control during execution of the budget. Adaptability to changing conditions is impossible if central direction is confined to the planning phase of budgeting.

This kind of current control must be a temperate one so that management prerogatives may be preserved and strengthened. Central direction can be cumbersome, unwieldy, and restrictive. This is a critical issue: the extent to which central or government-wide considerations are to be permitted to override and dominate departmental or program considerations. There are considerations which are central in nature and should be decided centrally, and there are considerations and accompanying decisions which may safely be moved away from the center. Overcontrol is a continuous hazard. Systems of budget execution undoubtedly tend to become inflexible over time, and if there is any

---

[1] A. E. Buck, *Public Budgeting*, Harper & Brothers, New York, 1929, p. 432.
[2] *Ibid.*, p. 452.

natural tendency here it would appear to be that of moving more and more decisions to the center. Re-examination of the machinery for budget execution to assure continued attention to the need for agency management control is periodically necessary.

Techniques for budget execution may be broadly divided into two groups, financial and administrative. The former are directed to the accounts established to record the various aspects of the transactions of a government, for both receipts and expenditures. Government accounts reflect budget execution; accounting procedures themselves may be used as a control over the execution of the budget. Accounting records must also be audited, as the phase of the budget cycle which follows execution. These aspects—accounting and auditing—will be examined in Chapter 14. The administrative techniques, which operate in a framework controlled by the legislature, will be the concern of this chapter.

I. OBJECTIVES OF A SYSTEM FOR BUDGET EXECUTION

The ideal system of budget execution can be defined simply, but it is difficult of attainment. Budget execution should preserve the intent of the legislature but at the same time should maintain flexibility at all levels of administration.

A. Preserving Legislative Intent

Legislative intent with respect to program is quantified in financial terms in the budget authorization. The legislature may also express intent concerning the administration of the program in terms other than financial. Program objectives may be redefined during budget hearings; members of the legislature may confer with administrators informally on occasions other than in the process of budget review; legislative intent may be expressed in committee reports on budget authorizations or in the work of special investigating committees (see Chapter 12).

In the execution of the budget it is generally the responsibility of program administrators to interpret and apply these expressions. There is little that can be accomplished by formal checks to assure that the feelings and wishes of legislators will be observed. The sanctions, nevertheless, are ever-present and reside in the condition that the legislature will, in the next year, review the program, and call the program administrators for questioning. This means that an administrator who wishes to maintain a pattern of harmonious working relations with the legislature will be most careful to secure an interpretation of legislative intent where he feels that this is not evident in the formal actions that were taken.[3]

In the absence of additional specified intent, budget execution necessarily proceeds in accordance with the financial and program plan as submitted to and reviewed by the legislature. The budget to be executed is the budget as submitted. If the legislature reduces the budget without specifying in detail where the cuts are to be made, the program administrator is left with a substantial margin of discretion. This may approach a vacuum. The central budget office may have no clear authority for rebudgeting the reduced appropriation, and the administrator has no guidelines in program terms.[4]

B. Observing Financial Limitations

Historically, systems of budget execution have been designed primarily to assure that the financial limitations expressed by the legislature are adhered to. Budget execution is traditionally conceived as almost wholly a matter of financial control, and its success is very often judged in terms of preventing deficiencies and effecting savings during the fiscal year.

Sundelson quotes the first director of the New York State Division of the Budget, Mark Graves, to this effect:

> It is not sufficient, as I see the situation, to attempt to control expenditures entirely through the instrumentality of the appropriation act. . . . I maintain that it is quite as important to control expenditures out of the appropriations as it is to exercise great care in making the appropriations in the first instance. It is virtually impossible for any spending official to anticipate twenty or more months in advance of the close of a fiscal year his financial requirements for that year. The result is that the official plays on the safe side, and if he errs at all, he requests more than will be needed. . . . It is essential to have vested somewhere authority to restrain the spending agencies; otherwise they are apt to view the appropriation as a command to spend rather than an allowance to spend.[5]

This kind of emphasis is significant and important, and just as budget preparation must be concerned, although not exclusively concerned, with

---

[3] For an illuminating case study of the relations between the U. S. Department of Agriculture and the appropriations committees during budget execution, see "Jump's Case," Committee on Public Administration Cases, Washington (undated, processed).

[4] For a discussion of this situation in the United States government see Charles S. Hyneman, *Bureaucracy in a Democracy*, Harper & Brothers, New York, 1950, pp. 339–342.

[5] J. Wilner Sundelson, *Budgetary Methods in National and State Governments*, J. B. Lyon Company, Albany, 1938, p. 618.

the efficient use of resources, so should budget execution be concerned with considerations of economy. But to suggest that the only concern of budget execution is to prevent overobligation is much too narrow a view. It would seem to imply that the legislature is the sole repository of judgment and jurisdiction over the effective use of public resources, and to ignore program considerations which are, or should be, of equal concern.

The issues here are well illustrated in the matter of deficiency appropriations. There are really only two kinds of deficiency appropriations, good ones and bad ones. The bad ones will come from faulty planning on the part of agencies and inadequate review by the central budget office—instances where, with the exercise of more care or more insight or better arithmetic it would have been possible to foresee that program costs would be greater than requested. Deficiencies can also arise from faulty management and inadequate cost control during the execution of a program. Or the legislature itself may force a deficiency, in the interests of temporary political advantage, by appropriating, with an overt display of economy, less than is known to be required.

But there is another kind of deficiency—that which arises from circumstances beyond control, as when costs increase because of inflation, when low-cost materials become unavailable and materials of higher cost must be substituted, or when personnel costs rise. In these circumstances, if the program intent of the legislature is to prevail, there is only one recourse; a deficiency will be incurred and the agency must return to the legislature with a request for additional funds. This kind of deficiency often reflects tight budgeting and could be avoided only by an original overestimate.

Traditional condemnation of all deficiency appropriations rests on an oversimplified and inadequate analysis of the needs of budget-making. Effective legislative review will extend to both program and finance. The able legislative budget-maker is one who can differentiate the sources of deficiency appropriations, tolerating the ones which arise from circumstances beyond control and condemning the ones which arise from faulty budget planning and management.

This will never be an easy task. In the United States government the history of budgeting prior to the enactment of the Budget and Accounting Act of 1921 is very largely the history of congressional efforts to control expenditures by the itemization of appropriations and by curbs on deficiencies. These efforts were notoriously unsuccessful, as Wilmerding has so ably documented.[6] The Anti-Deficiency Act of 1906,

[6] Lucius Wilmerding, Jr., *The Spending Power*, Yale University Press, New Haven, 1943, esp. pp. 137–153.

which was supposed to prevent all deficiencies by a system of apportioning appropriations through the fiscal year, was of no help in separating the needed from the unneeded, the good from the bad. It was not until the establishment of the Bureau of the Budget and the beginnings of a system of executive budget execution that significant control steps were taken. This experience strongly suggests that no system of budget execution intended to prevent deficiencies, or to effect savings as programs are administered, can be successful when imposed unilaterally by legislative authority. The cooperation and authority of the executive is a prerequisite.

Keeping the budget within prescribed financial limits is not solely a question of controlling expenditures. The income side must also be regulated, and again, this is a matter for executive authority, not for the legislature.

The executive must see to it that funds are available for the payment of bills as presented. To make sure that cash is on hand as required means that the executive—usually the treasury—must schedule anticipated income. Tax collections and their seasonal patterns must be known, and these must be related to payment patterns. This kind of cash planning may not be difficult if there is a single consolidated fund, but it is very much complicated by separate fund structures and earmarked revenues.

C. Maintaining Flexibility

Economic conditions and some program conditions inevitably change over time. The ability of a budget execution system to cope with these changes depends in large measure on the way in which budget authorizations are written by the legislature.

First of all, to ensure flexibility the budget authorization must be permissive, not mandatory. That is, it must extend the authority to incur obligations and to make expenditures, but not require that they be made. This means that legislative intent must be expressed in program terms, not alone in financial terms, and there must be accompanying authority for the executive to modify financial arrangements in the interests of program.

Second, the unit of voting must be broad. Lump sum appropriations can give to the executive the freedom to choose among the objects of expenditure in accordance with changing conditions.

Permissive expenditures and lump sum appropriations, in turn, must rest on a high degree of legislative confidence in the executive. These are broad grants of power and are capable of abuse. Their custodianship must be subject to review and, if they are to be properly safeguarded, should be accompanied by a careful legislative examination of performance in the postexecution phase of the budget cycle.

The history of budget execution systems in this country, particularly in the states, does not indicate that the need for program flexibility played a major part in their establishment. Many of the present state systems had their origins in the necessity for forcing realignment in budget expenditures during the depression of the 1930's. Rigid constitutional requirements for budget balance, in the face of declining revenues, forced legislatures to make wide grants of authority to state governors to effect drastic retrenchments. This, of course, is a kind of flexibility in response to changing economic conditions and is extremely effective in securing a balanced budget, but as Sundelson says, these

> . . . are the result of inadequate fiscal systems, violent economic crises, and defective budgetary mechanisms. Their existence is to be considered symptomatic of fiscal disorder rather than as a solution of any difficulties.[7]

Under these provisions, which were adopted widely by southern states, all appropriations were maximum, conditional, and proportional to revenue. As budget receipts dropped, the governor was required to slash appropriations across the board in proportion to available receipts. He was seldom given authority to make discretionary reductions, although in some states certain kinds of programs, as for institutional care, were exempt from the retrenchment process.

Other states, during the 1930's, instituted executive schemes for expenditure control which were much less rigid than those of the southern states. In Iowa, Maryland, Oregon, Utah, and West Virginia the executive was given increased authority to reduce appropriations during the budget year, but was given substantially more discretion in the selection of the programs and objects of expenditure to be affected.[8] In still other states the governor or a board of finance or department of finance was granted authority to make specific kinds of reductions under specific circumstances.

There is a vast difference between the "maximum, conditional, and proportional" authority over expenditures, and the carefully hedged grant of discretionary authority to the executive to control expenditures already voted. The former is a device for assuring budget flexibility in only one direction—downward. The latter can be an addition to an executive budget system, with a consequent increase in executive budget responsibility.

Very different in purpose are the budget execution techniques which national governments are coming increasingly to employ in the interests

---

[7] Sundelson, *op. cit.,* p. 562.

[8] *Ibid.,* pp. 577–602.

of broad economic management. If a national government budget is to have maximum potentiality as a device for economic stabilization, the budget may need to be modified as it is being carried out.

This means that during an inflationary period the executive may have authority to reduce certain items of expenditure in order to hold down the government's contribution to income-increasing expenditures. The authority to delay the starting of public works and to reduce the rate of construction for projects already underway will help to counter inflationary pressures. Conversely, where public works reserves are established, the executive may possess authority to initiate new projects to counteract a downturn in economic conditions. In a number of countries where balance of payments difficulties are perennial, the executive may possess authority to control the rate of expenditure on foreign goods and services during the budget year, again in the interests of maintaining a stable economy.

Flexibility may also be necessary in the interests of maintaining particular programs that are subject to cost fluctuations. During the budget year it may be possible to effect savings because of reductions in materials prices, or savings may be effected by a reorganization of work methods and procedures. These savings should be captured and either returned to the treasury or made available to other programs for which costs are increasing.

Cost fluctuations are not uniform among all programs. Public works projects are likely to be most affected by such changes; the operations of administrative departments, where personnel costs are a very large fraction of total outlay, are much less likely to be affected. A system of budget execution designed to permit flexibility should recognize these differences. It may be necessary to maintain considerably more current control over expenditure for materials and supplies than over wages and salaries. By the same token, a different kind of budget execution system may be applied to a police department than to a public works department.

The maintenance of flexibility in the execution of the budget should be undertaken in a way that will strengthen management control over operations. If budgeting is to be truly a continuous process, with next year's budget building on this year's operations, then management must come to regard budgetary control as a part of its responsibilities, and budgetary control patterns must not be separated from other management controls. In essence this means budget execution of a carefully devised work plan grounded in cost data. Current control is achieved by a comprehensive system of reporting on work progress and finance.

The central controls which may be established to prevent overobligation and deficiencies, or the controls which are used to vary the budget in accordance with changing economic conditions, should not be oppressive and stifling in their impact on those who have responsibility for operations. Somewhat more than a half-century ago Henry Carter Adams suggested that there could be extravagant parsimony as well as extravagant appropriations.[9] In discussing budget execution Adams said:

> . . . if no danger to political liberty lies in an extension of the functions of the administration it will, as a rule, lead to increased efficiency in public affairs. . . . Now it must be remembered that the development of budgets and of budgetary control resulted from a struggle of the people against the arbitrary exactions of an ambitious monarchy. That controversy, however, has been settled. The danger to which popular government is now exposed arises from deceptions practiced by legislators rather than encroachments designed by administrators. Moreover, the weakness of popular government shows itself in the inefficiency of administration, due in large measure to the petty limitations under which executive services are performed.[10]

The techniques available for assuring program flexibility within a framework of management control are conditioned by the nature of the legislature's budget authorizations. Their specific implementation may reside in the hands of a central staff such as the budget office, or in the hands of department and agency officials. These possibilities are discussed in the following paragraphs.

II. CONTROL BY APPROPRIATION

In Great Britain the system of budget execution rests on a longstanding informal tradition of Treasury control. In France it rests on formal institutional arrangements under the jurisdiction of the Minister of Finance. In governments in the United States, budget execution patterns are likely to be established by statutes that endow the executive with specified controls, but regardless of the formal pattern, the executive's responsibilities are exercised in relation to specific budget authorizations extended by the legislature. These authorizations may modify, in any one year or for any one program, the statutory powers generally possessed by the executive.

One means of assuring adaptability in the execution of the budget is to permit the executive to effect transfers among appropriation titles, within agencies, or among agencies. Appropriations by state legislatures

[9] Henry Carter Adams, *The Science of Finance,* Henry Holt & Company, New York, 1898, p. 26.
[10] *Ibid.,* p. 186.

in this country seldom permit such transfers, even within an agency. Similar restrictions operate in most city governments, except for city manager governments, in which case transfer power may be given to the manager, possibly with the proviso that he consult with the finance committee of the city council before taking action. In the United States government the tradition has long been to permit no transfer among agencies and very little within agencies, except on specific occasions and for specific purposes, as stated in annual appropriation acts; for example, a department might be permitted to transfer up to 5 percent from one title to another. In recent years somewhat greater flexibility within agencies has been assured by the consolidation of appropriation measures and a greater tendency toward lump sum appropriations.

The appropriation of an emergency fund will greatly increase the ability of the executive to meet unforeseen demands for expenditures during the budget year. A survey made in 1948 revealed that 25 states had established at that time some form of central fund to meet the emergency requirements of operating departments.[11] Ten of the states gave control over the fund to executive authority, sometimes to the governor or to a board of administrators. All of the states retained some form of legislative control over the use of the appropriation, usually through the finance committees of the legislature or specified members thereof. This would indicate that state legislatures do not uniformly regard budget flexibility as a prerogative of the executive and prefer to retain initial control over such special appropriations, in spite of the fact that the use of emergency funds is customarily restricted to programs originally authorized by the legislature, with the fund very often employed as a substitute for any transfer among line-item appropriations.

In the national government there are no appropriated general emergency funds comparable to those in the states. Specific funds are appropriated to the President, but these are available only for designated purposes. Mutual Security appropriations are made in this way; in addition, the President has control over such authorizations as disaster relief, defense aid, an emergency fund for international affairs, and an emergency fund for national defense. These authorizations are helpful in meeting emergency situations as they may arise within these areas, but the funds appropriated to the President are not generally available for the run-of-the mill operating contingencies of departments and agencies. In these cases flexibility in budget execution must be obtained by means of other techniques, operating within the appropriation limits.

[11] Daniel W. Tuttle, Jr., "The General Contingent Fund in Minnesota: Operation and Management, 1939–1947," *Public Administration Review,* Summer 1949, p. 194.

III. CENTRAL EXECUTIVE CONTROL OF EXPENDITURES

The close relationship between budget execution and government accounting very often permits the latter to dominate the former. Budget execution somehow becomes synonymous with fiscal control. And, as Millett says,

> The very term "fiscal control" has a negative connotation to many persons, suggesting that management is primarily concerned with placing limitations upon the expenditure of appropriations. This would appear to be an unfortunate, and an unwarranted, interpretation of management's authority and responsibility in conducting administrative operations. After all, the first job of management is to see to it that the basic work of an agency as authorized by law and as fixed by appropriations shall be carried out. The purpose in fiscal control is to help facilitate accomplishment of this basic task.[12]

The distinction may be subtle, as Millett points out, but there is a great difference between fiscal control in the spirit of facilitating operations and fiscal control in the spirit of restricting operations.

In most governments throughout the world not only does budget execution come to be dominated by accounting considerations, but the whole process tends to freeze into rigid routines. The national government of Great Britain is an outstanding exception to this tendency. Here budget execution is relatively free of negative connotations. "Treasury control" describes a pattern of relations between central executive authority and the operating departments which is much more fluid than the routinized systems of most jurisdictions.

Basil Chubb writes,

> The Treasury is the government's instrument for carrying out its financial policy and for supervising the activities of the departments. It stands in a unique position and its functions are difficult to define. "Treasury Control," wrote Henry Higgs, "is something that you live under, that you suffer from, that you profit by; and if you cannot define it, well—Lord Morley used to say that he could not define an elephant but he knew when he saw it."[13]

What makes Treasury control difficult to describe is that it is exercised informally and without codification; definite rules are avoided and it relies on tradition and common consent.[14] To the uninitiated American

---

[12] John D. Millett, *Management in the Public Service,* McGraw-Hill Book Company, New York, 1955, pp. 229–230.

[13] Basil Chubb, *The Control of Public Expenditure,* Clarendon Press, Oxford, 1952, p. 2.

[14] The best available treatment of this subject is Samuel H. Beer, "Treasury Control: The Coordination of Financial Policy in Great Britain," *American*

observer the British system of budget execution is confusing because of the way it is bound up with budget preparation—the phases of the budget cycle are not precise here.

Budget authorizations by the Parliament are extended in terms of Votes. For Army, Navy, and Air, these amount to 34 voted appropriations, and for Civil Estimates about 150 appropriations.[15] In the budget as presented to the Parliament there are further subdivisions of Votes, but final authorization does not incorporate the detail as presented. Legally, therefore, the executive is not bound by the subheads, but only by the Votes. This is lump-sum appropriation. The Treasury retains authority to control expenditure at the level of subheads, but may not shift appropriations from one Vote to another except, in unusual circumstances, for the armed services.

It is the Treasury's responsibility to follow the course of expenditure during the budget year, to effect savings where possible in one subhead and, if necessary, make them available elsewhere within the voted service. This is done by the Supply divisions, of which there are seven, each dealing with a group of related departments and services. In its exercise of control, the Treasury has a very definite economy orientation. Beer puts the matter this way:

> In one sense it [economy] is secondary; the main concern of Supply is not merely cutting costs and saving money. In a larger sense, however, economy is inseparable from the function of coordination. So to criticize expenditure as to provide the same service at a lower cost will reflect policy. . . . And to prevent extravagance in one sphere in order to have more funds available for pressing needs elsewhere follows from the attempt to balance expenditure. So understood, economy, now as in the past, is the principal purpose of Treasury control and is enforced by means of both the annual review of the estimates and the routine, day-to-day relations of Supply divisions and departments.[16]

Treasury control is exercised by means of more or less continuous consultation with the departments. No department may initiate any variation in its activities that involves financial implications without receiving prior approval from the Treasury. This may take the form of a specific sanction or it may take the form of a delegation of authority within certain limits. But approval there must be.

Political Science Review, March 1955, pp. 144–160.   See also R. G. Hawtrey, *The Exchequer and the Control of Expenditure,* Humphrey Milford, Oxford University Press, London, 1921, pp. 27–34.

[15] For a description of Parliamentary procedure in financial legislation see Eric Taylor, *The House of Commons at Work,* Penguin Books, Harmondsworth, Middlesex, 1951, pp. 189–225.

[16] Beer, *op. cit.,* p. 146.

Under the Treasury's continuous working relations with the departments, the annual review of the budget necessarily takes on a lesser significance as a means of policy formulation, financial and program. A great many of the issues which might be examined in annual budget hearings in governments in the United States will have been acted on by the British Treasury during the course of the year. Annual budget-making still retains significance, but as an occasion for over-all review. This kind of continuous control keeps policy matters always moving upward to the Cabinet for decision, and the Treasury is constantly placed in the position of interpreting and reinterpreting the Government's policy.

Treasury control preserves certain kinds of flexibilities in budget execution while limiting others. It is virtually the negation of the kind of flexibility that permits department heads and bureau chiefs financial autonomy in the management of their programs. It does provide flexibility at the center. In extreme cases the Treasury will even approve an overobligation when the Cabinet determines that this is necessary and if the Parliament has been informed; funds may be obligated before authorization has been obtained. And most evidently, Treasury control provides for a high degree of coordination between Government policy and financial policy.

Treasury control is the heart of the British system of budget execution, but it does not stand alone. It is paralleled by routines for accounting and auditing. The Permanent Secretary of each department is also its Accounting Officer.[17] He is responsible for maintaining the accounting system in his department, for liaison with the Treasury, and for reporting on the rate of expenditure. The Accounting Officer represents his department in all financial investigations, defends the department before parliamentary committees, and maintains a line of responsibility to the Auditor General. At the same time, the staff of the Department of Exchequer and Audit work continuously in the departments to provide a running check on legality.[18] There is no formal post-audit of accounts.

This extensive pattern of executive control is further supplemented by a system of parliamentary review and inquiry. The traditional committee for this purpose is the Public Accounts Committee, which dates back to 1861. The findings of the Department of Exchequer and Audit are submitted here, and the Committee, on the basis of these findings,

[17] Garry Armstrong, "The Accounting Officer," *Public Administration* (Australia), March 1948, pp. 5–10.
[18] Ursula K. Hicks, "The Control of Public Expenditure," *Public Finance*, Vol. VIII, 1953, pp. 20–21.

then interrogates the Accounting Officer of the department concerned.[19] In addition to the Public Accounts Committee, which examines the accounts after the close of the fiscal year, since 1946 a Select Committee on the Estimates has concentrated attention on current expenditure, that is, on the investigation of regularity and efficiency after the budget is authorized by the Parliament but before the close of the fiscal year.

There are highly developed systems of budget execution in the national governments of other western European countries, although nowhere is there as much emphasis on maintaining flexible central control as in Great Britain. And in no other jurisdiction is budget execution so closely meshed with budget review.[20] In France budget execution is more closely integrated with the control of accounts, with an emphasis on the prior control of expenditures in accordance with legality.[21] The Ministry of Finance has responsibility for all government accounting. Control a priori is exercised through the Comptrollers of Committed Expenditures, who are officials of the Ministry of Finance but are assigned to the ministries, and who must approve obligations in accordance with the availability of funds and their legal regularity. In the Netherlands the Minister of Finance controls the execution of the budget through an allotment system, in terms of time periods and programs.[22] Accounting controls are in the hands of fiscal officers appointed by the ministries but responsible as well to the General Auditing Court. This latter is independent of executive authority and answerable to the Parliament, and is generally restricted to a post-audit of legality.

In the executive control of expenditures in the United States government the emphasis is on procedural routines, generally more akin to France and the Netherlands than to the British system.

The control of expenditure during budget execution is under the authority of the Bureau of the Budget and its apportionment power. The only other important control which the Bureau has possessed was during World War II and in the immediate postwar years when it fixed personnel ceilings for departments and agencies. Within the limits of apportionment, expenditures are further controlled by department and

[19] For a thorough history and review see Chubb, *The Control of Public Expenditure;* Sir Frank Tribe, "Parliamentary Control of Public Expenditure," *Public Administration,* Winter 1954, pp. 363–381.

[20] In Canada, which might be expected to follow the British tradition, procedures are much more formalized. See A. E. Buck, *Financing Canadian Government,* Public Administration Service, Chicago, 1949, pp. 114–133.

[21] For a description see United Nations, *Government Accounting and Budget Execution,* New York, 1952, pp. 24–41.

[22] O. Bakker, "Budget Execution and Government Accounting in the Netherlands," *ibid.,* pp. 42–59.

agency heads by means of allotment (see Chapter 4). The Bureau's apportionment powers, dating back to the Budget and Accounting Act of 1921, were strengthened by executive order in 1940 and by the General Appropriation Act for fiscal 1951.[23] This Act also gave the Bureau precise legal authority for the establishment of reserves against appropriations to effect economies and savings during the fiscal year. There is no central pre-audit of expenditures in the United States government. Except for apportionment, budget execution is regarded as a responsibility of department and agency management.

Within departments the major technique for the control of expenditure is allotments.[24] These are based on the budget programs which served as the justification for requests for appropriations, as modified by congressional action. Allotments are a delegation of authority within a department, and are extended to designated persons—bureau chiefs or division heads—who may then proceed to obligate funds and enter into contracts. The allotment may be in lump sum, or may be specified in accordance with objects of expenditure. Allotment systems are not standardized in the federal government, but vary among departments and within departments in accordance with the nature of programs and their requirements for flexibility.

The allotment system is generally supported by a reporting system; where this is well developed, information on the status of allotments will be one part of a complete system of internal work progress reporting. Allotment control may be supplemented in some departments and agencies by a system of position control. This requires that the personnel office of a department clear all proposed appointments with the budget office of that department, to ascertain that the position is authorized and that it may be filled within the limits of program and funds. Where this control is in force, persons may not legally be entered on the payroll until appointment papers have been so certified.

In state and local governments there are innumerable variations in systems of budget execution; in fact, even the terminology is far from uniform. The term allotment is often used to describe the technique of central budget office control. Generally speaking, emphasis is placed on some type of precontrol in an accounting framework, with very little discretion available to operating departments and therefore with limited

---

[23] *Executive Order* 8512; *P.L.* 759, Sec. 1211, 81st Cong., 2d sess.

[24] See Chapter 10. The Department of the Army is a prominent exception to this, with budget execution patterns which require a hierarchal arrangement and which center on formal Budget Execution Plans and funding. See Frederick C. Mosher, *Program Budgeting,* Public Administration Service, Chicago, 1954, pp. 185–190; Arthur Smithies, *The Budgetary Process in the United States,* McGraw-Hill Book Company, New York, 1955, pp. 246–248.

flexibility.[25]   Even where appropriations are itemized in detail by the legislature, some kind of pre-audit may very often control legality and even propriety.

In New York State, for example, the budget is generally of a line-item type, specifying the objects of expenditure in great detail.   Some appropriations for maintenance and for public works, however, are in lump sum.   New York state practice requires that these be "lined-out" by the Division of the Budget before they may be obligated by departments.   This gives the budget office continuous control over the rate of obligations by departments, and extends to budget execution the highly centralized pattern which characterizes New York State budget preparation and submission.   Moreover, New York State enforces a pre-audit, restricted to legality, by an independent Comptroller.   The system apparently works with more dispatch than most of the pre-audit systems used in American governments.

In municipalities where there is a city manager, there are invariably strong central controls over budget execution.[26]   These will typically embrace the authority of the manager to establish an allotment system and an accompanying reporting system.   If the budget is of the line-item variety, the manager will frequently be given authority to transfer among the items and sometimes even among appropriation titles, possibly subject to prior consultation with members of the finance committee of the city council.   Position control will customarily center in the hands of the manager, very often to the extent of requiring that before an authorized position is filled the manager must ascertain that the work program of the department requires the employee.   In some city governments a part or all of the foregoing powers over budget execution are administered by a city comptroller in his capacity as an official appointed by the mayor.[27]

The rigidities in budget execution, like the rigidities in budget classification, will be relaxed as and if there is a further development of responsible administration in the public service.   With this can come a renewed and strengthened concern with program benefits and program consequences, and some abatement of the now too-frequent overconcern with financial control in a narrow sense.

[25] For an interesting case study of centralized expenditure control in a decentralized administration, see C. Beverly Briley, "Controlling Expenditures," *Municipal Finance,* August 1954, pp. 26–31 (Davidson County, Nashville, Tennessee).

[26] Frank P. Sherwood, "What is Behind the City's Budget," *Public Management,* April 1954, pp. 78–80.

[27] Richard W. Van Wagenen, "Financial Control: A Case Study," *Public Administration Review,* Winter 1942, pp. 40–49 (San Francisco).

Selected Bibliography

Adams, Henry Carter, *The Science of Finance,* Henry Holt & Company, New York, 1898, pp. 178–191.

Beer, Samuel H., "Treasury Control: The Coordination of Financial Policy in Great Britain," *American Political Science Review,* March, 1955, pp. 144–160.

Buck, A. E., *Public Budgeting,* Harper & Brothers, New York, 1929, pp. 431–550.

―――― *The Budget in Governments of Today,* Macmillan Company, New York, 1934, pp. 225–267.

Chubb, Basil, *The Control of Public Expenditure,* Claredon Press, Oxford, 1952, pp. 1–22.

Hicks, Ursula K., "The Control of Public Expenditure," *Public Finance,* Vol. VIII, 1953, pp. 7–28.

Jones, J. Weldon, "Accounting and Reporting from the Standpoint of Administration and Executive Budget Control," *Budgeting: An Instrument of Planning and Management,* Vol. VI, Catheryn Seckler-Hudson, ed., American University, Washington (undated), pp. 101–107.

Millett, John D., *Management in the Public Service,* McGraw-Hill Book Company, New York, 1955, pp. 229–252.

Robson, Lawrence W., "Management Accounting for Public Administration," *Public Administration,* Summer 1954, pp. 172–180.

Sherwood, Frank P., "What is Behind the City's Budget," *Public Management,* April 1954, pp. 78–80.

Sundelson, J. Wilner, *Budgetary Methods in National and State Governments,* J. B. Lyon Company, Albany, 1938, pp. 525–619.

14.

···

Accounting
and auditing*

Government accounting is a part of fiscal management, with objectives that are in some cases very close to budgeting and in other cases independent. Government accounts are used to record transactions as the budget is carried out. The techniques of central control over budget execution depend, for their implementation, on the accounts which record appropriations and obligations against those appropriations. Departmental allotment systems are likewise established in accounting terms, and specified persons are held responsible for financial transactions as recorded in government accounts. At the level of departmental and bureau management, accounting is linked with work planning and reporting. The accounts are used for the current administrative control of operations, and also serve for measuring past performance. This, in turn, is the basis from which future budgets must be planned and prepared.

In every government, accounting serves other purposes somewhat less closely related to the phases of the budget cycle. Cost accounting for management purposes may extend beyond that which is required for the preparation and execution of the budget. The settlement of accounts,

* Substantial portions of this chapter are reproduced from the author's staff contribution to United Nations, *Government Accounting and Budget Execution*, New York, 1952, pp. 3–23, 73–90. The author is indebted to Henry S. Bloch and Alfred H. Landau of the United Nations staff and Herschel C. Walling of the U. S. General Accounting Office for their contributions to the original manuscript.

while it may legally be conceived as the final step in budget execution, is very often discharged by persons and under arrangements that are wholly divorced from budget planning and execution. Similarly, the audit of accounts, while again a phase of budgeting, should be organizationally separate, in many of its aspects, from the other phases of the budget cycle.

In a modern government, particularly in national governments, it can be anticipated that accounting will be complex. This complexity arises because of the manifold purposes which must be served by government accounts and because similar types of accounts must be maintained at different levels of government. It is not practicable to have a single set of accounts or even to limit the types of accounts to three or four basic sets. Some duplication in accounting records may be unavoidable. A government needs the types of accounts which are adequate in relation to the purposes to be served.[1]

I. FUNCTIONS SERVED BY GOVERNMENT ACCOUNTS

The purposes which government accounts should serve may be generally outlined as follows.[2]

(1) Accounting systems should be designed to show compliance with legal provisions.

(2) Accounts that show the commitment and disbursement of monies must be related to budget accounts embodying requests for new expenditure authority. That is, budgeting and accounting must be components of an integrated system of fiscal control.

(3) Accounts must be set forth in such a way as to permit a determination of the adequacy of custodianship of monies and assets under the responsibility of administrative officials.

(4) Accounts must be maintained on a basis which will permit an independent audit extending to all records, funds, securities, and property.

[1] *Final Report of the Committee on the Form of Government Accounts* (Cmd. 7969), His Majesty's Stationery Office, London, 1950, pp. 9–11.

[2] For specific statements related to the United States government see General Accounting Office, *Statement of Accounting Principles and Standards for Guidance of Executive Agencies in the Federal Government*, Washington, 1952; Edwin J. B. Lewis, "Basic Principles in Federal Accounting," *Federal Accountant*, June 1954, pp. 8–10; Federal Government Accountants Association Research Committee, "Comments on GAO Statement of Principles," *ibid.*, pp. 6–8; Howard W. Bordner, "Federal Government Accounting Principles," *Federal Accountant*, September 1954, pp. 6–17. For a statement applicable to municipalities see Municipal Finance Officers Association, *Simplified Municipal Accounting*, Chicago, 1950, pp. 1–14.

(5) The accounting system should provide a full disclosure of financial results, including the measurement of revenue and the costs of activities, programs, and organizations.

(6) The accounting system must provide management at all levels with information for planning and direction. This includes, but is not restricted to, cost measurement.

(7) Accounting systems should incorporate effective procedures for internal audit and control of operations and programs.

(8) Government accounts must be maintained in such a way as to provide information necessary for the economic analysis and planning of governmental activity. This information should be presented in a form that is useful for both executive and legislative purposes.

It is possible to differentiate conceptually among the foregoing purposes of government accounting. In application, however, many of these purposes merge. In general, the first four of these may be described as the *accountability* function; these will be examined in section II. The last four may be described as the *management* function; these will be examined in section III.

It is evident that accountability and management purposes coincide at many points, but historically, in the establishment of government accounting systems, accountability has been given primary if not sole emphasis. Accountability means legal liability—the establishment of a pattern of control over receipts and expenditures that permits a determination, either by the executive or by the legislature (or both), that public monies have been used for a public purpose. Management considerations require that accounts be kept on a basis that permits the continued measurement and analysis of government programs and the efficiency with which they are performed. Management considerations may relate to the aggregate performance of the government as a whole and may therefore require accounting for the total financial transactions of the government. They may also, and increasing attention is being devoted to this phase of accounting, consist of the measurement of activities at the administrative unit level. It is in this latter connotation that accounting is most often referred to as a "tool of management."

In some governments there often appears to be a conflict in particular instances between accountability considerations and management considerations. Specifically, the accounting classifications which are useful for accountability purposes may not be the classifications which are useful for management purposes. But these conflicts are by no means irreconcilable. Both types of considerations are important; both can be contained in a workable system.

II. ACCOUNTABILITY

All modern governments have developed specific institutional arrangements to ensure, or attempt to ensure, accountability for the receipt and expenditure of public funds. Needless to say, there are very great differences in the nature of these institutional arrangements from one government to the next.

It is customary to apply to those agencies in the general government sector a different accounting and control pattern from that for agencies separately organized as trust funds or public enterprise. In fact, the term control itself has a different meaning in these cases. As a British authority has pointed out, control in the sense of "direction" ought to be distinguished from control in the sense of "reporting."[3] The latter consists of measuring and assessing what is happening, but control in this sense does not necessarily imply restraint, guidance, or stimulation. In the reporting sense, governments should establish a pattern of control over all agencies, including trust funds and enterprise. The degree of central direction, however, is another matter. Traditionally, much less direction is applied to commercial-type ventures than to conventional departments, but a system of control to ensure accountability is necessary for all operations.

For purposes of clarifying the varying applications of the principle of accountability, it might be well to abstract the procedural steps which may be followed in the execution of the budget, in order to indicate the role of accounting therein. This is intended to indicate the possibilities for control that exist in any system of budget execution, and is not intended to be representative of any particular government. The steps in a generalized procedure are as follows.

(1) The legislature authorizes the chief executive to make expenditure authority available to administrative agencies.

(2) The executive authority (president, cabinet, minister of finance, bureau of the budget) responsible for the execution of the budget, in accordance with legislative action, extends to the agencies authorization to incur obligations or opens credits to their account.

(3) The heads of agencies, in turn, extend to designated officials within the agency the authorization to incur obligations.

(4) Designated officials (fiscal officers) award contracts for goods and services and incur obligations for the payment of salaries.

(5) The central financial authority (treasury, ministry of finance) places money at the disposal of disbursing officers.

[3] Sir Geoffrey Vickers, "The Accountability of a Nationalized Industry," *Public Administration,* Spring 1952, pp. 71–80.

(6) Fiscal officers within agencies prepare and certify vouchers to show that obligations are due and payable by disbursing officers.

(7) Orders for payment are prepared by fiscal officers and submitted to disbursing officers.

(8) Disbursing officers provide for the payment of cash or check to satisfy the liability.

In practice, some of these procedures may be eliminated or combined. Some governments, for example, do not have disbursing officers but authorize administrative officials within agencies to direct payments by the central bank. In some cases considerable emphasis may be laid on the control of the budget at the point where obligations are incurred; in others, emphasis for control purposes may be centered at the point where vouchers are certified. But regardless of the point or points at which controls are centered, an effective system for ensuring accountability must be outlined in personal terms. Certain officials must be designated as accountable officers and required to assume and be responsible for certain specified procedures or transactions.

A. Pre-audit

In examining the pattern of budget execution in particular governments, it is usually possible to distinguish, at least on a functional basis, the enforcement of accountability by means of a pre-audit from the enforcement of accountability by means of a post-audit.

Pre-audit may assume a number of forms. It may extend to the advance determination of the legality of a particular transaction. This may be accomplished by countersignature of warrants or other documents authorizing the incurrence of obligations. Pre-audit may also extend to the examination of vouchers directing payment of obligations, and may embrace a determination that obligations were properly incurred, that goods were received, that the amounts certified are correct, that moneys are available for the specified purpose, and so forth. The term pre-audit is customarily used to describe an independent control, that is, one outside the jurisdiction of the spending agency.

Post-audit may be broad or narrow. It may consist in an examination of documentation for each step in budget execution. It may center attention at only one point in execution procedures. It is customarily, but not invariably, conducted by an agency independent of the administration, and its results are reported to the legislature.

Although both pre-audit and post-audit are means of ensuring accountability, they are based on quite different concepts of administration and have very different consequences for budgetary execution. The pre-audit tends to reduce the degree of responsibility exercised by departments and agencies. As is evident from the procedural steps listed, there are many points at which pre-audit control can be imposed. If statutes or practices require pre-audit at several stages, there is an inevitable tendency to duplicating effort, to excessive delay, and to resultant inefficiency in the transaction of the government's fiscal affairs. This condition of overcontrol seems to prevail in a number of South American countries, with resulting friction in relations between the *contraloría* and the administrative agencies.[4]

Experience in governments with reasonably efficient systems of budget execution would appear to justify the conclusion that post-audit should be external to the administrative agency, but that pre-audit should be a part of internal administrative responsibilities. Therefore, where standards of internal administration are well developed and accompanied by a high degree of responsibility, pre-audit and post-audit should not be combined in an independent agency.

B. Post-audit

The one feature which is most common to all systems of accounting and budget execution is the post-audit.

In most countries the post-audit is to be distinguished from closing the accounts. The latter typically refers to the procedures associated with the termination of the fiscal year—the summarization, formal balancing, and publication of the over-all budgetary results. Post-audit extends to the verification of legality of individual transactions and the accuracy of the accounts. In Great Britain the closing of accounts and their post-audit are combined in the annual report of the Comptroller and Auditor General. In the United States government the Comptroller General exercises both functions. In most other countries the accounts are formally closed by the ministry of finance, and the post-audit, conducted separately, is completed within a period of two or more years after that time. It can be forcibly argued that this is the preferred arrangement—that the settlement and closing of accounts is an administrative responsibility, but that post-audit must be external to the administration.[5]

The post-audit is generally conceived to be external to the administration in the sense that the agency responsible for the audit reports directly to the legislature. The independence of the audit is customarily rein-

---

[4] For a discussion of overcontrol and the consequences of intermingled pre-audit and post-audit, see *United Nations Mission of Technical Assistance to Bolivia,* New York, 1951, pp. 22–23. See also the recommendations in *Report of the United Nations Economic Mission to Chile,* New York, 1951, pp. 15, 22.

[5] See the extended consideration of this point in Lucius Wilmerding, Jr., *The Spending Power,* Yale University Press, New Haven, 1943, pp. 250–283.

forced by endowing the heads of the auditing agency with judicial or semijudicial power, and by protecting the tenure of the auditors. The Cour des Comptes in France, developed along these lines, has become a model for many countries, particularly in the Middle East and in South America. In France there is a sharp division between pre-audit as performed by the Ministry of Finance and post-audit as performed by the Cour des Comptes. The latter is a semijudicial body and enjoys a high prestige within the government. Its audit extends to the verification of accounts, the disclosure and prosecution of fraud, and the settlement and closing of accounts. In recent years, the jurisdiction of the Cour des Comptes has been extended to embrace the accounts of the social insurance institutions and a number of public enterprises.

The form and scope of the post-audit varies among countries and between countries. Three types of post-audit may be distinguished. First, there is what may be termed the traditional or legal post-audit, which extends to the verification of documentation and the ascertainment that receipts and expenditures have been treated in accordance with statutory requirements. This type of post-audit may be directed to an examination of the documentation (vouchers) that supports the receipt and obligation of moneys. It may also be directed toward an examination of the pay orders issued by fiscal officers. It may be conducted centrally or, preferably, at the site of agency accounting operations. The post-audit may be comprehensive in terms of the detailed examination of every transaction, or it may be undertaken in accordance with modern sampling techniques. In the latter form the post-audit becomes more an audit of the accounting *system* of an agency than an audit of its transactions. Although the scope and techniques of a post-audit vary in accordance with institutional requirements, it is evident that where accounting skills are reasonably well developed, the decentralized audit of the system can provide the most efficient and economical type of control.

Second, the post-audit may extend beyond its traditional scope to embrace an examination of transactions in their relation to the administrative rules of an agency. This type of post-audit is more likely to be conducted within an agency, by a unit attached to the head of an agency. It is useful for appraisal of internal administration.

Third, the post-audit may assume a substantive character—an examination of the effectiveness of administration as a whole, its efficiency and its adequacy in terms of the program of the agency. This type of post-audit may be conducted internally or externally; the findings may be reported to administrators or to the legislature. When the findings are available for internal administrative purposes, the substantive post-audit may be undertaken by the agency responsible for organization and methods analysis, which is typically an agency of the central staff. When the findings are to be directed to the legislative body, this type of post-audit may be conducted by an independent governmental accounting agency, as in the United States, where substantive post-audits are frequently made by the General Accounting Office, or as in France, where the Cour des Comptes may undertake special investigations at the request of the National Assembly. In some cases, substantive post-audit reports are subject to hearings before legislative committees, as in Great Britain, where the important work of the Public Accounts Committee depends on the annual audit findings of the Comptroller and the Auditor General.[6]

The post-audit is a flexible instrument of control. Properly used it can establish accountability and generally increase the effectiveness of government administration. As governments improve the efficiency and increase the responsibility of their administrators, it seems likely that post-audit will be strengthened but that external pre-audit, administered by an independent body responsible directly to the legislature, will diminish in scope. Pre-audit then becomes a matter of internal control and responsibility, subject only to the final reckoning of the post-audit. Post-audit itself should be strengthened and extended to provide the legislature with an authoritative analysis of the custodianship of public funds and public assets.

III. MANAGEMENT CONSIDERATIONS

In recent years it has come to be increasingly recognized that government accounting must serve the administrator's needs as well as the needs of the legislature. This concept of government accounting requires the following implementation.

(1) Control accounts at the management level must be related to, but more specific than, the accounts as set forth in the budget presented to and adopted by the legislature. The control accounts, or fiscal accounts, which record receipts, obligations, and disbursements, must embrace the detail that supports the budget.

(2) Responsibility for maintaining much of an accounting system should be decentralized. Decentralization of the accounting function is a corollary of the relation between control accounts and budget accounts. It may be necessary and desirable to maintain a high degree of

[6] See Basil Chubb, *The Control of Public Expenditure*, Clarendon Press, Oxford, 1952, pp. 169–197. A similar system is followed in Canada, where the Accountant General testifies before the Public Accounts Committee.

central control over the form of accounting records throughout all branches of the central government, but the routine of maintaining the records should be decentralized to the level of operational responsibility if financial information is to be continuously available to administrators. Central accounts will, of course, continue to be necessary for certain types of treasury operations, but even in this case—for example, when disbursement is centralized in the treasury—it is necessary to delegate operating responsibilities in order to avoid undue routine burdens on top officials.

(3) The accounting system within an agency should embrace a pattern of internal audit and control.[7] Administrators cannot be expected to personally supervise the maintenance of accounting systems, but they must be responsible for their accuracy. This responsibility can be discharged effectively and the administrator freed from the minutiae of supervision only by the establishment of a system that permits ready measurement of the financial results of program operations and incorporates a technique for cross-checking. A pattern of internal control is almost synonymous with good management. It requires an organizational structure that is linked with organizational responsibilities and a clear delegation of duties. Records for internal control should take the form of periodic financial reports on the status of receipts, obligations, and expenditures; where possible, these should be related to the performance of specific activities. Within any department or agency the periodic reports can provide higher supervisory levels with the informational basis for effective decisions. Internal reporting of operations greatly facilitates a post-audit, and can contribute to the audit of systems rather than the audit of transactions.

(4) Accounts maintained at the operational level should be based on a system which will reveal, so far as possible, actual costs. This is necessary so that an administrator can determine the character of changes in total outlay, to distinguish whether the cost of providing a unit of government goods and services is increasing or whether more units are being provided. The measurement of costs will require, in some circumstances, the application of commercial accounting techniques. In other instances the traditional cash basis of accounting will provide an adequate measurement of the costs of activities. The goal is the establishment of accounts that set forth an objective and quantified measurement of management's success or failure in the fiscal period. The realization of this goal requires a continued experimentation with new measurement techniques at the administrative level; no formal and mechan-

[7] E. L. Kohler, "Essential Elements in a Program of Internal Audit," *Accounting Review*, January 1953, pp. 17–24.

ical system of accounts can be expected to provide all the answers when programs are changing in scope and content.

(5) Flexibility in account classifications must be preserved, but within a pattern of over-all uniformity. Just as governmental programs differ from agency to agency, so must account classifications differ if management needs are to be served. The sharpest differences will arise between sectors. Classifications for the general government sector will differ from those which can be used for enterprise and for social insurance systems. For enterprise the classifications must permit the measurement of profit or loss on an accrual basis, with adequate provision for the maintenance of capital assets and of accounting for inventory. For social insurance systems the accounting basis must show receipts and expenditures and the condition and disposition of assets. At the same time there must be sufficient uniformity in the accounts maintained throughout the whole of government to permit certain types of aggregating. The summary accounts in the central government budget should provide the starting framework for account classification. Accounts maintained by the treasury, by departments, and by administrative units must be harmonious with the central budget accounts. A set of definitions should be employed so that the conceptual basis for certain distinctions (grant, taxes, transfers, loans, etc.) is uniform in application. To assure flexibility within a general pattern of uniformity, it is usually desirable to endow some central authority (the treasury, the budget office, the auditing department, or some combination thereof) with the power to prescribe or approve the account classifications to be employed throughout a government.

IV. OTHER ACCOUNTING PROBLEMS

A. FUND STRUCTURE

In the terminology of government accounting a fund represents the segregation of certain resources or monies, or the identification of certain types of transactions devoted to a special purpose. This purpose must be legally defined, and reflecting such definition, a separate set of accounts is maintained.

Separate funds are typically established for social insurance activities, and may also be used for commercial-type ventures. The legislature may create special funds from the proceeds of earmarked taxes, with the requirement that these funds be devoted to a specified purpose. Customarily, the term general fund applies to all receipts and expenditures not so earmarked.

Where possible, it would appear desirable to limit the establishment of funds in a central government to public undertakings, to social insurance accounts, and to monies held in trust for future payment (shared tax revenues, for example). For social insurance and monies held in trust, it is conceived that legal title rests elsewhere than in the government; these monies are not available for other governmental purposes, and a separate fund structure may be justified on this ground. Commercial-type ventures require a fund of working capital, replenished by operational receipts and depleted by operational outlays.

B. Cash and Accrual

The cash basis for government accounting records transactions at the time monies are received and expended. On an accrual basis, revenues are recorded as they are earned and expenditures are recorded as services or supplies are utilized. Inventories, for example, are posted as they are received, but are not booked as costs until they are used; that is, the accrual system requires that unearned revenues and unapplied resources shall be deferred in the accounts until they are earned and applied. The accrual basis makes fiscal reports comparable and lays the basis for the analysis of government costs over a period of time. The accrual basis accomplishes this by the accounting recognition of inventories, prepaid items, deferred charges, and capital outlay. This basis of accounting offers the greatest potentialities for government operations which involve the purchase and sale of commodities, the construction and operation of projects, and the lending of funds. It is in these operations that the discrepancies between actual costs and the receipt and expenditure of monies are likely to be greatest.

In practice, some governments have adopted what may be termed a modified accrual system. This approach seeks to incorporate accruals wherever it is quantitatively important and administratively practicable to do so. It is evident that for a governmental program whose outlays consist of wages and salaries to the extent of 95 percent of its total costs, the conversion of the accounts to an accrual basis may simply not be practicable in terms of the results to be accomplished. The maintenance of a cash basis of accounting in such circumstances will result in no serious distortion. But accrual accounting should be used where unearned revenues and unapplied resources are significant in relation to the total. The modified accrual system seeks to identify these circumstances and to change the basis of accounting where change is justified in relation to the expense involved and the accounting skills available.

It may be noted that the use of accrual accounting lays the basis for, but does not necessarily imply, cost accounting for governmental activities. The latter requires, in addition to accruals, the identification of units of work or performance, both organizationally and in an accounting sense, which permits measurement of unit costs over a number of fiscal periods.

The advisability of maintaining a system of depreciation accounts is a question related to the establishment of an accrual system. Where commercial accounting is used, as for separately organized government corporations, depreciation accounts will customarily be maintained as part of the commercial accounting (accrual) system. More difficult cases arise where enterprise activity is not separately organized but is conducted within the general government sector by administrative departments and agencies. In these circumstances there are three classes of cases for which depreciation accounting may be desirable. The first obtains where agencies engage in commercial-type operations and are intended to operate these at a profit or to avoid a loss. Since the measurement of profit (or loss) must include adequate allowance for the maintenance of capital equipment, a system of depreciation accounting must be used.

The second class of cases relates to those governmental operations which provide services at cost to other governmental agencies, such as a printing establishment. In this case the prices to be charged by the servicing agency should be based on the cost of providing the goods or services, and depreciation accounting in the servicing agency will be necessary for a complete measurement of costs (see Chapter 10).

The third circumstance embraces those cases in which the original capital must be retained intact, possibly as a means of maintaining the credit standing of a government, or those in which concepts of the custodianship of assets are firmly embedded in institutional practice. In such instances, capital costs must be captured, in the sense that reserves must be established for the replenishment of capital equipment as it wears out. Even in these latter circumstances, however, it is not generally appropriate to fund the reserve, that is, to maintain an offsetting investment in cash or securities, as is sometimes done in business firms.

Aside from these three general circumstances, depreciation accounting will usually constitute a refinement that does not justify the additional administrative costs involved. Possibly for public buildings, and certainly for military and naval installations, depreciation accounts may not be meaningful, and some of the functions ascribed to depreciation accounting, such as the determination of asset condition, may be more easily performed by other means.

In practice most governments use a mixture of cash and accrual accounting, and the question becomes whether relatively more or relatively less emphasis shall be placed on the development of accrual methods. The mixture of cash and accrual always poses problems for the summary accounts. A summary account can be one of two types. The first is an aggregate of items that have been previously recorded; the totals are posted in summary. The second type consists of items which have been previously recorded and are reclassified for summary purposes. If there were one single ideal account classification for all governmental purposes, the first type of summary account is all that would be required, although it would reflect greater or less distortion depending on the extent to which the cash basis failed to record the volume of governmental activity which actually took place in the fiscal period. The second type of summary account, requiring reclassification of recorded entries, can be uniformly presented on a cash basis, since an account maintained on an accrual basis may also be used to show the volume of cash transactions.

C. Closing the Accounts

It is customary for some governments to postpone the formal closing of accounts until some time after the end of the fiscal year. This feature, more frequently applied to expenditures than to revenues, permits an extended period for payment of obligations incurred during the fiscal year. In the Netherlands, for example, the books of account remain open for one year after the close of the fiscal year; and in France, for certain types of expenditures, the books are open for two months after the end of the fiscal year. In the United States government, however, accounts are closed at the end of the fiscal year, and all expenditures in liquidation of fiscal year obligations are carried forward to the following year and booked as expenditures in that year. Practices vary among state governments. The accounts may remain open for two or three months, or encumbered balances may be reappropriated by the legislature.[8]

The practice of keeping books open for a specified period has the advantage of bringing cash disbursements somewhat more into line with obligations in a given fiscal year. But no specific period will permit the liquidation of all obligations, and extending the period during which the cash accounts remain open inevitably delays the publication of the closed accounts. In general, it would appear to be a desirable practice to close the accounts as soon as possible after the end of the fiscal year. This would in no way limit the possibility for post-audit and the subsequent correction of entries.

D. Improvements in Government Accounting

Sir Henry Higgs, the British financial authority, once accompanied Lord Kitchener on a trip to Egypt in an attempt to improve the fiscal

[8] A. E. Buck, *Public Budgeting,* Harper & Brothers, New York, 1929, p. 526.

administration of that country. He discovered that a sample audit system was used; items numbered 1, 5, 9, 13, etc., were regularly checked, so regularly, in fact, that this had become known throughout the service; obviously, no defalcations were ever discovered. Sir Henry concluded:

> There you had the Audit Office, with its officials going round like squirrels in a wheel, producing nothing of value, but rather creating a false sense of security in the minds of those who were relying upon it. . . . [9]

Egyptian finances at the time of World War I may well constitute an extreme case, but there is always danger that accounts and procedures will appear to be important in themselves.

It is a safe generalization that inefficiency in government accounting most frequently stems from an institutional arrangement that sanctions repetitive accounting as a substitute for an adequate system to ensure accountability. The control points should be limited, and no one point should perform the same operations or record transactions in the same way as another control point. But at these points there is need for the application of what might be termed the principle of adequate documentation. Each control must be supported by documentary evidence. Inadequate documentation encourages the misappropriation of funds. Superfluous documentation inhibits effective administration.

The development of a higher level of accounting skills within a government will facilitate the utilization of modern techniques, such as machine tabulation and sample auditing. Only when such skills are available can there be important increases in efficiency and a corresponding reduction in the number of man-hours devoted to accounting functions.

In the improvement of accounting systems one of the most important factors is the development of adequate standards of responsibility in the lower echelons of administration. If the institutional pattern centers the responsibility for approving vouchers, for signing contracts, or for countersigning checks in the very top levels, delay and inefficiency are inevitable in the conduct of transactions with government. An improvement in accounting skills and an improved level of public responsibility can develop the increases in efficiency which derive from the delegation of financial responsibility.

V. RECENT ACCOUNTING AND AUDITING REFORMS IN THE U. S. GOVERNMENT

The lines of responsibility for the interrelated pattern of accounting, the settlement of accounts and the audit of accounts have been somewhat confused in the federal government of the United States since 1789.

[9] Henry Higgs, *Financial Reform*, Macmillan & Co., Ltd., London, 1924, p. 40.

Significant developments within the past decade have done much to clarify the nature of existing responsibilities; major improvements have been made in all their aspects.

A detailed history of accounting and auditing in the federal government and an analysis of the significant legal position of the Comptroller General and the General Accounting Office lie outside the scope of this volume. This subject has received extensive treatment in the literature.[10]

Experiences with central auditing and control date back to the beginnings of the Republic, but the present structure of the General Accounting Office (GAO) and the position of the Comptroller General are derived from the Budget and Accounting Act of 1921. This provided that the Comptroller General, as head of GAO, should be responsible solely to the Congress and that his appointment should be for a fifteen-year term, not subject to renewal. His principal duties, as established by statute and as they evolved over the next 20 years, were (1) to settle all claims and accounts in which the government was financially concerned; (2) to certify the amounts made available to agencies by the Congress; (3) to prescribe the forms, systems, and procedures for appropriation and fund accounting and for the examination of accounts and claims; (4) to investigate the receipt, disbursement, and application of public funds and make regular reports and recommendations thereon to the Congress.

The position of the Comptroller General and the work of the General Accounting Office thus came to combine a particularly awkward combination of responsibilities of an administrative nature—such as the establishment and maintenance of accounts and the settlement of accounts—and responsibilities that very properly should reside in the hands of an independent agency reporting to the Congress—the post-audit of accounts. Moreover, in his administration of the GAO the first Comptroller General (1921 to 1936) conceived his responsibilities broadly and aggressively. His authority to pre-audit expenditures gave rise to frequent conflicts with administrative agencies. His rulings on legal matters often conflicted with those of the Attorney General, resulting in litigation.

In 1937 the President's Committee on Administrative Management, on the basis of a searching task force report by Mansfield,[11] concluded:

[10] Wilmerding, *The Spending Power;* Harvey C. Mansfield, *The Comptroller General,* Yale University Press, New Haven, 1939.

[11] Harvey C. Mansfield, "The General Accounting Office," *Fiscal Management in the National Government,* President's Committee on Administrative Management, Washington, 1937, pp. 33–62.

The General Accounting Office has failed to achieve an independent audit of national expenditures. It has not supplied the Congress with comprehensive information concerning the financial administration of the Government which an audit should render . . . . the Comptroller General . . . . has rarely called attention to unwise expenditures or unsound fiscal practices. . . . The fundamental reasons why the Comptroller General has failed to provide the Congress with a complete, detailed, and critical audit of the fiscal accounts of the Government . . . is the anomalous and inconsistent position of his office.[12]

The Committee recommended that the anomaly be eradicated by giving the Treasury Department authority to prescribe and supervise accounting systems and to settle accounts, that the title of the General Accounting Office be changed to the General Auditing Office, and that its responsibilities be restricted to post-audit. Although the President supported the recommendations of the Committee and legislation was introduced to effect the changes, Congress took no action. The war years did not provide the occasion for a re-examination of the position of the Comptroller General. When Congress did come to its own Legislative Reorganization Act of 1946 (*P.L.* 601, 79th Cong., 2d sess.), the only change which was made was to strengthen the role of the GAO in its reports on the performance of administrative agencies and departments.[13]

Nevertheless, and in spite of the inaction of Congress in the immediate postwar period, a reorientation in the position and operations of the General Accounting Office began to emerge. The impetus was provided by the Comptroller General himself, working in cooperation with the Treasury Department and the Bureau of the Budget. This was formalized in 1947 as the Joint Program for Improving Accounting in the Federal Government (Joint Accounting Program or JAP). In 1949 the Commission on Organization of the Executive Branch of the Government (Hoover Commission) provided further stimulus to accounting reform by pointing out existing deficiencies and by commending the reform program already underway. The majority of the Commission, however, expressed doubt that the voluntary program, by itself, could be successful, and recommended that the Secretary of the Treasury be given authority to prescribe accounting methods and procedures.[14] The Congress did

---

[12] The President's Committee on Administrative Management, *Administrative Management,* Washington, 1937, p. 24.

[13] The Government Corporation Control Act of 1945 gave the Comptroller General authority to conduct comprehensive audits of wholly owned corporations. (*P. L.* 248, 79th Cong., 1st sess.)

[14] Commission on Organization of the Executive Branch of the Government, *Budgeting and Accounting,* Washington, 1949, pp. 35–44. Some members of the Commission wished to preserve and even strengthen the current control position of the Comptroller General. Others argued forcibly in terms of a reorganization

not adopt the Hoover Commission recommendations; instead, it approved and strengthened the Joint Accounting Program by the enactment, in 1950, of the Budget and Accounting Procedures Act (*P.L.* 784, 81st Cong., 2d sess.).

The Joint Accounting Program is predicated on the following principles:[15]

(1) The maintenance of accounting systems and the production of financial reports is the responsibility of the executive branch of government.

(2) There must be an audit independent of the executive branch, but one which gives appropriate recognition to the necessity for internal control and audit.

(3) The executive branch must participate in the development of accounting systems which serve the needs and responsibilities of both the legislative and executive branches.

The GAO, the Treasury, and the Bureau of the Budget joined in outlining a program for the review and analysis of the accounting needs of the federal government, and initiated studies of requirements in specific areas. These included: (1) the development of general accounting principles and standards; (2) the simplification and improvement of disbursement and collection procedures; (3) the improvement of central accounting and reporting; (4) the improvement of agency accounting and reporting; and (5) an examination of special accounting problems in particular agencies.

Under the Joint Accounting Program the Comptroller General, in effect, shares the responsibility for developing and installing accounting systems with the agencies that must maintain and operate them. At the same time, the Comptroller General must approve the systems developed and installed by the agencies.

Responsibility for the implementation of the Joint Accounting Program has been primarily in the hands of the Comptroller General. To this end, a new division was created in the General Accounting Office—the Accounting Systems Division. This division has initiated a large number of reforms extending through the whole range of accounting and

---

along the lines suggested by the President's Committee for Administrative Management in 1937 (*ibid.*, pp. 47–71). The task force report was generally in line with the recommendations of the majority. (See Commission or Organization of the Executive Branch of the Government, Task Force Report, *Fiscal, Budgeting, and Accounting Activities,* Washington, 1949, pp. 87–110.)

[15] Comptroller General of the United States, *Annual Report,* 1949, pp. 10–17; *Annual Report of the Secretary of the Treasury for the fiscal year ending June 30, 1949,* pp. 134–135; Walter F. Frese, "Recent Developments in Federal Government Accounting, *Municipal Finance,* November 1952, pp. 68–72.

auditing, affecting budgeting procedure as well. The major actions which have been undertaken under the Joint Accounting Program include:

(1) The participating agencies cooperated with congressional committees in the enactment of the Budget and Accounting Procedures Act of 1950, which gave wide latitude for procedural reform in government accounting. Cooperation has also extended to the enactment of legislation to reform the fiscal operations of the Post Office Department and the Department of Defense. Other legislation has provided for the establishment of working capital funds in particular agencies.

(2) The General Accounting Office has eliminated its central accounting functions. In some cases these accounting activities have been transferred to the agencies. In other instances the GAO has established appropriate safeguards and internal controls in the agencies themselves.

(3) The GAO has decentralized its auditing procedures to eliminate the necessity for shipping vouchers and records to the central office. An increasing number of audits are now conducted at the site of agency operations. The scope of audits has been extended beyond mere financial transactions, to embrace an appraisal of administrative practices. Sample audits have been employed as a substitute for a check on all financial transactions, and in general an effort is made to audit the bookkeeping procedures rather than the transactions.[16]

(4) Account classifications have been revised and simplified, and fund structures relating to accounts have been made more uniform for both receipts and appropriations.

(5) As agencies have been encouraged to revise and improve their accounting systems, a general effort has been made to decentralize accounting records to increase their usefulness for management purposes. At the same time, some agencies have been encouraged to create an office of central controller to maintain supervision over the decentralized accounting operations.[17]

(6) Accrual accounting has been extended to embrace the financial activities of an increasing number of agencies. These extensions are a part of the trend toward performance budgeting. As a part of accrual accounting, property records have been established in a number of agencies, and improved systems of property management have resulted.

(7) Disbursement procedure has been simplified in a number of agencies by eliminating overlapping cash controls maintained by disbursing officers and by the agency.

[16] See Robert L. Long, "Audit Activities Today in the General Accounting Office," *Federal Accountant*, March 1954, pp. 1–10.

[17] For a discussion of agency reforms see T. Jack Gary, Lindsley H. Noble, and Alfred R. Golze, "Improvements in Federal Accounting," *Public Administration Review*, Autumn 1950, pp. 270–280.

(8) The accounts maintained in the Treasury Department have been revised with a view to improving their usefulness for purposes of financial reporting.[18]

(9) The procedure requiring that warrants be countersigned by the Comptroller General has been largely eliminated.

The Joint Accounting Program is not regarded as a once-over affair, but as a permanent responsibility of the participating agencies. The success of the program to date is evidence that established routines can be changed and that those who exercise administrative authority will, if the occasion demands it, practice self-abnegation.

As might be expected, there continues to be considerable criticism of federal accounting procedures. The second Hoover Commission generally commended the Joint Accounting Program but contended that the rate of progress was too slow, and pointed to the need for revamping Treasury accounting and reporting, agency property accounting, and disbursement records.[19] Moreover, the Commission's report revealed that there is far from unanimity on the location of the accounting responsibility within the federal establishment. The majority recommended that the Bureau of the Budget create a new staff office of accounting, headed by an assistant director for accounting. The Bureau would then take over from GAO the task of installing accounting systems and supervising internal audit in agencies, and from the Treasury a part of its existing responsibilities for central reporting. But a dissenting Commissioner stated, "The report [of the majority] tends to exalt the role of the accountant in Government. . . . " (p. 70).

Whether or not the Commission's recommendations are adopted, the atmosphere of accounting reform generated by the Joint Accounting Program will very likely continue to bring substantial procedural improvements in the agencies. The neglected area is congressional review of the results of the post-audit. The Committees on Government Operations fall very short of their potential effectiveness. Improvements here must rest on recognition of the executive's role. Mansfield has put this point very well:

> When all is said, the vitality of administration is in operations. If the best talents of the country can be continuously recruited and held there, efficient government is assured and adequate powers can safely be delegated. To keep them there, the mechanisms of financial administration should coordinate and liberate their activities and not destroy their incentives. This

[18] See Harold R. Gearhart, "Integration of Treasury and Agency Accounts," *Federal Accountant,* December 1954, pp. 32–40.

[19] Commission on Organization of the Executive Branch of the Government, *Budget and Accounting,* Washington, 1955, pp. 29–49, 57–60; and the Commission's Task Force Report, *Budget and Accounting,* Washington, 1955, pp. 51–78.

means that the primary emphasis of the accounting system must be placed upon fostering administrative responsibility. On this foundation the super-structure of legislative control is secure.[20]

[20] Mansfield, *The Comptroller General*, p. 288.

Selected Bibliography

Bartelt, E. F., *Accounting Procedures of the United States Government,* Public Administration Service, Chicago, 1940.

Bordner, Howard W., "Federal Government Accounting Principles," *Federal Accountant,* September 1954, pp. 6–17.

Buck, A. E., "Financial Control and Accountability," *Fiscal Management in the National Government,* President's Committee on Administrative Management, Washington, 1937, pp. 21–27.

Commission on Organization of the Executive Branch of the Government, *Budgeting and Accounting,* Washington, 1949, pp. 35–71.

——— Task Force Report, *Fiscal, Budgeting, and Accounting Activities,* Washington, 1949, pp. 87–110.

Commission on Organization of the Executive Branch of the Government, *Budget and Accounting,* Washington, 1955, pp. 29–49, 57–60.

——— Task Force Report, *Budget and Accounting,* Washington, 1955, pp. 51–78.

Final Report of the Committee on the Form of Government Accounts (Cmd. 7969), His Majesty's Stationery Office, London, 1950.

Frese, Walter F., "Recent Developments in Federal Government Accounting," *Municipal Finance,* November 1952, pp. 68–72.

Gary, T. Jack, Jr., Lindsley H. Noble, and Alfred R. Golze, "Improvements in Federal Accounting," *Public Administration Review,* Autumn 1950, pp. 270–280.

General Accounting Office, *Statement of Accounting Principles and Standards for Guidance of Executive Agencies in the Federal Government,* Washington, 1952.

Kohler, E. L., "Essential Elements in a Program of Internal Audit," *Accounting Review,* January 1953, pp. 17–24.

Mansfield, Harvey C., *The Comptroller General,* Yale University Press, New Haven, 1939.

———"The General Accounting Office," *Fiscal Management in the National Government,* President's Committee on Administrative Management, Washington, 1937, pp. 33-62.

National Committee on Governmental Accounting, *Municipal Accounting and Auditing,* Municipal Finance Officers Association, Chicago, 1951.

——— *A Standard Classification of Municipal Accounts,* Chicago, 1953.

Selko, Daniel T., *The Federal Financial System,* Brookings Institution, Washington, 1940, pp. 383–553.

Wilmerding, Lucius, Jr., *The Spending Power,* Yale University Press, New Haven, 1943, esp. pp. 250–308.

Part IV

Specialized Budget Problems

15.

Revenue estimating

The day-to-day work of budgeting is very largely concerned with expenditures. Measured in terms of personnel, far more man-years will be devoted to the outgo side of the budget, its preparation and execution, than to the revenue side. Nevertheless, a budget is both revenue and expenditure. Revenue considerations will enter into budget-making at numerous points.

In the last century, as government budgeting became regularized and its literature formalized, something which might be called the principle of conservatism was advanced as an intended guide to budgeting.[1] Governments were supposed to underestimate their revenues and overestimate their expenditures. Then, when reality caught up with the estimators, there would be an automatic budget surplus. In some governments the revenue-estimating applications of this principle were written into the budget law.

In France, as early as 1823, "the rule of the penultimate year" was adopted. This required that revenues for the budget year must be forecast as identical with actual revenues for the fiscal year last ended.[2] The application of the rule accomplished two purposes, both in keeping with

[1] Henry Carter Adams, *The Science of Finance,* Henry Holt & Company, New York, 1898, p. 136.

[2] A. E. Buck, *Public Budgeting,* Harper & Brothers, New York, 1929, pp. 317–318; René Stourm, *The Budget,* translated by Thaddeus Plazinski, D. Appleton & Company, New York, 1917, pp. 171–176.

the spirit of the times. First, it eliminated any exercise of judgment or discretion on the part of the executive, thus restricting the scope of activities. Second, in an economy which was generally expanding—and the rule could not have been applied if this condition had not obtained —the national debt could be gradually retired. Budgetary equilibrium was thus assured. Although much criticized, the rule of the penultimate year continued to be practiced in France into this century.

A second technique for estimating revenues also had its origins in the budgetary practices of the last century. This is the method of averages, which consists of revenue estimates prepared on the basis of a three-year or five-year average of increases or decreases. A. E. Buck writes that this procedure was used briefly in France, and later in a number of American states. The method of averages requires simple projection of rates of change applied to each separate revenue source. Where the volume of revenue is responsive to changes in total economic activity, and where the economy is expanding, this method will most obviously permit a conservative increase in governmental expenditures or a modest reduction in tax rates, and will tend to hold down surpluses.

These two techniques of revenue estimating—the rule of the penultimate year and the method of averages—were the product of an era when there was little desire to increase executive authority in order to increase executive responsibility, and when there was apparent danger that revenues would be overestimated in order to justify unwarranted increases in expenditures. Where these conditions no longer obtain, it is possible to employ techniques of revenue estimating which will produce better results than the rigid application of rules, without at the same time incurring the risk of fiscal mismanagement.

All modern revenue estimating is done by the technique that is described in the older literature as direct valuation. This had its origins in British practice, and its use was encouraged there by the fact that the budget was presented to Parliament shortly after the beginning of the fiscal year to which it was to apply.[3] This meant that some of the elements which shaped the fiscal outlook were already known. Direct valuation then consisted of forecasting, for each major revenue source, its outcome for the remainder of the fiscal year.

I. OCCASIONS FOR REVENUE ESTIMATES

Revenue estimating is generally a staff responsibility of the central budget office, although this office may share its duties with the department of revenue or other agency charged with the collection of taxes.

[3] Buck, *op. cit.,* pp. 319–320.

Similarly, the central budget office may depend on operating departments and agencies for estimates of revenue from fees and incidental commercial-type activity, and on government corporations for estimates of their operating revenue.

Revenue estimates must enter at several points in budget preparation (see Chapter 4). In the initial stages of budget planning, before departmental expenditure estimates have been reviewed, a revenue estimate is needed to establish the over-all outlines of the budget for the guidance of the chief executive in initial fiscal decisions. The revenue estimate at this point must be translated, at least in broad outline, in the request for estimates which is transmitted by the central budget office to the agencies to constitute a part of the assumptions on which their budgets are to be prepared. Later, after departmental review, a final estimate of revenue is needed for inclusion in the summary budget statements, and to accompany any proposals for tax reductions or tax increases which the executive may submit as a part of the budget. This estimate is in two parts—the "short" or current year, which is not yet completed, and the "long" or budget year, for which new expenditure authorizations are proposed.

During the phase of legislative review there may be more or less continuous re-estimates of revenue, which will influence decisions on expenditures. Depending on the way in which the legislature is organized for its fiscal decisions, these estimates may be required by both appropriations committees and taxation committees. In some governments, revenue legislation must be enacted annually; the authority to collect taxes expires with each fiscal year. In other governments, which include most governments in the United States, the great bulk of revenue is collected under standing authorizations that require positive action only when rates or tax bases are changed.

After the legislature has completed its budgetary actions, there should be a set of revenue estimates to guide the executive in budget execution. As the fiscal year proceeds, the revenue outlook may require modifications in expenditures. These modifications are most likely to be downward. That is, if current revenues are falling short of the original estimates, the chief executive, given the necessary legal authority, will establish reserves against appropriations in order to prevent a deficit (see Chapter 13). Where revenues move in the other direction—that is, exceed the original estimates—the emerging budget surplus will influence proposed expenditures in the subsequent year but is not likely to be available for expenditure in the current year.

During the execution of the budget, revenue estimates are also necessary for planning cash requirements. Seasonal variations in receipts and expenditures may occasion short-term borrowing, and this must be anticipated if favorable terms are to be secured. In the United States government in recent years this kind of intrayear forecasting has been the basis for planning the refinancing of a large volume of both short-term and long-term debt obligations.

Revenue estimates are essential for executive and legislative decisions about new tax measures. Here revenue estimating is intimately bound up with tax research.[4] For example, as a part of budget preparation, the executive may find that there is a forecast deficiency in total revenue, and might recommend that this be made up by increases in the income tax applied to business firms. The revenue consequences of specific recommended changes would be estimated by those with responsibility for tax research within the executive or within the legislature. The estimate of aggregate revenues would thus be a part of budget-making. The estimate of specific revenue consequences of the tax law change would touch the budgetary process as such only at the level of fiscal policy formulation. Both kinds of estimates are essentially tax research, however, since both require an intimate knowledge of the peculiarities of the tax base.

The quality of revenue estimating in any government will depend, in some part, on the importance which attaches to it and the public attention which centers on it. The British Treasury for many years has had an enviable reputation for accurate estimating. There seems to be little doubt that this is directly due to the large volume of public attention and Parliamentary debate which centers on revenue, and the intimate relationship between the forecast of revenue and the possibility for increases or decreases in tax rates.[5] The Chancellor of the Exchequer has therefore taken steps to assure that the estimates of revenue are carefully prepared. A somewhat comparable situation obtains in American municipalities that have adopted a pay-as-you-go financial plan, requiring that all new capital outlays be financed from current revenue. The public interest in new schools or new roads will then come to center on the estimate of available revenue, with corresponding pressure on city budget officials to make the best estimates possible.[6]

Peculiarly enough, it is not always possible to judge the quality of revenue estimates. In some governments, revenue sources are so stable

[4] For a case study in this relationship see Walter W. Heller, "An Appraisal of the Administration's Tax Policy," *National Tax Journal*, March 1955, esp. pp. 26–28.

[5] J. Wilner Sundelson, *Budgetary Methods in National and State Governments*, J. B. Lyon Company, Albany, 1938, pp. 326–327.

[6] George N. Shaw, "Budgetary Crystal Gazing," *Municipal Finance*, February 1949, p. 10.

that even small errors are almost inexcusable. In other circumstances a bad estimate may be overcome by an unforseen increase in the tax base. Or the estimator may be fortunate in having his errors cancel out; the underestimates in some revenues are compensated by overestimates in others. A simple comparison of estimates with actuals will not indicate how well the task has been done.

II. THE SETTING FOR REVENUE ESTIMATES

The nature of the task of revenue estimating for budgetary purposes will be determined by the character of revenue sources and their stability, and by what Sundelson has called "time relationships."[7] This time factor relates to the period which elapses between the point when revenue estimates are made and the beginning of the fiscal year to which they will apply, and to whether taxes are collected currently or are based on transactions in a previous time period.

A. The Nature of Revenue Sources

The stability of revenue sources depends on the extent to which they are influenced by changes in the level of economic activity, and on the structure of intergovernmental fiscal relations. Many local governments in the United States receive a substantial part of their revenue as grants-in-aid from the state government. For example, a major share of the budget receipts of a New York municipality will be in the form of state grants for public education, per capita grants paid at a fixed amount in accordance with the decennial census of population, and grants for other purposes. The sums to be received as grants can be computed with a high degree of accuracy. This means that almost half of the budget revenue of a typical New York municipality is computed, not estimated, and is not subject to variation in accordance with changes in the level of economic activity. In fact, this is one of the compelling reasons for state grants-in-aid—to stabilize local budgets and eliminate the uncertainties which would otherwise result. State governments are in a far better position to withstand fiscal uncertainties than are local governments.

Revenue sources which are influenced by changes in the level of economic activity can be classified by categories in accordance with the degree of such influence and its operation over time. For example, property tax revenues from year to year are extremely stable, and this tax can be forecast with great accuracy for annual budgetary purposes. But even property tax revenues, over the long run, are determined by the level of economic activity. A prolonged depression will seriously

[7] Sundelson, *op. cit.*, pp. 326–330.

and adversely affect yields. A sustained period of full employment will tend to increase property tax revenues; as taxpayers' incomes increase, delinquency falls and the level of tax payments rises—regardless of the level of assessments and the rate of tax. But these changes are gradual and follow a trend. In any one year, revenue from the property tax can be estimated independently of anticipated changes in economic conditions, and for local governments this greatly simplifies the preparation of the revenue side of the budget. For longer periods, such as those involved in programing public works, an estimate of new construction and corresponding additions to the tax base will be required, and this will require a forecast of future economic growth in the area.

At the other extreme are the revenue sources immediately influenced by changes in economic conditions, such as personal and corporate income taxes. By and large, national governments and provincial governments throughout the world have tax structures based on revenue of this nature, taxes on personal and business income and excise taxes on commodities. The revenue sources of some provincial and most local governments tend to be based more largely on grants-in-aid and on taxes which are less responsive to changes in the level of economic activity.

These relationships, however, are by no means static. State governments in the United States have moved out of the property tax field since the turn of the century and have come to rely on revenue sources which are less stable, with consequent increased problems of revenue estimation. And local governments, particularly since World War II, have moved increasingly away from dependence on the property tax and have imposed levies on earned income and on retail sales and services, with a consequent increase in their revenue-estimating problems. These developments, while they tend to make revenue estimating more difficult, mean that the aggregate tax structure is more cycle-sensitive and thus serves increasingly as a built-in stabilizer to dampen fluctuations in economic activity. This fiscal policy advantage is of sufficient importance to more than counterbalance the resulting difficulties in revenue estimating—although this may be small comfort to the estimator.

B. The Organizational Role of the Estimator

Revenue estimates will necessarily be conditioned by the biases of the estimators. Very often, expenditure programs to be proposed by the executive depend on the availability of current tax revenues. The pressures for increased taxes or for reduced taxes may be influenced by the estimates of revenue from existing taxes. Estimators will be aware of these political realities, and this awareness may bias their findings. As Roy Blough says, speaking of the estimator, "Consciously or unconsciously, he is likely to choose data and methods that will lead toward the result he desires." In recognition of the essential fallibility of humans, including estimators, Blough proposes that, where possible, revenue estimation be isolated from " . . . the stress and strain of policy recommendation. . . . "[8]

This would suggest that revenue estimating be accorded a wholly expertise role and removed from the political economy of budget-making. An alternative would be to bring the revenue estimators closer to the budgetary process and make sure that their work is linked with that of economists and other staff who are charged with the preparation of budget assumptions and recommendations for the executive's fiscal policy. This would mean that the revenue estimators, even though their work partakes of the nature of tax research, would be located in the budget office, not in the treasury or department of revenue.

One means of assuring a reasonably prominent organizational role for the estimators is to include, perhaps in the budget message and certainly in the budget document, a description of the assumptions and techniques employed in estimation. This will tend to elevate the function of estimating and accord it greater prestige and greater respect. This, in itself, will strengthen performance and will make it more difficult for political leaders to tamper with the estimates in an unwarranted fashion.

The United States government, it may be noted, does not merge revenue estimating with budgeting; the former is located in the Treasury Department (see Chapter 4). The Budget Accounting Act of 1921 stated that "The President shall transmit . . . his estimates of the receipts of the Government during the ensuing fiscal year, under (1) laws existing at the time the Budget is transmitted and also (2) under the revenue proposals, if any, contained in the Budget. . . . " (*P.L.* 13, 67th Cong., 1st sess.). The President might well have chosen to implement this responsibility through the Bureau of the Budget. Instead, the Treasury estimates of revenue have traditionally been incorporated in the budget summary tables. Moreover, the budget message typically contains only the most casual reference to revenue estimates.

The budget document does contain an "Explanation of the Estimates of Receipts," but this statement is couched in generalities which provide no real clue as to the techniques employed or the economic assumptions used.[9] In fact, the U. S. Treasury Department has never published an account of its revenue estimating techniques.

[8] Roy Blough, *The Federal Taxing Process,* Prentice-Hall, New York, 1952, p. 300.

[9] See *Budget of the United States Government for the fiscal year ending June 30, 1956,* pp. 1146–1152.

Not all of the difficulties will be solved, however, by a properly assigned organizational role for the estimator or by more straightforward descriptions of the methods employed. Any estimator is subject to some almost natural biases. Blough has pointed to this in observing that there seems to be an inherent tendency to project the prevailing level of income into the future.

> When business is moving downward, the levels of national income used in revenue estimates are not likely to be forecast at much below those existing at the time. This reflects in part the normal optimism that prosperity is really just around the corner, the fear that to forecast a further downward movement may accentuate it, and perhaps unwillingness to forecast that under the administration in power business will sink to lower levels. On the upswing there may be an unwillingness to forecast an inflationary price rise.[10]

No matter how well developed the techniques of revenue estimation may be in any government, human frailty will remain.

C. Time Dimensions

Within the category of taxes which fluctuate in accordance with changes in economic conditions—generally income and commodity taxes —the task of revenue estimation will further vary in accordance with time relationships in collection procedure. The yield from a source of revenue such as the personal income tax may be an increasing function of changes in the level of economic activity. A given proportional change in the level of national (or state) income may produce a greater than proportional change in personal income tax revenues. However, if this year's tax collections are based on the taxpayers' income from last year, the estimating problem is considerably eased. When the budget is submitted, the current year's level of personal income may be known with reasonable accuracy. Therefore, the base of the estimate is available, and although the revenue source itself is inherently unstable, the lag in tax collections will mean that the volume of such revenue can be estimated with reasonable accuracy.

Where cycle-sensitive taxes are collected currently, as with the federal personal income tax and a number of state and local income taxes in the United States, the revenue estimating problem is severe. In these circumstances the base is unknown and tax yields must be forecast directly from the forecast of business conditions.

Time dimensions affect revenue estimates in other ways. It has been generally argued that the shorter the lag between the time of budget submission and the period to which the estimates are to apply, the

[10] Blough, *op. cit.*, p. 300.

greater the accuracy. There are some circumstances under which this has evident validity. In France, when the rule of the penultimate year was employed, and in a number of state governments in this country where the budget is for a biennium, revenues must be estimated for a period 30 months ahead. Experience indicates that accurate revenue estimating in these circumstances is rarely attained and that the practical expedient may be to assume that the second year will be like the first.

Apart from such obvious cases, where a shortened time span is preferable, there are some observations which ought to be made with respect to the generalization. It is not wholly evident that shortening the time span will, in every case, improve the result.

The validity of the generalization that shortening the time between the date of the estimate and the beginning of the fiscal year will make for accuracy rests on two assumptions: (1) that changes in the need for governmental programs and governmental revenues occur gradually, or at least in accordance with discernible trends over the short run; and (2) that total and structural changes in the levels of economic activity in a given jurisdiction occur in an orderly fashion in the short run. If this hypothetical short run could be entered by shortening the lag between preparation and execution, then the changes now in process could be assumed to be the changes which will continue, and more accurate estimating would be possible.

At mid-twentieth century it is hardly necessary to labor the point that this is not always the case. Governmental needs and the levels of economic activity in the forthcoming fiscal year are not uniquely determined by either the levels or the rates of change which are taking place in the months immediately preceding the fiscal year.

The limitations on and the uncertainties which attach to estimating, even for relatively short periods in the future, are well illustrated in the data in Table 18. This sets forth the errors in the short estimates of revenue and expenditure in the United States government over a 20 year period. That is, the percentage error shown in the table is that which is attributable to events in a six months' period, from the time the budget is submitted in January to the close of the fiscal year on June 30. This is the estimating error for the fiscal year already half-completed, with results for at least five months already known and, except for a few instances, with revenue and expenditure programs already determined by legislation. In spite of this reduction in the number of unknowns, the error is substantial for both revenue and expenditure.

The mean and the median in the table are computed without regard to sign. In terms of the median the error in the short estimate of revenue in this twenty-year period was 6.7 percent, ranging approximately from

TABLE 18

**Percentage Error in the Short Estimates of Revenue and Expenditure,
U. S. Government, Fiscal 1935–1954**

Fiscal Year	Revenue Error, percent*	Expenditure Error, percent*
1954	+4.6	+4.6
1953	+6.7	+0.8
1952	+1.0	+7.3
1951	−7.5	+5.8
1950	+1.9	+8.0
1949	+3.5	negl.
1948	+7.1	+11.5
1947	−7.0	+0.7
1946	−10.2	+5.5
1945	−1.6	negl.
1944	−6.7	+0.7
1943	+3.1	+2.8
1942	−6.7	−5.9
1941	−7.9	+3.9
1940	−4.1	+1.1
1939	+7.0	+9.0
1938	+1.3	−3.6
1937	+10.0	+6.0
1936	+7.3	−13.9
1935	−2.4	+16.5
Mean	5.4	5.4
Median	6.7	5.1
Range	−10.2 to +10.0	−13.9 to +16.5

* Percentage error is computed by dividing the difference between the estimate and actual by the actual. In computing the range, positive signs were given to estimates that exceeded the actuals and negative sign to estimates that fell short of the actuals; "negl." is less than 0.5 percent.

Source: Computed from data in *Budget of the United States Government*, selected fiscal years.

—10 percent to +10 percent. The average (median) error in the short estimate of expenditure is somewhat less—5.1 percent, but not as markedly less as might have been expected. The larger range for expenditures is attributable to the presence of just two years, fiscal 1935 and fiscal 1936. It may be concluded that expenditure estimates are subject to almost as great an error as revenue estimates. This would suggest that there are inherent limitations in attempts to refine the preparation of the expenditure side of the budget, even as for revenues.

The short estimate is for a six months' period, but the average error in the table is computed in terms of results for the whole fiscal year. The error for the period actually covered by the estimate is therefore much greater than appears from the data—approximately twice that shown in the table. This means that in the federal government, over these twenty years, the estimating error for a period six months ahead has been in the neighborhood of 10 percent.

Comparisons with the long estimates of revenue and expenditure are interesting, although these latter do not throw as much light on the inherent limitations in the estimating process, since both revenue and expenditure programs have not yet been reviewed and modified by the Congress at the time the long estimate is made. Computations of the long estimates for the same twenty-year period show that the average (median) error in the revenue estimate is 11.5 percent, and the average (median) error in the expenditure estimate is 15 percent. The estimating errors in the long estimates of both expenditures and revenues are therefore not very much larger than for the six-month estimates. Shortening the time period between the date of the estimate and the beginning of the fiscal year does not assure improved results.[11]

The foregoing computations emphasize, if further emphasis were needed, that there is still a wide gap between the needs of policy makers and the potentialities of our present tools of forecasting.[12] Recognition of this gap does not mean that he who enters the portals of estimating must abandon all hope, but the recognition should in itself encourage an improvement in existing techniques.

III. TECHNIQUES OF ESTIMATION

It has been said that "The basis of estimating is not forecasting and prophesying, but it is rather measurement and analysis.[13] If there are to

[11] This is substantiated by the experience of New York State. In 1943 the date of the fiscal year was changed, with the result that the forecasting period for the long estimate was reduced from 18 months to 15 months. This did not improve the accuracy of these revenue estimates. (See Robert S. Herman, *Revenue Estimating in New York State Government*, State of New York, Division of the Budget, Albany, 1952, p. 26.)

[12] For further relevant comments on this problem, directed to the postwar forecasts of unemployment, see Michael Sapir, "Review of Economic Forecasts for the Transition Period," *Studies in Income and Wealth*, Vol. XI, National Bureau of Economic Research, New York, 1949, esp. pp. 276–278; also comment by Lawrence Klein, *ibid.*, p. 357.

[13] J. Wilner Sundelson, "Techniques of State Revenue Estimating," *Proceedings of the 1939 Conference*, National Association of Tax Administrators, Chicago, 1940, p. 5.

be prophesies, they ought at least to be based on a knowledge of historical behavior. Important elements in revenue estimating can be quantified; careful research can convert guesses into insights. The most important research is the determination of the base subject to tax—the volume of transactions, or the volume of income, or the amount of property on which the levy is imposed. In addition, the estimator must possess a thorough knowledge of tax collection procedures and the pattern of receipts. This latter will be discussed first, with special reference to practice in the United States.

A. Collection Patterns

In every government the department of revenue has established routines for processing tax returns. In some procedures, for example, the checks in payment of tax are immediately taken from the returns and recorded as of that date; in other procedures the tax return may be subject to a preliminary office audit, and several weeks may elapse before the payments are recorded. Moreover, these procedures may not be uniform from one year to the next. A change in routine may suddenly bring in 13 months' revenue from a given tax in a 12 months' period, thus upsetting any revenue estimate. Indeed, in some American states there seems to be a tradition that the outgoing governor shall impoverish his successor, regardless of political party, by making every effort to accelerate tax collections in the closing months of his regime.

Changes in auditing procedure will also influence the volume of tax collections. The department of revenue, in one year, may concentrate its auditing attention on a particular type of tax return which is highly productive of deficiency assessments. In another year it may concentrate attention on a sample of all returns, regardless of productivity. The number of auditors employed will likewise influence the volume of collections, and these too are subject to variation with respect to skill. These factors are in addition to any statutory changes in the base, rate, or method of tax collection which may influence prospective tax yields.

Beyond a thorough knowledge of tax administration, the estimator requires a statistical analysis of the seasonal pattern for specific tax revenues. Every revenue source has such a pattern, which may or may not be constant from year to year. Seasonality may be determined by fluctuations in the base of the tax; revenue from a retail sales tax will follow the increases in sales at Christmas and Easter. Seasonality may be a function of the way in which the tax laws are written, requiring payments of liabilities on specific dates.

A careful study of seasonal patterns is particularly important in making the short estimate for the fiscal year about to close. Only an analysis of seasonality will give the estimator a basis for judging the fraction of the year's revenue which has been collected as of a given date.

B. DETERMINING THE BASE

In some cases the base of the tax, and hence prospective tax yield, is little more than a matter of sheer conjecture. For example, New York State has a tax on stock transfers; tax yields here are a product of the volume of transactions on organized stock exchanges. There is no way of estimating in advance the quantity of such activity. Somewhat the same situation obtains in estimating yields from state pari-mutuel taxes. In this case revenue is influenced by the number of racing days, the weather, competition from tracks in other states, the level of personal income and the personalized attitudes of bettors toward particular horses.

Estimates of revenues from inheritance taxes are subject to comparable difficulties. In some jurisdictions the taxes which might be collected from one or two large estates in a given year would make a significant difference in total revenue. But it is impossible to forecast with accuracy the number of estates that will be subject to the tax or the values that will be attached to such estates for tax purposes. The most that the estimator can do under these circumstances is to follow the progress of estates in probate courts in order to be able to approximate the probable volume of inheritance tax revenues. For the federal government the probability that an increase or decrease in the number of large estates will significantly alter the estimate is less than in the states, and no effort is likely to be made to follow the progress of estates in probate.

Most other sources of governmental revenue are related to the volume of private economic activity or to specific components thereof—the level of corporate income, the level of personal income, or the volume of sales of goods and services. In all such cases the determination of the base requires careful analysis of historical fluctuations in such revenues in relation to fluctuations in specific or aggregate measures of economic activity.

The estimate of revenue for a tax of this type proceeds in two steps. First is the determination of the tax base historically, that is, its measurement in relation to specific components or aggregates of economic activity. Second is the projection of the component or aggregate. These two steps may be put in the form of an equation, using personal income taxes as an example and assuming that their yield is closely related to personal income:

$$\frac{\text{Personal income subject to tax in prior periods}}{\text{Total personal income in prior periods}} = R$$

Then, if X represents total personal income for the forecast period, personal income subject to tax in the forecast period is equal to RX.

The ideal forecast will, of course, be accurate in terms of the *amount* of revenue. But the mayor, governor, or chief executive who must use the estimate for policy purposes may be satisfied with much less. The direction of change is perhaps as important as the amount of change. The executive must know, first of all, whether there will be more or less revenue available for expenditure requirements next year as compared with this year.

It is possible to forecast within a range, rather than to a single figure. The use of a range has the "public relations" advantage of convincing the user of the estimate that it is an estimate and is not precise. However, forecasting a range is of no statistical help to the estimator. Since he does not know the margin of error which attaches to any specific estimate, he does not know whether the range should be plus or minus 5 percent, or plus or minus 10 percent, or some other magnitude.

A. Personal and Business Income Taxes

The income tax is the most important source of governmental revenue in the United States, and the most difficult to estimate. Some of the difficulties are attributable to the lack of detailed statistical knowledge of the distribution of income by type and size class, and the changes in such distributions over time.[14]

The most difficult task, of course, is the forecast of the future base, which is so intimately bound up with the forecast of general business conditions. This difficulty is compounded because, unfortunately, there is no simple historical relationship between a change in national income and the resulting change in either corporate income or personal income tax yields, even when tax rates are constant. There are too many elements which intervene.

The composition and distribution of income does not remain constant. A given volume of increase or decrease in personal income does not affect all income brackets equally. Wage and salary income may increase in one year more than in proportion to the increase in total personal income. But wage and salary income is concentrated more heavily in lower and middle income brackets. Therefore, personal tax revenues will not rise as rapidly as total personal income. Conversely, dividend income may

[14] The best continuous source of information is *Statistics of Income,* published annually by the U. S. Treasury Department. The usefulness of these data is limited, however, by the fact that they are published several years late, and by the inadequate textual analysis of the information.

increase more than in proportion to an increase in total personal income, with a resulting concentration of income in upper brackets; tax revenues will rise more than proportionately. The taxation of capital gains under the personal income tax will also present formidable estimating problems, since the total volume of capital gains income will be a function of factors difficult to estimate, such as the trend of stock prices and the volume of stock market transactions.

In the absence of detailed knowledge about such changes in the composition of income and its distribution, reasonably good approximations can still be obtained when the average personal income tax rate is known.[15]

Different kinds of estimating problems are presented for the corporate income tax. Corporate profits are not a constant fraction of the national income. Even where the rate is proportional, corporate profits tax revenues are extremely volatile. Part of the difficulties here lie in the choices available to the corporate taxpayer. For example, under federal law the volume of corporate profits is affected by the choice of depreciation methods and by the choice among the options available for the valuation of inventory. And, depending on the inventory valuation method which is elected, corporate profits will vary in accordance with changes in the price level. In some cases tax yields will be affected by the establishment of private (deductible) pension funds.

These problems are compounded at the state level. Not only will there be variations in income by type and distribution, but, in addition, state personal and corporate income cannot be estimated directly from changes in the aggregate of personal and corporate income for the nation as a whole. A state's economic structure is not a computed fraction of the national economic structure. This point was well stated in the New York State budget message in 1951:

> . . . no formula exists by which changes in national personal income can be translated with exactness into changes in forthcoming revenue from the State personal income tax.

Robert S. Herman, in a detailed analysis of this relationship in New York State, observes:

> The statistical variance noted above can be explained generally on the basis of differences between the economy of the nation as a whole and that of

---

[15] One study shows that for the federal government, in spite of substantial changes in the composition of income, the average and the marginal tax rates remained reasonably constant in the years 1948–1953. See Joseph A. Pechman, "Yield of the Individual Income Tax During a Recession," *National Tax Journal,* March 1954, pp. 1–16.

New York State, but it has been impossible to measure these differences or to adjust the New York revenue estimates for their effect.[16]

In New York, and the same would be true of other states, it has not been possible to estimate personal income tax yields from the series on national personal income published monthly by the U. S. Department of Commerce. This is in spite of the fact that the New York tax is based on the calendar year which is closing. Most of the personal income subject to tax has already been received by taxpayers at the time the final revenue estimate is made.

The same kinds of problems emerge in the estimation of state corporate or business income tax revenue. The variations in a state's economic activity as a component of the national aggregate may be of sufficient magnitude to introduce major errors into the estimating process.

In the estimation of corporate tax revenues, for either national or state governments, it may sometimes be desirable to undertake sample surveys. The technique involved is that of selecting a number of corporations whose published financial reports are representative of the aggregate of corporations. If such a sample can be chosen with reasonable accuracy, its subsequent use is relatively simple. Financial reports published in the press, or the Federal Trade Commission reports on profits of manufacturing corporations, can be tabulated to provide a reasonably firm basis for estimating three of the four quarters of the calendar year. It may then be possible to project the fourth quarter with reasonable accuracy. For states whose corporate tax collections lag a full year, sampling techniques may be useful.[17]

In recent years the acceleration of corporate tax payments by the federal government has meant that budget-year revenues from this tax are increasingly determined by budget-year corporate profits. Under present legislation, half of corporate tax liabilities will be collected currently by the year 1959. The estimate of corporate income tax collections is thus increasingly a forecast of corporate net income for a future period.

B. Sales and Excise Taxes

In this country the revenue from retail sales taxes is the most critical of estimates for many state governments and for an increasing number of municipal governments.[18] Fortunately, there is available a considerable

[16] *Revenue Estimating in New York State Government*, p. 55.

[17] For a discussion of New York State experience with sampling, which has not been wholly satisfactory, see Herman, *ibid.*, pp. 84–86.

[18] For a discussion of experience in Illinois see Thomas Lee Smith, "A Problem in Revenue Estimating," *Proceedings of the 1939 Conference*, National Association of Tax Administrators, Chicago, 1940, pp. 3–5.

range of data on the volume and character of retail sales, data which can be related to past and prospective changes in the total volume of economic activity.

Estimating for a state retail sales tax might proceed as follows. First, the estimator would measure the volume of retail sales subject to tax in recent years. This measurement would be based on tax returns filed by retailers subject to the tax. Second, the estimator would secure measures of economic activity that would be expected to correlate closely with changes in retail sales subject to tax. These might include, but would not be limited to, the indexes of department store sales published by Federal Reserve Banks or state departments of commerce. The state income payments series published by the U. S. Department of Commerce should be studied to ascertain whether changes in income payments, or components thereof, have been closely correlated in the past with changes in retail sales. Third, the estimator should then be in a position to compute a ratio or a series of ratios, such as:

$$\frac{\text{Changes in state retail sales tax collections}}{\text{Changes in department store sales}}$$

or

$$\frac{\text{Changes in state retail sales tax collections}}{\text{Changes in state income payments}}$$

These ratios, computed on the basis of historical experience, provide a technique for projecting the base of the tax. For example, if it is found that state sales tax collections have correlated reasonably well with department store sales, it is now possible to analyze currently reported data on department store sales and to forecast these for the future. The application of the ratio to the projected base of department store sales will then serve as the starting point for the revenue estimate, which would be modified in accordance with changes in tax collection procedure or changes in auditing techniques, as described previously.

A forecast of specific excise tax revenues can utilize similar techniques. For some excise taxes, such as those on cigarets and alcoholic beverages, the historical records are reasonably adequate for both the federal government and state governments. Trends in consumer expenditures for these items can be analyzed, with particular emphasis on the rate of change, and in some cases they can be related to changes in personal income or to other factors peculiar to the consumption of particular products.

Where tax rate changes and resulting price changes are involved, it may be most difficult to estimate revenue consequences. An increase in the excise tax on distilled spirits will raise prices and induce consumers to substitute beer for distilled spirits; illegal production and sale of spirits may also increase. These effects may, within certain ranges, reduce rather than increase revenue from alcoholic beverage taxes when rates are increased. The same kind of substitution effect may occur between smoking tobacco and cigarets when taxes and prices are raised for the latter.

For some excises there is a further difficulty in ascertaining whether a tax increase is likely to be passed on to consumers, or a tax reduction reflected in lower prices. A reduction in the excise tax on automobiles might or might not mean lower automobile prices, and this in turn might or might not affect total sales.

Very little is known of the price elasticity of demand for particular commodities, or the incidence of a tax rate increase or decrease in particular circumstances. When these two problems are compounded, the estimating difficulties are extreme.

IV. REVENUE ESTIMATING IN NEW YORK STATE:
A CASE STUDY[19]

Considerable attention has been devoted to revenue estimating in New York State, particularly since 1943. The procedures adopted there illustrate that the elements of uncertainty indigenous to the process cannot be eliminated but can at least be held to a minimum.

The first budget law in New York, in 1927, contained a general requirement that the governor submit a plan of proposed expenditures and estimated revenues, but it did not require that the basis for the revenue estimates be explained in the budget message. In the early years of the budget system and on into the 1930's, New York governors paid little attention to revenues in their budget messages, and submitted no data to support the broad estimates that were incorporated therein. By the mid-1930's, as the state's fiscal affairs became critical under the impact of depression, the legislature became concerned with revenue estimates, and there was a mounting tide of dissatisfaction with the provisions of the budget law. These feelings were expressed in 1935, when the legislature requested a New York State Commission for the Revision of the Tax Laws to make independent revenue estimates. In 1937 a Joint Legislative Committee on State Fiscal Policies was sharply critical of the way in which the governors' revenue estimates had been presented.

These criticisms culminated, in 1938, in an amendment to the State Constitution requiring that the governor's budget contain "a complete

[19] This section is based on Herman, *Revenue Estimating in New York State Government*, pp. 9–33.

plan of expenditures proposed to be made . . . and all moneys and revenues estimated to be available therefor, together with an explanation of the basis of such estimates. . . . " (Article VII, Section 2). To implement this provision, the governor employed a professional economist as a consultant for revenue estimating, and in 1943 a special research unit was established in the Division of the Budget. This made revenue estimates the immediate responsibility of the Director of the Budget, and concentrated authority over revenue and expenditure estimates in the same agency. Since 1943 a well-articulated procedure for revenue estimating has evolved. The governor retains final responsibility for the estimates, but what this amounts to is that he satisfies himself that the estimates have been competently prepared. Revenue estimating has come to be regarded as wholly an expertise function.

In the establishment of estimating procedure after 1943 the first step was the preparation of a comprehensive historical and statistical record of monthly and quarterly collections for each tax. Adjustments were made for changes in tax rates and collection procedure, and the record has since been maintained to provide a basis for the continual comparison of current flows of tax receipts with the historical pattern.

The second step was the preparation of a form on which the collecting units of the Department of Taxation could return their estimates to the Division of the Budget. The use of this form has had the effect of regularizing and recording the estimates of the Department of Taxation and making these estimates continuously available to the Division of the Budget. At the same time, the Division retains responsibility for all final revenue estimates. Separate forms are used for the short and for the long estimate, and the Department of Taxation is asked to explain fully the basis for its estimates.

The third step was the preparation of a "Book of Revenue Estimates" for the use of the Division of the Budget. This contained the historical record for each fiscal year, with the successive estimates by the Department of Taxation and those by the research unit of the Division of the Budget. Finally, a separate historical record was prepared for each specific tax. At the close of each budget season all of these records are filed in the Division of the Budget as a guide for future estimators.

On the basis of these records, the formal estimating procedure has been as follows. First, by October 15 of each year the Department of Taxation returns to the Division of the Budget a revenue estimate based on collections as of October 1. Utilizing these returns and data on economic trends, the research unit of the Division prepares a preliminary revenue estimate by the end of October. This is reported to the Director of the Budget and to the Governor, and becomes part of the materials for major budget policy decisions.

Shortly after November 30, the Department of Taxation submits a revised set of revenue estimates, this time including October and November collections. With these revisions and additional information on business conditions, the research unit now prepares its final revenue estimates. These are discussed with the Director of the Budget, and by him with the Governor. On occasion, specific estimates may be challenged by the Director or the Governor and re-examined by the research unit, with subsequent revision. These cases are rare, and generally the final estimates of the research unit are unchanged.

Finally, the research unit prepares an analysis of the accuracy or inaccuracy of the previous year's revenue estimates. This is included in the budget message, together with a complete explanation of the estimate for the forthcoming year.

This procedure has provided responsible and improved revenue estimates. It has not, of course, produced perfect results. But New York State's record in this regard, in comparison with other states and with the federal government, is commendable.

V. IMPROVEMENTS IN ESTIMATING TECHNIQUE

There is a rather widespread impression that revenue estimating is an art, not a science; moreover, that it partakes of the nature of the occult. This impression may be attributable to the behavior of the estimating practitioners, who seem not to be particularly vocal and seldom write or talk about their activities.

This is an unfortunate state of affairs. The most important contribution which could be made to an improvement in revenue estimating would be to make explicit the techniques and assumptions employed. For example, in the United States government both the Treasury Department and the Joint Committee on Internal Revenue Taxation prepare a forecast of tax revenues. The former is printed in the budget and the latter is made available to congressional appropriations and revenue committees. Both of these agencies could contribute to public enlightenment by published descriptions of their work, including a discussion of the reasons for last year's errors.

At the state level there has been some attempt to share information on revenue estimating. Each year the National Association of Tax Administrators, at its research section, conducts a conference session on revenue estimating; it has been proposed that the NATA sponsor the preparation of a manual on standard revenue estimating techniques.[20]   This would be an important forward step in disseminating available information to those who must employ the techniques.

The limitations inherent in revenue estimating must be recognized and understood.   In every government, experience alone can determine the extent to which it is desirable to devote staff resources to a refinement of the estimates.   In this area, as in other aspects of budgeting, there is danger in getting carried away by a preoccupation with technique for its own sake.   There may be some virtue in the middle-of-the-road.   One extreme which should be avoided is the view that the economic future is so uncertain that any effort to do other than record the revenues from the most recent fiscal year is fruitless.   The other extreme, likewise to be shunned, is refinement and re-refinement of forecasts which are based on data inherently subject to a substantial margin of error.   Somewhere between these extremes lies the desirable middle ground.

[20] National Association of Tax Administrators, *Revenue Administration, 1953,* Federation of Tax Administrators, Chicago, p. 43.

Selected Bibliography

Arnold, James A., Jr., "Budget Estimates and Tax Policy: the New Jersey Experience," *National Tax Journal,* December 1953, pp. 386–392.

Blough, Roy, *The Federal Taxing Process,* Prentice-Hall, New York, 1952, pp. 287–303.

———— "The Nature and Importance of Revenue Estimating," *Proceedings of the 1939 Conference,* National Association of Tax Administrators, Chicago, 1940, pp. 1–3.

Buck, A. E., *Public Budgeting,* Harper & Brothers, New York, 1929, pp. 317–338.

———— *The Budget in Governments of Today,* Macmillan Company, New York, 1934, pp. 175–179.

Herman, Robert S., *Revenue Estimating in New York State Government,* State of New York, Division of the Budget, Albany, 1952.

Shaw, George N., "Budgetary Crystal Gazing," *Municipal Finance,* February 1949, pp. 10–13.

Smith, Thomas Lee, "A Problem in Revenue Estimating," *Proceedings of the 1939 Conference,* National Association of Tax Administrators, Chicago, 1940, pp. 3–5.

Stourm, René, *The Budget,* translated by Thaddeus Plazinski, D. Appleton & Company, New York, 1917, pp. 169–189.

Sundelson, J. Wilner, "Techniques of State Revenue Estimating," *Proceedings of the 1939 Conference,* National Association of Tax Administrators, Chicago, 1940, pp. 5–10.

———— *Budgetary Methods in National and State Governments,* J. B. Lyon Company, Albany, 1938, pp. 319–335.

16.

The budgeting and control of public enterprise*

Government undertakings which are financed wholly or in part by user charges may be broadly classified as public enterprise. Very often these activities are termed semipublic or quasi public to emphasize that they are conducted along private, commercial lines and are not customarily administered in the same pattern as the traditional departmental activity of governments. Public enterprise has economic characteristics which are different from those of general government. The latter does not sell a government product in the market; the former does, although very often the market in which government product is sold is a special kind of market, differing sharply from that in which private firms buy resources and sell product.

The special characteristics of public enterprise have been implicitly recognized by governments everywhere in their efforts to devise workable organizational arrangements for the conduct of commercial-type activity. The task of establishing such arrangements is not a simple one. Public enterprise is certainly not private enterprise; but the traditional patterns of political and financial control which are deemed applicable to general government are not as obviously applicable here. Programs are conducted in enterprise form so that their administration may be endowed with characteristics not possessed by general government. These char-

* A portion of this chapter was originally published in *Les Cahiers Economiques*, July–August 1954, and is reproduced here with permission of the editors.

acteristics are customarily described in terms of the desirability for greater flexibility in management.

It would not be safe to assert that public enterprise is increasing in importance in all governments. The role of public enterprise, at any one time, is most evidently shaped by the tides of political fortune and the accompanying attitudes toward the role and significance of private economic activity. In Great Britain, since 1951 there have been steps to reprivatize certain nationalized industries. In the United States, since 1953 the activities of a number of government corporations have been terminated, with considerable pressure to eliminate the commercial-type activities of federal departments and agencies.[1] At the same time, the American states have continued to experiment with and expand the number of public authorities for the conduct of public works programs. In underdeveloped countries, public undertakings have assumed a major role in developmental programs, but in some instances it is anticipated that this is not a permanent state of affairs, and that these governmental activities will one day be transferred to the private sector. Public enterprise will, however, persist in every government in varying forms and proportions.

I. CHARACTERISTICS OF PUBLIC ENTERPRISE

The purposes of public enterprise activities and the varieties of ways in which governments conduct them virtually defy classification. In some cases commercial-type activity may be so mingled with traditional departmental activity that its enterprise character is lost. Conversely, enterprise activity may be endowed with governmental authority but may in all other respects remain private in nature, outside political control, outside budgetary control, conducting programs with no discernible relation to other governmental programs.

At considerable risk of oversimplification, three organizational forms of public enterprise may be distinguished. First are the undertakings controlled by departmental administration, which may loosely be described as incidental commercial activity. These may be almost wholly integrated with departmental finances, or may be partially isolated and financed by means of a working capital fund.

A second organizational type is the joint stock company, which is established under general incorporation statutes with shares of common stock as evidence of ownership rights. The shares of stock may be owned by government, in whole or in part. Control over the company

[1] Commission on Organization of the Executive Branch of the Government, *Business Enterprises,* Washington, 1955.

may be exerted through exercise of the ownership rights attaching to the common stock; or the government may refrain from exerting its ownership rights, and control may, for all practical purposes, remain in private hands. In this latter case the undertaking may be as wholly private as if government had simply loaned funds to a private corporation.

A third organizational form is the public corporation. In its pure form it has the following legal characteristics: (1) it is created by a specific statute for a specific purpose; (2) there are no shares of common stock and therefore no shareholders; (3) the government (Administration) is ultimately responsible for its management; (4) a management group is appointed by the government and charged with its day-to-day affairs; (5) the corporation has an independent legal status, is a legal person in the eyes of the law; (6) the corporation is subject to specified standards of accountability, including financial accountability.[2]

Public enterprises may also be grouped in accordance with the kinds of economic activities they conduct. Here there are two broad classes, those involving financial transactions and those involving goods and service transactions. Financial undertakings may include banking, such as the central bank or commercial or savings banks conducted by government; lending activities, which may be organized and conducted outside banking channels, as with agricultural credit; and insurance, such as the underwriting of foreign loans or residential mortgages, or life insurance for veterans.

Goods and service activities may be roughly divided into production and sale programs and purchase and sale programs. The prototype of the production and sale activity is the government owned and operated electric power plant, or the nationalized railroad. An example of the purchase and sale type is a government marketing board, or a government stockpiling operation. An important kind of public enterprise in some western European countries is the fiscal monopoly, which may be either production and sale or purchase and sale. This is an undertaking organized to monopolize transactions in salt, or tobacco, or alcoholic beverages. The enterprise is conducted for revenue purposes and is expected to show a substantial surplus each year, which is then budgeted as a part of government tax revenue.

The foregoing classification, incomplete and nondiscrete as it is, may at least indicate that public enterprises possess no distinctive qualities other than that a part of their operating revenue is derived from transactions with the private sector. Certainly there is no rule, expressed or implied, that all public enterprise, in all countries, must break even or

[2] These characteristics are adapted from W. Friedman, ed., *The Public Corporation,* Carswell Company, Ltd., Toronto, 1954, pp. 164–165.

show a profit.   A recent survey of pricing practices by government enterprises in this country, for example, reveals that there is simply no prevalent uniformity.   In some cases the goods and services of public undertakings are priced in accordance with a vague standard of public welfare,
in other cases in accordance with the value of service or the cost of
service.[3]

In the literature of economics there is considerable discussion of the
principles which ought to be followed in pricing the output of government enterprise to achieve an optimum allocation of resources.[4]   This
discussion may have contributed to the development of welfare economics, but it is unlikely that it has been helpful to those responsible for
the prices charged by public enterprises.   Pricing policy has been and
will continue to be influenced by all manner of considerations, and the
possible attainment of an optimum point in the utilization of resources
will be only one of these.

In the phrase *public enterprise* it is the first word which is definitional.
The term enterprise does not have precise meaning, since all kinds of
activities, public and private, are of an enterprise character.   What is
important is that these are *public* undertakings, conceived for a governmental purpose.   That purpose, like all public purposes, may embrace a
number of goals.   These may very well include the subsidization of particular economic groups, or the maintenance of stockpiles in the interests
of national defense, or the control of foreign exchange.   The accomplishment of these goals may require that public enterprise incur a deficit or
that it earn a surplus.   The utilization by government of an organizational form characteristic of the private sector does not make the activity
less governmental in character.

II. EXTERNAL AND INTERNAL CONTROL

There are two conceptually separable aspects of budgeting for enterprise activity.   One is the internal budgeting which an enterprise does,
or should do, for management purposes.   When a government undertaking derives its income from the sale of product in a fluctuating market,
internal budgeting is very similar to that conducted by private firms, and
its objectives are not very different.   In these circumstances the preparation of the budget is a technique for coordinating the components of a

---

[3] Jules Backman and Ernest Kurnow, "Pricing of Government Services," *National Tax Journal*, June 1954, pp. 121–140.

[4] An excellent summary and appraisal of this is contained in I. M. D. Little,
A Critique of Welfare Economics, Clarendon Press, Oxford, 1950, pp. 180–210.

total program, and each component is geared to the forecast of operating revenue. Expense elements are analyzed in accordance with their functional relationship to changes in revenue. As the budget is executed, and as revenues change, expenses can be controlled accordingly. Here, as with private enterprise, and unlike general government, revenues are not assured by legislative action, but must be forthcoming from operations.

Where government enterprise is conducted in departmental form or as an adjunct of departmental activities, this kind of internal budgeting may be based on a working capital fund. This facilitates management control, and may also simplify budgetary review by the central budget office or legislature if departmental enterprise is subject to external control as well (see Chapter 10).

The second aspect of enterprise budgeting centers on the pattern of relationships running between the undertaking and the general government sector. Budgeting is, among other things, a control over governmental operations and may be used to influence and direct the components of a total governmental program. Budgeting may be used as a major tool for the centralized supervision of public enterprise—as a control external to the enterprise, and thus for a purpose differing from the budgeting which may be used as a technique for internal management.

Where enterprise is organized in the form of a public corporation, budgeting as an external control may involve the central budget office of general government, the chief executive, and the legislature. In this framework it is only a part of a larger pattern of relationships and controls, which may include personnel, accounting, auditing, and procurement.

It is this second aspect of budgeting on which attention is usually centered. The public corporation is generally the focus of controversy. The issue is customarily phrased as autonomy versus central control, or central direction.

A. Autonomy versus Central Direction

Viewed from the standpoint of public administration, the control problem may be stated as follows: the central direction of public corporations can produce a consistency in governmental policy and strengthen the whole of a government's operations; on the other hand, the effective management of public corporations seems to require freedom from the restrictions which are the frequent accompaniment of central control. Put in these terms, the issue is one of economy and efficiency in a broad sense. The alleged advantages of central direction and control must be balanced against the alleged advantages which come from the flexibility of decentralized management.[5]

It may be observed that the general controversy over centralized versus decentralized management is not confined to public corporations. All organizations, public and private, commercial and noncommercial, encounter this in their efforts to establish an organizational structure for decision-making. In the public sector the issue must be dealt with by every commission on reorganization and, in its routine applications, by every government administrator in almost every decision he makes. For many programs the choice of the level for decision-making is enormously complicated by the presence of interest groups who are affected and clientele groups who are served by the program. In other cases, complications emerge because some but not all parts of a government program express broader or national concerns, as against other parts which are more specialized or local.

The case for central control of public undertakings is most persuasive where the national government has assumed considerable responsibility for the direction and planning of the level and character of economic activity, and where major governmental programs are administered by public undertakings. In these circumstances the activities of undertakings must be brought in line with central government policies " . . . to the end that the policy of the government as a whole shall be free from contradiction."[6] To take a relatively simple example, the efforts of a government to reduce inflationary pressure may be partially nullified if public undertakings are free to incur deficits. A similar situation may obtain in efforts to implement a central government credit policy, or in a

[5] In the American literature the case for increased autonomy is presented by Marshall E. Dimock, "Government Corporations; a Focus of Policy and Administration," *American Political Science Review*, October 1949, pp. 899–921, and December 1949, pp. 1145–1164; Albert S. Abel, "The Public Corporation in the United States," in Friedmann, *op. cit.*, pp. 338–362. For contrary views see Harold Seidman, "The Theory of the Autonomous Government Corporation: A Critical Appraisal," *Public Administration Review*, Spring 1952, pp. 89–96; Arthur Smithies, *The Budgetary Process in the United States*, McGraw-Hill Book Company, New York, 1955, pp. 392–412. For British opinion see R. H. Thornton, "Nationalization," *Public Administration*, Spring 1947, pp. 10–21, a strong statement of the "autonomy" view; for a different approach, H. R. G. Greaves, "Postwar Machinery of Govenment," *Political Quarterly*, January 1945, pp. 67–77; see also the Mitchum Committee Report to the 1950 Labour Party conference, quoted in Andrew M. deNeuman, "Some Economic Aspects of Nationalization," *Law and Contemporary Problems*, Autumn 1951, p. 716.

[6] Leonard D. White, *Introduction to the Study of Public Administration*, quoted by Seidman, *op. cit.*, p. 94.

program to encourage certain types of industrial activity. In each case the activities of autonomous (noncontrolled) public undertakings may offset and nullify the efforts of the central government.

The argument for a high degree of autonomy in the management of the affairs of public undertakings is most persuasive in those circumstances in which central staff services are inflexible. A ponderous central government administrative machinery will hamper the day-to-day operations of undertakings. Specifically, a civil service system may make it difficult to obtain the flexibility in personnel administration that is appropriate for enterprise operations. The central control of finance, with its emphasis on strict accountability, may hamper an enterprise in its use of funds. If an enterprise must deposit its revenue with the treasury and can spend only from appropriated funds, it will be unable to adapt to changing market conditions. Patterns of central government accounting may not be adaptable to commercial-type ventures. Operating results cannot be evaluated if there is interference from central authority. The only way that initiative and imagination can be developed in the conduct of government enterprise is to give managers an opportunity to develop individual responsibility.

Judged by the recent literature on this subject in the United States and Great Britain, it is evident that partisans of autonomy and partisans of central control are to be found on both sides of the Atlantic. The practices of the two countries, however, reveal no such equivocation. The United States government has adopted a pattern for strict central control of corporations, but in Great Britain public corporations possess a high degree of autonomy.

B. A Contrast in Corporation Control: The United States and Great Britain

Before examining the important points of difference in the control patterns applied in the United States and in Great Britain, it should be noted that there is one major point of similarity. In neither country is there any uniformity in the treatment of those types of public enterprise which are organized in the corporate form. In the United States the Tennessee Valley Authority is organized as a government corporation, but the Bonneville Power Administration is conducted as a separate enterprise by the Department of the Interior. Similarly, the Alaska Railroad is operated in noncorporate form by the Department of the Interior, but the Inland Waterways Corporation, until its liquidation, was operated in corporate form by the Department of Commerce. In Britain the Agricultural Marketing Boards are conducted as corporate bodies within the Ministry of Agriculture, but the trading activities of the Ministry of Food and the Board of Trade are conducted in departmental form.

However sharply the two countries may differ in other aspects of their treatment of public corporations, they at least share in a nonuniform treatment of that which is to be deemed corporate in character.

1. CENTRAL CONTROL IN THE UNITED STATES. Federal corporations, in one form or another, have existed in the United States since its beginnings, although the device entered its modern growth phase after 1900. A large number of corporations were organized in World War I, many of which were later dissolved; this experience was repeated in World War II. Many of the corporations now in existence were established to administer antidepression programs in the 1930's.

Prior to 1945, the Congress of the United States permitted federal corporations to enjoy a substantial measure of autonomy. New programs and new governmental responsibilities seemed to require considerable freedom in administrative decision-making. Such undertakings as the Reconstruction Finance Corporation, the Tennessee Valley Authority, the Commodity Credit Corporation, and the Federal Housing Authority were initially granted wide latitude in matters of finance and personnel. They were subject to no central budgetary review by the Administration, and in practice, to little effective financial control by the Congress.

This situation began to alter even before World War II; the Congress and the Administration began to bring the corporations more and more into the central control pattern applicable to established departments and agencies. Civil Service Commission personnel rules were generally applied to corporations by executive order in 1938 (*E.O.* 7916), and by statute in 1940 (*P.L.* 880, 76th Cong., 2d sess.). A number of corporations were required to submit to a budgetary review of their administrative expenses by the Bureau of the Budget in accordance with an executive order in 1942 (*E.O.* 9159). And finally, in 1945, the Congress enacted the Government Corporation Control Act (*P.L.* 248, 79th Cong., 1st sess.), which consolidated and considerably extended the pattern of central executive and legislative authority over federal corporations.

The Control Act established two types of government corporations, "wholly owned" and "mixed ownership." The latter were defined to include specific organizations such as the Federal Deposit Insurance Corporation, the Federal Land Banks and Home Loan Banks, and certain credit institutions for agricultural cooperatives. In all of these cases the capital of the enterprise was partially owned by private persons.

Both classes of corporations were brought within the post-audit authority of the General Accounting Office, and the Secretary of the Treasury was given jurisdiction over all borrowing operations. In addition, and this was the heart of the legislation, the wholly owned corporations were required to submit annual budgets to the Bureau of the Budget, and these were subject to review by the appropriations committees of the Congress. Financial and operating flexibility was intended to be preserved by the use of the so-called "business-type" budgets; the corporations also retained considerable flexibility through their power to enter into contracts and to make expenditures from program receipts. In spite of these latter features, it is evident that since 1945 the degree of executive and legislative control over federal corporations in the United States is greater than that in any other western country.

The Corporation Control Act should probably be viewed as a manifestation of a trend toward the discouragement of additional government enterprise activity in the United States, even though this form of activity has not increased markedly—for the whole period 1900 to 1949, enterprise activity at all levels of government in the United States remained a constant proportion of total governmental activity.[7] Moreover, the Act has probably contributed to a specific discouragement of the use of the corporate form of organization. Both the Atomic Energy Commission and the Mutual Security Agency, which might well have been established as corporations, were created as independent agencies outside the corporate pattern, although the corporate form has been employed for the Small Business Administration (1953) and the Saint Lawrence Seaway Development Corporation (1954).

However, the Act did not fulfill the dire predictions of its critics, one of whom stated that it " . . . goes far toward completing the task of eliminating the features which have made government corporations useful instruments for enterprise purposes."[8] It has certainly been successful in providing more effective executive and legislative direction of the activities of government corporations. But there is no evidence that,

[7] Solomon Fabricant, *The Trend of Government Activity in the United States Since 1900*, National Bureau of Economic Research, New York, 1952, p. 108. (The relatives are measured in terms of the number of government employees.)

[8] C. Herman Pritchett, "The Government Corporation Control Act of 1945," *American Political Science Review*, June 1946, p. 509. Five years earlier Pritchett had predicted, somewhat overpessimistically, " . . . the attributes which marked the earlier federal corporations and made them representatives of a distinctive type of administrative organization have been disappearing before our eyes, like the Cheshire cat. Soon there may be nothing left but a smile to mark the spot where the government corporation once stood." ("The Paradox of the Government Corporation," *Public Administration Review*, Summer 1941, p. 389.)

in the process, it has stifled the initiative and enterprise of corporate managers.

2. AUTONOMY IN GREAT BRITAIN. In the year 1776 Adam Smith observed that no two characters seem more inconsistent than those of trader and sovereign.[9] The British have not exactly observed the letter and spirit of this dictum; the government has engaged in an increasing volume and variety of enterprise activity. But at least the sovereign and the trader are organizationally separated, although the sovereign may be the trader. In the national government of Great Britain, even where the corporate form is not utilized, enterprise activity tends to be isolated from traditional departmental functions and subject to a specific pattern of control. And where the corporate form is utilized, as is very frequently the case, the resulting public corporation is endowed with a high degree of autonomy in the shaping of its policies and in the management of its affairs.

The public corporations created in Britain during the 1920's had almost complete independence in relation to the central government. The British Broadcasting Corporation, the Central Electricity Board, and the London Passenger Transport Board were divorced from the central control pattern. Appointments to the corporate boards of directors were made by the ministers, but once appointed, the boards were largely autonomous. With the development of nationalization after World War II, central control was strengthened to the extent of requiring ministers to be responsible, not only for initial appointments of board members, but also for the major policy decisions of the corporation.

The independent legal status of the public corporation was set forth in 1949 by the English Court of Appeal, as follows:

> In the eye of the law, the corporation is its own master and is answerable as fully as any other person or corporation. It is not the Crown and has none of the immunities or privileges of the Crown. Its servants are not civil servants, and its property is not Crown property. It is as much bound by the Acts of Parliament as any other subject of the King. It is, of course, a public authority and its purposes, no doubt, are public purposes, but it is not a government department nor do its powers fall within the province of government.[10]

Actually, the control pattern which has emerged for public corporations in Britain implies, in practice, considerably more governmental

[9] *Wealth of Nations,* Modern Library, New York, 1937, p. 771.

[10] *Tamlin v. Hannaford* 1 K.B. 18 (C.A. 1949), quoted by W. Friedmann, "The Legal Status and Organization of the Public Corporation," *Law and Contemporary Problems,* Autumn 1951, p. 588.

character than is suggested in the foregoing decision. Those corporations that incur deficits and require an Exchequer grant each year are subject to a reasonably strict Treasury control. They must justify their operating results to the Treasury and before the Estimates Committee of the Parliament. For those corporations which are not grant-aided, however, there is no Treasury control over current operations, although capital outlay programs are subject to review and approval. Parliamentary control, with these exceptions, is restricted to a cursory review of the annual corporation report, together with whatever information may be provided by ministers who are willing to reply to parliamentary questions. Since 1951 this review has been supplemented by the work of a Select Committee on Nationalized Industries.[11] All public corporation employees are noncivil service. Full responsibility for the efficient management of the enterprise is vested in the minister, although he may be aided in the discharge of this responsibility by such devices as the consumers' councils and the consultative arrangements for labor which have been established to strengthen the nationalized undertakings in their accountability.[12]

The British pattern of control over public corporations seems to have emerged from a deep-seated desire to strengthen the authority and responsibility of the managers of the public corporations. This was put very strongly by Herbert Morrison in a parliamentary debate on the kinds of questions which the Government would answer regarding the affairs of the nationalized industries:

> I am certain that if we run these public corporations—highly commercial, highly industrial, highly economic—on the basis of meticulous accountability to political channels, we are going to ruin the commercial enterprise and the adventurous spirit of the public corporations in their work.[13]

In spite of a considerable volume of opposition to the views of Mr. Morrison on this point, and in spite of some general dissatisfaction with

[11] Ernest Davies, "Government Policy and the Public Corporation," *Political Quarterly*, April–June 1955, pp. 104–116. Davies concludes that the Conservative Party attitude toward the corporations does not differ substantially from that of the Labour Party. Ministerial supervision is somewhat stronger, veering from "pressure" toward "direction."

[12] For discussions of these techniques see Adolf Sturmthal, "Nationalization and Workers' Control in Britain and France," *Journal of Political Economy*, February 1953, pp. 43–79; Eldon L. Johnson, "Consumer 'Control' in British Nationalized Industries," *Journal of Politics*, February 1953, pp. 88–113, and "The Accountability of the British Nationalized Industries," *American Political Science Review*, June 1954, pp. 366–385.

[13] House of Commons, *Parliamentary Debates*, Vol. 444, March 3, 1948, p. 455.

the public accountability aspects of the control pattern presently applied to corporations and particularly to the nationalized industries, there is no evidence to indicate that this framework is likely to be altered in Britain in the immediate future.[14]   Public corporations will continue to enjoy far more autonomy than their American counterparts.

The differences between the British and the United States patterns for central government control of public corporations appear to present some anomalies.   The traditional British practice in financial administration, characterized by the phrase Treasury control, has long been synonymous with techniques for centralized decision-making.   One might expect, given a background of strong Cabinet leadership and central control of governmental operations, that the British would have been the first to bring public corporations within the orbit of centralized management. Similarly, one might expect that in the United States, where central executive leadership in government is a relatively recent development, government corporations would be permitted to operate with relative independence.   Furthermore, it might be supposed that in the United States, where freedom of entrepreneurship is presumably regarded as a desirable end in itself, government utilization of the corporate device would hardly take the form of restricting this freedom.   And for Britain, where civil service traditions are presumed to be very strong, it appears somewhat strange that every effort is made to grant maximum freedom to the managers of public corporations and to avoid all semblance of civil service patterns.

The sharply differing practices of Great Britain and of the United States in the control of public corporations may, however, not be as anomalous as would appear on first examination.   The explanation undoubtedly lies in the different kind of general economic situations faced in the two countries, and is illustrated most sharply by the conditions of the immediate postwar period.

The newly nationalized industries in Great Britain after 1945 were faced with critical problems centering on the effective utilization of extremely scarce resources.   The National Coal Board, to cite the most obvious case, was under great pressure to reduce costs of production and increase output in order to supply domestic needs and provide coal for export to ease Britain's critical balance of payments position.   The pressure, then, was on management, and management undoubtedly needed a

[14] For an impartial discussion see Raymond Nottage and D. G. Brunt, "The Public Corporation and Nationalization in Great Britain," *Revûe Internationale de Sciences Administratives,* No. 2, 1952, pp. 354–371; also William A. Robson, *Problems of Nationalized Industry,* Oxford University Press, New York, 1952, pp. 302–320; Lucille Sheppard Keyes, "Some Controversial Aspects of the Public Corporation," *Political Science Quarterly,* March 1955, pp. 28–56.

considerable degree of freedom and flexibility in order to work out its own solutions. The nationalized industries had clearly stated objectives and an important role to occupy in the British economy. Such rigidities as civil service would not be permitted to stand in their way.

The economic situation in the United States as the postwar period approached was quite different. There were no severe national pressures on the Tennessee Valley Authority, for example, to lower costs and increase output. The Reconstruction Finance Corporation was not administering programs important to the nation's economy. The situation had altered since the 1930's, when the government corporations felt it urgent to produce results in a short period of time. Then, as economic recovery proceeded, opposition to government enterprise became more effective, and federal corporations could not expect to enjoy freedom from central, and possibly restrictive, control. At the end of World War II, there were renewed efforts to limit government intervention in the private sector of the economy. The Government Corporation Control Act was an expression of this conservatism.

The important conclusion which emerges from this comparison of the experiences of Great Britain and the United States is that the pattern of central control over government corporation must be appropriate to the economic and political role which corporations are expected to play in a nation's economy. The greater freedom possessed by corporation managers in Great Britain fits the requirements there. It should be observed that in neither country is the pattern of control over public corporations in any important degree explained by the respective traditions of governmental administration.

III. A CASE IN AUTONOMY:
PUBLIC AUTHORITIES IN THE STATES

In the national governments of Great Britain and the United States considerable attention has been devoted to the administration and control of enterprise activity, and in particular to the operations of public corporations. Such is not the case with the public corporations known as authorities, established under the laws of the several states; attention has not focused on their administration and control. These, in fact, do not really inhabit the area between the public and the private sectors. Rather, they live in the shadow of government, endowed with governmental authority exercised, very often, without let or restraint; operating, very often, with public funds for which there is no accountability; free from their "owners," free from the restraints of the market, and free from established political authority.

According to the Council of State Governments, the distinguishing characteristics of authorities are two:

> First is the power to issue revenue bonds, payable solely from charges against consumer use of the agency's facilities, and the lack of dependence on taxes or power to levy them. . . . The second criterion is that the reliance on revenue funds, not taxes, is a *basic pattern* of the agency in question, not a characteristic only of certain of its secondary activities.[15]

Authorities come into existence by specific statute and corporate charter authorized by the state legislature.[16] They may be financed initially by specific appropriation. But at some point they are expected to secure their own sources of finance, through the issuance of bonds, and thereafter to exist on the basis of user charges. All expenses of operation, including the amortization of the bonds, is expected to be met from such charges. Authorities are seldom permitted to earn a profit, but they are expected to be self-liquidating.

The purposes for which authorities are established are legion, and their antecedents in the states go back to the early 19th century. In their modern version, authorities are commonly established for the construction and operation of toll roads, bridges, tunnels, ports, docks, and terminal facilities; for the development of water and power resources, public housing, airports, parking facilities; for marketing facilities; and for the construction and operation of public buildings. In some cases, authorities conduct operations which are of state-wide concern, such as the thruways. In other instances, although the corporation is created by the state, it is essentially local in character, as in the case of a county water authority or county sewerage authority.

There are manifold reasons for the creation of authorities, and these, of course, differ in accordance with time and place. Some of these reasons stem from constitutional and statutory restrictions imposed on the conduct of general government activity; the authority becomes a device for

---

[15] Council of State Governments, *Public Authorities in the States*, Chicago, 1953, p. 5.

[16] Pennsylvania appears to be the only exception to this. In that state a general enabling statute permits local governments to establish authorities on application to the Secretary of the Commonwealth. There are other unusual features in the use of authorities in Pennsylvania. Not only do their numbers exceed those of other states, but in addition, many of the authorities, such as those for public school buildings and state schools and office buildings, are supported from revenues appropriated from the general fund. (See George C. Lindsay, "The Municipal Authority in Pennsylvania," *Pennsylvania Department of Internal Affairs Bulletin*, August 1951, pp. 1–12; Joint State Government Commission, *Public School Building Subsidies*, Harrisburg, 1955.)

assuring greater "flexibility" than can be otherwise obtained. Or, to put the matter another way, authorities are created in order to evade restrictions which attach to other forms of governmental organization.

Therefore, most of the instant reasons for the creation of public authorities appear to lie in their special legal and operating characteristics.[17] Authorities can be used to finance public improvements without recourse to additional taxation in its conventional forms. In a great many states, opposition to increased general levies of any kind is intense. But conventional taxes are not increased by authority charges. The users of the facility appear to bear the burden, and even though this may ultimately be shifted to other persons or economic groups through higher prices, the shifting may not be obvious and the ultimate incidence may be difficult to trace. As a result, there may be little general awareness of the costs imposed by the authority.

Other reasons for the creation of authorities may be cited. (1) In their debt-creating capacity they will typically lie outside constitutional and statutory debt limits, and thus may not commit the general credit of the state or political subdivision. (2) The generally high regard in which private corporations are held in this country, as a form for the conduct of enterprise, carries over to government when it uses the corporate device. This is alleged to impart a freedom and flexibility which government conventionally lacks. (3) In accordance with prevailing attitudes which sometimes regard politics as a "dirty business," the authority is established outside political control and thus is thought to be cleansed of an otherwise undesirable taint. This, very often, is wholly illusory. The authority will end up by substituting a kind of private politics for public politics. (4) One of the most compelling and legitimate reasons for the establishment of an authority is to overcome existing governmental lines of jurisdiction, in order to provide effective service over broader areas than are encompassed by governmental boundaries. This was the rationale for the establishment of the Port of New York Authority, and its generally impressive record, financial and administrative, demonstrates the efficacy of the authority device under these conditions.[18]

Beyond the foregoing factors generally associated with organizational and legal arrangements, there are other elements which have contributed to the popularity of state authorities, particularly in the years

[17] See Temporary Commission on Coordination of State Activities, *First Interim Staff Report on Public Authorities Under New York State,* Albany, 1954, pp. 31–44.

[18] Frederick L. Bird, *A Study of the Port of New York Authority,* Dun & Bradstreet, New York, 1949; C. J. Kushell, Jr., "Operating Aspects of Revenue Bond Financing," *Journal of Finance,* May 1955, pp. 209–222.

since World War II. These additional elements are more closely linked with economic considerations, and in particular with the use of revenue bonds.

The interest on revenue bonds issued by public authorities is exempt from federal and state income taxes. The steeply progressive federal personal income tax rates of the postwar period have naturally stimulated a concern, on the part of taxpayers subject to these rates, for havens of refuge from their impact. The resulting preference for tax-exempts has improved the market for all state and local government bond issues, and the revenue bonds of authorities have participated in this. High income taxes on certain kinds of financial corporations have likewise encouraged their purchase of tax-exempt securities; commercial banks, for example, have become important holders of state and local bonds.

Data are not available which permit an analysis of the holdings of the revenue bonds of authorities, separated from other tax-exempts. It is reasonable to assume, however, that the patterns of holdings are not very different than for tax exempts as a whole. In a recent study, George E. Lent found, for the year 1953, that of tax-exempt bonds privately owned 40 percent were held by commercial banks, 16 percent were owned by other financial institutions, and 44 percent were in the hands of individuals.[19] The portion held by individuals is highly concentrated. Data for an earlier year (1941) show that two-thirds of individual holdings of tax-exempts are in the upper one percent of income recipients. It might be guessed that in the years since 1941 concentration in individual holdings has not diminished.

Apart from the tax-exempt feature, which makes the revenue bonds of authorities particularly attractive in the market for financial investments, an additional generalized condition has contributed to their success. High prosperity and full employment in the American economy generate a large volume of private and institutional savings. This liquid savings must find its way into earning assets. The increasing volume of such liquid savings imparts a general buoyancy to the demand for financial assets, a buoyancy advantageous to the revenue bonds of public authorities. Within limits, this is a self-feeding mechanism. Prosperity is assured by the continuation of expenditures on plant and equipment, private and public, including expenditures by public authorities.[20] At

[19] George E. Lent, *The Ownership of Tax-Exempt Securities, 1913–1953*, National Bureau of Economic Research, New York, 1955, pp. 2–3.

[20] The utilization of authorities by the states, and possibly by the federal government, has come to be regarded in some quarters as particularly appropriate for assuring the growth of the public sector in such areas as highways, schools, water, and other community facilities. (See *Economic Report of the President*, Washington, 1955, pp. 61–64.)

the same time, high levels of national income assure a market for the bonds of the public authorities.

The tax-exempt aspect of revenue bonds and the general availability of liquid savings for investment have been major factors contributing to the use of public authorities by the states in recent years.[21] These, added to the legal and organizational advantages which they possess, make for the popularity of authorities. On the surface at least, authorities are "operationally adequate." Their debts are not popularly regarded as a part of the public debt. Therefore, they may engage in deficit financing for public facilities without, at the same time, running afoul of prevailing antipathy toward public debt and deficits (see Chapter 17).

The state authority is truly a mixed creature, brought into existence by an unusual concatenation.[22] That it is capable of abuse is evident. At the same time, under favorable conditions, the authority can sometimes break free from a stultifying pattern of traditional behavior and from low levels of governmental morality to impart a new zeal and a new accomplishment to government programs.[23]

As a mixed creature, in but not of the government, state authorities have generally conducted their affairs with far more autonomy than national government corporations. The 1953 survey by the Council of State Governments analyzed in detail the control pattern in which 41 state authorities operated.[24] It was found that 13 of the 41 did not make any periodic report whatever to their state governments. In only 11 cases did the state post-audit the expenditures of the authority. In only 7 cases did the authority submit a part or all of its budget for approval by the legislature.

The traditional techniques by which government assures financial and administrative responsibility are thus very much lacking for authorities. Neither has there been an adequate substitution of other kinds of controls for those of the traditional governmental variety. The investment bankers who market the securities of state authorities assume some kind

[21] For further discussion see George W. Mitchell, "Economic Aspects of Revenue Bond Financing," *Journal of Finance,* May 1955, pp. 223–229.

[22] Joseph E. McLean has named this apparent magic remedy for governmental ills "authoritycin," which " . . . is guaranteed to overcome constitutional infirmities, such as debt limitations; to increase the leisure time of governors, legislators and other elected officials by delegating their worries to irresponsible parties; and, in general, to put the patient in such a state of well-being that even the medical bill can be taken painlessly." ("Use and Abuse of Authorities," *National Municipal Review,* October 1953, p. 439.)

[23] See Luther Gulick, " 'Authorities' and How to Use Them," *Tax Review,* November 1947, pp. 47–52.

[24] Council of State Governments, *Public Authorities in the States,* appendix Table V.

of responsibility for their "financibility." But the bankers' concern is necessarily with the maintenance of conventional standards of solvency and liquidity, not with the public policies which are formulated by the authority, nor with their impact on other governmental programs. Similarly, the bondholders, in so far as they have influence other than through investment bankers, will likely exhibit no concern for the affairs of the authority as long as interest is paid and the bonds are retired on schedule. The fact that the revenue bonds of authorities are subject to the test of the market, then, does not assure that the authorities' policies will be responsive and responsible with respect to the concerns of public policy—or even that they will be well managed.

At the same time, it appears somewhat quixotic to suggest that public authorities should be brought within the scope of traditional governmental policy and financial procedures. It is unrealistic to urge, for example, that all state authorities be required to submit their budgets for review by the central budget office and approval by the chief executive and the legislature. It was to escape controls of this sort that the authority was established in the first place. Legislatures are not soon likely to do an about-face.

To the end that sufficient public and legislative concern may some day be generated to reduce the degree of autonomy which authorities now enjoy, it would appear that first steps might well be taken in terms of financial and program reporting. There seems to be no good reason why, in most states, it should not be possible for the governor to assume a greater measure of responsibility for the authorities which the state has created. At minimum, this would mean that the governor would request from each authority a comprehensive annual report for transmission to the legislature. Beyond this, the governor's budget message might well contain a brief review of their financial and program activities. A summary statement, showing the operating results of authorities, together with their balance sheets, could be included in the budget document.

Public authorities are most obviously useful devices, and their usefulness should not be impaired by drastic reorganizations of their *modus operandi*. But most students of governmental affairs, after looking at their conduct, become concerned about their potentiality for irresponsibility, a concern no doubt reflected here. The increasing use of public authorities is a reversal of many of the significant trends in American government of the past half century. The short ballot, the reorganization movement among state and local governments, the budget system itself—these are all designed to increase the degree of responsibility in government. Authorities run counter to what, it may be hoped, is a long-run trend toward increased governmental responsibility.

IV. BUDGETING FOR CORPORATIONS IN THE U. S. GOVERNMENT

The Government Corporation Control Act of 1945 established the financial and budgetary framework in which federal corporations must operate. This Act was of a centralizing character—that is, it substantially reduced the degree of corporate financial autonomy.

The financial activities of United States corporations are fully reported each year in the budget document. In the first years after the Control Act, the corporations were given a separate section of the document. In recent years, perhaps to emphasize their greater integration with general government departments and agencies, they are reported, where possible, as a separate section of the departmental budget presentation. The impact of corporation activities on the government's financial position is shown for each corporation separately. The surpluses and deficits of corporations are brought into the summary financial accounts, although this is accomplished in such a way as to de-emphasize the importance of corporate activities in relation to the total of governmental activities (see Chapter 5).

Apart from their treatment in the budget document, the significant features of the Control Act and the procedures which have since emerged are as follows.[25] First, the corporation can conduct business in its own name, which gives it greater freedom in making contracts and in holding and disposing of property than is the case with general government departments and agencies. Second, a corporation's administrative expenses are usually fixed by annual congressional action, but there are no limits on its program outlays as long as they conform with the general statutory purposes for which the corporation was created. Third, accounts are set up along lines of traditional commercial practice, with statements of income and expense, and balance sheets. The corporation's accounting system must be approved by the General Accounting Office, but the corporation maintains its own books. Fourth, corporation accounts are subject to audit by the Comptroller General. This is called a commercial-type audit, and the Comptroller General does not have power to disallow specific transactions. Irregularities, however, must be reported to the

[25] See Sidney D. Goldberg and Harold Seidman, *The Government Corporation: Elements of a Model Charter*, Public Administration Service, Chicago, 1953, pp. 5–7.

CHART 10
Statement of Sources and Application of Funds
(Corporation Revolving Fund)

GOVERNMENT ENTERPRISE CORPORATION

A. Statement of sources and application of funds

PY—post year
CY—current year
BY—budget year

> Show program operations first and financing second. If there is more than one program, each program will be listed separately.

> Exclude inventories of goods to be manufactured, in process of manufacture, and finished for sale, and Treasury cash from the amounts of changes in working capital reported on these lines.

FUNDS APPLIED To operations	19PY actual	19CY estimate	19BY estimate
Loan program:			
Acquisition of assets:			
Defense plant expansion loans........	$12,000,000	$11,298,000	$9,358,000
Foreign aid loans.................	7,600,000	1,847,000	5,062,000
Other loans.................	400,000	1,355,000	580,000
Expenses:			
Interest on borrowings from U. S. Treasury...	1,106,175	993,000	809,000
Loan servicing fees..........	1,292,000	1,182,000	1,260,000
Research and development..........	646,000	875,000	851,100
Plant maintenance..........	1,900,000	1,940,000	1,546,200
Administrative expenses..........	1,100,000	1,050,000	1,250,000
Total, loan program.....	$26,044,175	$20,440,000	$20,716,300
Sales program:			
Acquisition of assets:			
Buildings, machinery and equipment......	....	1,075,000	537,000
Construction in progress........	....	....	530,000
Expenses:			
Purchases of commodities..........	18,350,468	10,697,100	9,191,000
Administrative expenses..........	460,000	430,000	380,000
Other expenses..........	75,000	50,000	40,000
Write-off of accounts and notes receivable....	9,000	1,500	5,000
Total, sales program.....	18,894,468	12,253,600	10,683,000
Power program:			
Acquisition of assets:			
Multiple purpose dams..........	5,203,000	....	8,297,000
Electric plant..........	2,560,000	710,000	1,061,000
Construction in progress..........	....	....	1,590,000
Expenses:			
Production..........	9,235,000	10,173,000	7,999,000
Transmission..........	4,795,000	5,610,000	3,205,000
General operating expenses..........	1,795,000	1,810,000	1,055,000
Distribution..........	450,000	546,000	1,395,000
Administrative expenses..........	800,000	954,600	750,000
Total, power program.....	24,208,000	19,810,600	24,347,000
Increase in selected working capital.....	....	644,500	....
Total applied to operations.....	69,146,643	53,148,700	55,746,300
To financing:			
Payment of dividends to U. S. Treasury.....	21,630,100	20,756,800	20,622,600
Repayment of borrowings.....	3,000,000	11,500,000	2,500,000
Increase in investment in U. S. securities held (par)...	....	2,200,000	....
Increase in cash with Treasury and in banks....	....	1,325,000	....
Total applied to financing.....	24,630,100	35,781,800	23,122,600
Total funds applied.....	93,776,743	88,930,500	78,868,900

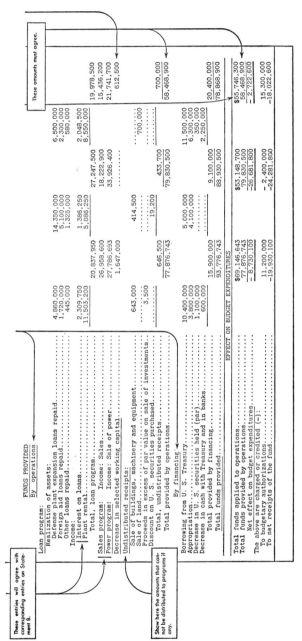

Source: U. S. Bureau of the Budget, *Instructions for the Preparation and Submission of Annual Budget Estimates*, Washington, 1954, Exhibit 57A.

CHART 11
Statement of Income and Expense
(Corporation Revolving Fund)

GOVERNMENT ENTERPRISE CORPORATION
B. Statement of income and expense

PY—past year
CY—current year
BY—budget year

Where an enterprise has more than one program show operations of each program separately.

Show depreciation as a separate item.

These amounts should agree with amounts shown on Schedule C-1.

	19PY actual	19CY estimate	19BY estimate
LOAN PROGRAM			
Income:			
Interest on loans..............	$2,309,750	$1,386,250	$2,048,500
Plant rental.................	11,503,200	5,086,250	8,550,000
Amortization of prepaid rent...	2,500	2,500	2,500
Total income...........	$13,815,450	$6,475,000	$10,601,000
Expenses:			
Interest on borrowings from U. S. Treasury......	1,106,175	993,000	809,000
Loan servicing fees..........	1,292,000	1,132,000	1,260,000
Research and development.....	646,000	875,000	851,100
Plant maintenance...........	1,900,000	1,840,000	1,546,200
Administrative expenses......	1,100,000	1,050,000	1,250,000
Depreciation...............	850,000	975,000	925,000
Write-off of loans receivable...	430,000	1,410,000	809,000
Increase or decrease (–) in allowance for losses on loans receivable......	570,000	-210,000	91,000
Total expenses............	7,894,175	8,115,000	7,541,300
Net operating income or loss (–), loan program......	5,921,275	-1,640,000	3,059,700
SALES PROGRAM			
Income: Sales............	26,958,600	18,222,900	15,436,200
Expenses:			
Cost of goods sold:			
Purchases of commodities......	18,350,468	10,697,100	9,191,000
Increase (–) or decrease in commodities inventory............	120,000	-270,000	227,000
Cost of goods sold.............	18,470,468	10,427,100	9,418,000
Administrative expenses......	460,000	430,000	380,000
Other expenses............	75,000	50,000	40,000
Write-off of accounts and notes receivable......	9,000	1,500	5,000
Increase or decrease (–) in allowance for losses on accounts and notes receivable......	- 6,000	425,000	500,000
			- 3,000
Total expenses............	19,608,468	11,335,600	10,340,000
Net operating income (or loss (–)), sales program............	7,350,132	6,887,300	5,096,200

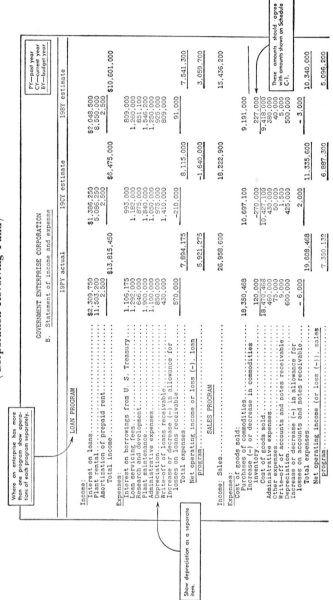

POWER PROGRAM

Income: Sale of power		27,786,693		33,926,400		21,741,700
Expenses:						
Production	9,235,000		10,173,000		7,999,000	
Transmission	4,165,000		5,617,000		3,205,000	
General operating expenses	1,795,000		1,810,000		1,050,000	
Distribution	450,000		546,000		935,000	
Administrative expenses	800,000		954,600		750,000	
Depreciation	1,150,000		1,050,000		1,200,000	
Total expenses		17,595,000		20,150,600		14,599,000
Net operating income (or loss (–)), power program		10,191,693		13,775,800		7,142,700
NONOPERATING INCOME OR LOSS						
Proceeds from sale of fixed assets:						
Buildings, machinery and equipment	643,000		414,500		....	
Land	....		....		700,000	
Net book value of assets sold (–)	–408,000	235,000	–552,000	–137,500	–600,000	100,000
Proceeds from sale of investments	1,103,500		....		....	
Net book value of investments sold (–)	–1,101,500	2,000	....	....	....	....
Amortization of premium or discount (–) on U. S. securities held		–5,000		–7,500		1,500
Net nonoperating income (or loss (–))		232,000		–145,000		101,500
Net income (or loss (–)) for the year		23,695,100		18,878,100		15,400,100

ANALYSIS OF RETAINED EARNINGS (OR DEFICIT (–))

Reserve for future contingencies:						
Balance at beginning of year		$10,000,000		$15,000,000		$15,000,000
Increase or decrease (–) during year		5,000,000		....		–3,000,000
Balance at end of year		15,000,000		15,000,000		12,000,000
Unreserved:						
Balance at beginning of year	$9,750,100		$6,815,100		$4,936,400	
Net income (or loss (–)) for the year	23,695,100		18,878,100		15,400,100	
Total		33,445,200		25,693,200		20,336,500
Increase (–) or decrease in reserve for contingencies	–5,000,000		....		3,000,000	
Payment of dividends to U. S. Treasury	–21,630,100		–20,756,800		–20,622,600	
Total		–26,630,100		–20,756,800		–17,622,600
Balance at end of year		6,815,100		4,936,400		2,713,900
Total retained earnings		21,815,100		19,936,400		14,713,900

Notes:
- If enterprise has more than one program, items not associated with program operations are shown here.
- Where portion of retained earnings is set aside as a reserve, divide this section of statement between reserved and unreserved.
- Amounts for these entries should agree with amounts on Statement C.

Source: U. S. Bureau of the Budget, *Instructions for the Preparation and Submission of Annual Budget Estimates,* Washington, 1954, Exhibit 58A.

CHART 12
Statement of Financial Condition
(Corporation Revolving Fund)

PY-1—year preceding past year
PY—past year
CY—current year
BY—budget year

GOVERNMENT ENTERPRISE CORPORATION

C. Statement of financial condition

Amounts here must agree with amounts shown for the fund in Combined Statement of Receipts, Expenditures and Balances of U. S. Government for 19PY-1 and 19PY years.

ASSETS	19PY-1 actual	19PY actual	19CY estimate	19BY estimate
Cash:				
With Treasury and in banks............	$4,250,000	$3,650,000	$4,975,000	$2,725,000
On hand and in transit...............	150,000	365,000	207,000	40,000
Total cash.....................	4,400,000	4,015,000	5,182,000	2,765,000
Accounts and notes receivable.........	2,450,000	2,625,000	2,350,000	2,565,000
Less allowance for losses...........	25,000	19,000	21,000	18,000
Net accounts and notes receivable....	2,425,000	2,606,000	2,329,000	2,547,000
Inventories:				
Commodities for sale.................	2,545,000	2,425,000	2,695,000	2,468,000
Supplies............................	30,000	25,000	27,000	30,000
Total inventories...............	2,575,000	2,450,000	2,722,000	2,498,000
Loans receivable:				
Defense plant expansion..............	23,245,000	30,155,000	26,103,000	28,261,000
Foreign aid.........................	10,195,000	15,875,000	12,212,000	14,874,000
Other...............................	210,000	165,000	195,000	186,000
Total loans receivable.........	33,650,000	46,195,000	38,510,000	43,321,000
Less allowance for losses...........	400,000	970,000	760,000	851,000
Net loans receivable............	33,250,000	45,225,000	37,750,000	42,470,000
Investments:				
United States securities – par value.....	3,600,000	2,500,000	4,700,000	4,350,000
Unamortized premium or discount (-) on United States securities...........	23,100	16,600	– 10,100	– 8,600
Net investments.................	3,623,100	2,516,600	4,689,900	4,341,400

Show investments in U. S. securities at par value with premium or discount as a separate item.

Item	19PY-1	19PY	19CY	19BY
Land, structures, and equipment:				
Land..	6,000,000	6,000,000	6,000,000	5,400,000
Multiple purpose dams.....................	75,317,000	81,342,000	81,342,000	89,639,000
Electric plant............................	12,510,000	14,760,000	14,160,000	15,221,000
Construction in progress..................	3,430,000	2,140,000	2,850,000	4,970,000
Buildings, machinery and equipment........	12,420,000	12,688,000	13,063,000	13,600,000
Total land, structures, and equipment....	109,677,000	116,930,000	117,415,000	128,830,000
Less portion charged off as depreciation....	14,305,000	16,803,000	18,505,000	21,130,000
Net land, structures, and equipment......	95,372,000	100,127,000	98,910,000	107,700,000
Deferred and undistributed charges...........	165,000	196,000	141,000	159,000
Total assets...............................	141,810,100	157,135,600	151,723,900	162,480,400
LIABILITIES				
Accounts payable............................	1,810,000	2,955,000	2,106,000	2,960,000
Accrued expenses............................	1,032,000	1,123,000	1,077,000	1,099,000
Trust and deposit liabilities...............	168,000	995,000	759,500	565,000
Deferred and undistributed credits..........	50,000	47,500	45,000	42,500
Total liabilities.......................	3,060,000	5,120,500	3,987,500	4,666,500
INVESTMENT OF U. S. GOVERNMENT				
Interest-bearing investment:				
Borrowings from Treasury.................	32,600,000	40,000,000	33,500,000	42,500,000
Non-interest-bearing investment:				
Appropriations...........................	86,400,000	90,200,000	94,300,000	100,600,000
Retained earnings:				
Reserve for future contingencies.........	10,000,000	15,000,000	15,000,000	12,000,000
Unreserved...............................	9,750,100	6,815,100	4,936,400	2,713,900
Total retained earnings................	19,750,100	21,815,100	19,936,400	14,713,900
Total non-interest-bearing investment....	106,150,100	112,015,100	114,236,400	115,313,900
Total investment of U. S. Government.....	138,750,100	152,015,100	147,736,400	157,813,900
Total liabilities and investment of U. S. Government.....	141,810,100	157,135,600	151,723,900	162,480,400

NOTE.—Selected working capital (other than cash with Treasury and in banks) included above is as follows: June 30, 19PY-1, -$215,000; 19PY, -$1,862,000; 19CY, -$1,217,500; 19BY, -$1,830,000.

Annotations:
- If there are any contingent liabilities, they should be stated in a footnote.
- Show Government's investment segregated between interest-bearing and non-interest-bearing items.
- Amounts shown here will agree with amounts shown on Statement B.

Source: U. S. Bureau of the Budget, *Instructions for the Preparation and Submission of Annual Budget Estimates*, Washington, 1954, Exhibit 59A.

Congress.[26] Finally, corporations present to the Bureau of the Budget what is known as a business-type budget. This is reviewed by the Bureau and the President. The corporation thereby seeks approval from Congress for its budget as a whole, in general and qualitative terms rather than in quantitative terms. This approval does not take the form of a specific annual congressional appropriation. The corporation is free to use its program receipts for further operations; these are not subject to control by appropriation. The corporation may, of course, request specific appropriations for the restoration of working funds or for capital expenditure.

Since 1945, budgetary routines for government corporations have been developed to the point where they do not differ in terms of procedure from those applied to the general government departments and agencies. The budget submissions of corporations have been made uniform; corporation programs move through the established channels of review and submission.

These procedures have centered on the development and utilization of three major budget schedules, designed as follows: (a) sources and application of funds, (b) income and expense, and (c) financial condition. All corporations subject to the Control Act must present their budgets in these terms. Model statements of three types are shown in Charts 10, 11, and 12. In addition, the budget presentation for any specific corporation may include a substantial number of supplementary schedules —an object classification, construction programs, changes in working capital funds, and, of course, the budget narrative.

The use of these statements has contributed to a very high degree of uniformity in the budget presentations of the United States corporations. They are used for review by the Bureau of the Budget, the President, and the Congress. Since they are grounded in the accounting systems of the corporations, budgeting and accounting are closely associated. Their accuracy for prior fiscal years is thus subject to verification through the audit process.

Although the form of the business-type budgets has been standardized, corporations retain flexibility in their definition of programs, in the degree to which they wish to employ cost accounting, and in their internal financial reporting and controls. The extent to which this standardization has jeopardized the budgetary freedom of corporation managers cannot be determined. Indeed, it is not possible to assess with any accuracy

[26] For a description see U. S. Senate, Committee on Government Operations, *Audit Reports of Government Corporations and Agencies, Senate Report* No. 861, 83d Cong., 2d sess. (1954).

the total managerial consequences of the pattern of central controls produced by the Government Corporation Control Act.

V. CONCLUSION: THE ABSENCE OF A GENERALIZED PATTERN

One would be either exceedingly brave or somewhat simple-minded, or both, to conclude that in any government there is a single "most desirable" pattern for the control, including the budgetary control, of public enterprise. The diversification in enterprise programs, their varying forms, their varying responsibilities, and their varying traditions prohibit such generalizations.

This is an area where governments need to take a fresh look from time to time to make certain that prevailing arrangements are adequate and that public purposes are served by existing institutions. In particular, it is an area where there is danger that clichés will serve as a substitute for analysis, and where attempts to transfer experience from one type of enterprise (public or private) to another are most hazardous.

The essential economic fact is that public enterprise derives its revenue from the sale of goods and services in the market. Starting with this differentiation between general government and public enterprise, Lucille Sheppard Keyes has recently suggested that it is possible to erect a philosophy for the control of enterprise:

> . . . the proper scope of direct political control depends in part on the intended significance of the market as a guide in the affairs of the corporation; that if the corporation is to be guided primarily by market considerations, public control in pursuance of other objectives can and should be limited and external in character. . . . [27]

Mrs. Keyes recognizes that the problem is complicated by the absence of the profit motive and by the ultimate identity of the regulated and the regulators, but nevertheless concludes that the need for maintaining responsiveness to the market requires flexibility and autonomy for the commercial activities of government.

This approach ascribes too much significance to the market as a conditioning element. Market considerations may not, in fact, require any flexibility whatever in decision-making. A toll bridge organized as a public enterprise is in a monopoly market, but one in which the demand for service is beyond its control. There is no evident case for flexibility here. The volume of traffic might increase twofold in a year's time; no sweeping managerial decisions would need to be made to adapt to this situation.

[27] Keyes, *Political Science Quarterly*, March, 1955, p. 28.

Neither can it be argued in general terms that public enterprise operates in a more uncertain framework than does general government. What is more uncertain than next year's appropriation? There are a great many governmental programs in politically sensitized areas where the need for flexibility and wide management descretion is much greater than in the case of government enterprises conducting their activities in a controlled market.

Similarly, the market for government enterprise product is very seldom the kind of market that enforces an efficient allocation of resources. It is very often a market with few or no substitutes for the product. The only test of efficiency here is the avoidance of a deficit. But the absence of a deficit may only conceal a prodigious volume of waste and inefficiency.

There are undoubtedly a few circumstances in which control by the market is stringent, rigorous, and adequate. But market control is not a *general* substitute for the political control of government enterprise. The established channels for the enforcement of public responsibility must somehow be adapted for application to public enterprise.

Recognition of the need for strengthening governmental responsibility over government enterprise is the first step. Beyond this, there are manifold possibilities for experimentation with various kinds of administrative and financial control patterns. These may be described in terms of an array moving from lesser degrees of control to greater degrees of control.

At the minimum level of control comes financial reporting to the chief executive, to the legislature, and to the citizenry at large. A step beyond this is ministerial control, as in Great Britain, where each corporation is subject to the authority of a politically responsible government official. In Britain this has operated to leave a great range of significant management and policy decisions in the hands of the public corporation.

A further step is to require central government control over all capital outlays of government enterprise. This means that when the enterprise is expanding, it must come to the executive and to the legislature for a program review and authorization. When its operating revenue covers its total outlay, it is immune from control. This approach argues that the general taxpayer will be represented and given an opportunity to be heard, through his elected representatives, at the time when tax revenues are employed in behalf of the enterprise. A control over capital expenditures might also be used to encourage expansion at a time when it was important to raise the level of national income and employment.

A still further step is to control the administrative expenses of enterprises, leaving their program operations outside the purview of the central government. This is sometimes easier than it sounds, since very often the dividing line between administrative and program expenses is rather inconstant.

Finally, on the budgetary side, administrative, program, and capital outlays may be reviewed and authorized by central budget authority and by the legislature. This is the high point of control and represents the least degree of autonomy which is likely to be possessed by public enterprises.

To the foregoing may be added, in varying combinations, central controls over purchasing, personnel, accounting, and auditing. The latter may also include a review of performance by the legislature.

The variety of enterprise activity in government is matched by the variety of possible control patterns. Stereotypes need not prevail here.

Selected Bibliography

Commission on Organization of the Executive Branch of the Government, Task Force Report, *Revolving Funds and Business Enterprises of the Government,* Washington, 1949.

Commission on Organization of the Executive Branch of the Government, *Business Enterprises,* Washington, 1955.

Council of State Governments, *Public Authorities in the States,* Chicago, 1953.

Davies, Ernest, *National Enterprise,* Victor Gollancz, Ltd., London, 1946.

Dimock, Marshall E., "Government Corporations; a Focus of Policy and Administration, I," *American Political Science Review,* October 1949, pp. 899–921; II, December 1949, pp. 1145–1164.

Friedmann, W., ed., *The Public Corporation,* Carswell Company, Ltd., Toronto, 1954.

Goldberg, Sidney D., and Harold Seidman, *The Government Corporation: Elements of a Model Charter,* Public Administration Service, Chicago, 1953.

Gulick, Luther, " 'Authorities' and How to Use Them," *The Tax Review,* November 1947, pp. 47–52.

Johnson, Eldon L., "The Accountability of the British Nationalized Industries," *American Political Science Review,* June 1954, pp. 366–385.

Key, V. O., Jr., "Government Corporations," *Elements of Public Administration,* Fritz Morstein Marx, ed., Prentice-Hall, New York, 1946, pp. 236–263.

Keyes, Lucille Sheppard, "Some Controversial Aspects of the Public Corporation," *Political Science Quarterly,* March 1955, pp. 28–56.

Law and Contemporary Problems, Autumn 1951 (whole issue on nationalization in Great Britain).

McDiarmid, John, *Government Corporations and Federal Funds,* University of Chicago Press, Chicago, 1938.

Pritchett, C. Herman, "The Government Corporation Control Act of 1945," *American Political Science Review,* June 1946, pp. 495–509.

———— "The Paradox of the Government Corporation," *Public Administration Review,* Summer 1941, pp. 381–389.

Robson, William A., *Problems of Nationalized Industries,* Oxford University Press, New York, 1952.

———— "The Public Corporation in Britain Today," *Harvard Law Review,* June 1950, pp. 1321–1348.

Seidman, Harold, "The Government Corporation: Organization and Controls," *Public Administration Review,* Summer 1954, pp. 183–192.

———— "The Theory of the Autonomous Government Corporation: A Critical Appraisal," *Public Administration Review,* Spring 1952, pp. 89–96.

Street, Sir Arthur, "Quasi-Governmental Bodies Since 1918," *British Government Since 1918,* Macmillan Company, New York, 1950, pp. 157–192.

Sturmthal, Adolf, "The Structure of Nationalized Enterprises in France," *Political Science Quarterly,* September 1952, pp. 357–377.

Temporary State Commission on Coordination of State Activities, *First Interim Staff Report on Public Authorities Under New York State,* Albany, 1954.

Thornton, R. H., "Nationalization," *Public Administration,* Spring, 1947, pp. 10–21.

17.

The balanced budget*

In a world in which Keynesianism abounds, one might reasonably expect that balancing the government's budget would be regarded as an outmoded policy goal. A great many other pre-Keynesian fiscal notions have pretty well gone by the boards. One seldom hears these days that a dollar of government expenditures causes a corresponding reduction of a dollar of private outlay, or that government expenditures cannot raise the level of national income, or that we can never achieve full employment by government spending. But amidst the wide acceptance of the goals and tools of Keynesianism, even in those circles where the name is still anathema, there is remarkable persistence in the notion that government budgets ought to be balanced, even balanced annually.[1]

This chapter proposes to examine our intellectual heritage in the mat-

* This chapter originally appeared in *The Quarterly Journal of Economics*, May 1954, and is reproduced here with permission of the publisher.

[1] Documentation is everywhere evident. For example, "The first order of business is the elimination of the annual deficit. . . . A balanced budget is an essential first measure in checking further depreciation in the buying power of the dollar. . . . As the budget is balanced and inflation checked, the tax burden that today stifles initiative can and must be eased. . . . " (President Eisenhower in the "State of the Union Message," February 1953.) And, although somewhat more guarded, "We should make it the first principle of economic and fiscal policy in these times to maintain a balanced budget, and to finance the cost of national defense on a 'pay-as-we-go' basis." (President Truman in the *Economic Report of the President,* January 1951.)

ter of budget balancing. The first section will be devoted to the views of the classical economists on national debt and deficits. Here it will be pointed out that while there is a common body of doctrine which may be characterized as the classical view of debts and deficits, this doctrine changed substantially, in accordance with the changing nature of the problems, from the time of Adam Smith to that of Alfred Marshall. The second section will review briefly the major characteristics of Keynesian thinking about national debt and deficits, and attempt to analyze the reasons for the relative positions of the classicists and Keynesians. The third section will attempt to explain the failure of Keynesianism to influence the practical nature of the problem and will assess the degree to which the classical heritage is real and the extent to which it is folklore.

"Practical men, who believe themselves to be quite exempt from any intellectual influences, are usually the slaves of some defunct economist," said Keynes. This chapter is devoted to an examination of the degree of enslavement.

It should be noted at the outset that this subject is not marked by conceptual clarity either in the writings of economists or in public policy. Considerations relating to balanced budgets are tied to considerations relating to increases in national debt. Annual increases in debt, in turn, are tied to problems of the size of the debt and the annual payment of interest thereon. And all these are linked, in the literature and in past and current public policy, with notions about the role of the state vis-à-vis the private sector.

In the review of classical doctrine, only the writings of the major classical economists will be examined; the work of others, including important and influential writers on government finance, will be neglected. This neglect, however, may be justified on the ground that the main stream of classical economics has defined the character of our intellectual and technical heritage in governmental financial practice. Also, the term "classical" will be used here as it was used by Keynes, to include both the classical and neoclassical school.

I. THE CLASSICAL APPROACH

It is commonly held that the classicists assumed that the economic role of the state must necessarily be limited, and they then adduced certain rationalizations regarding the nature of governmental fiscal operations to support this assumption. It seems more likely that such economists as Adam Smith looked first at the objective requirements of the

economic order and then proceeded to theorize about the proper role of
the state therein.[2]

Adam Smith's views on balanced budgets were conditioned very
largely by his views on national debt.[3] And his views on the latter are
a clear and direct product of his antimercantilism. It is difficult to dissociate Smith, the antimercantile polemicist, from Smith the economist.
His often quoted passages defining, in restrictive terms, the proper and
legitimate functions of the state should probably be viewed less as an
evidence of his pro-laissez-faire position than as an evidence of his antimercantilism. Smith was an antimercantilist because he saw that the
state apparatus as it then existed was an inefficient organization from
the standpoint of wealth and income creation. It was the bulwark of a
pattern of special trading privileges, grants of monopoly, and tariffs.
More importantly, the state was wasteful; it took funds from merchants
and industrialists and spent these funds in riotous living. This deprived
industry and commerce of capital badly needed for the furtherance of
production and trade, by diverting the national product toward consumer goods and away from capital goods.

This was the major reason for Smith's opposition to unbalanced budgets: governments would borrow from industry and commerce and thus
deprive a capital-poor society of revenue which could be productively
reinvested.[4] From this major ground for opposition to public borrowing stemmed other arguments. Once the sovereign started to borrow,
his political power was increased, because he was no longer dependent
on tax exactions from his subjects. Therefore, borrowing encouraged
the sovereign to wage needless wars. On the other hand, if taxes were
raised to meet current costs, "Wars would in general be more speedily
concluded, and less wantonly undertaken."[5] In short, the ability to engage in loan finance makes for irresponsibility in the sovereign.

England's experience with national debt after the beginning of the
18th century adequately justified Smith's concern. In the years from
1713 to 1739 the South Sea Bubble and the war with Spain had added
to the national debt. The war of 1739–1748 raised England's debt from

[2] See Harvey S. Perloff, "Budgetary Symbolism and Fiscal Planning," *Public
Policy,* Harvard University, Cambridge, 1941, pp. 40–44.
[3] For a discussion of pre-Smithian practices and views on these matters see
C. F. Bastable, *Public Finance,* Macmillan & Co., Ltd., London, 1922, pp. 611–657;
Gustav Cohn, *The Science of Finance,* translated by T. B. Veblen, University of
Chicago Press, Chicago, 1895, pp. 691–703.
[4] Adam Smith, *The Wealth of Nations,* Modern Library, New York, 1937,
pp. 409–411.
[5] *Ibid.,* p. 878.

£47 million to £78 million. At the end of the Seven Years' War in 1763, the debt stood at about £136 million. Furthermore, the intervening peacetime years did not bring important debt reductions.[6]

For Smith these increases in debt were most serious when they were *created;* the burden of an *existing* debt, although important, was much less significant. The most important loss came when industry and trade lent their funds to the state. Contemporaries of Smith had pointed out that an internally held debt occasioned no loss through the annual interest transfer from taxpayers to bondholders. Smith replied, "This apology is founded altogether in the sophistry of the mercantile system . . . "[7] In confounding the sophistry Smith contended that the public creditor was not a good manager. Unlike the private creditor, he " . . . has no interest . . . in the good management of any particular portion of capital stock." Further, the annual tax burdens occasioned by the interest payment may drive capital from the country. "The industry of the country will necessarily fall with the removal of the capital which supported it, and the ruin of trade and manufactures will necessarily follow the declension of agriculture."

And, finally, there is a long-run danger in the debt. Once "accumulated to a certain degree," it leads inevitably to national bankruptcy. Since the days of Rome, sovereigns had resorted to all manner of juggling and trickery to "liberate the revenue." Bankruptcy had been disguised by "pretended payments" in debased currency; sovereigns adulterated the coin.

Jean-Baptiste Say, conditioned no doubt by a French debt experience which was even more irresponsible than the English, was as vehement as Smith in opposition to debts and deficits. He was very much impressed with the wastefulness of government outlay, and cited example after example to the point.[8] The sovereign is engaged in pomp and circumstance; the preservation of etiquette and custom is a very expensive affair. The wealth which passes from the hands of the taxpayer to the taxgatherer is consumed and destroyed.

Say based these views on the argument that public consumption is not, in principle, different from consumption by individuals or families. In either case there is a destruction of values and a loss of wealth. The limitation of public consumption, like the limitation of private consump-

---

[6] Bastable, *op. cit.,* pp. 630–632.

[7] *Wealth of Nations,* pp. 879–885.

[8] "It would be curious to calculate the time wasted in the toilet, or to estimate, if possible, the many dearly paid hours lost, in the course of the last century, on the road between Paris and Versailles." (J. B. Say, *A Treatise on Political Economy,* translated from the 4th ed. by C. R. Prinsep, Lippincott, Grambo & Co., Philadelphia, 1853, p. 428.)

tion, is necessary to provide capital for industry and trade. Public borrowing is not only unproductive, because the capital is consumed and lost, but in addition, the nation is burdened by the annual interest payment. It cannot be argued that the annual circulation of interest payments is a net addition to capital. "The tax-payer would have spent what is now spent by the public creditor; that is all."[9]

A national debt of moderate amount which had been judiciously expended in useful public works might be attended by the advantage of providing an investment outlet for the minute forms of capital that might otherwise be squandered by individuals.

> This is perhaps the sole benefit of a national debt; and even this is attended with some danger, inasmuch as it enables a government to squander the national savings. For, unless the principal be spent upon objects of permanent public benefit, as on roads, canals or the like, it were better for the public that the capital should remain inactive, or concealed; since, if the public lost the use of it, at least it would not have to pay the interest.[10]

It is irresponsible government which is to be feared. When the government credit is strong, Say said (apparently quoting with approval from contemporary political scientists):

> . . . they are too apt to intermeddle in every political arrangement, and to conceive gigantic projects, that lead sometimes to disgrace, sometimes to glory, but always to a state of financial exhaustion; to make war themselves, and stir up others to do the like; to subsidize every mercenary agent, and deal in the blood and the consciences of mankind; making capital, which should be the fruit of industry and virtue, the prize of ambition, pride, and wickedness.[11]

It is not surprising that David Ricardo, writing at the end of the Napoleonic Wars, should have generally shared the antipathy of his classical predecessors to national debt. By 1816 England's debt stood at about £500 million, approximately double what it had been at the turn of the century. It was appropriate, in these circumstances, for Ricardo to refer to the debt as " . . . one of the most terrible scourges which was ever invented to afflict a nation . . . "[12] However, by this time the industrialization of England was much further advanced than it had been in 1776. Irresponsible sovereigns, in league with merchant princes, were no longer the threat to economic progress that they had been in Smith's time. The national debt was a significant problem, but in his

[9] *Ibid.*, p. 480.

[10] *Ibid.*, p. 481.

[11] *Ibid.*, p. 483.

[12] David Ricardo, "Funding System," *The Works and Correspondence of David Ricardo,* Vol. IV, Piero Sraffa and M. H. Dobbs, eds., Cambridge University Press, London, 1951, p. 197.

"Principles," Ricardo did not devote the attention to this subject that
Smith had. When he did discuss it, Ricardo made important modifications in the arguments of Smith and Say.

Ricardo pointed out that the important burden of the national debt
was not in the annual interest transfer, but in the loss of original capital.

> When, for the expenses of a year's war, twenty millions are raised by means
> of a loan, it is the twenty millions which are withdrawn from the productive
> capital of the nation. The million per annum which is raised by taxes to
> pay the interest of this loan, is merely transferred from those who pay it to
> those who receive it, from the contributor to the tax, to the national creditor.
> The real expense is the twenty millions, and not the interest which must be
> paid for it.[13]

The effects of the annual interest transfer, Ricardo argued, would depend on what A and B, taxpayer and creditor, did with the revenue.
Either A or B might squander the revenue; either might employ it productively. The annual transfer was in no sense lost to the economy.

Once a nation has incurred a debt, no great *economic* advantage accrues from retiring it. The presence of the debt does not affect the nation's ability to pay taxes. There is the same taxable capital with or
without the debt.

> It is not, then, by the payment of the interest on the national debt, that a
> country is distressed, nor is it by the exoneration from payment that it can be
> relieved. It is only by saving from income, and retrenching in expenditure,
> that the national capital can be increased; and neither the income would be
> increased, nor the expenditure diminished by the annihilation of the national
> debt.[14]

Neither does the presence of the debt place the nation at any particular
disadvantage with respect to foreign countries. Taxes will be higher,
it is true, and the price of labor will be increased, but the real capital
of the nation is unchanged; the only problem it a transfer problem.

Why, then, should the national debt be retired? Why does it justify
the appellation of "scourge"? Here Ricardo shifts ground and abandons
aggregative analysis to contend that, even though there is no loss of
capital in the aggregate, the particular taxes which may be levied to pay
the interest will encourage every individual contributor to "withdraw his
shoulder from the burthen," and,

> . . . the temptation to remove himself and his capital to another country,
> where he will be exempted from such burthens, becomes at last irresistible,
> and overcomes the natural reluctance which every man feels to quit the place

[13] Ricardo, "Principles of Political Economy and Taxation," *The Works and
Correspondence of David Ricardo,* Vol. I, p. 244.

[14] *Ibid.,* p. 246.

of his birth, and the scene of his early associations. . . . That which is wise in an individual, is wise also in a nation."[15]

Ricardo's most important writing on the national debt was the essay on the funding system contributed to the *Encyclopedia Britannica*. Dr. Robert Hamilton, his contemporary, had authored *An Inquiry Concerning the Rise and Progress, the Redemption, and Present State of the National Debt of Great Britain*, which included a critical attack on the debt retirement schemes that had been in force since 1716. The sinking fund schemes had not proved efficaceous in eliminating the debt; ministers always abused the arrangements. Ricardo was apparently in essential agreement with Hamilton in his criticism of these schemes, and in this essay he elaborated Hamilton's arguments and discussed at some length the distinctions between annual revenue paid as interest on the debt or as contribution to the sinking fund, and the capital of taxpayers which was available for productive investment.[16] Although in his "Principles" Ricardo had pointed out the limitations in the arguments of those who advocated retirement of the debt, in the *Britannica* article he simply assumed that debt retirement was desirable.

Ricardo proposed that in future (war) emergencies the government adopt a pay-as-you-go financial plan. Thus, "When the pressure of war is felt at once, without mitigation, we shall be less disposed wantonly to engage in an expensive contest, and if engaged in it, we shall be sooner disposed to get out of it, unless it be a contest for some great national interest."[17] A pay-as-you go plan might encourage a higher level of current saving, in order to meet the temporarily heavier taxes. At the termination of hostilities there would be no continued interest (and taxation) burden. Further, to extinguish the outstanding debt, Ricardo proposed a once-over special levy of two or three years' duration on property. Thus, "by one great effort" we should get rid of this "terrible scourge."[18]

The dissenter, whose views on public debt ought to be examined before continuing the main stream of classical development, is Thomas Robert Malthus. The national debt is not the evil which it is generally supposed to be, said Malthus. Those who live on the interest from the national debt, like statesmen, soldiers and sailors, " . . . contribute powerfully to distribution and demand . . . they ensure that effective consumption which is necessary to give the proper stimulus to production. . . . "[19] Therefore, the debt, once created, is not a great evil.

[15] *Ibid.,* pp. 247–248.
[16] "Funding System," *op cit.* pp. 149–200.
[17] *Ibid.,* p. 186.
[18] *Ibid.,* p. 197.
[19] Thomas R. Malthus, *Principles of Political Economy* 2nd ed., William Pickering, London, 1836, p. 409.

It is, I know, generally thought that all would be well, if we could but relieved from the very heavy burden of our debt. And yet I feel perfectly convinced that, if a spunge could be applied to it tomorrow, and we could put out of our consideration the poverty and misery of the public creditors, by supposing them to be supported comfortably in some other country, the rest of the society, as a nation, instead of being enriched, would be impoverished. It is the greatest mistake to suppose that the landlords and capitalists would either at once, or in a short time, be prepared for so great an additional consumption as such a change would require; . . . and I feel very little doubt that, in five years from the date of such an event, not only would the exchangeable value of the whole produce, estimated in domestic and foreign labour, be decidedly diminished, but a smaller absolute quantity of corn would be grown, and fewer manufactured and foreign commodities would be brought to market than before.[20]

Since the greatest powers of production are comparatively useless without effective consumption, Malthus argued, " . . . it would be the height of rashness to determine, under all circumstances, that the sudden diminution of the national debt and the removal of taxation must necessarily tend to increase the national wealth, and provide employment for the labouring classes."[21] But having made his case as forcibly as possible, Malthus almost immediately modified his position to bring it closer to that of his classical colleagues. There are, after all, evils in the debt. The taxation which is required to meet the interest payments may be harmful; people think the debt should be paid off, so the interest on it is always to some degree "insecure"; the presence of the debt aggravates the evils arising from changes in the value of money. These disadvantages must be weighed carefully against the advantage of maintaining a body of "unproductive consumers" who encourage wealth by maintaining a balance between production and consumption. The need for the unproductive consumers, in turn, varies with time and place and the skill and tastes of a people.

In 1848 John Stuart Mill could appropriately suggest some further modifications in the body of classical thinking on national debt and deficits. Apparently, by this time industry's need for capital was not as pressing as it had been earlier. In some circumstances, Mill said, government loans are not charged with pernicious consequences.

. . . first, when what is borrowed is foreign capital, the overflowings of the general accumulation of the world; or, secondly, when it is capital which either would not have been saved at all, unless this mode of investment had

[20] Notes on Malthus's Principles of Political Economy, *The Works and Correspondence of David Ricardo*, Vol. II, pp. 434–435. To this Ricardo replied, "I should think that Mr. Malthus must be the only man in England who would expect such effects from such a cause."

[21] Malthus, *op. cit.*, p. 411.

been open to it, or, after being saved, would have been wasted in unproductive enterprises, or sent to seek employment in foreign countries.[22]

Further, Mill suggested an "index" for determining whether there are pernicious consequences stemming from government loans. If the loan raises the rate of interest, it could be concluded that capital is taken which could have been productively employed, and " . . . those loans are chargeable with all the evils which have been described."[23] But if interest rates are unchanged, the pernicious consequences are not evident.

Mill continued to stress that government borrowing is harmful if it destroys capital which could otherwise be used for productive employment. However, he finds it somewhat paradoxical that in these years of capital destruction—mainly war years—there is apparent prosperity. He concluded that this occurs because loan finance is an effective subtraction from the portion employed in paying laborers, and the laborers suffer accordingly. But if production is the same, the country is no poorer. "The breach made in the capital of the country is thus instantly repaired, but repaired by the privations and often the real misery of the labouring class."[24]

Regardless of whether a country has wisely or unwisely incurred a national debt, it is expedient to pay it off as rapidly as possible. Mill discussed the two methods available—immediate payment by a general contribution and gradual payment with surplus revenue—and concluded that the former was preferable but that the latter was more practicable. It seems to be characteristic of Ricardo, Malthus, and Mill that after partially destroying the "scourge concept" of the national debt they embrace it in their policy conclusions. It is almost as if they are arguing, "The debt is not so bad as is supposed, but nevertheless we ought to pay it off."

After J. S. Mill, the major classical economists devoted less and less attention to problems of the national debt. This is evidently a direct reflection of the fact that from this time until 1914 the outstanding British debt remained almost constant. The increase at the time of the Boer War was wiped out by debt reduction in the immediately subsequent years. At the same time, the level of national income increased tremendously; Britain grew out of her debt. The writings of the classicists of this period reflected the lesser significance of the debt. Cairnes, in 1874, has no organized discussion of national debt or government

[22] John Stuart Mill, *Principles of Political Economy*, Ashley edition, Longmans, Green & Co., London, 1929, p. 874.
[23] *Ibid.*, p. 874. Mill obviously assumed that there is a "free" market in funds and that supply is relatively inelastic.
[24] *Ibid.*, p. 76.

financial problems. Sidgwick, writing in 1883, briefly discusses the effects of government borrowing, but adds little to the views of J. S. Mill.[25]

The culmination of the classical tradition—Marshall's *Principles*— devotes no attention whatever to the subject. And, significantly enough, the passing references to national debt in Marshall's *Money, Credit and Commerce* exhibit almost no concern for the problem, even though this book appeared immediately after World War I. Marshall's attitude toward the possibly wasteful spending practices of the sovereign is strikingly different from Smith's:

> The work of credit in the modern age differs from that of earlier times. . . . Formerly a great part of it was given by professional money-leaders to spendthrift heirs; now it is chiefly given by people who are living within their incomes to States which do not spend recklessly; and to strong businesses. . . . Monarchs used to be large borrowers: chiefly for the purposes of war; largely to support extravagance on the part of themselves and their favorites; and occasionally for financing expenditure on good roads, and other requisites of national well-being.[26]

At about the turn of the century public finance dropped out of the main stream of classical economics and developed as a partially inde-

---

[25] Sidgwick incorporates in his discussion the distinction between productive and unproductive government debt, a distinction observed but not fully developed by his predecessors, and also suggests that borrowing tends to increase inequality in the distribution of national wealth. (Henry Sidgwick, *The Principles of Political Economy*, 3rd ed., Macmillan & Co., Ltd., London, 1901, pp. 549–553.)

The main body of American writing on governmental financial policy did not differ in general outlook from that of the British classicists in the last half of the 19th century. Henry C. Adams, for example, was as strong as but no stronger in his condemnation of public debts and deficit financing than his British contemporaries. (Henry C. Adams, *Public Debts,* D. Appleton & Company, New York, 1895, p. 78.) The prevalence of these views in the United States indicates not only the strength of the classical outlook but also the triumph of Gallatin's position over Hamilton's. The latter had contended forcibly that any evils inherent in the debt were more than offset by the advantages derived from a high level of federal expenditures and from the resulting stability of private credit. Gallatin, however, had apparently been more influenced by *The Wealth of Nations* and was in general agreement with Jefferson's pungent phrase that the national debt was "swindling futurity on a large scale." (For a summary of this controversy see Paul Studenski and Herman E. Kroos, *Financial History of the United States,* McGraw-Hill Book Company, New York, 1952, pp. 69–71; also, George Rogers Taylor, ed., *Hamilton and the National Debt,* D. C. Heath & Company, Boston, 1950; Henry Adams, ed., *The Writings of Albert Gallatin,* Vol. III, J. B. Lippincott & Co., Philadelphia, 1879, pp. 143–152.)

[26] Alfred Marshall, *Money, Credit and Commerce,* Macmillan & Co., Ltd., London, 1923, pp. 69–70.

pendent "science of finance." The views of Bastable are representative of this approach.[27]

It seems likely that Bastable, writing the first edition of *Public Finance* in 1892, was influenced by the German and French writings and experiences in government finance, and possibly by the financial practices of private industry.[28] Whatever the reason, Bastable now presses the " . . . fundamental difference between two classes of debt, the one contracted for non-economic ends, the other for purposes of reproductive employment."[29] This distinction should not be stretched, however, to embrace nonrevenue-producing assets. "National culture, education, the promotion of social progress are all most desirable; but their promotion is not so urgently required as to need the use of borrowing by the public powers."[30] It is appropriate to finance the purchase of the Prussian railways or the English telegraphs by borrowing, but not the construction of school buildings. The latter may be generally and indirectly productive, but the results of such expenditure are " . . . hard to trace or measure, and any statement respecting them must rest in a great degree on conjecture."

Unless there is an equivalent revenue obtained from the application of the proceeds of borrowing, Bastable argued, there will inevitably be a curtailment of the future power of spending. Heavy borrowing cripples the ordinary revenue and compels retrenchment in the future. How-

---

[27] The style of writing on this subject altered drastically from the time of Smith and Say to the time of Bastable. For the former, the history of governmental financial practice was cited for purposes of drawing a moral or citing a horrible example of malpractice. With Bastable, history is history—this happened, and that was said. The issues are no longer burning. One can afford to be dispassionate.

[28] A wholly different view of the role and function of public credit was developed by the German economists in the last half of the 19th century. This approach stressed the "productive" character of much public expenditure and the role that public credit had played in the development of private credit instruments. It further argued that governments could appropriately borrow for permanent improvements that would benefit future generations. For an excellent discussion of this literature, and German national and state financial policy which accompanied it, see Cohn, *The Science of Finance*, pp. 718–726.

This approach seems to have had very little impact on the literature or practice of fiscal policy in Great Britain and the United States, unless it can be contended that the distinction between productive and unproductive debt came from this source. However, in the Keynesian attack on classical fiscal principles, some inspiration was apparently derived from the most prominent of the German writers of the 19th century. See Walter F. Stettner, "Carl Dietzel, Public Expenditures, and the Public Debt," in *Income, Employment and Public Policy*, Lloyd A. Metzler, ed., W. W. Norton & Company, New York, 1948, pp. 276–299.

[29] Bastable, *op. cit.*, p. 627.

[30] *Ibid.*, p. 670.

ever, there are conditions under which loan finance is to be preferred to heavy taxation. Nonrecurrent and large expenditures may be financed by loans with less disturbance than if heavy taxation were used. Where the expenditure extends over a period of years, there may be limits to the productiveness of specific taxes and of the tax system as a whole, so that borrowing is necessary. And, in some circumstances, it may not be politically expedient to press heavily on the taxpayers. In developing an adequate financial policy for a government it is of greatest importance to have a budget system, and a strong minister of finance who will undertake "prudent reduction of outlay" and "skilful adjustment of resources." " . . . the creation of the budget is therefore a work of administrative art, in which the use of proper methods will very materially improve the financial position, and contribute to the public advantage."[31]

A final and important addition to this body of doctrine developed from the application of the principles of marginalism to public finance. Marginalism in public finances seems to have been first elaborated as a conceptual framework for analyzing the distribution of tax burdens, then applied to the distribution of government expenditures, and finally utilized to bring together the revenue and expenditure activities of government.[32] Dalton's is one of the first complete elaborations of this approach.

> Public expenditure in every direction should be carried just so far, that the advantage to the community of a further small increase in any direction is just counterbalanced by the disadvantage of a corresponding small increase in taxation or in receipts from any other source of public income. This gives the ideal total both of public expenditure and of public income.[33]

It may be assumed that public income from borrowing involves no disutilities to the lender. Therefore, utilities and disutilities are balanced when the budget is balanced.[34]

[31] *Ibid.*, pp. 678–679, 734–736.

[32] Emil Sax is credited with being the first to apply marginalism to public finance. For an excellent discussion of the development of this approach see Mabel L. Walker, *Municipal Expenditures*, Johns Hopkins Press, Baltimore, 1930, pp. 28–51.

[33] Hugh Dalton, *Principles of Public Finance*, Alfred A. Knopf, New York, 1923, pp. 18–19.

[34] Smithies has pointed out that the application of marginalism to the division of resources between public and private use does not require a balanced budget where there is a defined fiscal policy goal of raising the money level of national income and where tax reduction is one of the means available for reaching this goal. However, this possibility was not considered by the marginalists; for them, budget balancing was the end product of the application of their principles. (See Arthur Smithies, "Federal Budgeting and Fiscal Policy," *A Survey of Contemporary Economics*, Vol. I, Howard S. Ellis, ed., Blakiston Company, Philadelphia, 1948, pp. 192–195.)

From this summary account of the classical approach to budget balancing and national debt, it is evident that attitudes and analyses changed substantially from the time of Smith to the time of Bastable and Dalton. Perhaps the greatest change is that the degree of antipathy to debts and deficits was modified sharply downward.

In spite of the changes, it is possible to summarize the classical doctrine in a set of propositions, intermingled though the propositions are. In some cases these are clearly set forth in the writings of the classicists. In other cases they must be inferred. Parts of the doctrine were accepted by some writers but rejected by others. These propositions on debts and deficits, together with an assessment of their current validity, are as follows:

(1) Government loan finance withdraws funds from productive private employment.

Where this point is interpreted to mean that an economy has an aggregate funds shortage, it is a generalization which has no applicability whatsoever in an advanced industrial economy possessed of a fractional reserve banking system and central banking techniques. Government bonds sold to commercial banks and to the central bank do not absorb funds which would otherwise be invested in the private sector. Indeed, J. S. Mill, as noted, did not attempt to support this generalization so long ago as 1848. Where the argument is advanced, as it was by Say, to mean that funds should be expended on capital goods by industry rather than on consumer goods by the state, what is really implied is that government expenditures do not add to productive capacity and that there are unfulfilled investment opportunities in industry and trade. This makes the point much more complex and eliminates any general validity which it may possess.

(2) Deficits are less painful than current taxes. Unbalanced budgets therefore expand governmental activity and invite irresponsible governmental action.

There is no doubt that deficits are relatively painless, as compared with increased taxes, but it is much less certain that deficit spending necessarily leads to irresponsibility, unless it has been defined in advance as equivalent to irresponsibility. In a modern budgetary system it would be most difficult to demonstrate that the legislature scrutinizes less closely the outlays financed by loans than the outlays financed by taxes, or that wartime deficits or deficits incurred to combat a depression represent a fiscal policy which is more irresponsible than that indicated by peacetime surpluses.

The point at issue here is the general one of securing a responsible and democratic government. The emergence of such government over the last several hundred years is not at all equivalent to the avoidance of governmental deficits. Modern budgetary systems have been most important in the development of responsible government, but their contribution is not to be judged solely in terms of the elimination of deficits.

There is another point which remains in this argument, the point which Adam Smith was most concerned about. Deficit finance expands the relative power of government vis-à-vis the taxpayers. Where governments can control resources without immediately diverting them from private incomes, there is, beyond doubt, an augmentation in the political and economic power of the sovereign. If the sovereign is irresponsible, he will resort to loan finance under conditions where it is not justified; loan finance, in turn, will increase his power. Strict adherence to the limitations of a balanced budget will operate to restrict the growth of the public sector.

(3) Government borrowing makes future financing more difficult by increasing the proportion of the budget which must go for fixed charges and by increasing the amount of taxes which must be paid to finance the transfer of interest on the debt.

This proposition is applicable and important to the extent that governmental revenues are restricted by constitutional, statutory, or economic factors. Therefore, it is more applicable to state and local governments than to a national government. Moreover, for a strong national government the increase in fixed charges and accompanying taxes may be offset by lowered interest rates, unless there are institutional barriers which require orthodox financial practices. Additions to government debt need not bring higher tax rates, even with the level of national income unchanged, if interest rates are continuously brought down by central monetary authority.

Where interest payment do increase, together with taxes, to support these payments, the possibly deleterious consequences depend, as Ricardo pointed out, on the pattern of taxpaying and the pattern of bondholding. A domestically held debt is burdensome in so far as the transfer is burdensome. Economic burdens will obtain only where the additional taxes levied to finance the interest payments discourage economic activity more than the receipts of interest encourage it.[35]

[35] This subject received much attention in the years immediately after World War II when public and professional concern over the national debt was at its height. In one careful analysis of the problem it was concluded that interest on the federal debt, and the corresponding pattern of tax payments to support that interest, operated moderately in the direction of reducing concentration in the distribution of total income, a consequence which is desirable if the economy is tending toward underconsumption. See Henry C. Wallich, "The Changing Significance of the Interest Rate," *American Economic Review,* December 1946, pp. 770–775; Jacob Cohen, "Distributional Effects of the Federal Debt," *Journal of*

(4) Loan finance is costly; public outlays financed in this way must be paid for twice, one in meeting interest charges and once in amortizing the debt.

Viewed as a matter of arithmetic, this proposition cannot be doubted. Where debts are amortized, the finance of capital outlay by means of borrowing entails an increasing volume of annual charges, which soon mount to the point where less outlay is possible than if all financing had been undertaken out of current revenue.[36] However, as in the case of budgetary inflexibility, the importance of costliness must be judged in relation to the nature of the governmental receipts and expenditures.

The costliness of governmental borrowing, again, is most serious for governmental units with limited tax and credit resources. It is not hard to convince city officials that a pay-as-you-go plan for municipal improvements is to be preferred to loan finance; the latter is too expensive. The interest payments may be a serious drain on a city's financial resources, and the interest payments are likely to be made abroad, that is, to bondholders outside the city's jurisdiction.

But costliness in these terms does not apply to the federal government of the United States. Here the interest payments are not made abroad; instead, they are transfer payments within the economy.

Of these propositions the first and fourth appear to possess little validity. The second—that deficits expand the scope of governmental power —is significant, particularly where government officials and legislators are irresponsible and require the fiscal discipline of rigid rule-making. The third—that debt finance raises the level of future tax payments— is important in those cases where governments choose to make it so, that is, where policy decisions are limited by fiscal orthodoxy.

The two remaining propositions in the classical doctrine can be evaluated only after an examination of the Keynesian contribution to the theory and practice of government debts and deficits. These are:

(5) Unbalanced budgets lead to currency deterioration.

(6) Balanced budgets provide a guide for the transfer of resources from the private to the public sector.

II. KEYNESIAN VIEWS

The Keynesian attack on the classical principles of budgeting and public finance was a logical extension of the Keynesian attack on the view that the economy tends to equilibrium at full employment. If

---

Finance, September 1951, pp. 267–275; Jesse V. Burkhead, "Full Employment and Interest-Free Borrowing," *Southern Economic Journal,* July 1947, pp. 1–13.

[36] For a demonstration of this point see James A. Maxwell, "The Capital Budget," *Quarterly Journal of Economics,* May 1943, pp. 454–456.

there are unemployed resources which the private sector cannot or will not employ, these resources may be put to work by the state by means of additional public outlay, which need not be matched by additional government revenue. Orthodox financial rules must be abandoned, even as orthodox economics must be abandoned.[37]

Keynes himself did not elaborate the role of fiscal policy in the maintenance of full employment. This remained for Alvin Hansen and the Keynesians. Writing at the end of a decade of depression, Hansen, in *Fiscal Policy and Business Cycles,* made a number of significant contributions.[38] He attempted to restore public finance, as fiscal policy, to its place in the main stream of economics. He reinterpreted the 19th century experience of national governments in their debt-creating capacity. And he attempted to establish a new set of guide lines for government borrowing and deficit financing.

The general outlines of Hansen's contribution are well known and need be summarized only briefly. Hansen argued that fiscal policy had been forced to serve as a compensatory device more by accident than by design. Public finance had been broadened by the political necessity of coping with unemployment. Most of the principles intended to cover public debt policy had been borrowed from private finance, but the analogies were misleading. "If one adopts wholeheartedly the principle that government financial operations should be regarded exclusively as instruments of economic and public policy, the concept of a balanced budget, however defined, can play no role in the determination of that policy."[39]

Hansen contended that success or failure of public debt policy can be determined only in relation to the aggregates of national income and its distribution. Whether or not the public debt should be reduced depends on the general economic situation, not on principles applicable to private commercial accounting. Economic activity in the government sector is not sustained out of private economic activity; it is an independent sector in the production of goods and services. Government outlay financed by debt creation will increase the level of national income, regardless of the productivity of the assets which may be acquired. Moreover, the importance of the public debt in the establishment of the credit system in

---

[37] "The logical corollary of orthodox economics is orthodox finance. If it is believed that all factors of production are normally and inevitably utilized by private business it follows that the State can obtain the use of such factors only by preventing private business from using them. . . . From this it follows that the first principle of 'sound' Public Finance is that the budget should be balanced." (E. F. Schumacher, "Public Finance—Its Relation to Full Employment," *The Economics of Full Employment,* Basil Blackwell, Oxford University Institute of Statistics, Oxford, 1946, p. 86.)

[38] W. W. Norton & Company, 1941, esp. pp. 135–222.

[39] *Ibid.,* p. 188.

western European countries and in the United States had not been fully appreciated.

Hansen pointed out that the limits to the public debt must be determined in relation to a nation's taxable capacity, the danger of price inflation, and the distribution of income; the limits are flexible and not fixed. The implementation of compensatory fiscal policy required a recasting of traditional budgetary policy, in order to view the expenditure and receipts side of government budgets in relation to the total level of economic activity.

The attack by the American Keynesians on the classical principle of budgetary equilibrium was accompanied by numerous suggestions to improve budgetary techniques with a view to making the federal budget more flexible and of greater usefulness in a compensatory fiscal policy. Many of these contributions, evidently inspired by Hansen, appeared in the 1941 volume of *Public Policy*.[40]

Experience with capital budgets in the Scandinavian countries had impressed Hansen with their usefulness as tools of fiscal policy. By varying the rate of expenditure for capital outlay, the Swedish government had apparently made a major contribution to economic stabilization. Although he did not recommend that the United States adopt this technique, he did suggest that the experience be carefully examined. The capital budget might offer means for the expansion of governmental expenditures, loan financed, but in accordance with a set of rules and procedures which could be readily understood.

The Hansenian contribution is not, however, the whole of the development of Keynesian fiscal theory. The culmination is A. P. Lerner's functional finance.[41] This approach to fiscal policy views government revenue and expenditure and government debt solely as instruments for the control of aggregate community expenditure. These are the tools, and the goal is the maintenance of stable employment at constant prices. Taxes and expenditures should be increased or reduced solely to affect the community's rate of spending; debt instruments should be sold to the public to absorb their idle balances and reduce liquidity in times of inflation, and redeemed to increase liquidity in times of depression. Perhaps to gain currency for his views Lerner formulated his propositions in terms of "laws."

Unfortunately, the enactment of the "laws" of functional finance would provide no workable guide for the formulation of budget policy.

[40] Yearbook of the Graduate School of Public Administration, Harvard University, Cambridge, 1941.

[41] A. P. Lerner, *The Economics of Control*, Macmillan Company, New York, 1944, pp. 302–322; "Functional Finance and the Federal Debt," *Social Research*, February, 1943, pp. 38–51.

The policy-making official would have three instruments of stabilization available for use—taxation, expenditures, and the purchase and sale of debt instruments. But he would have no criteria available for choosing among them. Beyond this, functional finance provides no guides for the selection of alternative government expenditures. Lerner gives no assistance to the budget-maker who must determine both the aggregates of receipts and expenditures and their components. Government responsibility for stable full employment is substituted for government irresponsibility in the determination of the kinds of programs which are undertaken.

From this brief examination of the Keynesian impact on budgetary theory certain conclusions may be drawn.

It is evident that the major difference between the outlook of the classicists and the Keynesians turns on their analyses of the nature of economic society and the role of the state therein. The classicists, particularly Adam Smith, were completely explicit on this point: economic society is characterized by a fundamental harmony of interest. The invisible hand, operating in a competitive society, will reconcile all conflicts. The role of the state must and should be narrow. With fundamental harmony prevailing, there is no need for extensive intervention.

The Keynesians have not been so explicit—modern economists appear to shun political theory. But running through almost all of the Keynesian literature there appears to be an unstated assumption that the economic order is harmonious *except for* its inability to achieve stability. This defect can be overcome by governmental fiscal action. The enlarged role of the state is necessitated by the requirement for erecting a balance wheel for economic activity. Stable full employment is identical with the general welfare, and this general welfare is greater, *Gestaltische,* than the aggregate of specific interest groups and economic class welfares.[42]

The Keynesians conceive the state to be primarily ameliorative, but with a program of its own and an internal dynamic of its own making. The state operates with a high degree of independence above and beyond the interest groups which comprise it. The government is not a pawn in the hands of these groups, nor does it merely serve as a device for reconciling conflicting pressures. Rather, governmental organizations contribute to policy-making as an independent force.[43]

[42] For a critical dissent see Paul A. Baran, "National Economic Planning," *A Survey of Contemporary Economics,* Vol. II, Bernard F. Haley, ed., Richard D. Irwin, Homewood, Illinois, 1952, pp. 355–377.

[43] For an excellent statement of this position in terms of the administrator's role in policy formulation see Emmette S. Redford, *Administration of National Economic Control,* Macmillan Company, New York, 1952, pp. 220–236.

III. THE PREVAILING PHILOSOPHY

Two questions remain for consideration. First, why has there been so little Keynesian impact on prevalent attitudes toward government debts and deficits in this country? Second, what are the reasons, whether practical or folklore, which explain the widespread acceptance of the doctrine of balanced budgets for the federal government?

The answer to the first question is undoubtedly to be found, in good part, in the behavior of the American economy since World War II. Full employment has been maintained almost consistently, and the federal cash consolidated budget has been generally in balance. It may be that the high level of federal expenditures has been a major factor in maintaining prosperity, but the fact is that these high expenditures have been matched by high receipts. From 1947 to 1952 the economy did not require deficit spending for the maintenance of prosperity; only in 1953 did a substantial deficit appear.

Since full employment has been maintained without compensatory spending, it is not surprising that American Keynesians have devoted little attention to the development of workable concepts and techniques for flexible budgeting. The importance of the federal budget in economic stabilization is widely recognized, but this recognition has not been accompanied by implementation.

An implementation would require two things. First, there must be a more or less official adoption of flexible concepts of budgeting, with a view to the use of the budget for stabilization purposes. Second, there must be a classification of governmental receipts and expenditures which will provide at least an approximation to the measurement of the economic effects of governmental activity. This classification must be useful and used in budgetary planning.

Sweden is an outstanding example of a country where the national government has abandoned the budget-balancing philosophy. This abandonment has evolved gradually. The capital budget used in that country in the 1930's required a balance in the current account, but capital expenditures could be varied for purposes of stabilization. By 1937 there was official abandonment of annual budget balancing for either the current or capital account, and balancing over the cycle was substituted therefor. Since 1944 cyclical budget balancing is no longer regarded as important; the total impact of state finances on the level of national economic activity is now the major determinant of budgetary policy.[44]

The second requirement involves a thoroughgoing reclassification of

[44] United Nations, *Budgetary Structure and Classification of Government Accounts,* New York, 1951, pp. 68–81. Also, see Chapter 8.

governmental activity—an economic character classification.   This classification should, at minimum, provide estimates of the net effect of current and proposed government activities on private income accounts. Such a classification was proposed for Great Britain by J. R. Hicks, and one has been set forth in generalized terms by the Department of Economic Affairs of the United Nations (see Chapter 9).   To be useful and used an economic character classification should be developed in the process of budgetary formulation, at a time and place in the governmental hierarchy where it enters into budgetary decision-making.

In this country neither of these developments has occurred.   Rigid and inflexible concepts of budget balancing have the greatest influence on public policy, and there has been no government effort to introduce alternative and more flexible concepts.[45]   Further, there has been no development of an economic character classification to accompany the United States budget, although there have been important developments in other areas of budgeting technique in the federal government in recent years.   The budget message continues to be a review of agency and departmental programs, rather than a document reflecting an analysis of the economic character of governmental operations.

The practical influence of Keynesian economics on budgeting concepts and procedures in the United States has been almost nil.   We continue to be dominated by adherence to the goal of a balanced budget buttressed by the phrases and arguments of the classical economists.

The answer to the second question—the explanation for the adherence to balanced budgets—would appear to be provided by a combination of considerations, some of which relate to the economics of debts and deficits, and others which are the product of popular attitudes.   These may be labeled "real" and "attitudinal."   The real considerations are those previously summarized in the review of classical doctrine.   These are:

---

[45] For one important set of suggestions for more flexible budget concepts see Morris A. Copeland, "The Capital Budget and the War Effort," *American Economic Review*, March 1943, pp. 38–49.   The Committee for Economic Development has proposed a budgetary policy which would set tax rates at a point to provide a surplus for debt retirement at an agreed high level of income and employment.   These rates would be unchanged except in a severe depression or critical inflation.   (*The Stabilizing Budget Policy*, New York, 1950.)   This proposal, if adopted, would serve to reduce, not increase, flexibility in the use of the budget as a stabilization measure, since variations in expenditures for stabilization purposes would be almost precluded.   For a critical examination of the CED and similar proposals see Paul A. Samuelson, "Principles and Rules in Modern Fiscal Policy: A Neo-Classical Reformulation," *Money, Trade, and Economic Growth,* Macmillan Company, New York, 1951, pp. 157–176.   This argument is developed further in an exchange of comments with Herbert Stein, *Quarterly Journal of Economics,* February 1955, pp. 153–156.

(1) Unbalanced budgets contribute to currency deterioration.

There is no doubt that, from the time of Adam Smith to the present day, unbalanced budgets have evoked great concern on this ground. History, even recent history, is replete with cases of corrupt or inefficient governments which went to their ruin in a shower of paper currency.

Unbalanced budgets could conceivably lead to inflation in one of two ways. Either the deficit itself could be inflationary, as governments made net contributions to levels of demand, or the accumulated deficits, by their additions to money supply, could contribute to inflationary pressure. These influences are not always separated in popular discussion.[46]

It is almost a truism that government deficits add to levels of effective demand, and that unless the supply of resources is elastic at current price levels, prices will rise. However, from this relationship it should not be concluded that an increase in the federal deficit will inevitably lead to an increase in prices. Examination of the behavior of the wholesale price index and federal deficits since 1930 shows that it has not worked out this way. In only eight of the twenty-three fiscal years from July 1, 1930, to June 30, 1953, was there a positive association between an increase in the federal deficit and an increase in the price level. In fifteen of these years changes in the deficit and changes in wholesale prices moved in opposite directions. In some recent years the inverse association has been striking. In fiscal 1951 the budget moved from a deficit of $3.1 billion to a surplus of $3.5 billion, that is, a *decrease* in the deficit of $6.6 billion. In the same fiscal year there was an *increase* in the wholesale price level by 15 percent. In fiscal 1953 the budget deficit increased from $4.0 billion to $9.3 billion, but the level of wholesale prices dropped slightly.

It is evident that in any one year currency stability cannot be assured by balancing the budget. It can be assured only by balancing the combined operations of the government and the private sectors. If the outlook is inflation, then, clearly, a balanced or overbalanced budget is not out of order. But there can be no assurance that the surplus will not be offset by activities in the private sector.

It is very frequently contended that accumulated deficits (debt) are an inflationary force. The additions to money supply occasioned by the

[46] For Adam Smith it was the debt itself which produced the currency deterioration, as sovereigns attempted to reduce its crushing burden by clipping coins and printing paper money. This view, surely, was the product of an age of irresponsible sovereigns, and of a time when, at least in part, the debts of the state were the personal debts of the crown, to be retired in depreciated currency when the crown could temporarily gain an advantage over the merchant bondholders with whom it was engaged in a more or less continual struggle. Smith did not argue that there was a causal relation between current deficits and currency depreciation.

debt may add to bank reserves, which, in the absence of countervailing action, may encourage banks to extend loans to business firms and households. Debt holdings by persons, by adding to the stock of liquid assets, may conceivably lead to a higher consumption ratio out of current income. Business firms may liquidate their debt holdings to bid up the price of inventory or producers' durables. Debt holdings by the public are thus an inflationary potential, which, if not offset by other controls, may be a destabilizing influence. But again, the point to be stressed is that accumulated deficits and the concomitant increased liquidity do not, in themselves, generate an inflationary movement. They may feed it but they do not start it. Liquidity is significant only in relation to its distribution among those who are motivated to make their demands effective. It is not significant in the aggregate. Liquid asset holdings did not prevent the 1949 recession.

(2) A balanced budget provides an easily understood rule to guide the transfer of resources from the private to the public sector.

Here the advocates of budget-balancing appear to be on firm ground. Whether or not this proposition is grounded in the economics of marginal utilities and disutilities, there is no doubt that budget-balancing, particularly annual budget-balancing, has a definite and precise character which is lacking in any other available guide to fiscal policy.[47] The concept of "balancing over the business cycle," for example, always generates uncertainty as to the precise point in the cycle where one finds oneself. Moreover, budget-balancing is a practicable guide for policy-making officials, who can roughly gauge the amount of taxation which the community can stand and then trim expenditures to fit the revenue.

Unfortunately, however, this guideline is valueless when there are unemployed resources which may be put to work producing goods and services. The employment of such resources is virtually costless to the economy as a whole. In the vocabulary of the marginalists, there are only utilities—no disutilities.

The remaining possibility is that it is not economic factors but attitudinal factors which account for the prevalence of the balanced budget doctrine.

(1) It may be that popular thinking about government budgets is based on popular thinking about household budgets.

It matters not that, as Hansen pointed out, the analogies are all faulty. Household budget balancing is in accord with the kind of Poor Richard economics which has made up the code of conduct of the American

[47] For the limitations which attach to a strict application of marginalism in this area see A. C. Pigou, *A Study in Public Finance,* 3rd rev. ed., Macmillan & Co. Ltd., London, 1951, pp. 31–34; also see Chapter 2.

economy for many generations.   Thrift and frugality in personal affairs; economy and efficiency in government.   Saving is a virtue; for governments as for individuals, the rule is "waste not, want not."

(2) It may be that there is a fear of the economic and political consequences of government spending rather than direct concern over the debt itself.

This is a variant of the argument that deficits expand governmental authority.   Those who are most vocal in opposition to an increase in the debt may, in reality, be opposing only the increase in expenditures.   Certainly, conflict over whether activities shall be conducted collectively by government or by firms in the private sector is one of the most persistent in the history of economic systems.   Those who are in a position to feel government competition directly, as in electric power or housing, will diligently oppose the extension of governmental expenditures in these areas.   It is understandable that in seeking to combat such competition, those who are most affected thereby will both oppose the expenditure directly and utilize the concern over the national debt and deficits to bolster their case.   The extent to which this type of attitude is significant is, of course, impossible to determine.

(3) The opposition to an increase in debt may be explained by opposition to compensatory fiscal policy.

If the adherence to balanced budgets is based on opposition to what its opponents call "a managed economy," the practical nature of the problem is likely to force this kind of folklore out of the sanctuary.

Undoubtedly, there are difficulties in applying government compensatory action.   Forecasting techniques are not well developed; governmental programs cannot be administered with sufficient rapidity to prevent either rapidly moving inflation or rapidly moving deflation; the increase in governmental authority which is required for compensatory action may be difficult to control—policies may be irresponsibly conceived.

Nevertheless, and in spite of the difficulties, it can hardly be doubted that any modern and responsive government will use the weapons at its disposal, including budgetary policy, for purposes of economic stabilization.   The government may act less promptly than some would like; expenditures may be increased when some would prefer that taxes be reduced; pyramids may be built when some would prefer that resources be developed.   But, surely, compensatory fiscal policy will continue to be used by the federal government for purposes of stabilizing levels of economic activity, even as it has been used since the 1930's.

To summarize.   The classical case for budget-balancing rests on a series of interrelated propositions, some of an economic nature and some of a political nature, reflecting attitudes toward the role of the state and the responsibilities of sovereign authority. Two of these propositions possess at least a limited validity for budget-making in strong national governments: (1) deficits may encourage irresponsibility and contribute to the growth of the public sector, and (2) deficits may require a higher level of future tax rates. In addition, one of the propositions—that current deficits contribute to inflation—has validity, although recent United States experience would indicate that a federal government deficit is by no means a sufficient condition for inflation. Accumulated deficits may contribute to inflation through effects on the money supply, if the inflationary movement is already under way and unless offset by the actions of monetary authority. Finally, the classical proposition that balanced budgets provide an automatic rule-making authority for government budgeting is significant and important and at the basis of the practical nature of the problem. The prevalence of the balanced-budget philosophy is, however, not fully explainable by the propositions of the classical case. Beyond doubt, the attitudinal factors are at least as important as the real factors.

The Keynesian contribution to budgetary theory and practice is reducible to the proposition that government activities should be used to stabilize the level of total economic activity. The classicists stressed the control of the budget; the Keynesians the effects of the budget. Unfortunately, the Keynesian attention to budgetary effects has been accompanied by inattention to the problem of control.

This would seem to be the remaining and challenging task for the critics of conservative fiscal policy: to provide a guide to governmental budgeting which will serve two purposes simultaneously. The first purpose is to guide the transfer of resources from the private to the public sector; the second is to guide the selection of the aggregate level of receipts and expenditures, with a view to stabilization. The guidelines must be widely understood and capable of political implementation. Until this task is done, we can confidently anticipate a continuation of discussion over national debts and deficits, a discussion which will abound in semantic confusion.

Selected Bibliography

Adams, Henry C., *Public Debts,* D. Appleton & Company, New York, 1895, pp. 3–101.

Committee for Economic Development, *The Stabilizing Budget Policy,* New York, 1950.

Hansen, Alvin, *Fiscal Policy and Business Cycles,* W. W. Norton & Company, New York, 1941, pp. 135–222.

Malthus, Thomas R., *Principles of Political Economy,* 2nd ed., William Pickering, London, 1836, pp. 398–413.

Mill, John Stuart, *Principles of Political Economy,* Ashley edition, Longmans, Green & Company, London, 1929, pp. 873–880.

Perloff, Harvey S., "Budgetary Symbolism and Fiscal Planning," *Public Policy,* Harvard University, Cambridge, 1941, pp. 36–62.

Pigou, A. C., *A Study in Public Finance,* Macmillan & Co., Ltd., London, 1951, pp. 30–34, 231–251.

Say, Jean-Baptiste, *A Treatise on Political Economy,* translated from 4th ed. by C. R. Prinsep, Lippincott, Grambo & Co., Philadelphia, 1853, pp. 412–487.

Schumacher, E. F., "Public Finance—Its Relation to Full Employment," *The Economics of Full Employment,* Basil Blackwell, Oxford, 1946, pp. 85–125.

Smith, Adam, *Wealth of Nations,* Modern Library, New York, 1937, pp. 859–900.

Sraffa, Piero, and M. H. Dobb, eds., *The Works and Correspondence of David Ricardo,* Cambridge University Press, London, 1951, Vol. I, "Principles of Political Economy and Taxation," pp. 243–250; Vol. IV, "Funding System," pp. 143–200.

18.

Budgeting for
economic development*

The evolution of the modern budget system, in both its procedure and
techniques, accompanied the growth of responsible and democratic government (see Chapter 1). The development of budgeting in western
Europe and in the United States was part and parcel of the economic
development of these countries—of industrialization, of the growth of
the national government, of the development of skills in accounting,
finance, and administration. Public budgeting has paralleled the political and economic changes in the structure of societies. In some cases,
as in governments in the United States, it has reflected and formalized
changes which have already occurred. In other cases, the development
of government budgeting has assisted and accelerated economic and
political changes which were in progress. Japan is a case in point here.
As early as 1889 this rapidly developing country introduced a budget
system as a means of rationalizing and controlling governmental activities; government budgeting in Japan would appear to have led, not
lagged, in the process of economic development.[1]

In the underdeveloped countries of today, experience with functioning

---

* This chapter has benefited greatly from discussion in the faculty seminar on
economic development of the Maxwell Research Center of Syracuse University.
The author is indebted to his colleagues in this seminar: Messrs. Eggers, James,
McIsaac, Mosher, Stainbrook, and Sufrin.

[1] A. E. Buck, *The Budget in Governments of Today,* Macmillan Company, New
York, 1934, pp. 35–36.

budget systems is limited.   Very few Latin-American countries had any more than rudimentary budgeting in the 1930's.   In Asia and Africa, budget systems prior to World War II were either nonexistent or designed solely to serve the limited governmental responsibilities of the colonizing powers.   In only a very few countries, as in India, was there a development of budgeting and accompanying administrative skills that exceeded the basic level of economic development.

On the surface it would appear that economic development would require and provide the incentive for a rapid improvement in the systems and techniques of governmental budgeting.   In every underdeveloped country, governments, and particularly the national government, play leading roles in planning and implementing programs for development. The budget and the budgetary process are major instruments for such purposes.   Their importance should facilitate the transfer of budgeting experience from countries which have reached a higher stage of economic development, and the adaptation of this experience to the needs of developing countries.

Unfortunately, the adaptation may be extremely difficult.   The public sector and the private sector are even less sharply divided than in developed countries, and the pattern of relationships between the two is likely to be intricate.   Government enterprise is not clearly defined, and private enterprise is supported by government loans, grants, and subsidies. Revenue structures are complicated by special taxes and special funds. This makes for difficult budgeting.

So often, in underdeveloped countries, the basis from which budgeting should proceed is lacking.   There is a shortage of accounting and administrative skills; there are gaps in the hierarchy of government organization; there is an inadequate sense of personal moral responsibility for the conduct of government affairs.   In this situation it is not possible to build a budgeting system on the basis of established techniques and with existing skills.   Budgeting must help to create the situation which it is called on to serve, not merely formalize and strengthen an existing political, social, and economic structure.   The challenging task is to make budgeting a catalyst that will improve and strengthen the developmental program.

The manner in which a nation grows and expands, raises its living standards, alters its social patterns, democratizes its culture, and adopts new goals embraces the whole of the social, economic, and political process.   A study of even one aspect of this must necessarily involve knowledge and insights into the whole of what we call social science.   Moreover, social science must be brought into contact with at least some insights customarily employed only by natural scientists and engineers.

The process of development is, among other things, the interplay between the social order and the requirements of technology.

The aim of this chapter is to abstract a very small segment from this complex. Even this segment—budgetary policy and procedure—is too broad to be examined here in its entirety. First of all, those operations of government which the budget is expected to describe and control reflect a pattern of myriad influences. It is not possible to trace all the interrelations between the public sector and the process of economic development. Further, the task of examining budgeting for developmental purposes in terms of generalizations with wide applicability is complicated by the economic, social, and resource heterogeneity of what is so frequently put into the taxonomic pigeonhole as an "underdeveloped country." There are as many degrees of development and of internally different development patterns and cultures as there are underdeveloped economies.

I. THE PROCESS OF ECONOMIC DEVELOPMENT

To lay the basis for an examination of those aspects of budgeting that are most important for economic development, it seems desirable to set forth, in terms of generalizations, relationships which have historically characterized the developmental process.

First, industrialization is the key to economic development and, in fact, is virtually synonymous with it. Development requires, at some stage, an increase in the amount of accumulated capital per head of population, in industry, in agriculture, in the distributive trades, and in government. It may be that in a number of countries economic development must begin by strengthening and improving the agricultural sector without, initially, an increased capital accumulation. This may even take the form of strengthening subsistence agriculture—the nonmarket sector of the economy. But at some point, growth requires capital, and this will inevitably mean industrialization in the sense of increased fabrication, with a concomitant shift of economic activity and the labor force away from agriculture and into other activities.

In most countries this is what economic development has come to mean, and it is this that commands widespread support—industrialization to strengthen the nonagricultural sector of the economy. It is only through industrialization that an underdeveloped country producing raw materials can gain economic independence in relation to the more advanced countries on whom it depends for markets. It is only through industrialization that an economy can become both specialized and diversified, developments which have come to be associated with progress.

Second, economic development can be operationally defined in terms of (a) an increase in real output per capita, including the output of the nonmarket sector, and (b) consequent increase in real income per capita.

The emphasis on both output and income is necessary in establishing a usable criterion for judging the rate of development. Progress in the economy as a whole can generally be gauged solely on the basis of output per capita. The consequences of almost all policies, public and private, can be examined and appraised in relation to the output criterion. But economic development has come to mean more than this. Historically, as western European countries and the United States have developed, increases in income have been enjoyed by larger numbers of the population. In an underdeveloped economy the distribution of income is typically more concentrated than in developed countries. At some point in the process of development, there appears to be a reduction in income concentration.[2]

This emphasis on the distribution of the "fruits of development" distinguishes modern programs from the programs of colonial development. Total output, and even output per capita, may well increase in the colonies, but the income counterpart may be exported, with no resulting improvement in the distribution of income through the whole population. Economic development should be judged not only by the increases in output but by the extent to which there is an increased participation in economic activity and in the income derived from it.

Third, population pressure need not prevent development. It may intensify the need for development; it may slow the rate of development; it does not necessarily preclude it. The histories of Belgium, the Netherlands, and Japan, among others, suggest that high ratios of population to land area do not in themselves stifle economic growth.

There is little historical evidence to confirm the view that the Malthusian specter condemns countries to poverty until birth rates are reduced. In fact, the experience of developed, industrialized countries would suggest quite the contrary. As industrialization and urbanization proceed, and as the proportion of families engaged in agriculture declines, birth rates also decline, until at some point the rate of population growth declines. It is reasonable to expect that a successful development program will in itself, over time, contribute to a solution of the population problem.[3]

[2] Simon Kuznets, "Economic Growth and Income Inequality," *American Economic Review*, March 1955, pp. 1–28. Kuznets' data indicate that the initial stages of industrialization tend to increase the concentration of income, but he concludes that this will not necessarily occur in contemporary underdeveloped countries.

[3] For a more detailed consideration see Norman S. Buchanan and Howard S. Ellis, *Approaches to Economic Development*, Twentieth Century Fund, New York, 1955, pp. 92–116.

Fourth, economic development, in the foreseeable future, is primarily a task for the developing countries themselves, not for the outsiders. The kind of development which is wanted today by the peoples of Latin America, Asia, and Africa is not the kind that occurred in the 18th and 19th centuries, when mines, railroads, and ports, and sometimes schools and hospitals, were built in the colonies.[4] What is now demanded is a widespread popular participation in the process of development. This means that for many countries a new system of economic values must be internalized, with new patterns of behavior and expectation. Development must command the efforts and the moral support of increasing numbers of persons. Broadly speaking, the task is to assure that there is a demand for capital—the prerequisite to development—by a societal organization and structure necessary for its utilization.

As Buchanan and Ellis put it:

> Unless the habits of consumption and saving, the institutions and legal framework for accumulation, lending and investing can be adapted to the building and maintenance of capital, foreign aid can bring only transitory benefits. A permanent basis for higher living standards must be created *within* the society; indeed, this is the very meaning of economic development. Unless the chief nurture of growth is indigenous, the society is constantly exposed to retrogression.[5]

Economic development with widespread participation by large numbers of persons cannot be imported.

There are, of course, many ways and means by which outsiders can help, particularly in the transmission of skills and techniques from their own cultures and economies. The presence, side by side, of highly developed economies and very much underdeveloped economies does not make for a stable world. The recognition of this, it may be hoped, will encourage assistance from the developed countries.

Fifth, economic growth must be viewed as a learning process. New skills are acquired and old skills abandoned, with a resulting increase in the specialization and interdependence of the total system. Capital formation itself, the physical accompaniment of growth, may be conceived at a broad level as an increase in learning. The skills implicit in an increase in the volume of physical capital per head of population are technical, financial, managerial, and organizational.

---

[4] For an illuminating examination of the consequences of outside economic development see the discussion of U. S. efforts in Haiti in the 1920's in Marian Neal, "United Nations Technical Assistance Programs in Haiti," *International Conciliation*, February 1951, pp. 81–85.

[5] Buchanan and Ellis, *op. cit.*, p. 301.

Economic growth not only increases the specialization and complexity of an economy, it also increases certain kinds of internal mobility. These mobilities are two, geographic and social. As economic development proceeds, persons and families will move from the farms to the villages, from the villages to the cities, from the already developed areas to the frontiers of development. This will be accompanied by social mobility —the up-grading of persons in the hierarchy of skills and prestige, or the new creation of such hierarchies. Old occupations acquire new status, challenging the established power positions which have hitherto inhibited and resisted the growth process. In every society there are persons and interest groups resistant to change. Where these are in command of the power structure of a society, there will be no evident impetus to economic development until new persons and organizations are in a position to challenge the existing order.

Growth processes are frequently painful and often have a shattering impact on existing cultural values. This impact must be recognized and dealt with, but an overconcern with the preservation of existing folkways partakes of the romantic. It may safely be assumed that the elimination of poverty, ignorance, and disease is a worthwhile objective, for which it is necessary to pay a price.

The present examination of budgeting and development will necessarily emphasize the *economics* of development, although in full recognition that this involves an incomplete separation of elements from the whole. Economists have a basic contribution to make to the study of economic growth, but theirs is not the only contribution which can be made.

An emphasis on the economics of growth is handicapped by the deficiencies of formal theory in providing tools of analysis for dealing with process and change. Until very recent years this has been a backward and underdeveloped area of economic analysis.[6] Even in the years since World War II it would be difficult to contend that the breach has been fully repaired.

The reason for this inadequacy is not hard to find. Most of modern economic theory presupposes a specific organizational character for society. This is an outgrowth of attempts to describe and understand the behavior of advanced industrial market structures. Much less attention has been devoted to precapitalist organization and to the factors

[6] An excellent review of the work that has been done in formal economics is contained in Moses Abramovitz, "Economics of Growth," *Survey of Contemporary Economics,* Vol. II, Bernard F. Haley, ed., Richard D. Irwin, Homewood, Illinois, 1952, pp. 132–178. See also James Baster, "Recent Literature on the Economic Development of Backward Areas," *Quarterly Journal of Economics,* November 1954, pp. 585–602.

which accompanied the transition from one kind of economic order to another.

Underdeveloped countries do not conform to the presuppositions of modern formal economics. The prevailing theory of income determination will serve as an example.

Keynesian theory teaches that when there is a favorable schedule of the marginal efficiency of capital in relation to the schedule of the rate of interest, investment will proceed. This is assumed to occur automatically, without additional intervention from public or private authority. Such an approach, with such an assumption, is not unrealistic for an advanced industrial economy. There, it is usually safe to conclude that if profitable investment opportunities are present, the entrepreneurial organization will also be present to avail itself of the opportunities. No special attention to the organizational structure through which investment takes place is required.

The case in underdeveloped countries is much different. Here the organizational assumptions are by no means applicable. Adequate opportunities for private investment may exist on every hand, but investment does not proceed, because there is no entrepreneurial zeal, because the social structure does not encourage investment, because available funds are spent on ostentatious consumption to maintain status, because managerial skills are not available. The organizational structure of the underdeveloped country is the inhibiting factor, not the hiatus between the schedules of the marginal efficiency of capital and the rate of interest.

In this situation economic analysis must be adapted backward as well as forward, and should include a re-examination of the history of advanced economies and the history of developed sectors of economies which are otherwise underdeveloped. It may well be that important insights can be gained by looking once more at the development of the steel industry in France, or the textile industry in India, or the dairy industry in New Zealand.

Insights which may be provided by economists must be supplemented by the studies of political scientists, sociologists, geographers, and anthropologists.[7] These skills are particularly needed in the study of the organizational character of society and its relation to economic growth— the interaction between resources and organization, the ways in which groups are organized for the conduct of economic activity, the leadership patterns which develop within groups.[8]

[7] For a discussion of the integrated approach see Shepard B. Clough, "Strategic Factors in Economic Growth," *Political Science Quarterly,* March 1955, pp. 19–27.
[8] See, for example, Margaret Mead, ed., *Cultural Patterns and Technical*

Economists from developed countries are prone to think of organization for economic activity in terms of business firms (corporations, partnerships, proprietorships), governments, households, and possibly cooperatives. But in underdeveloped countries, growth must proceed on the basis of what there is—which may be a tribal structure, or a feudal structure, or a community organization. Sociologists and anthropologists should be able to contribute to an analysis of the ways in which these structures and organizations can be used as the carriers of economic change or, alternatively, the degree to which they must give way and be supplanted by other organizational forms and structures.[9] Similarly, there is need for further investigation of the prestige which attaches to certain kinds of occupations and activities in underdeveloped countries, in particular the prestige or lack of it which attaches to entrepreneurship; and, in a number of countries, the behavior of "out-groups" which now conduct the bulk of commercial and financial activity.[10]

II. GOVERNMENTAL RESPONSIBILITIES

There are three broad problems of development, all of which are at least partially economic in character, to the solution of which government budgeting can make a major contribution. The first of these is the organizational problem—the initiation of patterns for the conduct of public activity. Second is the task of channeling economic activity into the acquisition and utilization of increased amounts of capital goods. The third is the requirement that development programs be conducted within a price structure that is reasonably stable. That is, substantial inflation should be avoided.

These three broad problems will shape and condition budgeting and the budgetary process. The applicability of particular fiscal techniques must be judged in their context.

Change, UNESCO, Paris, 1953; Preston E. James, "An Assessment of the Role of the Habitat as a Factor in Differential Economic Development," *American Economic Review,* May 1951, pp. 229–238; Roscoe C. Martin, "Technical Assistance: The Problem of Implementation," *Public Administration Review,* Autumn 1952, pp. 258–266.

[9] The special need for research in community growth problems has been recognized in other connotations. See Joseph J. Spengler, "IBRD Mission Economic Growth Theory," *American Economic Review,* May 1954, p. 588.

[10] Charles Wolf, Jr., and Sidney C. Sufrin, *Capital Formation and Foreign Investment in Underdeveloped Areas,* Syracuse University Press, 1955, pp. 11–33; Yale Brozen, "Entrepreneurship and Technological Change," *Economic Development,* Harold F. Williamson and John A. Buttrick, eds., Prentice-Hall, New York, 1954, pp. 198–226.

A. THE DEVELOPMENT OF ORGANIZATION

The achievement of responsiveness and responsibility in governmental organization is not a problem which arises solely in underdeveloped countries; some developed countries continue to struggle with difficulties along these lines. But the problem has particular importance where the governmental machinery is encumbered with new and major tasks at a time when the performance of routine functions is a strain.

Burma, Indonesia, and the Philippines are cases in point—where newly gained independence with its consequent demands for the conduct of foreign relations, national defense, *and* economic development are piled on an administrative structure barely able to sustain the weight of programs for the administration of justice, the maintenance of transportation facilities, and the provision of minimum education. In these circumstances the governmental machinery may simply lapse into inactivity, and the tendency of administrators to seek safety in quiescence may predominate.[11] Alternatively, aggressive administrators, in their zeal to encompass new responsibilities, may resort to authoritarian techniques and to the creation of political and economic power centers outside the framework of public responsibility. Either eventuality can be almost fatal to the process of economic growth. Somehow, ways and means must be found to keep in touch, to maintain channels of communication and control back and forth between the governmental administration and the citizenry. Only in this way can a developmental program capture the imagination and enlist the efforts of large numbers of people.

The absence of responsiveness and responsibility in the governmental structures of a number of underdeveloped countries is symbolized, very often, by the prevalence of more obvious types of graft and corruption, legal and illegal. Bad organization breeds immorality, but an attack on the latter by means of fulmination and exhortation is likely to produce little improvement without strenuous attention to the organizational weaknesses which permit the immorality to flourish.

A good many of the organizational difficulties of underdeveloped countries arise because the national government is both overburdened and overcentralized—overburdened with the responsibilities which have been assumed, overcentralized because there is an inadequate number of well-trained persons, and those who are possessed of training and experience are given the tasks of review and coordination at the center. This results in an organizational structure staffed much better at the top

---

[11] For comments on this state of affairs see Lynton K. Caldwell, "Technical Assistance and Administrative Reform in Colombia," *American Political Science Review*, June 1953, pp. 494–510.

and at the lower echelons than in the middle.[12] The absence of the middle management group perpetuates the overburden on the top officials. The pressure of day-to-day work does not permit reorganizations in structure and responsibilities or the training of new administrators. The existing organizational pattern is continued, even though its weaknesses are as evident to the insiders as to outsiders.

Like so many other development problems, this is a vicious circle. The lack of skills perpetuates the weaknesses in administrative structure, and the lack of an adequate structure fails to call forth the development of new skills. Like most vicious circles, this one can be broken only by a frontal attack on the twin evils—in this case, skills and systems.

The circle cannot be broken simply by decentralization of administration in the conventional sense. A diffusion of responsibility downward through the ranks is certainly required, but this does not mean that final responsibility in decision-making is moved either outward (geographically) or downward. The need for a centralized review and coordination of public policy decisions is at least as great in an underdeveloped as in a developed country. The budgetary process can serve this purpose as well in the former as in the latter.

A systematic effort to relieve the pressure on the center requires a careful examination of those decisions which must be made by the coordinators and those which may safely be left partially or wholly uncoordinated. For example, the control of imports and exports and the use of foreign exchange must be centrally administered, but decisions about the development of an economy's transportation system can be reviewed at the center and implemented at lower and broader levels of governmental organization. Similarly, decisions about agricultural credit can probably be moved almost wholly outside the central government orbit once the basic program is established.

The relief of pressure on the center also requires ingenuity in the application of existing and projected organizational patterns. For example, the public corporation need not be wholly owned and operated by government; there are many variations in form and structure, some of which are capable of utilizing personnel and capital not typically available to a governmental organization.[13] At the same time, given a degree of ingenuity, it is possible to retain in governmental hands the responsibility for general direction over the corporation and for the supervision of those things which may be matters of public responsibility —such as the rate of capital formation (see Chapter 16). Similarly,

[12] Paul H. Appleby, *Public Administration in India,* Manager of Publications, Delhi, 1953, pp. 23–30; Walter R. Sharp, "Some Observations on Public Administration in Indochina," *Public Administration Review,* Winter 1954, pp. 40–51.

[13] See United Nations, *Some Problems in the Organization and Administration of Public Enterprises in the Industrial Field,* New York, 1954.

developmental programs can often be effectively conducted by cooperatives,[14] by the extension of credit facilities to existing organizations such
as provincial and local governments, and by the encouragement of new
types of private entrepreneurship. The lines between the public and
private sector in underdeveloped countries are not now and should not
be expected to be as sharp as in such countries as the United States and
Great Britain. Economic development requires experimentation with a
multiplicity of organizational forms, in an effort to find those which will
most quickly develop effective management.

B. Programs for Capital Formation

Even with the most careful attention to the organizational and decision-making pattern, governments will be faced with complex problems
in economic policy. The contrast with economic decision-making in the
development of colonies by the major powers in the 19th century points
up the complexity. There, as Frankel has contended, the question of
developing a whole community or a whole economy did not arise. The
role of government was clear-cut and consistent. Its responsibilities were
confined to political security, the maintenance of law and order, the
conduct of a limited fiscal and monetary system, and the provision of
adequate communications. In this framework,

> . . . the entrepreneur was freed from the necessity to choose between different
> and therefore necessarily conflicting goals of action. As far as he was con-
> cerned the purpose of investment was the production of additional net income.
> He was not distracted by such questions as whether the pursuit of that ac-
> counting objective would or would not bring about an increase in welfare,
> social efficiency, or happiness.
>   When he subscribed to a loan for or made a direct investment in an under-
> developed country he, as an investor, was not concerned with whether the loan
> would have good or bad effects on the welfare, health, or social structure of
> the borrowers. All such matters were not his responsibility, but were as-
> sumed, often indeed all too conveniently assumed, to flow from the hidden
> hand of providence, given only that each man "calculated" correctly in regard
> to that which it was his responsibility to calculate about.[15]

Today the task is more difficult. A responsible government in an underdeveloped country must both choose among the conflicting goals of
action and make entrepreneurial decisions about resource allocation.

The major economic responsibility facing the government of an underdeveloped country is to increase the volume of capital formation. This
may be done by direct government investment in the construction and

---

[14] For the experience of Ceylon see P. T. Ellsworth, "Factors in the Economic
Development of Ceylon," *American Economic Review*, May 1953, pp. 122–124.

[15] S. Herbert Frankel, *The Economic Impact of Under-Developed Societies,* Harvard University Press, Cambridge, 1953, p. 71.

operation of facilities; by encouraging private investment through tax concessions, subsidies, protective tariffs and the like; and by combinations of government and private effort in accordance with the organizational multiplicity previously noted. The relative importance of the public and the private will differ, of course, among countries and over time within the same country.

It may be asserted without qualification that in an underdeveloped country capital formation can proceed without the sacrifice of existing standards of consumption. It is true that income is equal to consumption plus investment in any economy, primitive or advanced. But this does not mean that consumption must be cut in order to provide investment. What is required is that increases in consumption be limited, so that as national product per capita increases, a part of that increase, perhaps a major part, will be devoted to goods for other than immediate use.

The pervasive characteristic of an underdeveloped economy is mass poverty and subsistence living; any effort to depress consumer expenditures results in further degradation and squalor. This is self-defeating because there is a link between consumption standards and the productivity of labor; reductions in the former are likely to be matched by further reductions in the latter. Very often, increases in output must come from longer hours of work and a reduction in the "preference" for leisure. Basic levels of living must be adequate to withstand the additional work requirements.

At the same time, an underdeveloped economy is faced with the necessity for applying rigid controls to the increase in incomes generated by an increase in output. With the distribution of income concentrated, with savings ratios low and consumption ratios high, an increase in income tends to be spent. The marginal propensity to consume is high and the marginal propensity to save is low, with correspondingly high multiplier values. This can quickly generate inflationary pressures, which are likely to be most serious in those sectors of the economy where mass consumption items are in demand. In many underdeveloped countries this brings immediate pressure on foodstuffs, where supply may be relatively inelastic, with resulting inflation in a strategic sector of the economy. In some instances the higher levels of demand generated by moderate initial increases in income will bring pressure on imported luxury goods, with resulting balance of payments problems.[16] In a de-

---

[16] Ragnar Nurkse has noted that the world-wide tendency to copy American consumption standards tends to limit the supply of investible funds ("Some International Aspects of the Problem of Economic Development," *American Economic Review*, May 1952, pp. 577–578). On the other hand, increases in income in the agricultural sector are undoubtedly less affected by pressure for respending on

veloped, industrialized country with a relative shortage of investment
outlets, high consumption ratios would be most desirable; in an underdeveloped country they are anathema because they make for instability.

In every economy an expenditure for capital goods is inflationary at the
time it is undertaken.   It matters not that the capital goods will some
day yield substantial increases in total product.   In developed countries
these inflationary pressures can be more easily absorbed than in underdeveloped countries, where high multiplier values may make capital expenditures dangerously income-increasing.

The capital formation problems which face the government of an
underdeveloped economy are twofold: mobilizing the surplus and directing the surplus.   These are quite separate matters.

Directing the surplus consists of the allocation of resources to effect
maximum long-run increases in output.   But there must be a surplus to
direct.   This is the task of mobilization—to assure that savings increase
with an increase in economic activity, that the marginal propensity to
consume is lowered, that multiplier effects are dampened down.   The
surplus to be mobilized consists of income and product above that necessary for the consumer sector.   The surplus comes from increases in
economic activity.   Its mobilization occurs as households are induced to
hoard their additions to income, to reduce the pressure of spending on
limited resources.   This makes it possible for governments or private
firms to expand capital formation without inflationary consequences.
The amounts so hoarded need not be loaned directly to government or
to business firms.   The hoarding itself will reduce spending pressures
and permit the expansion of bank credit.   Alternatively, with a decline
in the marginal propensity to spend on consumer goods, the government
may safely resort to deficit financing for additions to money supply.
These additions are not inflationary, as long as the hoarding continues.

Government efforts to mobilize the surplus are not likely to stop with
an increase in the volume of idle savings, but will generally seek to attract the savings directly into investment in financial institutions or in
government bonds, or to secure them through the taxing process.[17]   If

---

consumer goods.   Here conventional living standards are more likely to be influential, and savings ratios may increase, with reinvestment in additional capital
assets.

[17] For a discussion of experience in Southeast Asia see United Nations, Economic
Commission for Asia and the Far East, *Mobilization of Domestic Capital in Certain
Countries of Asia and the Far East,* Bangkok, 1951, pp. 78–230, *passim;* Maurice
Zinkin, "What the Underdeveloped Countries Have to Do," *Economic Problems of
Underdeveloped Countries in Asia,* B. K. Madan, ed., Indian Council of World
Affairs, New Delhi, 1953, pp. 34–39; Benjamin Higgins, "Development Financing,"
International Conciliation, March 1955, pp. 299–303.

the surplus is immobilized, substantial economic power remains in private hands. If the surplus is captured by taxation, the economic power of the private sector is reduced.

1. MOBILIZING THE SURPLUS. As things now stand, underdeveloped countries tax less heavily in relation to national income than do developed countries. Tax ratios in the countries of Southeast Asia generally run from 7 to 14 percent; in South America, from 10 to 15 percent. These are far behind the ratios of taxation to national income, 33 and 40 percent, in the United States and Great Britain.[18]

There seems to be a generally positive relationship between the degree of development and the ratio of taxation to national income, but the reasons for this are not at all obvious. Walter Heller has pointed out that, conceptually at least, the ratio of taxes to national income expresses what a country decides to spend collectively in relation to what it decides to spend privately. The upper limit to this ratio is determined, or ought to be determined, by the effectiveness with which a government uses the funds which it collects.[19] A country embarking on a development program ought to be able to raise taxes to finance it. But in fact, tax ratios increase slowly and the possibilities for government investment are thereby limited.

For developed countries, apart from special taxation to control inflation, the volume of tax revenues is generally determined by the volume of expenditure to be undertaken. Expenditure decisions set the stage for and precede tax decisions. In underdeveloped countries the sequence of decision runs from taxation to expenditures.

The low ratios of taxation to national income in underdeveloped countries mean, however, that modest increases in the aggregate of taxes can make substantial increases in developmental expenditure. In a country in which the ratio of taxation to national income is 12 percent, with one-third of these taxes channeled into development, an increase of only two percentage points in the ratio of taxes to national income could raise the government's developmental expenditures by 50 percent.

---

[18] Data from E. M. Bernstein and I. G. Patel, "Inflation in Relation to Economic Development," International Monetary Fund, *Staff Papers*, November 1952, pp. 392–393; Walter Heller, "Fiscal Policies for Underdeveloped Countries," *Report on the Technical Assistance Conference on Comparative Fiscal Administration*, United Nations, New York, 1952 (mimeo), p. 19; "Taxation and Economic Development in Asian Countries," *Economic Bulletin for Asia and the Far East*, United Nations, November 1953, pp. 3–4. (The last two are also contained in Haskell P. Wald and Joseph N. Froomkin, eds., *Papers and Proceedings of the Conference on Agricultural Taxation and Economic Development*, Harvard Law School, Cambridge, 1954.)

[19] Heller, *op. cit.*, p. 20.

In their efforts to expand tax revenues for the mobilization of the surplus and the prevention of inflation, underdeveloped countries find that they must select revenues in relation to their effects on incentives to work, save, and invest. But, as Richard Goode says,

> These two objectives are conflicting in the sense that too much emphasis on one is likely to interfere with progress by complicating the attainment of the other. But they are complementary in that too little attention to either consideration may give rise to conditions that are an obstacle to economic development.[20]

Faced with the conflict between incentives and expanded revenue sources, such countries are likely to show a strong preference for taxes on consumption rather than for taxes on income and profits, since the latter may be assumed to be the more detrimental to private incentives to save and invest. This preference is further strengthened by the fact that in most developing economies there is continuous inflationary pressure, which may be partially relieved by mass-consumption taxes, and there is little risk that depression or stagnation will result from the lack of consumer markets. Furthermore, income taxes are most difficult to administer in an economy where nonmarket activity is significant, where literacy is low, and where persons and firms maintain inadequate accounting records.[21] These conditions make a persuasive case for consumption taxes, but there are limits. Where large numbers of persons are poverty-stricken, further taxation of necessities may bring not only hardship but an impairment of health and working efficiency.

There are some kinds of selective taxes which may be particularly useful. One of the most attractive of these is a betterment tax, modeled along the lines of the special assessments used to finance sidewalks or streets and roads in local governments in the United States. A betterment tax seeks to capture a part or the whole of the increase in private asset values which accrues as a result of specific governmental expenditures. A flood control project may restore lands to cultivation; owners of such lands may appropriately be required to pay a betterment levy. The construction of improved transportation facilities may give rise to incremental increases in land values along the right of way; these may be appropriately subject to special taxation.

A capital gains tax may also perform a specific and useful function

[20] Richard Goode, "Taxation and Economic Development," *Proceedings of the 46th Annual Conference on Taxation,* National Tax Association, Sacramento, 1954, p. 226.

[21] Richard Goode, "Reconstruction of Foreign Tax Systems," *Proceedings of the 44th Annual Conference on Taxation,* National Tax Association, Sacramento, 1952, pp. 213–215.

in an underdeveloped economy. A great many countries, particularly in South America in the years since World War II, have experienced a construction boom in urban centers. Much of this new construction has gone into luxury hotels, apartment houses, and office buildings. Once constructed, the buildings are bought and sold by speculators, and real estate prices mount, encouraging further construction. Available capital and entrepreneurship tend to be attracted into this kind of speculative activity.

The funds invested in the speculative purchase and resale of such existing assets are not lost to the economy. The problem here is to make both construction and speculative activity in real estate less attractive, in the hope of diverting activity into other, more socially productive kinds of entrepreneurship, with a resulting improvement in the allocation of resources. A selective capital gains tax may be used in some circumstances to discourage speculative construction and redirect private investment.

Revenues imposed for special purposes may also acquire a usefulness in an underdeveloped economy that they do not possess in a developed economy. Earmarked taxes on soft drinks, on electric energy, or on agricultural land, for " . . . governmental activities important and vivid in the community would make such taxes more acceptable in whatever dimensions are in fact possible and equitable."[22] Earmarked revenues very often destroy the flexibility and comprehensiveness of the government's budget, but where developmental programs and their financing are the paramount concern, these considerations take on a lesser significance. On the other hand, assigned revenues for development, like most special-purpose arrangements in government finance, need periodic re-examination. Statutory allocations of taxes may exceed requirements for the purposes originally assigned, and the revenues may thus be effectively lost or squandered. Earmarking, like other fiscal arrangements, should not be permanent.

Betterment taxes, capital gains levies, and earmarked revenues by no means exhaust the possibilities for the adaptation of specialized techniques to the revenue structures of developing countries. Selective excises for the control of luxury consumption, export taxes, and the much-debated tax concessions to investment are other possibilities.[23]

There are other techniques available. Some underdeveloped countries, particularly in South America, have reasonably well established

[22] Appleby, *Public Administration in India,* p. 35.
[23] Heller, *op. cit.,* pp. 23–26; Goode, "Taxation and Economic Development," *op. cit.,* pp. 225–236, and "Reconstruction of Foreign Tax Systems," *op. cit.,* pp. 212–222.

governmental or quasi-governmental systems of social insurance. Employer and employee contributions are used to build reserves for the payment of sickness and disability benefits, unemployment benefits, and old age pensions. Very often, these systems can be strengthened, the rate of contributions modestly increased, and the accumulations made available for government investment purposes.

Land reform may also fall in this category, although its social and economic implications usually extend far beyond the connotations of surplus mobilization. Where large landholdings predominate and landowners fail to use their income and accumulation for investment in product-increasing outlays, the redistribution of land holdings may be accompanied by an increase in agricultural taxation, with a net accretion of a part of the landowners' income to government.

All of these techniques, and others which may be devised, are of little use if the surplus so mobilized is not properly channeled into investments which make a maximum contribution to the developmental program. In some cases the channeling will be done through the private sector, either directly by means of government loans, or indirectly as government captures the surplus and simultaneously permits an expansion in private bank credit. In other cases, funds may be made available to semi-governmental development corporations or to cooperatives, or to provincial and local governments.

2. DIRECTING THE SURPLUS. Regardless of the channels through which the surplus is moved to investment, it may be assumed that central government direction of the kinds and volume of capital formation will, to a greater or lesser degree, be necessary. Government planning for capital formation has come to be increasingly significant in programs for development.

Where investment decisions are made or influenced by public policy, choices should be guided by the "trigger-off" principle. That is, the best investment which can be made at any one time is the investment which will set the stage for and encourage additional investment and additional increases in total product. The first investment makes succeeding investments either more productive or less costly, or both. The Sears Roebuck and Company experience in department store merchandising in Mexico City is illustrative.[24] In its first years most of the commodities sold were imported from the United States. But over a period of years domestic fabrication increased, with a corresponding substitution for imports. The fabricators were not required to make outlays for merchandising facilities; these were provided by Sears.

[24] Richardson Wood and Virginia Keeper, *Sears Roebuck de Mexico, S.A.,* National Planning Association, Washington, 1953, pp. 39–45.

Very often, external economies can be provided for both the public and private sector by additions to social capital.[25] Improved roads and rail transport will lower the costs of shipping goods and open up private investment opportunities which would not otherwise be profitable. Electric power projects will attract additional private investment and make further government investment less costly. But agricultural improvements and the development of extractive industries seldom produce such external economies.

Attention to the importance of external economies means that major emphasis should not be placed on the income-producing aspect of direct investment by government. The construction of a publicly owned steel mill to be operated at a loss may produce more external economies, and indirectly and in the long run more government revenue, than the construction and operation of a self-liquidating toll bridge.

Economic growth is an uneven process; one sector advances at a faster rate than other sectors, and each builds on the developments which have preceded. Attention to these differentials and a continued search for the bottlenecks which, if removed, will trigger-off another round of capital formation does not assure a balanced developmental program in the sense that all sectors of the economy advance simultaneously. But it probably assures the maximum rate of long-run growth.

At the same time, the search for the ideal government investment which will provide maximum stimulus to further investment is complicated by the large number of additional elements that must be taken into account. At any one time the determining factor may be the shortage of foreign exchange, the need to produce commodities for export or commodities which are substitutes for imports, the need to provide employment for off-season labor, or the necessity for making expenditures that are labor-intensive rather than capital-intensive.[26] The balancing and weighing of these considerations is influenced by social and political pressures. In fact, the complexity of the choices has encouraged many underdeveloped countries to establish development boards or autonomous corporations, or planning commissions partially isolated from the political framework. This tends to simplify the choice-making and gives greater authority to expert staff. It also runs the risk of weakening central executive authority (see Chapter 16).

[25] John H. Adler, "The Fiscal and Monetary Implications of Development Programs," *American Economic Review*, May 1952, pp. 584–592; Ragnar Nurkse, *Problems of Capital Formation in Underdeveloped Countries*, Oxford University Press, New York, 1953, pp. 152–154; United Nations, *Measures for the Economic Development of Under-developed Countries*, New York, 1951, pp. 49–60.

[26] Spengler, *American Economic Review*, March 1954, p. 596.

C. Programs for Stabilization

There are two general kinds of inflationary pressure to which the economies of underdeveloped countries are exposed. The first arises from the development process itself; this was examined in connection with the mobilization of the surplus. The second kind of inflationary pressure arises from increases in price and demand in world markets, influences largely beyond domestic control. Many underdeveloped economies depend heavily on raw materials exports, the prices of which fluctuate more than the prices of imported manufactured goods. The combined influences of domestic pressures and foreign trade, the separate effects of which cannot always be disentangled at any particular time, may give rise to persistent inflationary pressures in underdeveloped economies.

The extent to which inflation is detrimental to development, and the extent to which public policy should be geared to its suppression at all costs, have been hotly controverted in public, private, and professional debate. Only the major outlines of this controversy will be set forth here.

Those who contend most forcibly for strong anti-inflationary programs in underdeveloped countries point out that inflation leads to a misdirection of resources. Rapidly rising prices tend to encourage speculative activity in urban real estate, in commodity inventories, in foreign exchange. This serves to channel entreprenurial talent to the "get rich quick" kinds of activities that are the antithesis of the needed investment outlays. Inflation further tends to destroy the income and asset position of bondholders, and to increase the difficulties which governments face in selling their obligations and in the establishment of a capital market. Domestic inflation puts a cost-price squeeze on exporters, and unless devaluation proceeds concomitantly with domestic price rises, which it almost never does, exporters are at a severe disadvantage. Inflation also produces increases in interest rates, offering a further impediment to certain kinds of domestic investment. All of these arguments are quite apart from the humanitarian considerations. An increase in the price of foodstuffs may not have a severe impact on subsistence agriculture, but it wreaks great hardship on urban wage earners and is often catastrophic for government officials, public school teachers, pensioners, and other semifixed income recipients.[27]

---

[27] The staff and officials of the International Monetary Fund have probably presented the most consistent and forceful case for a strong anti-inflationary program in underdeveloped countries. See *Staff Papers:* Bernstein and Patel, November 1952, pp. 363–398; Felipe Pazos, "Economic Development and Financial Stability," October 1953, pp. 228–253; "Economic Development with Stability, Report to the Government of India," February 1954, pp. 313–386, esp. pp. 316–319.

On the other side, there are none who argue that a severe inflation produces anything other than chaos in developed and underdeveloped countries alike. But it is contended that a mild inflation, on the order of a general rise in prices of 3 to 5 percent a year, will encourage development. A gradual rise in the price level shifts income toward entrepreneurs and away from fixed income groups. The higher profit margins will encourage entreprenurial activity and tend to wash out business losses that would otherwise occur. Where governmental authorities have control over additions to monetary supply through central bank borrowing or the printing press, they are able to command the resources needed before the price rises are fully effective. The development program becomes an engine for forced saving, and a higher rate of capital formation results.[28] A gradual inflation may also induce a larger volume of work output for the same or an even lower level of real wages, a condition which reflects a "money illusion."

It is a counsel of perfection to suggest that it is posible to enjoy the advantages of inflation and at the same time avoid all of its disadvantages. Nevertheless, this may be very nearly possible as long as the rate of inflation is kept within narrow limits. Quantities are important here. A 10 percent annual increase in the level of prices may lead to serious misallocation of resources; a 5 percent increase may provide the necessary stimulus to investment and the encouragement to increased employment of available resources. The best of all possible worlds is always something to strive for!

To let inflation proceed slowly, keeping it always within reasonable bounds and averting its cumulative effects, is a most difficult task, and one for which few underdeveloped countries are equipped. Revenue systems based on income-inelastic levies such as commodity taxation do not automatically dampen down inflationary movements. The lack of emphasis on income and profits taxes in the revenues of underdeveloped countries means that this built-in stabilization device, which helps to curb inflation in a developed country, is largely inoperative.[29] The lags in tax collection delay the anti-inflationary effects of those levies which are imposed.

The inflationary impulses that arise from abroad as a consequence of increased demand for the exports of underdeveloped countries (with a corresponding rise in domestic income), may be easier to control than those initiated internally. A careful manipulation of export duties

[28] See Martin ᴅronfenbrenner, "II—The High Cost of Economic Development," *Land Economics*, August 1953, pp. 209–210.

[29] Henry C. Wallich and John H. Adler, *Public Finance in a Developing Country* (El Salvador), Harvard University Press, Cambridge, 1951, pp. 220–209.

may help to capture some of the increases in domestic income. Imports may be increased to offset demand; monetary controls may be tightened. The techniques of control are available, but administrative skills need to be enlisted for their application.

In spite of the very real danger that inflation cannot be kept in bounds, where countries are faced with a choice between more inflation and more development or less inflation and less development the former is very likely to be elected. An adequate quantity and quality of budgetary information can help to assure that these choices are made rationally— that the rate of development is known and the stabilizing or destabilizing consequences of governmental action are adequately assessed.

III. APPLICATIONS OF FISCAL TECHNIQUES

The needs of developing countries for modern fiscal systems encompass the whole range of techniques and procedures examined in previous chapters of this book. Governments in underdeveloped countries should have a strong central budget office, a well-articulated budget procedure, a thorough classification system, central control over budget execution, and a responsible post-audit of accounts. In some countries none of these exist; in others, certain kinds of budgeting techniques are reasonably well developed. Meaningful generalizations applicable to large numbers of countries as to "first steps" and "where to begin" are possible only in broad terms. Reforms must proceed differently in different countries.

A. THE BUDGETING FUNCTION

The technical assistance mission reports of the International Bank for Reconstruction and Development and of the United Nations Secretariat reveal the diversity of the conditions encountered in the budgeting systems of underdeveloped countries.[30] In spite of this diversity, there has been an almost unanimous conclusion that the first fiscal reform required is a strengthening of the scope, power, and prestige of the budgeting function. Budgeting needs to be elevated in the hierarchy of governmental decision-making and placed under the direct supervision of the chief executive or the minister of finance. A strengthened and expanded central budget office will result. To accomplish this it may be necessary

[30] Nine of these mission reports, including two reports of missions sponsored by the United States Economic Cooperation Administration, are summarized in *Report on the Technical Assistance Conference on Comparative Fiscal Administration*, pp. 63–138. One of the most extensive examinations of fiscal administration and budgeting is contained in *Report of the United Nations Mission of Technical Assistance to Bolivia*, New York, 1951, esp. pp. 18–44.

to draw personnel from other agencies or from the central accounting office, and to institute training programs at several levels.

At the same time, budget responsibilities need to be made more comprehensive. Proliferation of governmental authority represents, in many cases, a desirable state of organizational multiplicity, but for budgetary purposes these activities must be brought under review, although probably not under control, of the central administrative structure. This is particularly important where autonomous agencies have major responsibilities in a developmental program, and where their capital outlay programs may impinge on other government and private capital requirements.

With the strengthening of the prestige of the budgeting function and the extension of budgetary review to public enterprise activities, it may be possible to utilize these enterprises more fully and completely as instrumentalities for development. The pricing practices of publicly owned utilities, for example, may be altered to encourage surplus accumulations which may be made available for developmental purposes. This would transform the enterprise from a commercial-type venture to one which is both commercial and tax-gathering in nature.

In the process of broadening and deepening the responsibilities of the central budget office, a pattern of coordination with the agencies in charge of developmental planning must be established. The coordination task here is not very different from that faced in American municipalities which use a capital budget. At some point in the process, the multi-year projects incorporated in the capital improvements plan must be annualized for inclusion in the government's budget. The current budget is adjusted to reflect the impact of the expense of operating the projects; over-all financial requirements, both current and capital, are harmonized.

These are probably the first and most important steps in the establishment of the budget function in underdeveloped countries. Beyond this, where personnel are available, the central budget office may wish to undertake studies of management and organization, or may institute a system for the control of budget execution. In most cases these are in the nature of things desirable but postponable until program review and coordination has been firmly established.

B. The Statistical Basis for a Development Program

A realistic appraisal of development projects and a careful analysis of the intricate relationships between the needs for capital formation and the needs for stabilization require an extensive data base for economic planning and budgeting. This means national income accounts, supplemented by an economic character classification of government activity and by other significant data.

In the connotation of economic planning, "other significant data" does not mean all the information that can conceivably be assembled, but rather the data on factors which are strategic at any one time. This may be foreign exchange, and the data base for planning will require information on imports and exports, their quantity and composition and the forecasts of these magnitudes. The limiting factor may be skilled construction labor, and data with accompanying analysis will be necessary for effective planning. The data base for planning and budgeting must adjust to changing requirements.

In recent years national income accounts have become highly useful for developmental planning. Social accounting permits an appraisal of possible growth rates. The accounts are benchmarks by which developmental programs can be assessed to determine whether they are realistic, and to determine by how much per capita output can be raised, annually and over a period of years. This serves to eliminate the more grandiose and emphasize the more feasible. National income accounts also facilitate an examination of the extent of foreign control over the economy of an underdeveloped country, and can thus contribute to a relatively dispassionate appraisal of the character and extent of outside participation in the internal economy.[31]

The usefulness of national income accounting in an underdeveloped country is well established and generally recognized, but the construction of the accounts may be very difficult. It may be almost impossible to maintain national accounts on a basis that permits forecasting and the use of a Nation's Budget for policy recommendations. The difficulties arise not only from the absence of data, but from underlying conceptual problems that have not been fully resolved, such as the relationship of the market to the nonmarket section. However, substantial progress has been made in recent years.[32]

Where national income accounts can be used as a basis for develop-

[31] Such an appraisal is said to have been one of the major consequences of national income accounting in Puerto Rico. See Daniel Creamer, "Uses of National Income Estimates in Under-Developed Areas," *Income and Wealth,* Series III, Bowes & Bowes, Cambridge, 1953, pp. 214–222.

[32] See Harry Oshima, "The Price System and National Income and Product," *Review of Economics and Statistics,* August 1951, pp. 248–254; V. K. R. V. Rao, "Some Reflections on the Comparability of Real National Incomes of Industrialized and Under-Developed Countries," *Income and Wealth,* Series III, pp. 178–210. For a somewhat different view of the significance of national accounts see S. Herbert Frankel, "Concepts of Income and Welfare—in Advanced and Under-Developed Societies—with Special Reference to the Intercomparability of National Income Aggregates," *ibid.,* pp. 156–168.

mental planning but the supply of skilled statisticians is limited, it is often desirable to select the income and product magnitudes which are most crucial and direct attention toward their improvement and refinement. This kind of selectivity would stress the improvement of data on capital formation, public and private, and the sources of savings available for investment. Less attention might be directed to the refinement of the components of personal consumption expenditure, and more attention to the components of investment. This approach might be directed to a regrouping of those transactor units which can be specifically influenced by governmental policy. Rather than lumping together the public and private enterprise sectors, as is typical of most national income accounting schemes, these two might be separated. Public enterprise may be presumed to be susceptible to direct governmental influence, and it is therefore important to possess adequate factual knowledge of its operations.

An adequate data base is a prerequisite for development planning; it is not the planning itself. As Frankel has stated:

> No system of accounts and no statistical calculations can in themselves yield aggregates which will obviate the need for detailed individual and social decision as to the activities which society should pursue or the social framework within which they should be conducted.[33]

Improvements in the data are not a substitute for government officials skilled in policy formulation.

C. Budgetary Classification

Budgetary information can make a major contribution to the data base necessary for planning and executing a development program. Moreover, a reform in budgetary classification can bring an improvement in the whole machinery of government and its administration. A classification system must serve simultaneously the needs of developmental planning, budget program formulation, execution, and accountability. Improvements in classification designed to accomplish this can be a part of the process by which administrators and citizenry come to understand the character of and the possibilities for general improvement in the quality of administration.

As a matter of technique, budgetary classification is not very different in underdeveloped than in developed countries. But in the former, at the outset, the application of techniques should be undertaken with a minimum of refinements.

Where anything resembling a budgetary system is in operation, the

[33] *Ibid.,* p. 168.

classification will necessarily be based on organizational units, usually with object detail. An improvement in classification does not always mean an abandonment of the existing system, although very often needless detail can be eliminated. It may mean a supplementation by additional classification patterns—a functional grouping for the summary accounts, an economic character classification, and attention to performance budgeting in selected programs.

In the development of supplementary budget classifications it will generally be desirable to re-examine the definition of that which is governmental. The budgets of most underdeveloped countries are far from comprehensive, in part because of the intricate patterns of public-private fiscal relations. A major objective of supplementary classifications should be an extension of the system of budgetary reporting. These extensions may embrace a number of undertakings in which the government has substantially less than total control.[34]

A major possibility for utilizing budgetary classification as a means for centering attention on the development program lies in the establishment of a separate category of budget expenditures specifically called "developmental." This designation can be part of a functional classification to group expenditures or parts of expenditures which would otherwise fall under such headings as education, transportation, or health. A category for development expenditures could also be incorporated in an economic character classification.

A budget category labeled developmental would necessarily be broader in scope than the definition of capital expenditure for purposes of an economic character classification (see Chaper 9). As was contended earlier, economic development must bring, at some point, an increase in the ratio of physical capital to population. Government may contribute to the encouragement of capital formation by current expenditures for health and education. Developmental expenditures would thus include the improvement of human capabilities, broadly defined. Yet the extension of the category of development expenditures to include such outlays poses the familiar problem of drawing a line. Social services such as unemployment benefits or disability benefits may also conserve and improve human resources, but these may be less closely related to development than new programs for the training of public administrators or schools for agricultural technicians.

[34] It has been suggested that the scope of budgetary classification of government enterprise for those undertakings where the government owns less than 100 percent of the stock be determined on the basis of whether or not a governmental purpose is served by the enterprise. (United Nations, *Budget Management, Report of the Workshop on Problems of Budgetary Classification and Management,* New York, 1953, pp. 7–8.)

In the United Nations publication, *A Manual for the Classification of Government Accounts*,[35] It is suggested that the developmental category be defined to exclude most of the traditional government services, such as national defense, the administration of justice, and outlays for fiscal administration, and also to exclude the great bulk of traditional social services. The subdivisions of development expenditure would then include the following:

1. Education and research
2. Health
3. Housing and slum clearance
4. Agriculture, forestry, hunting and fishing
5. Industry and commerce
6. Transport and communications
7. Other

Flexibility is most obviously necessary; any such classification must be adapted to the particular projects which are regarded within a country as developmental in character.

The utilization of a broad category called development expenditures does not preclude the possibility of measuring additions to government physical capital. Information on government capital formation is a significant part of the data necessary for developmental planning. Within the category of developmental expenditure, it will be desirable to separate outlays which add to physical resources from those which do not.

In the utilization of an economic character classification in an underdeveloped country there may be other differences, apart from the use of a category of developmental outlays. Where an economic character classification embraces a consolidated account intended to measure additions to private incomes, some differences in treatment may be called for (see Chapter 9). Sales of government bonds directly to persons, for example, may very well be classified as a current account revenue of government not very different in economic impact from tax revenue. This is the conceptual basis of the balancing item in the budget of the Government of India. Only where borrowings are financed by the sales of bonds to banks is there conceived to be a deficit. Borrowings from the public are classified as a part of the revenue which reduces the deficit. This is an appropriate classification where it can be assumed that the sales of bonds to individuals and business firms in itself operates to restrict private expenditure on goods and services. There may be other differences in the application of an economic character classification to an underdeveloped economy. Distinctions between at-home and abroad receipts

[35] New York, 1956.

and expenditures of government will probably be important; within the public enterprise sector it may be necessary to establish separate categories for trading ventures and for financial institutions. Social insurance funds may engage actively in outlays for capital formation and may therefore require a separate capital account.

The application of certain types of performance budgeting in underdeveloped countries offers considerable potentiality. It has the advantage of being capable of introduction in a step-by-step sequence. Those agencies having adequate budget staff may be in a position to undertake performance classification; this may encourage other agencies to make similar efforts.

Applications of performance budgeting that require the measurement of full costs per unit of governmental product are undoubtedly overrefined for application in most underdeveloped countries. But performance classification which seeks only to measure broad program costs over time, supplemented by performance reporting, should be able to make a valuable contribution to improved management and to public understanding of the activities of government.

The potentialities of this type of performance budgeting would appear to be greatest for specific developmental projects, such as in public health or education. Square miles of swamps drained, numbers of persons inoculated, adults enrolled in basic literary programs, and similar kinds of data, are both measurable and sufficiently homogeneous to represent accomplishment under specific programs. These measurements may be most useful in dramatizing governmental operations and thus enlisting support both inside and outside the governmental structure.

The requirements for developmental planning and program execution may also call forth a type of project classification, which in turn may be supported by performance classification and performance reporting. A great many development programs are likely to be conducted across the lines of established departments and agencies. The air force may spray the swamps with DDT; the army engineers may construct transportation facilities; the ministry of health may conduct education programs for technicians. Where interdepartmental activities assume major proportions in themselves, or are of particular significance in the total of developmental activities, specialized administrative organizations and staff, described and controlled by a separate budget authorization, may be called for. The activities of such interdepartmental organizations may very well lend themselves to performance classification.

D. GOVERNMENT ACCOUNTING

In most underdeveloped countries the operating efficiency of government is greatly hampered by an inadequate and cumbersome accounting system. These systems were often devised primarily to serve the interests of accountability in a very narrow sense, that is, to prevent the misappropriation of public moneys.[36] In practice this has come to mean repetitive accounting, an overcontrol enforced by a pre-audit system that requires extensive patterns of documentation. This state of affairs, particularly prevalent in South American countries, serves to limit the effectiveness of all of the administrative operations of government. For example, Caldwell found that:

> The waste of time involved in these procedures is not an inevitable concomitant of official accountability. And after attempting to guard against all eventualities of official carelessness or misconduct, the government of Colombia still lacks many of the most useful records and procedures for genuine control —particularly for managerial control.[37]

An improvement in accounting procedures requires explicit recognition of the multiple purposes which must be served by government accounts. The prevention of stealing is not the sole consideration; management needs for program information, and executive and legislative needs for information on which to review and approve programs must also be met.

As levels of skills are raised and as administrative systems are improved in underdeveloped countries, government accounting can also be improved. A general rise in the level of administration permits the abolition of detailed pre-audit controls and provides a framework in which program administrators can be given greater authority over their own accounting systems. The post-audit can then be employed to check on the operation of the system, rather than on the manner in which each transaction is documented. The activities of the central accounting office can be moved out into the agencies. This would facilitate management use of accounting records for internal purposes, and would strengthen both budget formulation and program planning. The decentralization of accounting should facilitate the development of accounting skills.

There is no doubt that a reform in governmental accounting, in most underdeveloped countries, can make as much contribution to operational effectiveness as a reform in budgetary procedure and classification. When undertaken together, these two can be mutually reinforcing.

E. Conclusion: The Cumulative Nature of Reform

Government service, in most underdeveloped countries, probably enjoys more prestige than in developed countries—or at least more than in

---

[36] United Nations, *Government Accounting and Budget Execution*, New York, 1952, p. 22.

[37] Caldwell, *American Political Science Review*, June 1953, p. 502.

the United States. The government employee may be underpaid and overworked, but he commands the respect of his fellow citizens.

The prestige of government service can be put to use in marshalling support for an improvement and extension of governmental activities. Here it should be possible for government to take the lead in raising the standards of performance for the whole social and economic organism so that the peoples of underdeveloped countries may enjoy the increased material well-being necessary for the establishment of human dignity.

This places a high degree of responsibility on government officials and on organization and procedure. Government must attract the most able and industrious of persons interested in the national welfare, persons capable of instilling a high standard of responsibility in all aspects of national life.

Even as a well-ordered program for capital formation can give rise to cumulative waves of further investment, so it may be hoped that budgetary reform will be a cumulative process. A reclassification of budget accounts should lead to improvements in government accounting; improvements in the data base for economic planning will bring better decisions about resource allocation; the introduction of performance reporting will raise the level of public interest in and support of a developmental program.

To capture the imagination of a society, to instill a motive for innovation, to mobilize the latent energies of a people—these are the fundamentals. Fiscal and budgetary reforms are a small but nevertheless important part of this task.

Selected Bibliography

Abramovitz, Moses, "Economics of Growth," *Survey of Contemporary Economics,* Vol. II, Bernard F. Haley, ed., Richard D. Irwin, Homewood, Illinois, 1952, pp. 132–178.

Alder, John H., "The Fiscal and Monetary Implementation of Development Programs," *American Economic Review,* May 1952, pp. 584–600.

Alder, John H., Eugene R. Schlesinger, and Ernest C. Olson, *Public Finance and Economic Development in Guatemala,* Stanford University Press, Stanford, 1952.

Appleby, Paul H., *Public Administration in India,* Manager of Publications, Delhi. 1953.

Baran, Paul A., "Economic Progress and Economic Surplus," *Science & Society,* Fall 1953, pp. 289–317.

Bernstein, E. M., and I. G. Patel, "Inflation in Relation to Economic Development," International Monetary Fund, *Staff Papers*, November 1952, pp. 363–398.

Bloch, H. S., "U. N. Technical Assistance in Public Finance," *Proceedings of the 44th Annual Conference on Taxation*, National Tax Association, Sacramento, 1952, pp. 202–207.

Bronfenbrenner, Martin, "II—The High Cost of Economic Development," *Land Economics*, August 1953, pp. 209–218.

Brozen, Yale, "Entrepreneurship and Technological Change," *Economic Development*, Harold F. Williamson and John A. Buttrick, eds., Prentice-Hall, New York, 1954, pp. 196–241.

Buchanan, Norman S., and Howard S. Ellis, *Approaches to Economic Development*, Twentieth Century Fund, New York, 1955.

Creamer, Daniel, "Uses of National Income Estimates in Under-developed Areas," *Income and Wealth*, Series III, International Association for Research in Income and Wealth, Bowes & Bowes, Cambridge, 1953, pp. 211–223.

Finer, Herman, "The Role of Government," *Economic Development*, Harold F. Williamson and John A. Buttrick, eds., Prentice-Hall, New York, 1954, pp. 365–426.

Frankel, S. Herbert, *The Economic Impact on Under-Developed Societies*, Harvard University Press, Cambridge, 1953.

Goode, Richard, "Reconstruction of Foreign Tax Systems," *Proceedings of the 44th Annual Conference on Taxation*, National Tax Association, Sacramento, 1952, pp. 212–222.

———— "Taxation and Economic Development," *Proceedings of the 46th Annual Conference on Taxation*, National Tax Association, Sacramento, 1954, pp. 225–236.

Heller, Walter, "Fiscal Policies for Under-developed Countries," *Report on the Technical Assistance Conference on Comparative Fiscal Administration*, United Nations, New York, 1952, pp. 12–40 (mimeo).

Hoselitz, Bert F., *The Progress of Underdeveloped Areas*, University of Chicago Press, Chicago, 1952.

Martin, Roscoe C., "Technical Assistance: The Problem of Implementation," *Public Administration Review*, Autum 1952, pp. 258–266.

Nurkse, Ragnar, *Problems of Capital Formation in Underdeveloped Countries*, Oxford University Press, New York, 1953.

———— "Some International Aspects of the Problem of Economic Development," *American Economic Review*, May 1952, pp. 571–583.

Rostow, W. W., *The Process of Economic Growth*, W. W. Norton & Company, New York, 1952, esp. pp. 218–257.

Singh, Baljit, *Federal Finance and Underdeveloped Economy*, Hind Kitabs, Ltd., Bombay, 1952.

Spengler, Joseph J., "IBRD Mission Economic Growth Theory," *American Economic Review*, May 1954, pp. 583–599.

United Nations, *A Manual for the Classification of Government Accounts*, New York, 1956.

———— *Budget Management, Report of the Workshop on Problems of Budgetary Classification and Management*, New York, 1953.

Wallich, Henry C., and John H. Adler, *Public Finance in a Developing Country*, (El Salvador), Harvard University Press, Cambridge, 1951.

Wolf, Charles, Jr., and Sidney C. Sufrin, *Capital Formation and Foreign Investment in Underdeveloped Areas*, Syracuse University Press, Syracuse, 1955.

Author index

485

Subject index

Accountability, 112, 359–361
  and object classification, 130
  in underdeveloped countries, 480–481
Accounting classification, defined, 131
Accrual accounting, 319–320, 367–369
  and performance budgeting, 145n, 151–152
  in economic classification, 236
Accuracy, principle of, 107
Activity measurement, 144–147
  in Los Angeles, 178
  in T.V.A., 161–162
Administration, supervision of, 312–316, 324–326
Administrative budget, U. S., 118, 120
Administrative expenses, 417, 426–427
Administrator, general role, 45–48, 51–57
Aggregative classification, defined, 131
Agriculture, U. S. Department of, 134, 145–146, 150–151, 250, 256–258, 343n
Aldrich, Senator, 17
Allocation of resources, 43–44, 402, 425–426, 450, 464–467
Allotments, 102, 174, 353–354

Alternative budgets, 252–253
Alternatives, examination of, 249–251
  in business budgets, 274, 276
Annuality, principle of, 107
Applicable receipts, 121–124
Apportionment, 101, 353–354
Appropriations, and agency budgeting, 262
  in U. S. Government, 97, 316–317
  itemization of, 313–314
  language, 324
  limitations on, 324
  lump sum, 345–346
  permanent, 317
  structure of, in Department of the Army, 167
    in Richmond, 173
  supplemental, 94–95
Appropriations committee, 11, 309–310
  in U. S. Congress, 97–99, 164, 324–326
Army, U. S. Department of, appropriation structure, 167
  budget execution, 354n
  program budgeting, 162–170

491